George W. Liebmann is a lawyer and hi... ...
and international diplomatic history. His publications include *Diplomacy between the Wars: Five Diplomats and the Shaping of the Modern World* (I.B.Tauris, 2008).

'A detailed account of this remarkable career. [Liebmann's] book will be valued by all serious students of American foreign policy.'
TLS

'Well-informed and objective.'
Robert Earle, *American Diplomacy*

'Meticulous.'
Donald Devine, *The American Conservative Union*

'Liebmann's book will leave the reader with a deeper understanding of US foreign relations.'
The Washington Independent Review of Books

'A true masterpiece.'
John Lukacs, author of *The Future of History*

'A major contribution to diplomatic history.'
Mary Ann Glendon, Learned Hand Professor of Law, Harvard University and former US Ambassador to the Holy See

'Liebmann is able to demonstrate empathy with a man so impenetrable.'
Kenneth Weisbrode, *The National Interest*

'The volume shows the shifts and tides, ideological underpinnings, and personal agendas of US foreign policy makers over this span and the ways a consummate professional diplomat worked within the vicissitudes.'
J. P. Dunn, *Choice*

'In this book, [Negroponte's] remarkable career is the lens through which we gain a sharper understanding of not just the man, but the diplomatic history of the Cold War and its aftermath.'
Foreign Service Journal

'An original, important book, not just about the career of one able diplomat, but about America's foreign policy.'
A. W. Purdue, *Salisbury Review*

THE LAST AMERICAN DIPLOMAT

JOHN D. NEGROPONTE AND
THE CHANGING FACE OF AMERICAN DIPLOMACY

GEORGE W. LIEBMANN

I.B. TAURIS

LONDON · NEW YORK

SOMERSET CO. LIBRARY
BRIDGEWATER, N.J. 08807

New paperback edition published in 2014 by I.B.Tauris & Co Ltd
6 Salem Road, London W2 4BU
175 Fifth Avenue, New York NY 10010
www.ibtauris.com

Distributed in the United States and
Canada Exclusively by Palgrave Macmillan
175 Fifth Avenue, New York NY 10010

First published in hardback in 2012 by I.B.Tauris & Co Ltd

Copyright © 2012 George W. Liebmann

The right of George W. Liebmann to be identified as the author of
this work has been asserted by him in accordance with the Copyright,
Designs and Patents Act 1988.

All rights reserved. Except for brief quotations in a review, this book,
or any part thereof, may not be reproduced, stored in or introduced
into a retrieval system, or transmitted, in any form or by any means,
electronic, mechanical, photocopying, recording or otherwise,
without the prior written permission of the publisher.

ISBN: 978-1-78076-694-2

A full CIP record for this book is available from the British Library
A full CIP record is available from the Library of Congress

Library of Congress Catalog Card Number: available
Printed and bound in Great Britain by Page Bros, Norwich

*For the members, past and present, of the
United States Foreign Service*

EPIGRAPH

As life is action and passion, it is required of a man that he should share the action and passion of his time, at the peril of being judged not to have lived.

— Oliver Wendell Holmes, Jr.

Are you a member of the Society of Jobbists or do you know that guild? If not, let me tell you of it. It's an honest craft, gives good measure for its wages, and undertakes only those jobs which the members can do in proper workmanlike fashion. It demands right quality, better than the market will pass.

— Learned Hand

CONTENTS

LIST OF ILLUSTRATIONS

PREFACE

This is a book about a boyhood friend whose life has followed a very different trajectory from my own and who possesses attributes, including an infinite capacity to suffer fools gladly and to survive and ascend in large organizations, in which I have always felt myself to be deficient. It is in essence a book about an "insider" by an "outsider," albeit an outsider who has sometimes been successful in influencing large events. It is a book about maturation—the John Negroponte of 1960 is not the John Negroponte of 2010—about the maturation not only of a man but of a nation, for the bombast of President John F. Kennedy's inaugural speech would be inconceivable today, even from our last president. It is a book about a nation that has been "mugged by reality," which no longer occupies, as it did in 1960, the position of an undamaged economic colossus amid other nations struggling to recover from a war in which they had bombed one another into smithereens. If our national leadership still proclaims American exceptionalism, the best of our diplomats know better. No president has expressed for America what Bonar Law, British statesman and prime minister, said of Britain in 1922: "we cannot alone be the policeman of the world," but the time is not distant when one will. Recent events, including some of those recounted here, have taught us that our vast mechanical superiority in the technology of war—in ballistic and cruise missiles, bunker-busting bombs, and the like—is almost as irrelevant to the nature of modern conflicts as the possession of thousands of nuclear weapons was to the postcolonial wars of the 1950s, 1960s, and 1970s. Technology can provide immunity from invasion, although not from destruction, but it cannot provide the means to dominate and occupy. In that respect, our time has seen the democratization of war. War, in its modern forms, is dominated by infantry and by the morale of infantry. In an age of improvised explosive devices, the defense has the same advantage that it was given by the machine guns and trenches of World War I. Military collapses, when they occur, are the product of ideas and examples, including economic examples. A mercantile republic, with great absorptive capacity and a constitution framed with due regard for human frailty and the realities of human nature should feel itself advantaged by this change; it is a mark of the failure of our political leadership that it does not.

Until very recent years, I interested myself only in domestic policy. My earlier writings deal with the uses and possibilities of sublocal institutions; the appropriate role of the law, seen as a branch of mechanics and not of theology, in structuring orderly change, and with the process of social reform as seen in the lives of six mostly forgotten social reformers. Recent events, however, with their impact on the possibilities of rational reform, have led me to write about foreign policy, first with a book of biographical sketches of five interwar diplomats who displayed in their thought and work professionalism and intellectual autonomy rare in their successors. Second, this book, about a contemporary diplomat, makes many of the same points in a different way. It is a book about a bureaucratic politician, but one who at some points has been a risk taker; a man who has sometimes made hard choices but otherwise whose characteristic weapon has been the gentle nudge.

John Negroponte and I grew up in the same apartment building in New York City. Contrary to many articles about him, it was located on Lexington and not Park Avenue, although the difference was not significant. Until the first grade, we attended the same school, the Town School, run by a half-dozen women from a brownstone on East 76th Street; now a much more elaborate establishment at a different location. One of my earliest political memories goes back to an occasion when my parents had two of my teachers to dinner on the evening of the Czech *coup d'état* in 1948, an event that caused a sudden change in the outlook toward the Soviet Union on the part of at least one or two of those present. Although John and I were good friends while we were in knee pants, our lives thereafter went in different directions. John, who, with his remarkable siblings, had the advantage of an intact family, went first to the fairly conservative Allen-Stevenson and Buckley Schools and then to Exeter and Yale. At Allen-Stevenson, he was presented in 1948 with a plaque for being second in the class. Years later, when Negroponte was giving a speech in Paris, he recalled having written a paper on Clemenceau while in the eighth grade. When his former colleague at the United Nations, Jean-David Levitte, asked for a copy of it, Negroponte replied, to general merriment, "It's classified!"

The 1940s New York in which we grew up has been described as

Among the best of times. An era of turmoil without social upheaval, a time of transition made quietly behind a façade of normality. Almost every major corporation had or wished it had its headquarters in Manhattan. Businesses were attracted by the vast pool of skilled clerical labour waiting in the city... mobility away from the neighbourhood and into the suburbs was limited. The city was the country's richest market for plays, musicals, movies and nightclub entertainments as well as the staples of publishing—newspapers, magazines, and books.[1]

As for the following decade,

the fifties are a badly researched and badly reported time. There was more social action and more sense than we're given credit for. Subsequent generations have politicised every emotion and believed it was happening to them for the first time... we set out essentially to be spectators and reflectors on life. A dogged kind of centrism came out of this... we had no desire to shout political slogans or march with banners, because we had seen the idealism of the radical thirties degenerate into the disillusionment of Stalinism and the backlash reaction of name-calling anti-communism.[2]

It was a cycle that was to repeat itself in the 1960s and after.

Some 50 years after our paths diverged, my mother, then in her late 80s, noticed an obituary of John's mother, and suggested that I might write to him, admonishing that she had watched her friends die off and would not have any had she not renewed old acquaintanceships. I took this advice, which I had no qualms about doing, as John had then "retired" and gone to McGraw-Hill and I was not in the position of clutching at a great man's garment. We saw each other several times since then. At one of these lunches, I gave John the manuscript of my book on five diplomats, and as we were leaving he made a remark, about not having kept a diary or planned an autobiography, which I took, accurately or not, to be an implicit suggestion that I might want to write something about him. I thought this might provide a way of exploring the last 50 years of American history. When I told him of this conclusion, he was back in government, as Director of National Intelligence, and properly took the view that he could not talk to me until his anticipated retirement on January 20, 2009.

John Negroponte was not, in any literal sense, "The Last American Diplomat."

The technology of rapid communication over great distances doomed old-fashioned diplomatic negotiation ... modern diplomats, no matter how intelligent or resourceful can seldom have an impact on the making of policy unless they have direct access in their own right to the nation's leaders in Washington ... their ideas must coincide with those of the leaders or at least be congenial to the prevailing wisdom.[3]

However, it may be fairly said that no recent American diplomat *en poste* has wielded a comparable influence. For the North American Free Trade Agreement (NAFTA) and the ozone treaty, both involving new forms of American engagement with the outside world unlike, for example, the more conventional Dayton and Northern Ireland agreements were not the work of special emissaries but of initiative by a regularly assigned diplomat, who also wielded more than ordinary influence in Honduras, Iraq, and the United Nations and as Director of National Intelligence and Deputy Secretary of State.

ACKNOWLEDGMENTS

In addition to Ambassador Negroponte, a number of persons gave helpful interviews to the author including Richard Benedick, Raymond Burghardt, Robert Earle, David Engel, Sir Jeremy Greenstock, Michael Kennedy, W. Anthony Lake, Herbert Levin, Jean-David Levitte, Thomas Lovejoy, Shepard Lowman, Nicholas Negroponte, General Colin Powell, Susan Schwab, Judge Laurence Silberman, and David Young.

I am indebted to President Gordon Johnson and the Fellows of Wolfson College, Cambridge, UK, for a visiting fellowship during the period that this book was written. I am also indebted to David and Alma Engel for hospitality in Florence, Italy, and to Richard Meade for hospitality in Cambridge.

I received assistance from Margaret Grafeld in obtaining documents from the State Department Archives and am also indebted to the staffs of the Cambridge University Library, the Liddell Hart Collection at Kings College, London, the National Archives at College Park, Maryland, and the Ronald Reagan Presidential Library, Simi Valley, California, for their support.

I am also grateful to Dr. Lester Crook, the commissioning editor for the book, and to Priya Venkat, his skilled copy editor.

1

EARLY YEARS

A true natural aristocracy is not a separate interest in the state, or separable from it. It is an essential integrant part of any large body rightly constituted. It is formed out of a class of legitimate presumptions, which, taken as generalities, must be admitted for actual truths. To be bred in a place of estimation; to see nothing low and sordid from one's infancy; to be taught to respect one's self; to be habituated to the censorial inspection of the public eye; to look early to public opinion; to stand upon such elevated ground as to be enabled to take a large view of the widespread and infinitely diversified combinations of men and affairs in a large society; to have leisure to read, to reflect, to converse; to be enabled to draw and court the attention of the wise and learned, wherever they are to be found; ... and to possess the virtues of diligence, order, constancy, and regularity, and to have cultivated an habitual regard to commutative justice: these are the circumstances of men that form what I should call a *natural* aristocracy, without which there is no nation.

— Edmund Burke, *Appeal from the Old to the New Whigs* (1771)

In an interview in 2006, John Negroponte stated:

I always wanted to be involved in diplomacy. I was fascinated by history; political science. I liked foreign languages...I'd taken my junior year abroad when I went to college and I was pretty set on joining the Foreign Service right from the time I went to college...I took the exam while I was still in college and entered...several months after graduation.[1]

He had been influenced in this aspiration by Jacques de Thier who had been Belgian ambassador to Mexico, Canada and Britain and who married Negroponte's aunt. In 2008, Negroponte told a group of District of Columbia school children that he had traveled abroad in the summers while a teenager; he urged them to develop the habit of daily reading of a good newspaper. "Once you've got past understanding and speaking and learning another language, then the concept of learning additional languages becomes really rather easy; you've sort of broken the code."[2] In the meantime, he had enrolled in the Harvard Law School. After a week, Negroponte went to notify Dean Erwin

Griswold of his acceptance by the Foreign Service and was told: "Well, you have arrived in time to get your tuition refunded." His later approach recognized that

> there's no substitute for hard work and studying your situation very carefully... none of these things can be accomplished by one single individual through a virtuoso performance... I've always put a great deal of weight on people, recruiting good people to collaborate with.[3]

Negroponte came from a family of Greek expatriates. His great-great grandfather had left the island of Chios following a massacre there in connection with the Greek War of Independence in 1822, which consumed or exiled 90 percent of the population, a decimation in reverse that left the same impress as the Holocaust on the few survivors, Negroponte's grandfather was born in Tagenrog and moved to Switzerland before World War I. In Russia before World War I, Negroponte's grandfather had a fleet of about seven steamships. Negroponte's father was born in Lausanne, Switzerland, in 1915; his grandmother at one point was treated for tuberculosis in Davos. Negroponte shared Chios ancestry with another notable student of diplomacy, the British historian Peter Calvocoressi.[4] Dimitri Negroponte, John's father, was brought up in Francophone Switzerland and went to boarding school in Klosters and then to the École des Sciences Politiques in Paris, where his son was later to spend his junior year abroad. He was one of the two members of the Greek Olympic ski team at the 1936 Olympics in Berlin, Germany. He wanted to enter the Greek Foreign Service but was told that he could not do so without a Greek university degree, although he was fluent in French, English, Greek, and German. Dimitri had inherited about $600,000 from his mother in 1933 and in 1936 started a small shipping business in London. After marrying in 1938, he came to the United States in September 1939. During the war, he worked for Stavros Niarchos, a cousin of his wife; at the end of the war, he resumed trading for himself with four or five ships under the name of D. J. Negroponte and Company. The ships were Liberty ships, acquired from the US government with the aid of Greek government guarantees. By 1958, he had 7 ships, rising to 11 in 1965. In the 1970s, the fleet diminished to three vessels. In 1973, he returned to London from New York.[5] John Negroponte observed that he would have done better financially if he had put his money in the stock market in 1933. Negroponte's mother, the former Catharine Coumantaros, was born in New York of Greek parents but was raised in Greece from the age of three onward and was married in Paris in 1938. She was active in relief programs for the Greek underground during the war and ran a Friends of Greece shop at 52 East 57th Street in New York.[6] Two cousins endowed the Dimitri and Maria Negroponte-Delivanis Award in International Affairs. From this background, Negroponte gained the view that there were political causes worth fighting for. After the war, the family remained in New York where the children were in school.

Negroponte characterized his father as

> the liberal in the family... he saw our political process here through the lens of his anti-fascist perspective on Europe, so I think he misread some

things—like Nixon, for instance. He exaggerated. [He] was a little horrified that I went to Vietnam, and a bit more horrified that I went to Central
America—to Honduras.

Finally, when Negroponte became Ambassador to Mexico, Dimitri voiced
approval. He died in 1996, followed in death by Negroponte's mother in 2000.
"Neither lived to see me come back into government."[7]

Our milieu was one that has vanished, that of the Manhattan upper middle-class
in the 1940s and 1950s, when persons with moderate but not grand earned or
inherited incomes could still afford to live on the Upper East Side and pay private
school tuitions for their children, which had not reached their present astronomi-
cal heights, when the massive flight to the suburbs was just getting under way,
and when one live-in domestic servant was customary and two or more not
infrequent. The region has now become the preserve of UN diplomats, the very
wealthy, and an expense-account aristocracy. We lived within walking distance
of our early schools. The ground floor of our apartment building included an
old-fashioned drug store, the Wilcox Pharmacy, with a soda fountain; a small sta-
tionery store; a branch of Gristede's Grocery in which bills were written out and
added by hand and merchandise was brought down from the shelves by the manager using an enormous hook; across the street was the Montauk Market, an old-
fashioned butcher shop, familiar with the idiosyncrasies of its customers. A block
away, the Third Avenue El was still standing, with its stations heated in winter by
pot-bellied stoves; beneath it was an array of antique stores and ethnic restaurants.

Most people who were young in the Manhattan of the 1950s do not doubt the
reality of global warming: sleigh riding in Central Park, all but vanished today,
was a part of their youth. Most also are sympathetic to environmental controls;
clear skies over any large city were rare in that era. Many apartment buildings
were heated by soft coal, delivered down chutes across sidewalks, while many
others had incinerators to burn their garbage, emitted over Manhattan from a
myriad of smokestacks.

Negroponte attended the Town School in New York (where the writer was
his classmate); and then the Allen-Stevenson School, where a classmate remembered "at that age you can see the intelligence of someone. It hasn't got the
varnish of pretension yet." He then went to Exeter for his high school years,
where he participated in the debating society, varsity soccer, golf, and swim-
ming and where he won the French prize. At Yale (where one of his friends
was William H.J. Bush, the brother of the elder President Bush), he belonged
to Psi Upsilon, otherwise known as The Fence Club, along with William Bush
and Porter Goss (who was the last Director of Central Intelligence following
the passage of the 2004 Intelligence Reform and Terrorism Prevention Act), and
pursued his language studies, spending his junior year, 1958–9 at the Institut
d'Études Politiques in Paris. It was said that he and William F. Buckley, Jr, were
the only students to achieve an A in the political science course given by the
conservative scholar Wilmoore Kendall.[8] He was also influenced by Professor
Cecil Driver's emphasis on the nonpartisan nature of the British civil service (a
course on the English political system was required of all Government majors),
as well as by Charles Lindblom's course on comparative political systems and

a course on quantitative political analysis taught by Karl Deutsch. His closest faculty friend was Roulon Wells in the philosophy department, who wrote his principal letter of recommendation to the Foreign Service; he took almost as many philosophy as government courses.

John Negroponte had three brothers, all with notable careers. Nicholas, the best man at his wedding in 1976, was about five years younger, and is known for his writings on computers and intellectual property and as the leader of a program to place inexpensive computers in the hands of all school children in underdeveloped countries. The other two brothers are identical twins, fourteen years junior to him. Michel is a filmmaker and the author of *Jupiter's Wife*; the fourth brother, George Negroponte, is an artist who lives in Sweden with his Swedish wife. Two of the brothers went to Yale, and two went to the Massachusetts Institute of Technology (MIT). A cousin, Anthony Lyiardopoulous, recalled that "His dad taught him how to eat, how to ski, how to be a good athlete. His dad would have made a sensational diplomat." As one of his brothers observed, "Our father spoke at least five languages fluently. John has his genes." In his youth, he displayed "a feeling that one must handle problems privately"; he was mortified in college when he "had to call his father to bail him out [of a poker debt]. I don't think John was too happy about that." He had "a propensity for reaching out to other students, especially those from foreign cultures, engaging them in conversation, asking them questions…it was an outstanding trait."[9] While he was at McGraw-Hill, John Negroponte was active in the French-American Foundation.[10]

On entering the Foreign Service, he took the basic officer's course from October 1960 to January 1961. He did not excel in the written Foreign Service exam, passing it because of an added five points given to him for his foreign language proficiency. His oral exam was a happier experience; he had spent the summer after Yale as an intern at Lazard Freres. On a shelf behind his desk was a study on the Federal Reserve System that he leafed through in idle moments. He was delighted when the oral examiners asked him to describe the Federal Reserve System. He was also asked what to do about the new Castro Government in Cuba and recommended a policy of engagement. After he was told that he passed the exam, he was also told that he passed notwithstanding his ignorance about the Foreign Service and his answer about Cuba: "you'll get over it!" He initially wanted to be an Africa specialist and applied on the State Department's annual request sheet, the so-called "April Fool" sheet because of the date of circulation, to be assigned to Francophone sub-Saharan Africa; he expected to study Arabic with a view to ultimate assignment in the Maghreb region in northern Africa. As John Negroponte recalled at his retirement reception in January 2009, he was instead sent to Hong Kong and, after two years, was assigned to the Bureau of African Affairs as a junior administrative aide. Bored with administrative chores after two months, he volunteered to study Vietnamese in August 1963, a career-defining move. At this time, he was an admirer of Roosevelt and Truman: "if they hadn't lost my absentee ballot somewhere in the bowels of the State Department, I would have voted for Kennedy. I considered myself a Democrat until Ronald Reagan came along, and then I switched political affiliation."[11]

2

HONG KONG

I look forward to an American world empire, whose long-term chances
are poor, with more fear and less enthusiasm than I look back on the
record of the old British Empire, run by a country whose modest size protected it against megalomania.

— **Eric Hobsbawm**, *Interesting Times: A Twentieth Century Life*
(London: Allen Lane, 2002), 418

The Hong Kong to which John Negroponte was assigned in 1961 was important less as a commercial center than as a listening post. America's relations
with China were at their nadir in 1960. The McCarthy period was not long in
the past, and although the Sinologists in the Consulate longed to visit China,
there was little talk about normalization of relations. Few remember the high
hopes invested in China by the Roosevelt administration with its vision of four
or five "world policemen" under which China, the Soviet Union, Britain, and
perhaps France were to share in the maintenance of world order, a vision of a
revived Holy Alliance not, as it is frequently misrepresented, a Wilsonian world
parliament or world government. The government of Chiang Kai-Shek was thus
given the veto power of a permanent member of the Security Council. Fewer
still remember that in 1945 and 1946 there were some 200,000 US troops in
China concerned with supply of the Chungking Government and the taking
of the Japanese surrender. The recurrence or continuation of civil war and the
corrupting effect of US aid on the Westernized nationalists made the Communist
victory almost inevitable. Notwithstanding our substantial aid to Chiang, given
despite the prescient warnings of General Stilwell and the diplomat John Paton
Davies, among others, the Chinese Civil War was not really a proxy war, and
both American and Soviet aid were limited, the Russians giving the Communist
Chinese little assistance during the era of "socialism in one country," although
the Russians gave more after the second world war. The decision of Harry
Truman, George Marshall, and Dean Acheson embodied in the China White
Paper of 1949 in favor of American withdrawal was a prudent decision, resting
on three premises: that a society of enormous population, however ramshackle
its armies, could bleed and absorb large numbers of American troops; that the
United States despite its victories and its 12 million men under arms, was war
weary; and finally, as made most explicit in the writings of George Kennan,

that China, unlike Germany, Britain, Russia, or Japan, did not have even a medium-term industrial potential with the capacity to seriously hinder American interests.

China, nonetheless, cast a large shadow over American politics and foreign policy. The Truman administration was charged with having "lost China," although some Republicans, including Senator Robert Taft and General Dwight Eisenhower, certainly knew better. The Nationalist *émigrés*, aided by Senator William Knowland, who succeeded Taft as Senate Republican leader, made any revision of policy by the Eisenhower–Dulles administration difficult. The Communist victory rendered the United States more sensitive to any communist threat to Japan, hence the prompt American intervention on the North Korean invasion of South Korea. The Chinese intervention in the war in turn was prompted not only by General Douglas MacArthur's semiauthorized march on the Yalu River, but also by the Japanese peace treaty in which Dulles was heavily invested and which firmly rooted Japan within the Western alliance. All this took place during the waning hours of the Stalin regime, in which there was little communication among the great powers.

When Negroponte was assigned to Hong Kong as a visa officer in the Document Verification Center after his brief internship, he was remembered by the journalist and historian Stanley Karnow: "He came in there, a kind of classy guy. Very amiable, you know, hanging around. He quickly became one of the cast of characters." Theodore Heavner recalled that during the Vietnam period Negroponte

> had continuing friendships with…Stanley Karnow. And they used to spend a lot of bull sessions talking about the situation. I am sure that John did not entirely agree with Karnow or vice-versa but they did have a relationship.[1]

Negroponte later described the work as "things like attending to American seamen who had gotten put in jail, we had to defend their interests in Hong Kong. It was very much of a people-related kind of work."[2] His supervisor in Hong Kong was Herbert Levin; the consuls under whom he served were Julius Holmes, who had earlier been in the shipping business; Sam Gilstrap; and ultimately Marshall Green, later ambassador to Indonesia and Assistant Secretary of State for Far Eastern Affairs. One of the consuls advised him to "get a good Chinese cook boy and read good books on China and you'll be made." He remembered Green as a determined punster, who later declared himself "mortarfied" by Vietcong (VC) attacks. Levin was a humorous taskmaster who required memoranda about arcane commercial problems to be translated into plain English on the premise that the readership of reports declined by 10 percent for each additional page. Negroponte, being tall, was sought out as the escort of the daughter of the then British Governor General, Sir Robert Black. Negroponte was later impressed by the Levins' relationship with their adopted daughter, which may have made him receptive to the idea of adoption later in his life. In this period, Levin talked Negroponte out of becoming an Arabic specialist and was thanked for doing so by Negroponte's father, Levin facetiously alleging to Negroponte that his impression of Arabs was derived from the Lebanese Christian girls he met on nudist beaches in the South of France.

Negroponte's work as a visa officer together with his provincial reporting in Vietnam was an eye-opening experience. He had had a sheltered life in private schools and Yale; his encounters with impoverished people in varied states of desperation were illuminating. They gave him a respect for the importance of consular work that later informed his conduct of two very large embassies in Mexico and the Philippines.

He ultimately served as commercial officer, and at one point was charged as quarantine officer with arranging inspection of ships destined for Cuba at the time of the American embargo accompanying the Cuban missile crisis. He learned rudimentary Cantonese Chinese sufficient to conduct visa interviews of persons claiming to be wives and children of Chinese immigrants to the United States. Prior to the late 1940s, many such immigrants sold the identities of their relatives to others in China; knotty problems frequently resulted when the actual relatives sought family reunification visas after 1949. Negroponte became economic defense officer in the commercial section and was impressed when, as a humble vice-consul, he received a visit from the then chief executive officer of Xerox. He wrote a report on transistor radio imports.

Although Green was, like Negroponte, a graduate of Exeter and Yale, his family, like that of his superior, U. Alexis Johnson, had been seriously scarred by the Depression; Johnson had in addition been interned by the Japanese after Pearl Harbor. Neither of them were ideologues; both held views about the vulnerability of the United States that were not shared by the triumphalist postwar generation. For the expatriate Negroponte, as for them, history was not a series of inevitable triumphs.

Little about America's relations with Hong Kong during the period 1961–3 suggested that China would be America's largest trading partner in 40 years. The only significant issue confronting American diplomats was that presented by American political pressure to curtail textile imports from Hong Kong, fostered by the then secretary of commerce, Terry Sanford of North Carolina. The British had a three-year agreement for "voluntary" curtailment of Hong Kong textile exports that the Hong Kong Government refused to renew. In a meeting with Prime Minister Harold Macmillan in April 1961, President John F. Kennedy complained of a 400 percent increase in textile imports from Hong Kong, causing them to equal those from Japan: "Something must be done or there could be a disastrous effect on the reciprocal trade legislation" being renewed by Congress. Macmillan was not too sympathetic:

> If the West gives aid to new countries to set up industries, they are bound to manufacture ... Lancaster [in England] had shifted from the manufacture of textiles to high-grade machinery. A problem arises when a new source comes so quickly into the market. This upsets things politically.[3]

The Hong Kong textile boom was a consequence of the curbs on imports from the People's Republic. In a meeting with Japanese Prime Minister Ikeda on June 20, 1961, Secretary of State Dean Rusk and Undersecretaries Chester Bowles and George Ball indicated that the swelling of Hong Kong's textile exports to a size greater than those of Japan was an inducement to American promotion of a multilateral pact.[4] "Hong Kong always scrupulously observed its commitments and was now able to concentrate on the problems of improving efficiency in production and expanding sales by diversification." Clothing exports increased 233 percent during the period 1962–9; sales of blended goods increased 15-fold. By 1969, total Hong Kong textile exports were of $3.826 billion.[5]

There was a substantial influx of refugees to Hong Kong in 1962, leading to defensive troop movements and a closing of the Chinese frontier by the British. A cable from the consul, Marshall Green, later ambassador to Indonesia, indicated that the refugees from communism owed no particular loyalty to the Chinese Nationalists. The Communist pressure on Quemoy and Matsu was thought to be in part due to a desire of the Communist government to distract attention from recent economic setbacks and to combat the "two China" policy of the Nationalists.[6]

The existence of the peculiar enclave at Hong Kong was due not only to Britain's annexation of Hong Kong Island as a crown colony in the mid-nineteenth century and the subsequent leases of areas on the mainland, but also to the legitimacy Britain gained from its spirited though foredoomed resistance to the Japanese occupation, which allied it with the Chinese, Nationalists, and Communists. The postwar development of both Hong Kong and Singapore owed much to the coexistence in these enclaves of a trustworthy legal system, *laissez-faire* economic policies no longer stressing colonial monopolies, and the social stability provided by the Confucian family system and neighborhood institutions. In Hong Kong, development was initially fostered by the sale of crown lands in Singapore by forced savings and investment in housing. These developments excited the admiration even of some Western Marxists.[7] Later, there was much Japanese investment. Japan, in East Asia, and Germany, in Central and Eastern Europe, ultimately achieved through peaceful commerce many of the economic aspirations of the New Order and the Greater East Asian Co-Prosperity Sphere. Britain also benefited greatly from its traditional policy of recognizing *de facto* governments. Although China behaved as a hermit kingdom during the aberrations of the Cultural Revolution and the Great Leap Forward, she profited by the example of successful Chinese capitalist development furnished by Hong Kong, which ultimately influenced its internal policies. The ultimate opening of the American market to Chinese exports, like its earlier opening to Japanese trade, had a liberalizing effect on the governments of both of the great Pacific powers.

It is important to realize that most of the work of the Foreign Service involves foreign relations, not foreign policy. To those who believe that policy should be empirically rather than ideologically driven, this is an important distinction. A denizen of a think tank or presidential subcabinet whose experience of the world is confined to book learning, especially book learning about international relations theory rather than about history, is a person with a different and less humane outlook than one who has spent one or two of his formative years looking into the faces of desperate or disappointed visa applicants. Consular work, whether having to do with visas or with commercial relations, or with the criminal justice system of the country to which a novice is accredited, provides knowledge in depth of a society not easily acquired in other ways; it is where the moment of truth appears

After Hong Kong, Negroponte spent a short period in Washington on the Africa Desk, an assignment from which he sought to be relieved in the summer of 1963. In September 1963, he was sent to study Vietnamese at the Foreign Service Institute in Arlington, Virginia, where he remained until May 1964.

3

VIETNAM

'I hope to God you know what you are doing there. Oh, I know your motives are good, they always are.' He looked puzzled and suspicious. 'I wish sometimes you had a few bad motives, you might understand a little more about human beings. And that applies to your country too, Pyle.'

— Graham Greene, *The Quiet American*
(London: Heinemann, 1973 ed.), 148

The Vietnam to which John Negroponte came in 1964 was an unpropitious candidate for successful Westernization. The French colonial regime dating from the mid-nineteenth century had been notoriously dirigiste and exploitative. The educational system was not highly developed and was largely a function of the Christian minority. The Vichy French, unlike the British in Hong Kong, had not offered serious resistance to the Japanese invasion, and their return thus lacked perceived legitimacy, particularly as it was carried out in a gratuitously brutal manner by the French commander, Admiral Thierry d'Argenlieu, who had previously bombarded the principal port in Madagascar with similar political results.

The fact that most educated Vietnamese were Catholics, that they had been accorded limited opportunities to gain political experience, and that there had been a large migration of Catholics to the south at the end of the French war, all militated against development of a representative polity in South Vietnam. The Americans similarly dismissed the insights painfully gained by some of the more capable Frenchmen, including the French vice commissioner, Jean Daridan; General Charles de Gaulle himself; and some French writers on unconventional warfare whose writings were belatedly adopted as standard texts by the Americans in Iraq.

The limited nature of American interests in Vietnam at the inception of US involvement is attested to by a memorandum by William Gibson as American consul in Hanoi written in January 1949, which remained classified for 50 years until 1999 and was then reclassified Top Secret in 2001 until it was finally declassified in 2008 at my insistence.

Hanoi today is a vastly different city from what it was before 1946. At that time, the city had a population of 200,000 including 15,000 Chinese and 10,000 French. Today, according to a recent unofficial census, Hanoi has a population of 130,000 Vietnamese, 12,000 Chinese, 7,000 French, and

1,000 Indians, a total of 150,000. In the three months' fight for control
of the city, approximately 60 percent of the houses in the Vietnamese
and Chinese sections were destroyed and many of those in the European
suburban area were either destroyed or damaged. Virtually all useable
dwellings are now in dire need of major repairs and even public buildings remain unpainted. The city's water supply is inadequate, the pressure being too low to reach above the street level. Streets are unpaved,
badly rutted, and poorly lighted if at all. Hanoi is surrounded by Vietminh
guerrilla forces. It is unsafe to leave the city limits at all times and despite
the claimed French control of the town, the throwing of grenades and
other terrorist practices are pursued in broad daylight, often resulting in
fatalities.... The railway is mined and sabotaged frequently and the daily
military truck convoy [to Haiphong] is subject to regular attack.... There
are only two American firms (Standard Vacuum Oil Company in Hanoi
and California Texas Oil Company in Haiphong) now doing business in
Northern Indo China. All of the employees of these two firms are either
French or Vietnamese.... There are only four Americans residing in this
consular district other than the three members of the Consulate staff. All
four are missionaries, two of whom live in Hanoi and two in Haiphong.
Of the two missionaries in Hanoi, one, a Catholic priest, has stated infor-
mally that he would not leave under any circumstances and the other, an
aged and bedridden nun, probably would not leave even if arrangements
were made for her to do so... in the event of an evacuation, the Consulate
would have to deal with only two missionaries, man and wife, resident in
Haiphong... it is questionable whether they would agree to leave.[1]

By 1963, the year before Negroponte's arrival, the United States was closely
linked to the cause of Ngo Dinh Diem, who had effectively been installed by
the Americans against the advice of the French. The American regard for Diem
and the roots of it are suggested by Senator John Kennedy's tribute in a campaign book: "Despite the chaos, despite the universal doubts, a determined
band of patriotic Vietnamese around one man of faith, President Diem, began
to release and to harness the latent power of nationalism."[2] The warnings at the
time of his installation were vociferous and prescient. Gibson, who was First
Secretary (later Minister-Counselor) in Paris at the time of the Geneva talks,
spoke with the journalist C. L. Sulzberger in June 1954:

The new prime minister just chosen for Vietnam, Ngo Dinh Diem is a
virtually unknown individual. By sheer chance, Gibson knows him well
and is probably the only Westerner who does. Ngo Dinh Diem is a rather
mystical Catholic of an impractical sort. He has been studying in a Catholic
retreat in Bruges recently and is now in Paris very much incognito. The
ministry of the Associated States here didn't even know a thing about
him when he was named. He is staying at a third-class hotel in Paris and
Gibson is his only contact. He calls up Gibson under a code name and
they meet in places like park benches. He is a completely unreal figure,
but at least he is scrupulously honest.[3]

Later, Gibson sent an unusual top secret memorandum to Ambassador to France Douglas Dillon, Minister Achilles, and Counsellor of Embassy Joyce in November 1954, reporting on a conversation with the French Deputy High Commissioner for Indochina, Jean Daridan, who, Gibson said, "enjoys the respect and friendship of virtually all American officials who have been associated with French affairs…. they would agree with me that there never has been reason to question his honesty and integrity."

Daridan told Gibson he had just refused the French high commissionership for Indochina because he could

> no longer agree to support a policy which no intelligent Vietnamese or Frenchman with any knowledge of Indochina believed in, which had no basis in reason, which had been invented by the 'American Special Services'… and which would result in the absorption of Free Vietnam by the Viet Minh in the near future…. Our attachment to Ngo Dinh Diem, apparently on the ground that he was the only honest man in Vietnam, had, he said, become a fixation. Daridan said that, although Diem himself was honest his advisers, in whose power he was, were not so the end result was the same…. He referred to Ngo Dinh Diem's family advisers with contempt. Diem, a religious fanatic, was putty in the hands of the crafty Vietnamese, Daridan claimed.

The memorandum met with immediate bureaucratic sabotage, K. T. Young minuting to Assistant Secretary Robertson that Daridan "has grossly exaggerated and distorted the situation in so far as the Americans are concerned," whereas Ambassador Donald R. Heath from Saigon, although acknowledging Daridan's integrity, depicted Daridan as one of "the French in Indochina [who] have a very bitter inferiority complex."[4]

Gibson had acquired an enemy in the person of Wesley Fishel, a Michigan State University professor who played a highly important role first as a sponsor of Diem and then as an advisor to him.[5] A report on a telephone conversation with Fishel in July 1954, referring also to Diem's Foreign Minister Ngo Din Luyen observed that "Fishel appeared to dislike Gibson and said Luyen had told him Gibson was pro-French, patronizing toward the Vietnamese, an 'hypocrite' and 'dishonest'."[6]

In September 1954, heavy American intervention had saved Diem from a French attempt to get rid of him. An unsigned summary of events noted that

> On September 13, (French General) Ely told (American Ambassador) Heath of Bao Dai's intention to replace Diem Government. Heath recommended that Embassy Paris sound out Bao Dai and tell him that in our opinion it would be a mistake to replace Diem at this time. On September 17, Daridan told us that unless something positive were done to strengthen the government, Diem would have to go. Nguyen Van Tam was the French candidate to replace Diem. French were now determined that Diem must go and were telling (Vietnamese General) Hinh to 'sit tight.' Heath thought that only the exercise of extreme US pressure on Paris would now save

Diem and thus a nationalist government capable of obtaining support in the country. Message to La Chambre opposing the forcing of Tam in the cabinet was delivered in Paris. On (September) 22 and 23 made clear to Cao Dai and Hoa Hao (sects) that we continued to support the Diem government...strongly urged French to give Diem another chance.

provided the new government included the Binh Xuyen sect and the Army. On September 24, there was a new Diem Government including two generals and seven Cao Dai and Hoa Hao representatives but no Binh Xuyen.[7]

By May 1955, according to Gibson,

The [US State] Department still adamantly insists that the only way to save the southern part of Indochina is to support the Diem government. This is lunacy. Everyone is against him. But apparently the CIA has for the moment bought Diem the support of the sects, including the Cao Daists.... The odds in favor of the Communists gaining all of Indochina no matter what we do, Gibson says, are at least ten to one. And the process will probably succeed before elections are ever called in 1956 as provided for by last summer's Geneva settlement. US policy hopes vaguely to establish a strong enough government in the South (with its larger population) to influence the North favourably prior to the 1956 elections. But Diem, the instrument chosen to carry out this policy, is a failure. We are disillusioned but reluctant to admit it. So we have prolonged this dead-end policy to a point beyond repair. Meanwhile, the French have sourly agreed to go along with us for the present in order to avoid a major split with the United States. But they would prefer to make a working arrangement with Ho Chi Minh, saving Tonkin (the North) from China.[8]

"Gibson is fed up with the reputation that Diem has for incorruptible honesty. He says the Diem family is profiteering heavily. Large restaurants have been bought by their interests in Paris. Bribery and corruption and the sale of jobs are rampant. American aid is being used by the Diem family."[9]

In fact, the United States had marginalized the French by transferring American aid "from the French to the Diem government from the first day of 1955."[10] Diem was not blameless in the subsequent outbreak of further hostilities, although the Viet Minh had left behind arms caches when they withdrew from the South,

[d]espite American pressure, Diem had refused to supply food to North Vietnam in the mistaken belief that the northern regime was about to collapse under the weight of peasant revolts. Thus Ho was given an economic as well as a political motive for reopening the war.[11]

The decision to do so is said by some to have been made by the North Vietnamese in May 1959.[12]

Five years earlier, twenty-five years ahead of his time, Gibson had seen American relations with the Communist Chinese as one of the keys to resolution of the Vietnam problem. In August 1949, in common with most American diplomats in Southeast Asia, he had received a circular letter from Dean Acheson, then Deputy Secretary of State, seeking his advice on whether the United States should recognize Communist China, a subject about which Acheson had a persistent ambivalence.[13]

> If the Vietnamese … have any hope left it is directed to the Anglo-Saxons to whom he looks both to oblige French to grant him full independence and at same time somehow forestall domination of Vietnam by the Chinese as they did with the Japs. In considering all this it is strange that no one locally at least has appeared to consider possibility that Western recognition of Chinese commies might alter military position and threat to Indo-China border … any US step re recognition will probably not influence opinion here one way or another provided it is not taken too hastily and is taken jointly with UK and France. Any independent action would doubtless lead to further confusion and misunderstandings.[14]

This echoed the insight of George Orwell in a newspaper article written at the end of World War II:

> there is very little awareness … of the strategic dependence of the French Empire on other powers. Large portions of it would be quite indefensible without American or British help, and Indo-China, in particular, is very unlikely to remain in French possession without the agreement of China as well.[15]

In fact, it was Chou En-lai's assistance to Pierre Mendes-France at the Geneva Conference, along with Soviet assistance deriving from Mendes-France's neutrality on the European Defense Agreement then before the French National Assembly, that resulted in a demarcation line 200 miles north of that expected when the conference began, and the evacuation by the North Vietnamese of about a quarter of the territory that they held.

In August 1955, the American diplomat John Gunther Dean composed a prescient memorandum entitled "Crystal Balling on the Political Future of Vietnam." In it, he observed:

a) South Vietnam cannot afford to hold free elections or refuse free elections since both alternatives will lead to ultimate Viet Minh control of entire Vietnam.

b) An independent South Vietnam state can only be created with the expressed consent of Communist Russia and China which might be obtained at some future international conference on Far East.

c) If the *de facto* partition is recognized by the major powers as a long-term solution, President Diem may have to broaden his cabinet and to bring in more representatives of the South and eliminate some of the Northern leaders in order to reflect the popular sentiment of a predominantly Buddhist South.

Dean went on to observe that the North Vietnamese estimated that an election would give the Viet Minh 80 percent support in the North and 55 percent in the South. Refusal of an election "would undoubtedly lead to the Viet Minh resuming their guerrilla warfare in the South at which they are so proficient." Diem had estranged the mountain tribes and arms were either "hidden or can be obtained from the North." Negotiations, Dean thought, were realistic. The failure to agree on German reunification at the Geneva Conference suggested that another partition might be acceptable to the Communists. "A predominantly Buddhist Southern state must be governed by its own people to enjoy popular support."[16]

Despite his prescience, Dean found himself the American ambassador to Cambodia 20 years later at a time when the Lon Nol Government collapsed for want of congressional appropriations; this he regarded as a betrayal of a nation "with whom the American people had mingled their blood and had died."[17]

Negroponte's early political reporting in Vietnam is distinguished by its focus on religious differences and tensions between the South Vietnamese and the new arrivals from the north.

Gibson's memorandum was not the only warning about the probable characteristics of the Diem regime. Joseph Alsop, a conservative, indeed "hawkish" commentator, wrote in the *New York Herald Tribune* on March 31, 1955 that Diem was

> narrow, obstinate, and petty … out of contact with the broad mass of his people and the political realities of his country…. The roots of Diem, moreover, are in the dead and gone court of Hue. In modern Indo-China, except for his connection with the small Catholic minority, Diem is effectively rootless.[18]

Diem's ascendancy, like that of many foreign politicians before and after him, owed much to American susceptibility to the blandishments of exiles, particularly those with religious and other allies in the United States, including Chiang Kai-Shek, Jorge Mas Canosa in Nicaragua, and Ahmed Chalabi in Iraq.

The historian Joseph Buttinger charged Diem with "brazenly favouring Vietnam's Catholic minority" and described him as "opposed by the intellectuals, despised by the educated middle class, rejected by businessmen, hated by the youth and by all nationalists with political ambitions, and totally lacking in mass support."[19]

Assistant Secretary of State William P. Bundy writing in 1965 following Diem's overthrow observed that

> Diem's increasingly personal and ingrown methods were well under way as early as 1958. The inside story here is that the State Department attempted to do a lot but was largely undercut by the special and preferred position of the hard-headed and utterly conventional military assistance chief, Gen. Williams.[20]

By 1965, Undersecretary of State George Ball declared: "The 'government' in Saigon is a travesty. South Viet Nam is a country with an army and no government."[21] Diem however had firm control of rural areas, especially those with large Catholic populations.

In August 1963, President Charles de Gaulle invited all parties to the Vietnam conflict to a conference in Paris to negotiate its end, an invitation rejected by the Kennedy administration a month before the president's assassination. This action gives the lie to assertions by Kennedy's hagiographers that Kennedy was looking for a way out of Vietnam. Certainly there was no purpose to seek a way out before the 1964 elections. But the world did not wait on the American political calendar, any more than it did in 1916, when Wilson deferred mediation efforts until after the presidential elections, by which time militarists were in the ascendancy in Germany.

There was fear in Washington that Ngo Dinh Nhu would enter into negotiations with the Communists, one of the forces driving American support of a coup against Diem.[22] By December 1963, shortly after the American-tolerated coup against Diem, the deterioration of his regime was described by a British academician:

> Somehow things had gone wrong. In the name of "defeating Communism" President Diem had flouted the constitution and turned his regime into an authoritarian, single-party government. The national parliament was reduced to little more than a rubber stamp and all political opposition was ruthlessly suppressed.... The opposition movement in the pagodas had undoubtedly been smashed, but only at the cost of disturbing the conscience of every Vietnamese no matter what his religious denomination. Whatever political advantage might accrue, the irruption of armed troops into sacred buildings and the physical maltreatment of religious men and women which few Vietnamese could either condone or forgive may well prove to have lost President Diem the right to rule.[23]

Some, including Roger Morris, who resigned from the Foreign Service at the time of the Cambodia incursion in 1969, blamed the State Department's lack of historic perspective on Vietnam on the purges of the McCarthy era: "the absence of such men during the early decisions on the Vietnam policy left unchallenged the cultural and political ignorance of Asia that made possible the American intervention."[24] This misidentifies the reason for the loss of Indochina expertise. Most of the Indochina experts were involuntarily retired during the Kennedy administration by enforcement of the State Department's "up or out" rule. Several of them, including Gibson, were slated to receive embassies in the newly independent countries of Francophone Africa in the last days of the Eisenhower administration. With the advent of the Kennedy administration, seven embassies in Francophone African countries, those in Cameroon, Gabon, Guinea, the Ivory Coast, Morocco, Niger, and Senegal were parceled out to deserving Democrats from outside the career service.[25] The eminent defrocked diplomat John Paton Davies, a friend of George Kennan and the most prominent victim of the McCarthy purges, noted the true reason for the loss of Indochina expertise: "in a rather novel transaction, some 200 senior Foreign Service officers were brought into premature retirement in mid-1962, while there continued the politicization of the Department of State with pedagogues and politicians."[26] This was "another, but genteel, purge, this time from the liberal center. That the Foreign Service did not win the confidence of the New Frontiersmen is not surprising. Crusading activism touched with *naïveté* seldom welcomes warnings of pitfalls and entanglements."[27] Negroponte, throughout his career, took for granted recurrent such purges at the start of each new administration. He had a high regard for the State Department assignment and personnel system, which, left to its own devices, functioned well apart from the wastage resulting from these periodic bloodlettings.

The plunge into Vietnam was explained by McGeorge Bundy, National Security Advisor to Presidents John F. Kennedy and Lyndon B. Johnson, in rhetoric about American exceptionalism unmatched until similar expressions by Madeleine Albright 30 years later: "The United States is the locomotive at the head of mankind and the rest of the world is the caboose"... "We like Caesar have all things to do at once."[28] In this period, Negroponte shared Eisenhower's view that "the Vietnamese could be expected to transfer their hatred of the French to us."[29]

Prior to becoming engaged in the Vietnam peace negotiations

I was a political reporting officer... almost four years, I spent in Vietnam travelling around the countryside, reporting on political, economic, and military developments; generating literally hundreds, if not thousands, of pages of reports... an overt intelligence collector, just like... a military attaché.[30]

At the time, President Johnson had ordered that every entering Foreign Service officer serve a tour in Vietnam; several decades later, as Deputy Secretary of State, Negroponte came close to enforcing a similar rule with reference to Iraq.

He was assigned to cover seven provinces in the lowlands of central Vietnam for 18 months. Among his associates at the embassy during that time were Richard Holbrooke, Anthony Lake, Frank Wisner, David Engel, and Peter Tarnoff. James Rosenthal, one of the groups, referred to them as "the greatest group I ever worked with. And there wasn't this great demoralization or feeling that everything was going to hell in a handbasket. I think there was still the feeling we would prevail."[31] He flew about on Air Vietnam DC-3s or "space available" military orders. He was initially impressed by the American military's "can do" spirit. It was said by the journalist Georgie Anne Geyer that in this period: "He disagreed fervently with American generals arrogantly keeping the South Vietnamese in the back of the fight." Forty years later he was to similarly note that the Afghans "have not exactly taken well in the past to outside forces."[32]

His former mentor Herbert Levin thought that American impressions of Vietnam were distorted first by French-speaking ambassadors like William Trimble and Frederick Nolting who spoke only to the Christian minority and then by an influx of academic Sinologists who spoke only to the Chinese minority. Negroponte recalled leaving a briefing conducted by General William Westmoreland explaining the frontline role assigned to American forces with the feeling that it meant perpetual war and was later to regard President Johnson's

choice of Westmoreland over Creighton Abrams as commander in 1964 as decisive for the future of Vietnam. His colleague Robert Oakley observed of this
period that "Westmoreland was going to remove all Vietnamese troops from the
front lines; they would be exclusively devoted to the pacification efforts. The
front would be manned entirely by American and South Korean troops." The
replacement of Westmoreland came too late: "by that time there were no effective Vietnamese fighting forces left." Ellsworth Bunker also was to observe "we
were slow in training the Vietnamese .... It really wasn't until Abrams got out
in 1967 that we did it intensively as we should have done."[33] U. Alexis Johnson
concurred in the view that for Vietnamization to have worked, "we should have
started it in the early 60s."[34] In this period, Negroponte also learned of the powerful role that religion can play in politics. "In authoritarian countries, religion
can be one of the safest ways of advocating political subjects." In the spring of
1965, he succeeded Anthony Lake as vice-consul at Hue, returning there again
for a month in the spring of 1966.

He became a friend and tennis partner of Richard Holbrooke, who later
recalled:

> A few months into his tour, John returned home one night to find a
> drunken American seaman prowling his apartment with a knife, looking
> for more of the demon rum. This was not as unusual in those wild days
> in Saigon as it may sound today, but it was dangerous and so, quite unex-
> pectedly, John showed up at my house a few blocks away shortly after
> midnight, took the spare bedroom and stayed for the next year. For the
> record, he was the neat one, Felix to my Oscar.

Holbrooke also characterized him as "the second best Vietnamese speaker in the
Foreign Service [the best being David Engel]."[35] "He could sing in Vietnamese.
He could tell jokes in Vietnamese."[36]

John Negroponte arrived in Vietnam in May 1964 on the same Cathay Pacific
flight from Hong Kong as Engel, a fellow Vietnamese language specialist who
had been a class ahead of him at Exeter, and was detailed as a political officer to
write a series of reports based on visits to a number of Vietnam's 47 provinces.

Negroponte's first visit was to Phu Yen province in July 1964; he reported
that there had been an abrupt change in the province's political leadership,
that there were 2,400 Vietcong there, and that the situation was deteriorating.
Although there was a good new province chief and some successful resettlement efforts, there were bad relations between the 5 percent Catholic minority and the rest of the population, a theme that was to recur in further reports
on other provinces.[37] In early August, he reported on Long Khanh province.
It had French rubber plantations, a Catholic majority that was militantly anti-
Communist and only about 200 Vietcong, giving the government a 20:1 force
ratio advantage. The provincial government was ineffective; there was need for
more police as distinct from troops.[38]

Later in August, Negroponte prepared a report on Phuoc Tuy province.
The government had completely abandoned some hamlets to the Vietcong.
At least two more battalions were needed to pacify the province. The pay of

civil servants was too low. The province was 18 percent Catholic.[39] His next visit, in September, was to Binh Thuan province. The province was 8 percent Catholic and quite poor. There was an able province chief, combatting about 700 Vietcong. There was a rice deficit. There was need for a year-round water supply to allow for cultivation of more than one crop per year.[40]

In early October 1964, Negroponte visited Khanh Hoa province. The deputy province chief had a bad reputation among Buddhists, although the government troops were adequate. There were about 800 Vietcong.[41] Later in the month, he visited Binh Dinh province, a former Viet Minh stronghold that he viewed as the most important and populous of all the provinces. The situation there was deteriorating; the Vietcong were perceived as calling the shots, and more than 200,000 people were under their rule. There were as many Vietcong as government troops and much change in provincial leadership, as well as dissatisfaction with the Vung Tau constitution and the feeling of persecution on the part of the Catholic population.[42] Negroponte viewed his Binh Dinh reports as especially prophetic.

In November, 1964 he revisited Phu Yen and found worsened security, harassment of roads and railroads, political agitation, and an incompetent deputy province chief; the government army "uses artillery excessively, improperly, and to its own detriment."[43] In March 1965, he revisited Binh Dinh province. He recounted a conversation with a Buddhist leader holding unusual views: that the bombing raids against the north were an encouraging development.[44] In May and June 1965, he reported on the provincial elections in Quang Tri, noting the former Viet Minh affiliation of some successful candidates, and that 25 years of turbulent history had created "political nuances…often difficult for a foreigner to comprehend."[45]

In July 1965, Negroponte again visited Phu Yen. There was resentment of conscription and of the overuse of artillery. Captured rebels were stripped and obliged to sit or lie in the sun for several hours, with anti-Vietcong slogans daubed on their backs with enamel paint. Access by road or rail was impossible; there was no gasoline, and there was a shortage of diesel fuel. The Vietcong were undercutting the government rice prices, which "must be impressing local inhabitants." "The Viet Cong can make no further gains…without help from main force units." He bemusedly related a conversation with a local official: " 'Why don't you take us over as a 51st State? It would be so much better than Communism.' In all, a rather disconcerting remark."[46] In October 1965, he revisited Long Khanh. He found the administrator to be incompetent, the provincial council not useful, and road travel to be unsafe. There had been Vietcong successes and there was also a Vietcong tax system.[47] North Vietnamese successes in the later Tet offensive were no surprise to Negroponte and the State Department field officers, who had accurately reported on the deteriorating security situation.

In the same month, he met with Henry Kissinger and South Vietnamese General Nguyen Van Chuan, who criticized the Americans' failure to screen the residents of fortified hamlets. On the following day, he and Kissinger (then a State Department consultant) met with the Buddhist leader Tri Quang, who urged a return to the Geneva settlement with its election provisions and an end to the payment of American troops in dollars.[48] Earlier, Tri Quang had taken refuge in the American embassy during a coup, where he had been debriefed by James Rosenthal. Kissinger, who had a marked dislike of helicopter travel, went on the tour after the legendary Deputy Ambassador Philip Habib, with characteristic bluntness, had refused to see him until he completed his tour, telling him: "You don't know a god damned thing about this place."[49]

In November 1965, Negroponte visited Phuoc Long province, reporting on "devastating" Vietcong attacks, disabling three of the four major plantations. Access could be had only by air or in government convoys. Plantation employment was one-sixth that of the previous year. A provincial civil servant, frozen in place by his draft exemption, complained that he had not had a pay raise since 1952 and that he earned far less money than he would earn with a planter.[50]

By early 1966, as Negroponte's dispatches revealed, in consequence of the Buddhist uprising, central Vietnam for practical purposes was no longer under the control of the central government. Negroponte recalls an episode in which a truckload of Marines with their bayonets in the air inadvertently tore down some overhead banners. When a local leader threatened to burn down the consulate unless an apology was received, Negroponte found himself on the phone with Philip Habib, "the mentor of us all" and Ambassador Henry Cabot Lodge. Lodge saw no reason for anyone to be aggrieved by the tearing down of banners: "When I campaigned [in Massachusetts] they used to write 'Fuck you,' all over them!" Ultimately, after Lodge made American transport available, the central government restored order.[51]

Conditions of life of the provincial reporting officers were described by Joseph P. O'Neill, who was one of them:

> we did everything by road. There were no helicopters. There were no short trips. So you would leave, and it would be four days, five days, depending on convoys and the rest. We would go to Da Nang through the Hai Van Pass, a long, dangerous, and torturous ride. Jeeps. No armoured jeep, but we carried sidearms.[52]

David Engel suffered shrapnel wounds in his arm from what in Iraq was called an improvised explosive device; his experience was not unique. Negroponte had no similar misadventures but recalled being a passenger on a helicopter that was detoured to a battlefield to pick up casualties. He was in a military hospital with a back problem at the time of the embassy bombing on March 30, 1965.

The reporting officers were part of a 26-man political section of the Saigon Embassy under Philip Habib. The unit had been created at the behest of U. Alexis Johnson, "after I concluded during a 1962 inspection tour that [the Embassy] was too isolated from the countryside."[53] According to Robert Oakley, "we lived in a compound of five houses; Habib occupied the one in the middle and his acolytes lived around him." Although the reporting officers were at one point commended by Secretary of State Rusk, the

> reports were largely ignored at the policy level in Washington. In fact, according to Alexis Johnson, worse than ignored, they were denounced by

agencies other than State that found them too pessimistic. Eventually the US Pacific Command and the Pentagon succeeded in having the provincial reports stopped and the section disbanded on the spurious grounds that the reporting was too subjective. They were replaced by a new objective measure of the situation in the countryside, which came to be called the Hamlet Evaluation Program.

This measured the security of hamlets by the number of hamlet officials killed by the Vietcong, an inaccurate measure in many circumstances, such as when none were killed because all had fled. "Everyone recalls that it measured the provinces as over 95 percent secure and stable just before the Tet offensive."[54]

Negroponte, in an unpublished memorandum written in 1969 while he was at Stanford, decried

reliance on reports by the very same persons who consider themselves responsible for progress…. At the risk of sounding immodest, I would say that reports on developments in the provinces prepared by a small group of Embassy political officers—called provincial reporters—were, and perhaps still are, the best narrative accounts by Americans of what was going on in the provinces. I served as a provincial reporter for 18 months and from personal experience would say that the strength of these reports rested in the technique of our work, the absence of any responsibility for the progress of programs and the breadth of our samples…we would talk to as many people as possible—American and Vietnamese—on how things were going, politically, militarily, and diplomatically. We focussed the bulk of our efforts on various local Vietnamese leaders, seeking out parish priests, labour leaders, military officers and others in an effort to get a feel for the situation…it took several and sometimes even a half dozen trips to a particular province before you developed useful contacts…spending about half our time in Saigon we were in a position to relate local problems to regional or national ones. In the summer of 1964, for example, we were the first to report on a consistent and timely basis the rapid deterioration in security conditions in the northern half of the country. The remainder of the official community recognized this deterioration but much more reluctantly and was only firmly convinced of it at the end of 1964 when the war was literally at the point of being lost…our samplings of opinions were normally confined to literate, middle-class Vietnamese in the province and district capitals. None of us had a feel for Vietnamese peasants and it is doubtful that any westerner, except perhaps a missionary, really could. Because of our provincial orientation, we tended to neglect what was happening in Saigon itself…the political and particularly administrative decay in Saigon itself.[55]

When Secretary of Defense Robert McNamara visited Saigon in June 1965, Westmoreland arranged a dinner at which he was seated at a table with an assortment of junior officers from the Foreign Service, the Agency for International

Development (AID), the Central Intelligence Agency (CIA), and the military services. All agreed that Vietnam was at the brink of disaster following the overthrow of Diem and that more American troops were needed.

John Helble, a personnel officer, believed that

> there were only a few people in our Embassy in Vietnam over the years whose Vietnamese was adequate to conduct any serious discussion. John Negroponte, David Lambertson, Dave Engel, perhaps the best, Spence Richardson later on and Hal Colebaugh also. I recall John Negroponte's file.... It was clear that he was a superior officer who would succeed.[56]

In July 1964, Helble, while he was consul in Hue, reported that two North Vietnamese in uniform had been captured in the south, the first such confirmed incident. He was instructed to forward future reports to Saigon rather than directly to Washington; LBJ wanted no disturbing influences on his reelection campaign.

Another reporting officer, William Harrison Marsh, recalls the Military Assistance Command Vietnam (MACV) office "blowing up" over a report that a provincial South Vietnamese militia force was inadequately trained. When Habib attempted to propitiate the military by telling the State Department reporting officer to go down to the affected province to take another look, it was found that "his flight could not land at the provincial capital because the Viet Cong had overrun it." Nonetheless the military "would not change a word of the neutered version that they wanted." The field personnel got little support in their pessimism from Secretary of State Dean Rusk, who was prone to invoke the analogy of Munich over and over again.[57] Bunker's dispatches were filled with body count and other statistical information from the military, leading Richard Holbrooke to later reflect that "almost everything they believed and told Washington turned out to be wrong."[58]

Robert Oakley recalled

> John Negroponte and I spent a lot of time playing badminton. It was a healthier form of exercise than bar-hopping or finding female companionship. Sometimes we would find two other officers and play tennis. Most Embassy officers, including Ambassador Lodge, belonged to Cercle Sportive Saigonnais.

This portrait of innocence is balanced by David Lambertson's recollection of all-night poker games once a week including Negroponte, Habib, Barry Zorthian, and one other.

Negroponte served for two brief periods in 1965 and 1966 as acting consul in Hue, his first independent posting. Forty years later, while Deputy Secretary of State, he was to foster the creation of more small posts in the Third World, for their value both in information gathering and in training of Foreign Service officers. While Negroponte was vice-consul in Hue, there was a potentially violent mass demonstration of several thousand people outside the vice-consulate. O'Neill related: "No marine guards. We all had our weapons sort of sitting around. We hadn't decided what we were going to do, all of us travelled throughout South Vietnam without guards.... All of us were shot at. They did not come in. I still don't know why they didn't come in, but they didn't."[59] The normal security personnel had joined the Buddhist demonstrators. When on leave shortly thereafter, Negroponte was awakened by his father, who announced "They've burned your consulate."

O'Neill deplored the fact that

> we would have an American sitting with almost every Vietnamese official above the rank of deputy district officer. It was foolish. I ascribe this primarily to Westmoreland who by this time had taken over both the political and military side of the war. He did not understand either the US military on the ground or the Vietnamese.... Westmoreland was as narrow-minded as any general I've ever read about.

The French Consul in Da Nang told O'Neill "you have more administrators in my consular district than we had in all of Indochina prior to 1954."

On June 30, 1965, after Nguyen Van Thieu and Nguyen Cao Ky had taken power, Negroponte, functioning as acting consul in Hue, reported that their appearance in Hue had occasioned demonstrations in which placards were borne charging Thieu with being "Diem's Pet" and charging them with complicity in the coups of September 13, February 19, and May 20: "Thieu and Ky could have gotten off to a much less shaky start in Hue if the entire session had been out of doors and more oriented toward the people rather than a select group of guests."[60] In the same month, William Bundy described the Ky–Thieu Government as "absolutely the bottom of the barrel," and George Ball declared that "politically South Vietnam is a lost cause. The country is bled white from twenty years of war and the people are sick of it.... South Vietnam is a country with an army and no government."[61]

Anthony Lake, whose tenure at the consulate in Hue partially overlapped with Negroponte's, remembered him as "an honest hawk, an intelligent hawk, and an affable hawk." It is doubtful that Negroponte would have thus labeled himself.

The ouster and assassination of Diem in 1963, the first of which took place with the acquiescence of Lodge and the Kennedy administration following Diem's alienation of the Buddhists, was followed by a series of short-lived civilian and military governments, several of which fell victim to sectarian tensions. Negroponte saw the assassination of Diem as a turning point and believed that the Kennedy administration's interest in the removal of Diem was an outgrowth of a felt need to be assertive following the Kennedy/Khrushchev meeting. Ambassador Frederick Nolting, who was replaced by Henry Cabot Lodge before the coup, "knew Diem's shortcomings, but he was concerned that if anything went awry, the result would be more chaotic. Of course he was quite right." David Nes, later Deputy Chief of Mission in Saigon, ascribed to CIA directors John McCone and William Colby the view that "to have succeeded in Vietnam we would have had to have had public support for the occupation of the North."[62] That would have raised the specter of Chinese intervention

on the Korean pattern. The British consultant Sir Robert Thompson had similarly cautioned "without Diem we would probably lose within six months.
The quality of the opposition was very poor."[63] The junior officers before
Negroponte's arrival had favored "the devil you know"; Lodge was viewed as
"a distant, rather arrogant, cold, famous person."[64] William Jeffras Dieterich, a
colleague of Negroponte in Mexico, reflecting on Central American experience
was later to observe that "it is fairly easy to overthrow a stupid authoritarian
government, what is hard is to get something to replace it. We proved that in
Guatemala."[65]

Joseph O'Neill discounted the notion that Kennedy would have withdrawn
from Vietnam: "He could not have carried the Catholic clergy if he 'lost' or abandoned 'Catholic' Vietnam, even though Vietnam was not Catholic but Buddhist."
John Sylvester similarly attributed Kennedy–Johnson policy to "the abuse the
Democratic party took for 'losing China.' They were not going to lose another
divided, partly Christian, country to the Communists."[66] Strategist Walt Rostow
by way of justification referred to "the decay of Diem's mind, almost, and capacity, and the attempt by brother Nhu to take over the establishment."[67] William
Colby was to allude in his oral history to "the compulsion that I think President
Johnson felt that he had because of our involvement with the Diem overthrow
to send in our troops; [otherwise] he could have let the thing go down and said
it wasn't his."

Because of Diem's very insularity, Negroponte doubted that Diem would
have acquiesced in the Americanization of the war with 550,000 foreign troops.
Diem's resistance is suggested by the statement that senior American officials
were "primarily interested in getting US combat units into Vietnam, with the
training mission as a possible device for getting Diem to accept them."[68] Diem
was quoted as saying of the advisors: "All those soldiers, I never asked them to
come. They don't even have passports."[69]

General Maxwell Taylor, though eventually acquiescing in the buildup of
American troops, initially expressed the fear that it would "sap the government's
initiative…we think we're winning and will continue to win unless helped to
death."[70]

The Americans welcomed the overthrow of Duong Van (Big) Minh, who
favored exploring neutralization, by General Nguyen Khanh in January 1964.
William Colby observed of Minh that "his only decisive act was to decide to
kill Diem and Nhu," and considered that "the overthrow of Diem was the
worst mistake we made."[71] Reporting on a meeting with the Buddhist leader
Tri Quang in January 1966, Negroponte related Tri Quang's complaints about
Catholic coup plotting, describing them as "probably an accurate reflection of
what certain Catholics would like to do if they could muster sufficient support."[72] In March 1966, Negroponte recorded that another Buddhist leader
"remarked gloomily that the political situation is going from bad to worse.
Corruption increases every day and the masses preoccupied by the rising
cost of living are fed up. Recent appointments of Catholics [were a] rever-
sion to Diem."[73] In June 1965, the day before the Phan Huy Quat government
relinquished power into the hands of the military, the Saigon embassy had
prepared a cable to the American Embassy in Rome asking it to intercede with

the Vatican to relieve Catholic pressure on the Quat government. The Vatican had a keen interest in Vietnam; in 1969, Pope Paul VI told Nixon and his interpreter, Vernon Walters: "You are doing the right thing. You cannot abandon the Christian community or it will be destroyed."[74] This prophecy turned out to be largely accurate.

Negroponte, James Rosenthal, and Engel were the embassy's principal contacts with the Buddhist leader Tri Quang.[75] After Quang had taken refuge in the US Embassy after one of the coups, "a junior embassy official, John Negroponte, was assigned to keep an eye on him," according to Vice President Ky's memoirs, which were inaccurate in that James Rosenthal had the initial contacts with Quang.[76] Reporting on other conversations with Tri Quang, Negroponte noted his observations that the Vietcong repressed Buddhists, that there had been severe repression of them by the government military, and that American aid "was lining the pockets of a handful of high ranking officers and civil servants." Tri Quang considered the newly created advisory council to be inept, and viewed the elected municipal and county councils as the only legitimate bodies. Military self-interest gave rise to the consultative council, as opposed to an assembly drawn from the provincial assemblies. Tri Quang objected to the arming of private groups, Catholic or otherwise, and suggested that announcements of American troop increases should be made at a low level in Saigon rather than a high level in Washington. He thought that the Chinese would intervene and that the Americans would be at war with them for 10–15 years. "Ky and Thieu could not conduct a social revolution."

Engel found Tri Quang to be a "Buddhist nationalist ... a very smart and clever person" with a sense of humor and in no sense a sympathizer with the Viet Cong. When Engel appeared before him after being wounded, Tri Quang used expletives about the Vietcong that would not have been used by a sympathizer. Engel was the interpreter at a disastrous meeting between Tri Quang and Lodge. Tri Quang arrived in a jeep, wearing a baseball cap. Lodge responded to him with "a lot of silence"; there was essentially no communication. Tri Quang had suggested a Buddhist peace initiative; Lodge said this was not necessary; the US Government of Vietnam (GVN) position was getting stronger, and the onus for refusing peace talks was already on the North Vietnamese.[77] In a dispatch to Washington, Lodge described Tri Quang as "brilliant, dynamic, deeply interested in politics, totally ignorant of democratic methods, with a capacity for debate and demagoguery."[78] Negroponte defended Tri Quang as a misunderstood nationalist, earning glares at a meeting that included Lodge, William Porter, and Westmoreland. He also had conversations with another An Quang monk, Nhut Hanh, who now lives in France and indeed accepted an offer from Hanh to buy his Austin Mini car.

Negroponte also reported on a meeting with a Hue University official Bui Tuong Huan, who urged a popularly elected national assembly and said that American aid should involve technical and educational skills as well as commodities. Lodge derided him as an "extremist."[79] There is no indication that Negroponte shared the view of the Buddhists of McGeorge Bundy, who reported to President Johnson in February 1965 that "the dominant Embassy

view is that 'the Buddhists' are really just a handful of irresponsible and design-
ing clerics and that they must be curbed by firmness."[80]

Richard Teare, later an ambassador, observed of the period that

> Someone observed in 1965 or 1966 that we had as ambassador a politician
> from a predominantly or heavily Catholic state, and then under him a
> Deputy Ambassador, a Political Minister-Counselor, a Political Counselor,
> and the Chief of the Internal Unit, John Burke, all of whom were Roman
> Catholics themselves … this was sort of a built-in bias. Certain others, nota-
> bly John Negroponte were caught up in a vague sort of way as more
> sympathetic to the Buddhists, also David Engel. I think there was even a
> term "Bud symp reporting."[81]

Engel recalls that essentially no one among the reporting officers viewed Tri
Quang as anything but a Buddhist nationalist, albeit one skilled at public relations and happy to make trouble for the Catholic-dominated South Vietnamese
government.

Alexis Johnson took the view that "Lodge had a reputation in the embassy
for not immersing himself too deeply in details of South Vietnam's intricate
political structure," relying heavily on Habib. Lodge nonetheless had a sense of
humor, once solemnly telling Negroponte that he would have a chance to "defy
the Viet Cong" by organizing an Embassy New Year's Eve party, an unpopular
festivity from which all the guests fled at the stroke of midnight.

The Buddhists regarded Lodge as no friend:

> While he was packing [to leave] a delegation of Buddhist monks from Tri
> Quang's group had come around to the residence bearing a gift. When
> Cabot opened it, there was a nicely framed picture of a monk burning
> himself to death in the middle of a street. It was later reported in the press
> that after a look of total shock, Cabot politely thanked the group and
> returned to packing.[82]

Although a number of journalists including Robert Shaplen, Marguerite Higgins,
and Richard Critchfield and a 2004 academic study by Mark Moyar[83] urged the
proposition that Tri Quang was a communist agent, a recent thorough academic
study by Mark McAllister rebuts this conclusion and urges that "Tri Quang was
in fact strongly anti-communist and quite receptive to the use of American military power against North Vietnam and China."[84] "The fact that Tri Quang was
later tortured by the communist regime and has spent his life under house arrest
in postwar Vietnam is just one of many reasons to doubt the Higgins/Moyar
thesis." "Tri Quang's intended targets [for his anti-communist and hawkish senti-
ments] were not gullible peace activists or idealistic academics opposed to the
war, but veteran analysts committed to winning the war in Vietnam such as John
Negroponte and George Carver."[85]

In 1966, Negroponte again helped organize a visit by Kissinger[86] and helped
organize the elections to the Vietnamese Constituent Assembly. During this
period, he lived in what Engel described as "a wonderful apartment on the

road leading to the [Presidential] palace." The Assembly, however, unlike the later similar body created by the Americans in Iraq, could not elect a provisional government; the incumbents remained in power, impairing their legitimacy. It was said of the Assembly that:

The Constituent Assembly elected in Sept. 1966 drafted a new constitution to replace the 1956 one suspended on 1 Nov. 1963; it was promulgated on 1 Apr 1967, amid no public enthusiasm but in fulfilment of promises to the US administration, desirous of justifying its support for the RVN against charges at home that the Saigon was a military dictatorship .... The American model is followed more closely, with an executive President and an almost sinecure Vice President, a bicameral National Assembly (Senate and House of Representatives) and hopes for a two-party balance of power. A Prime Minister and other ministers are appointed by the President, answerable to him, not to the Assembly. Either left over for further legislation or ignored are (a) procedures for insuring independence of the Judiciary, (b) responsibilities of ministers—especially in regard to the henceforward decentralized territorial administration—and (c) the powers of the Armed Forces, National Security, and Cultural Councils. The President is C-in-C, but relations between army and Government are not spelled out. He may take emergency powers as before but, this time, subject to ratification by the National Assembly.[87]

Negroponte viewed the process of constitution-making as a credible one for a third-world country. The Americans had imported a New York University (NYU) constitutional scholar, Gisbert Flanz, who had been an advisor on the South Korean constitution. Negroponte deplored a provision which had no purpose but to disqualify Big Minh from political office.

Ambassador Bunker, in his oral history of his tenure, forthrightly declared: "I remember calling in the military and making it very clear to them that we couldn't go along with any division in military ranks at the time of war." The choice between Thieu and Ky was left to the Vietnamese military; Bunker "expected and hoped the Thieu-Ky ticket to win." He thought "Ky was more articulate, rather flamboyant and much more voluble. But Thieu had a certain solidity about him which I think Ky lacked." Bunker was unperturbed at fostering military dominance; "all these countries are more accustomed to authoritarian rule than we are."

Robert Oakley was even more blunt about the thin facade of Vietnamese democracy.

Ambassador Lodge received orders from the White House to transform Vietnam into a democracy. This seemed highly unrealistic, but President Johnson insisted. We did it because we were instructed to do so ... we had hoped that a fine civilian Mr. Huang would step up and become a candidate. But Washington felt that we could not afford to take any chances .... We received word from the White House that either Thieu or Ky would be Vietnam's next President.

Both Oakley and Negroponte "were certain it would be Thieu because he was much more Vietnamese. Ky appeared to be much more Western.... Our policy of democracy was not an 'exit strategy,' it was a cynical move dictated primarily by US domestic politics."

Negroponte was the coauthor of voluminous dispatches about the work of the Constituent Assembly, sent to Washington over the signatures of Ambassadors Lodge and Bunker.

Negroponte seems to have been no enthusiast for the new constitution, viewing it as a facade for presidential dictatorship. Reporting on a speech by a Catholic leader, Hung, Negroponte observed that his speech was "weak and reflects his own prejudice for a presidential system...glosses over possible dangers posed by adoption of a Presidential regime."[88] David Lambertson, former ambassador to Thailand, recalls that "Negroponte and I were basically the embassy's lobbyists. We spent all day in the old opera house advising these Vietnamese politicians on how to draft a really good constitution," with special concern about emergency provisions. They unsuccessfully urged deletion of Article IV disqualifying all former Vietcong from participation in political life. Lambertson regarded Negroponte as "the most sophisticated junior officer I ever came across."[89] Lambertson deplored the American practice of convening meetings of the South Vietnamese cabinet in the American Embassy; Negroponte in Iraq was to be particularly deferential to the new government there.

Lodge's successor, Ellsworth Bunker, sent a series of dispatches to Johnson, two of which reflected the views of Negroponte and Ambassador Eugene Locke, Bunker's deputy for civilian matters. In May 1967, Bunker noted that the Constituent Assembly made

> no provision for a run-off election and the budget allocated to presidential candidates is too small...the military believe that in a single election the 'civilian vote' will be scattered among a number of candidates, thus giving a military candidate a better chance.[90]

A week later, Bunker quoted the An Quang Buddhists led by Tri Quang as complaining that

> We want peace, but we cannot have peace without independence. In reality, what do we see at present? We become more and more dependent in every field: military, political, diplomatic and economic. It is a blatant dependence that nothing can cover up. An American freighter transporting rice fails to arrive on time, and the price of rice visibly increases!"

Bunker noted that in the elections "the military and the refugee Catholics...will insist that peace be defined as victory over the communists."

By May 17, Bunker, expressing his own preferences, noted "the growing separation between Ky and Thieu," and observed:

> If it appears that their rivalry threatens serious damage to the progress toward constitutional government or that the unity of the armed forces is

in jeopardy, we will want to consider using the various means available to us for influencing events here.

After discussing the famous self-immolation of a Buddhist woman, Bunker made clear his hostility to the An Quang group:

the call for a halt in bombing and the withdrawal of American forces without any reference to communist attacks or the need for communist actions to bring peace is a clear echo of Hanoi's demands. The militant Buddhists played Hanoi's game by extreme anti-American propaganda and their efforts to bring down the government in 1966.... This latest action can only deepen the suspicion that the Buddhist militants are infiltrated if not controlled by the Viet Cong.

A week later, Bunker was vehement in refusing to contemplate an election that would pit Thieu against Ky:

If it is necessary to move in, I intend to make it clear to both Thieu and Ky that political manoeuvres which may split the armed forces and further fragment the competing political groups in this country are entirely unacceptable. I will make it plain that the welfare of the country must come ahead of personal rivalries and that we cannot have our enormous investment of men, money and world prestige put at risk by such rivalries.[91]

By May 24, Bunker defined his priorities as "(1)...elections...(2) the pacification program...(3) the revamping and restructuring of the Vietnamese military forces...and (4) the determination of the optimum use of available manpower." Building up the Vietnamese civil service was nowhere on this list. By June 28, Bunker took the view that "Big Minh's return would, in my opinion, be likely to further divide and confuse the military," while lamenting that "we lack adequate means of finding out what the Vietnamese people are really thinking."

On July 5, Bunker reported that Minh was "viewed by most senior officials as a common threat." Earlier, in December 1966, William Bundy had noted that Colonel Edward Lansdale "mentioned Big Minh as having the widest popularity in the country but totally hopeless in terms of effectiveness."[92] By then, Thieu and Ky had reached agreement. Bunker noted "Under the new constitution, the president holds virtually all executive power." "I fear that Minh's return might face us with the problem of a divided military. Despite his considerable popularity, he proved incapable of providing strong leadership and of uniting the military in 1963–4."[93] On July 12, Bunker was even more explicit:

Minh's candidacy could pose a serious threat to military unity. His bid for the presidency might also divide the nation in other ways. The Catholics are strongly opposed to his candidacy and would probably react vigorously if he continues to be a candidate...a clear threat to the essential degree of political stability without which we cannot get further progress toward democratic government in this country.[94]

Bunker overestimated the popularity of Thieu and Ky, projecting that Thieu and Ky would obtain 35–45 percent of the vote in 1967; in the event, they got 34.8 percent of the vote. The most antiwar candidate, Dzu, though "off the chart" for Bunker, got 17.2 percent of the vote; three other major civilian candidates shared 28 percent. On August 30, Bunker lauded Thieu's "dignity, restraint, moderation, and good nature." While he may not have been President Johnson's "Churchill of Asia," he seems to have been the Bunker of Vietnam.[95]

The war prior to 1968 was characterized by optimistic field reporting by the American military and civilians in the AID agencies. An AID official, Robin Pell, noted that "John Negroponte used to say 'Everyone lies a little.' He meant that everyone lies to make what they're doing look a little better than it is."[96] The strategy pursued by the Americans was General Westmoreland's "search and destroy" strategy, productive of large American and Vietnamese casualties and great disillusionment with the war in the United States.

> Westmoreland often predicted that the enemy was going to run out of men but in the event it turned out to be the United States that did so … "Pacification bored him." Westmoreland in effect pushed the South Vietnamese out of the way, thus also abdicating his role as the senior advisor to those forces and essentially stunting their development for a crucial four years.[97]

Ambassador Lodge's misgivings about the attrition strategy led him to the verge of resignation in 1967. In this dispirited period, hawks like the academic John Roche advised President Johnson to "buy time and hopefully do something with it, namely, make the Army of (South) Viet Nam (ARVN) into an army."[98]

The Tet offensive in January 1968 was the decisive event discrediting the war with the American public, although it proved a disaster for the North Vietnamese. Negroponte was on leave at the time it took place. Their overoptimism caused the Vietcong cadres to emerge from hiding and be decimated, whereas the city populations turned against the North Vietnamese. In June 1969, with the replacement of Westmoreland by General Creighton Abrams, who had nearly been appointed in place of Westmoreland in 1964, an entirely different war began with emphasis on pacification of villages by South Vietnamese troops rather than pursuit engagements by Americans. The thinking leading to Vietnamization is said by Anthony Lake to have begun in the Johnson administration, its advocates ultimately including Leslie Gelb, former correspondent for *The New York Times*; Paul Warnke, a former ambassador; and Secretary McNamara. Kissinger had doubts because gradual American withdrawal whetted the North Vietnamese appetite for more withdrawals. Lake thought that serious negotiation should have preceded rather than followed the start of withdrawals, a judgment vindicated by the four-year stalemate in Paris while withdrawals continued. Alexis Johnson agreed: "I thought taking them out would not convince Hanoi to be less belligerent—'feeding the crocodiles' would only whet their appetite … decisions were being made on domestic political grounds."[99] It is accurate to say that "most of the better-known treatments of the Vietnam war have given relatively little consideration to these later years."[100] A similar pattern, in which inept was replaced by competent military leadership only after the American public had turned against the war, was also to manifest itself 30 years later in Iraq.

The American academic George Kahin, writing after Negroponte had become famous and controversial, reminisced about a visit he made to Vietnam in December 1966, encountering Negroponte as a "bright, well informed but cautious and reserved embassy political officer whom Bill Bundy had asked to meet me".

In 1968, in recommending a strategy of "Vietnamization" and "fortified hamlet" pressure on the Viet Cong guerrillas, Sir Robert Thompson estimated, with great accuracy, that "it would take about three to five years of this strategy to force Hanoi to give up and negotiate. For a while, the DRV would continue to hold out by trying to protract the warfare."[101]

Negroponte was actively engaged in the Vietnam peace negotiations from their inception in the Johnson administration. He had been assigned as a political officer at the US Mission to the UN, but a necessary appropriation had not been received, and during the period of delay Negroponte was recruited for the Paris talks by Habib and Holbrooke. A reporter covering the proceedings noted that he and Engel were the Vietnamese translators for the American delegation. (In fact, Negroponte served as liaison officer and Engel as interpreter.)

> The strapping extroverted Mr. Negroponte is one of the youngest [29] Class 4 officers in the US Foreign Service, holding a rank comparable to that of an Army Lieutenant Colonel.... an expert on Saigon's labyrinthine politics [who] knows scores of politicians in Saigon.

Engel was later referred to by his colleague William Harrison Marsh as one "whose efforts for many years went unrewarded by the Service, a self-effacing kind of man but whose contributions were colossal." While they were in Paris, the interpreters lived at the Crillon; most of the talks took place at the former Hotel Majestic.[102] Negroponte appreciated that the war was a "drain on the United States psychologically, politically, morally and in terms of loss of blood and treasure."[103] From May 1968 to August 1969, Negroponte discharged three functions: as recordkeeper for the plenary sessions, notetaker for the secret meetings, and liaising officer; he was assigned as notetaker because he was regarded as trustworthy and Johnson feared leaks. As liaison officer, Negroponte was on one occasion presented with several hundred dollars by Harriman to buy caviar as refreshments for the two delegations at afternoon meetings. Knowing the Vietnamese, Negroponte purchased sweet cakes as well. The Vietnamese descended on the sweet cakes, leaving the caviar to the Americans. By 1970, all of Kissinger's aides were in varying degrees pessimists looking for a Vietnam exit strategy. *The New York Times* bureau, in arranging interviews for the visiting James Reston, placed him in touch with "their best sources, men whose judgment they all respected, Holbrooke, Peter Tarnoff, Tony Lake, John Negroponte, Pete Dawkins."[104]

Some of the meetings coincided with the 1968 disturbances in Paris. Harriman upset his security detail by insisting on going "where the action was."

Negroponte and Holbrooke, despite their lack of French citizenship, participated in the huge parade on the Champs Elysees organized as a counterdemon-
stration by supporters of General de Gaulle.

Earlier, it was said that Negroponte was a skeptic of America's Vietnam
involvement and of its tactical and defoliation bombing raids; as a reporting
officer, he had criticized the overuse of artillery. He was the embassy's expert
on Vietnamese Buddhists and on the Constituent Assembly. By 1970, he was
thought to be a supporter of the Cambodia bombing, though in fact he was on
leave when it occurred.[105] In spite of what are alleged to have been its dread-
ful indirect consequences for Cambodia, some students of the Vietnam War
regarded it as a military success: the long, nearly 1,000-mile frontier separating
Vietnam from Laos and Cambodia rendered South Vietnam virtually indefensi-
ble if there were sanctuaries there, and the North Vietnamese had been allowed
to operate quite freely, with limited protests from the Cambodian government.

> The incursion greatly disrupted North Vietnamese Army operations in
> Eastern Cambodia, setting them back some six to nine months according
> to estimates by the Joint General Staff in Saigon and the Military Assistance
> Command, Vietnam…that it caused grievous damage to Cambodia, the
> Cambodian people and the Cambodian government was not, as [William]
> Shawcross shows, really relevant to the purposes of the policy.[106]

In a candid interview, given in 1976 while he was in exile in Thessaloniki,
Negroponte told Shawcross:

> I never knew very much about Cambodia, I don't think anybody did. I am
> a Vietnam expert, and I always thought of Cambodia as just an adjunct
> to the whole damn thing. I knew what I had to know, but I didn't get
> involved in the gory details.[107]

Some Foreign Service officers such as John Sylvester believed that "The whole
thing in Cambodia happened for Cambodian reasons, the Cambodian elite
had gotten tired of Sihanouk's petty tyrannies and were distressed at how the
Communist Vietnamese were essentially governing on the border areas of
Cambodia."[108]

Anthony Lake and Roger Morris had resigned from Kissinger's staff over the
Cambodian incursion, stating in an unsent draft of their ultimately rather anodyne joint resignation letter that "the costs and consequences of such an action
far exceed any gains one can reasonably expect." Their grievances, however,
went deeper; they were "appalled by the attitudes of leaders of the administration on racial issues" and regretted an "atmosphere of suspicion, manipu-
lation, and malice which we have seen over the last year."[109] According to
Winston Lord, Kissinger "thought that Lake and Morris were being hypocritical
[in linking their resignations to Cambodia] because they planned to leave anyway." Lord regarded Lake as "a puzzling and secretive person to deal with."
Young recalls that Morris, who had become something of an African specialist,
was highly exercised about American policy toward Biafra, acquiescing in the

bloody suppression of a secessionist movement. Nixon was said to believe that the negotiations would go nowhere, the "North Vietnamese were revolutionaries and…there was little prospect we would achieve much." Negroponte was likewise a skeptic about the negotiations.

Richard Holbrooke in June 1969 recommended "reduction in force levels to keep [US] domestic discontent in check—something may give on political front," whereas Anthony Lake and Roger Morris in October 1969 observed that the Democratic Republic of (North) Vietnam (DRV) was "waiting for the enemy's domestic collapse. Vietnamization will become unilateral withdrawal." They counseled a "mad dog" strategy later embraced by Kissinger and Nixon: "we are cornered. We are therefore dangerous—we really care so deeply about a humiliation that we would first act irrationally toward the Soviets as well as North Vietnam."[110] The picture painted by the journalist Theodore H. White is not altogether accurate:

> The [McCarthy] purge ended with a State Department full of junior diplomats who knew that prediction of a Communist victory would be equated with hope for a Communist victory; and who learned to temper their dispatches of observation in the field with what their political superiors in Washington or in the Congress wanted to hear. No field-grade American diplomat, in the long period between 1964 and 1975 had the courage flatly to predict the potential for disaster in Vietnam.[111]

On June 28, 1968, Negroponte along with Deputy Secretary of State Vance and Ambassador Philip Habib attended the Paris peace talks as the American interpreter.[112] Habib said of the younger members of the American delegation: "these guys were all my boys. I took them all with me, most of them were with me in Paris."[113] The North Vietnamese had been successful in conditioning start of the talks on cessation of bombing; their leading historian observed: "It was strategically significant that we caused the US to de-escalate the war."[114] The bombing halts were conditioned only on "the assumption that the North Vietnamese would not attack the cities of South Vietnam."[115] Negroponte described the 1968 negotiations as desultory:

> one side or the other would make a prepared statement and then the other side would reply with a prepared statement, and then there would be a little bit of give and take…not negotiations as you or I would think of them.[116]

Negroponte was frustrated by his role in a place where nothing was happening; this, together with exhaustion, accounted for his willingness to take a year off at Stanford. Johnson had forbidden any concessions that would displace Thieu, which greatly frustrated Harriman, who wanted a visible settlement before the American election "to avert the greatest disaster—Richard Nixon."[117] Negroponte attended a dinner with Davidson and Holbrooke and a North Vietnamese delegate on August 14. In September, he accompanied Harriman and Habib in further discussions. His role was that of liaison officer; in the same month he accompanied Vance at two meetings with the Soviet charge in Paris. Further meetings with the Vietnamese ensued on October 11 and November 3. Vance, like Habib, was a person inspiring great loyalty from his subordinates. The delay in consummating an agreement was due to recalcitrance by Thieu, who opposed any agreement before the election on the accurate premise that he would get more support from a Nixon administration.[118] Negroponte was also present at Harriman and Vance's farewell meeting with the Vietnamese on January 14, 1969 and at the introductory meeting with them of Henry Cabot Lodge on March 8.[119] Harriman was embittered by his experience, considering that Rusk "has done more damage to America than anyone in our time," that Maxwell Taylor was "a fool" and that Bunker "regards the preservation in power of...Thieu and Ky as the central object of American policy."[120] Between the farewell of Harriman and the introduction of Lodge, there continued to be discussions in Vietnamese among junior officers, the United States being represented by Negroponte and Engel.[121]

4

STANFORD INTERLUDE

A university should be a place of light, of liberty, and of learning.

— Benjamin Disraeli, *Parliamentary Debates,*
House of Commons, March 11, 1873

John Negroponte continued as liaison to the North Vietnamese in conjunction with an abortive conference held in July 1969. He was physically exhausted by his liaison duties, marathon all-day shifts as an interpreter being followed by evenings typing minutes and cables to Washington. Robert Oakley recalls that Negroponte had an additional duty: "John Negroponte was both the interpreter and the food caterer—he had to get it so the negotiators could eat in our apartment so that the meetings might be less exposed to public observance [sic]" At Oakley's request, Negroponte was given an assignment as the first State Department fellow at the Hoover Institution at Stanford University from September 1969 to May 1970 where he wrote six lengthy unpublished memoranda about his Vietnam experience under the supervision of Professor David Potter, an historian of the American South and author of a book on the American character. Negroponte also helped teach a course on disarmament with Wolfgang Panofsky. One of these memoranda he circulated to his colleagues in Iraq 35 years later. Donald Norland of the Foreign Service, who was his office mate and tennis companion[1] at Stanford, recalls that Negroponte "had just come out of his Vietnam experience highly frustrated. He had run into Henry [Kissinger] and taken issue with him…. We lived on campus in student housing called Escondido Village." The campus atmosphere was dominated and distorted by the Vietnam War and by the Cambodian bombing in the spring of 1970; Negroponte left Stanford early because of the disruptions, which included the breaking of windows at the Hoover Institution. He had no input into the decisions about Cambodia but would not have been enthusiastic about the bombing. He had been opposed to purely tactical bombing because of its impact on civilian opinion, and regarded all bombing below the 17th parallel demarcation line as tactical rather than strategic. His time at Stanford, in the wake of being at the Paris talks, was one of pessimism about the Vietnam outcome.

The memoranda Negroponte produced in this academic interlude are of continuing interest for the light they shed on our Vietnam experience as well as for their discussion of ongoing institutional problems. They are also personally revelatory; except for a few guarded interviews and some published papers on environmental questions written under diplomatic constraints, they are among the few exemplars of Negroponte's own voice.

The first memorandum,[2] one of the four written during his first month at Stanford, which gave the appearance of each being part of a pent-up flood, was entitled "The Negotiated Solution." It noted that during the period 1964–8, both the Americans and South Vietnamese had assumed a successful outcome of the war and avoided talking about a negotiated solution at all. Our goals in the South were unlimited; the war was a limited war only in that we did not seek to unseat the Northern regime.

In South Vietnam, this picture was shattered by the 1967 presidential elections. The provisional national assembly had "rejected the candidacy of the popular anti-Diemist general 'Big' Minh on the grounds that his declared running mate had once held French citizenship." It permitted the candidacy of a "lawyer of ill repute" named Truong Dinh Dzu, even though "it could probably have also rejected Dzu's candidacy on the grounds of his rather murky financial past." When Dzu ran an unexpectedly strong second to Diem, after promising to negotiate with the Viet Cong National Liberation Front (NLF), he and other candidates contested the selection, and were aided by Vice President Ky as a means of strengthening his bargaining position with President Thieu. After Thieu's election, Dzu was prosecuted for old financial irregularities. "[A]s Dzu languishes in jail, few if any Americans believe he is there for anything but political reasons and I think they are right even though Dzu probably is a bona fide crook."

Johnson's partial bombing halt in 1968 led the South Vietnamese to fear "a quick and unfavourable settlement." "It was clear as daylight that once the bombing question was resolved both the US and the South Vietnamese would have to work out joint and/or separate positions on the whole range of issues affecting the outcome of the war. Little of this kind of thinking was being done in Saigon and certainly not in the right places." Prior to the bombing halt, there were 13 consultation meetings between Bunker and Thieu: "quite sterile and rather typical of high-level US-GVN contacts over the years. Thieu and his colleagues listened politely.... but their responses were not forthcoming."

There were prolonged discussions in Paris on the shape of the table, resulting in an "our side–your side" formula. The GVN balked at the implication "that the VC would be assured a significant role"; there was greater concern about Hanoi's willingness to sit down at the same table with representatives of the GVN.

A tacit understanding was reached about the bombing halt: "[i]n effect we told the North Vietnamese we would stop the bombing if certain actions followed on their part, namely: stopping the flow of men and materials into, through and across the DMZ; stopping artillery and gunfire" at the DMZ; cessation of rocket attacks against major South Vietnamese cities such as Saigon, Hue, and Danang. "On at least one occasion they said that if we stopped the bombing they 'would know what to do.'.... What Hanoi agreed to most explicitly was the participation of the GVN in the ensuing conference."

In Negroponte's view, the risks of cessation could have been taken much sooner, in July or August rather than on the eve of the American election. "[T]he bombing was not significantly hampering Hanoi's war effort in the South ... there weren't many risks involved in the first place." The only way we could have gotten explicit concessions was by "(1) the infusion of additional US troops into the South and/or (2) the resumption of bombing of all of North Viet Nam. Both of these possibilities were unthinkable ... at the time."

There were breaches of the tacit understanding as to military action by the North and because of GVN recalcitrance talks did not get under way promptly; "those opposed to cessation saw each breach as confirmation of their views."

Negroponte went on to speculate as to whether the "tacit understanding" approach could be used to foster "the mutual withdrawal of external forces." Negroponte's conclusion was that

> Hanoi's purpose is not merely to drive out US forces .... Communization and reunification is the ultimate goal ... Hanoi could withdraw some troops in response to US withdrawals but it would never withdraw so many as to jeopardize its political interests in the South.

Negropointe flatly stated his pessimism about the possibilities of a reasonable negotiated solution:

> virtually all the reasonable options facing us in the coming months or years lead to outcomes sharply difficult and less favourable than those to which we committed ourselves several years ago ... we have no real lever- age working for us.

Hanoi was disappointed by negotiations in 1946, 1954, and 1956 and was not ready to be disappointed again.

> Any so-called negotiated solution will likely be a face-saving camouflage of our inability to achieve in Vietnam anything resembling our initial objectives. The principal reason for this failure was precisely our underes- timation of Hanoi's resources and patience and a converse overestimation of our own.

In his second memorandum,[3] Negroponte declared that

> my conversational ability [in Vietnamese] was limited to the most basic discussions of political or economic matters. Because of the specialized nature of my language training I could hardly speak about other matters at all. This was and is a serious problem. At most there are 20 officers in the Department with capabilities in Vietnamese similar to mine. In addition there are two officers whose knowledge of Vietnamese could be charac- terized as good to excellent, almost measuring up to standards expected of linguists at important international conferences. These officers [one of them Engel] were in Paris.

In that era, as Negroponte was later to note, "When the Foreign Service Institute opened its doors, it offered instruction in only 13 languages…. Now every desktop is a learning platform."[4] Later, at a conference at the State Department in late 2010, he recalled that "it took about ten years for a missionary to get to the point where they really felt they could teach religious scriptures."

The military had given hundreds of officers a three to six month course in Vietnamese and a few a full-year course at the Army Language School in Monterey. Vietnamese, like Chinese, requires "at least 18 months to 2 years of full-time study to acquire a solid basic knowledge." Negroponte himself had nine months of formal language training. "A little bit of Vietnamese is a very danger-ous thing since…an incorrect inflection can change the entire meaning of a sentence." French was useful with elite groups educated prior to departure of the French. The Vietnamese spoke bad English; many Americans with some French spoke it badly: "many high-level meetings turned out to be dialogues between the deaf and the dumb…we have never been able to establish with any degree of satisfaction what the Vietnamese really think of us." Negroponte was to return to concern with inadequacy of language training while Director of National Intelligence, finding that linguistic competence at the CIA was less than even that in the State Department. American training in third-world languages bears little resemblance to that once required of British entrants to the Indian Civil Service.[5]

Negroponte then addressed himself to what he saw the shibboleths of "coun-terinsurgency warfare" as initially fostered by the Kennedy administration.[6]

> Before, when we involved ourselves in a war, direction of our efforts in the war theatre was turned over to the military, American press reporting was closely censored and civilian agencies of the US government were relegated to minor supporting roles.

In theory, the Vietnam war was to be run by a "Mission Council" presided over by the Ambassador. In practice, there was "no effective machinery to ensure that orders emanating from the Mission Council were effectively implemented." Bunker lacked

> his own communications with the field—that is to say with the representa-tives of various US agencies operating at the Corps, Province, and District levels. Inter-agency rivalries were rampant…and the degree to which many US officials, including some of the highest, viewed the Vietnam situation almost exclusively in terms of their own personal careers was appalling.

There was complete inconsistency in the field on the question of aid to religious groups: some offices gave subventions to Buddhists, some to Catholics, some to both, and some to neither. Varying opinions were expressed as to the benefits of civilian versus military rule.

> Americans serving in Vietnam associated and spoke freely with US cor-respondents knowing little about such ground rules as "on the record,"

"off the record," "background," and so forth and they were willing to offer quotes on just about any subject no matter how far from their own expertise.

The root problem was that "We could never decide among ourselves what our purposes in Vietnam were. This indecision gave rise to the diffuse and confused nature of our efforts there."

In the fourth memorandum of his opening salvo,[7] Negroponte deplored our failure to define objectives or appreciate the nature of our adversary: "underestimation of his resolve and to a lesser extent, his capabilities. We lack even the most rudimentary information on the workings of the Viet Cong. Our knowledge of North Viet Nam is equally or more limited."

To Americans operating in Vietnam, the conflict had an overriding ideological content and few saw our commitment in qualified terms such as support against an externally supported insurgency or as an effort to help the South Vietnamese freely determine their own future, irrespective of what that decision was.

There was a division between those who saw the war as a police effort requiring the rooting out of Communists from every village; those who saw it as a competition in economic development; and those who saw it as a military conflict requiring the defeat of main-force units.

For Negroponte, the war arose from North Vietnam's determination to reunite Vietnam by force. Diem's success in creating a somewhat viable state had forestalled the North's hope that South Vietnam would collapse. Diem was not going to agree to elections, though he erred in failing to have consultations concerning them, which "would have broken up shortly thereafter in disagreement or dragged on inconclusively for years." The ensuing insurgency and invasion were the products of a single leadership. While

[a] number of American activists both in Vietnam and the US (Bobby & Jack Kennedy figure prominently on the list) saw the war as something special, new, and requiring new techniques … [t]here is nothing new about the Vietnam war. We made the mistake of confusing the tactics used at by the Communists at any given time with the overall nature of the war itself…. a simple look at the remaining manpower resources available in the North could have persuaded any fool that they could eventually have even doubled their effort in the South—and without the kind of political constraints that operate in the US

As a result, we frittered away resources on "a series of frivolous programs" and "excessive reliance on improvisation." What was required was

a more global approach to the whole Indochina question than we have ever been prepared to undertake. To dissuade North Vietnam from pursuing

their objectives we would probably have had to wage war against the
North Vietnamese regime itself—something we have never been prepared
to do and the consequences of which are at this point incalculable. Instead
we chose not to wage war against the source.

This analysis, as we will see, was shared by General de Gaulle and explains
Negroponte's support for the so-called "Christmas bombings" in 1972 and ultimate opposition to the Paris Agreement.

Negroponte's fifth memorandum, produced a month after the first four, dealt
with the vagaries of statistics, and is discussed above in the context of his provincial reporting.

Negroponte's most ambitious paper was produced in March 1970,[8] six months
after the first four. It appears to have been provoked by an article by Barry Zorthian
in the February 1970 issue of *Foreign Service Journal*. Zorthian, Negroponte said,
"somehow manages to infer positive and encouraging lessons from more than a
decade of agonizing and tragic involvement in the Vietnam conflict."

Negroponte declared unequivocally, in terms later derided by neo conservatives as "the Vietnam Syndrome":

> That the United States should avoid future entanglement of this sort at all
> costs short of a clear, immediate and direct threat to our national security—
> to use a ludicrous hypothetical example—say the threat of a Communist
> Chinese takeover of Mexico. We are not a nation with the necessary colo-
> nial experience to conduct effective interventions of this type overseas and
> there is little question in my mind but that we are incapable of the sophis-
> ticated types of counterinsurgency efforts to which Mr. Zorthian refers.

Negroponte's language was a distant echo of the cautionary words of the
American diplomat Lewis Einstein in warning against acceptance of a mandate
over Armenia in the 1920s:

> The same reasons will prevent us from withdrawing in 50 or 100 years as now
> induce us to accept the mandate. We shall in self-defence have to become
> the leading military power in the Near East ... hostages of any power able
> to cut our lines of communication across the Mediterranean ... diversion
> of economic resources which could be better employed in the Western
> Hemisphere [not in] a new and greater Philippines in a land so inacces-
> sible to ourselves and so accessible to our enemies .... [We would be
> required to] devise religious policies alien to our experience. The essence
> of the democratic spirit is little favourable to the assertion of one man over
> another necessary to make the successful administrator of an alien race.
> We have no wide colonial experience. We fortunately possess no particu-
> lar traditions of class domination .... The most certain way to keep a daily
> casualty list in our newspapers would be to accept an Armenian mandate.[9]

Negroponte went on to stress that as of 1970 the Vietnam war was a limited
war—limited in our non-resort to nuclear weapons and the limited use made

of conventional bombing and in that "we have never sought to overthrow the government of North Vietnam." The limitations were largely "in order to avoid unacceptable risks of total, thermonuclear war." The North Vietnamese, by contrast, waged total war, restrained only by "their apprehension of some sort of 'irrational' retaliation by the US such as the bombing of Hanoi, the mining of Haiphong or the use of nuclear weapons." Our initial objective of a militant anti-Communist state on the South Korean model was unlikely to be realized:

> the situation in South Vietnam will gradually evolve towards a state which the North Vietnamese will consider less hostile to their interests and perhaps eventually, say in five or ten years, opt for federation or even outright unification with the North...the period of intervention of 500,000 US troops and massive doses of civilian aid will turn out to have been an interlude which delayed but did not significantly change the final outcome.

To Negroponte, Diem's downfall was the major turning point in the war. It was produced by "the cutting off of our massive commodity import program upon which South Vietnam depended and President Kennedy's statement on nationwide television that Diem had gotten out of touch with the people."

> US officials are [not] capable of determining the proper mix of leverage against and in support of any given regime to elicit certain behaviour on its part without running the risk of encouraging that same regime's adversaries to plot its overthrow.

Prior to Diem's overthrow, the economy was not disrupted in any cataclysmic way, and casualties were at a low level. By the summer of 1964, the Communists determined to move in for the kill. The situation was rescued by the arrival of American troops, and the ascendency of conventional forces on both sides.

> I believe that, faced with a deteriorating security situation such as that which actually materialized in late 1964, [Diem] would have sought a political accommodation with the Communists. I do not think that Diem would have wished to contemplate the disruptive, and indeed destructive, effects of 500,000 US troops operating in his small country, not to mention some 9 North Vietnamese divisions and the Viet Cong regular and irregular forces.
>
> Any accommodation which Diem might have sought would likely have resembled the kinds of compromises the South Vietnamese government will be forced to consider once we have withdrawn all our combat forces. When you get down to the nitty-gritty of the thing, it seems to me an unavoidable conclusion that without massive US presence in South Vietnam, it is impossible to expect a militantly anti-Communist, anti-North Vietnamese regime to survive there. The South Vietnamese need not throw in all their cards in one fell swoop—and they do hold some—but they must come to terms with North Vietnam's superior power position in Indochina...

[J]ust because a war is a limited war it is [not] any the less cheap in terms of conventional military outlays... we deluded ourselves into thinking that a bit of hocus pocus and counter-insurgency gimmickry would do the trick.... Present and future wars must continue to be limited—limited primarily in terms of means but in terms of geography, objectives and number of belligerents as well. For an escalation in any of the latter three can quite logically create unacceptable risks of escalation in the first.

As for the lesson of Vietnam, five years before its end:

counter-insurgency techniques became irrelevant rather early in the game and now we are faced with the difficulty of salvaging enough faith in the doctrine of flexible response so that future interventions will not automatically be discredited... in the coming years we are more likely to let nature take its course in the relations between smaller nations and place more emphasis on the restraining influence we might exert on local conflicts through quiet diplomacy rather than armed interference.

There is no reason to think that Negroponte has altered this general view. His somber view of the prospects in Vietnam was revised somewhat when Kissinger's engagement with the Russians and Chinese made possible strategic bombing that would not have been dared four years earlier, and when General Abrams had been somewhat successful in equipping the South Vietnamese to stand on their own, but not without American economic support.

The Foreign Service historically lacked mid-career training and opportunities for reflection like those provided by the National War Colleges and the Industrial College of the Armed Forces. The creation of a "diplomat in residence" program at some universities has too often provided a means of getting rid of or side-lining unwanted or controversial officers for whom appropriate assignments cannot be found. Negroponte was an extreme skeptic of the value of the Paris negotiations, and his year at Stanford provided a way out of what he saw as a dead-end street. His language proficiency together with the Lake, Morris, and other resignations caused the year to be not a detour but a road to a promotion which caused him at the age of 30 to be designated the desk officer for America's most pressing foreign policy problem. Later, as Director of National Intelligence and Deputy Secretary of State, he fostered new opportunities for mid-career training, suggesting that he found his Stanford interlude of great value.

5

KISSINGER AND THE NATIONAL SECURITY COUNCIL

Saying Peace, peace, when there is no peace.

— Jeremiah VI, 14

In the summer of 1970, John Negroponte briefly served as part of the US delegation to the Disarmament Conference at Geneva, Switzerland, having been reassigned to the Arms Control and Disarmament Agency. He was expected to become expert in chemical and bacteriological warfare. There were parallel negotiations at Vienna concerned with the SALT (Strategic Arms Limitation Treaty) agreement; the Geneva negotiations, which bore fruit, were concerned with the narrower question of banning the use of nuclear weapons on the ocean floor, and resulted in a treaty.[1] Negroponte received his baptism of fire on law-of-the-sea issues writing a long comprehensive memorandum that he shepherded through the bureaucracy and that became the foundation of later American policy,[2] which was to again engage his attention as political officer in Ecuador, Deputy Assistant Secretary for Fisheries, Assistant Secretary for Oceans and Environment, Ambassador to Mexico, and Deputy Secretary of State.[3]

Negroponte was enthusiastic about the arms control assignment and about life in Geneva. He had turned down an offer to be personal assistant to Secretary of State William Rogers. As a result of the resignations of Roger Morris, Anthony Lake, and others in the wake of the Cambodian incursion, Negroponte was called to the West Wing, where he was greeted by Kissinger and former Secretary of State Cyrus Vance. "There's Negroponte!" Kissinger exclaimed. "I'm going to hire him so he can resign from the White House in protest." Vance declared "Well, you couldn't be getting a better man." Negroponte was assigned to the NSC staff under Kissinger, rising to become the principal officer for Vietnam, then the central concern of US foreign policy. Philip Habib recalls "when he came back [from Stanford], Henry asked me to have him for the NSC and I gave him a high recommendation."

Kissinger brought five staff people into the NSC, including Anthony Lake, Roger Morris, Winston Lord, Bill Watts, and Larry Lynn. David Young, a lawyer and not a Foreign Service officer who was also brought by Kissinger to the

NSC in an administrative role, recalls Negroponte as being "unflappable" and the least outwardly egotistical of Kissinger's staff members; he did not behave as someone with an exaggerated view of his own importance. Nonetheless, he stood his ground with Kissinger, who was frequently given to making wounding remarks to his associates. Young regarded him as a "civil servant of the highest caliber." When Negroponte joined the staff, owing in part to a demand for his interpreting skills and in part to the Lake and Morris resignations, together with that of Watts, he, Lord, and Richard Smyser prepared briefing books for Kissinger as well as strategy papers for Nixon's approval, as well as opening statements, responses, and contingent proposals for the secret talks. They were periodically flown to a French military airfield in central France, the cover story being that the flight was a training flight for the Air Force. From there, a French military plane took them to a military airfield outside Paris, where they were joined by Vernon Walters, military attaché in Paris. They were then taken in a rental car to Walters' apartment, where they were given code names to disguise their identities from Walters' French cleaning lady.[4] After 4–10 hours of meetings, they were taken to a nearby safe house; on the trip back to Washington, they prepared verbatim transcripts and memoranda for Nixon. There were 19 such trips in the course of the negotiations.[5]

Negroponte had gone real estate shopping for a "safe house," the requirement being that it had to have two separate wings for delegations. He had a hard time explaining why he wanted such a large house, finally declaring that his uncle was a *bricoleur* (fixer upper).

Kissinger's known practice of wiretapping members of his staff, supposedly to respond to Nixon's obsession about leaks, did not improve staff morale. Lake was convinced that he was tapped because Kissinger knew he was discreet and that taps would not reveal indiscretions. Engel later realized that he was probably tapped when Kissinger asked where he was staying and later asked "what are you going to do, give that to your mother?" thus revealing awareness of Engel's frequent conversations with her. Negroponte appears not to have been tapped, but he had some general suspicions of what was going on, once waving his hand at the Old Executive Office Building and saying: "they're doing funny things in there." Young had been commissioned by Kissinger to plug "leaks" after the publication of the Pentagon Papers. Kissinger, rather than the much-maligned H.R. Haldeman, Nixon's White House Chief of Staff, was responsible for the Nixon administration's violent reaction to this development; Haldeman regarded publication of the papers as an aid to the Nixon administration, as they dealt entirely with the Kennedy–Johnson policies. Kissinger has justified his concern on the basis of the possible effect of leaks on the secret start of negotiations with China; whether this concern or mere self-importance fuelled the lawsuits and wiretaps is a matter of some dispute. Negroponte in his later career had a somewhat philosophical attitude toward "leaks": "in Washington, everything leaks eventually." What is certain is that Kissinger's obsession had a highly deleterious effect on the Nixon administration and many of its members, including the president. The suits over the Pentagon Papers caused the leading newspapers to devote more resources to the Watergate break-in than they otherwise might have; a break-in at the office of Daniel Ellsberg's psychiatrist implicated both John Ehrlichman, Nixon's counsel and assistant, and David Young; the latter was spared prosecution by a grant of immunity in exchange for testimony. He redeemed his almost inexplicable youthful misstep, on which he reflected in a lecture at Yale 25 years later,[6] by an especially useful later career—as the founder of the private open-source intelligence service Oxford Analytica.

With the advent of the new administration in 1969, the Paris talks had taken on a new seriousness. Johnson, until the end of his administration, had thought in terms of military victory. The Foreign Service officer Robert Duemling observed that "This [Nixon] administration decided to go for a negotiated settlement. The whole policy changed and [Marshall] Green was part of that."[7] There were further discussions with the North Vietnamese in 1971; on May 30, for the first time, Kissinger abandoned a demand for mutual withdrawal.[8] The abandonment was ambiguous; an October 1971 proposal stated that armed forces must remain "within their national frontiers," which meant different things to the north and south; a similar ambiguous statement had been made in a presidential speech on October 7, 1970 and later in a speech on January 25, 1972, as Kissinger pointed out in his memoirs.[9] The so-called "leopard spot" approach to the delineation of ceasefire lines allowing North Vietnamese troops to remain in enclaves in the South was said to have originally been thought of by Cyrus Vance during the Johnson administration but was not then proposed because Harriman thought it would make no difference.[10] Kissinger's former aide, Roger Morris, who resigned in protest against the "fishhook shaped" Cambodian incursion, was not alone in his uncharitable assessment:

> To both the Russians and North Vietnamese he [Kissinger] formally renounced the old tenet of mutual withdrawal, a point he had been coyly ignoring but never making explicit for some months. Without bothering to consult his ally in Saigon, General Thieu, Kissinger now agreed to the presence in the south of at least 100,000 North Vietnamese troops. It was a surrender that forever haunted his diplomacy, became an important factor in Alexander Haig's rise (Haig was US Secretary of State under President Ronald Reagan and White House Chief of Staff under Presidents Richard Nixon and Gerald Ford), and would sooner or later doom any postsettlement non-Communist regime in Vietnam.[11]

"The blunder was one of the worst among many in America's diplomacy in Asia."[12]

The approach contrasted markedly with that of Pierre Mendes-France at the Geneva conference in 1954, which, as a North Vietnamese history acknowledged, focused on the "adjustment of regions in each country and each battlefield based on the exchange of land" and which was accompanied, even as the French withdrew from Hanoi and Haiphong, by the transfer to them of areas in the South with a population of more than two million,[13] and the movement of about 130,000 North Vietnamese troops to the north. The French, with the aid of Chou En-lai, first premier of the People's Republic of China, negotiating from a position of weakness in the wake of Dien Bien Phu, secured a border at the 17th parallel, and a two-year delay in elections and in the final withdrawal of French troops, which did not take place until April 28, 1956. The French also secured a provision for free emigration, benefiting more than a million Catholics; the North Vietnamese thereafter ruefully observed of it "we thought that this provision concerned government functionaries, troops, and their families only. We did not guess this was a proposed scheme to force Catholic people to South Vietnam."[14] It was not until February 1955 that the border was closed to emigration by the North Vietnamese.[15] The significance of this was appreciated by the independent and astute Senator George Aiken of Vermont (also a former governor of that state):

> there are altogether too many candidates and others who are going too far in taking the position that Hanoi is right and the United States is wrong. They completely overlook the fact that North Vietnam slaughtered an estimated 200,000 people after the French evacuated Dien Bien Phu in 1954 and undoubtedly would have killed as many more had the United States not seen fit to transport the refugees, nearly all Catholics, to South Vietnam where they would have at least temporary security.
>
> There was so much persecution and actual killing of the Catholic population at that time that the United States finally sent ships to move close to one million persons to South Vietnam. Of course when they got there we felt responsible for their welfare, and that responsibility led to our involvement in the Vietnam War, which lasted for ten years. This was just another example of the saying that "the road to Hell is paved with good intentions."[16]

Alexander Haig was later to observe:

> My own mental model of a peace agreement was the Korean settlement, which removed all communist troops from South Korea and even banned the communist party there. This had been achieved after years of stalemate through the threat of using overwhelming force against the enemy.[17]

The somewhat parlous state of the South Vietnamese government during this period is suggested by a memorandum "used for ideas by John Negroponte" in drafting [a] proposed memorandum to the president in September 1971. The memorandum, prepared by Josiah Bennett, noted that Thieu had held only one meeting with the foreign press in 15 months; suggested that military district chiefs be gotten rid of, that provincial and municipal chiefs be elected, and that a decree authorizing the prime minister to remove provincial counselors be revised. The memo also urged removal of the more notoriously corrupt generals, a withdrawal of the military from economic management of a military bank, and army transportation companies "which detract from the basic mission, open opportunities for corruption, and make bad economics." The memo also urged that there not be a wave of arrests after the elections, that some of the more blatantly rigged elections be invalidated, and that there be wage increases for civil servants and soldiers and a more just tax system in the interest of "improving the reputation and performance of the administration during President Thieu's second term."[18]

Kissinger was steadfast in refusing to make Thieu's removal the price of an agreement. Negroponte agreed with this, pointing out rather paradoxically "that Minh as President would have difficulty in making moves of accommodation to the enemy because he was not trusted by the northern Catholics and senior military officers."[19] Beginning in June 1969, Averell Harriman, a diplomat and former governor of New York State, held a series of meetings with Kissinger in which he promoted the cause of Big Minh. On June 14, Harriman told Kissinger and Anthony Lake that they should strive for an agreement that would postpone the unification of Vietnam for five years.

> Mr. Kissinger stated that we are not wedded to President Thieu and had avoided personal commitments to him at Midway.... But he saw no purpose in taking actions now which would damage Thieu's position.... Governor Harriman warned that Ambassador Ellsworth Bunker would complicate efforts to achieve a political settlement and urged his removal.

On July 8, Harriman urged "an advisory council consisting of army officers and civilians representing all non-communist groups might be useful, but with only advisory functions, not executive. The chairman of this group might be Big Minh." On September 19, Harriman told Kissinger and Lake

> that we should cease wedding ourselves so closely in public to Thieu. He criticized Thieu's failure to rally non-Communist forces, described his recollections of Thieu's past "trickiness", and argued that Thieu is not a good negotiating instrument.... Returning to the importance of broadening the government in Saigon, Governor Harriman suggested establishing a council of notables including men like Big Minh (Duong Van Minh, a Vietnamese general and politician) and General Tran Van Don (a general in the army of the Republic of Vietnam). The council should be given authority and advice with respect to the negotiations. Harriman did not mean to imply that the Thieu government should be dropped.

In September 1969, Harriman reported on a conversation with Senator Tran Van Don.

> He underlined the need to bring into the government representatives of the religious groups—Buddhist, Catholic, Hoa Hao, Cao Dai—and the labor unions...into a "government of unity" either as ministers or as a Council of Notables with real power. He considers Big Minh the obvious man to head such a group.[20]

In January 1971, Averell Harriman held another meeting with Kissinger in which he promoted the cause of Minh:

> Harriman felt that we should back Big Minh because he was one of the ways by which we could get out. If Minh won the election against Thieu, he would then come to an agreement and we could then get out. The only

other way out would be for Thieu to put some new players in Paris and in his Cabinet. Kissinger said that he had heard that Big Minh was not that bright. Harriman said, "Yes, everyone has always said that—i.e., he is a nice guy, but lazy. Yet I've gotten more and more indicators from Vietnam that he is likely to win. In any event, I don't see how we are going to get out otherwise." Kissinger mentioned that he had sent Negroponte and some other people out to see what their impressions were of Thieu's chances and Negroponte had come back quite impressed. He thought Thieu would beat Big Minh. At this point Harriman seemed to lose his composure a bit. He said that the most important thing was that we get out of Vietnam. He would not take a cut and run attitude but would advocate a definite schedule.[21]

Negroponte thought that Harriman's view was shaped by his success in negotiating the neutrality of Laos under Prince Souvanna Phouma.

William Bundy later wrote of Big Minh: "Given every chance of leadership after the overthrow of Diem in 1963, he had failed miserably".[22] Lodge in 1964 had similarly disparaged him: "Khanh is definitely the best bet in this country."[23] Ellsworth Bunker for his part, as Harriman understood, took the view that "the current incumbent is far more qualified than any other candidate on the scene."[24] The American journalist Arnold Isaacs described Thieu's chief defect: "For Thieu, the Army and the Americans were allies enough."[25] In early 1972, Bunker acknowledged that

> Lack of stirring leadership and abuse of power are no doubt major contributors to South Viet Nam's persisting inability to develop a viable political consensus. The body politic, although clearly non-communist, remains split and divided along religious, racial, personal and philosophical lines.[26]

The instability following the American-encouraged ouster of Diem weighed in this decision; it would have been bad to have first overthrown Diem and then Thieu.[27] Both Diem and Thieu were Catholics with appeal chiefly to an influential and embittered minority within the South Vietnamese population, although Thieu had the advantage over the nominally Buddhist Ky of not being from the North. Diem was credited with having built a structure in the countryside which came unraveled after the coup.[28] According to Bunker, Lodge felt that Ky was the more dynamic of the two; Bunker preferred Thieu. In September 1971, in a meeting at which Negroponte was present, Vice President Ky had warned Haig that

> if Thieu remains in power and continues his present policies it will be very difficult for South Viet Nam to survive, not in the next five to six months but over a period of several years. When the United States has withdrawn, then the power struggle with the Communists will begin. Ky said that with Thieu in power he saw no hope for success in such a struggle.[29]

In 1972, Negroponte was heavily involved in preparations for Nixon's summit conference with the Russians. An atmosphere of interdepartmental intrigue surrounded preparation for these negotiations; it was later found that the Joint Chiefs of Staff were using Yeoman Charles Radford, a Naval clerk attached to the State Department, to obtain information on the State Department's attitudes.[30] In February 1972, Negroponte recommended against a suggestion by Deputy Ambassador to South Vietnam William Porter that the Paris talks be suspended unless there was access to prisoners by a neutral body and an exchange of sick and wounded prisoners. Negroponte found some merit in the idea, "very much in keeping with his innovative style" but recommended against "rocking the Paris boat."[31] Negroponte attended meetings of the Washington Special Action Group set up to prepare for the summit as one of the National Security Council (NSC) representatives along with Haig and others, including John Irwin, Deputy Secretary of State at the State Department, and Richard Helms, director of the Central Intelligence Agency. On March 30, 1972, Negroponte speculated that Hanoi was indicating willingness to talk in April because it expected to derive benefit from its new military offensive.[32] He also cautioned against "excessive emphasis on the prisoners of war (POW) issue, if we get a settlement we'll get our POWs back anyway."[33] On April 22, 1972, he was present at Kissinger's first meeting with Leonid Brezhnev, General Secretary of the Communist party, and Andrei Gromyko, minister of foreign affairs, at a guesthouse outside Moscow, along with Helmut Sonnenfeldt, Winston Lord, and Peter Rodman.[34] At that meeting, Nixon

> told an astonished Brezhnev that the United States would be willing to accept a ceasefire in place in exchange for the departure of the North Vietnamese forces that had entered South Vietnam since the start of the offensive on March 31. This was a veritable diplomatic bomb; Washington had never before explicitly agreed to let any North Vietnamese forces stay in the South.[35]

Negroponte stayed in a Politburo dacha. When he asked to swim, he was escorted to a Politburo locker room with the names of the members on the lockers. When a Xerox machine broke down, Kissinger held a SALT modification up to a chandelier and pretended to command General Yuri Andropov, head of the KGB, to produce seven copies of it. Relating his failure to Foreign Minister Gromyko, Kissinger was met with the reply that "that camera in the chandelier was installed by Ivan the Terrible and broke down a long time ago!"

On April 24, Alexander Haig passed on the President's compliments to Sonnenfeldt, Negroponte, Lord, and Rodman for their work in Moscow.[36] However on April 30, Nixon, in a memorandum to Kissinger, voiced displeasure with a memorandum in one of his briefing books prepared by Negroponte entitled "Possible Flexibility in Our 8 Point Plan":

> Under no circumstances in talking with them is the term "reduction of the level of violence" to be used. I saw it in one of the papers that someone on your staff prepared prior to your trip to Moscow. This is the kind of gobbledegook that Johnson used at Manila and also that was talked about at the time of the 1968 bombing halt. It means absolutely nothing at all

and is too imprecise to give us a yardstick for enforcement. Now is the best time to hit them. Every day we delay reduces support for such strong action.[37]

A second memorandum: "What Do We Demand of Moscow and Hanoi" prepared by Negroponte and Winston Lord urged: "Our stick is our bombing of the North and our naval deployments, with specific reference to Haiphong. Our carrot is a conciliatory posture on summit-related topics."[38]

Negroponte was present along with Kissinger and Lord at Nixon's meeting with Brezhnev in Moscow on May 24, after a comic opera episode in which he and Lord were left behind with Nixon's briefing papers and talking points and were driven at 85 miles per hour by a cooperative Soviet police chief to the dacha where the meeting took place.[39] According to Winston Lord, "we had visions of losing our jobs due to a disaster at the meeting or holding up the meeting while they waited for us." Brezhnev had taken Nixon out on a boat, but Lord and Negroponte nonetheless were "just frantic for about 45 minutes." "The session gave us some interesting insights into just how mildly the Soviets are playing the Vietnam issue." "Acceptance of the communist political proposals [for a three-segment South Vietnam government including neutralists] would result in a communist takeover in the South and reunification with the North in very short order." Lord speculated that North Vietnamese delegates might appear in Moscow during the summit:

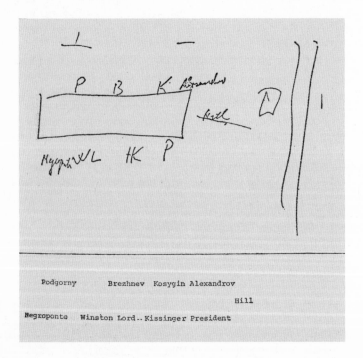

Kissinger Sketch of Brezhnev Meeting

I come down hard against the President's seeing either of these two men for the obvious reasons—there's a shooting war going on with an ally and the President has never met Thieu, at least not while in office. This is not to mention the military, political and psychological reverberations of such a meeting on what we are attempting to accomplish in the South.[40]

He went on to suggest:

I think a proposal to resume plenaries at this stage might even be a useful initiative on our part. It costs us nothing, provided it is unconditional and does not inhibit our military options. It would also be a minimum achievement which both sides could point to in the absence of any greater Vietnam breakthrough...if we agreed to resume the meetings say two weeks from now—June 8—I suspect the military situation will be well enough in hand to press the ceasefire theme in all earnest.[41]

In the Kissinger files there appears a draft memorandum from Kissinger to Nixon implementing Negroponte's proposal, presumably prepared by Negroponte, not initialed by Kissinger; there is no indication that the Nixon saw it.[42]

On May 6, Kissinger organized a meeting in the White House Situation Room on a "Contingency plan for operations against North Vietnam". Present were Kissinger, Haig, various military and CIA personnel, and Negroponte, Lord, John Holdridge, Richard Kennedy, and Jonathan Howe from the NSC staff. Seymour Hersh, journalist for *The New Yorker* magazine, noted that the NSC staff under Haig's direction had been militarized; Howe, Holdridge, and Kennedy all had military backgrounds.[43] Negroponte emphatically supported the proposed blockade, interdiction of rail lines, and mining of ports:

the actions would have a major impact on ARVN morale and thereby greatly increase their fighting effectiveness. He stressed that the Government of North Vietnam was in a fairly precarious position and that mining and all-out bombing could result in a shake-up of the current power structure.... He felt the result would be quicker and more decisive than others anticipated. The morale factor would be a key to the success of the ARVN.

Nothing like this strategic bombing had been considered earlier. Walt Rostow during the Johnson administration had toyed with the idea, but it had been rejected because memories of Chinese intervention in the Korean War were still fresh. Two things had changed during the intervening period: Kissinger's opening to China, made possible by China's fear of Soviet interference with its nuclear program, and the Soviet Union's need for American wheat.

Winston Lord opposed the proposal: "losses would exceed gains."[44] Secretary of Defense James Schlesinger later also expressed his agreement with Negroponte's evaluation: it was necessary to go for the heart of the opponent's power. As noted, the United States had taken no military action prior to 1972 to shut off the flow of *matériel* into the war zone[45] because of fear of Soviet or Chinese intervention. Afterward, Kissinger called Negroponte and

George Carver into his office. According to Seymour Hersh, "Kissinger was surprised at Negroponte's strong endorsement; he had been known to oppose the earlier bombings of North Vietnam. This escalation was different, Negroponte explained; now the White House was going for the jugular."[46] Kissinger delightedly reported to the president that "all but one of his staff were for the blockade, including his Vietnam expert, who is something of a dove."[47]

Interestingly, at the outset of serious American involvement in the war in 1964, General Charles de Gaulle had indicated to Ambassador Charles Bohlen that the United States would have French understanding, though not support, if the United States "adopted a more vigorous policy that had some chance of success, that is attacking North Vietnam" to quote a memorandum from Ball to Rusk reporting on a conversation with French Ambassador Herve Alphand. Walt Rostow during the Johnson administration had speculated that

> could he have used military power in a way that would have forced the
> go-no-go decision on Hanoi, Moscow, and Peking at some higher risk of
> a larger war—how much—notably with respect to mining the harbors or
> trying to cut the infiltration routes on the ground north of the DMZ but
> not very far north?[48]

However, as noted by Alexis Johnson, memories of Korea and General Douglas MacArthur's "March to the Yalu" were still fresh.[49] Bohlen confirmed that de Gaulle had been explicit in indicating understanding, but at no point pledged support.[50] De Gaulle's overall assessment of the American enterprise in Vietnam was expressed to Bohlen the following year:

> It was not detrimental to the interests of the free world, including the
> US if all of Vietnam, Thailand and Laos were to have Asiatic communist
> regimes. Asiatic communism in his view would not be either Chinese
> or Soviet communism but would follow its own patterns and emergent
> nationalisms would control the future of these countries.[51]

In March 1969 at the time of President Dwight Eisenhower's funeral, de Gaulle met with President Nixon and Vernon Walters, and advised that "when it was clear that the US was going to leave, [the Vietnamese factions] would get together and form some type of transition government."[52]

After bombing of the rails and a port blockade began, it could accurately be said that "the new strategy was working. In 1971, it was estimated that North Vietnam imported over two million tons of war materiel. By the end of May 1972 imports were down to a trickle.... Rail traffic was virtually stopped."[53] To a greater extent than was realized by public opinion in the United States, the Vietnam War had the attributes of a conventional rather than guerrilla war. The strategic hamlet program and its successor, the famous or infamous Phoenix Program,[54] a counterinsurgency led by the CIA, reduced the power and influence of the indigenous South Vietnam guerrillas, the Vietcong. As Negroponte once put it, contrasting Vietnam with Iraq, "In Vietnam, the cities were secure; the province capitals were secure. I walked around that country as an unarmed civilian for almost four years without having any serious brushes.... Whereas, in Iraq, even the capital is highly insecure."[55]

On May 8, Negroponte was the notetaker at a NSC meeting at which the proposed escalation was discussed. Secretary of Defense Melvin Laird entered a partial dissent, alluding to diversion of funds and observing, "If you are to have a viable policy, you can't break down your whole force position, you've got to have the support of the people and the Congress."[56]

On May 23, Negroponte attended a meeting with Gromyko at which Kissinger gave his consent to a tripartite electoral commission including the Government of Vietnam (GSV), the Vietcong, and "third force" neutrals, and at which Kissinger proffered that the bombing might end before the return of all prisoners of war. Negroponte expressed concern about the acceptability to Thieu of the tripartite electoral commission, leading Kissinger to exclaim: "Well, they [the North Vietnamese] bought it, didn't they? They're going to help us."[57] On July 14, Negroponte cautioned Kissinger that

> the Communist side continues to reject any kind of ceasefire which does not assure them military and political superiority in South Vietnam ... [they] still intend to use their bargaining leverage—principally over POWs—to achieve both of these objectives.[58]

In August and September, Haig and Negroponte went to Saigon to discuss this proposal with Thieu; on September 13, Negroponte urged Kissinger to go to Saigon for this purpose, leading him to respond "I don't want your stupid State Department advice on going back to South Vietnam."[59]

In July 1972, Negroponte effectively brokered a difference of opinion between Kissinger and the Defense Department concerning the future use of draftees in Vietnam. "We don't know whether this decision [exempting draftees] is firm or not. Laird's fall-back position is as the announcement is phrased, i.e. no draftees after Sept. 1." In September of the previous year, he reported on a luncheon in Washington with a Polish diplomat, noting that "the Pathet Lao had conveyed the strong impression to the Poles that American prisoners in Laos would be dealt with as part of an overall Vietnam settlement." He also rebuffed a complaint from the Pole that the United States had not responded to a seven-point Vietcong proposal that "was simply designed to cut out the GVN [government of Vietnam]. This we could not accept."[60]

By August 1972, Negroponte had earned Kissinger's high esteem. Kissinger addressed a memorandum to the President with a letter of commendation annexed, reciting that Negroponte had

> made a particularly valuable contribution in the development of our Vietnam policy. Although he is a relatively junior Foreign Service officer, I think it would be appropriate to recognize his significant contribution as we enter another intense phase of negotiations.

Kissinger was grateful for Negroponte's support on the strategic bombing issue. The letter signed by Nixon lauded the counsel you provided during the volatile period of the last South Vietnamese Presidential elections, the knowledge and conviction you displayed during deliberations concerning my decision of May 8 and the outstanding work you have done in assisting Dr. Kissinger in preparing for his negotiations in Paris …. That you could demonstrate such deep understanding and professional excellence at your age is indeed a high compliment.[61]

The advice about the elections referred to was Negroponte's recommendation that the elections not be postponed after the withdrawal of Ky; Negroponte saw

REPRODUCED AT THE NATIONAL ARCHIVES

DECLASSIFIED
Authority *EO 12958*
By *MWB* NARA Date *5/7/08*

THE WHITE HOUSE
WASHINGTON

August 4, 1972

Dear John:

Your contributions during the past year in developing our Vietnam strategy have been invaluable, and I want you to know how grateful I am. I have been particularly impressed by the counsel you provided during the volatile period of the last South Vietnamese Presidential elections, the knowledge and conviction you displayed during deliberations concerning my decision of May 8, and the outstanding work you have done in assisting Dr. Kissinger in preparing for his negotiations in Paris.

That you could demonstrate such deep understanding and professional excellence at your age is indeed a high compliment, and is especially gratifying to all of us who look forward to working with you in the future.

With warmest regards.

Sincerely,

Richard Nixon

Mr. John D. Negroponte
National Security Council Staff
Washington, D. C.

Commendation from Nixon: Age 33

Ky's demand for postponement as an illegitimate ploy that should not be permitted to succeed. Negroponte subsequently sent Kissinger a memo urging that the State Department, which had been "out of the loop," be informed at least of the broad outlines of what was taking place in Paris:

> the texts of our various proposals—the text of the DRV 9-point proposal. You may also want to consider providing them with the summary memos to the President which followed each of last summer's meetings although I recognize that this is a more sensitive area. I am not suggesting that the foregoing documents be spread all over town ... essentially to Bill Sullivan, Walter Cutler, and the staff people in the Secretary's office.

Kissinger approved the recommendation with the caveat "Let me see [the documents] first."[62]

On August 18, Negroponte participated in a meeting with Thieu in Saigon along with Kissinger and Bunker at which Kissinger declared:

> our strategy is that we are prepared to step up the military pressure on the DRV [Democratic Republic of Vietnam] immediately drastically and brutally one or two weeks after our election.... If we can move quickly after the elections we can destroy so much that they will not be in a position to come back and harm you for a long time to come. At some point, we may have to accept the prisoners of war for an end to the bombing. But if so, it will be at a point where we have severely weakened them. At some point we may have to stop the bombing for this. Maybe in the second half of next year. But what they want is for us to also stop economic and military aid. If we agreed to stop such aid, we could settle now but we will not do this. We have to get to a point where you can continue to fight with a minimum of direct US military involvement but with continued military and economic assistance. We can also try to influence their allies not to arm them in such a way that they are capable of repeating military activities on the scale of the past few months.[63]

In the event, Kissinger delivered six months' less bombing than he had promised.

On the previous day, Thieu had foreseen the actual endgame: "What if they propose a ceasefire in North Viet Nam for an exchange of prisoners. You would cease the bombing and pull out." Kissinger offered in return candor followed by bombast:

> I will be honest. If they propose this during the election campaign, we will be in a very difficult position ... the US will not end the war in which it lost 45,000 men by joining our enemy against our friend, or destroying a government allied with us for 400 prisoners of war, or even to win an election ... The history books will last longer than the election.[64]

On October 8, 1972, Negroponte was in attendance at the meeting in Paris, where Kissinger tendered a ceasefire in place, without a withdrawal north of

Negroponte and Chou En-lai in Beijing

the demilitarized zone (DMZ). At an ensuing meeting, Le Duc Tho took a proposal out of his pocket that became the basis of negotiations thereafter. In it,
the North Vietnamese agreed in form to the continued partition of Vietnam at
the DMZ and the survival of the Thieu government, no longer insisting on an
immediate coalition government. As Winston Lord recalled it, "John Negroponte
was very skeptical on Thieu's reaction, more pessimistic. Among other factors
was the fact that North Vietnamese troops would remain in South Vietnam.
Negroponte was very uneasy and unhappy. He wasn't a mindless hawk, he
understood the pressures on the President and he knew that this was a better deal than *The New York Times* and other newspapers were calling for. The
rationale of the agreement was that there was supposed to be no further infil-
tration across the DMZ and that over time the North Vietnamese presence in
the south would therefore wither." Kissinger and Lord are said to have felt
that in the event of North Vietnamese violations, "the American people and
Congress would approve a substantial bombing offensive" and that the Chinese
would tolerate some bombing near their southern border, Kissinger enthusiastically declaring: "on the basis of your ideas and your way of presentation, I
think you have opened a new page in the history of our negotiations." When
producing his document, Le Duc Tho observed: "'you are in a hurry, are you
not?' I [Negroponte] recall Dr. Kissinger nodding affirmatively."[65] Kissinger also

repeatedly disclosed that the president "didn't want to begin…a second term of office still having to read battlefield reports every morning after breakfast." Negroponte recalled Kissinger making the same statement to Chou En-lai at a meeting in Beijing in June 1972:

> Prime Minister Chou: If after you withdraw and the prisoners of war are repatriated, if after that civil war again breaks out in Vietnam, what will you do? It will probably be difficult for you to answer that.
>
> Dr. Kissinger:…if after a longer period it starts again after we were all disengaged, my personal judgment is that it is much less likely that we will go back again, much less likely…they demand immediately what we might be prepared to have happen over a period of years.[66]

Negroponte had been involved in the preparatory work for the "opening to China," as had his one-time mentor Herbert Levin. Levin saw the initiative, long sought by State Department Sinologists like himself, as coming from Nixon rather than Kissinger, Nixon interesting Kissinger in it as a way to balance or "bug" the Russians. Rusk had regarded China and the USSR as an indivisible monolith. Negroponte recalled from his days in Hong Kong a cable from Hayward Islam, a diplomat who was later ambassador to Haiti, persuasively arguing the contrary. Chou sounded unenthusiastic about Chinese aid to North Vietnam, but said "we have to help."

On October 8, "Kissinger had us sit up virtually the entire night to draft what was, in effect, a counterproposal."[67] Negroponte regarded this as an atrocious mistake and considered that Kissinger should have said that he had to go back to both the president and the South Vietnamese. "Try to avoid negotiating in October of an election year." At a conference on the Vietnam War at the State Department late in 2010, Kissinger declared that he regarded Le Duc Tho's agreement to let the South Vietnam government survive a peace treaty as "my most moving moment"; Negroponte declared "I did not believe that was a particularly hopeful moment." Kissinger blamed the ultimate fall of South Vietnam on a "combination of Watergate and domestic divisions which cut aid to Viet Nam by two-thirds while oil prices were rising." Assistant Secretary of State Richard Holbrooke rejected this as "a popular myth that's gained great currency over the last thirty years…whatever we did, the long-term outcome would have been the same." Holbrooke acknowledged the view of Negroponte and others that "more force more rapidly applied might have brought a greater willingness by Hanoi to agree to end the war on what might have appeared to be better terms." Negroponte acknowledged that he "found myself pretty much all over the place over the years in terms of how I felt about the war" but nonetheless maintained his ultimate view that the North Vietnamese could have been induced to withdraw from the South, and that the South was not terminally corrupt but "a perfectly normal developing country government" that might have survived.

Negroponte recognized that Thieu would object, and along with Winston Lord drafted a tough set of demands, leading Kissinger to declare: "You don't understand. I want to meet their terms. I want to reach agreement. I want to end this war before the elections." In another version, Kissinger further declared: "It can be done and it will be done. What do you want us to do? Stay there forever?" One Kissinger critic observed that:

> this was an unfair accusation by a man who barely six months later was to blame the Congressional cut-off of aid to Cambodia for aborting his scheme to have the Chinese broker with the Khmer Rouge a hypothetical negotiated peace in that country to which he devoted 34 pages of his memoirs.[68]

Richard Holbrooke said of Negroponte's breach with Kissinger: "I think that was the decisive event in his life. He felt Kissinger had abandoned the people of South Viet Nam." Stanley Karnow, an American historian and journalist, observed: "Negroponte was smart in saying that once the North Vietnamese troops stay in South Vietnam, it'd be like a death warrant for the South Vietnamese."[69] Negroponte protested against Kissinger "trying to do too much with too much risk" and later observed: "the scenario was almost more important than the words. He got so excited about going to Saigon and then going to Hanoi to announce the signing."

> [H]is commitment to the North Vietnamese was that we wouldn't change a word of that agreement—scheduled to go to Hanoi and initial the agreement just prior to our election and the ceasefire was going to go into effect two or three days before the 1972 election. Instead of taking that agreement back to Washington and consulting with all the different governmental agencies concerned and with the President and the Secretary of State, Dr. Kissinger chose to respond immediately, "tomorrow morning." The real negotiation of the Paris peace agreement took place over a four or five day period.[70]

Tad Szulc, former foreign and Washington correspondent for *The New York Times*, later quoted Negroponte, referred to as an "American official, familiar with the events of that week" as saying "Henry was rushing things too much; it was getting too sloppy."[71] Negroponte has acknowledged that he was that official; the Szulc article,[72] rather than the earlier article by writer Joseph Kraft in which Negroponte denies involvement, was the cause of his breach with Kissinger. The *Time* magazine summary of the Szulc article observed that:

> Some of Kissinger's aides have told Szulc that they doubted that Kissinger really believed an agreement was at hand but that he wanted to commit Nixon to a quick peace. Kissinger seemed worried that after the elections Nixon might reopen the whole diplomatic situation; he feared that given Nixon's natural inclinations, the president might revert to toughness after being reelected.

It is important to bear in mind in understanding Negroponte's uncharacteristic willingness to talk to journalists that at this point South Vietnam had not yet fallen, and that a full public account might still enhance American willingness to aid South Vietnam and enforce the agreements, but his action was, by his own account, primarily due to anger and exasperation. His conversation with Szulc took place while Negroponte was at the Foreign Service Institute in early 1973, nearly a year before Szulc's article was published.

Negroponte, although intensely loyal in nearly all his dealings, did not share McGeorge Bundy's abhorrence of criticism directed by staff assistants at their former superiors, saying "they have taken a gun provided by someone else and aimed it at him."[73] Provided the motivation is not self-aggrandizement, such criticism where the public stakes are large may be demanded by a recognition of whom both superior and assistant work for. It reflects a recognition that public offices, in the words of Associate Justice of the Supreme Court Joseph Story, are "not for cringing favourites or court sycophants but to give dignity, strength, purity and energy to the administration of the laws." Nor, despite the claims of exponents of the "unitary executive," are officers to be the "obsequious instruments of the president's pleasure," as explained by Alexander Hamilton in *The Federalist* 76.

Kissinger vehemently disputed Szulc's criticism, declaring that it was "fiction" and "pure nonsense" to suggest that North Vietnam would have unilaterally withdrawn from what it had gained in the March 1972 offensive.[74] Kissinger did, however, insist on provisions allowing both sides to replace existing military goods, which benefited the GSV because of its superior arsenal; he also resisted any provision for releases of Vietcong cadres held by the GSV at the time of release of American prisoners, as the cadre prisoners were one of the few sources of leverage the GSV possessed.[75] Negroponte was credited by Kissinger with using a half-hour break to point out flaws in the North Vietnamese proposals.[76]

Earlier, Negroponte had drafted a cable from Haig to Kissinger giving his considered, and in the final event prescient, judgment on Kissinger's proposals:

> It appears we may conceivably be moving towards framework of a settlement which will enable us to disengage militarily get our prisoners back and leave the Vietnamese to slug it out between themselves in a context of reduced main force violence but continued political struggle of intensive brutality. Hanoi … recouped a number of their base areas in the South from which it may prove more difficult to dislodge them than in the 1969–70 period, and they are patient. Besides, no matter how effective the ARVN has become, one practical effect of our diminished presence—not to mention the psychological ones—is that there are hardly any of us around anymore to prod the ARVN and GVN to high levels of performance. Assuming continued fighting at a reduced level, but without our air [power], the GVN would be totally hamstrung without a continued flow of aid.[77]

It was not until October 12, 1972, that Negroponte learned that Kissinger proposed to make a secret visit to Hanoi at a time when Thieu had been kept in complete ignorance of an almost completed document, the American Embassy and Ambassador Bunker being equally ignorant of it. Negroponte thought that Thieu would resist "like a trapped tiger," whereas Kissinger noted that "All of us except John Negroponte thought that Thieu would be overjoyed by the agreement" because it allowed survival of his government. Kissinger grudgingly conceded that Negroponte "proved to be more prescient than the rest of us."[78] "The one thing Thieu was sure of was that he wanted to find a way to delay."[79] The Embassy staff referred to their required effort to sell the agreement to the South Vietnamese as "Operation Big Lie" and viewed the agreement as a "formula for defeat" because of the unclear lines of demarcation and the provision allowing the North Vietnamese to keep troops in the south.[80] Negroponte held the view that Kissinger's

> mistake was to proceed hastily and on his own without taking a break to consult with the two presidents for whom he was supposed to be negotiating.... Thieu had been treated shabbily and would likely balk, even though the deal was the best he could expect.[81]

Thieu's objections centered on the continued presence of North Vietnamese (NV) troops in the south, the legal status given the National Liberation Front (NLF), the failure to obtain immediate and ironclad ceasefires in Laos and Cambodia, and the reference to "one nation"[82] Szulc's "American diplomat" explained:

> We could have insisted [in October] on a ceasefire throughout Indochina and we had reason to believe Hanoi was thinking of meeting us halfway. We had a secret agreement with them that a ceasefire in Laos would be signed thirty days after the Vietnam ceasefire and subsequently we got this down to twenty days...we could have gotten the Cambodian ceasefire. We had a hell of a lot of leverage...by January [Kissinger] felt that Cambodia was too much trouble. He was psychologically exhausted and willing to believe that Hanoi didn't control the situation in Cambodia. Hanoi had told us in October that foreign troops should leave Laos and Cambodia and that of course was put in the formal agreement—but we did not negotiate a ceasefire there on that basis although we could have. By January there was too much haste and un-interest on our part. We never had a clear-cut perception of what we wanted politically.[83]

Thieu's attitude toward coalition governments of any kind was expressed by him to Haig: "In 1967 when I was asked by Ambassador Lodge to absorb the NLF I said 'we are a sick man. Please don't give us another spoon of microbes. It will kill us. We must get better first.' "[84] In his last statement to the North Vietnamese in January, Kissinger recorded his understanding that the United States would be free to bomb in Cambodia until a *de facto* ceasefire occurred there. In the three days following October 12, Haig and Negroponte objected to the plan for an October 31 signing, considering that some provisions were "too favorable to Hanoi" and required renegotiation.[85] They both "objected to the speed with which it had been drafted which they felt was the result of Kissinger's eagerness to get agreement before the election."[86]

To this day, Negroponte is uncertain whether the push for an agreement before the start of Nixon's second term came from Kissinger or Nixon; Kissinger's reports to Nixon throughout the negotiations were confined to highly general three-sentence cables at the end of each day. Kissinger had told Chou En-lai that Nixon wanted to be out of Vietnam by the beginning of his second term. Earlier, on October 13, Negroponte, at Kissinger's direction, informed the North Vietnamese in Paris: "The President has reviewed the agreement. He is pleased with it" except for some technical issues requiring changes "relating to ceasefires and prisoners in Laos and Cambodia.[87] Of this and another communication by Kissinger, John Ehrlichman was to write, "twice he cabled the North Vietnamese in the President's name to accept their October proposal. Henry did that over Al Haig's strong objection and beyond any Presidential authority."[88] It seems clear, however, that at least as of October 12 that Haig found the deal acceptable, although it did not require North Vietnamese withdrawal from the south.[89]

On the eve of the 1972 election, after the North Vietnamese had disclosed the October draft, Kissinger gave a press conference minimizing the remaining difficulties and declaring "peace is at hand." Nixon later asserted that this pronouncement eroded negotiating leverage, although it is less than clear that he was displeased with it at the time it was made.[90] The North Vietnamese for their part viewed it as a statement that "further laid bare Nixon's face,"[91] whereas Nixon's aide John Ehrlichman later observed: "Nor did it take much negotiating experience to predict that Le Duc Tho would take advantage of such comments as 'peace is at hand,' 'just one more session,' and 'I'm the lonesome cowboy.' "[92] Haig said of it that

> It is hardly possible to imagine a phrase so redolent of Neville Chamberlain and the effete 30s cult of appeasement more likely to embarrass Nixon as President and Presidential candidate, inflame Thieu's anxieties or weaken our leverage in Hanoi. The President regarded Kissinger's gaffe as a disaster.[93]

Negroponte was more indulgent, regarding "peace is at hand" as "one of the most widely misinterpreted statements of that era...[its] real content was to reassure Hanoi that we had not abandoned the negotiating table," given that Kissinger reneged on his contemplated flight to Hanoi to initial the agreement. There was concern that Hanoi would find the agreement less attractive: the "element of surprise had been removed and we had committed to sending Saigon one or two billion dollars worth of military supplies, advanced fighter aircraft, and so forth." At the same time, the United States embarked upon two resupply operations designed to enhance South Vietnamese armaments before any restriction on enhancements took effect; all the hardware promised for 1973 was sent in a three-month period before the ultimate agreement.[94] Between November 1 and January 27, South Vietnam received 266 warplanes, 277 helicopters, and military aid amounting to at least $1.23 billion, and title was transferred to military bases. The Military Assistance Group newly forbidden by the agreement had been transformed into a defense attaché office, part of the embassy, with 1,345 civilians; in addition, there were thousands of "civilian" contractors. By May of 1974 there were still 9,000 American civilians in Vietnam. On November 11, Nixon told Thieu that "It is unrealistic to assume that we will be able to secure the absolute assurances which you would hope to have on the troop issue"; on November 14, Nixon reiterated that "the United States was not prepared to scuttle the agreement or to demand such amendments as would have that result."[95]

Nixon also sent the first of several unpublished assurances to Thieu that the United States would retaliate against violations of any agreement.[96] Of these, Bunker observed that

> I gave Thieu personally three letters from President Nixon committing us in case of a violation of the Paris agreements by the other side to come to their assistance. The President obviously hadn't consulted sufficiently with Congress when he made these commitments to Thieu.[97]

Negroponte was unaware of these assurances, although he was present when Kissinger gave similar oral assurances to Lon Nol, prime minister of Cambodia. These promises were not publicly disclosed until a public statement by an embittered former member of the South Vietnamese government in May 1975,[98] leading to publication of *The Palace Files* by Jerrold and Leona Schechter describing the peace negotiations and their aftermath from the South Vietnamese side. According to Admiral Elmo Zumwalt, the Joint Chiefs of Staff, who would have had to carry them out, were not advised of these assurances.[99] In early November, Negroponte and Haig had visited Phnom Penh and had similarly assured Lon Nol that the United States would maintain "a massive air and naval presence in the area...even more at your disposition." They made it clear, however, that the agreement could not guarantee the end of the Khmer Rouge, a ban on training of Cambodians in North Vietnam, or the removal of arms caches, although the United States would try to obtain North Vietnamese withdrawal and the evacuation of Cambodian sanctuaries.[100] Nixon was said to have held the view that only six months' appropriations for aid to South Vietnam would be forthcoming from Congress if bombing were resumed; John Ehrlichman thought that aid would be cut off in half that time if Congress blamed the South Vietnamese and that they would be doomed without aid.[101] Negroponte's view was that it was not unlikely that the situation would deteriorate so rapidly given the presence of North Vietnamese troops in the south that there would be no way of saving the situation other than reinvolving ourselves in ways that would be unacceptable to the American people.[102]

In November and December 1972 when Kissinger attempted to improve on the October terms, the North Vietnamese retreated from them, their style being characterized by Negroponte as "clumsy, blatant and essentially contemptuous of the United States...tawdry, petty and at times transparently childish,"[103] although Kissinger reported to Haig some movement by the North Vietnamese on troop relocation, there having been some discussion of removal of some NV troops from Region 1.[104] During this period, when the Americans at the behest of the South Vietnamese complained about 10–15 differences in the meaning of the English and Vietnamese drafts, the North Vietnamese responded by saying that Negroponte's knowledge of Vietnamese was remarkable and the translations had been mutually agreed on.[105] On November 15, Negroponte, at Kissinger's request, drafted a bilateral agreement excluding the

South Vietnamese and containing no military or political provisions relating to South Vietnam except provisions for a ceasefire, release of prisoners, reconciliation, and a process for composing a new government, and also providing for no international supervision except for Laos and Cambodia.[106] In mid-December 1972, Negroponte was summoned from Paris by General Haig to accompany him to Vietnam, Cambodia, Laos, and Thailand:

> Broad backs get ever-increasing burdens. Henry and myself are convinced that you must accompany me to the Far East.... Pace will be hectic so be sure and leave Paris in sufficient time to give you a good rest before Sunday night's departure.[107]

Negotiations were broken off and a revived bombing campaign, including interdiction of railroads and mining of Haiphong harbor ensued. Serious efforts were made to avoid civilian targets. Reportedly, 40,000 tons of bombs were dropped, resulting in 1,318 civilian casualties in Hanoi and 305 in Haiphong. As many as 93 pilots were lost, of whom 31 were captured. Surface to Air Missiles (SAMs) shot down 26 aircraft, although almost all missiles had been disabled by the time the bombing ceased.[108] Another accounting listed 2,196 civilians killed and 1,577 wounded, 28 lost aircraft, and 121 crewmen shot down.[109] The bombing was bitterly denounced in the United States, James Reston, columnist for *The New York Times*, referring to it as "war by tantrum," Joseph Kraft as "Senseless Terror," and Anthony Lewis as the act of a "Maddened Tyrant."

Kissinger took the view that the four-month delay in completing negotiations was necessary because had an agreement been forced on the South Vietnamese days before the presidential election, "we would have been justly accused of playing politics with the destiny of millions,"[110] a charge that could equally well be levied against the rush to complete an agreement before the presidential inauguration three months later. In May 1972, Kissinger had more clearly explicated the roots of his policy at a meeting with the Ivy League college presidents (excluding Kingman Brewster of Yale, who had rendered himself *persona non grata*). On being asked by President John Kemeny of Dartmouth, a mathematician by training, "After a year or two, if you expect South Viet Nam to fall, what do we say to the younger generation about all the cost?" Kissinger responded:

> What do you say to them if it happens that in addition we did for the opponents what they couldn't do for themselves? It is one thing if Saigon fell from its own incompetence but another thing if we brought it about by our action.

To this, Kemeny said, "If we're willing to stop later, why not today?" to which Kissinger's response was "It has partly to do with the prisoners of war."[111] The "Christmas bombing" did not disrupt the summit with the Russians, who wanted détente to settle their Lend-Lease debt, limit armaments, and obtain wheat shipments. Negroponte felt "that the bombing had indeed produced a condition where the [North Vietnamese] would finally accept American demands to withdraw their forces" from the south.[112] Although the bombing resulted in the loss of 100-odd American aircraft and the downed pilots aggravated the prisoner of war problem, American intelligence indicated that the North Vietnamese were down to their last three (SAMs) when the bombing ceased. Negroponte was on leave at the time and was not consulted about the cessation.

Kissinger justified cessation by saying that President Nixon had set a deadline of January 20, 1973. The war must be over when his second term began. Bitter, Negroponte told friends "We bombed the NVS into accepting our concessions."[113] This view was also ascribed to Haig,[114] who echoed Negroponte's sentiment "My own view was that we should keep on bombing as the only hope of inducing the enemy to remove his troops from the South."[115] Haig elsewhere said, however "the President probably could not have continued to pound Hanoi without provoking a showdown with Congress that might well have led to his impeachment."[116] Richard Holbrooke held essentially the same view, regarding the January agreement as "just a camouflaged bug-out. We could have gotten essentially the same deal anytime after the 1968 bombing halt."[117] A North Vietnamese historian happily observed:

> We were always in a victorious posture. Public opinion in the world and the US did not criticize us for intensifying the fighting in the South but continued to demand the cessation of US bombing in the North and the withdrawal of US troops from the South. Our diplomacy had been doing well.[118]

The British military consultant Sir Robert Thompson, a veteran of the British suppression of a colonial revolt in Malaya, held the view even more emphatically that the bombing should have continued until a final agreement was arrived at:

> In my view, on December 30, 1972, after eleven days of these B-52 attacks on the Hanoi area, you had won the war. It was over. They had fired 1242 SAMS. They had none left, and what would come in overland from China would be a mere trickle. They and their whole rear base at that point were at your mercy. That ceasefire agreement restored complete security to the rear bases in North Vietnam, in Laos, in Cambodia and in the parts of South Vietnam that it held. It subjected the South Vietnamese rear base again to being absolutely open to military attack. We won the unconventional war in that the South Vietnamese and American joint effort had largely eliminated the Vietcong as a serious contender for power by 1972.[119]

Furthermore, Thompson declared:

> You had the war won; you did not have to do it again. But you had to be in a position to say that you could and would do it again….Because the opposing forces would remain in place, there could be no separation of forces as after the Geneva agreements of 1954 and therefore no chance of a real peace.[120]

There were also less consequential flaws, including the absence of deadlines for withdrawal as to Laos and Cambodia and the fact that the restriction on introduction of additional manpower was effective not immediately but only from "enforcement of the ceasefire," leading to the last-minute seizure of 350 hamlets by the North Vietnamese.

Negroponte was apparently not bashful in asserting his disagreement with what had happened. *The New York Times* correspondent Tad Szulc referred to him as an unnamed source in an article in *Foreign Policy* for September 1974: "Behind the Vietnam CeaseFire Agreement." Intimations of Haig and Negroponte's differences with Kissinger also appeared in an article by Joseph Kraft in *The Washington Post* for January 9, 1973, while the revived negotiations were ongoing, observing that in addition to Ambassador Ellsworth Bunker "Two members of Dr. Kissinger's own staff, Gen. Alexander Haig, the deputy who moved to the Pentagon last week and John Negroponte, a Vietnam specialist, also believe the agreement is too loose." "Negroponte assertedly believed his remarks to press friends were necessary because the United States had to keep its moral commitments if it were to remain a great power."[121] Negroponte told Neil Sheehan that Kissinger's terms "helped to insure that we did lose the war,"[122] declared that Kissinger had "a death wish for South Vietnam,"[123] and is said to have apologized to Thieu's press secretary, Hoang Duc Nha, declaring "We really screwed you guys,"[124] when Negroponte accompanied Vice President Spiro Agnew on a visit to Saigon on January 30, 1973.[125] Negroponte also gave interviews to the Cold War History Project of the Liddell Hart Military Archive at Kings College, London, and to Jerrold and Leona Schecter, the authors of a book on South Vietnam's role in the talks.[126] For his part, Kissinger is said to have told Hoang Duc Nha "the past is behind us. I realize that I moved too fast and that October was a mistake," to which Nha is said to have replied: "I would make a lot of money if I released your admission of a mistake in October to the press right now." "I know you wouldn't do that sort of thing," said Kissinger.[127] Kissinger later told a Senate Committee that ten divisions was the number of North Vietnamese troops allowed to remain in the south under the peace agreement.[128]

However, the North Vietnamese terms in 1968 insisted on the removal of Thieu. By January 1973, the North Vietnamese acknowledged that the bombing had "completely obliterated our economic foundation."[129] It is doubtful that many Americans realized the new dependence on imports that resulted from Hanoi's dependence on its regular army rather than the guerrilla forces of the Vietcong: "Gone [were] the days when human porterage could meet the needs of the army."[130] However, it had also "made re-intervention far less likely. It aroused strong public opposition and provoked Congressional moves to cut off funds for any further bombing."[131]

Further bombing, as the December 1972 bombing showed, would also have resulted in a new, if smaller, tranche of prisoners of war. These numbers, in turn, contributed to the haste in negotiating the terms of the agreement.[132] As William Colby acknowledged, "We signed the peace treaty in order to get our POWS out more than anything."[133] When the agreement was finally signed in January 1973, there was a secret agreement by which the North Vietnamese agreed to provide an accounting of Americans missing in Laos in exchange for a promise of $2.5 billion in economic aid, later increased to $4.75 billion in a

Nixon letter of February 1, none of it authorized by or discussed with Congress, as the North Vietnamese well knew. The accounting was found to be inadequate and the aid was accordingly withheld.[134] Negroponte felt that "The peace treaty did nothing for Saigon—there were no ostensible benefits for Saigon to justify all of the enormous effort and bloodshed of the previous years."[135] In September 1973, Congress enacted a prohibition of further bombing, which Lord regarded as "a truly dishonourable and reckless act…. all the sticks and carrots were effectively removed" that had been relied upon for enforcement of the agreement.

There were only cosmetic differences between the draft October and January agreements: the tripartite council was no longer referred to as an "administrative structure," the demilitarized zone though still not a border was to be respected, there was no linkage of release of cadres held by the South and American prisoners held by the North, and the two agreements were "within give or take a dozen words or so."[136] These concessions were accurately characterized as "minor and soon to prove meaningless," as North Vietnam controlled both sides of the DMZ and the National Councils never came into existence. As a North Vietnamese historian observed, "the matter was overvalued because the Liberation Forces would completely control the demilitarized zone."[137] There were secret agreements or declarations allowing American civilian advisers, enlarging the number of international supervisors from 250 to 1,160, and allowing South Vietnamese police to carry rifles. In both the October and January agreements, but not in earlier negotiations, the north did not require dissolution of the Thieu regime and did not bar continued US aid to it; its chief negotiator later declared, "since the military balance of forces had been fundamentally altered [by the American withdrawal], no puppet administration could remain firmly in place."[138] Sir Robert Thompson concurred in this judgment, "there is no single country in the world, given the shape and topography of South Vietnam, which could have withstood such an invasion without massive air support."[139] U. Alexis Johnson took a contrary view as to the feasibility of obtaining North Vietnamese concessions: "we could not obtain on paper for Vietnam what we had not been able to win in battle,"[140] although the French at Geneva had obtained evacuation of a quarter of the land held by the Viet Minh.

After meeting with Kissinger, Nixon, and Haig at San Clemente, Thompson told Thieu that Nixon would find a way around the bombing ban.[141] In a memorandum to Walt Rostow on January 5, 1973, Kissinger acknowledged that "we have no illusions but that enforcement will ultimately depend on our own vigilance."[142] Bunker, as noted, had delivered three secret written assurances from President Nixon. Thieu, however, did not secure any public American commitment to enforce the Paris treaty. "He thought if he could just keep the arms coming and the airplanes, he'd be able to hold the next attack off."[143] Alexis Johnson referred to "Al Haig's skillful twisting of Thieu's arm as well as the President's assurances."[144] Bunker bitterly observed that "we let the thing fall apart by our refusal to continue assistance while the Soviets and the Chinese kept on supplying the North fully, we didn't."[145]

Negroponte thought that given the permitted presence of North Vietnamese troops in the south, American aid or bombing would have made no difference to the final outcome. He attended the initialing of the treaty, where his services were required, but declined to attend the signing or to accompany Kissinger on his subsequent visit to Hanoi.

This contrasted with the success of Korean President Syngman Rhee, who torpedoed a peace agreement in June 1953 by releasing North Korean prisoners required to be repatriated under a draft agreement, declaring that

> The South Korean government has argued that while American promises never to desert Korea are very pleasant, it would be more satisfactory to have something in black and white…to allow the Chinese Communists to stay in our country is similar to accepting a death sentence.

In the final event, the 1953 armistice was accompanied by a defense treaty between South Korea and the United States, and followed by gradual withdrawals of American and Chinese troops extending into 1955, with a residual American presence thereafter.[146]

Although Eisenhower had made the case for a Korean mutual security treaty, and Reagan and the Kissinger Commission were to later make the case for US involvement in Central America, neither Nixon nor Ford disclosed, let alone made the case for, the obligations assumed toward the South Vietnamese at the time of the Paris agreement. By contrast, as was later trenchantly pointed out by the Special Inspector General for Iraqi Reconstruction:

> Those who developed the Marshall Plan methodically and successfully cultivated widespread bipartisan Congressional and public support, even though opposing parties controlled the White House and Congress. Secretary of State George C. Marshall made an extensive speaking tour of the country…. The head of the Economic Cooperation Administration (ECA) in Washington was auto industry executive Paul Hoffman, a Republican party leader; his deputy in Paris was former ambassador and businessman Averell Harriman, a Democratic party leader. Hoffman gave some 150 speeches about the Marshall Plan's value.[147]

The collapse in Vietnam, former Vice President and former Ford Chief of Staff Cheney to the contrary notwithstanding, was not due to statutory or constitutional weakness of the executive, but to its failure to even attempt to lead public opinion to support the secretly promised appropriations and air support.

Whether the preservation for a time of the Thieu regime was worth the 20,552 Americans who died in Vietnam between 1968 and 1973 has been questioned. As early as 1971, Kissinger recognized that the relaxed terms he was seeking would provide only a "healthy interval for South Vietnam's fate to unfold."[148] He had, as even Thompson conceded, secured some concessions: the separation of the ceasefire and a political settlement, eventual withdrawal of the North Vietnamese from Laos and Cambodia, preservation of Thieu, elections under international supervision, continued receipt of American economic aid and military aid on a replacement basis, and an international conference. These provisions effectively required Hanoi "to continue fighting until American will had been so eroded that the terms of the settlement would not be enforced against the North."[149] As Larry Berman more charitably put it: "Permanent war (air war, not ground operations) at acceptable cost is what Nixon and Kissinger anticipated from the so-called peace agreement."[150]

Deputy Secretary of State Elliot Richardson, looking back in 1988, observed, "had Nixon not been weakened by Watergate, he might well have gotten the Congress to support some US reaction against the invasion of South Vietnam by regular North Vietnamese forces after the peace agreement had taken effect."[151] It is said that he had decided to resume bombing in March 1973 because of truce violations but "lost his nerve and decided it was politically difficult if not impossible to do this."[152]

In May 1974, when Kissinger remonstrated about truce violations with the North Vietnamese, he was assertedly told: "you don't know what is going on in your own Congress." William Stearman, of the Foreign Service, says that Kissinger responded: "'This is of no concern to you, this is a domestic issue.' At that point, I knew that it was all over."[153] On April 5, 1975, just before the final collapse, Kissinger advised Ford against resumption of the air war: "If you do that, the American people will take to the streets again."[154] A commentator has observed: "Kissinger was probably right, but so was Negroponte. The situation would ultimately prove disastrous for South Vietnam."[155] Kissinger later explained his soft position to President Ford: "to ask them to withdraw when the North had agreed not to reinforce or add equipment would have been impossible. I don't think Congress would have stood for continued fighting under these conditions."[156] Kissinger had to concede, however, that "the entire North Vietnamese Army is in the South at the present time. There has been a terrible violation of the Paris Peace Accords."[157] The journalist Jerrold Schecter concluded that "Nixon was more concerned about the fall of South Vietnam than Kissinger was...we had to move toward a great power condominium and balance of power, and that the end of the Vietnam War would achieve that."[158]

Negroponte continued to believe that continuation of the bombing would have secured full withdrawal by the North Vietnamese on the Geneva Conference pattern and that the war could thus have been won, as the Korean War was won. Fairness to Kissinger requires the observation that the strategic bombing fostering a possible victory was made possible only by his détente with the Russians and Chinese. He is fairly chargeable with abandoning through haste what his squaring of the great powers made possible. He himself has written:

> what did torment me was my own role in the next-to-last act: the accelera-
> tion of negotiations after Le Duc Tho's breakthrough offer on October 8,
> 1972.... Did the demoralization of the Saigon structure which led to its col-
> lapse in 1975 start with the pace of negotiations we imposed back in 1972?[159]

Adviser and diplomat George Kennan, who had opposed American involvement in the war, supplied one of the better descriptions of the victors, possessed of

> a driving lust for power for which ideology and nationalism served as con-
> venient disguises. The iron rule they have subsequently fastened on the

peoples who fell under their power is many times worse from the political standpoint and that of human freedom than anything we ever tried to bring to those same people.... [They] will indeed eliminate some of the seamier aspects of life...will produce a certain floor in living standards beneath which the common people cannot fall, and will afford to these people, if not political freedom, then such satisfactions as a puritanical egalitarianism and the absence of any conspicuous foreign presence may afford.[160]

Elsewhere Kennan observed:

I can't see them as any [danger]. This is a feeling I've had ever since the late forties and have stated since the late forties. For the time being, we won't have the same opportunity of sending Congressmen and missionaries and all sorts of busybodies to this area. I don't think we're going to suffer very greatly from that. They're going to need trade, just as all Communist countries do. We'll trade with them eventually to the extent that we want to.[161]

Kissinger's later apologia for the four-year delay asserted that

our decision in 1965 prevented Indonesia from falling to communism and probably preserved the American presence in Asia.... Our friends including Japan did not feel that they had to provide for their own defense—we gained ten years of time.[162]

British intelligence officer Peter Calvocoressi has observed that the "domino theory" "turned out not to be valid, [but] seemed the more plausible in the 50s and 60s owing to the strength of the communists in the huge country of Indonesia and the introduction there of Sukarno's Guided Democracy."[163] However, the connection between Vietnam and Indonesia was tenuous at best. Writing in 1966, the historian Richard Lowenthal took a different view of the war:

To cooperate with...indigenous forces of national mobilization and modernization is the only form of "matching" Communist political warfare open to the West in the Third World, and the West has learnt it remarkably fast. Nor can American inexperience be blamed for the unfortunate fact that in some countries, including Viet Nam, such forces do not exist. But where their absence has given a native Communist movement a decisive advantage, it seems to me a wiser course, in the present age of Communist pluralism, to encourage its independence from the Communist Great Powers by coming to terms with it than to cement its dependence on them by trying to bomb it out of existence.... the relative weight of Chinese power today, because of the radically different level of industrial-military development, is in no way comparable with the relative weight of Japanese power in 1941 and would not be decisively increased by the addition of further millions of "underdeveloped" humanity.[164]

William Bundy, despite his own role, declared, well after the event, that

> a strong "heroes and villains" tendency [existed] in the thinking of both
> Nixon and Kissinger. Such thinking can have its place; the generation
> that knew Hitler and then Stalin had reason to look at the possible dark
> side of regimes and their relation to like-minded regimes. [The State
> Department was more] conscious of the often ambiguous influence of
> historical parallels.[165]

An Indonesian Ambassador to the United States, Soedjatmodo flatly said
in 1971 to a gathering of former Johnson Administration officials including
William Bundy, Harriman, and McNamara as well as Senators Frank Church,
John Sherman Cooper, and Edward Kennedy that "Removal of the Communist
apparatus in Indonesia and evolution of post-Sukarno Indonesia owes nothing to US involvement in Vietnam."[166] The American Foreign Service officer
William Stearman asserts that "Malik and Suharto gave us credit for morale"
of the Indonesians suppressing the Communist coup attempt in Indonesia in
September 1965; by 1973, the only place the North Vietnamese even arguably wanted to expand was into the portions of northeastern Thailand with a
Vietnamese population.[167] American diplomat Marshall Green took the view that
after the events in Indonesia ending in April 1966, the "domino theory thereafter
lost whatever validity it had once had."[168] The CIA's Board of National Estimates
in 1964 doubted that Vietnam's fall would lead to "the rapid successive com-
munization of the other states of the Far East."[169]

By the end of 1965, when the Communists had been suppressed in Indonesia,
there were only 1,594 American dead in Vietnam as against an eventual total
of 58,191. General Westmoreland's strategy was explicitly one of attrition.
However, the journalist David Halberstam, later the most vociferous of "doves,"
in 1965 assailed withdrawal on the basis that

> those Vietnamese who committed themselves fully to the United States will
> suffer the most under a communist government.... It means a drab, lifeless
> and controlled society for a people who deserve better...and it means that
> the pressure of Communism on the rest of Southeast Asia will intensify.[170]

Nixon had effectively given up on Vietnam:

> I put it to Henry quite directly that even if we could go back to the
> October 8 agreement, we should take it, having in mind the fact that there
> will be a lot of details that will have been ironed out so that we can claim
> some improvements over that agreement.[171]

"Nixon," one later historian observed, "had concluded that direct American
involvement in the war must end, because of Congress, because of public opinion, and because he was weary of it."[172] "Only in Vietnam", Kissinger observed,
"did the United States, driven by internal dissent, agree to leave no residual
forces; in the process, it deprived itself of any margin of safety when it came to

protecting the agreement that was eventually reached."[174] However, recrimination about what happened afterward does not answer Thompson's point that
"all the operating pressures must be maintained at full force throughout the
negotiation until a satisfactory agreement is reached and signed."[175] The side too
eager for an armistice almost invariably loses the peace. Kissinger and Nixon
were charged with not having shown "the 'courage' necessary to defy the will of
others."[175] In extenuation of Kissinger, it may be noted that on January 3, 1973,
he was encouraged in his course by two men of infallibly bad judgment, Robert
McNamara and McGeorge Bundy. He received a telephone call from McNamara
in which McNamara observed:

> All this crap about the task being loose and ambiguous—look, Henry you
> know and I know there is only one way to resolve this and that's to have a
> conscious ambiguity in the damn thing ... a lot of this is put out by jealous
> bureaucrats ... what you're doing is the right thing, Henry, and if it weren't
> for you I'd be deeply pessimistic about getting out of there ... this is not
> just my view, I should say all also it's the view of some others of you[r]
> friends and well McBundy for example and a lot of others that I know, so
> don't feel that everything's dark and bad.... Not everybody is as critical as
> some of these damn columnists and others.[176]

As Bunker rightly observed, neither Nixon nor Kissinger "level[led] with
Congress or the American people about what was essential to preserving [an]
imperfect peace."[177] In the view of the North Vietnamese after the agreement
was signed, "the diplomatic task during the period of the offensive and liberation of South Vietnam was to prevent the possible re-intervention of the US"[178]
The political fallout from the Christmas bombing operated to make reinter-
vention difficult. In the view of John Sylvester of the State Department, the
south "was always dependent on a relatively constant relatively large amount
of assistance from the United States both material and psychological."[179] The
flaws in the agreement, together with a threefold increase in the oil price, 65
percent inflation, a drop of 25 percent in ammunition stocks, and threats to
American aid leading to the inability to replace helicopters and fixed-wing
aircraft, all demoralized the South Vietnamese army, which overextended itself
and failed to adopt an enclave strategy.[180] As did the Polish generals in 1939,

> Faced with agonizing choices between attempting to hold and defend all
> the people and territory of South Vietnam—a nearly impossible task while
> the enemy held the initiative, and one that became ever more difficult as
> support from the US continued to erode—or pulling back to a more con-
> stricted and defensible perimeter [Thieu] could not bring himself to give
> anything up.... It proved simply impossible to abandon that position,
> psychologically or physically.[181]

Such arms and fuel as South Vietnam retained from that shipped before the
cutoff were conserved against what was viewed as the certainty of a Communist
offensive in 1976. The historian Peter Calvocoressi observed:

With hindsight, it could be said that they would have been wiser to
have adopted Gen. Sagan's strategy [in Algeria] of holding the centres
of population from which no enemy could have dislodged them and of
securing and sealing off the rich, easily defensible and ethnically distinct
Cochin-China.[182]

The last-ditch defense of Thieu also produced a government that was nar-
rowly based. The Americans had trained the Vietnamese field leadership but not
the Vietnamese generals. John Sylvester observed of Thieu, "We should have
pressed him harder on his appointments of the division commanders. [Thieu's]
decisions at the end were disastrous—pulling Airborne out of I Corps and
allowing General Phu to lead the retreat out of the highlands."[183]

There was little American political oversight of the implementation of the
Paris agreement: Negroponte, who might have provided it, was sent to Quito,
Ecuador. The last American ambassador, Graham Martin, despite his personal
gallantry at the end, "strengthened the South Vietnamese in their own intransigence and in their dependence on the United States…our protégés in Saigon
had been tolerated in their most self-defeating policies." Kissinger, asked to
estimate the durability of the South Vietnamese after the agreement was signed,
is said to have declared: "I think that if they're lucky, they can hold out for
a year and a half."[184] Negroponte believed that given the permitted presence
of North Vietnamese in the South, the situation was beyond hope, no matter
what Congress did. Nonetheless, as late as August 1972, a Harris poll revealed
a majority of 74–11 percent in the United States for the proposition that "it is
important that South Vietnam not fall into the control of the communists," the
prevailing mood, as later described by Senator James Webb of Virginia, being
that "the national goals in Vietnam were commendable, even though the policies that evolved to carry them out were acutely flawed."[185]

The main features of what Kissinger did had been urged five years earlier
by George Kennan in a variety of speeches and publications: "Americans' willingness to extend support [is] dependent upon the ability of other people to
make effective use of that support". Bombing might be justifiable "as a means
of gaining elbow room and bargaining power for a satisfactory disengagement."
"Defeat" would be "a six-month sensation." What was needed was "total withdrawal, followed by silence and detachment."[186] By this standard, Kissinger
was successful, declaring of the prisoners of war: "We got them home without
destroying those who relied on us."[187]

Twenty years of repression and stagnation in Vietnam followed the end of
the war. The repression was not as bloody as the disaster in Cambodia, or even
that which followed the French war in 1954–5, which is said to have included
50,000 executions and the imprisonment of another 50,000–100,000 people, as
well as the flight to the south of 600,000 Catholic refugees. In 1968, 4,000–5,000
government supporters in Hue were massacred during the Tet offensive. In
South Vietnam following the collapse in 1975, there were some executions,
500,000 to a million dissenters were sent to "reeducation" camps, some for a
few years and some for as much as 16 or 17 years, the first two to three years
involving hard labor in camps with meager food and no medical care, and there

were hundreds of thousands of refugee "boat people," a substantial fraction of whom died at sea. In Laos, 10 percent of the population fled and 30,000 were "reeducated."[188] There was also a famine, a not untypical consequence of agricultural management by Marxist governments. "Although no revenge killing or bloodbath took place in Vietnam, the Communist Party relied on incarceration and indoctrination to bring the country under its control."[189]

In the early 1990s, with normalization of relations with the West, resisted during the earlier Carter administration by the usual suspects, a process of economic liberalization began. By April 2008, Negroponte was to observe that Vietnam had reduced the percentage of its people living in poverty from 58 percent in 1993 to under 14 percent in 2007.[190]

Negroponte's reflections on the subsequent demise and resignation of Nixon were not recorded. There is no reason to think that he would have disagreed with a remarkable letter that Daniel Patrick Moynihan, then Ambassador to India, sent to Nixon just before his resignation:

> it is not really been evil that has brought on the present shame but innocence. What struck me most, and alarmed me most, about the almost always decent men who came to Washington with you, or in your train, was how little they knew of government, and especially of the standards of personal behaviour required of men in power. They had acquired in their youth or, as was sometimes the case, in long years excluded from national affairs, an oppositional frame of mind which much too easily assumed that squalid behaviour was common rather than rare in Washington, and they were all too ready to judge what would be required of them by reference to what they thought others did, rather than what they knew ought to be done. There was a failing of education and imagination. As a teacher in an elite school I live with it daily from the opposite political perspective: The government is fascist: what then is wrong with us blowing up a building. But this is innocence not evil.

(On this, Nixon annotated "A very thoughtful note.")[191]

Negroponte "had been with State for a decade in Hong Kong and South Vietnam, one of relatively few American officials to learn Vietnamese. He had served at the embassy with General Maxwell Taylor, Henry Cabot Lodge, and Ellsworth Bunker and then had gone to Paris to work on the early Vietnam negotiations with Averell Harriman and Cyrus Vance. He is said to have asked to return to the State Department in January 1973, when he was overworked and his relationship to Kissinger was in a shambles,"[192] but instead "Negroponte's reward would be a dismal posting to Quito, Ecuador," Kissinger by then being Secretary of State.[193] "John just said 'I want out,' and went off to the Embassy in Ecuador as economics officer," said Robert C. Oakley, a diplomat who shared an office with him in Saigon. "His approach has always been to work from within."[194] Foreign policy expert Peter Rodman thought that Negroponte's parting with Kissinger was amicable,[195] but if so the Tad Szulc article changed that. The kindest approach to this change is that of Peter Swiers of the State Department: "John Negroponte went on to Ecuador where you might say he was laundered a bit and he wouldn't be blamed for aid problems."[196] Vietnam had different effects on different Foreign Service careers. Habib's career was enhanced by his experience there, not so the career of Ambassador Colby Swank. David Lambertson, Joe Mendenhall of the State Department, and Negroponte were perceived as survivors.[197] Richard Holbrooke, reflecting on the melancholy fate of many of his Vietnam colleagues, observed that "even John Negroponte had a huge argument with Kissinger and was exiled to Greece."[198] Negroponte had been director for Vietnam at the NSC from the summer of 1971 to February 1973, reporting directly to General Haig, the Deputy NSC Director, but nonetheless was left to his own devices by Kissinger in finding his next assignment. He was assigned to Ecuador where a vacancy as political officer had arisen due to a falling about between the-then ambassador and Negroponte's predecessor as political officer. After six months of Spanish language training, he arrived in Quito in August 1973.

In December 1976, during his Greek assignment, Negroponte married Diana Villiers, who he had first met nearly 10 years earlier in Vietnam when she was only 18; they had a long plane ride together to Paris in the late 1960s while returning from Vietnam and met again through the efforts of Negroponte's mother in London. Diana was a graduate of St Mary's in England and of the London School of Economics and later took a law degree at American University and a doctorate at Georgetown, her thesis being on the settlement and aftermath of the Salvadoran Civil War. She is the daughter of Sir Charles Villiers, the socially conscious former chairman of British Steel,[199] and has been active in a number of organizations concerned with international relations, including the British–American Project for the Successor Generation. Her mother, a Belgian aristocrat and friend of Queen Elizabeth II, was similarly not a naïf in international relations, becoming the subject of a book entitled *Granny Was a Spy*, dealing with her activities in the Belgian underground during World War II.[200]

Negroponte's detours did not end until July 1977, six months after the start of the Carter administration, when Cyrus Vance, then Secretary of State, returned him to Washington as Deputy Assistant Secretary of State for Oceans and Fisheries with ambassadorial rank, followed by an assignment as Deputy Assistant Secretary of State for East Asian and Pacific Affairs under Richard Holbrooke, where he served from January 1980 to September 1981. The fisheries appointment came at the instance of Ambassador Bob Brewster, his superior in Ecuador, who was then Deputy Assistant Secretary for Oceans and Environment. Notwithstanding his clash with Kissinger, looking back after 20 years, Negroponte felt that "President Nixon and Dr. Kissinger will be very well remembered for the major openings they made to both the Soviet Union and the People's Republic of China. Détente was irreversible."[201]

The lessons Negroponte derived from his Vietnam experience significantly colored his approach to subsequent assignments. Certainly, the Vietnam negotiations gave him an ineradicable suspicion of standstill ceasefires, affecting his attitude toward Central American negotiations. In addition, he learned some things about the intractability of human nature in politics, affecting his attitude toward Iraq and Iran:

I became fairly wary about foreign engagements and foreign involvement and very mindful of the importance of gauging one's moves very carefully before becoming involved, on a large scale, in a foreign situation of this kind ... situations tend not to resolve themselves as quickly as one might like ... an objective that looks like maybe it'd take maybe a few months to a year to accomplish, sometimes, is a matter of many, many years indeed ... some of them endure to this day. The Korean War, we still have thousands of troops there.[202]

In 1988, Negroponte was one of a number of Vietnam War figures asked by an Oklahoma schoolteacher to comment on its lessons for schoolchildren. He "wants them to know that 'the US lost,' to 'ensure that we pick our fights more carefully in the future.'"[203]

There are those who consider the claim that South Vietnam might have survived but for the withholding of congressional aid as akin to the "stab in the back" legend perpetrated by German Chiefs of the General Staff Paul von Hindenburg and Erich Ludendorff to explain the German defeat in World War I. In this view, the South Vietnamese government and army were so decrepit that their survival was a hopeless cause. This undervalues the effects of the Christmas bombing of Hanoi and Haiphong and the extent to which the war by 1973 had become a conventional war. Negroponte's view was that the exhaustion of North Vietnam's SAMs might have produced an agreed withdrawal from the south, but that once the United States had failed to insist on withdrawal, South Vietnam's cause was hopeless, a view which somewhat relieves Congress of blame for its posttreaty actions. Negroponte had little doubt that such a withdrawal even if temporary would have spared South Vietnam much: 20 years of drownings of boat people, poverty and famine, followed by a turn toward capitalism that left Vietnam well behind its Southeast Asian neighbors. Whether American public opinion would have sustained such a policy is itself unclear; the nondisclosure of Nixon's three promises to Thieu made it clear that a serious effort to persuade the public of the case for intervention was not made. For Nixon and Kissinger, a "decent interval" was enough. This may have accurately assessed their nation's interests. One's judgment on Negroponte's position, both in Vietnam and Iraq, depends on whether and to what extent the United States holds itself responsible for the consequences of interventions that should not have been undertaken in the first place. There will always be diehards quick to proclaim the loss of honor in any "advance in another direction" from a doomed position. It is hard to characterize most of the supporters of continued "Christmas bombings" in Vietnam and supporters of a delayed American withdrawal from Iraq as defenders of a form of "humanitarian intervention"; but for at least a few of the Americans among them, including Negroponte, a reasonable case can be made. Continued American foreign intervention has frequently been driven by the plight of particular ethnic minorities in foreign countries; it is hard to avoid the conclusion that these concerns might frequently more usefully and cheaply have been assuaged by the granting of visas and in some circumstances the revision of boundaries rather than the dispatch of expeditionary forces. This was ultimately the path America followed in the wake of the Vietnam War, and it was the course adopted in the Treaties of Potsdam and Lausanne, for all their cruelties. It was not the path followed in addressing the Holocaust, the claims of the European displaced persons after the war, the claims of Palestinian refugees, and the effects of perverse provincial boundaries in Yugoslavia and the former Soviet Union.

John Negroponte began his involvement with Vietnam as a "dove" and ended as a qualified "hawk," a parallel to his later experience in Iraq. There was, however, no contradiction in his outlook. He regarded both interventions as improvident, but considered in both instances that the United States could not abandon the local populations to the predicament it had created, and that time, together with intelligent engagement with neighboring great powers, could make possible a reasonable future. His conviction that the United States could not walk away from the consequences of its military interventions also colored his outlook toward Central America and Afghanistan, where the attention span of American policy makers proved woefully limited.

6

ECUADOR

Where is the promise of my years
Once written on my brow?
Ere errors, agonies and fears
Brought with them all that speaks in tears,
Ere I had sunk beneath my peers;
Where sleeps that promise now?

I stand a wreck on Error's shore
A spectre not within the door,
A houseless shadow evermore,
An exile lingering here.

— Adah Isaacs Menken, *El Suspiro*
(Infelix) (1868)

The Ecuador to which Negroponte was relegated was indeed a backwater in the development of a State Department career. The Latin American Division was historically regarded as a world unto itself, and historically did not attract much of the Foreign Service's top talent. Latin America was not one of the world's five great centers of industry. For reasons summarized in a famous or notorious memorandum by adviser and diplomat, George Kennan, whose publication was suppressed for 30 years, its industrial and educational development was and remains seriously stunted alongside that of North America, Europe, and East Asia. Ecuador is one of the most isolated and small Latin American countries, with its capital in the Andes and its dominant industries agriculture, fisheries, and more recently petroleum production and illicit drugs. Oil production, although minor in international terms, was sufficient to provide inflation, weakening industrial competitiveness.

Negroponte felt that Ecuador was the most beautiful country in which he served and accompanied personnel of the Defense Mapping Agency on helicopter tours of its lesser-known regions.

The "Dutch Disease"
Negroponte's tenure in Quito began in August 1973 after five months of language training beginning in March. The salient feature of Ecuador for him was its isolation. Prior to the construction of the Panama Canal, it had been a long

voyage from both America and Europe; an inland capital at 9,300 feet added to its isolation and resultant xenophobia. Among his duties was that of narcotics officer. Ecuador's antinarcotics efforts were modest but increasing, involving expenditures of less than $1 million per year; at one point, Negroponte arranged for shipment of nine US vehicles for this purpose.[1] An oil boom based on new discoveries in the Amazon had just begun; by 1974, oil exports had increased to $900 million from $500 million in the previous year.[2] The oil boom had serious social effects, accentuating existing economic divisions. In October 1974, Captain Gustavo Jarrin Ampudia, an anti-American personality who was also president of the Organization of Petroleum Exporting Countries (OPEC), was dismissed as Minister for Natural Resources.[3] Jarrin had terminated and renegotiated the Texas/Gulf Oil concession, acquiring a 25 percent government stake in it in June 1972.

The oil companies had boycotted bid invitations for exploratory rights, and the United States had excluded Ecuador and other OPEC members from preferential treatment under a new trade act, as well as threatening to cut off military aid to Ecuador. Ecuador and Venezuela, in turn, had threatened to boycott a meeting of the Organization of American States in Buenos Aires, but Negroponte reported that the Ecuadorian press was having second thoughts about the implications of OPEC participation, quoting a satirical weekly as saying that

> The Arabs consider us "little brothers" since our petroleum, compared with that of Saudi Arabia or Iran, is hardly enough to refuel a cigarette lighter. The other Latin American states who are victims of the energy crisis…and who have to lessen the contents of their pots in order to lengthen the flame of their stoves, have begun to look on Ecuador as an Emirate full of camels and oil derricks…. For no reason at all we find ourselves involved in the war in the Middle East…we are no better than little Arabs.[4]

Jarrin's downfall, however, was largely a product of a worldwide fall in oil prices. The oil boom had produced greatly increased foreign investment while it lasted, accompanied by a deteriorating trade balance and increasing foreign debt and interest charges. Ecuador was a classic victim of the "Dutch disease," a concept that purportedly explains the apparent relationship between the increase in exploitation of natural resources and a decline in the manufacturing sector, afflicting most countries that "get rich quick" on new natural resource discoveries: the strength of the currency chokes off exports, resulting in a single-product economy. Manufacturing output quadrupled between 1970 and 1976, and there was a rush of population to the cities, as well as considerable corruption and extravagant imports of luxury goods. The government had nationalized telephone, electrical, and airline companies, as well as banks. It maintained its popularity by heavily subsidizing basic goods, to the extent of 23 percent of its budget, although 65 percent of the rural population was said to be below the poverty line in 1975, and 45–75 percent of the urban population was employed in the "informal" non-tax-paying sector.[5]

In September 1973, early in his tenure in Quito, Negroponte expressed the view that the government's policies on oil and fish were generally popular and preempted two of the major issues around which any opposition might coalesce.[6]

The "Tuna War"

Virtually all of Negroponte's significant activity involved the "tuna war," reintroducing him to fisheries and law-of-the-sea issues that he had addressed during his work under Henry Kissinger at the National Security Council and that he was later to revisit as Deputy Assistant Secretary for Fisheries and again as Assistant Secretary for Environmental and Scientific Affairs. Negroponte took the part of the Ecuadorians with respect to the underlying issue of the right to charge license fees to vessels within the 200-mile limit, while laboring for the prompt release of American transgressors and their ships. In January 1975, Negroponte sent to Washington a lengthy memorandum urging repeal of the Fishermen's Protective Act (FPA), a US statute under which the government reimbursed American fishing vessels for fines paid to foreign governments. He referred to the FPA's absurdities: which, in effect, subsidized conflict between our tuna industry and that of Ecuador. Reimbursement to our industry by US taxpayers was more expensive than if the owner had paid for a license in the first place. The license fees represented only about 10 percent of the typical catch. To the objection that repeal of the act would be a law of the sea concession, Negroponte replied that if the United States wished to maintain its theoretical purity on the issue, it did not have to encourage buying licenses; all that was necessary was to take away the built-in incentives for not buying them.

> I can think of no single step which USG could take to solve current situation in respect to "tuna wars" than the repeal of the FPA, as long as it is on the books it is hard to see how our industry can be persuaded to come to a durable modus vivendi with countries which claim fisheries jurisdiction beyond the twelve miles.[7]

In a separate memorandum, Negroponte had cautioned against retaliatory measures against Ecuadorian tuna boat seizures. There had been changes in Ecuador's own situation that mitigated against renewed seizures; the significance of $3–$4 million a year in revenues from fishing licenses and fines paled next to the hundreds of millions in annual oil revenues that began to accrue in 1973. The local Navy no longer needed fines, as it got an earmarked share of oil revenues; the new seizures appeared to reflect a legitimate conservation policy. Seizures may also have been provoked by the US retaliation in its trade act against Ecuador's OPEC participation and discriminatory policy toward Inter-American Development Bank soft loans to Ecuador. The United States was doing well in military sales: it was negotiating for sale of $150 million in construction equipment and had $300 million in oil investments that

> loom far larger than any other concern of ours in Ecuador … we now have enough things going well for us here that it should be possible to prevent

an incident in one relatively minor area of interest to us from threatening the entire fabric of our relationship.[8]

In February 1975, there were high-level discussions with the Ecuadorians that included Negroponte, Ambassador Robert Brewster, and American law-of-the-sea negotiator John Norton Moore looking to an agreed position on the pending law-of-the-sea negotiations in which both sides agreed on a regional approach to management of listed migratory fish including tuna and to expanded coastal state authority within a 200-mile zone, on bonding procedures for violators, and on avoidance of arrest of crews; these principles could serve as the basis for interim bilateral agreement.[9] These discussions followed agreement by the United States to the resumption of military assistance.[10] In March 1975, the US Consul in Guayaquil reported to Negroponte about a colorful incident involving a tuna vessel known as the *Neptune*. After a seizure, the American crew had disarmed the Ecuadorian guards; the Ecuadorians then boarded the vessel and removed the crew, two of whose members were injured. The American consul attempted to have himself imprisoned with the crew, who were released after a night's detention and after giving statements, except for one crew member who was sentenced to five days' detention, a potentially dangerous incident being thereby defused.[11]

Under the terms of the Fishermen's Protective Act, it was the duty of embassy personnel to inventory the seized fish. Anne Patterson, then a junior officer at the embassy, complained that, unlike the embassy's male personnel, she had not been detailed to count fish, an unusual, if not valuable, entry on a Foreign Service resume. Negroponte sent her to count fish, encountering her again while he was Deputy Secretary of State when she was ambassador to Pakistan, she having previously served as ambassador to El Salvador and to Colombia.

Negroponte departed from Ecuador in August 1975; an attempted military coup against the populist president, Rodriguez Lara, was crushed in December,[12] but Gonzales Lara resigned in favor of a military junta the following month. This was a rather civilized coup, the president being allowed to delay his departure by three days so his daughter could have her wedding reception in the presidential palace.

Ecuador's Indian population was largely isolated from the rest of the economy.[13] Foreign aid had been suspended because of the expropriation of properties of ITT Corp. pending a controversial study of expropriation policy launched by the Nixon administration.[14] Douglas Watson, who served under Negroponte, described Brewster as "very competent" and credited him with "a lot of attention to detail."[15]

In Ecuador, Negroponte displayed a willingness to take issue with established American policies, particularly the absurd policy of indemnifying violators of local fishing regulations against fines embodied in the Fisherman's Protective Act. If Ecuador was a backwater, and a particularly insular one, it gave Negroponte further experience of international negotiations and of navigation of the Washington bureaucracy, and an interest, carried forward in later assignments, in international environmental problems. It also gave him knowledge of the petroleum industry of value in both Mexico and Iraq.

A Noteworthy Blunder

At the conclusion of two years in Ecuador, Negroponte sought another assignment, and was slated to gratify his Francophile tendencies by becoming Executive Assistant to the Ambassador to France, Kenneth Rush. An uncharacteristic indiscretion derailed this aspiration. In April 1975, Negroponte addressed an "Official–Informal" letter to Henry Kissinger from Quito, prompted by the naming of two CIA agents in Ecuador in Philip Agee's book, *Inside the Company: CIA Diary*, "blowing the cover" on a multitude of agents, which is shown in the image below.

DECONTROLLED/UNCLASSIFIED
RELEASED IN FULL
P370034-0749

EMBASSY OF THE
UNITED STATES OF AMERICA
Quito, Ecuador

April 14, 1975

(276)

OFFICIAL-INFORMAL

(EI)

Dr. Henry A. Kissinger
Secretary of State
Department of State
Washington, D.C.   20520

LIMITED OFFICIAL USE

Dear Henry:

I was delighted to see the April 14 cable from the Department announcing your visit to South America. It is, if I may say, long overdue; and I think this Continent is an area where a bit of direct involvement by yourself through visits such as these can go a very long way (as opposed to parts of the world where a hell of alot of effort got us practically no where).

In preparing for your trip, I do not know if anyone has raised with you the subject of CIA involvement in the domestic affairs of other countries. With the publishing of Phil Agee's book, this topic seems to hang over many of our relations with contacts here in Ecuador, and I would not be surprised if that is not the case in the countries you plan to visit. It occurred to me that there might be an opportune moment during the course of your tour to state publicly just what the CIA is and what it isn't, with suitable noises about our non-involvement in internal affairs. Believe me, if we leave the field to Phil Agee, John Marks, Marchetti and the like, it will become increasingly difficult for us to do business around here. I think the time has come for someone at your level to again make publicly clear that we are not engaged in a massive conspiracy to prop up reactionary regimes.

I am being transferred to Paris in August as Kenneth Rush's Executive Assistant. I plan to come through Washington for a week or so on consultations and hope that at that time you will have a few minutes to receive me.

DECONTROLLED/UNCLASSIFIED

Sincerely,

LIMITED OFFICIAL USE

John D. Negroponte

UNITED STATES DEPARTMENT OF STATE
REVIEW AUTHORITY: ADOLPH H EISNER
DATE/CASE ID: 18 MAR 2009 200803282

A Fateful Blunder

This could not have been better calculated to strike raw nerves, both about Vietnam and about Kissinger's elaborately denied role in the overthrow of the Allende government in Chile.[17] Unbeknownst to Negroponte, Kissinger was still angry about Tad Szulc's article, and announced "I don't want Negroponte to be anywhere where I might run into him." Kissinger was advised by Kissinger's deputy Lawrence Eagleburger that under State Department procedures, the only way to alter Negroponte's assignment to Paris was to abolish his job, which Kissinger duly did. Negroponte learned of this development from Assistant Secretary of State Carol Laise and from James Lowenstein, the Deputy Assistant Secretary of State for European Affairs. Laise, the Director General of the Foreign Service and the wife of Ellsworth Bunker, then sought to assign Negroponte as consul general at Izmir, only to have the ambassador to Turkey, William Macomber, object to Negroponte's appointment because of his Greek descent. Instead, Negroponte was made consul general at Thessaloniki, Greece, a cockpit in both world wars and a listening post with respect to Yugoslavia and Bulgaria. The post had added importance because of an outpost there of the Strategic Air Command and the presence there of a largest Greek military base. The Ambassador to Greece, Jack Kubisch, had another candidate but was told by Washington to take Negroponte.

7

THESSALONIKI

Such is the aspect of this shore;
Tis Greece, but living Greece no more!
So coldly sweet, so deadly fair
We start, for soul is wanting there
Shrine of the mighty!
Can it be
That this is all remains of thee?

— George, Lord Byron, *The Giaour* (1813), lines 90, 106

As a Foreign Service post Thessaloniki, Greece, had the advantage of not being as isolated from modern history as Quito, Ecuador. In World War I, Thessaloniki had been the site along with Gallipoli in Turkey of a bloody and abortive British invasion of the Balkans. In World War II, it had been occupied by the Germans and Bulgarians who carried out a massacre of the long-established Greek Jewish community even though the Bulgarians had been notably protective of their native Jews, a situation somewhat resembling that in Vichy France. After the war, the city was important because of the Yugoslav and Bulgarian assistance to the Greek communists, and thereafter because of the tensions between America's Greek and Turkish allies, the fact that it was the leading Greek military base, and the presence there of a little-known outpost of the Strategic Air Command. It was a cosmopolitan port city but not an especially broadening experience for a diplomat with roots in the Greek shipping industry. Certainly, consular rank in Thessaloniki was a far cry from near-ambassadorial rank in Paris.

John Negroponte's assignment as consul general in Thessaloniki from September 1975 to June 1977 was even less eventful than his stay in Ecuador. There were student demonstrations against a new constitution shortly before his arrival,[1] as well as the establishment of a "sister cities" relationship with Odessa in the USSR.[2] Richard Benedick, who was economic counselor in Athens, recalled massive anti-American demonstrations in the wake of US refusal to impose sanctions on Turkey after its treaty-authorized invasion of Cyprus. In November 1975, there was a demonstration outside the consulate in which the demonstrators carried signs reading "Out Americans," "Out of NATO," and

"They Killed Our Children," the last referring to alleged American complicity with the former junta. Negroponte reported on labor unrest resulting from bus fare increases, and on a visit by the conservative Prime Minister Constantine Karamanlis, whose political position Negroponte thought was secure but whom he bemusedly charged with hyperbole for characterizing a nearby industrial area as "the Ruhr of the Balkans." Negroponte reported on a visit by an unenthusiastically received opposition leader and on the content of his speech urging nationalization of the education and health systems; he also fostered American commercial interests in connection with an exhibition of pollution control equipment and development of the local lignite industry, and reported on the opening of a local office by the Palestine Liberation Organization.[3] At one point, he wrote an elaborate dispatch on the Mt. Athos monastery suitable for an anthology of travel writing.

Negroponte had the good fortune to depart a year before the earthquake measuring 6.5 on the Richter scale that struck the city in June 1978.[4] Negroponte married the former Diana Villiers in December 1976; her father, Sir Charles Villiers was chairman of British Steel from 1976 to 1980; he did not regard Thessaloniki as an ideal honeymoon site. After the assassination of the CIA station chief in Athens, Richard Welch, on Christmas Eve 1975, the Negropontes were followed by four Greek security men who they labored hard to lose.

One of his subordinates dealt with the issues presented by the flight to Thessaloniki from Turkey of a small-time American student drug dealer, who subsequently earned renown as the author of the book and film *Midnight Express*.[5]

Thessaloniki provided Negroponte with an introduction to post management. Although Negroponte did not have a passionate interest in either the theory or the details of administration, and had avoided relegation to the Africa Desk on this ground, he later urged the multiplication of small posts, in part for their value in the education of Foreign Service officers.

8

DEPUTY ASSISTANT SECRETARY
FOR FISHERIES

That which is common to the greatest number has the least care
bestowed upon it. Every one thinks chiefly of his own, hardly at all
of the common interest, and only when he himself is concerned as
an individual. For besides other considerations, everybody is more
inclined to neglect the duty which he expects another to fulfill; as in
families many attendants are less useful than a few.

— B. Jowitt (trans.), *The Politics of Aristotle*
(Oxford: Clarendon, 1885), Book II, Chapter III, 1261b

In June 1977, John Negroponte became Deputy Assistant Secretary of State for
Fisheries with the rank of ambassador. He had a notably cold interview with
the Commerce committee chairman, Senator Warren Magnuson of Washington
State, who announced that he had another candidate, thought that Negroponte
knew nothing about fish, and did not invite him to sit down. At his confirmation
hearing, another senator complained that he did not know enough about fish,
despite his involvement in tuna disputes with Ecuador.

The post of Deputy Assistant Secretary for Fisheries was also some distance
outside the diplomatic mainstream. Negroponte was already familiar with fisheries issues from his tenure in Ecuador and from his authorship while serving with
Henry Kissinger of a comprehensive memorandum on law of the sea issues that
still defines American policy. It is nonetheless true that fishing is not a major
American industry, accounting in 2006 for $8.4 billion of a gross national prod-
uct of $13.2 trillion. The post was still important to his career; he conducted
negotiations under his own authority. Kissinger was no longer Secretary of State
when the appointment was made; it appears to have been the product of the
State Department's own assignment system, for which Negroponte had respect.

Fish and the Pacific
Although, as mentioned above, fishing is not a major industry in the American
scheme of things, this unpromising portfolio proved to be quite lively.
Negroponte's tenure began with a quarrel with Canada about tuna fishing
off the Pacific coast. On August 20 and 31, 1979, the Canadians seized some

American fishing vessels off the port of Victoria. Canada claimed the exclusive right to fish within a 200-mile limit; the United States had a similar limit but contended that migratory fish such as tuna were the subject of exclusive rights within only a 12-mile limit by reason of an international treaty. On September 4, the United States banned imports of Canadian tuna. On September 12, talks were broken off, but the negotiators agreed to meet again.[1] Finally, in July 1981, a treaty allowing unlimited American and Canadian albacore tuna fishing was unanimously approved by the Senate. Negroponte was also credited by Senator Ted Stevens of Alaska, who became a good friend, of being "very much involved in the negotiations with the Government of Japan to protect our Alaska salmon stocks."[2]

The 200-mile exclusive jurisdiction policy introduced under the Magnuson Act had large consequences: in this case, nationalism and enclosure operated to prevent overfishing of a commons:

The 200 nautical mile exclusive fishing zone established by the US and Canada in 1977 reduced the number of fishing vessels of several foreign deep-water fleets, particularly the Soviet Union, by as much as 45 percent in the two nations' fishing grounds. Other distant water fleets affected were those of Japan, Spain, South Korea, and Poland—distant-water factory trawlers are gradually phasing out of service. [The 200 mile zone is] the home of 85–95 percent of the world's fishing...fishing on the world-wide scale is more diffused with a larger number of smaller vessels over a wider expanse of world oceans.[3]

The leviathan ships once hailed as fishing technology's greatest leap forward are proving too costly to operate under the low quotas assigned to them by coastal states around the world...the richest meadows of the sea, the continental shelf and slope waters that are home to eighty-five percent of the world's harvestable fish—are now a staked plain. Almost everywhere, moreover, the stake lines that nations draw out to 200 miles fully encompass this plain. The fishing commons of the ocean have been enclosed...instead of intense Northern Hemisphere concentration there is now a diffusion of fishing effort: a great global diaspora. The greater the diffusion, the less is the probability of dangerous over-fishing, or the kind of "targeting" on a few key species that characterized the factory trawler era.... What the decline of factory trawling has meant, therefore, is that the threat of commercial extinctions no longer exists.... Iceland, the first and most vigorous of the good stewards, has benefited most. In the eight years since the establishment of a 200-mile zone, the island republic has seen an overall catch increase of 58 percent. The United States has had almost equal success. The endangered haddock has risen five-fold from its 1974 low, and the cod catch has almost doubled. Even the Atlantic herring once so coveted by foreign trawlers are coming back strongly from what Maine fishermen, who catch them as juveniles for packing as sardines, thought was the end of their inshore fishery.... The sea, as a result, seemed newly alive.[4]

The country director for Canada during Negroponte's tenure, Richard J. Smith, concurred in the view that "the ability of the great factory ships was over-taxing the capacity of the sea to replenish itself." He was later to rejoin Negroponte as principal deputy when Negroponte later became Assistant Secretary for Oceans and Environment.[5]

Fish and the Atlantic

There was an even more lively controversy over Atlantic fisheries. Two treaties were negotiated with Canada during Negroponte's tenure, one settling a boundary dispute and providing for international arbitration of any disputes arising from the settlement, while the other establishing quotas for the cod, haddock, and scallop fisheries; the United States was to have 83 percent of the cod, 79 percent of the haddock, and 27 percent of the scallops. The treaties aroused Senate opposition,[6] further aggravated when Ronald Reagan, first as presidential candidate and then as president, opposed quota arrangements.[7] Ultimately the quota treaty fell by the wayside and the boundary treaty was ratified by the Senate in May 1981, a year and a half after Negroponte's departure from the fisheries assignment.[8] The boundary was ultimately determined under the arbitration clause by the International Court of Justice.[9]

Negroponte during this period received criticism from environmentalists for a whaling treaty that, while banning some factory ships, reduced quotas only from 16,000 to 14,500; there was also an agreement limiting the dolphin catch to 20,500; and differences among the American negotiators of an Atlantic salmon treaty just before his departure.[10]

The Law of the Sea Treaty

During his tenure on Kissinger's staff at the National Security Council, Negroponte prepared a comprehensive review of law of the sea issues that ranged well beyond fisheries. In June 1971, he had prepared a memorandum summarizing a study of an Interagency Law of the Sea Task Force headed by the State Department, with his own comments in brackets.[11] He succinctly defined the objectives of US policy as to ensure mobility of our military forces, to protect economic and environmental interests, and to avoid political and armed conflict over rights to use ocean space.

Existing US positions were defined as a 12-mile territorial sea, a military right of free transits through international straits, carefully defined preferential rights for coastal states in fisheries, a 200-mile seabed boundary for the continental shelf, a trusteeship regime for coastal states up to the remainder of the continental shelf, licensing by an international organization in other areas, controls over pollution from seabed activities, and maximum freedom for scientific research. A note by Negroponte indicated that the fisheries position thus described was a "non-starter.... This NSSM (National Security Strategy Memorandum) exercise is in large measure due to the need for a new and better defined fisheries position."

Negroponte went on to note that the seabed proposal lacked appeal to Latin American countries seeking to enhance their own 200-mile thesis and that

African and Asian countries, in order to maintain developing country solidarity, frequently support the Latin position. The oil and gas industry had been opposed to the trusteeship concept and international zone, but this was established US policy that would not be reopened. Indonesia and the Philippines had made archipelago claims that might be accepted if they recognized military rights of free transit. Negroponte noted that the most important reason for US opposition to unilateral claims limited to natural resources relates to the assumption that unilateral claims of jurisdiction for one purpose tend to expand into claims for other purposes," Negroponte urged the granting of exclusive resource jurisdiction to coastal states up to, say, 200 miles in exchange for acceptance of a 12-mile territorial sea.

Negroponte opposed any immediate pressure on recalcitrant states: use of pressure tactics before we had decided our negotiating strategy was putting the cart before the horse.

On fisheries, the paper recommended a 200-mile trusteeship zone in which control would be exercised by regional organizations, or in their default by coastal states, and within which unspecified special arrangements would be made for migratory fish. While this would be initially opposed by the nations, notably Japan and the then Soviet Union, with distant fleets, they might be mollified by reasonable license fees. The overall State Department recommendation, largely reflected in the 1982 Law of the Sea treaty, was for this option that

> should capture the imagination of other countries, disarm the Latin Americans and would lead to an agreement that protects our vital security interests because coastal states would be offered means to satisfy their interest in resources off their coast without resorting to unilateral assertions of territorial jurisdiction.

The 1982 treaty was widely ratified; however, the Reagan administration declined to do so because of concerns with the seabed mining regime. After the level of mandated royalties was curtailed by amendments to the treaty negotiated in 1994, the United States began to support its ratification, which Negroponte was still struggling with Congress to secure as late as 2008, 37 years after his memorandum, an illustration of the value of continuity in the conduct of foreign relations.

9

DEPUTY ASSISTANT SECRETARY
FOR EAST ASIAN AND
PACIFIC AFFAIRS

Remember that when you say
"I will have none of this exile and this stranger
For his face is not like my face and his speech is strange"
You have denied America with that word.

— Stephen Vincent Benet, *Western Star*
(New York: Farrar Straus, 1943), Book 1, 189

Negroponte owed his appointment as Deputy Assistant Secretary for Far Eastern and Pacific Affairs to his friendship with Richard Holbrooke. As a former Kissinger aide reputed to be to the right of Kissinger, Negroponte possessed no attributes commending him to the new Carter administration. Holbrooke's tenure as assistant secretary was distinguished by the Indochina refugee program, which had started in the Ford administration but which was fueled by Holbrooke's passion about the Holocaust. Holbrooke, unlike Negroponte, was not a pure career man; he had left the Department for the think-tank world and was restored to power by his links with Democratic foreign policy advisors. Despite markedly different temperaments, they remained good friends; Holbrooke testified in favor of Negroponte's confirmation as his successor at the United Nations and acknowledged Negroponte's presence in the audience at his own swearing in as a special emissary at the start of the Obama administration. It is not clear that Negroponte would have joined Holbrooke in taking issue with George Kennan's opposition to North Atlantic Treaty Organization expansion (Negroponte thought that expansion had been carried too far in the case of Romania and Bulgaria), and Negroponte's approach to the Yugoslav Civil Wars is more likely to have built on the arrangements contrived by the parties themselves and embodied in the abortive Lisbon and Vance–Owen agreements, which were more favorable to the Bosnian Moslems than the ultimate Dayton Agreement.

Cambodia, China, and Proxy Warfare
Negroponte's service as Deputy Assistant Secretary for East Asian and Pacific Affairs from January 1980 to September 1981 involved some reinvolvement with the Indochinese peninsula. The Ford administration, guided by

Henry Kissinger, had little to do with the victorious Vietnamese, rebuffing requests for economic aid, demands for which were dropped in 1978, and twice vetoed their admission to the United Nations. The Carter administration sent Leonard Woodcock, former US ambassador to the People's Republic of China, on an abortive mission looking toward restoration of diplomatic relations; the Vietnamese had firmly allied themselves with the Soviet Union. In Holbrooke's view, a united Indochina led by Hanoi would represent a power bloc that the Association of Southeast Asian Nations (ASEAN) could not hope to equal. It was imperative that Hanoi not be allowed to consolidate its hold on Cambodia.[1] Negroponte attended an international conference on Kampuchea in July 1981 at a time when both the United States and China, intent on containing Vietnam, refused to recognize the Vietnamese-installed government of Hun Sen in Cambodia, a position that benefited the Khmer Rouge. Although Secretary of State Alexander Haig and his deputy, John Holdridge, walked out of a speech by a Khmer Rouge representative, they sent Negroponte to pressure ASEAN to adopt China's position, even asking the heads of the Philippine, Singapore, and Thai governments to compel their foreign ministers to knuckle under.[2]

> That bit of theatrics made the front page of *The New York Times*, but behind the scenes they pressured us to adopt the Chinese position.... Haig carried his Sino-philia to the extent of siding with Peking against America's non-communist allies and friends.... Holdridge and...Negroponte went around the ASEAN missions urging ASEAN foreign ministries not to push China for concessions since the pragmatic leader Deng...was under pressure from the left.[3]

When Negroponte visited ASEAN capitals in March 1981, he urged Indonesian officials to be sensitive to Thailand's distinctive front-line situation. Negroponte also assured ASEAN leaders that the United States felt that it was important to retain the Khmer Rouge's UN seat, thereby reaffirming US solidarity with China on this issue and indicating that the United States did not intend to follow Australia's lead in derecognizing Democratic Kampuchea.[4] The upshot was that the ASEAN countries gave up their insistence on disarmament and an interim administration pending elections in favor of vaguer appropriate arrangements to ensure that armed Kampuchean factions would not be able to prevent or disrupt elections.

In June 1982, a coalition government was formed in Cambodia; its non-Communist members received $15 million in American assistance through ASEAN. Shortly earlier, Richard Armitage of the State Department had resumed US contact with the Vietnamese, visiting Hanoi to discuss Americans missing in action during the war.[5] In 1980, Negroponte visited Vientiane, the capital of Laos, urging Laotian adherence to the 1925 Geneva Protocol against chemical warfare that had been adhered to by France; he also had a conversation in late March urging Vietnamese adherence with Ha Van Lao, Vietnamese Ambassador to the UN. Chemical weapons had reportedly been used in the war between Vietnam and the Khmer Rouge.[6]

One of Negroponte's subordinates, Desaix Anderson, wrote of this episode that we were heavily engaged with ASEAN seeking a solution that would end the occupation of Cambodia by Vietnam. The focus of US efforts was on denying Cambodia's ex-UN seat to the Heng Samrin regime (implanted by Vietnam by force to replace Pol Pot) and constructing a solution that would end Vietnam's occupation without the return of the Khmer Rouge.[7] The Vietnamese rejected the plan. In 1991, many years later, there was a formal agreement, not implemented by the Vietnamese; finally in June 1997, they staged a coup giving them complete control.

This episode has not gotten rave reviews, though the US position was devised by Vance and Haig, not Negroponte, and there was little difference between the policy directed by Richard Holbrooke under Carter and that directed by John Holdridge under Reagan. As the Ambassador to South Korea, Daniel O'Donahue, noted in an oral history: "paradoxically, in the case of the Carter administration you went from a tremendous, verbal focus on human rights to supporting the Khmer Rouge in Cambodia in the UN."[8] By the end of the Carter administration, as was the case with Central America, foreign policy was in a shambles. When the Vietnamese invasion of Cambodia occurred in 1979, there developed a greater interest in security in these countries, with refugees growing as a separate policy issue.

> Secretary of State Haig had a very Kissinger-esque view of China. He favoured very close relationships with China .... Regarding Southeast Asia, when the Reagan administration entered office, my predecessor as Deputy Assistant Secretary (DAS), John Negroponte, had been charged by Secretary of State Haig with doing what he could to find a role for the United States in supporting the non-communist Khmer resistance groups.... To a very great degree this seemed to be driven by Haig's desire to make a gesture toward the Chinese rather than overwhelming interests in the Southeast Asian context.... This policy of support for the Khmer Rouge continuing to occupy the Cambodian UN seat was certainly supported by all of the ASEAN countries.... CIA, the NSC staff, the Vice President's office all had grave doubts about our ever becoming re-engaged in any way in Indochina. After this conference the Chinese concluded that the non-communist resistance in Cambodia was more of a nuisance to them than they expected.

Haig was explicit in his view that in Southeast Asia, we had abandoned our influence almost totally, and "if it had not been for the Chinese, who were doing America's work for it in this region, the rest of the dominoes might have fallen after South Vietnam and Cambodia and Laos. The Chinese, strategically the most important nation on earth, had been promised much by both Democratic and Republican administrations and had been given little."[9]

Much later, during the period 1990–2, the issue of aid including military aid to the Cambodian resistance flared up again.[10] US aid to the opponents of Vietnam was not confined to economic assistance but included modest amounts of military aid pursuant to presidential findings. This aid went to the Sihanouk and Son Sann factions then allied with the Khmer Rouge. Most of the military aid was nonlethal, including uniforms. Ray Burghardt, then Deputy Director for Vietnam, Laos, and Cambodia looked on this as an anti-Soviet proxy war similar to that which Negroponte was later to help wage in Honduras and the still-later aid to the Mujaheddin in Afghanistan and the Savimbi faction in Angola. These proxy wars took bizarre turns, not least in the efforts of private citizens, including Lewis Lehrman, Grover Norquist, Jack Wheeler, and others to arrange something in the nature of an American Comintern at a conference in the African bush in 1985.[11] The left-wing historian Eric Hobsbawm referred to Cambodia in the 1970s as "one of the more depressing episodes of diplomacy—both China and the US bloc continued to support the remains of the Pol Pot regime on anti-Soviet and anti-Vietnamese grounds."[12] The compromise was a pragmatic way of minimizing conflict between Washington's Chinese and ASEAN partners.[13]

Efforts to propitiate the nation that is now the United States' largest trading partner took other forms as well. When Assistant Secretary of State for Human Rights Patricia Derian testified before Congress in 1980 about China's arrests and prosecution of dissidents, Holbrooke sent Negroponte to assert that "an encouraging trend has begun to emerge in the direction of liberalization."[14]

The United States cannot be accused of running after the Vietnamese, and established diplomatic relations with them only some years later. At the conclusion of the Indochinese wars, George Kennan had cautioned:

> There is no reason why we should be in a hurry to conclude relations of any kind with the respective governments or to manifest any particular interest in what they are doing…. Let us be content if the period that ensues before we find it necessary to have anything more to do with them is a good long one.[15]

Refugee Relief

In the same period, according to Negroponte's testimony at his Senate Foreign Relations Committee hearing to be Deputy Secretary of State, he was "strongly committed to relief efforts for the thousands of refugees in camps in the Indochina region." Richard Holbrooke at Negroponte's confirmation hearing as UN Ambassador credited him with a "burning sense that we could not walk away from the human beings whose lives were now at risk before the victorious communists."[16] Holbrooke himself was strongly committed to refugee relief, being driven by recollections of the Holocaust; the Chios massacre of 1822, more damaging in percentage terms to the affected population than even the Holocaust, helped shape Negroponte's sensibility. (The Chios massacre was the slaughter of tens of thousands of Greeks on the island of Chios by Ottoman troops during the Greek War of Independence.) At one point, Holbrooke directed Negroponte not to come back from Capitol Hill with less than 14,000 visas per month.[17] In the final event, the United States admitted some 1.3 million Indochinese refugees, 60 percent of them from Vietnam,[18] in a period when it was seriously neglecting its returning war veterans. Robert Oakley later declared

"I think in the final analysis our refugee policy was wiser than we anticipated because over the long run it has helped Canada and Australia change their total approach to immigration."[19]

It is hard to think of any comparable episode in American history in which a policy of such importance was initiated and carried through by a group of mid-level Foreign Service officers with only limited political support from the administrations in power or from American interest groups.

Shepard Lowman, then Deputy Assistant Secretary for Refugees and later Negroponte's Deputy Chief of Mission in Honduras, confirms that Negroponte was highly supportive of the refugee relief effort, which was a generous one. Lacy Wright, one of Lowman's deputies, also recalled in 1998 that the East Asia Bureau was very involved, particularly in the person of Negroponte."[20] The budget in 1975 exceeded a half billion in then-current dollars. None of the Southeast Asian nations other than the Philippines would grant permanent visas. Aid was granted to all refugees who came out by boat without a particular strike against them. Large retraining camps, largely financed by the Japanese, who declined to accept any refugees, were set up in Thailand, the Philippines, and Indonesia, providing high school instruction and three to six months of language training. (The failure to regularize Mexican and Central American immigration has militated against any similar preparation of America's millions of immigrants from Latin America. In an interview given in connection with the writer's last book, the late Turkish Foreign Minister Erdal Inonu regretted the failure of the Turkish and German governments to provide Turkish guest workers and migrants with similar training.)

In addition to the initial wave of 125,000 refugees in 1975, more were created two years into the new Vietnam regime with the herding of small businessmen into so-called "new economic zones" and thereafter when the Vietnamese in 1978–9 sought to forcibly deport a large portion of their Chinese population, putting refugees 2,000 at a time on tramp steamers for Southeast Asian ports. The Thais, in turn, pushed ships out to Malaysia, and Malaysia began to reject boats. This led to a UN High Commissioner for Refugees (UNHCR)-sponsored conference in Geneva that enlarged quotas. At the peak, beginning in June 1979, the United States was accepting nearly 14,000 refugees per month, double the number accepted during the Ford administration; large numbers were accepted by France, Canada, and Australia, the United States accepting about half the total in all.[21] A high proportion of the refugees were Catholics. Negroponte and Lowman enjoyed the support of the House Committee on Foreign Affairs, then presided over by Congressman Stephen Solarz of New York.

The first wave of refugees consisted almost entirely of American employees and their relatives and persons deemed at high risk. They went almost entirely to the United States and were admitted pursuant to executive parole authority contained in the 1952 Immigration and Nationality Act (also known as the McCarran–Walter Act), the maximum number being set at 200,000 on April 19, lowered to 129,000 two days later. In 1978, parole authorization was given for an additional 53,000 refugees plus 25,000 per year thereafter, raised to 84,000 per year in 1979 and to 14,000 per month in June 1979. The refugee flow in this period was driven by the movement of 800,000 urban dwellers to rural "new economic zones" and their attempts at flight by boat. In 1978, a campaign was launched to control urban economies and to drive ethnic Chinese out of cities, the effects of which were exacerbated when the Chinese in July 1978 closed their border to Chinese refugees from Vietnam. Finally, in the years following 1987, some 50,000 Amerasian descendants of American servicemen were driven out of Vietnam.[22] In July 1979, there was a conference in Geneva at which the nations present pledged to accept 260,000 refugees. American refugee policy was finally regularized by the enactment in March 1980 of the Refugee Act creating a federally funded Refugee Resettlement Program providing for up to 36 months of assistance to refugees.

In 1981, the *Far Eastern Economic Review* published a rather mean-spirited group of articles suggesting that the program was an ideologically fueled program for economic migrants:

> certain elements within the State Department quite seriously believe that a continuing exodus from the Indochinese countries is a "good thing" and should be discreetly encouraged. It helps to prevent the stabilization of the Communist regime in Indochina, provides a useful source of intelligence information on the situation inside these countries, and appears to demonstrate to the world that Indochinese continue to "vote with their feet."

Another writer alluded to "Saigon cowboys":

> State Department officials with long experience in Indochina many with Vietnamese wives and an emotional conviction that the US has an obligation to provide through the refugee program a non-Communist alternative for those abandoned to the Hanoi Marxists six years ago.[23]

Negroponte, to be sure, was involved only with the later stages of the refugee program. Author Carl Joseph Bon Tempo has noted that the most amazing aspect of the 1975 refugee admissions was that they occurred at all. The American public wanted nothing more than to wash its hands of Southeast Asia. The lower levels of the State Department and the military forced action.[24] Most of the impetus for the Indochinese admissions program came from Shepard Lowman, Herb Cushing, and Lionel Rosenblatt, supported by a number of senior State Department officials. Lowman had served for six years in Vietnam, had married a Vietnamese woman, and had many good friends there. In the final days of the evacuation, he personally arranged for the departures of hundreds of South Vietnamese, including the mayor of Saigon, with whom he was airlifted from the country on April 29.[25] Within the US government, the Bureau of East Asian and Pacific Affairs assumed the leading advocacy role for a larger Indochinese admissions program."[26] Lowman recruited the assistance of economist Leo Cherne and the International Rescue Committee to organize the support of business, labor, and church leaders.

A Harris Poll in May 1975 indicated that Americans were opposed to admitting Vietnamese by a 3–2 majority, 54–36 percent, proportions that remained constant over the life of the program.[27]

In May 1980, Negroponte had become involved in a dispute with the International Committee of the Red Cross (ICRC), which was reluctant to deliver seeds to Cambodia because of the perception that it was aiding Khmer Rouge combat forces. Negroponte thought that the ICRC presented a cogent argument. Washington, nonetheless, directed that the aid should continue.

By June, the United States had effectively abandoned as futile efforts to keep food aid out of the hands of Khmer Rouge combatants. Negroponte in Washington on July 3 called in diplomats from several donor countries and urged them to make parallel demarches to the international relief organizations, stating that

1. The basic objective of the feeding program from the outset had been to feed all needy Cambodians regardless of political persuasion.
2. The border was needed because of deficiencies of the Phnom Penh side.
3. The United States and international organizations were always aware that distribution would be carried out in a war situation and that diversion was possible.
4. Diversion should certainly be kept to a minimum—it was happening on both sides.
5. The United States, despite assertions, had never asked the ICRC to be more lenient on the border than inside Kampuchea.
6. The United States in no way supported Pol Pot's return but wanted to get food into Cambodia in the most effective way.
7. The Thai track record was not perfect, but their constraints must be recognized. After all, they had allowed Thailand to be used as a base for the entire operation and had permitted refugees to stay in Thailand.

Thailand's justification for its collaboration in food aid to the Khmer Rouge was that it wanted the Cambodian population to survive so that one day it could rebuild an independent Cambodia.[28] The then Ambassador to Thailand, Morton Abramowitz, recalled that our purpose was not to undermine the Vietnamese regime in Cambodia, although it was a rotten one, but to make sure people were fed.[29]

Alexander Haig was more concerned with maintaining the viability of the Cambodians as a guerilla force than with moving them out of Thailand to the United States.[30]

The Indochinese refugee experience had more than a little to do with America's ensuing proxy wars in Central America, President Ronald Reagan being driven not only by concern about Soviet and Cuban encroachment near Mexico but with the prospect of feet people arriving in the United States being driven out by political instability caused by Communist leftist insurgencies.[31]

Introduction to the Philippines

In this period, John Negroponte had his first involvement with the affairs of the Philippines. In late 1980, Holbrooke ordered the audience to be restricted at a presentation at the State Department by Philippine opposition leader Benigno Aquino out of a desire to protect his aides, principally John Negroponte, who would have to work for the incoming Reagan administration. Vice President George H.W. Bush attended Marcos' third inauguration. In 1981, Negroponte passed on the complaints of Filipinos protesting against an American antitrust investigation of price fixing in the coconut oil industry; to the distress of the prosecutors, the government settled for a civil consent decree prohibiting future violations.[32] Investigative reporter Raymond Bonner observed that "Reagan's State Department had made a choice: Marcos and monopoly rather than competition and the free market."[33]

Although the Indochinese refugee program was well established at the time of Negroponte's assignment as Deputy Assistant Secretary of State for Far Eastern and Pacific Affairs, through the efforts of Richard Holbrooke, Shepard Lowman, US official Julia Taft, and others, Negroponte rendered it valuable service in budget matters. (Thirty years later, shortly before her death, Julia Taft was to urge greater generosity to Iraqi refugees, particularly those who had assisted Americans as interpreters.[34]) Negroponte was no nativist and no exponent of an American version of the former "white Australia" policy. His approach to the claims of foreign refugees and migrants was consistently liberal, as is sufficiently suggested by his adoption with his wife of five Honduran children. The essence of the United States was not found in an ethnic inheritance but in principles that subdivided and checked arbitrary political power while providing freedom of establishment and economic opportunity to new entrants.

10

HONDURAS

The Christian faith ought to persuade us that political controversies are always conflicts between sinners and not between righteous men and sinners. It ought to mitigate the self-righteousness which is an inevitable concomitant of all human conflict. The spirit of contrition is an important ingredient in the sense of justice. If it is powerful enough, it may be able to restrain the impulse of vengeance sufficiently to allow a decent justice to emerge.

— Reinhold Niebuhr, "Why the Christian Church Is Not Pacifist," in R. Brown (ed.), *The Essential Reinhold Niebuhr: Selected Essays and Addresses* (New Haven: Yale University Press, 1986)

Honduran Prelude

Honduras revealed John Negroponte as a vigorous executor of policy. The policy of proxy war designed to contain the growth of Soviet and Cuban influence in North America was one of which Negroponte approved. He regarded Central America as an area of vital American interest; it is doubtful that he shared the enthusiasm of others in the Reagan administration for support of further-afield anti-Communist forces in places like Central Africa or Afghanistan. He also wanted, however, to contain the American commitment, restraining Honduran ambitions for an invasion of Nicaragua or the provision of large quantities of offensive weapons, and also working to preserve constitutionalism in Honduras.

Negroponte became ambassador to Honduras in November 1981, serving until May 1985. He had not sought the appointment; he had wanted to go to Thailand, a post for which he had been recommended by the State Department and Deputy Secretary. In a highly unusual development, the Thailand post went not to a political appointee but to another career officer, John Gunther Dean, as a result of intervention on Dean's behalf by a personal friend, White House aide Michael Deaver. Thereafter, Negroponte was offered appointments in Zaire and in Lebanon, which he avoided, as he did not want an unaccompanied tour.

His appointment to Honduras may have owed something to his association and alliance with Alexander Haig in the controversies over the Paris agreements on Vietnam but was directly due to an offer from Thomas Enders, the Assistant Secretary for Latin America, whom Negroponte had known when Enders was Deputy Chief of Mission in Cambodia. Negroponte managed to retain the confidence and patronage of persons as divergent in outlook as Haig and Richard Holbrooke owing to his reputation for competence, speed, and discretion. While waiting to be confirmed, Negroponte and his wife were living at the Kenwood Country Club in two rooms as was a similarly situated Vietnam colleague, David Miller, and his wife.[1] On his appointment, he wrote in his class notes in the Phillips Exeter alumni magazine that

> there is so much more at stake in Central America than seems to come through in our media. So writing to you from one of Central America's potential dominoes, I urge fellow classmates to get more than superficially interested.... It's a helluva lot closer to home than Saigon.[2]

Negroponte's embassy wall was said to have been decorated "with paraphernalia from his days as a political officer in Saigon and with an autographed photo of Haig that read "Good luck in your challenging new assignment."[3] He was widely, though not very accurately, perceived to be President Reagan's proconsul in charge of combatting the spread of communism in Central America.

Honduras was no garden spot. Columbus is said to have declared "Thank God we've left these Honduras." Theodore Wilkinson, one of Negroponte's aides there, referred to it as "not an uplifting place to be, it was the poorest in the Americas while I was there, except for Haiti...a very pathetic country, very backward." His colleague Chris Arcos called it "a cesspool, because it dragged everybody down" in behavior. Twenty years later, when the population had doubled to 7.4 million, another American diplomat, James Mack, spoke of the deforestation, the migration of the population to large cities, and the traditional 80 percent illegitimacy rate, which meant that after the migration "social controls have broken down...a traditional society with a lot of poor people living all over the mountainside in little communities farming small plots of land."[4] On the other hand, another Foreign Service member, Dr. Howard Steele, observed "there were 25 families that ran [El Salvador]. They controlled everything. I didn't see that in Honduras." There were two large American companies running fruit plantations and many small coffee-growers.

Historically, Honduras had been run by its military. As observed by Fernando Rondon, who served at the American Embassy before Negroponte's arrival: "The military officers became quite wealthy; being in government was a profitable enterprise...Honduras was run by a junta of colonels who had a reputation for alcoholism." During the Carter administration, the first ambassador was Mari Luci Jaramillo, a political appointee from New Mexico who was generally credited with doing a good job and who was able to get US military assistance increased. When concern grew about the Sandinistas in Nicaragua, she was replaced by the more experienced Jack Binns. Successful elections were held in Honduras, won by the Liberal candidate, Dr. Roberto Suazo, who did not enjoy the support of the military but who rapidly made his peace with it. "[T]hey were both free and fair and both liberals and conservatives celebrated the outcome in the streets of Tegucigalpa—some cried joyfully."[5]

In the waning hours of the Carter administration, Marxist guerrillas in El Salvador on January 10, 1980, had launched a general offensive, hoping to take advantage of the "lame duck" period in Washington. This led the outgoing

administration to resume military aid to El Salvador on January 14.[6] At the outset of the Reagan administration, Secretary of State Alexander Haig had urged
blockades of both Cuba and Nicaragua to prevent the shipment of arms to
Central America. Because of the reaction this might provoke from both Cuba
and the Soviet Union, he found himself in a minority of one among the then
high-ranking principals of the Reagan administration, although similar suggestions were later made by Robert Gates of the Central Intelligence Agency (CIA)
and, at least implicitly, by Reagan's Ambassador to Costa Rica, Curtin Winsor,
Jr., who typified a "hard-line" view in decrying

> A two-track policy which has us wanting to negotiate with the Sandinistas
> on the one hand to hit them with a weak stick if they don't negotiate on the
> other. The idea of negotiating Communists into becoming good democrats;
> Tom Enders' masterpiece, then sending a group of non-politically rooted CIA-
> controlled commandos to blow up bridges if they don't do it I consider...to
> be one of the dumbest policies the United States has pursued since Vietnam.[7]

Haig was much less enthusiastic about covert aid. He observed "covert aid is
a contradiction in terms—there were no secrets." He also did not want to "tell
others what form of government they must have."[8] National Security Council
(NSC) Director Bud McFarlane had an intermediate view:

> covert action is supposed to be a marginal kind of activity to enhance a
> foreign policy goal, not to be its foundation...if it was important, you
> shouldn't go with covert action as the core of your policy.[9]

The war against the Sandinistas stayed covert because the White House apparently believed that if it was brought out into the open, Congress would refuse
to go along. During the Carter administration, the Argentines had trained about
1,000 Nicaraguans; Reagan's CIA director William Casey met with General
Leopoldo Galtieri of the Argentine junta on November 1, 1980, before the new
administration took office.[10]

The outgoing American ambassador to Nicaragua, Laurence Pezzulo,
regarded covert action pressure as "some sort of circus." The issue [of aid to El
Salvador] should have been "played out at a different level with Fidel Castro,
with the Soviets. But you needed pros to do it, not ideologues." He viewed the
Contra effort as "a mindless crusade...we've become a banana republic...."[11]

Fernando Rondon believed that "the facts as we reported them [about
Nicaraguan and Cuban aid to the rebels in El Salvador] would have required
the imposition of sanctions on Nicaragua. I thought the Carter administration
wanted to bury its head in the sand." The Honduran military, abetted by the
Argentine trainers, had begun a crackdown on internal dissidents: "People were
beginning to disappear, not a major issue during my two years there but just
beginning as I left." The London *Economist*, in September 1981, two months
prior to Negroponte's arrival, referred to two such "disappearances."[12]

In November 1981, coincident with Negroponte's arrival in Honduras, the
president and NSC had adopted a formal finding, reported to the Intelligence

Committees of Congress pursuant to Section 501 of the National Security Act of 1947, as amended, directing the CIA to:

> "in cooperation with other governments, provide support…to Nicaraguan paramilitary resistance groups as a means to induce the Sandinistas and Cubans and their allies to cease their support for insurgencies in the region…"[13] On December 1, 1981, President Reagan issued National Security Decision Document (NSDD) 17, authorizing expenditure of $20 million in appropriated CIA funds for a 500-man Contra force.

Negroponte was not happy with the draftsmanship of the finding, declaring "the more complete the finding, the broader the likely Congressional support…one of the principal objections to the finding is that it does not accurately or completely describe what is happening on the ground."[14] Curtin Winsor, the "hard line" Ambassador to Costa Rica was similarly of the view that "the administration in effect lied to the Congress or shall we say told partial truths to the Congress and the resulting breakdown in credibility has…adversely affected American interests."[15] In March 1982, the Contra war got seriously under way with the destruction of two bridges in Nicaragua. In September 1983, the administration transmitted a second finding authorizing pressure on Nicaragua "to enter into negotiations and cease provision of arms." In February 1982, Negroponte cautioned UN Ambassador Jeane Kirkpatrick: "Beware of stand-still ceasefires."[16]

In April 1982, the NSC prepared a working paper on Central America, which was leaked to the press by the administration a year later. It declared a purpose of "not allowing the proliferation of Cuban model states which would provide platforms for subversion, compromise vital sea lanes, and pose a direct military threat at or near our borders."[17] Reagan's National Security advisor, William Clark, grew increasingly impatient with Assistant Secretary Enders because of Enders' view that the behavior of the Nicaraguan government could be moderated, and that negotiations would ultimately be necessary with the Salvadoran rebels, and pushed for a new Assistant Secretary. His candidates were Negroponte and ambassador to Guyana Gerard Thomas, a former admiral. When Secretary of State George Shultz and Deputy Secretary Lawrence Eagleburger bridled at being told whom to appoint, Ambassador to Brazil Langhorne Motley became the compromise choice. Clark, Deputy Assistant Secretary of Defense Nestor Sanchez, Constantine Menges, formerly of the CIA and then on the NSC staff, and UN Ambassador Jeane Kirkpatrick continued to exert important influence.[18]

Negroponte plainly believed in the policy of support for the Contras as a means of containing Cuba and Nicaragua. The bitter aftermath in Vietnam, with millions of "boat people," firmly established in his mind the character and behavior of Marxist regimes and their indifference to individual personality. He had also received a deep introduction into Communist negotiation tactics including an artfulness in playing on Western public opinion through exploitation of the atrocities almost inevitably attendant on war, a willingness to repudiate the territorial limits set out in agreements, and peace plans appealing to the susceptible which left existing military advantages unaltered. Although cautious about the wisdom of American direct intervention for any purpose short of the hypothetical threat to Mexico mentioned in his Stanford writings, Negroponte considered Honduras to be uncomfortably close to Mexico.

This anxiety had rational origins. As writer William Pfaff observed:

In the past, the conventions of Communist internationalism imposed certain restrictions on Soviet behaviour, notably in barring the employment of troops. Forms were observed that allowed the Soviet government to disclaim responsibilities that might prove inconvenient to Soviet national interest.

However, Soviet or Cuban troops and East German aid were employed in Angola, in Ethiopia, in Afghanistan, and in various African states.

[T]hese forms, under Brezhnev in the 1970s were abandoned. The conflict in the Third World thus was sharpened, just at a time when the United States had drawn back, as a consequence of its Vietnam experience, and when serious progress in arms limitation agreements had begun to seem possible. The change exploited American uncertainty in the post-Vietnam and Watergate period in a way that made the ripostes of the Reagan administration—in Grenada, Nicaragua, and El Salvador—all but inevitable.

The proxy wars, as Pfaff points out, allowed the superpowers to

evade a suffering that was imposed on others on their behalf. The moral meaning and consequence of this use of others has not been edifying, but it had the usefulness of sparing the world (as well as the two superpowers) the risks of an engagement from which there might be no retreat.[19]

Facilitator of Military Aid

The United States was concerned with Nicaraguan aid to insurgents in El Salvador. As author and diplomat Anthony Lake described it,

In November and December 1980…US intelligence agencies reportedly found evidence of a significant increase in the arms flow to El Salvador and of Sandinista involvement in the smuggling operation. In its last month in office, the Carter administration suspended—but did not cancel—the aid program, one fifth of which had not yet been provided…the November 1980 US presidential election led the Sandinistas to conclude that the hard line which Reagan would almost certainly follow when he took office called for preemptive action of their own. They therefore gave more aid to the Salvadoran rebels in preparation for the rebels' January 1981 offensive (which failed, in the event, to secure the victory the rebels had predicted.[20]

Former Ambassador to El Salvador Robert White conceded that

Most of the killings [in El Salvador] occurred in the period between the election of Ronald Reagan as President and his taking office. [The Carter administration] had lost a lot of its coherence, a lot of its ideals, and basically was concentrating on how to get re-elected. One thing I admire about the Reagan administration was their ability to put coherence into foreign policy even though I thought the policy was totally wrong-headed.[21]

Beginning in 1981, before Negroponte's arrival, the CIA had begun recruiting veterans of the Nicaraguan National Guard of the former Anastasio Somoza Debayle regime, the so-called "Contras"; support for non-Sandinista political groups had begun during the Carter administration.[22] By the spring of 1983, there were 5,000–7,000 Contras in place.

Negroponte's role was the subject of a sensational article in *Newsweek* for November 8, 1982.[23] This article he attributed to the influence of opponents of the Contra support policy in the State Department. A sidebar to the article was filled with personal aspersions:

> his deliberate, pause-filled conversation prompts a strong desire for coffee … a Machiavelli, only shrewder … "his obsession to get to the top fast will be the very thing that brings him crashing down" concludes a foreign diplomatic colleague in Honduras. The question is whether he might not bring a policy and the fragile government of Honduras down with him.

The article itself suggested that Contra support

> threatens … to destabilize Honduras, to fortify the Marxists in Nicaragua, and to waste US prestige along the tangled banks of the Coco River … "This is the big fiasco of this administration," says one US official. "This is our Bay of Pigs."

Negroponte responded to the article with a statement that "I have the impression that this article … was written by someone who is not in favour of our policies here in Central America."[24] Before the article appeared, Negroponte advised the State Department that Beth Nissen of *Newsweek* "armed with a series of extremely thorny questions" had interviewed him on October 30. "We would not be surprised if former Colonel Leonidas Torres Arias were one of *Newsweek*'s principal sources."[25] Leónidas Torres Arias, a former chief of Honduran intelligence, was alleged by some to have been exiled by the Honduran Chief of Staff General Gustavo Alvarez because of excessive involvement with drug traffickers; he, in turn, charged Alvarez with "a madness to physically annihilate and disappear, as they have already done, all those who do not share their radical ideas."[26] Alvarez was said by him to have declared: "Everything you do to destroy a Marxist regime is moral."[27] In another cable to Shultz, Negroponte noted that he would not try to correct the numerous errors in the article: "at least they spelled my name right" but wanted the secretary to know that he was not "personally hurt" when President Reagan refrained from stopping in Tegucigalpa.[28]

At a later time, Reagan offered to meet Suazo in Costa Rica. Suazo refused to go: "If I am summoned, my name is mud." Negroponte succeeded in arranging a Reagan visit in December 1982. The meeting took place at San Pedro Sula, Air

Force One being too large for the Tegucigalpa airport. The Pope later had a similar experience; Suazo, an irrepressible politician, asked the departing Pope to have his plane fly low over Suazo's native village. In a letter to *The Washington Post* chairman Katharine Graham, Negroponte reproached the *Newsweek* writer for wrongly alleging that he was an avid student of Shakespeare, from whom he got "my alleged imperiousness and my supposed proconsular role. In other words, a cheap shot." "I expressly request that this letter not be published [and] that it be considered for your information and that of your colleagues only."[29] Several of Negroponte's friends protested the article, one of them, Peter Rosenblatt, responding to a defense of it by one of its authors by observing:

> I really cannot think of a more mealy-mouthed excuse for the publication of a personal attack upon a public servant than "the views expressed were those of Negroponte's fellow envoys or officials he's worked with in Honduras".... Was there no editorial discretion involved.? Supposing your informants had also expressed the view that Negroponte was gay, suffered a loathsome disease, or was a vampire? Surely you have some obligation to consider the impact of what you print.[30]

Negroponte rarely responded to this extent to press criticism, coming to view responses later in his career as counterproductive "rising to the bait."

A contemporary *The Washington Post* story depicted the embassy as a nest of Vietnam retreads. Lowman, who with his Vietnamese wife had entertained the *Post* reporter in his home, took umbrage at the journalist's reference to their chopsticks.

Negroponte further denied to the *Post* that he had conveyed a paper on the economy, phrased in the imperative, to President Suazo on his inauguration day; the paper was prepared at Suazo's request, was phrased in the subjunctive, and was given to him a month before his inauguration. Theodore Wilkinson credited Negroponte, mindful of his Vietnam experience, as "hand[ling] [the Hondurans] with great dignity and care. [Foreign Minister Paz Barnica] was treated like a foreign minister of another sovereign state should be." The American economic recommendations reflected the so-called "Washington Consensus," including fiscal discipline, trade liberalization, tax reform, a competitive exchange rate regime, privatization, liberalization for foreign direct investment, market determination of interest rates, and deregulation. Two state responsibilities, those for education and for enforcement of property rights, tended to be neglected in the doctrine as propounded to most Latin American countries, at least until the mid-1990s.

US military aid in the Negroponte era increased from $4 million in fiscal 1980 to $77.5 million in 1984. By that time, there were 11 airfields and base camps spread out over 450 square miles, from which 12,000 Hondurans had been removed. Negroponte had assisted the Army's Special Operations Division, which used Beechcraft and other aircraft based in San Pedro Sula, and later La Ceiba, to monitor Salvadoran rebel communications; later, data about Nicaraguan troop movements from the same source was given to the Contras. Negroponte is said to have protected the division from subordination to General Paul Gorman's Southern Command.[31]

The *Newsweek* article had been preceded by two articles in *The New York Times*, the first of which alleged that Secretary Shultz was "fuming over the mess," and the second of which accurately acknowledged that "Negroponte as the chief of mission oversees the operation, but nothing is done without clearing it in Washington first ... [a] limited covert operation designed to sting but not incapacitate [the Sandinistas]."[32]

"'It was Negroponte who began dealing with the guardsmen and the Somozistas' says one US official. 'That wasn't the original plan. He had to improvise.' Sources in both Washington and Honduras say the ambassador has been careful to deal with the Somozistas through intermediaries to preserve his deniability. Asked about US support for Somozistas or other Contras last week, Negroponte said: 'No comment, no comment, and a big fat no comment.' Of his own contacts, he said 'The only Nicaraguan I know personally is the Nicaraguan ambassador to Honduras. The only Nicaraguan I deal with in any official way is the ambassador.' After Negroponte began to deal with the Somozistas, any chance of recruiting Edén Pastora probably was lost: 'the orders came from Alvarez himself that our American friends did not want this guy to have any part of the game.' 'Haig and Enders gave Negroponte full autonomy' said one high-level insider." "The whole idea, as explained by Ambassador Negroponte among others, was to have the local forces do the work. But the problem, perfectly evident by June was that the local forces were not, in fact, doing what they were supposed to do."[33] Later, Negroponte asserted that only about 15 percent of the Contras were Somozistas. It was said that after the *Newsweek* article, "the Ambassador met with the Honduran president on November 4 to coordinate how each side would comment on the revelations. Even at that early date, the Hondurans cautioned Negroponte that the Contras would never amount to much."[34]

Shortly after Negroponte's arrival, General Gustavo Alvarez, who had been trained by the Argentine junta, was installed as chief of the Honduran armed forces over the head of older rivals, reportedly on the recommendation of the CIA station chief, Donald Winters (viewed by some as almost a caricature of the CIA agent of fiction), and the embassy defense attaché.[35] An indication of Winters' closeness to Alvarez was that Winters became the godfather of one of Alvarez' children. (The Honduran Minister for the Presidency, Carlos Flores, whom Negroponte held in high esteem, was the godfather of one of Negroponte's adopted children, but contrary to some reports Negroponte had no such relationship with Alvarez.) In the 1970s, Alvarez had reportedly been paid by Standard Fruit to assist in the repression of a fruit cooperative.[36] In a dispatch to Washington in January 1982, Negroponte reported on a meeting with President Suazo over rumors that the defeated Nationalist candidate in the recent elections was seeking to have General José María Paz remain as the military commander. Negroponte noted that Suazo favored the appointment of General Alvarez, which Negroponte thought "would be most convenient to our mutual interests here."[37] Negroponte in a dispatch in February 1982 urging

additional aircraft for Honduras lauded "his [Alvarez'] customary drive and justified sense of urgency."[38]

Alvarez' ascent was almost providential in light of the purposes of American
policy. He was a committed anti-Communist. He was not perceived as having
been promoted by drug cartels. He was a man of zeal in a country noted for
its lassitude.

Alvarez was unhappy with US support of Britain in the Falklands War,
demanding of Negroponte, "Where is the Monroe Doctrine? Is South America
part of Europe?" and declaring that the United States had "its mind in Washington,
its heart in Great Britain and its feet in Latin America."[39]

In November 1982, disillusionment with Alvarez' excesses had set in. The
Honduran bishops issued a statement decrying "terrorism, disappearances, the
mysterious discovery of bodies, assaults, thefts, kidnappings, individual and
collective insecurity all appear to have grown over the last two years … a sort of
Religious War." "The bishops particularly criticized [Alvarez'] new civil defense
committees as instruments of repression normally used by governments of
'extreme right or extreme left'."[40]

Opposition to Premature Ceasefires

The stiffness of Negroponte's attitude toward peace negotiations is suggested
by an early dispatch in May 1982 urging nonacquiescence in premature plans

> in their domestic and international Marxist orientation … we can visualize no
> such negotiated arrangement capable of insuring that Nicaragua would not
> come back to cause trouble to its neighbours some other day. Indeed, such a
> negotiated outcome would be a Trojan horse not unlike the 1962 Cuban mis-
> sile arrangements which facilitated consolidation of the Cuban revolution.[41]

In the wake of the *Newsweek* article, Senator Patrick Leahy of Vermont and
other congressional representatives visited the embassy in Honduras: "officials
told Leahy and the others that the embassy was staking the outcome on some
kind of negotiations. They expressed concern about the small war that was
being ginned up around them."[42] The embassy received an extraordinary influx
of congressional visitors, and was a favorite weekend destination for congressional delegations. In the first four months of 1983 there were eight congressional delegations, including Congressman Michael Barnes; Senator Leahy and
four staff members; four staff members of the House Foreign Affairs Committee;
Congressmen Stephen Solarz and Leach and a staff member; Congressmen Long,
McHugh, Dixon, and Mervyn Dymally and two staff members; Congressmen
Berkley Bedell and Robert Torricelli and four staff members; Congressman
G. William Whitehurst and four staff members; and Congressmen Hamilton,
McCurdy, Whitehurst, Young, Stump, and Norman Mineta and five staff mem-
bers. During the rest of the year, there were 23 more visits including 10 sena-
tors, 35 congressmen, and 41 staff members.

The portrait of Negroponte as a proconsul for Central America appears over-
drawn. Negroponte's tenure at the embassy, from November 1981 to May 1985,
overlapped with that of Colonel Gerald Clark, defense attaché at the embassy

from 1981 to 1986. Barry Rubin noted that from the time of his arrival in May 1983, General Paul Gorman "eclipsed Negroponte as the major player in the field";[43] Roy Gutman observed that after October 1983, Gorman was more powerful than any of the American ambassadors on the scene.[44] "Gorman is even over-shadowing John Negroponte. Negroponte received the CIA cables but not those of the military." Shortly after his arrival in Honduras, Negroponte allowed the visiting Duane Clarridge, the CIA "point man" for Central America, to meet alone with outgoing President Paz, an action he regarded as a mistake, and one which he never made again.

It was said that "What Gen. Gorman stands for is the Centralamericanization of any intervention."[45] Apart from Gorman's role, with which Negroponte had no quarrel, Negroponte was also subjected to supervision by, and aggravation from, an active "war party" in the State Department which at various times included Jeane Kirkpatrick, Constantine Menges, Richard Burt, William Middendorf, Fred Ikle, Nestor Sanchez, and Jacqueline Tillman; Nicaraguan policy was also influenced by Attorney General Edwin Meese, CIA chief William Casey, and National Security Advisors William Clark and Bud McFarlane and from the outside by Republican Senator Jesse Helms of North Carolina and an influential staff member of his, John Carbaugh. Oliver North in the White House frequently acted for this group. The second-tier officials in this group were irreverently referred to as "the pygmies."

> The tensions generated by this unorthodox power arrangement appear to have shortened the tenure of top officials at the State Department including Enders and his successor Motley as well as some of the hardliners' key operatives on the scene—the US Ambassador to Honduras, John Negroponte and Nutting's successor as commander of the Southern Command, Gen. Paul Gorman... Negroponte had to be a chameleon to satisfy the hardliners, but his "action" orientation and his devotion to Reagan's goals endeared him to the war party, although he was never really a member.[46]

Raymond Burghardt, who was Menges' deputy at the NSC before becoming Negroponte's political counselor in Honduras, described the lineup as pitting Kirkpatrick, Menges, and Weinberger on the one hand against George Shultz, Robert McFarlane, and John Poindexter on the other. When Menges was made to resign, Burghardt replaced him.

Langhorne Motley declared his premise in a blunt oral history:

> I was not going to let the Central America issue get out of hand... become an adversarial or pejorative 1984 campaign issue. We don't want another Cuba. We don't want another Vietnam. We would not use US troops. We would tolerate, even though distastefully, people like the contras... bullying, pushing and shoving and hoping there would be an internal collapse... anything to keep the pressure on without becoming militarily involved... a practical approach. The end game was to prevent the consolidation of the Sandinista regime. It took six years, but it worked.... I knew that using American troops would go beyond the limits of the American popular will.

This declaration was made with the benefit of hindsight; Negroponte perceived Motley as having been less than consistently supportive of the Contra effort and even as possibly complicit in the *Newsweek* article. Motley, however, was no fool. He quoted General Gorman as estimating that an invasion of Nicaragua would require 125,000–150,000 troops, 4 to 6 weeks, and 4,000–6,000 American casualties. He took the view that Americans would not stand still for six weeks.[47] In addressing himself to Negroponte's successor, John Ferch, he is said to have observed: "John, always remember that you are playing with other peoples' lives down there (meaning that we are not putting our troops on the line, we are putting Central Americans on the line)."[48]

Negroponte's role involved informing Washington on Honduran attitudes toward the Contras, on ploys that might work, on talking points to use with the Hondurans, and on military aid to ferry Honduran troops by helicopter to blocking positions along the borders of either El Salvador or Honduras.

Negroponte's writ did not run far beyond Honduras. While Deane Hinton was Ambassador to El Salvador until May 1983, only once did Negroponte receive his clearance to enter the country, and that was on a weekend.[49] It must also be remembered that Alvarez' rise, although not his appointment, preceded Negroponte's arrival:

> Both are strong-willed ambitious individuals. Both are anti-communists and believe in the need for a vigorous military defense. Thus despite the fact that they do not always agree on issues, they seem to complement each other nicely. However, notions that Alvarez is Negroponte's man are mistaken. Alvarez' position was made possible by his relationship with President Suazo Cordova.[50]

The American military favored Alvarez: "He was dynamic, aggressive, and disciplined. He had a clear chain of command. He fit our mold of military leader. He was our candidate."[51] In July 1982, Alvarez expressly declared that he was "in agreement with US intervention in Central America because we now confront an armed aggression from the Soviet Union via Cuba."[52]

Suazo, in turn, though a country doctor and convinced anti-Communist, was not a pillar of strength: "he is a libertine, he lies, he conspires, he is incompetent, he plays cards, he is a reformed alcoholic."[53] Negroponte's aide, Theodore Wilkinson, described Dr. Suazo as "about as much as a small-town country hick President as I've ever run into," alluding to his first lady who ran the country's charities," but crediting him with "tremendous grasp of the politics of the country…. Everybody looked forward to the day when Honduras would have a slightly more dignified President, but while he was there, he was our guy."[54]

The United States conducted joint exercises with Honduras near the Nicaraguan border, leaving equipment behind.[55] There were six airfields, a port, and a base area for the Contras on the Atlantic coast of Honduras, and 50 members of the American air force at a radio station. Sixteen hundred American military participated in Operation Big Pine I in February 1983. From August 1983 to February 1984, 5,500 American troops took part in Operation Big Pine II, said to be "the biggest single US military operation in the history of Latin

America and to have wiped out 100 Honduran rebels." The abandoned equipment was a means of circumventing congressional restrictions on aid to the
Contras. In the period 1982–9, the United States supplied Honduras with $1.2
billion in economic and military aid; 350 members of the Peace Corps were
sent to Honduras, and there were American civil action teams devoted to combatting the AIDS (Acquired Immunity Deficiency Syndrome) epidemic.[56] There
were 15,000–20,000 Contras in place by 1986.[57] Negroponte was alleged to have
rebuffed the disenchanted Sandinista leader Edén Pastora who had declared
that he would not work with the CIA or former members of the Nicaraguan
National Guard.[58] Curtin Winsor conceded that "unlike the poor Contras in the
north, who had no political root, [Pastora] had a political root." The difficulty
was: "The man is tremendous in front of the press, but as a guerrilla he lived up
to his name, Comandante Zero."[59]

The ostensible purpose of aid to Nicaraguan Contras was prevention of
the flow of arms from Nicaragua to El Salvador and to put pressure on the
Sandinista government without overthrowing it. There were claims, however,
that there had been no arms shipments from Nicaragua to El Salvador since
1981.[60] On May 19, Negroponte addressed an unusual six-page memorandum
to Shultz urging that

> Nicaragua's anti-social regional behaviour is after all a mere symptom
> of a deeper political disease.... The evolution of our position appears,
> however, to have shifted progressively and almost in imperceptible incre-
> ments toward a severe reduction of our first two objectives (pluralism
> and non-alignment), half-hearted pursuit of the third (reduction of forces
> and reduction of defense spending) and elevation of the fourth objective
> (end to support for insurgencies) to such a prominent position that many
> impartial observers could easily infer that if satisfied on this point we
> would be satisfied completely ... a requirement that military/security levels
> be "kept" to levels commensurate with security needs does not fully deal
> with the asymmetry that has developed since 1979 and the corresponding
> need for a reduction of forces on Nicaragua's part. Nicaraguan forces are
> already twice the size of Honduras' and ... their military budget, not count-
> ing arms donations, may be three times Honduras'.[61]

In the same period, Negroponte supported Honduran pressure on the Salvadoran
military to ensure Christian Democratic participation in the next Salvadoran government.[62] In July, he urged increased military and economic aid, noting that
there were Honduran advocates of a rapprochement with Nicaragua accompanied by "substantial economic assistance from unspecified Middle Eastern state."[63]
In August, he cautioned against a commitment proposed by General Wallace
Nutting to "neutralize any Nicaraguan offensive military action outside sovereign
Nicaraguan land, sea, and air space," suggesting that there be added the words
"beyond the capacity of Honduras to meet with its own conventional forces" to
"raise the threshold of possible direct United States military involvement here as
high as possible."[64] Throughout, Negroponte, unlike many of the "hardliners,"
regarded support of the Contras as a means of avoiding direct American military

intervention, which he was leery of by reason of his experience in Vietnam. In October 1982, Negroponte and Shultz, over the objection of "hardliners" in the Reagan administration, embraced the San Jose Principles put forth at a conference in San Jose[65] attended by representatives from Belize, Columbia, El Salvador, Jamaica, and the Dominican Republic, including general disarmament, reduction of foreign advisers, multilateral observers, reduced arms traffic, respect for borders, and continued negotiation,[66] and in November 1982 urged that they be reaffirmed when President Reagan visited San Jose.[67] He also urged redoubled efforts to enact the Caribbean Basin initiative, and a visit by President Reagan to Honduras. At this time, Negroponte was, nonetheless, of the view that Nicaragua was becoming another Cuba.[68] In June 1983, he again returned to the San Jose principles in warning against a peace initiative by the Salvadoran rebels:

> Dust off the old National Liberation Front of South Vietnam political platform or the South Vietnam Provisional Revolutionary Government seven-point peace plan and one finds an uncanny similarity with the "fundamental points for negotiations … they wish to complement their aggressive military strategy on the ground, masking themselves to extent possible behind veil of willingness to negotiate … they want to bait us into direct talks with them or into playing intermediary role either of which course could have potentially fatal consequences for Government of El Salvador (GOES). They certainly don't want to talk about elections or anything resembling terms GOES is thinking about."

The objective should be to have "Nicaragua to negotiate with them [San Jose signers] not us, on basis of San Jose principles."[69] This cable was sent not only to the Department but also to the UN delegation, then headed by Jeane Kirkpatrick, and to the embassies in Bogota, Caracas, Guatemala, Managua, Mexico, Panama, San Jose, and San Salvador.

A Nicaraguan Disinformation Campaign

In February 1983, Negroponte was the subject of a lengthy article, in Spanish and English, in the Managua magazine *Soberania*. The article sounded familiar propaganda themes, some of them picked up on by American writers, charging that he was a CIA informant in his years in Hong Kong, a "security adviser" in Saigon and "liaison in establishing relations between the United States and the bloodthirsty government of Pol Pot in Cambodia." The article went on to accuse him of links to the overthrow of the Lara government in Ecuador and Pinochet's military coup in Chile and with a "Honduran Anti-Communist movement … to follow and assassinate all revolutionary leaders." For good measure, it described him as "a complex-ridden man who enjoys projecting false and prefabricated images of himself as a cold-blooded person with great self-control or as a yoga contemplative." He was "a sagacious Machiavellian," whose conversation was "lengthy, tedious, and filled with pauses that exasperate the listeners." Having just received a note containing a death threat,[70] Negroponte took alarm at the last sentence of the article, predicting that he may have "his final experience as a diplomat," and requested added security from Washington.

A more detached observer in this period declared that Negroponte was "well-versed in the art of obfuscation…the master of the pointless interview." Nonetheless,

> the truth [as to Negroponte's role] is closer to the Negroponte- [Shepard] Lowman account than to the other. Both the Contras and the Hondurans loved to gossip, especially about their contacts with the gringos. Negroponte had made enemies within the bureaucracy. Personalizing the issue was a way for dissenters to discredit policy that they hoped to sink.

Unquestionably, Negroponte "helped work out arrangements for [Contra] support with the Honduran military…the Hondurans were particularly resistant to some of the embassy's economic advice."[71] One of his aides, Robert Pastorino, later ambassador to the Dominican Republic, observed that "The strategy was never to win on the ground…. We couldn't because they had Russian support. The strategy was to give the Sandinistas enough of a problem so they couldn't consolidate like Castro did, and so we could use diplomacy."[72]

A critical US Senator, James Sasser of Tennessee, described the conditions of Negroponte's life in Honduras:

> I rode with him in his armed car through the city…we were accompanied by a dozen heavily armed security troops. Each time the caravan was forced to stop in traffic, the doors of the vans carrying the security troops swung open and the troops brandished machine guns, positioning themselves against any would-be attacker.[73]

A similar description of the life of the Ambassador to El Salvador was provided by William Jeffras Dieterich of the State Department: A "big, big security package. The ambassador had an armored Cadillac, a follow car, a lead car, probably four American security agents with him and another six Salvadorans riding in both those cars."[74]

Assessing Honduras' Problems

In April 1983, the ambassador delivered a wide-ranging speech before the Tegucigalpa Rotary Club.[75] After lauding the advantages of democracy and Honduras' record, he pointedly noted that "the United States has been known, perhaps too often in recent history, to withdraw vital support from authoritarian governments even at the expense of other very important interests…having a democracy sure helps." He noted that glaring social inequalities do not exist in Honduras "on the scale apparently known in some of the neighbouring countries." He pointed out that the AID assistance program amounted to $90 million and was the third largest in the Western Hemisphere, and that Honduras had the second largest Latin American peace corps contingent. He lauded the trade provisions of Reagan's Caribbean Basin initiative providing for a "twelve year one way duty free zone." He commended recent sound economic policies on the part of Honduras while bemusedly noting that if Honduras' population continues to grow at the present rate of 3.6 percent per year, your country will have 21 million inhabitants by the year 2025, one generation from now. For purposes of comparison, I will mention that this figure represents approximately the same population as the entire United States had in 1850.

He asked for thought as to the "social pressures this will create," without making any direct suggestions about birth control, a subject anathema to the American religious right. He then compared Honduras' military mobilization of one-half of 1 percent of its population with that of Nicaragua "with the avowed intention of mobilizing almost ten percent of its population." He noted that American military aid had tripled to $30 million in 1982. He also referred to joint military exercises and a new radar installation.

It has been said that in that month

the Honduran ally began to waver. John Negroponte reportedly warned of this disastrous possibility, which he feared would convince Managua that the Sandinista revolution had become irreversible. In April 1983, Negroponte advocated pushing Edén Pastora hard to activate the southern front, raising the visibility of US contacts with Calero and doing more to gain the confidence of the intelligence committees of Congress, encouraging members to visit Central America.[76]

The Contra leader Adolfo Calero did not arouse universal enthusiasm; Robert Duemling of the Foreign Service, who was placed in charge of $27 million in humanitarian aid to the Contras voted by Congress in 1985, although having the "highest regard for the [Contra] rank and file" thought that Calero was "out of the classic Central American caudillo mold," and "didn't think the contras could hack it."[77]

In July 1983, Negroponte lauded the re-deployment of the US fleet, "a very positive step which tends to bottle the problem back up into Nicaragua."[78] In the same month, he noted of a new Sandinista peace proposal that "all the obligations fall on our side and none on theirs."[79] Earlier, he had noted that "Nicaragua has developed and continues to develop armed forces in excess of any reasonable defensive need…in 1981 Comandante Ortega said Nicaragua intends to develop a regular force of fifty thousand men and a militia of two hundred thousand."[80]

In August 1983, the Ambassador published an op-ed piece, "Honduras Is Well Worth Saving" in the *Los Angeles Times*, pointing out that during the 70s, Honduras enjoyed a 7–8 percent annual economic growth rate and that because of Nicaragua "Growth was estimated at –1 percent in 1982—under the circumstances viewed as something of an economic triumph. Unemployment stands at 25–30 percent of the work force, and there has been no significant new foreign investment for the last five years." The much disparaged American fruit companies

are excellent corporate citizens…the best paid earning several times the per capita average. Both companies have been pioneers in the diversification of Honduran agriculture; the large majority see political stability and export-led economic growth as the long-term answer to their problems.[81]

A less sanguine foreign diplomat took the view that "This place is too vulnerable and disorganized to play the role it is being assigned in Washington. You can't destabilize Nicaragua any more from here without also destabilizing Honduras."[82]

In October, 1983, Negroponte denied that the Grenada invasion was designed to put further pressure on Nicaragua to change the course of its revolution. Joint American-Honduran military exercises were helping to restore an equilibrium that has been distorted by the military buildup in Nicaragua.[83] In January 1984, an American helicopter reportedly inspecting Honduran road construction landed inadvertently in Nicaragua; the pilot was killed by the Nicaraguans, apparently the first American military casualty of the "Contra war."[84] In April 1984, a helicopter was forced down, reportedly over Salvadoran air space, whose passengers included two US Senators, Lawton Chiles and J. Bennett Johnson.[85] Another helicopter carrying Diana Negroponte, who had been active in Honduran and Salvadoran charitable work, was fired upon.[86] Even Mrs Negroponte's charitable work had aroused controversy; she had been obliged to respond to an article in *Mother Jones* magazine, reprinted in the *Miami Herald* for April 3, 1983, alleging that she was working for a Christian evangelical group that ran supplies to anti-Sandinista Indians on the frontier.[87] In fact, she was a volunteer with the Evangelical Christian charity World Relief administering the UNHCR office in Tegucigalpa.[88] Two historians of the Contra conflict, writing in 1994, observed that "Even today, Mrs. Negroponte is fondly remembered for her social work, some of which was done at no small risk to herself."[89] On her departure from Honduras, a plaza (since demolished) was named in her honor.[90]

Disillusioned Diplomats

In spite of Negroponte's reputation as a "hard liner," he, unlike his colleague Ambassador to El Salvador Deane Hinton, confirmed that a serious massacre of Salvadorean villagers had been carried out at El Mozote by the Salvadoran military or death squads supplied by it. Hinton asserted that "a lot of people believed these incidents were manipulated, that they didn't take place";[91] on January 25, 1982, Hinton said that allegations of massacres by death squads were "an impossible charge to sustain," though two weeks later he publicly cautioned the Salvadorans: "there is a limit, and at times this government has trended dangerously close to that limit."[92] After the massacre had been disclosed in *The New York Times*, *The Wall Street Journal*, relying on the US embassy in El Salvador, and statements by foreign policy adviser Elliott Abrams in Washington, questioned the veracity of *The New York Times* report. A Negroponte cable written a week after the *Times* story noted that the

> most significant element in refugees' reports is their decision to flee at this time when in the past they had remained during sweeps. This lends credibility to reputed greater magnitude and intensity of the [Government of El Salvador's] military operation in Northern Morazan.[93]

The American diplomats in Central America were increasingly dissatisfied with the Salvadoran government; in October 1982 Hinton, earned the disfavor of the Washington hardliners by declaring in a speech in El Salvador that "since 1979 perhaps as many as 30,000 Salvadorans have been MURDERED, not killed in battle, MURDERED." This utterance was repudiated by Deputy Secretary of State William Clark, and was watered down when published to read "illegally, that is, not in battle."[94] Later, Vice President George H.W. Bush on a visit to El Salvador warned the Salvadoran colonels that any more such incidents would result in the reluctant withdrawal of American military aid.[95] In December 1982, Congress passed the Boland amendment forbidding the use of funds "for the purpose of overthrowing the government of Nicaragua." In April 1983, Negroponte urged Nicaraguan participation in Central American peace talks instigated by the Costa Rican President, Oscar Arias. Senator Robert Torricelli (D-NJ) accused Negroponte of declaring to him, apropos of assistance to the Contras, "we can't let legal trivialities get in the way of our objectives."[96]

In May 1983 in advance of a visit by General Alvarez to Washington, Negroponte noted his concern that half-hearted American support of the Contras might generate "a Bay of Pigs (their phrase)." He urged assistance to Honduras in acquiring transport aircraft: "It can hardly be characterized as offensive weaponry…and makes enormous sense in terms of keeping his armed forces relatively small, but mobile, rather than seeking to match Nicaragua's build-up man for man." Apropos of the Contras, Negroponte noted "this thing is starting to work and is building up a momentum. It wouldn't surprise me if size of force could be doubled in next five months if we provided necessary weapons."[97] The outfitting of the Contras sometimes gave rise to amusing incidents. Theodore Wilkinson was surprised on one occasion to receive a call from an unknown person announcing "your boots are ready." "What boots?" asked Wilkinson. "Seven thousand pairs," was the reply. In the preceding month, Negroponte had to warn Alvarez against overambitious plans to overthrow the Sandinista regime, hence the emphasis on provision of defensive weapons.[98]

Alvarez and the Death Squads

Battalion 316, over which Alvarez had presided before being named Chief of Staff, was alleged to have committed 247 political killings. Negroponte complained of them without avail in 1983, as he made clear in later hearings before the Senate Foreign Relations Committee. It was the successor to a Directorate of Special Investigations trained in Texas by the CIA.[99] This in turn had been preceded by a military intelligence operation with 10 or 12 advisors supplied by the Argentine junta, including Israeli advisers.[100] Duane Clarridge, the regional CIA operative, observed that the first 500 Contras had been organized by the Argentines during the Carter administration

> why because the Argentines had a messianic idea in their head that, that they were gonna take on communism, wherever they could find it and because the US had basically backed out of the whole war during the Carter administration.[101]

On his arrival in Honduras in early 1980, two years before the advent of Negroponte, President Carter's Honduras ambassador, Jack Binns "suspected these advisers might be helping the Hondurans set up an extralegal counter-subversion operation that would resemble and emulate that of Argentina." These concerns, it turned out, were well grounded.[102] Binns concluded that initially

> the Argentines were already involved without US Government (USG) knowledge or support and had been working with the Contras since at least mid-1980 .... Although I was at the time certain we had little infor-mation regarding the activities or plans of the Nicaraguan exile groups in Honduras, and even less about what the Argentines were doing, the CIA's later involvement with both groups has shaken my confidence in that regard. What is clear ... is that following the change in administration the CIA engaged in a wide range of covert activity in Honduras that was not shared with me or, perhaps the State Department. And the Tegucigalpa station was an active player.[103]

Negroponte's aide Theodore Wilkinson similarly observed:

> some of the things that were being done back in Washington by Ollie [North] and the so-called Regional Interagency Group and Elliott Abrams and Dewey Clarridge were almost certainly being done without the knowl-edge of, I expect, even the ambassador.[104]

Human Rights Reports

In 1982, the initial draft of a human rights report to Congress ascribed respon-sibility to the government for disappearances, but Negroponte, who had only been in Honduras for three months, ordered the reference deleted, replacing it with a statement that

> There have been allegations of a number of mysterious disappearances during 1981. In the majority of instances these allegations have involved nationals of other Central American countries who may have entered Honduras illegally or who may have engaged in illegal activities resulting in their deportation.[105] In the few cases of allegations of disappearance of Honduran nationals, the government has consistently denied any involve-ment by security services.

Negroponte later declared: "I recall focussing on the introductory passages because of my interest in placing Honduras' human rights performance in an appropriate regional context." "I believe that the Honduran law enforcement officials did at times badly mistreat suspected terrorists and on a number of occasions may have killed them." "Could I have been more vocal? Well you know in retrospect, perhaps I could have been. But that is the way I handled it at the time."[106]

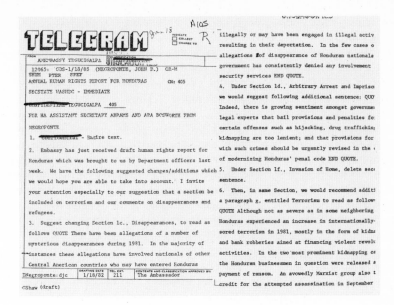

See No Evil? The 1982 Human Rights Report

The bombing of the Tegucigalpa power plant by Honduran insurgents shortly after Negroponte's arrival in 1981 was a landmark event:

> banks and businesses had to convert to hand calculators…some patients undergoing operations died on the operating tables…traffic became congested, snarled and generally unmanageable…broadcasts could no longer be enjoyed by the people at night…life after sunset appeared to be governed by just how many candles you could find…meat and dairy products were now spoiling in the supermarkets and in household refrigerators…one does not want to have the local housewives arrayed against you…blame was placed squarely on the guerrillas.

Negroponte was successful in getting Washington to provide an emergency power generation facility in a bit more than a week—something that the Honduran government and its people would not forget for quite a while.[107]

In April 1982, Negroponte had a conversation with President Suazo in which he referred to information that

> various communist factions here have concluded their unity talks and have made threshold decision within the last month to move from "oasis of peace" approach to revolutionary violence for Honduras…. We urged that strongest possible pre-emptive measure be taken now in effort to preclude problem from taking on unmanageable proportions later on. Suazo was aware of these reports and expressed agreement with our suggestions.[108]

This might have been taken as an incitement to further arrests and "disappearances."

The same month, Honduran insurgents machine-gunned the US Embassy, the US Agency for International Development (USAID) office, and the US Information Service office.[109] There ensued, in the candid words of Colonel Sewell Menzel: "kidnappings, assassinations, disappearances, torture, secret detention centers, ambushes and murders on the part of both sides [which] involved the innocent as well as the guilty."[110] In September 1982, Negroponte asserted in a letter to the London *Economist* that "it is simply untrue to state that death squads have made their appearance in Honduras."[111] The US Department of State Country Reports on Human Rights for 1983 submitted in 1982 was, therefore, benign as it related to Honduras.[112] Negroponte at his confirmation hearing as DNI director later declared: "I believe my characterization of Alvarez' 'dedication to democracy' was overstated and with hindsight would not have used that phrase…. I do not believe, however, that Alvarez himself aspired to political office."[113]

His action in editing the 1982 memorandum submitted to the State Department is the most-criticized action taken by Negroponte in the course of his long career. A number of points, however, can be made in his defense. The requirement of human rights reports was created by Congress in the wake of the Helsinki agreement less as a way of informing itself than as a means of allowing the executive branch to bring pressure on foreign governments to improve their human rights practices. The reports were conceived of as a tool of foreign policy, not as an information-gathering device, and had been so treated by administrations of both parties. Thus, for example,

> [President] Carter's hands-off attitude toward the Democracy Wall move-ment [in China] was merely one part of a larger pattern of behaviour by his administration in dealing with China. At the beginning of 1980 the administration was obliged for the first time to include China in its annual report to Congress about the human rights situation around the world. The question of what to say about China led to open warfare within the Washington bureaucracy. "Richard Holbrooke and Pat Derian had a brawl over the human rights report for China," says Stephen B. Cohen, a Georgetown University law professor who worked as an aide to Derian. 'He [Holbrooke] tried to understate human rights issues because we had a new relationship with China and he didn't want to offend China.' Although Holbrooke and his staff watered down the text, they were forced to include some critical material when the US embassy in Beijing submitted a detailed report candidly describing some of China's repressive policies.[114]

The journalist Barry Rubin has provided other examples of the "fudging" of human rights reports by diplomats resentful of being required to publicly criti-cize regimes with which they are trying to maintain good trade and military relations. Thus

> the Philippine mission sent cables ignoring corruption and overstating improvements in living standards under dictatorial President Ferdinand

Decorating a Colonel: Negroponte and Sewall Menzel in Honduras

Marcos. Glowing reports were sent from Zaire in the midst of a repression campaign. Human rights officials had to battle the Iran desk, just before the revolution, on whether internal documents should say there was "discontent" rather than "dissatisfaction" with the Shah's rule.[115]

Assistant Secretary for Latin American Affairs Langhorne Motley referred to "155 ambassadors who have to clean up the mess that the report makes every year."[116]

A more spectacular example, little commented upon by Negroponte's critics, related to El Salvador, where "death squads" killed thousands. As summarized by Diana Negroponte:

From 1981 the administration certified progress on human rights in El Salvador in order to sustain Congressional funding. The hearings were held every six months if not more often until President Reagan's pocket veto at

the end of 1983. The Certification Hearings acquired a theatrical quality with
the administration claiming progress in order to sustain funding and the
Congress contesting their report, aware that their criticism was inadequate
to cut or terminate financial support for the Salvadoran government.[117]

There is some justice in Elliott Abrams' comment: "The certification process
is ridiculous...a product of Congress' refusal to make decisions or let the
President make them."[118]

The Salvadoran conflict dwarfed that in Honduras, resulting in 75,000 dead
in a population of 4 million. At one point, it was estimated that 41,048 casualties
had been inflicted by supporters of the government, as against 776 by the rebels;
Assistant Secretary Enders acknowledged that the bullets killing all but a handful
of dead came from American-made rifles.[119] On the other hand, the applicable
legislation was tightened up over time. A finding that there are no "disappearances" is now an express precondition to AID assistance, absent a finding that
assistance "will directly benefit the needy people," congressional committees
being empowered to demand further details. Military aid requires similar findings, absent a finding of "special circumstances" by the president.[120] Although
such findings could have been sought in the Honduran situation, they were not.

As Peter Rodman later observed: "The administration sometimes laid itself
open to charges that it did not aggressively anathematize, or gear its whole
policy to the pursuit of, individual military officers linked to atrocities."[121]
George Shultz in his memoirs was to observe: "The governments of El Salvador,
Honduras and Guatemala contained and tolerated many unsavoury characters.
Still, serious people in those governments were engaged in a stalwart effort to
move toward democracy and the rule of law."[122]

Years earlier, George Kennan had urged on American diplomats a course
directly the opposite of that supposed to be demanded by the provisions for
human rights reports:

> I think it urgently desirable that there be enforced upon our entire official
> establishment a form of discipline that would cause its members to desist
> from all sorts of moralizing public judgment about the internal quality or
> propriety of Latin American governments.[123]

One critic observed of the embassy Americans: "their attitude was one of tolerance and silence...they needed Honduras to loan its territory more than
they were concerned about innocent people being killed."[124] By August 1983,
Negroponte's statements on this subject were less unqualified. In an article in
the *Los Angeles Times*, he acknowledged:

> If there is a soft spot in Honduras' otherwise positive political record, it is
> in human rights. There have been arbitrary arrests and credible allegations
> of some disappearances. The Honduran press has been free to publish
> what it wishes about such cases, no doubt contributing to the satisfac-
> tory resolution of some of these cases.... Moreover, there is no indica-
> tion that the infrequent human rights violations that do occur are part of

deliberate government policy. Indeed disciplinary action has been taken against members of the police and military (including officers) who have abused their authority.[125]

In September 1982, Negroponte advised the State Department that

San Pedro [kidnapping] incident and growing terrorism in Honduras generally brings home urgent need to improve Honduran anti-terrorist capability [redaction] there is much that can be done in the area of training and making available the kinds of equipment Hondurans [are] likely to need in future crisis situations.[126]

In November 1982 reporting on a meeting with Minister for the Presidency Flores, Negroponte reported that

Ambassador agreed that human rights abuses are a problem and suggested that Government of Honduras (GOH) consider coming up with urgent plan to improve Honduran judicial system. This requires joint effort of executive, judicial, legislative branches as well as National Police...without such an action plan, creation of a Congressional Committee could turn out to be another pressure point without a remedy. [Redaction].[127]

In later testimony, Negroponte alluded to an

archaic penal code,...a complex, ill-trained, and over-burdened judicial system,...a law enforcement system whose members, frustrated by light sentences and numerous loopholes sometimes found it expedient to take extra-legal means to ensure the punishment of known criminals.[128]

The Honduran press reported remarks by him on this theme.[129] The United States itself, in the late 1960s and again in connection with post-2001 terrorist threats, modified its criminal codes to include new inchoate offenses relating to such matters as possession of explosives and financing of terrorist acts.

In February 1985, Negroponte reported to the State Department on a meeting with General Alvarez' successor, General Walter Lopez. Negroponte referred to a February 4, 1985, *Newsweek* article alleging

more than 200 disappearances in Honduras since 1981 and...that the anti-Sandinistas were responsible for many of these...[Lopez] noted that there have been only one or two alleged disappearances of any sort in the last eleven months. Also, talk of the existence of "death squads" is totally without foundation. He did say that the armed forces had been conducting an investigation into alleged violations over the last four or five years. Testimony had been taken from many military personnel and there was confirmation of some human rights abuses going back as far as the time when Col. Leonidas Torres Arias had been the G-2 of the armed forces.... He promised to apprise us of conclusions.

Negroponte further commented that

> It is not beyond the realm of possibility that some have in mind blam-
> ing the "Contras" for violations they themselves carried out in the past.
> Others may be more focussed on discrediting the anti-Sandinista program
> itself.... On top of all this, we can only assume that the propagandists and
> disinformation specialists in Havana and Managua are having a field day
> building on stories which initiated from GOH military inquiry into these
> alleged human rights problems.[130]

Data derived from interrogations was turned over to the embassy according
to classified congressional testimony by a CIA official in 1988, and Honduran
investigations in 1984 and 1985 confirmed the "disappearances." A Honduran
report entitled *The Facts Speak for Themselves* concluded that

> the State Department failed to recognize and respond to credible reports
> of human rights violations in Honduras, particularly the increasingly com-
> mon phenomenon of disappearances.... The number of disappearances
> increased dramatically between January 1982 and March 1984, [131] while
> General Alvarez was commander-in-chief of the armed forces.[132]

In Negroponte's view, 1981 was the peak year for "disappearances"; he arrived
in Honduras in November, 1981. Another account asserts that they reached their
peak in February 1983, with 22 in that month alone, and that many were the work
of Contras rather than Hondurans.[133] Negroponte contrasted the 100–150 unex-
plained disappearances in Honduras with the 50,000–75,000 in El Salvador. "There
were instances where General Alvarez could reasonably have been suspected of
acquiescing in a disappearance, but I do not recall seeing any evidence to such
effect."[134] Negroponte was said to have viewed Alvarez as "a hard man but an effective officer."[135] Alvarez was awarded the American Legion of Merit in 1983 during
Negroponte's ambassadorship.[136] In 1988, an Amnesty International report noted
the role of the CIA in training the Hondurans, though acknowledging that "US
Government officials had sought to discourage the practice of physical torture as
ineffective... disappearances and summary executions were carried on deliberately
and systematically by the security forces notably in the period 1981 to 1984."[137]

In June 1988, *The New York Times* ran an elaborate article on Honduras
under Alvarez, declaring that:

> According to American officials who served there, Mr. Negroponte did pri-
> vately protest some of the worst abuses, and embassy human rights reports
> of the period note a few of the most egregious cases. But in the main the
> Americans appeared to have helped organize an army intelligence machine
> they could not control, or perhaps did not want to control. American offi-
> cials who spoke to me about these matters seemed deeply troubled by the
> political and moral meaning they held. Ambassador Negroponte warned
> me in an interview in 1983 that "Marxist guerrillas are organizing here" and
> went on to say that Alvarez was a hard man but an effective officer.

The article quoted a former member of the Honduran military intelligence brigade as saying "We hid people from the Americans, interrogated them, then gave them to a death squad to kill. [Alvarez] decided it was time to kill them all before they got stronger in Honduras."[138]

A heavily redacted report issued by the CIA Inspector General in 1997 contained a redacted statement that a CIA official investigating death squads learned:

> On November 22, 1983 that the Ambassador was particularly sensitive regarding the issue and was concerned that earlier CIA reporting on the same topic might create a human rights problem for Honduras. Based on the Ambassador's reported concerns [blank] actively discouraged [blank] from following up the information reported by the [blank] source. [Blank] justified this action by noting that the information regarding executions by the Honduran Army had already been reported [blank] in the two October 1983 reports.[139]

"The CIA had nothing to do with picking people up. But they knew about it and when some people disappeared, they looked the other way."[140] "Some US officials were deeply disturbed at the morality of what was happening, but more than one argued that the Honduran strategy 'worked'—it broke up the Salvadoran rebels' support infrastructure and demolished the small Honduran left."[141] A journalist present at the embassy party that welcomed Negroponte in 1981 described conversational remarks of then Col. Alvarez:

> When you capture one subversive you must find out quickly where his comrades are, before they have time to escape. The colonel did not say exactly how one did this. A couple of journalists took deep sips of their drinks and said nothing.[142]

When the president announced his intention to nominate Negroponte to be ambassador to the United Nations in 2001, transmission of his nomination encountered protracted delays while an investigation proceeded relating to allegations of complicity in Honduran human rights violations, further inflamed by the discovery in 2001 of corpses of "disappeared persons" at the El Aguateate military base.[143] (Senator Robert Byrd of West Virginia later disingenuously criticized the president for delaying the nomination and credited the Senate with acting on it within ten days after its transmission.[144]) Negroponte was denounced in a lengthy article in the *New York Review of Books*, prompting rejoinders by three members of the Foreign Service. The article contained little new material, except an allegation that a former commander of Battalion 316, Luis Discua Elvir, had his residence permit withdrawn just before Negroponte's confirmation hearings, as did another battalion veteran Juan Hernandez Lara; a third veteran, Jose Barrera, was said to have been deported from Canada. None of the three made charges against Negroponte, although Elvir on returning to Honduras said that "I think you as journalists can draw your own conclusions" as to the reasons for his deportation. Elvir's permit in fact was withdrawn before Negroponte was nominated.

The article also charged that Negroponte, Suazo, and Alvarez had met with three justices of the Honduran Supreme Court to secure the nullification of the election of Juan Almendares as rector of the Autonomous University of Honduras. This allegation was derided as "hilarious" by Shepard Lowman; in his rejoinder, he also observed that Negroponte's "opposition to Kissinger was the act of a courageous young Foreign Service officer taking on the man who would become the secretary of state"; replying, the author of the article, Stephen Kinzer, asserted that in addition to making the allegations in a news-paper column, Almendares

> has appeared on nationally broad-cast radio interviews in Honduras in which he and radio hosts have appealed to surviving Supreme Court jus-tices of that era, and to…Suazo, to deny the allegation if it is not true. So far, the justices have not done so nor responded to direct requests for comment.[145]

Almendares, a political activist and man of the left, had hurled similar accusations of complicity in human rights violations at Jack Binns, the Carter administra-tion appointee who had been Negroponte's predecessor, leading to criticism of him in *La Prensa* as "assum[ing] unjust and sectarian positions which can only lead to the destruction of the relative peace in which we live."[146] Prompted by Negroponte's press secretary, Alfred R. Barr, Theodore S. Wilkinson in addition to Lowman pointed out that during Negroponte's ambassadorship, in Barr's words,

> Honduran officials wisely chose to use generous US economic assistance to subsidize many of the consumer goods needed by Hondurans in their daily lives. Life in the second-poorest country in the hemisphere did not get worse; social strife was avoided partially by a conscious effort by the government to maintain minimum standards of living for the people.

Furthermore, as pointed out by Wilkinson,

> a public denunciation by the US ambassador of the Honduran military on human rights grounds would also have jeopardized a still-fragile constitu-tion, under which the military had just turned over government to civil-ians, with adverse consequences for democracy and development.[147]

Negroponte's nomination was rapidly confirmed after the 9/11 attacks after the CIA provided the Senate Foreign Relations Committee with a series of stipula-tions, drafted by committee staff from the fruits of its investigation and revised by the CIA. These stipulations recited that beginning in 1980, well before Negroponte arrived on the scene in November 1981, the public security forces maintained a secret unit known as the Honduran Anti-Communist Liberation Army (ELACH) which, among other things, tortured and executed prisoners. In 1984, based on recommendations of a joint United States–Honduran mili-tary seminar, the unit was placed under the Armed Forces General Staff and renamed the Military Intelligence Battalion (Battalion 316); it was dissolved in

1987. CIA reporting linked Honduran personnel to death squad activities, but CIA personnel were not directly involved. CIA reporting on such activities was spotty. In August and September 1983, a guerrilla group entered Honduras from Nicaragua and was subdued by the Honduran military, most of them being executed in what an American reporter called "a period of rationally directed state terror against an identified enemy who was also willing to kill to change the system of government."[148] On September 28, Negroponte met with the family of an American priest, Father James Carney, who had been travelling with the group and who was missing.

In September 1983, Negroponte asked for American assistance in the debriefing of captives belonging to the group, and "urged Embassy personnel to exploit the failure of the guerrillas from a broader regional standpoint." In October 1983, the Embassy learned that nine guerrillas had been executed. At the urging of Deputy Assistant Secretary of State Craig Johnstone, Negroponte met with Alvarez, who denied the reports; in view of the conflicting accounts, Negroponte "urged that the United States not pursue the specific matter further with Alvarez"; "it should be made certain that prisoner executions had occurred." Negroponte told the CIA Inspector General that he suggested "methods, such as the Administration of Justice Program, to prevent further abuses." Negroponte said that even though there were doubts about Father Carney's citizenship, the Embassy energetically pursued his case and the Consul General concluded he had died for want of nourishment.

Honduras subsequently suffered an adverse decision before the new Inter-American Court of Human Rights, the first exercise of that court's jurisdiction,[149] the case had arisen during Binns' tenure before Negroponte's arrival. George Shultz was to fairly summarize Negroponte's record on the "human rights" issue:

John Negroponte wouldn't get blindsided by anybody. He's too smart for that.... There are a lot of positive things to be said. You go to a country and not everything that happens there is your fault, but you do your best and you work toward democracy, which John did, superbly.[150]

In an interview with Cable News Network (CNN), Negroponte said:

Some of these regimes to the outside observer may not have been as savoury as Americans would have liked. They may have been dictators or likely to become dictators, when you would have been wanting to support democracy in the area. But with the turmoil that was there, it was perhaps not possible to do that.

The controversy revived in August 2001, when excavations at the El Aguacate air base revealed 185 corpses, including those of two Americans.

In November 1983, the CIA learned that Alvarez had specifically approved the execution of guerrilla leader Reyes Mata. On November 25, while Negroponte was away from the embassy, the Embassy Charge Shepard Lowman said that his reports contradicted those of the CIA and urged that dissemination of further reports on the subject be "by memorandum restricted to designated addresses only." Negroponte said "that his position at the time was that it should be made certain that prisoner executions had occurred before taking further action such as publicizing the information or confronting President Suazo." Negroponte acknowledged that the 1982 human rights report did not mention this case, but noted that it had been separately reported to the State Department.[151] "The US government cannot rule out the possibility that Father Carney was executed by the Hondurans."[152] A Honduran officer linked to the so-called death squad was dismissed in 1984 after death of a prisoner. Negroponte conceded that the embassy used restricted channels of communication "to prevent broad distribution in light of the volatile political environment concerning Central America."[153]

On this subject, Jack Binns, Negroponte's predecessor as ambassador, who was replaced by the Reagan administration, observed of the early activities of Assistant Secretary of State Thomas Enders respecting Honduran human rights violations: "He was afraid it would leak and make it more difficult for us to continue our economic and security assistance." As for Negroponte,

> In Honduras he told these guys to cut it out, but he wasn't going to say that publicly.... This is the problem with most of Washington, you tell political bosses what they want to hear and don't let the truth get in the way of policy.

Binns also later declared: "I think he was complicit in abuses. I think he tried to put a lid on reporting abuses, and I think he was untruthful to Congress about those activities." Binns, a career officer, had been replaced "out of cycle" after barely a year in Honduras, and was resentful of his treatment. Two of Negroponte's then subordinates defended him. Raymond Burghardt, the political counselor in Honduras from 1982–4, "remember[ed] very difficult conversations with Alvarez on the treatment of prisoners."[154] Rick Chichester, a political adviser, was highly critical at the time and was a source for highly critical articles in the *Baltimore Sun*, but later moderated his views: "Should we have done more? Obviously. But I think it would have been tough for anyone to be Ambassador during that period without controversy."[155] Negroponte had other detractors, being described by Jose Vivanco of Human Rights Watch/ Americas as "the ostrich ambassador."[156] The 1984 human rights report, however, "cannot be said to pull any punches," according to Negroponte's colleague Theodore Wilkinson.[157]

Aiding the Contras

In April 1984, General Alvarez, with whom Negroponte was accused of collaborating on Contra-aid matters, was ousted as commander;[158] he was replaced by Air Force General Walter Lopez Reyes, whose planes had buzzed the Legislative Palace to produce the downfall of Alvarez. Alvarez' removal was due to his disregard of the Superior Council of the Armed Forces; an increase in time for promotions between ranks from three to five years; Alvarez' alleged use of a Battalion 316 as a "death squad" to repress dissidents; the view that he was a puppet of the United States; his failure to share the fruits of corruption by drug dealers; his evangelical Christianity;[159] and the unpopularity of the training of "enemy" officers from Salvador at the Regional Military Training Centre.[160]

The Defense Department, in the persons of Sanchez and Gorman, was upset by the Alvarez removal; Negroponte viewed it with relative equanimity. Negroponte claimed to have only limited contact with Alvarez, seeing him only four times in the last three months of his tenure, three of these occasions involving the introduction of visitors.

One writer asserts that

> General Lopez demanded that the United States be informed of the coup and met Ambassador Negroponte one week before the crisis unfolded. Washington received the information and let things run. Alvarez' messianic warmongering was proving inconvenient for Reagan in his re-election campaign.[161]

Others dispute that any prior notice was given and Negroponte has denied that it was.[162] Alvarez had been scheduled to go to Washington on the day after his ouster. Negroponte is said by his political counselor Raymond Burghardt to have become progressively more disillusioned with Alvarez on account of Alvarez' exaggerated view of Honduran military competence and his character as a potential "putschist." Theodore Wilkinson regarded Lopez as "very enlightened and honest, a straightforward general who wouldn't tolerate that kind of [death squad] activity and probably didn't unless it was being done behind his back by the Army." Lopez proclaimed: "I'm not, and we're not, and I'm clean."

Lopez insisted on a lower profile for American advisors, who had virtually taken over the leading hotel, the Hotel Maya; some of them wandered about wearing weapons, or even in fatigue uniforms. The Contras were kept in the border areas.[163]

Alvarez had reportedly boasted that he would spend his birthday in Managua. It was said that he

> was influenced by the national security doctrine espoused by various military regimes throughout Latin America which holds that the world is divided into just two blocs—Western Christendom and communism...according to this doctrine, the former is in a state of permanent war against the subversion by the latter; subversives are defined to include many of those who are simply opposed to the government; and the security forces are above scrutiny from any civilian government or judiciary.[164]

(Recent events suggest that this affliction is not limited to Latin America.) In August 1982, Alvarez had been warned off a plan "to build up the Contras in order to provoke the Sandinistas into an attack thus providing the US with a pretext for military intervention"; he was "reminded [by the embassy and US military] that they were not in the business of trying to foment a regional war."[165] It is universally agreed that "neither Negroponte nor Suazo had been behind the coup."[166] Negroponte endeavored to preserve a façade of constitutional government by suggesting that Alvarez had been dismissed by President Suazo.

In exile, Nestor Sanchez and Fred Ikle provided Alvarez with a $100,000 con-sultant's contract.[167] He was later assassinated in January 1989 after returning to Honduras.

Peace Negotiations

In May 1984, after a contentious summit meeting with Mexican President Miguel De la Madrid, President Reagan agreed to reconsider bilateral talks with Nicaragua. On June 1, Secretary of State Shultz stopped in Managua on return-ing from President José Duarte's inauguration in El Salvador and met for two and a half hours with Daniel Ortega. His objective in negotiation was reduction of the size of Sandinista armed forces and an end to Soviet and Cuban sup-port of them, with little emphasis on democratization. On September 21, the Nicaraguans unexpectedly agreed to a proposal by the Contadora group, which also avoided requiring democratization and also provided for disbanding of the Contras but only weak controls on further Cuban assistance to Nicaragua or further Nicaraguan assistance to the rebels in El Salvador.[168]

On September 24, Negroponte cautioned that

> United States obligations to disengage militarily from Central America would take effect upon signature and would not depend on final ratifica-tion; the disarmament provisions are utterly deficient, and the draft does not deal in any way with...the continued fighting in El Salvador which we know Nicaragua (and at least some Contadora countries) have in mind as a completely separate negotiation once our disengagement has been arranged...Nicaraguans see draft treaty as their own form of a "decent interval", to use a phrase from a different era.[169]

Negroponte had expressed similar views about an earlier draft in September 1983, suggesting that the Contadora drafts had been unduly influenced by Mexico and that Venezuela had not furnished the counterbalance the United States had hoped for. "We cannot entrust the defense of our position to other countries." He suggested that four working groups be formed to negotiate a treaty: "one political, one military, one economic, and one for verification."[170] In the same month, he urged enhanced economic aid for Honduras, pointing out that it got less aid than Costa Rica, although it was far poorer. He also rejected as a "nonstarter" a suggestion by an Admiral that a US flag naval base be sought in Honduras.[171]

Sometime in the fall of 1984, apparently in early October, Negroponte had lunch in Washington with Constantine Menges, an NSC "hardliner," referred to by some of his adversaries as "Constant Menace" or "Menges Khan."[172] In mid-October, Secretary Shultz was to make a swing through Central America, beginning with Panama, to seek changes in the Contadora proposal. In seek-ing to enlist Negroponte's aid in resisting negotiations based on the Contadora draft, Menges inquired whether the initiative in instituting Vietnam negotiations in 1968 and 1972 came from the President or the State Department. Menges reported the ensuing conversation as follows:

"In both cases," Negroponte is said to have declared,

the pressure for using the opportunity of an election eve peace agreement came from State…the State Department negotiators knew they could find allies on the White House staffs—people who just wanted to win the election and didn't care much about the fine print in any peace treaty. And they made their White House coalition in 1968 and they did it again in 1972. I don't have to tell you what a blunder it was, both times. The communists understood our political timetable and they tried to exploit it to get the agreement they wanted. In Paris in October 1972 the chief North Vietnamese negotiator brought their completed draft of a treaty to the first meeting with Kissinger. He said to Henry "You are in a hurry, aren't you?" Very considerate!

Menges, further summarizing, alleged that

Negroponte went on to say that at Kissinger's insistence, he and several others stayed up all night, in spite of jet lag, trying to rework the very one-sided communist draft treaty instead of starting the negotiation on a more even basis. Ultimately Negroponte had refused to go along with what he viewed—correctly as history grimly proved—as a very bad Vietnam peace treaty (for which the Nobel Peace Prize was awarded). He was punished by being "exiled to Ecuador and commercial issues." I asked John what he knew about Shultz's imminent meeting in Panama. "Something's up", he said, "but I really don't know what. I'm not part of Motley's in-group and they don't tell me these things."[173]

This summation has the ring of truth about it. The "hardliners" as well as Negroponte had reason to be alarmed at the one-sided terms of the Contadora draft, presented by Nicaragua on a "take it or leave it" basis. The State Department, however, well appreciated its flaws. By the time the "hardliners" as well as President Reagan had weighed in, the instructions given to the American negotiator were summarized in a memorandum from Deputy National Security Adviser Poindexter to McFarlane: "Continue active negotiations but agree to no treaty, and agree to work out some way to support the Contras either directly or indirectly. Withhold true objectives from staffs."[174] Professor Leo Grande's summary of this episode seems just: "Within the administration, the hard-liners were not strong enough to prevent pragmatists at the State Department from launching a diplomatic foray, but they retained enough influence to veto any real US concessions at the bargaining table."[175] General Gorman was said to be of the view that the Contras could not win, and that theirs was a holding action; more aggressive and optimistic views were said to have been held by Abrams, Casey, Kirkpatrick, and North.[176] In general, there was a confusion of purposes, noted by several commentators, about the American effort. Some sought overthrow of the Nicaraguan government; some sought to stress it until it would fall; some sought merely to deter Cuban and Nicaraguan aggression; and some sought to provoke the communists into acts which would generate Congressional consent to retaliation.[177] Peter Rodman took the view that "the confusion about motive was a ticking time bomb." All were agreed that the interdiction of arms shipments to El Salvador was in substance a cover story. In fact, the last three objectives were reached; a Nicaraguan retaliatory raid in 1986 after Negroponte's departure produced a renewal of congressional authorization of aid to the Contras.[178]

In October 1984, after Congress adopted the second Boland amendment cutting off aid to the Contras, the Honduran government expressed doubts about its commitment to them. In February 1985, President Reagan sent a letter to Suazo committing to release $174 million in economic assistance funds that had been held up due to differences over economic policy (devaluation and tax reform) and to pressure Suazo not to violate the constitution by seeking a new term, and committing $4.5 million in covert support from the CIA for Honduran internal security forces. Separately, the administration would thank Suazo for support for the Contras and assure him that appreciation would involve "more than just words." On March 16, 1985, Vice President Bush met with Suazo and discussed both aid and Contra support, though without stating a quid pro quo.

> Negroponte, who had attended the meeting between Bush and Suazo said that while Bush "may well have alluded to" the expedited aid to Honduras "there was no discussion of a quid pro quo." Former Assistant Secretary of State Motley, who was also present, tried to make a delicate semantic distinction: "You don't have to be a clairvoyant to understand you do things to expedite stuff…It shows good faith and the guy knows what you are interested in. That's a step back from a quid pro quo."[179]

However, shortly thereafter, the Hondurans endeavored to keep for themselves a shipment of air defense missiles en route to the Contras. On April 23, at McFarlane's suggestion, President Reagan called Suazo and got him to release the missiles, though not without listening to an appeal for more US aid, which was granted some weeks later.[180] "At his confirmation hearings as US Ambassador to Mexico in 1989, Negroponte disclosed that he had heard about President Reagan's telephone call to Suazo from Suazo."[181] On April 25, National Security Adviser McFarlane recommended that Reagan again call Suazo to assure him of forms of American support not requiring congressional approval, the House of Representatives having taken adverse action on the previous day.[182] The congressional report on the Iran–Contra investigation contained as one of its findings that

> On April 26, US Ambassador Negroponte notified McFarlane that President Suazo had called Negroponte immediately after Suazo's conversation with President Reagan to say that Suazo was satisfied with the US commitment to continue support for the Resistance. President Suazo told Ambassador Negroponte that he (Suazo) had assured President Reagan of his full support and had promised that he (Suazo) would check into the interdicted munitions shipment, which he did immediately after the conversation with President Reagan by calling a senior Honduran military official.[183]

McFarlane was remembered by Negroponte for a disastrous visit to Honduras, in which he walked out on the entire Honduran political establishment after suggestions were made that Reagan's oral commitments to Honduras were not good enough.

Reagan, Negroponte, and Suazo at San Pedro Sula

In November 1984, Alvarez' chief of staff, General José Bueso Rosa was arrested by the Federal Bureau of Investigation (FBI) while he was in possession with coconspirators of $10 million worth of cocaine to be used to finance a coup against Lopez and a plot to kill Suazo. Negroponte had been kept apprised of the investigation and had warned Suazo of the plot. Bueno Rosa's sentence was reduced at the behest of North, Gorman, and Elliott Abrams, among others, in consideration of his services in aiding the CIA in organizing Contra logistics in Honduras.[184] A memorandum released in connection with the congressional Iran–Contra investigation from Oliver North to John Poindexter appealing for lenient treatment for Bueno noted that Gorman, North, Negroponte, and Dewey Clarridge of the CIA have been subpoenaed to testify at Bueno's trial and that:

"the problem w/the Bueno case is that Bueno was the man with whom Negroponte, Gorman, Clarridge and I worked out arrangements [redacted].... Only Gorman, Clarridge and I were fully aware of all that Bueno was doing on our behalf."[185]

Negroponte at his DNI confirmation hearing declared

I was not in a position dealing with Central America at the time the Iran-Contra scandal developed.[186]

Negroponte was reassigned from Honduras in May 1985. Shortly thereafter, in June, Congress authorized $27 million in nonmilitary aid to the Contras, ending the drought on American government assistance that had begun at the end of 1984, with the adoption of a congressional prohibition of aid to the Contras on October 12, 1984; that prohibition led to the Iran–Contra affair in which the NSC staff, disregarding the prohibition, raised $37 million in private and foreign funds for the Contras in 1985–6. In June 1986, aroused by Nicaraguan reprisal raids into Honduras, Congress authorized $100 million in military aid for Honduras. This was ascribed to General Gorman's influence.[187] While Negroponte in his early days had a close relationship with Alvarez, once acclaiming him as "a model professional,"[188] "Negroponte's usefulness in Honduras diminished after General Alvarez was deposed…because the new government would not confide in him."[189]

Lopez' first message to Negroponte was "We're anticommunist but we're nationalistic." Lopez began treating Negroponte as an appendage of a previous regime. "He refused to confide in him and preferred to let him discover major decisions in the press."[190] Negroponte had been responsive to requests from the new government that the number of Salvadorans at the training center be scaled down, and that there be no more obtrusive American military exercises of the "Big Pine" type. This, one commentator observed, "raises the question of whether the Hondurans…just never bothered to drive a harder bargain." The new government was tight-lipped about the Contras. After being kept waiting in Lopez' anteroom for four hours, a reporter submitted a list of written questions. "His response, made through his secretary, was 'ask the Americans.' "[191] In January, when word of the impending transfer arrived, President Suazo lauded Negroponte as "a source of understanding between our two countries. He has immersed himself in our society and has identified with the fears and expectations of our government and our people."[192]

"Battle of the Ambassadors"

According to Constantine Menges' version of the controversy, Negroponte was a victim of a "Battle of the Ambassadors" in which Secretary Shultz and his allies in the State Department undertook to purge or reassign the Reagan appointees in Central America, being resisted by the Ambassador in Costa Rica, Curtin Winsor. Winsor reportedly told Menges

> I've spoken to five of the ambassadors scheduled for removal and…all of us want to stay on.

After pressure from the usual hardliners, including Meese, Kirkpatrick, Casey, and Faith Whittlesey, no changes other than the departure of Winsor were immediately insisted on by Shultz, who thereafter achieved his purpose by adopting a rule requiring rotation of all but a handful of the most important ambassadors after three years in post in the case of career officers and 2½ years in the case of political appointees.[193] At the time of his departure, Negroponte had been in Honduras for three and a half years.

There were varying explanations. Assistant Secretary Motley invoked "an ongoing requirement for rotations that have been backlogged since last June," also President Reagan's version "just rotations. The individuals are going from one place to another." Curtin Winsor in Costa Rica was moved at the same time by Motley.[194] Others claimed that Negroponte asked for his new assignment in Washington. An anonymous Democratic Senate source alleged that Negroponte "blotted his copy-book badly when he failed to predict the military coup: Negroponte spent a good deal of time promoting Alvarez, bringing him to Washington and parading him all over, just before he was deposed." Another version alleged that

> What has nettled Shultz the most has been behind-his-back collusion...by Meese, Clark and Casey...with certain hard-line envoys to Central American countries, of whom the hardest and most free-wheeling is John Negroponte. Shultz believes that there is at least a fair possibility of defusing tensions in that region through negotiation and conciliation...the secretary has found that envoy's ways high-handed to the point of arrogance and is reassigning him to a somewhat obscure assistant secretary-ship.

This last account may have an element of truth; Shultz may well have been put off by Negroponte's spontaneously declared skepticism about the possibilities of peace negotiation with the Sandinistas;[195] later he was to bestow high praise on Negroponte for his work on environmental treaties. Soon thereafter, in 1986, Colonel Gerald Clark, the defense attaché was also forced to leave. It was alleged that

> He wasn't being allowed to do what he wanted to do about corruption...because he thought the White House was afraid their Contra program would be harmed [he had] little doubt that [Oliver] North would sacrifice Honduras to ensure the Contras' survival.[196]

One matter of concern was a contract for a million rounds of ammunition and other supplies for the Contras awarded by the State Department to a group with asserted involvement with the drug trade.

Curtin Winsor ironically observed: "whenever John gets into trouble, they throw him into tuna. They did that after Southeast Asia; they made him the tuna negotiator. And now in Central America they put him over the OES (Oceans, Environment and Scientific Affairs) Bureau." One of his aides, Sarah Horsey, observed: "many people's careers got ruined by Central America–how often these jobs were going vacant because nobody would bid on them." Raymond Burghardt felt that his career suffered by association with Honduras, an effect partially ascribable to the process of self-selection that later took place in the Central American embassies as the wars dragged on in the late 80s. Negroponte's Deputy Chief of Mission (DCM), Shepard Lowman, was described as "splendid [and] upright...a cold warrior of the old school" by the more liberal Theodore Wilkinson. In Negroponte's time, people in the Embassy, as Sarah Horsey put it, "thought the Sandistas were pretty awful people." Later, however, according to Ward Barman, they were succeeded by further-out advocates of invasions, bombings, embargoes, and sanctions.[197] The Iran–Contra affair, which took place after Negroponte's time, cast a pall over those who served in Central America.

Last Days in Honduras

In October 1983, Negroponte had summarized Honduras' situation:

> The promising aspects of the Honduras scene are its democracy and social
> peace. The security situation is manageable but difficult…. The economy
> is going from bad to worse and needs a strong injection to buy time for
> Honduran democracy while the problems of regional political instability are
> sorted out. This is a holding operation and Honduras is muddling through.
> But there are those who ask at what point the limits of Honduran stoicism
> might be exceeded and pressures develop for more desperate solutions.[198]

In February 1984, Negroponte fended off Honduran appeals for a formal security treaty: "There aren't going to be bases for us because we aren't planning
to station huge contingents of US forces in them…the facilities are there for
contingency use." As a critic of American policy observed, "Washington avoided
the slippery slope in part just by knowing it was there."[199] Negroponte thought,
however, that a joint naval facility "ought to be seriously considered…it would
require much more planning and negotiations for access rights." At this time, a
poll revealed that 63 percent of Hondurans thought that the military was more
influential than the civilian government.[200] In May 1984, 60,000 demonstrators
sought an end to aid to the Contras, as did 126 Honduran signers of a newspaper advertisement.[201] In June 1984, at a National Security Planning Group
meeting, Secretary Shultz indicated that he had just conferred with Negroponte,
who indicated that Suazo was concerned with "what Honduras can do with the
Nicaraguan freedom fighters who return. President Suazo is also bothered by
the sharp decline in the US military presence." This led to a discussion of a need
for third-country funds, and to James Baker's famous warning, later partially
retracted, that their solicitation might be an impeachable offense. In August 1984,
the Hondurans demanded more American aid and reduction of the number of
Salvadorans to be trained in Honduras; Negroponte told Suazo that the Contras
had funds from private sources.[202] Because the training of Salvadorans was the
primary purpose of the training center, it was closed in June 1985 just after
Negroponte's departure.[203] In December 1984, a meeting took place at the officers' club in Honduras between General Lopez and Negroponte, Gorman, and
visitors from Washington including National Security Adviser McFarlane and
Oliver North, at which Lopez demanded of the Americans: "what guarantees do
we have the Contras can win?"[204] Honduras' continued demands for US aid in
exchange for tolerating displacement of thousands of its citizens by the Contras
led an opposition newspaper to declare that "Everything, including honour, has
been lost"[205] and another commentator to characterize Honduras as "a whore
who doesn't know how to sell herself."[206]

Negroponte on three occasions responded with letters to *The New York
Times* to criticisms of American policy.[207] In September 1982, he responded to
a *New York Times Magazine* article by former US Ambassador to El Salvador
Robert White; he disputed allegations that the Honduran government was bel-
licose; denied that US pilots were flying military helicopter missions, and denied
that Honduran troops were fighting in El Salvador.[208] In September 1984, the

United States sought to forestall a military coup, while inviting opposition leader José Azcona to the United States and opposing a second term for the government. Negroponte was quoted as regarding Honduras as "an important model for democracy and tranquillity."[209] In October, El Salvador refused to allow the United States to train more of its troops after the United States declined to become involved in a border dispute between Honduras and El Salvador. Congress had limited American military advisers to 57 in El Salvador and 114 in Honduras, which received $141 million in aid for 1985, double the 1984 aid; $18.5 million for a joint training center was withheld pending agreement on the training center.[210]

In January 1985, the United States boycotted the World Court proceedings on the CIA's mining of Nicaraguan harbors, which ultimately resulted in an adverse judgment, and also broke off negotiations with Nicaragua.[211] The mining scheme had been originally proposed in May 1983 and had been killed by Reagan after Shultz opposed it; its revival involved an end run by NSC and CIA staff.[212] Negroponte had no advance notice of it, and ascribed it to a "lack of adult supervision." In March of 1985, shortly before Negroponte's departure in May, there was a constitutional crisis involving the new government and the Honduran Supreme Court.[213] This led a jaundiced commentator to observe:

In what other country could a new Chief Justice be sworn in one morning, arrested that afternoon, and formally accused of high treason the next day. Where else could half the Supreme Court be in hiding, three fourths of the Congress under criminal indictment, and the lame duck President under attack from a political faction of his own parties called the Bambuistas?[214]

The embassy "applied substantial pressure to ensure that Suazo... would not succeed in his efforts to extend his tenure as President." Negroponte thus bequeathed "a string of successful elections and a vibrant party system but with an enfeebled presidency shadowed by a domineering military."[215] Questions about his role in the Iran–Contra affair delayed his later confirmation as Ambassador to Mexico four years later.[216] Negroponte later testified that he cooperated in the Walsh investigation, had never been called to testify before a grand jury, met only four times with civilian leaders of the Contras, and engaged in no talk about circumventing the Boland amendment.[217] It was alleged that in early 1984, two Americans, Thomas Posey and Dana Parker, contacted Negroponte offering to supply arms to the Contras after the congressional ban on further military aid. Negroponte reportedly put them in touch with the Honduran military, an action which by itself would not appear to have violated the Boland Amendment. Shortly thereafter, President George H.W. Bush's Chief of Staff, John Sununu, cited a Negroponte cable to refute charges that Vice President Bush had sought aid to the Contras at his meeting with President Suazo of Honduras in March 1985.[218]

Early in 1985, a report that the Sandinistas intended an attack on the Contras in Honduras aroused alarm in Washington, though it was received calmly in Honduras. National security adviser McFarlane reporting that "no Honduran units have been put on alert or moved to the area and there are indications that the Honduran government has ordered nearly all of the resistance personnel to vacate their base camps by next week." A crisis planning group concluded that it was necessary to "encourage the Hondurans to remain firm in their support of the Nicaraguan Democratic Force (FDN) during the coming weeks" before Congress votes on US aid. Negroponte delivered a cable reading:

> We have recently been apprised of Sandinista military attacks on the territory of Honduras using material provided by the Soviet Union.... Should such an attack on your territory occur, please be assured that the United States is fully prepared to meet its responsibilities for collective defense under the Organization of American States (OAS) Charter and the Rio Treaty.

A presidential letter was also sent "to provide several enticements to Honduras in exchange for its continued support of the Nicaraguan resistance." The quid pro quo was not otherwise made explicit. Negroponte was also instructed to make oral points that the two nations were working in harmony on "Contadora issues" and that the United States wanted "not to appear intrusive in your internal affairs during an election year."[219] In April 1985, Negroponte reported to NSC Director Robert McFarlane that Suazo was satisfied with Reagan's commitment to Honduras.

Negroponte had considerable awareness of US efforts to generate third-country and private support for the Contras. The Hondurans had repaired Contra aircraft at cost, allowed government aircraft to bring in aircraft parts for the Contras, loaned them ammunition, and provided them with false end-user certificates. The CIA reported to Negroponte and others that a ship would arrive in Honduras in February 1985 bearing $2 million in foreign supplies. In September 1986, Colonel Oliver North told NSC Director John Poindexter that a Honduran General Bueso Rosa should be dissuaded from testifying about arrangements for Contra support reportedly worked out between Negroponte, Clarridge, Gorman, and North; whether this was an effort by North to diffuse his own part in it is unclear.[220]

During Negroponte's tenure, economic assistance to Honduras had risen from $50.7 million in 1980 to a high of $168.7 million in 1984; military assistance rose from $4.0 million in 1980 to a high of $78.5 million in 1984.[221]

On May 18, 1985, the month of his departure, Negroponte reported on incursions by two companies of Sandinista troops into Honduras, noting that since the cutoff of US aid to the Contras in 1984 and the defeat of Contra aid in Congress in April 1985 that the Contras' presence in Honduras had become "a truly neuralgic point" in US–Honduran relations. The Hondurans felt

> exposed and carrying what it believes to be an undue share of the burden of confrontation with Nicaragua ... [they] squirm over anything which contributes to a reputation of contributing to regional tensions or serving as a cat's paw for the United States

and delivered the "not-so-subtle message ... that a negotiating option" was available "if sufficient help for the FDN and assurances of various kinds were not forthcoming from the United States."[222]

Honduran Epilogue

Negroponte had begun to think that the Contra effort was creating problems as well as solving them; his later nomination as Ambassador to Mexico was not enthusiastically supported by Senator Jesse Helms, who "had been critical of the nominee's advice to Reagan to quit pushing for Congressional support of the Contras,"[223] and was delayed by Senator Christopher Dodd of Connecticut, acting for the critics of the Honduran policy on the left. By 1989, American aid accounted for 50 percent of Honduran government revenue; the Contra war had produced severe economic dislocations, including a higher defense budget, erosion of investor confidence, inflation and reduced purchasing power, a negative trade balance, and 40 percent unemployment or underemployment.[224] Military aid amounted to $77.4 million in 1984; by 1992, it was down to $16.2 million. Economic aid amounted to about $34 million in 2004 and 2005; new Millennium Challenge funds raised the amounts to $74.9 million in 2006 and $68.5 million in 2007.[225] Military spending, which had accounted for 8.4 percent of gross domestic product (GDP) in 1989, was down to 1.3 percent by 1996. Exports as a percentage of gross product rose from 32 percent in 1990 to 47 percent in 1996; the increase was accounted for by maquiladora plants and the processing of primary products. Although Honduras remained under civilian rule, it had serious governance and crime problems and low levels of investment in education.[226] The growth rate in 2004 was 3.8 percent; per capita gross domestic product was $850, the lowest in the Americas save for Haiti, Bolivia, and Nicaragua. Negroponte and those like him finding value in the creation of evanescent democratic forms is frequently derided, and not only by the Marxist left. Robert D. Kaplan, best known as a celebrant of American "boots on the ground," has asserted the view that "Social stability results from the establishment of a middle class. Not democracies but authoritarian systems, including monarchies, create middle classes."[227] To this, the Peruvian writer Mario Vargas Llosa responded:

> market dictatorships are now gathered on their knees before the IMF, the World Bank, the United States, Japan, and Western Europe, asking to be saved from total ruin. Open societies in which information circulates without impediment and in which the rule of law governs are better defended against crises than satraps.[228]

After Negroponte's departure, three of the embassy's CIA officials were moved to other Latin American posts, and John Ferch, the former head of the American interest section in Havana, became ambassador; he was to serve only a year before being forced out by the hard-line faction in Washington, it being said that "the Hondurans didn't like him and the Contras didn't like him." In addition, Ferch was disliked by embassy staff and was charged with mismanaging a visit by Vice President George H.W. Bush. He viewed Latin American issues as of low consequence in the larger scheme of things. Gorman had been replaced as head of Southern Command in January 1985 as Shultz gained authority to try negotiations. A State Department team did a postmortem on the embassy's failure to anticipate the coup; a report on this alleged that "Embassy reporting was viewed as terribly out of sync with what the Hondurans were doing.... The State Department first became aware of Honduras' desire to renegotiate the 1954 military cooperation pact from press reports." These allegations were implausible; as previously shown, the Embassy may have had advance word of the coup and there were press reports about the Honduran government's desire for guarantees and Negroponte's rebuff of them a year earlier.[229] Among the brickbats hurled at Negroponte on his departure was a demand for his expulsion by a new Honduran human rights commission[230] and the allegation that the coup

initiated by the military's expulsion of Alvarez, resulted in part from the general's quirky character and, according to press reports too numerous to be discounted, the imperiousness of US Ambassador John Negroponte, whom many in Honduras believed better suited for the British colonial service in the days when its representatives ruled over more than a few large rocks.[231]

The Radicalism of Gates

The extent to which Reagan's policy, which Negroponte supported, can be deemed moderate and can be gauged by considering one of the alternatives. In December 1984, the then Deputy Director of Central Intelligence, Robert Gates (now the Secretary of Defense) addressed a memorandum to Director William Casey outlining the consequences as he saw them of the congressional withdrawal of support from the Contras:

Without further assistance by February, all the information we have suggests that the Contras are going to begin heading into Honduras. The Hondurans will then be faced with some 12,500 armed fighters (whom the Hondurans see as closely allied with Alvarez), thereby potentially unsettling Honduras itself.

Flight of the Contras into Honduras will be followed not only by their families but presumably by a second wave of refugees and others who, seeing abandonment of American efforts...determine that their personal futures are in peril and leave the country...[and] the complete reopening of the channels of arms support to the Salvadoran insurgency.... In 1958–60 we thought that we could reach some sort of accommodation with Castro that would encourage him to build a pluralistic government in Cuba. We have been trying to do the same thing with the Nicaraguans, with the same success...the only way that we can prevent disaster in Central America is to acknowledge openly...that the existence of Marxist-Leninist regime in Nicaragua closely allied with the Soviet Union and Cuba is unacceptable to the United States and that the United States will do everything in its power short of invasion to put that regime out.... Any negotiated agreement simply will offer a cover for the consolidation of the regime.

Gates went on to urge, in language echoing Haig's suggestion of four years' earlier:

> Withdrawal of diplomatic recognition…and the recognition of a government in exile,…overt provision to the government in exile of military assistance…economic sanctions…[and] the use of air strikes to destroy a considerable portion of Nicaragua's military build-up (focussing particularly on the tanks and the helicopters). This would be accompanied by an announcement that the United States did not intend to invade Nicaragua, but that no more arms deliveries of such weapons would be permitted….
> If we have decided totally to abandon the Monroe Doctrine…then we ought to save political capital in Washington…. Economic sanctions surely would have an impact in the initial months, but…we will find ourselves with a Nicaragua even more closely attached to the Soviet Union and Cuba than we have now…relying on and supporting the Contras as our only action may actually hasten the ultimate unfortunate outcome.[232]

Reagan's Secretary of the Navy, John Lehman, alleged that

> There was a major effort recruiting more educated young men and women and they were sent first to Cuba for basic military training and indoctrination then on to the Soviet Union for several years of more sophisticated training and indoctrination. Cadres for the leadership of future Central American satellites were being built.[233]

Looking Back on Honduras

The Honduran–Nicaraguan conflict and the internal conflicts in El Salvador proved to be artifacts of the Cold War. A communiqué issued at the conclusion of the Bush–Gorbachev meeting in May 1989 announced that the Soviet Union would no longer supply arms to Nicaragua.[234] In 1990, elections and programs of internal reconciliation followed in both Nicaragua and El Salvador. Negroponte ascribed the change in American policy to Secretary of State James Baker, who sought to bring an end to the mistrust between Congress and the White House. A Soviet official, Yuri Pavlov, took the view that

> each year the Sandinista government would assure us that okay we'll deal a final blow to the Contras. So they dealt some blow, then the Contras would melt away into Honduras and they would infiltrate back and every year it was a repetition of what happened before…the determining factor was when the US Congress banned any further military aid to the Contras. This enabled us in Moscow to overrule the objections of the Soviet military and some political leaders against stopping or reducing and then stopping our military aid to Nicaragua.[235]

While serving in Honduras, Negroponte and his wife

> adopted…two Honduran girls. They're now [2006] ages 24 and 23 and then, after we left Honduras, my wife went back to visit the country several

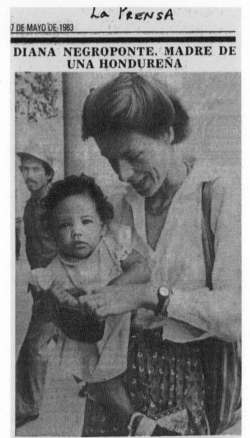

"Diana Negroponte: Madre de Una Hondurena"

times and as a consequence, of which, we adopted three more children, over the years, from Honduras so we now have five, ages 24 all the way down to 13 and like any other parents of children we're very very proud and they are the joy of our lives.[236]

Of Mrs Negroponte, Stanley Karnow wrote: "She was a one-woman Peace Corps. I was down in Honduras once. She was out in the refugee camps and she came back to the capital all covered with chiggers. She's absolutely formidable." Nicholas Negroponte observed: "She did more for diplomatic relations by adopting those children than anyone in the world."[237] Ultimately, the Negropontes adopted five children from Honduras, three of them after his ambassadorship there, John Negroponte explaining "These children were all orphans. Life was going to be complicated enough without having siblings from all over the world. Adopting them from the same country ensured that they would have a natural bond to each other."[238] The adoption of the first child to be adopted received much attention in the local press.[239]

Looking back after 15 years, Negroponte was generally unrepentant about the usefulness of American involvement while conceding that "we did not devote necessary effort to achieving consensus—people had already taken positions based on their reaction to our covert action policies…before we had convinced the American people of the need to mount an overall strategy." It was "not until 1983…that Reagan came and spoke to a joint session of Congress about our Central American policy."[240] Here he echoed the early writing of his onetime mentor Kissinger, who did not always practice what he preached: "The Statesman must therefore be an educator; he must bridge the gap between a people's experience and his vision, between a nation's tradition and its future."[241]

Intervention began in the context of the Vietnamese invasion of Cambodia in 1978 and the Soviet invasion of Afghanistan in 1979.

> I had no doubt these conflicts were being funded by Cuba and by implication the Soviet Union…they sort of let Cuba have the lead on this and basically said to them have at it boys and see what you can accomplish.

> It would have been hard to foresee in the early 80s what was going to happen to the former Soviet Union in the late 1980s and the early 1990s and of course I think that had a fairly significant impact on the outcome in the region.[242]

Central America was vulnerable because of "their social structure, excessive dependence on a very small number of products for export, [and] because of the disparities in wealth between rich and poor." The Kissinger Commission in 1982–3 played a valuable role in building consensus, and also recommended some useful scholarship and other programs; Gorbachev's visit to Cuba, quite late in the game, set the stage for the final settlement. "The poverty, the inequality, all that still needs a lot of work." Nonetheless, Honduras had "a reasonably strong labour movement, discrepancies between rich and poor were not so great."[243] The Kissinger Commission's suggestion for 10,000 scholarships for Central American university students to attend American universities and for a 3,500 member teaching corps recruited from Spanish-speaking Americans have not been effectively implemented; this was part of Kissinger's avowed strategy to move away from military remedies in Central America.[244] (The Commission had also provided a resounding denunciation of the Salvadoran death squads with their "systematic use of mass reprisals and selective killing and torture."[245])

Negroponte did not "consider myself a Cold Warrior." As for the carnage of war,

the immediate suffering [in the absence of intervention] could have even been considerably greater, through population movement, the loss of human freedom, the degradation of economic conditions...even in con-ditions of peace they don't seem to be able to figure out how to support their people and the human suffering is enormous...[there was] actually less suffering than there would have been had we just folded our arms and done nothing.[246]

The economic record of the Sandinista government in Nicaragua somewhat bears out this view. As summarized by Peter Calvocoressi

the government had nationalized the banks and taken control of wages, prices, and imports with disastrous results. Foreign aid, most of it from the USSR and East Germany, was considerable but wasted. Real wages fell during the 1980s by nine-tenths of their value, industrial output declined by a fifth each year, and domestic product per head sank to $300 per year, the lowest in the region.[247]

In 1997, Negroponte told CNN

It was a Central American domino theory if you will: so that if it hap-pened at first in Nicaragua then in El Salvador and if they succeeded in El Salvador then presumably they would try to finish off the situation in Guatemala, which was rather ripe at the time, you may recall. And then maybe Honduras would have fallen of its own volition, without necessar-ily even having to make that much effort. That was the theory in any case and it seemed a plausible hypothesis at the time...we bent over back-wards to press for elections and for democratic reform.[248]

The Contra effort was disparaged as not an indigenous movement, in spite of the fact, pointed out by a critic of American press coverage, that "The contras were four times larger than the Salvadoran guerrillas in a country with fewer than two-thirds the people."[249] They were "Not a tropical Hell's Angels...but a legitimate political-military movement." Those who assisted them "suffered some damage to their careers through their involvement in a program that ulti-mately proved a political pariah."[250] "At its peak," Negroponte later pointed out, "refugee presence in Honduras was about 80,000, which would be proportion-ately equivalent to almost 6 million refugees in the US"[251]

The most even-handed and thorough assessment of American involvement concluded that

Whatever else one may think about the Reagan administration's Central American policy, it must be pointed out that the United States had a great deal to do with the preservation of Honduran stability. Had it not been for US enticements and pressures, elections probably would not have been held in 1980 and 1981. The perpetuation of the military dictatorship would have undermined the legitimacy of the political order, making it far more vulnerable to revolutionary turmoil. By the same token, strong North American opposition to President Suazo's attempt to remain in power in 1985 helped preserve the fragile legitimacy that had been built over the previous five years. At the same time, massive economic aid prevented the economy's collapse, whereas military aid considerably strengthened the armed forces' capability of maintaining order. One can criticize the Reagan administration for its Contra policy and the attendant militarization of Honduras (which limited the development of democracy and diverted scarce resources from pressing social and economic problems) but the fact remains that without the United States, it might well have disintegrated into chaos.[252]

Senator Bill Bradley, of New Jersey, looking back in 1996, referred to the whole episode as "a minor issue—the supply of arms to the Nicaraguan Contras, a policy that took on monumental proportions inside the Beltway and among those liberals who saw another quagmire in every exercise of military power."[253] British author Peter Calvocoressi observed that

> The US was able to keep the Contras in the field in Honduras but in spite of a strength of 15,000–20,000 and lavish modern equipment they took no sizeable town in Nicaragua. Honduras, which harboured them and was well paid for doing so received no support from any other Central American government.[254]

Congressman from Michigan David Bonior's assessment seems a just one:

> Ronald Reagan gave more speeches on Nicaragua than on any other issue of his Presidency. During the eighties we had fifteen major debates on the House floor on this contentious issue, voting three times to cut off military assistance to the Contras. Secretary of State Jim Baker accurately noted, and I quote "The war in Central America was the Holy Grail for both the left and the right in the United States. It was the divisive foreign policy issue." .... The Reagan doctrine and the Monroe Doctrine were colliding with self-determination and with liberation theology.[255]

Negroponte was again involved with Honduras during his tenure as deputy to Colin Powell at the NSC from November 1987 to January 1989, at which time the Contras were still in action. At that point, the hard-liner Elliott Abrams was Assistant Secretary of State for Latin America, however:

> shar[ing] influence over Nicaragua policy with three officials who, administration officials say, act as his supervisors: NSC Deputy Director John Negroponte, Deputy Secretary of State John Whitehead, and Undersecretary of State Michael Armacost. Negroponte ... has emerged as rival to Abrams within the inter-agency structure in which policy is debated and implemented, often contradicting his assertions and predictions.

Abrams was said to have earned disfavor by inaccurate forecasts that Ortega would not join in proposing a peace plan and would not agree to a ceasefire; he also earned the disfavor of the military with a suggestion that American bases in Panama be used to foster an insurrection against the Noriega government, leading to military concerns that nations around the world "would just throw us out."[256] At the same time, Negroponte was said to have driven José Sorzano, a Cuban émigré, off the NSC staff because Negroponte considered his views on the Contras "too hard-line," and "too simplistic and doctrinaire." It was also alleged that in March 1988 Negroponte, on a private visit to Honduras to adopt a child, transmitted a memorandum from Abrams to the Hondurans demanding the extradition of a drug dealer named Matta, a contention denied by Negroponte.[257] When Abrams departed, Negroponte was mentioned as a possible replacement, the post ultimately going to Bernard Aronson: "Some conservatives oppose [JN's] appointment, contending his support for the Nicaraguan Contras is only lukewarm."[258] As late as 1991, Ambassador Philip Habib was complaining that his efforts toward a Nicaraguan settlement were being frustrated by Elliott Abrams and Oliver North.[259]

Nathaniel Davis, who was ambassador to Guatemala from 1968 to 1971 and to Chile from 1971 to 1973 took a broader view:

> looking back on the result in Eastern Europe and in the Soviet Union I think that the outcome of the cold war was decided there, it was not decided in the fields of Nicaragua or Central America, and so that in that sense if we had been able to avoid the human tragedies and human costs it would have been a good thing. But also the same thing could be said of course in a greater extent in Vietnam, because in Vietnam, once again the Vietnam did not turn out to be the determining event in the unfolding relationship of the superpowers and it was Vietnam in that sense was looking back on it, could have been regarded as something that we would have been better off to avoid it.[260]

Another postmortem was that of the CIA's Duane (Dewey) Clarridge, who expressed the view that:

> Well I think we had to take them on in Nicaragua, because they weren't gonna let up in El Salvador, they thought they had the easy one, alright? So you had to do something, alright, now did it have to be of the dimension it was? Probably not, had we come to the economic approach to warfare earlier and gone for the point. I think we could have finished it off a lot earlier, probably with a lot less lives lost you know…. I think we could have reduced the number of casualties, had we just decided the economic was the way to go a little earlier. And certainly if we had been allowed to continue the mining, it would have been all over by 85, and we know that from special information that the Sandinistas had, that this was really choking, and so its too bad, because we went on for another 4 years.[261]

This view was not universally shared. The mining was denounced not only by the International Court of Justice but by Senator Barry Goldwater of Arizona: "This is an act violating international law. It is an act of war. For the life of me, I don't see how we are going to explain it." It was characterized by a defender of the Contras as "one of the most catastrophic covert actions in the history of US intelligence."[262] Motley regarded the mining as "a great idea until it went public, then it became a terrible idea…[the] most successful mining operation in naval history…shut down Nicaraguan imports."[263] The specially constructed small mines were compounded at a CIA garage in Virginia and were designed to frighten insurance companies rather than to sink ships.

Fidel Castro's perspective on the ultimate outcome of the "Contra war" was an unexpected one:

> Imperialism launched an internal war and an internal war can't be fought, as I say, with regular soldiers, soldiers who have been drafted, as it were. Given the law of compulsory military service, you take a boy, you train him, you send him off to fight and he dies and then the family thinks that the State or the Revolution or the laws have sent him to his death…the highest price of a dirty war may have been paid by the Sandinistas because they instituted compulsory military service which is something we never did to fight our dirty war…. If you allow yourself to be persuaded by the dogma in books, you're lost.[264]

Joseph O'Neill in Vietnam had shared Castro's insight:

> You cannot fight a guerrilla war with a conscript army. Most of the army were ticket punchers.[265]

As late as 2006, Castro continued to denounce Negroponte:

> the sadly well-known John Negroponte, a close friend of that terrorist they intend to protect and who bears the repugnant name of Posado Carriles…. His first statement [as DNI] was not directed…against terrorism, against torture, against extra-judicial executions.[266]

Nicaragua, unlike Vietnam, was in an area of at least arguable vital interest to the United States. Neither Nicaragua nor Cuba nor Brezhnev's Soviet Union was pursuing in Central America a policy of "socialism in one country." George Kennan observed in 1984, having urged the surrender of the Panama Canal and the containment of Cuba: "Beyond the questions of Cuba and Panama, and of the security generally of Central America, we have no really vital interests in that part of the world."[267]

Diana Negroponte's assessment of the Central American conflict is set out in her 2005 doctoral thesis for the Georgetown History Department,[268] which supplied one of the more balanced retrospectives on American policy in Central America. The Salvadoran refugees in Honduras who she assisted at a refugee camp in Colomoncagua, Honduras, from 1982 to 1984 were refugees from government counterinsurgency sweeps of the countryside.[269] Violence, though probably inevitable, "was exacerbated by the presence of the United States and the Soviet Union, each seeking to take advantage of local actors and the context of a protracted social conflict."[270] "A level of heightened internal destruction would have occurred with or without the United States. Whether that level of violence would have amounted to a civil war that endured for twelve long years without the US presence is doubtful."[271] The Soviets likewise sought to replicate Nicaragua in El Salvador, provided transshipped weapons, and trained cadres.[272] Settlement required "internal recognition that a 'hurting stalemate' existed and that neither [of the] military forces could win."[273] Her husband's role was candidly acknowledged: "So long as Washington sought to undermine the efforts of the Contadora group, the capacity of the four regional governments to end the civil wars was minimal."[274]

> [I]ndividuals within the US State Department set out to wreck the process. (The US government was divided in its approach to the Contadora peace process. Assistant Secretary of State for Latin American Affairs Thomas Enders supported the Contadora process. However, US Ambassador to the Contadora negotiations, Harry Shlaudeman, together with the US Ambassador to Honduras, John Negroponte, were determined to prevent the Contadora process from achieving its stated goals. Both considered that the US had a critical role to play in defeating the Sandinista government. Honduras became the US government's strongest ally in pursuit of this policy.[275])

In El Salvador, she noted, American critics thought that "the Embassy made insufficient effort to find the masterminds [of atrocities] within the military High Command. They were correct: a countervailing issue, surrounding the survival of the civilian presidency, was at stake."[276] Here also El Salvador mirrored Honduras.

Substantial contribution toward settlement came from the greater self-consciousness of a business class as a counterweight to the traditional landed oligarchy and army, itself a development consciously fostered through massive American economic aid while fighting continued.[277] "USAID intended to create a social class that was compatible with Washington's political purposes for El Salvador."[278] The group known as FUSADES (Salvadoran Foundation for Economic and Social Development) in El Salvador had its counterpart in Honduras in an organization known as APROH (Association for the Progress of Honduras).

> Within two years, the...people expressed their disillusionment with the peace process; their sense of insecurity and lack of economic opportunity. The rise of criminal gangs and the failure of the economic restructuring policy to improve the lives of ordinary citizens led to disillusionment...it was a mistake to pursue both the economic and political reforms at the same time and around different green baize tables. The negotiations with the International Monetary Fund (IMF) and World Bank to introduce a

liberal, free-market, macro-economic system should have taken into account the political process and the costs associated with making a politico-military peace.[279]

"[People] harbored their resentments and went back to work. When there was no work, they joined criminal gangs and made a living through violence, or migrated northward."[280]

[t]he productive capacity…cannot absorb…growing population and unemployment remains endemic. Disparity in wealth and income continues. The underlying socio-economic causes of the civil war remain…. The willingness of young men and women to take the dangerous journey to Chicago, Los Angeles and Fairfax County has provided the safety valve for a restless people. Also the remittance of their wages to urban and rural communities…has injected much-needed funds for the men and women who stay behind. A new dependency upon the United States has been created…. Migration and remittances have provided the glue upon which…fragile peace depends.[281]

Although written about El Salvador, these observations apply in substantial if reduced measure to Nicaragua and Honduras also. One of the defects of the ultimate Salvadoran peace accord, in Diana Negroponte's view, was "omission of the process by which the Salvadoran National Liberation Front (FMLN) combatants would be reintegrated into society, the transfer of land, and the availability of credit and training in new skills."[282] "Elite negotiators on both sides…brought no social benefits to impoverished rural peasants and urban slum dwellers."[283] A second failure derived from the fact that "Internal parties looked outwards for funding and support only to find that international priorities had shifted away from Central America to the Balkans."[284] As Peter Calvocoressi put it, "attempts to find a livelihood (outside crime) for demobilized fighters were not very successful."[285] The legacy of the wars in Central America was "overcrowded housing, suburban development, air pollution, and rising crime rates."[286]

Thomas Carothers, international expert on international democracy support, has observed that

the military and the economic elite maintained their position as dominant forces beyond the reach of direct governmental control…the Reagan administration's Honduran policy was not a Honduran policy per se; it was one part of the administration's militant Nicaraguan policy.[287]

Contrary to the preferences of Haig, Gates, Winsor, and others, Reagan did not want direct intervention, remembering its consequences in the 30s, when he was a young man. "That's why we did the covert stuff that we did."[288] For similar reasons, Reagan later declined to intervene in Panama. Negroponte in Honduras was in agreement with this policy, and carried it out. William Harben, a Vietnam colleague, echoing the cautionary words of Kennan and Haig about covert action, observed: "Our Constitution precludes efficient management of proxy conflicts that last more than a few months";[289] others, notably Andrew Bacevich, professor of international relations at Boston University, have more starkly suggested that we have a choice between democracy and empire and unlike the British and French have made the wrong choice.

Honduras after Negroponte

The history of Honduras after Negroponte's departure was not altogether happy. The memorandum relating to economic matters which Negroponte had given Suazo shortly after his arrival had recommended a rapprochement with private international banks, encouragement of private sector exports and of a private rural land market, new sales and income taxes, removal of restrictions and tariffs on foreign investment, particularly mining investment and budget cuts including cuts in price subsidies for basic goods, as well as deferral of new social programs until the economy had been righted. The Hondurans were in no hurry to embrace most of this program. They rejected devaluation; the artificially high value of the lempira required the maintenance of import controls. In 1983, an export promotion law was enacted; in 1984, export firms were exempted from import duties, and in 1986, after Negroponte's departure, were allowed to use their foreign earnings to settle their import bills without requiring permits. This produced a positive trade balance by 1984 and greatly reduced inflation, which had been at the 42 percent level, but also produced a fall in real wages of 12 percent in 3 years and a 64 percent rise in unemployment, which reached 10.7 percent in 1984. Much of this was the product of the war, and of about $1 billion in resulting capital disinvestment in the period from 1980 to 1984. This was partially offset by more than $700 million in US aid during Suazo's term of office, which allowed a postponement of devaluation. As a result of the removal of protection from import-substitution industries, manufacturing as a share of the economy fell from 22 percent in 1980 to 16 percent in 1984. By 1984, per capita GDP was $314, almost exactly what it had been in 1970.[290] In 1985, the Suazo Government balked at deflationary measures but was brought to heel by a threat to withdraw $147.5 million in American economic aid.

By 1990, GDP was up to $531 in constant dollars and $822 in actual ones, but as a result of disputes between the fruit companies and independent growers and resulting failure of banana exports collapsed to $205 (in constant dollars) in 1992.[291] The neoliberal program of devaluation, tax increases, and free alienability of land was not introduced until 1990–2, by which time Honduras had been blacklisted by the IMF and World Bank because of its large budget deficits. The government continued food subsidies and froze mass transit rates, but the agricultural economy suffered a series of disasters, both natural and man-made, including strikes in 1991; a curtailment of coffee exports in 1993, conforming to an international cartel; a hurricane and drought affecting the banana crop in 1993; and a plant disease in 1994. Nominal per capita income was $825 in 1993; there was 89 percent inflation over a 3-year period. In 1993, about 60 percent of the cash incomes of both urban and rural populations were spent on food.[292]

The Clinton administration withdrew aid from and otherwise seriously neglected Central America, whose countries were plagued by gang warfare, crime, and difficulty in assimilating former rebels.[293] As Theodore Wilkinson observed, economic aid "dried up because of the lack of strategic interest in Honduras." In 1998, Hurricane Mitch devastated the country, leaving 2000 dead and $3 billion in damage, and leading one commentator to allege that the "formal economic sector hardly exists."[294] As a gesture of personal solidarity, Negroponte, who was then at McGraw-Hill, visited Honduras, meeting with President Carlos Flores. In 2001, author Anna Arana was to write in *Foreign Affairs* that

> in the case of El Salvador and Nicaragua we just went in and closed the book on them…[leaving] the scars and open wounds of traumatized societies…flourishing smuggling, car theft, and kidnapping industries…. Recent US policy toward Central America has been essentially limited to the issues of immigration and drugs.

Stephen Kinzer, a chronic critic of Negroponte, observed that many Hondurans fled from the civil war to Los Angeles, where "large numbers of Honduran teenagers joined violent street gangs. In the 1990s many of these youths were deported back to Honduras, causing violence and gang warfare there."[295] This continuing problem was adverted to in Diana Negroponte's monograph on the Merida agreement, elsewhere discussed. A UN aid mission in Nicaragua departed in 1990.[296] The words of the historian Tony Judt about Africa apply in some measure to Central America also: "It is precisely those African countries most corrupted by the 'proxy wars' of the later cold war that were to become the 'failed states' of our own time."[297]

By 2008, both Nicaragua and Honduras were recipients of Millennium Grant assistance from the United States, and both were members of the Central American Free-Trade Agreement. Negroponte observed:

> We can't be against left-of-center governments if they were properly elected by their own people. I didn't think I would be sitting with you 25 years after being Ambassador to Honduras talking about a major assistance program we have in Nicaragua with Daniel Ortega in charge.[298]

In mid-2008, he was able to point with pride to a doubling by the second Bush administration of development assistance to Latin America and the Caribbean.[299] By 2006, Honduras, according to the State Department's own figures, had 7.3 million people (as against 3.7 million in 1980); there were a million Honduran migrants in other countries, and remittances of $2.5 billion per year represented a 5th of the gross national product. Per capita GDP at the official exchange rate was $1,635 or $3,130 according to the International Monetary Fund. Manufacturing accounted for 19.7 percent of GDP and 15.3 percent of the workforce; agriculture accounted for 13.8 percent of GDP and 35.9 percent of the work force. Thirty-eight percent of the work force was said to be unemployed or underemployed. The pattern of under-investment in education continued; the literacy rate was 76.2 percent (as against 40 percent in 1980); only 88 percent of the age cohort attended elementary schools and only 31 percent junior high schools. The public health statistics were a bit more respectable; life expectancy was 66.2 years (as against 56 years in 1980) and the infant mortality rate 29.6 per thousand births, as against 117 per thousand births in 1980.[300] The economic growth rate was 6.3 percent.

The leftward turn of Honduras' elected president, Manuel Zelaya, and his quest for constitutionally unauthorized re-election led to his expulsion from the country in mid-2009. Diana Negroponte urged a negotiated solution, cautioning against the danger of an alliance between the exiled president and powerful drug cartels.[301] A monograph published by her on *The Merida Initiative and Central America: The Challenges of Containing Public Insecurity and Criminal Violence*[302] contained searing descriptions of contemporary Honduras: a Gini index of economic inequality of 54, one of the 18 highest in the world; an incipient "narco state" with judicial and police institutions open to purchase by cartel members and criminal networks; 36,000 gang members, the largest number in Central America; a 44 percent crime victimization rate among students; 65 percent drug consumption by gang members; and dedication of only 2.5 percent of GNP to education, resulting in a failure to construct an "information highway" fostering distance learning. She saw four measures as necessary: larger police forces, wealth redistribution, and reduction of drug demand in both Central America and the United States.

Honduras permanently scarred Negroponte's reputation. The principal wound was not inflicted by a dis-information campaign from Managua nor by the criticism in *Newsweek* inspired from within the State Department, but from his crude editing of a single "human rights report," that for 1982, which impaired Congressional trust in his candor. George Kennan had once observed of clandestine operations that they cause their authors "to lose all realistic understanding of the interrelationship, in what they are doing, between ends and means." Human rights reports, also deplored by Kennan, placed the ambassadors contributing to them in an inherently false position. Nonetheless the report, written by an energetic 43-year-old who had just arrived in Honduras, was a blunder, as was his allowing the regional CIA chief, Duane (Dewey) Clarridge to meet with President Paz without the ambassador being present. Negroponte profited from both lessons. As Director of National Intelligence, he was careful in his statements to Congress, on several occasions making disclosures that his colleagues would have preferred not to have been made. His congressional interlocutors did not find him a font of information on highly contested questions but were left with a clear understanding of the constraints on his testimony.

11

ASSISTANT SECRETARY FOR OCEANS, ENVIRONMENTAL AND SCIENTIFIC AFFAIRS

Europeans insist they approach problems with greater sophistication. They try to influence others through subtlety and indirection. They are more tolerant of failure, more patient when solutions don't come quickly. They generally favour peaceful responses to problems, preferring negotiation, diplomacy and persuasion to coercion. They are quicker to appeal to international law, international conventions, and international opinion to adjudicate disputes. They try to use commercial and economic ties to bind nations together. They often emphasize process over result, believing that ultimately process can become substance. Europeans because of their unique historical experience of the last century—culminating in the creation of the European Union—have developed a set of ideals and principles regarding the utility and morality of power different from the ideals and principles of Americans, who have not shared that experience.

— Robert Kagan, *Paradise and Power: America and Europe in the New World Order* (London: Atlantic Books, 2003), 5

A Smorgasbord of Issues

From May 1985 to November 1987, Negroponte served as Assistant Secretary for Oceans and International Environmental and Scientific Affairs (OES), increasing the size and influence of the office, and earning widespread praise on his departure.[1] He had sought the appointment in late 1984 in a conversation with Michael Armacost, who later called to offer it to him. He was credited with improvements in OES morale and in the Bureau's standing.[2] His confirmation had been momentarily delayed by a "hold" placed on his nomination by Senator Jesse Helms, who was seeking leverage to obtain a choice appointment for Negroponte's conservative predecessor, James L. Malone.[3] Malone was described by Theodore Wilkinson, who came with Negroponte to OES, as "one of the least loved and desirable appointments of the Reagan administration in the State Department." Negroponte also engaged a black Foreign Service officer, Allen Sessoms, later his political counselor in Mexico, whom Negroponte helped enter the Senior Foreign Service by dark of night, in Wilkinson's words. Sessoms, a scientist, is currently the president of the University of the District of Columbia.

In two speeches in 1987, Negroponte described the extraordinary sweep of the agency's activities, extending even to the harmonization of auto emissions standards among the United States, Canada, and the European Economic Community (EEC),[4] and ongoing negotiation of the Law of the Sea Treaty.[5]

On global warming, Negroponte urged extensive monitoring needed to develop a scientific consensus. "Instilling environmental values in economically deprived societies [is] a task [we] can only begin to appreciate." This approach had also fostered the successful Montreal Protocol on Substances That Deplete the Ozone Layer, with its requirement for ratification by countries representing a large majority of countries "making it impossible for a major player to sit out while others bear the burden of restraint." Negroponte secured swift congressional action on the ozone convention and an agreement on conservation of wetlands but not on protocols to the 1969 Civil Liability and 1971 Compensation Conventions relating to oil pollution damage. The ozone convention partly refutes the pessimism of John Gray of Oxford and others: "Global regulation of environmental standards, though an inspiring ideal, is a Utopian prospect. It is not enforceable where it is most needed—for example, there are few effective measures of environmental protection in Russia or China."[6] In all, Negroponte executed 13 treaties during his tenure.

Negroponte followed up his earlier work on fisheries by promoting a UN agreement barring driftnet fishing on the high seas, the agreement providing for payment of compensation costs to Japan.

Cultural Exchanges

In the course of his tenure, he clashed with the neoconservative Richard Perle on the subject of international scientific cooperation.[7] Perle asserted that lax review of exchange programs was "Like Putting the KGB Into the Pentagon," to use the title of an alarmist op-ed article published by him; Negroponte noted that review was careful, that Perle himself while in the government had approved programs relating to civil space research and fusion energy, that the State Department had vetoed programs involving ocean drilling and applied systems analysis because of their national security implications, and that it had properly approved cooperation relating to environmental protection, housing, atomic energy, cancer research, oceanography, agriculture, and public health. He told the relevant congressional committee that

> a good case can be made that scientific exchanges provide opportunities for an articulate and politically sensitive sector of Soviet society to be exposed to Western methods, ideas and values in ways that would not otherwise be possible. I cannot help but believe that such opportunities, steadily sustained over the years, could make a contribution to the gradual opening of Soviet society, with attendant benefits to the human rights situation.[8]

In his testimony, he noted that by the 1970s, there were 11 separate exchange agreements, but that tensions arising from the Afghanistan invasion and the declaration of martial law in Poland had by the end of 1983 reduced exchanges to

20 percent of their 1979 level. In speeches in June 1984 at the Smithsonian and in April 1987 to the Los Angeles World Affairs Council, President Ronald Reagan called for renegotiation and extension of the bilateral agreements. In 1985, the ocean research and atomic energy agreements were renewed, followed by the Geneva General Exchange Agreement and entry into an agreement for cooperation on fusion energy. In 1986, an agreement between the respective National Academies of Sciences was renewed.

However, Perle successfully blocked a grant by the National Science Foundation to the International Institute for Applied Systems Analysis and caused the Soviet Union to be "disinvited" from the International Ocean Drilling Program, being credited with "having won another round in the political battles between Defense and State."[9] A framework agreement for US–Soviet cooperation in international space research was signed in 1987; it was extended to human space flight in 1992. The framework agreement revived a 1972 agreement that the Reagan administration had permitted to lapse in 1982; the United States is said to have derived important benefits from it in the design of docking devices, in which the Soviets were ahead of American technology. Negroponte was supported at the hearings by Victor Rabinowitch of the National Academy of Sciences, who declared that "carefully managed exchanges can bring substantial scientific benefits to the US"[10]; he was also aided by a statement in support of exchanges by the commonsensical President Reagan.[11] "The greatest benefit we derive from these arrangements," George Kennan had earlier observed,

> lies in the field of the intangibles: the greater mutual acquaintance between experts on both sides of the line—the breakdown of unreal stereotypes in the minds of both parties—the discovery that not all those on the other side are inhuman and that we actually have a good deal in common.[12]

Space Stations

Negroponte negotiated an agreement on space exploration after negotiations with the Europeans, Canadians, and Japanese. The agreement provided that the space stations could not be used as weapons platforms but that each country could do defense-related research in its own modules. President Reagan had to over-rule objections by the Defense Department on this issue. Negroponte noted that the Soviet Union had the world's largest group of scientists and engineers, who were in the forefront in some fields, notably mathematics and theoretical physics. There had been valuable cooperation as a result of the agreements on such matters as drugs preventing sudden cardiac deaths, laser technology for glaucoma, construction techniques for earthquake zones, marine navigation and housing in the Arctic, the control of agricultural pests, ozone research, investigation of the gene pools of animals, space research, and nuclear reactor safety.[13]

The Ozone Protocol

Negroponte's bureau played an active part in the formulation of an international agreement relating to ozone at Montreal in August 1987. The ozone agreement was a pathbreaking accomplishment, and one achieved against the odds. Suzanne Butcher, Deputy Director of OES observed: "Ozone was not easy at the time. At the time we did ozone, it was incredibly groundbreaking, new. If Ronald Reagan hadn't had skin cancer, I don't know what we would have ended up with." The agreement owed much to Secretary of State George Shultz and Environmental Protection Agency (EPA) Administrator Lee Thomas. It involved what was for the time an unusual degree of official cooperation with environmental groups: "Non Governmental Organizations (NGOs) were just getting established as players in international negotiations." Industry participants in talks, including Du Pont, stressed that "We need predictability to make the investments we need to make."[14] The Clean Air Act expressly vested responsibility for ozone control in Negroponte: "the President through the Secretary of State and the Assistant Secretary of State for Oceans and International Environmental and Scientific Affairs shall negotiate multilateral treaties for these purposes." Negroponte initiated American participation in the Montreal negotiations.[15] When Negroponte took office in 1985, major nations had just signed the Vienna Convention pledging them to cooperate in the study of the effects of chlorofluorocarbon (CFC) and other aerosols on the ozone layer. One official justified this approach on the basis that, without it, "We are trying to make a risk management decision before conducting a risk assessment." At the time, the United States and USSR wanted agreement on terms which would have required very small reductions, and Japan completely denied the existence of a problem. "There were a lot of nay-sayers in the administration. Some of these people didn't believe the science. I believed the science."[16] In successfully urging ratification of the Vienna Convention, Negroponte told Congress:

> For almost ten years, we have not had reliable worldwide data on CFC production. Since 1976, the Soviet Union, a major CFC producer, has not supplied production data .... Other countries such as China may be producing CFCs but they are not reporting this information. Once the [Vienna] ozone convention enters into force, perhaps within the next two years, it is expected that more countries, including the USSR. will provide CFC production data .... [The Vienna Convention] does not commit the United States to additional regulatory undertakings.[17]

He also observed: "This is a difficult and complex negotiating process—we have made substantial progress but we have a long way to go to reach an effective agreement with broad participation."[18]

At the opening of the Protocol discussions in December 1986, the US Delegation had sensed that the Soviets were unfamiliar with the latest science on the potential danger of CFCs. Therefore, taking the occasion of an informal lunch two weeks later with a visiting Soviet minister at Washington's Cosmos Club (appropriately an institution founded in the nineteenth century to promote scientific endeavours) Negroponte and the US Chief Negotiator [Richard Benedick] proposed a collaborative research effort on ozone and climate. The resulting meetings of Soviet and US scientists in the spring of 1987 contributed to a gradual weakening of Soviet opposition to international controls on ozone depleting compounds—relations between the Soviet and American delegations were unusually cordial and marked by frequent informal consultations. One such exchange in Montreal led to the resolution of the base-year problem that had threatened to stall the negotiations.[19]

In January 1987, serious negotiations began at Montreal; in the intervening period there had been dramatic research results from Antarctica showing the seriousness of the problem. Negroponte began by suggesting "that a phase-out of up to 20 years might be required—twice as long as the US had originally proposed." The EEC had no initial position; the US had reduced its contribution to the relevant UN agency from 36 percent of its total budget in 1973 to 22.7 percent in 1983. In February, the US proposed a 10–14-year phaseout; the EU asked for 20 years. Even this proposal met with opposition from Reagan's Interior, Energy, and Commerce Secretaries and the Office of Management and Budget; the Department of the Interior Secretary, Donald Hodel, at one point suggesting that no government action was needed since people could protect themselves against skin cancer by wearing hats and using sunglasses and sun cream. Remarkably enough, this observation was leaked by Hodel's staff on the premise that it would help the opposition; it unleashed a host of derisive articles and cartoons. Negroponte enjoyed the support of the Economic Affairs Section of the State Department, which had originally been skeptical even of the Vienna Convention, as well as of the Environmental Protection Agency, the Council of Economic Advisors, and the Trade Representative. Environmentalists "reminded [George H.W.] Bush's Presidential campaign that an international ozone policy would be about the only good thing the Vice President could claim for the [Reagan] administration's environmental policy." The State Department's efforts were assailed by right-wing critics of the Reagan administration.[20] Reagan, to the great surprise of the European opponents of a treaty resolved all but one of the disputed issues on the side of the administration agencies fostering it.

The United States offered to freeze existing production by 1990 and to have a 20 percent production cutback by '92 and a 50 percent cutback by the end of the 1990s. The Senate adopted by a margin of 80:2 a resolution calling for a 50 percent cutback plus added phaseouts. The United States insisted that any treaty be ratified by nations possessing a total of at least 90 percent of world production, a measure to force the response of Japan and the Soviet Union, each of which had more than 10 percent of world production. The accession of Japan and the Soviet Union outflanked opposition from within the European Community. Ultimately it was agreed to freeze production at 1986 levels by 1990, to have a 20 percent reduction by January 1994 and 30 percent more by January 1999, with a freeze on halon production by the mid-1990s; the United States agreed that the treaty would be operative when nations with two-thirds of production rather than 90 percent ratified it. The treaty was ratified by the Senate unanimously in March of 1988 and became effective only shortly thereafter, only three months after the Vienna Convention had secured the necessary ratifications. After the Du Pont Company agreed to cease CFC manufacture well before the deadline, an overwhelming number of other chemical companies followed suit.[21] It was pointed out that

[b]y then the US, notably the giant Du Pont company, was the world leader in developing substitutes for CFCs, and the counter-accusation flew back that all this concern about the environment was simply a smoke-screen, that Americans actually wanted a ban on CFCs so that they could move into the marketplace and clean up with sales of substitutes.

The initially recalcitrant British were likewise charged with altering their position at the urging of William Waldegrave, the Environment Minister, on the premise that "it would cost almost nothing to restrict the use of CFCs whereas controlling emissions of sulphur dioxide from power stations would cost millions."[22] Twenty-nine nations with 83 percent of production had ratified the treaty by December 1988; it took effect in January 1989. As an inducement to underdeveloped countries to participate, the developed countries made available a $1.3 billion multilateral transition fund for their benefit; the fund had been initially opposed by Bush's then Chief of Staff, John Sununu.

The treaty was spectacularly successful; worldwide consumption of CFCs fell from 1 million tons annually in 1986 to 10,000 tons by 2002; production fell by at least 85 percent. There were almost immediately measurable declines in CFC compounds in the lower atmosphere; the hole in the ozone layer in Antarctica which excited so much alarm is projected to disappear by 2050. Without the Montreal Protocol, it is said that atmospheric CFC concentrations would now be at five times their present level and ozone depletion at 10 times its present level. A commentator described Negroponte as a "strong supporter of ozone protection."[23]

The compensation fund and the almost universal participation of underdeveloped countries was not a part of the original American design, Negroponte initially acknowledging that "developing country representation at Geneva was sparse," being limited to Argentina, Brazil, and Egypt. Although the universality of the agreement owed much to UN officials, the impetus was heavily American: "According to John Negroponte's congressional testimony, the US had three objectives for the protocol negotiations: 1) reduce risk of ozone depletion, 2) come up with a long-term strategy, 3) periodic reassessment."[24]

The success of the treaty is said to be due to the fact that each nation was left free to devise its own strategy, to the availability of the compensation fund, and to the open-ended nature of the treaty, Article 2, paragraph 9 of which provided for

> adjustment of control measures based on scientific and technical assessments carried out under Article 6 ... in the one instance in which the United States took the lead [in environmental protection] ... the US deployed significant diplomatic capabilities and side payments to those important states without which it could not secure the agreement it sought.[25]

The relevance of the Montreal Protocol to later controversies over global warning has been disputed: "CFCs are one of any number of chemicals that can be used for cooling, so substitutes exist; carbon dioxide, however, is the respiration of our fossil-fuel powered civilization."[26]

Twenty years earlier, I had played a minor part in the ozone controversy. At the behest of a schoolteacher, Kenneth Grief, a client of the law firm with which I was associated, I sought out means by which he could indulge his interest in combatting air pollution, and thereby became the organizer and secretary of the Coalition Against the Supersonic Transport (SST). That confederation of groups deployed a variety of both environmental and economic arguments against the proposed aircraft; my principal contribution was to urge, in deference to the Republicans in Congress, that economic arguments be given at least equal place with environmental ones, which was done. Some days before the congressional votes, a study was published suggesting that 800 supersonic aircraft would lead to a 4 percent decrease in the ozone layer, and that each 1 percent decrease would translate to 6,000–8,000 fewer skin cancer cases in the United States each year. This study was said to have provided the "straw that broke the camel's back" when the Senate rejected the aircraft by a vote of 51 to 46.[27] President Richard Nixon had endorsed the SST proposal at the urging of Henry Kissinger, who in April 1969 had characteristically urged considerations of national prestige:

"I must admit that many of the arguments against going ahead with the project are extremely persuasive. I cannot dispute the technological or economic cases against the program. My concerns center on an unrelated (and perhaps irrelevant) consideration.... We will have run from one of the major scientific challenges of the day. And it is this latter point that most concerns me, for it seems to me that we, as a nation, are increasingly losing our verve for challenge and adventure. The US will neither stand nor fall on what we do about the SST, but the broader issue of our national spirit and sense of purpose deserves some thought."[28] These passages were underlined by the President.

This calls to mind Ambassador Sir Horace Rumbold's definition of nationalism as "patriotism plus inferiority complex."

The Antarctic Treaty

George Kennan, writing 10 years earlier, had urged in place of the UN treaty mechanism governing Antarctica creation by the leading industrial powers of

an international environmental authority, which would have in certain fields (and notably in the great international media of the high seas, the Arctic and Antarctic, the stratosphere, etc.) its own power of decision and enforcement... the sponsoring and supervising agencies of this authority should be [not governments but] major scientific bodies of the respective countries.[29]

Kennan's suggestion reflects his frequent impatience with democratic politics. Nonetheless, the tortuous pace of the law of the sea and Kyoto agreements gives some force to his suggestion, if the major powers could summon the political will to authorize such a delegation to an international body, at least for fact finding and recommendatory if not for enforcement purposes.

Negroponte opposed proposals by the New Zealand government and Greenpeace to make Antarctica into an international park, expressing the view that "If it ain't broke, why fix it? We think the Antarctic treaty system is working very well." He noted ongoing negotiations over a mineral agreement and was criticized because raw sewage and scrap metal were being disposed of into McMurdo Sound and there was a garbage dump onshore.[30] In a speech in Charlottesville in March 1987, Negroponte pointed out that the 55 signers of the Antarctic Treaty represented two-thirds of the world's population; that it was a major arms control treaty, providing for unrestricted inspections; and that it allowed scientific research to go forward in spite of the conflicting territorial claims of seven nations: "a wonderfully imaginative stroke." He acknowledged that time may have revealed some exploitable minerals in Antarctica, though quoting Antarctic researcher Dr Larry Gould's earlier statement: "I would not give a nickel for all the mineral resources I know in Antarctica." Negroponte alluded to new minerals negotiations, as well as to agreements on Antarctic seals in 1972 and on fisheries in 1980. The mineral negotiations gave rise to an agreed moratorium on exploration in 1988; Australia and France favored complete prohibition of mining; the United States and Britain a moratorium. He alluded to the treaty as an "open system" that allows the parties to undertake mineral exploration activities. He warned against overconcentration of exploration efforts in a few locales, urged pooling of efforts, greater information sharing and cooperation with international organizations, and the possible creation of a permanent Antarctic Treaty secretariat to replace the duties of the rotating chairmen of the biennial treaty meetings. He noted that the treaty was up for review in 1991, describing it as "an eminently successful basic charter [which] should only be modified in the most compelling of circumstances" and which should persist "into the next century."[31] This prophecy was realized.

Acid Rain

During Negroponte's tenure, a new International Committee of the Federal Coordinating Council for Science, Engineering, and Technology was established under the chairmanship of John McTague, the acting Presidential Science Advisor, other high-level members including Negroponte, and National Science Foundation executive director John H. Moore. Negroponte was also involved in discussions with the Canadian government about the still-vexing (2009) subject of acid rain. A meeting produced little except an agreement to "accept" an inconclusive report; however Negroponte and the Reagan administration supported a $5 billion technology demonstration program to facilitate coal washing and other clean coal technologies, half the funds for which were to be supplied by the federal government. Negroponte told the Senate Foreign Relations Committee that Reagan "agreed to a process, not a specific outcome [which] could have serious and unnecessary socio-economic consequences...billions a year.... The need for, or form of, additional emissions reductions cannot be defined at this time."[32] However, a cutback on sulfur emissions using a system of emissions trading was agreed to by Congress as part of clean air legislation in 1988–9, and an agreement was signed with Canada in 1990. Richard Smith, his principal deputy, credited Negroponte with taking the view that

You have to get your own act together…you can't negotiate beyond it, because you won't be able to deliver…. By workshops with industry, we helped change minds…you've got to have workshops with them.

Smith, who had gotten to know Negroponte when Smith was head of the Canada desk while Negroponte was at Fisheries, regarded Negroponte as "one of the giants of the Foreign Service, a very fast-moving, brilliant officer," and referred to him and Richard Benedick as "good and high-flying officers who wanted to devote time to it." Negroponte delegated most personnel matters to Smith.[33]

Chernobyl

Negroponte also was charged with ascertaining the facts about the Chernobyl nuclear disaster.[34] In May 1986, in advance of a summit meeting, he sent a memorandum to Secretary Shultz outlining talking points urging a convention for reporting of nuclear accidents, and seeking post-accident review by the International Atomic Energy Agency. He cautioned against "overt demands for USSR participation," and also cautioned that "mixing safeguards inspections with safety evaluations could detract from the effectiveness of international safeguards, which are critical to US nonproliferation and national security objectives."[35] In May 1987, he described American efforts to the Orange County World Affairs Council, noting concerns with both reactor safety and nonproliferation. He noted that since the early 1960s, only India had become a new nuclear power in spite of dire prophecies of 25 new powers. As for Chernobyl, he noted that the reactor had no true containment vessel and produced a surge of power with loss of coolant, a condition not replicated elsewhere, not even in the Soviet reactors projected for Cuba. In the wake of Chernobyl, two new international conventions on notification of nuclear accidents and emergency assistance in connection with them had been drafted and opened for signature in the record time of five months.

Negroponte alluded to the Nonproliferation Treaty and the similar Tlatlelolco Treaty with reference to the Americas by which signers bound themselves not to transfer weapons technology and not to assist others in manufacture of nuclear weapons. He also alluded to the facilitation of nuclear commerce for peaceful purposes and to US participation in the Nonproliferation Treaty Exporters Committee and the Nuclear Suppliers Group.[36]

In an earlier speech before the Rotary Club of Detroit, Michigan, in November 1986,[37] Negroponte stressed the nation's stake in nuclear energy in light of the "severe impacts on our national well-being of [the] oil shocks of 1973 and 1979." He observed that "standardized reactor designs…seem to be making out best"; noted that nuclear plants do not contribute to the acid rain problem, and that while "we have much to learn about the greenhouse effect…nuclear power plants do not contribute in any significant way."

He noted that the United States and the Reagan administration "have deliberately resisted any temptation to make political capital from the Soviets' misfortune." He lauded creation at Stanford of a pilot program for a new nuclear safety training academy, and referred to the Nuclear Waste Policy Act of 1982 resulting from recommendations of President Carter's State Planning Council on Nuclear Waste Management [on which I was an alternate representative]. As to nuclear wastes, he said, with understatement that "questions of public and political acceptance must still be resolved." As late as the 2008 election campaign, several presidential candidates, whenever they approached Nevada, surrendered on this question. Negroponte alluded to substantial American exports of nuclear technology, amounting to $250 million annually in the case of Japan, and stressed that these "must be safeguarded so that there is minimal risk of their serving as a subterfuge for nuclear explosives development."

Nuclear Nonproliferation

Although Negroponte was not the sole official responsible for efforts to curtail nuclear proliferation, his office, represented by Theodore Wilkinson, was active in that field. A Latin Zone agreement curtailing proliferation in the Western Hemisphere was a forerunner of the later International Atomic Energy Agency (IAEA) agreement. Wilkinson regarded Hans Blix, later the IAEA director, as "a first-rate international civil servant." The Taiwanese were discouraged from engaging in nuclear development; the United States looked the other way with respect to development in Pakistan, and there was little stress on North Korea. A decision was made not to include missiles in the IAEA treaty because of their importance as an export commodity to some of the nuclear powers.[38]

Population Affairs

Population affairs was a subject which Negroponte addressed gingerly in the Reagan years as he had in Honduras, declaring in a speech in 1987: "clearly there is a relationship between demographic pressure and environment which is evident in such issues as the destruction of tropical forests to accommodate population growth or the pollution and health problems created by urban over-crowding." He appointed Nancy Ostrander as Coordinator for Population Affairs, a "position that had drawn a lot of flak from some very conservative congressmen and other groups." Richard Benedick had been relieved of his duties for this issue after a political flap arising from a conference in Mexico City. The Reagan administration had begun by supporting international population control efforts; a reference to population problems was included in a G-7 communique. CIA Director William Casey was concerned with population pressures in places like Kenya, Pakistan, and Central America. In the runup to the 1984 presidential elections, the administration's position hardened in response to pressure from the religious right. In Mexico City, a policy allowing support of NGOs funding abortions as long as funds were kept in separate accounts was abandoned at the instance of James Buckley, head of the US delegation; this resulted in an end to US funding of UN population control efforts. While holding the position, Ostrander told the oral history project that

> they're frightened of this subject, they just wish it would go away. In the current [Reagan] administration, if you say "family planning" everybody is a hundred percent in back of you; if the shadow of abortion comes up first, no one will even look at it.

This was so even though "not since the early seventies have we had anything to do with any program overseas that involved abortion." Ostrander, with Negroponte's support, adopted a policy of working through non-governmental organizations:

> if the President is going to have to choose between [the state] and church…he's not going to make that choice…. Best thing to do is to let the people alone. There's just no one solution. You have to go to every culture and each one is different.[39]

AIDS

Negroponte conducted a study, only recently declassified,[40] on the foreign policy implications of AIDS. This study resulted in a four-page memorandum drafted by Chas Freeman, later his colleague at McLarty and Associates, and also signed by Negroponte, to Secretary of State Shultz and Deputy Secretary John Whitehead in April 1987.[41] In it they cautioned that a

> calamity is unfolding in a swath of a half-dozen countries across Central Africa, including several important and influential friends and allies such as Zaire, Zambia and Tanzania…By the mid 1990s two thirds or more of the modern educated elite and perhaps half of the overall urban population in highly infected countries such as Burundi, Rwanda, Tanzania, Uganda, Zaire and Zambia will probably have died. In Africa, AIDS has the potential to devastate entire societies, erasing the hundred-year-old impact of modern European technology and thrusting whole nations back into the early iron age…. There is no point in debating where AIDS came from. The relevant question is where it is likely to take us and what we can do about it.

This alarmist description of the problem was accompanied by cautious recommendations urging the cultivation of local responsibility among Africans: "It is we believe imperative that the US not give the impression that we can through a massive 'task force' approach to the problem deal with it by hurling resources into the void." The conclusions of the study were echoed in a Special National Intelligence Estimate prepared by the CIA in June 1987 on "Sub-Saharan Africa: Implications of the AIDS Pandemic," concluding that

> In the short term at least, the United States and Western countries appear to offer only the future hope for a vaccine or cure while currently denying the massive assistance that would be needed to care for the victims and raise health services to developed-world standards.[42]

A very modest AIDS Technical Support Program was launched by the Reagan State Department in late 1987 involving expenditures of $68 million by 1992; another $30 million was provided by State for AIDS research in 1989.

Negroponte also, together with his former mentor Herbert Levin, worked to stave off congressional legislation that would have barred AIDS carriers from entering the United States, pointing out that there was no accurate test for AIDS and that such a provision would invite a witch hunt.

They were successful in defeating the restrictive proposal, which had been supported from within the administration by John Bolton and Gary Bauer, among others, after Negroponte and Levin enlisted the aid of the Surgeon General, C. Everett Koop, a favorite of social conservatives, who appeared at the hearings looking like an Old Testament prophet with his beard and gold-braided uniform. Negroponte prepared a report at the direction of Deputy Secretary John Whitehead. The report recommended against the denial of visitors' visas to persons testing HIV positive. It took a different view with respect to permanent visas, by analogy to the provisions with respect to tuberculosis, there being concern about the burdens on the American health system. The report similarly recommended against the admission of HIV carriers to the Foreign Service, as the necessary medical care might prejudice the principle of universal assignment dictating in theory that Foreign Service officers be available for assignment to all countries.

Global Warming

Unlike many in the second Bush administration, Negroponte regarded the Kyoto climate change negotiations with sympathy, although seeing a need for firmer commitments by developing nations along the lines of those in the Montreal Protocol. At OES, he had participated in an Intergovernmental Panel on Climate Change. After his departure, OES participated in a summit on sustainable development at Rio in 1992. Thereafter, global warming discussions fell on hard times. Thomas Macklin, Jr., the Deputy Director of the Office of Global Warming in 1992–3 referred to the office's director, Dan Ritesnyder, as a "nice guy unable to delegate"; the office was besieged by coal and oil industry lobbyists from the Global Climate Coalition. During the Clinton administration, the OES became a backwater in the State Department; the percentage of Foreign Service officers among its professional staff declined from 85 percent to 10 percent under an executive director who did not understand recruiting.[43]

In 2008, Negroponte took a long view, looking forward to negotiations for an Action Plan on global warming scheduled for Bali in 2012. While he decried "attributing all manner of ills to global warming," he felt that as with ozone, solutions would be found and that "technology is going to be a major part of the answer, clean coal technology and others."[44]

> I think it's real. I do have an issue with how you go about it ... if you're going to deal with these issues, you have to deal with them discretely. You can't try to be too sweeping. One of my philosophical beefs with the environmental community generally is, when they see an issue, they immediately want to take a global approach to it. They throw in everything but the kitchen sink; they try to solve everything all at once .... if you want to deal with the greenhouse gas issue, you could have done it 25 years ago. You could have done something about preserving tropical forests. You take individual components.[45]

Negroponte regarded the Montreal Protocol along with The North American Free-Trade Agreement as his most significant accomplishment.

The position of Assistant Secretary for Oceans Environment and Fisheries was especially well suited to Negroponte. It involved complex, multifaceted and low-key negotiations, mostly conducted outside the public eye. The ozone treaty was a notable achievement, Negroponte and Benedick undertaking to crack the hardest nut—Russian and Chinese resistance—first, thereby outflanking the Europeans. The post-Chernobyl treaties on notification and reporting of nuclear accidents were also important, and derived from the Reagan administration's care to not exploit Chernobyl for propaganda purposes. Similarly, sensible policies with respect to AIDS were adopted without either surrendering to or seriously offending the "religious right." The so-called "Mexico City policy" adopted by the Reagan administration with regard to population control programs was of more symbolic than real importance; most birth-control programs, including those of Mexico, did not involve provision of free abortions but nurse counseling and the promotion of contraceptive use and were carried out by governments, not the more controversial private NGOs.

12

DEPUTY NATIONAL SECURITY ADVISOR

No great society can survive if its policies toward others are dominated by passion or ideology…American hegemony would not be a return to the peaceful state of nature. Omnipotent rulers are rarely popular; we would be plagued by minor wars and revolutions throughout the world. To maintain our position of dominance, increased governmental control over the private lives of American citizens would be called for. The spirit of individualism and free enterprise would continuously be contradicted by demands for centralized governmental planning, and the combination of national pride and enormous wealth could as easily corrupt our populace as it did the Athenians and Romans after they rose to empire…even the most unexpected success of our nineteenth-century outlook on foreign affairs would decisively contradict and undermine our political traditions.

— Roger Masters, *The Nation Is Burdened: American Foreign Policy in a Changing World* (New York: Knopf, 1967), vii, 313

Cleansing the NSC

From November 1987 to January 1989, John Negroponte served as Deputy National Security Advisor under Colin Powell. Explaining his appointment, Powell wrote:

I needed to spike any perception that the NSC was a wholly owned subsidiary of the defence establishment. I found just the man…in the unlikely outpost of Assistant Secretary of State for Oceans and International Environmental and Scientific Affairs. Negroponte…had the management style I liked, toughness applied in an easygoing manner, a rare combination.[1]

One of his functions at the National Security Council (NSC) was coordinating intelligence support for it.[2] Powell succeeded Frank Carlucci, to whom he had been deputy, who in turn had succeeded John Poindexter. Carlucci and Powell had conducted a general housecleaning of the NSC staff, closing Oliver North's former bailiwick, the Office of Politico-Military Affairs. The Iran–Contra affair very nearly led to Ronald Reagan's impeachment, although Reagan owed his election in part to the action of the Iranian regime in making hostages of American

Briefing Reagan with Powell

diplomats. Reagan's fixation on limiting Communist influence in Central America led him to authorize arms sales to the Iranian regime even at a time when the United States was providing aid to its Iraqi adversary.

Powell and Carlucci "got rid of all…the principal conduits to the CIA… a 100% turnover was required in light of the events of the previous two years. They did the same thing for the Latin American office."[3] Negroponte's mandate extended across the board to everything but arms control. Negroponte chaired the Policy Review Group. He had an active role in Central American matters, according to some accounts forcing out the "hardliner" José Sorzano as the agency's Latin American specialist,[4] although he attributed Sorzano's resignation to his frustration over the failure of Contra aid in Congress and irresolution over Panama. Negroponte briefed President Reagan at 9:30 each morning on intelligence matters, most particularly on the Iran–Iraq war, in which the United States was assisting Saddam with intelligence sharing and commodity credits. William Stearman, an NSC veteran, said of Powell that he was "not a genius in national security affairs but the best organized person I have ever worked for in my life…. He had common sense and looked after his troops," in addition to responding to all memoranda within 48 hours. Stearman regarded Brent Scowcroft as the intellectually best qualified of the NSC heads, although he was slow in moving papers, William Clark as the most personally pleasant of them, and Henry Kissinger as the most powerful operator.

Panama and Noriega

Negroponte participated in an abortive effort to induce Manuel Noriega to voluntarily leave office as president of Panama by "plea bargaining" an indictment for drug trafficking[5] that was vigorously supported by Secretary of State George Shultz and President Reagan and that failed due to delays resulting from election-year politics and opposition from administration "hardliners."[6] At one point, one of Negroponte's aides demanded of a Florida prosecutor eager to pursue a Noriega indictment "since when do district attorneys make foreign policy?"[7] The decision to return an indictment was said to have been "laid in cement" at a meeting presided over by Negroponte. Negroponte is said to have declared to the prosecutor: "You sit at this table. You are the reason we are having this meeting." The prosecutor took a jaundiced view of the proceedings:

> no one even wanted to talk about it…. In government you learn that no one makes the hard call. We were allowed to go ahead, not because every official thought it was a good idea, but because those who didn't like it wouldn't dare argue against it.

Attendees at the meeting knew that the prosecutor had leaked word of an impending indictment to the press and that the probable Republican presidential candidate, Vice President George H.W. Bush would be pilloried by his political opponents if the indictment was discouraged. The controversy allowed Bush to appear tough and to distance himself from Reagan. The indictment was supported by Elliott Abrams and William Weld and was opposed by the CIA, the Defense Department, and Nicholas Rostow of the NSC staff.[8] One commentator observed:

> after the meeting, officials complained to each other that the indictment was the height of foreign policy folly, and one guessed that it would paint them and Noriega in a corner…none dared speak out for the meeting's note-taker, fearing he would be quoted…as having backed a drug-dealing dictator.[9]

After the indictment was returned, there were meetings concerning a plea bargain with Noriega, pursuant to which he would resign from office and go to a third country in exchange for dismissal of the indictments. This approach was supported only by President Reagan and Secretary Shultz but was opposed by Vice President Bush, James Baker, the Defense Department, the National Security Agency staff, and the intelligence agencies in a discussion in which political considerations loomed large. President Reagan took the view that "indictments are worthless as long as Noriega's in Panama" and charged that prosecutors "overlooked the fact that the Panamanian Constitution makes it impossible to extradite this man in response to indictment."[10] Reagan feared that failure of negotiations meant "I can start counting up the bodies." In the event, the negotiations failed, both because of Noriega's mercurial nature and because of procrastination and divided counsels on the American side. A period ensued in which economic sanctions were applied to Panama, one participant in the discussions observing, in terms with wider applicability than merely to Panama,

> It's the one decision that no one sitting around the table in the room has to pay for. Economic sanctions have become a weapon of choice because no one in the decision-making group is directly affected... .It's people outside the room—Panamanians, American businessmen, and bankers...who get hurt.[11]

Negroponte appears to have kept his head down during these discussions: "Chastened as a result of Oliver North's schemes, the NSC acted as a broker that avoided any role even vaguely operational." "General Powell, the current national security adviser and an officer accustomed to giving orders, was forceful," said *The New York Times* in a postmortem. "Mr. Negroponte, a career diplomat, was more cautious, more conciliatory, more reluctant to make crisp decisions if they would offend agencies involved in the secret deliberations."[12] Negroponte's view almost certainly was one of pessimism as to the prospects of an agreed resolution with the devious and stubborn Noriega.

Negroponte knew that Noriega was the conduit for messages from Fidel Castro to Honduran leaders. Noriega was as close to Leonidas Torres Arias, the head of Honduran intelligence and a key facilitator of Contra aid, as he was to then Cuban Interior Minister Jose Abrantes, who led Castro's effort to undermine the Contras: "He has always played both sides," said Negroponte of Noriega. He also observed of Noriega: "this wasn't a question of intelligence failure. It was a question of not listening to the intelligence." The CIA had warned of Noriega that "based on his psychological profile, he would fight even harder when cornered."

Reagan, according to Powell, did not find Noriega to be a sufficient problem to warrant war and was fearful of the effect on Latin America of a perceived revival of "gunboat diplomacy."

The butcher's bill in Panama that Reagan feared did not fall due until the advent of the first Bush administration, by which time Negroponte was ambassador to Mexico. It involved the loss of about 25 American lives, 1,000 Panamanian fatalities, and $1.5 billion in property damage. On the night of the invasion, Negroponte received a call from White House Chief of Staff John Sununu that led him to cancel a meeting at which he was to introduce Senators John Mitchell and Paul Sarbanes to Mexican President Carlos Salinas; he foresaw that the meeting would not be pleasant. A critic observed that "Noriega, distasteful as he was, wasn't endangering American lives, US property, or national security interests."[13] Negroponte, during the Reagan administration, also presided over an interagency meeting discussing a scheme to reinstall Noriega's predecessor, Eric Delvalle, as Panamanian president on a corner of an American military base, a notion rejected at the urging of Admiral William Crowe because of its potential effect on the willingness of other foreign countries to accept American military bases.[14] Shultz had favored the use of force; Carlucci, Crowe, and ultimately Reagan opposed it.

Iran

In late 1987 and early 1988, as Powell's deputy, Negroponte headed a Policy Review Group that held three meetings for every one National Security Planning Group session in response to an episode in which a tanker in the Persian Gulf was struck by an Iranian antiship missile. The United States at the time was covertly aiding the Iraqi regime of Saddam Hussein to limit a possible threat by the revolutionary Iranian regime to Persian Gulf oil supplies. The group recommended retaliatory air strikes:

> When Iranian flyboats and larger naval vessels appeared to react to the strikes, American helicopters and ships sank or damaged a number of them ... Secretary of the Navy [James] Webb [now US Senator from Virginia] resigned "out of concern at the seemingly open-ended requirements of the Gulf neutrality patrols."

Soon thereafter, the United States was embarrassed by the accidental American military attack on Iran Air Flight 655, with the loss of 290 lives, an episode the memory of which, nurtured by the Iranian government, continues to bulk large in US–Iranian relations.[15] In April 1989, Negroponte presented to Reagan a request by Secretary Frank Carlucci for authority to board an Iranian ship suspected of laying mines in the Persian Gulf, and to sink it if boarding was refused, a request granted by Reagan. In October, he presented to the President a Drug Enforcement Agency request that military involvement in Peru be doubled by reason of the asserted production in a valley there of 40 percent of the world's cocaine, the requested commitment being of $20 million and a survey team to work with Peru's National Guard.[16] Negroponte also participated in a meeting on the cancellation of elections in Haiti.[17]

Negroponte was considered along with Rozanne Ridgway for the post of Undersecretary for Political Affairs, the highest career position in the State Department, in November 1988; the post finally went to Robert Kimmitt. Thomas Pickering and Paul Wolfowitz had also been mentioned for the position.[18] He was again considered in 1991, the post going to Arnold Cantor. Negroponte had indicated he wanted to remain in Mexico to complete the North American Free-Trade Agreement negotiations.

13

MEXICO

There is ... pretty conclusive evidence that an uncontrolled economy does not make for justice, and that a compounding of political and economic power, according to collectivist programs, will threaten both justice and liberty. The classes which prefer liberty to security are those which already have a high measure of security through their social and professional skills and who do not like to have their economic power subjected to political power. The classes which prefer security to liberty on the other hand are on the whole devoid of special skills and therefore individual securities; they are exposed to the perils of a highly integrated technical society, and therefore fear insecurity more than they fear the loss of liberty.... It is probably true that the health of a democratic society depends more upon the spirit of forbearance with which each side tolerates the irreducible ideological preferences of the other than upon some supposed scientific resolution of them, because the scientific resolution always involves the peril that one side or the other will state its preferences as if they were scientifically validated value judgments.

> — Reinhold Niebuhr, "Ideology and the Scientific Method,"
> in R. Brown (ed.), *The Essential Reinhold Niebuhr*
> (New Haven: Yale University Press, 1986), 207, 215

Appointment and Reception

After George H.W. Bush was elected president, he inquired of Negroponte as to what he wanted to do, and asked him to see James Baker. Colin Powell advised him not to give Baker a list, but to ask for a particular assignment. Negroponte sought and got Mexico. In December 1988, as Deputy National Security Advisor, he had attended the inauguration of President Carlos Salinas. Negroponte's nomination as ambassador to Mexico was greeted with criticism from the Mexican left, who charged that it indicated that the United States regarded Mexico as a national security problem. A cartoon on his arrival bore the caption "It seems that Mr. Negroponte is arriving," depicting an aircraft with claws instead of landing gear.[1] In addition, there was resentment at news of his appointment having been leaked to the press before the agreement of the Mexican government had been sought.[2] Manuel Clouthier, the conservative National Action Party (PAN) candidate for president in 1988, inquired

Just why has John Dimitri Negroponte been sent here? Surely, as is his
specialty, to engage in covert action and, what is more important, to make
the Mexican government pay for refusing to join a common market with
Canada and the United States.[3]

The commentator Jorge Castenada declared, "this is not a reserved, soft-spoken,
discreet individual from Washington," although he was "unquestionably a professional." A newspaper published a three-part series, "The Path of an Ultra-
Hawk." The American columnist Jack Anderson referred to him as "Ambassador
G.I. Joe" and declared he was "a natural-born meddler and not the type to
spend his tenure in an armchair at the Embassy." Larry Binns of the Council
on Hemispheric Affairs said he was "the worst possible candidate"; the commentator Adolfo Aguilar charged him with "intervention in domestic affairs,
espionage, and links to the military"; and Adolfo Zinser, who was to again cross
his path as Mexico's ambassador to the United Nations said that he "symbol-
izes all that Mexico has always considered injurious to cooperation and good
relations." There were "scathing news stories, bitter editorials, cartoons, and
sarcastic puns on his name, which can be translated as 'black bridge.'" The
Mexican government's agreement had a bit of a sting to it, expressing the hope
that his appointment meant "equality and strict respect for the sovereignty of
both countries." The government newspaper *Nacional* said he was "a faithful
executor of the instructions of a government blackened by apocalyptic ideological visions" and that he "simply complied, like a good ambassador, with orders
from Washington." The Honduran liberal Ramon Benitez, a critic of American
policy, conceded that he was "an efficient and prudent ambassador who acted
with great intelligence."

Two scholars of Central America, both critics of American policy, were the
kindest. One unnamed scholar at a California university said that he is "not a
State Department flunky or fifth-rater. He is ambitious and capable." Another,
Mark Rosenberg, said he was

> a first-rate professional diplomat, a very good sense of American inter-
> ests and knows how to articulate and defend them…a heavy-duty
> professional diplomat…knows the US bureaucracy…understands
> Congress…a pretty good manager—people who worked with him may
> have disagreed with some of his decisions, but they knew he would back
> them up.[4]

The London *Economist* drily observed: "he is not a retiring man."[5]

Negroponte, however, had an easy act to follow. He had been preceded
by Charles Pilliod, a business executive who left little impression; Pilliod's
predecessor, Reagan appointee John Gavin, a former movie actor, was viewed
as contentious and combative to the point of being bizarre.

Negroponte's family suffered some misadventure in Mexico. His wife was
seriously injured in a horseback-riding accident. One of his daughters was
found to have elevated levels of lead as a result of lemonade consumed at
an embassy party and thereafter; it was found that the source was a ceramic

urn. She recovered completely; her classmates, who had less opportunity to be enthusiastic about the lemonade, were tested and found to be unaffected.

Negroponte took with him to Mexico Theodore Wilkinson and Allen Sessoms. The latter eventually became his second DCM, and was charged by Wilkinson with not paying

> a great deal of attention to what was going on on the administrative side of the Embassy and there was some unaccountable missing property and some other administrative problems…he didn't pay as much attention to running the largest chancery in the world as they might have and the inspectors noticed…. I don't think that Negroponte was fully aware of how little attention his DCM was paying to his job.

Robert Pastorino, who previously served as DCM, observed that

> We had a very good relationship, [he] asked advice in [his] first year—allowed me to run the Embassy—turned over the drug problem [to me]…. People warned me about Mrs. Negroponte who people thought would be the real DCM. On trade issues we worked together very well. She went out and made speeches, but we always coordinated on them…. There was one corruption problem within the Embassy in which several articles of furniture disappeared and I didn't catch it.

Pastorino was later appointed ambassador to the Dominican Republic on Negroponte's recommendation.[6]

Negroponte Children: 1999

Negroponte also burned his fingers in an unsuccessful effort to close the Guadalajara consulate as an economy measure.

He viewed interest in environmental questions as a part of confidence-building between the two countries. The environmentalist Thomas Lovejoy organized two week-long tours for the Ambassador. On the first of these, which examined deforestation problems in Oaxaca and Chiapas, he was accompanied by Senators David Boren and Orrin Hatch, who were en route to the Amazon in connection with further examination of deforestation. The second trip focussed on whale habitats in Baja California and butterfly habitats in Michoacon.

Cuba and Central America

Prior to Negroponte's assumption of his post in June 1989, George H.W. Bush and Salinas had met in Houston, Texas, in November 1988. "Salinas and Bush decided from the very beginning, from the outset, to create the mechanisms to stop having Central America as key issue between the two countries. And they accepted that the UN should play a bigger role." The Mexican Minister of the Interior, Fernando Gutierrez Barrios thereafter prevented the large-scale transfer of arms from Cuba to El Salvador or Guatemala through Mexico. Salinas' chief of staff, José Cordova, reported to Negroponte the substance of a meeting between Castro and Salinas at Cancun in 1990, at which Castro admitted his incapacity in light of Mexican and Soviet pressure to continue supplying the FMLN in El Salvador.[7]

It has been observed that

in a subtle diplomatic role, Mexico served for several decades as a communications bridge (and security and buffer zone) between Cuba and the United States…Mexico was able to make it through the Cold War, from beginning to end, without suffering the continental plague of guerrillas financed and trained by the Cubans. Given that the United States put years of concern and billions of dollars into fighting the guerrilla movements in Central America, one can imagine the alarm that similar movements in Mexico would have caused.[8]

The Origins of NAFTA

In an early speech to an American audience after his nomination to Mexico, Negroponte lauded the Salinas government's privatization of the airline and telephone company, crediting it with an 180-degree opposite economic policy from that previously practiced. A free-trade agreement (FTA), not yet promoted by the Salinas government, was conceivable; we don't want to provoke resistance by stating overly ambitious goals. He doubted that the left-wing opposition in Mexico would gain power soon: free markets and liberal democratic ideas, as we understand them, seem to be the ones that are on the march in Mexico, as in so many other places in the world.[9] The Bush administration was highly supportive of Salinas, providing a $3.5 billion bridge loan before his election was finalized and later a $1.5 billion Export–Import Bank of China loan a week after an allegedly fraudulent election in the State of Mexico.[10] Salinas for his part first hesitated before embracing the project of a FTA, in February 1990. In an early meeting with Negroponte in August and September 1989,[11] he referred only to a liberalized regime for textiles and steel and expressed hope for regularization of the movement of Mexican migrant workers. He also expressed an aspiration to stamp out drug traffic, noting that seizures of cocaine by the Mexicans were triple in volume to seizures by the Americans. He later declared:

> When you are introducing strong economic reform, you must make sure you build the political consensus around it. If you are at the same time introducing additional drastic political reform, you may end up with no reform at all. And we want to have reform, not a disintegrated country.[12]

On his departure four years later, Negroponte was credited with leaving American–Mexican relations in the best condition they had been in since 1910 as a result of his fostering of the NAFTA. During the NAFTA negotiations, Negroponte met President Salinas once or twice a month; he had a telephone conversation with Salinas' powerful chief of staff, Jose Cordoba Montoya, almost every day. In contrast, the Mexican ambassador to Washington in the late 1990s met President Bill Clinton only in ceremonies.[13] "We both conceived and negotiated the North American Free-trade agreement."[14] At the swearing in of trade representative, Carla Hills, although Bush had quoted Macaulay in saying that "Free trade is one of the greatest blessings that a government can confer on a people," the impetus toward response to Salinas' proposal came not from the Office of Trade Representative but from the State Department. "The opportunity arose, and the State Department understood it, and pushed the [US] government process to respond,' says a senior aide to Hills." Hills wanted to focus on the forthcoming Uruguay Round of negotiations; when in August the Bush administration asked Congress for fast-track authority for NAFTA, Hills and Labor Secretary Elizabeth Dole were said to be initially opposed to making such a request. Former trade representative Clayton Yeutter is quoted as saying "I think they [officials in the White House and State Department] called Carla and said 'We want to do this…Is it okay with you?' She couldn't say 'I don't want to do this.' "[15]

The decision to promote NAFTA was made at a meeting between Negroponte, Bush, James Baker, and Tom Johnson (the National Security Council deputy for Latin America), at which Bush, after listening to the arguments, said simply "Go ahead." Baker initially did not want a trilateral agreement: having been through the earlier Canadian free-trade negotiations, he preferred not to negotiate with Canada again. Canadian Prime Minister Brian Mulroney made a personal appeal to President Bush at Kennebunkport, Maine, his summer home, to be included in the negotiations. Niceties about the difference between trade creation and trade displacement did not enter into these discussions, which partook of the crudeness frequently associated with decisions on matters of high policy. No reader of any FTA can consider that it involves free trade in the nineteenth-century sense; instead, it is about perceived reciprocal advantage and political alliance.

In April 1991, a leaked memorandum from Negroponte to Assistant Secretary of State Bernard Aronson inspired some adverse comment from Mexican nationalists but accurately reflected Negroponte's view. In it Negroponte declared that the

> economic reforms begun in the mid 80s were dramatically accelerated by Salinas when he came to office in 1988. The proposal for a Free Trade Area is in a way the capstone of these new policy approaches…. [The] Free Trade Area would institutionalize acceptance of a North American orientation to Mexico's foreign relations…an instrument to promote, consolidate, and guarantee continued policies of economic reform beyond the Salinas administration. The fact that the preponderance of Mexico's foreign dealings were with the United States was carefully masked through various defensive mechanisms. In a way, therefore, adoption of a free-trade agreement would help put on an open and legitimate footing what should have been the reality of US/Mexico relations a long time ago. A growing economy and increased employment in Mexico translates into a stronger boost to US exports than virtually anywhere else abroad. A NAFTA will help insure the permanence of…visionary new economic directions. A vibrant North American partnership for open trade and investment greatly strengthens our leverage in fostering an open global economy to counter the troubling tendencies toward regionalism in Europe and Asia.[16]

Negroponte lauded new Mexican policies that were "pragmatic, outreaching, and competitive," rather than "ideological, nationalistic and protectionist."

"Every so often," a commentator observed 20 years later,

> there comes to light a document revealing the foresight of a public servant who grasped the full consequences and implications of a particular government measure or policy. Such a document was written in the Spring of 1991 by the-then US Ambassador to Mexico, John Negroponte.[17]

For a president self-admitted to "lack the vision thing," this supplied an appealing agenda, leading one commentator to write about "Bushism Found: A Second-Term Agenda Hidden in Trade Agreements."[18] That writer foresaw "an economically polarized society, with a powerful executive and a weak Congress. It is Mexican President Carlos Salinas de Gortari—a strong President in a laissez-faire state—who knows how the world should be won." Persons close to Negroponte ascribed the leak to Democratic staffers on Capitol Hill, who hoped that the leak would arouse Mexican nationalist opposition to the treaty that would complement the opposition of US labor unions.

The dispatch was one of the few that Negroponte wrote personally, leading him to exclaim to his public information aide Robert Earle: "One time I do it, look what happens!" In September 1993, in an interview with United Press International, he predicted that NAFTA could lead to economic unification throughout the Western hemisphere by the next generation.[19] Diana Negroponte took the view that "By its decision to pursue a North American free trade agreement (NAFTA), Mexico had lost its historical independence of action in foreign affairs."[20] That loss, however, proved only momentary, as is suggested by Mexican resistance to the American-sponsored Security Council resolution on Iraq 10 years later, although, according to Robert Pastorino the new relationship helped to change a Mexican vote on a UN resolution relating to human rights in Cuba.

The NAFTA initiative was forced through by Salinas. Pastorino noted, "if the Cancelleria [Mexican Foreign Office] would have been the NAFTA policy maker, we wouldn't have a NAFTA even today."

Although embracing and promoting a bilateral agreement, Negroponte displayed a general awareness of the perils of bilateralism. Although NAFTA did not include clearing, barter, or compensation agreements, its rules of origin provisions and safeguarding of Mexican Petroleums (PEMEX) had somewhat similar effects.[21]

> Modern economic arguments pro and con preferential trade agreements spring from Jacob Viner's classic distinction between trade creation and trade diversion. (The former results from a shift in production from a high-cost member to a low-cost member of a PTA [Preferential Trade Agreement], and the latter from a diversion of imports from a low-cost nonmember to a high-cost member of a PTA.)[22]

The bilateral provisions did not partake of the rigidity of the textile quota and semiconductor agreements with Japan. Even purists regarding unilateral liberalization as generally preferable to trade negotiations concede that "unilateral free trade is not exactly a political movement in this country. The cause of free trade rests entirely on the fate of trade negotiations, the Uruguay Round and of course NAFTA."[23] The American Preferential Trade Agreements (PTAs) were said in part to be a response to EU "spokes" extending the reach of its free trade, such as the Lomé agreement. PTAs are said to be biased through choice of products toward specific regions of political interest. Furthermore, many of the FTAs have been dictated principally by security concerns, including those with Singapore, Jordan, Morocco, and South Korea.

The Mexican Institutional Background

The condition of Mexican society at the end of the nineteenth century had been described by Alberto Vargas Llosa: "95 percent of the rural population in Mexico owned no land at all, and one-fourth of all the land in that large country was in the hands of 200 families."[24] "Every new government appointed or removed judges at will, rewrote the constitution, and rewrote or extended the codes."[25] The revolution changed little: "in the corporatist structure rights were collective. The capitalist Mexico of Porfirio Diaz and the revolutionary Mexico of Plutarco Calles, Lázaro Cárdenas, and Luis Echeverria had more in common than either party would care to acknowledge."[26] In Mexico, there were

> new corporate satellites of political authority–local industrialists, government functionaries controlling the import of capital goods and state enterprises, worker movements in certain areas of industry…. The protection of the domestic market created conditions in which industrial producers

could export part of their output…. Mexico's economy could boast a 6 percent annual growth rate in those three decades [1945–75]…statistical results did not reflect comparable improvements in standards of living and in consumption levels…incubat[ing] a crisis that was subdued by massive foreign lending in the 1970s but that eventually exploded in the 1980s…. What incentive could there be for efficiency and the use of new technology in companies that operated in highly protected markets?[27]

By the 1980s Latin America's GDP per capita had fallen to less than one third the level in the core countries of the Organization for Economic Cooperation and Development (OECD) from a level of 45 percent in 1950…in the 1970s…investment rates did not exceed 16 percent of GDP whereas other underdeveloped zones such as Asia, were already approaching 25 percent.[28]

Meanwhile "Franklin D. Roosevelt protected agriculture, Dwight D. Eisenhower protected oil, and the successive presidents by and large maintained tariff and nontariff barriers that did not help make the case for Latin American free trade."[29]

Vargas Llosa further noted the absence in Latin America of the checks on administration supplied by the Conseil d'Etat in France, judicial review in Germany, and localism and decentralized property rights in the United States a culture of immediate gain on the part of those with access to wealth in a context they knew to be unstable, never permitted…capital formation.[30] Thus informal employment accounts for 50 percent of the working population in Mexico.[31] "Without repealing the mountain of norms responsible for the black market, distributing ownership papers amounts to attacking merely a symptom…entrepreneurs are not able to capitalize the present value of future expected profits."[32]

The impetus to modernize Mexico was neutered by the same liberals who enacted reform…. What good was it to divest the church of its highly concentrated ownership of land if the same laws forced Indian communities to get rid of their property, thereby creating other enclaves of privilege through the transfer of vast amounts of land to a handful of haciendados or big creole landowners?[33]

Former US State and Treasury Undersecretary Kenneth Dam, in discussing Mexico, refers to the "predatory ruler problem". Mexico, despite its proximity to a rapidly growing US market, was held back by this coalition between autocratic rulers and what today might be called "oligarchs."[34] Justice in Mexico is heavily politicized: by Mexican tradition; sitting presidents have dismissed sitting judges whenever it suits their purpose to do so.[35] Lawyers with uncompetitive institutional pedigrees, undistinguished records of professional experience, and/or modest socioeconomic backgrounds tended to pursue careers on the bench.[36]

In a rule of law index prepared by the World Bank in 2003 in which nations were rated on a scale of +2.5 to –2.5, Mexico scored –0.22, well below Chile and on a par with several African and Central Asian states.[37]

Under the *ejido* system, investment fell, the work became more labour-intensive, and even crop choice was biased toward short-term pay-offs...farmers have been reluctant to take advantage of tilting, in part because taxes on privatized land rise sharply, surely a counterproductive approach to improving productivity and farm incomes.[38]

Mexico had no widely-held corporations among either the 20 largest or the medium-sized corporations...family-controlled corporations accounted for a large percentage of publicly-traded corporations...100 percent in Mexico. Families that controlled the firms also participated in their management...95 percent in Mexico...minority shareholders run the risk of expropriation both by controlling shareholders and by management separately...the combined efforts of controlling shareholders and management were devastating for minority shareholders.[39]

In 2005, a typical Mexican insider transaction was uncovered only by virtue of an Securities and Exchange Commission filing in the United States:[40] Dam alludes to Mexican life, where one can encounter great wealth (often behind high walls) but also millions upon millions of impoverished citizens.[41] The Mexican regime thus is characterized by a high degree of both political and economic imperfection and thus does not implicate the arguments of those who urge that while both political and economic freedoms are important to development, the Chinese and other experience suggests that economic freedoms, as in the robber baron era in the United States, are more important.[42]

It has been said that:

A fiscal system cannot rest on the weak foundations of a complex set of rules and decisions that gives rise to uncertainty, for example, regarding property rights, state confiscation of deposits or the composition of releases on the debt issued by the state itself. This gives rise to an institutional counter system not very apt to have an equity effect on income distribution.... Nor is it good to have a "swarm" and "maze" fiscal system that juxtaposes in a kind of set-up provoked by short-term financial shortages, payments upon payments, emergency upon emergency...a situation made up artfully to confuse...fiscal policy should embody the characteristics of generality, simplicity, proximity and transparency.[43]

Mexican federalism is said to have been unsuccessful because of the ability of the states to run fiscal deficits.[44]

In June 1991, Negroponte and the Mexican government are said to have forestalled a planned meeting in Mexico City of members of the US and Mexican congresses and Mexican citizen organizations. The Mexican government restricted its consultations about NAFTA to the heads of Mexico's Institutional Revolutionary Party (PRI)-affiliated trade unions and small farmers' leagues and an organization known as the Coordinator of Business Organizations for Foreign Trade, made up of the largest Mexican business conglomerates.[45] Negroponte had few meetings with the Mexican opposition and declined ever to comment on the political situation in Mexico, "I have a lot of thoughts on the Mexican political situation...but I didn't say anything...we didn't talk much about internal political developments in Mexico."[46] The opposition leader, Cuauhtémoc Cárdenas, was said to be somewhat reclusive; Negroponte's numerous embassy receptions were among the few places where government and opposition leaders met. Negroponte also held much-appreciated meetings with Mexican journalists, including Julio Scherer, the founder of the left-wing *Proceso*.

Another subject off the table was the Mexican political system: "For us to impose political conditions would be counterproductive, a red flag...that might even jeopardize the free-trade agreement." "The cost you pay for being openly, publicly critical is you risk harming interests in other areas."[47] Similarly, "the FTA process can...be helpful in dealing with environmental, labor and other 'flank' issues but within carefully defined limits."[48] The enthusiasm for regional rather than multi-lateral trade agreements derives from the fact that they "seemed more manageable, more likely to work, more in accord with the interests of countries which knew one another; they gave states the feeling, valid or not, that they were still running their own affairs."[49]

Robert Pastorino recalled receiving word from Negroponte of Salinas' sudden interest in an agreement: He drafted a cable "spelling out the tariff and quota adjustments we should bargain for, making educated guesses as to what terms the Mexicans would take, accurately predicting that oil and immigration wouldn't be on the table."[50]

NAFTA was the result of an initiative by Mexican President Salinas, who rejected the idea of a North American Common Market as incompatible with the national objectives of sovereignty. From the war until the late 1960s, Mexico had followed the "import substitution" model of economic development, including high industrial tariffs, recommended by economist Raúl Prebisch and the UN Economic Commission for Latin America and once practiced by Alexander Hamilton in the United States and Friedrich List in Germany. This produced, as Eric Hobsbawm has noted, "bureaucracy, corruption, and much waste—but also a 7% rate of growth...for decades."[51]

By the late 1960s, Mexican industry was circumscribed by the lack of a domestic market with much purchasing power and with its own lack of innovativeness and dependence on government preferences. The domestic market was small because of a strong disparity of income, not large enough to make the protected industries competitive.[52] The Mexican economy by 1990 suffered from collapse of the oil boom and from the consequences of the irresponsibility of two Mexican presidents, Luis Echeverría and José López Portillo. The former had tripled government spending as a percentage of Gross National Product and had increased foreign debt sixfold; the latter allowed inflation and luxury imports resulting from the oil boom to run unchecked and had nationalized the banking system.[53] Salinas had privatized much of the Mexican economy, but the country suffered from massive short-term foreign debt and an overvalued currency; Salinas was intent on making the best deal he could before the economy imploded, which it did a few months after NAFTA was ratified. In Negroponte's view, Salinas concluded he needed something dramatic. He wanted something to consolidate domestic reforms.[54] Susan Schwab, later US trade representative, remarked on the unusual number of trained economists in the higher ranks of the Mexican government. Trade agreements, in her view, were inspired as much by political as economic purposes, allowing domestic political constraints to be by-passed. One of their principal economic advantages to less developed countries was their provision of secure access to foreign markets, fostering investment in export industries to a greater extent than unilateral tariff concessions that might be withdrawn.

At the inception of the negotiations, Salinas hoped to obtain provisions guaranteeing Mexicans certain rights to work in the United States, but this demand was given up rather quickly. Negroponte regretted the demise of the Bracero Program for temporary workers, which had been abolished in 1965 in the Johnson administration under pressure from the AFL-CIO labor union. The elder President Bush did not want to defy the unions by attempting to revive it. Salinas had been disappointed with the result of a European trade-promotion tour, the Europeans preferring to devote their attention to the newly liberated countries of Eastern Europe. French President François Mitterrand is said to have told him: "We are not your option." He saw little hope in the suggestion of the Mexican left for a Latin American Free-Trade Area and believed that NAFTA would give rise to new investment, technology transfers, and ultimately improvement in Mexican wage levels.[55] He almost immediately conceded, in Houston in 1990, that Mexico would not be treated as a developing country, meaning that it would not receive preferential treatment in matters such as transition periods for the elimination of tariffs. This rendered the impact of NAFTA on Mexico far more profound than the immediate impact of European Economic Community (EEC) enlargement on the economies of Spain, Portugal, Greece, and Ireland. The Mexican delegates were young economists with glittering academic records from the best universities, one of whom later observed: "there were many economists on our team who could not give the protectionist arguments."

Final signature of the NAFTA treaty with its necessary side agreements on labor and environmental issues took place on August 13, 1993; the crucial vote approving the treaty and its "fast track treatment" was that in the American House of Representatives on November 17, 1993, two months after Negroponte's departure from Mexico. The side agreements are said to be not very meaningful; a Mexican trade negotiator analogized President Clinton's position on NAFTA to that of British Prime Minister Arthur Balfour on free trade, as satirized in a contemporary couplet:

> I'm not for free trade and I'm not for protection
> I approve of them both, and to both have objection
> So in spite of all comments, reports and predictions
> I firmly adhere to unsettled convictions.[56]

This does some injustice to Clinton, who fought hard for the NAFTA treaty; Vice President Al Gore's debate with H. Ross Perot was a political turning point.

Negroponte's role in the detailed NAFTA negotiation was limited, trade matters having been largely removed from the State Department and vested in a cabinet-level trade negotiator ever since the Trade Expansion Act of 1962. The late Julius Katz was the American coordinator of the negotiations. The American Embassy at the time was second in size only to that in Cairo; there were 400 American employees, but only 60 from the State Department. They were said to have provided to the trade negotiators "a 'concierge' service, providing advice and logistical support."[57] Other issues with which Negroponte had to deal included debt renegotiation under the so-called "Brady Plan,"[58] discouraging Mexican participation in a "debtors' cartel," increased oil shipments, and environmental problems along the border,[59] Mexican protests against temporary American steel tariffs,[60] the deportation of Central Americans from Mexico,[61] the deportation to China without asylum rights of refugees apprehended off the Mexican coast by the US Coast Guard,[62] increased US investment, and the "drug war"[63] and its consequences.

At the beginning of Negroponte's tenure, military assistance credit programs were providing $40 million in equipment a year to Mexican security forces, in addition to another $45 million in State Department and Drug Enforcement Agency (DEA) grants. From 1988 to 1992, the US exported about $214 million in arms to Mexico; it is said that American intelligence services assisted in identifying Zapatista leader Subcomandante Marcos after the Chiapas rebellion broke out just after Negroponte's departure as US Ambassador; at that time, about 150 Mexican military officers were trained each year in the United States and there were about 50 paramilitary police advisers from the American DEA in Mexico.[64] The embassy employed approximately 1,000 people, and was the largest in the world. It received 600 official visitors a week and housed 19 agencies, including the Immigration and Naturalization Service (INS), Federal Bureau of Investigation (FBI), Customs, DEA, Bureau of Alcohol, Tobacco, and Firearms (BATF), and Internal Revenue Service (IRS). It was responsible, among other things, for 13 consulates, the issuance of a million visas a year, and the protection of 600,000 American citizens resident in Mexico, as well as dealing with thousands of arrests of American citizens, 25 percent of them in Tijuana. It was a post requiring "political talents as well as enormous managerial skills."[65] Negroponte was credited by his critics with the smoothest, most discreet covert operation and with vigorous effective carrying out of policies that haven't enjoyed widespread support.[66] To virtually everyone's surprise, Negroponte hardly created a ripple. He so vigorously supported Mexican interests that he was dubbed "the Mexican Ambassador." In 1990, writer Carlos Monsiváis commented that he "has the most intense low profile that has ever been seen in Mexico."[67] He pressed for improved treatment of Americans by the Mexican criminal justice system, and diplomatically declined to describe what he had done to foster Mexico's new multi-party system.[68]

Negroponte's premises dismissed Senator Daniel Patrick Moynihan's concern about "a free-trade agreement with a country that is not free." "The FTA process can also be helpful in dealing with environmental, labor and other 'flank' issues, but within carefully defined limits."[69] The perception of the leader of the Mexican left-wing opposition, President Lázaro Cárdenas' son, Cuauhtémoc Cárdenas, was exact and accurate: "the new Mexican administration offered the US an implicit deal; Mexico would implement the economic reforms the US always wanted, but the US would accept the existing political system, warts and all."[70] Wilkinson, who hosted a dinner for Negroponte and Cárdenas, viewed Cárdenas as "a nice person. He is not a brilliant intellect. He's decent. He is the prisoner of the ideology of the left, but his instincts are Institutional Revolutionary Party (PRI) centrist." Negroponte's aide Robert Pastorino also hosted a breakfast for Negroponte and Cárdenas.

The upshot, after the advent of the Clinton administration, were two side agreements, of which US trade negotiator Katz said: "Labor was only a memorandum of understanding.... The environments [sic] was really agreements." The labor side agreement referred to minimum wage and child labor laws, but not to collective bargaining and the right to strike; it presaged no change in Mexico's system of government-dominated unions. The Clinton administration's efforts to obtain it were treated by a Mexican negotiator with scorn, as the product of "lack of governmental experience and the exhilaration of victory as well as simple political greed ... [a] supremacist attitude under the guise of moralistic principles."[71] Broadly speaking, the American approach was that taken toward China—one of allowing economic agreement to precede political development, in the hope that economic improvements would generate a middle class that would demand democratization. However, even "Chinese decision-makers have begun to recognize that a strategy of 'grow now, distribute later' is inconsistent with the adequate expansion of productivity-based domestic markets" and have begun to provide state support for infrastructure and education in impacted areas.[72]

A combination of developments fostered some liberalization of the political order notwithstanding an absence of overt American pressure for it. Salinas' equivocal electoral victory gave rise to creation of an impartial national electoral agency and to the recognition of victories of the left opposition in a Mexico City election and of the right opposition in some state elections and ultimately a national election. In that sense, Negroponte's method of the gentle nudge may have borne fruit.

The Mexican tax system also had grave flaws, a common phenomenon in Latin America. The seven major Latin American states are said to derive about 14 percent of government revenues from taxes on income, profits, and capital gains, as against 40 percent in the 10 leading economies and 67 percent in Japan.[73] In the period 1988–96, the economically active population increased by 10.7 million while the economy created only 4.1 million new jobs. The remainder either migrated northward, became unpaid laborers on family farms, or entered the informal sector or drug trade. The government attempted to maintain social expenditures as a percentage of total government spending, but the total volume fell by reason of various crises and an inadequate tax system. By 1998, real wages were at 57 percent of their 1980 levels, whereas the share of the top two deciles in national income increased from 49.5 percent to 53.7 percent and there were several dozen new Mexican billionaires, leading a critic to ask

how much further can real wages be flexibilized? Are there any political, social or even ethical minimum levels? .... A small section of Mexico's

economy has been able to integrate itself successfully into world markets...the operation was successful but the patient died...the learning
process of the Mexican government in the past decade as well as that of
multi-lateral agencies, particularly of the IMF and the World Bank has been
very slow in the best of cases.[74]

In 2002, an index of global competitiveness prepared by the World Economic
Forum in cooperation with Harvard's International Development Center
ranked 75 of the world's nations. Mexico was 10th in total GNP, but ranked
from 38th to 49th in indices of per capita income, protection of intellectual
property, government interference in business, antimonopoly policies, com-
puter ownership, confidence in government, and internet access. In three
categories, Mexican rankings were abysmal: women in the economy (60th),
influence of organized crime (64th), and time necessary to start a new business
(71st).[75]

Another critic observed that

A Mexico with increasing GDP and exports, segments of Mexico's economy linked to global commodity chains with state of the art factories,
stable inflation rates and high foreign investments, but with little or no
impact on the majority of Mexico's firms and regions, with falling real
wages and employment, and a worsening income distribution. Such an
economic, social and political scenario, the continuation of polarization,
should worry not only Mexico but neighboring nations such as the United
States.[76]

But perhaps it does not worry the United States because it describes the United
States.

Benefits of NAFTA

Vargas Llosa did not denigrate the trade liberalization and privatization of industry that accompanied NAFTA in Mexico. Mexican tariffs were reduced from a
maximum of 100–120 percent; by the end of the 1990s, 85 percent of Mexican
exports were manufactures, twice the level of the 1950s. By 2003, intra-NAFTA
trade was $600 billion, half the three nations' exchange with the world. By
2007, bilateral trade between the United States and Mexico was $351 billion;
there was a substantial trade balance in favor of Mexico, US exports to it
amounting to $140 million. Mexico accounted for 29 percent of US auto parts
imports, 15 percent in vehicles, 34–35 percent in electrical, audio, and visual
equipment, and 14 percent of agricultural imports. Mexican GDP per capita was
a bit less than $10,000 in 2007, 4 times that of China and 10 times that of India,
and greater than that of Brazil and Argentina. John Gray, a critic of NAFTA,
concedes that by 1993 "Mexico bought as many American goods as Russia,
China, and most of Europe together."[77] Restrictions on foreign investment were
removed in most industries, 1,000 companies were privatized for $38 billion.
Profitability and production in privatized firms are said to have increased by
40 percent and 80 percent, respectively.[78] Sixteen million Mexicans shared

in thirteen billion dollar in private pension funds.[79] Privatization, however, involved transfers to huge private corporations. Mexico's Telmex recovered its investment in two years; its banks were an oligopoly, costing taxpayers $68 billion in deposit guarantees. High utility and communication costs helped foster the flight of Mexican manufacturing jobs to China. Privatization is said to have had a negative effect of 36 percent on formal employment in Mexico.[80] "In Mexico, it takes 112 business days and 15 different procedures at a cost of almost 60 percent of per capita GDP just to be able to operate a start-up company."[81]

As for Latin American education, according to Vargas Llosa,

> Between 30% and 40% of public funding is concentrated at the university level, a form of bottom to top wealth distribution. The relatively few skilled workers earn much more than the rest, making the educational system a vehicle for the inequality it is supposed to correct.[82]

Later in 1991, Negroponte said that US–Mexican relations had reached a "critical mass," pointing to 240 million border crossings a year and the fact that 50 percent of Mexicans have a close relative in the United States. He also expressed the belief that the end of the Cold War would give rise to greater focus on North–South relations, a cause that largely perished after September 11, 2001.[83] A later commentator observed:

> The dynamic of US-Mexican relations since the signing of the free-trade agreement proved Negroponte right. The Clinton administration's support of a financial rescue package for Mexico's flailing economy in early 1995 strengthened US leverage over Mexican affairs, including drug and immigration policy.[84]

Enthusiasts for the agreement like Senator Bill Bradley welcomed enhanced cultural integration toward "a distinctly North American … society."[85]

There can be no doubt that NAFTA more closely bound the United States and Mexico. Mexican exports to the United States increased from $43 billion in 1993 to $144 billion in 2002; imports from the United States from $42 billion in 1993 to $97 billion in 2002 and $292 billion in 2008.[86] Intra-NAFTA trade increased 106 percent during those years, while NAFTA trade with the rest of the world increased by only 42 percent. American direct investment in Mexico, which had averaged $3 to $5 billion a year in 1980–93, rose to an average of $13 billion annually in 1994–2002. Mexican oil exports as a percentage of all exports continued a dramatic fall from 78 percent in the early 1980s to only 8 percent in 2002. It was said that in the decade following 1987 that "the gap between American and Mexican median manufacturing wages has been cut in half, from 13:1 to 6:1," and that in border areas American wages are a third lower and Mexican wages a third higher, yielding a ratio there of 3:1.[87] At the time of the treaty, there were estimates (which proved overoptimistic) that it would take 20 years for Mexico to achieve half of the US per capita income.

Another assessment noted that

> although mechanization and modernization of industry and poor education
> kept unemployment high and privatization enriched only a privileged oli-
> garchy, Salinas pruned foreign debt and the state's overblown investment in
> inefficient enterprises, reduced inflation below ten percent, and turned the
> budget deficit into an unprecedented surplus … [NAFTA] benefits were une-
> venly distributed geographically and barely apparent to smaller businesses.

The regime was not uninvolved in

> corruption, torture, political murder, and the use of Mexico by Colombian
> drug dealers … problems although massive were also easily intelligible
> since they proceeded not from inherent poverty but from the mismanage-
> ment of potential wealth and the sclerosis of nearly a century of one-party
> rule. In which the PRI "never grasped the nettle of taxing the rich and
> reforming a notoriously inefficient agriculture."[88]

Looking back in 2008, Robert Pastor noted that US trade with Canada and
Mexico tripled between 1993 and 2007, whereas inward direct investment in the
three countries quintupled and in Mexico increased tenfold between 1990 and
2005. Foreign direct investing in Mexico dramatically fell from $27.2 billion in
2007 to $18.6 billion in 2008 as a result of the financial crisis in that year.[89] On
the other hand, annual trade growth since 2000 has increased by only 3 percent
as against nearly 10 percent in the previous seven years, there has been little
investment in road construction, truck shipments are impeded at the border,
and the rules of origin provisions make some of the tariff concessions for textiles a dead letter and have rendered Mexican manufactures uncompetitive with
direct imports from China. Intra regional exports rose from 43 percent in 1990 to
57 percent in 2000 but have since remained unchanged. The effects of NAFTA
on Mexican per capita income were modest; according to World Bank estimates
an increase of 4–5 percent spread over a 10-year period, although NAFTA is said
to have increased Mexican exports by 50 percent and inward investment by 4
percent. "Since NAFTA was put in place, the northern part of Mexico has grown
ten times as fast as the southern part because it is connected to the Canadian
and US markets," leading to proposals from Pastor for an infrastructure fund.[90]
It was said that

> By relieving the state of many of its long-standing inefficient and oner-
> ous responsibilities in managing the economy, the NAFTA has contributed
> decisively to the process of political liberalization. Zedillo consolidated the
> Federal Electoral Institute … gave full independence and autonomy to the
> judiciary; put in place the conditions for a true separation of powers, and
> welcomed an opposition Congress. Bush proclaimed that the top issue on
> his agenda was to consolidate the relationship with Mexico. Unfortunately,
> five days after fireworks were set off over the Potomac to honour Mexico,
> terrorists set fire to the Twin Towers.[91]

Limitations of NAFTA

The substantive effect of NAFTA was to encourage maquiladora factories on the Mexican border, which had also been fostered by earlier trade concessions, whereas the elimination of tariffs damaged Mexico's import-substitution industries in the interior: the factors that encourage cross-border labor migration are the growth of the export-assembly industry along the US–Mexican border, the liberalization of agriculture in Mexico, and pressures from NAFTA itself.[92] "Capital will inevitably move south…if the United States is going to…move ahead in terms of prosperity, it must massively increase its savings and investment."[93] The existing maize tariff was 250 percent, to be phased out over a 15-year period, with sharp reductions beginning in the seventh year; average maize yields were 2 tons per hectare in Mexico as against 7.4 in the United States.[94] Large-scale migration to the border cities, also fostered by an end to the low-yield subsistence agriculture fostered by the *ejido* system curbed by the Salinas government[95] resulted in pressure on border controls. Guaranteed prices for maize were reduced by 20 percent in 1984–9 and by another 10 percent in 1989–92; the corresponding reductions for beans were 50 percent and 30 percent.[96] Salinas'

> program did not offer a single measure for temporary protection to Mexican industry…[the] recognition of asymmetry was insufficient. In NAFTA there does not exist such things as investment funds established in favour of weaker nations…as in the European Union (EU).[97]

There was "no sign of any such initiatives involving the governments of the two countries. All that exists are mechanisms run by [Mexican] state governments."[98] Theodore Wilkinson wondered "whether Salinas also understood the social consequences—tremendously accelerated migration. I personally believe that in the long run it did Mexico good."[99]

One of the opponents of NAFTA, Senator Ernest Hollings (D-SC) had diffidently suggested that a fund similar to the European Regional Development Fund and the European Social Fund (ESF) should be established. The proceeds from it would be used to upgrade Mexico's infrastructure and to clean up the environmental mess along the border.[100] Unlike in the EEC, there was no institutional framework to deal with issues such as decentralization (subsidiarity); labor mobility; compensatory arrangements; social, labor, and environmental standards; and supranational institutions.[101] There was no political will in Washington for that kind of aid (the fact that Mexico collects so little tax revenue from its citizens would make it hard to justify anyway).[102] Nor was there attention to the recommendations of a Commission on American Workplace Skills that reported a year before the ratification of the NAFTA agreement.[103]

NAFTA had major effects, some positive, some negative. From 1992 to 2000, exports rose from 10 percent to 26 percent of GDP. Firms with more than 500 workers accounted for 57.2 percent of Mexican employment, in 1998 up from 50 percent in 1988. Per capita GDP in the southern province of Chiapas was 25.5 percent of that in Mexico City in 1988 but only 17.5 percent in 1996. There was widespread sympathy for, and consequent mild government reaction to, the rebellion that broke out there. Wages as a percentage of total income are said to amount to 15 percent in Mexico as against 55 percent in the United States; Mexican wages approximate 20 percent of value added, as against 35 percent in the United States.[104] William Jeffras Dieterich, one of Negroponte's colleagues in the Mexico City embassy, observed: "the human rights and political cost of stamping out a rebellion like that simply isn't worth the game ... the Mexican government is smart enough not to turn Chiapas into El Salvador."

The percentage of Mexicans living in poverty rose from 1981 to 1996 according to three different indices, the figures improving somewhat later but not back to the original level. According to the World Bank, the percentage in poverty nearly doubled; according to the UN Economic Commission for Latin America, it increased by about 25 percent. Salinas, choosing his years carefully, claimed a fall in the percentage in extreme poverty from 14.9 percent in 1989 to 13.6 percent in 1992. Between 1989 and 2000, Value Added Tax (VAT) yields increased by 50 percent but income tax yields by only 30 percent, there being severe defects in Mexican tax collection. Exports of vehicles and television sets from Mexico greatly increased; by 1998, there was a $6 billion trade balance in favor of Mexico. Corn imports as a percentage of total agricultural imports tripled between 1982 and 2000; coffee exports sharply dropped and those of fruits and vegetables sharply increased. Hourly wages for workers in the formal work force fell by nearly 20 percent for those with 6 years of education or less, and rose by more than 20 percent for those with more than 12 years of education in the 1987–98 time period. There were 5 million more rural residents in extreme poverty in 1994 than there were 10 years earlier, and about 100,000 fewer urban residents in that state.[105]

The Salinas government sought to mitigate the worst hardships by a program of supporting the food expenditures of the groups most adversely affected. Salinas claimed to devote a day a week to the supervision of social programs, which were administered on a decentralized basis but tended to be concentrated in areas where his party was dominant. These measures, however, did not fully offset the effects of the withdrawal of production subsidies from agriculture or the progressive elimination of tariffs on American corn and soybeans. The approach of NAFTA differed dramatically from that of the EEC: the OECD countries massively support agriculture to avoid the social and political effects of the dislocation that exposing this sector to competition would entail.[106] The recent US FTAs are characterized by

> weaker disciplines or carve-outs for some politically sensitive sectors (particularly in US agriculture); no World Trade Organization (WTO)-plus disciplines on agricultural subsidies or anti-dumping measures; and often complicated or restrictive rules of origin ... NAFTA rules of origin may be equivalent to a tariff of 4.3% and they could be the main factor in the limited effect of NAFTA on Mexican exports.[107]

Mexico typified the 1990s experience with liberalization of the economy in underdeveloped countries:

For the decade as a whole growth was little more than half of what it had been in the 1950s, 1960s or 1970s…. And of that growth, a disproportionate part went to the upper third or even the top ten percent of the population…unemployment rose by 3% each year, and an increasingly large fraction of workers found themselves in the informal sector, without the normal protections offered by formal sector jobs.

Trade agreements, while opening up financial services in Mexico, did little to promote Mexican access to American construction and maritime markets and interfered little with American farm subsidies and antidumping laws; the latter were far more severe than their domestic counterpart, the Robinson–Patman Act.[108]

By 2008, considerable disillusionment had set in. *The New Republic* writer John Judis noted that

the treaty's problems stem from its unforeseen effects on the Mexican economy—particularly its agricultural sector…as American agribusiness moved in, 1.1 million small farmers—and 1.4 million other Mexicans dependent on the farm sector—were driven out of work between 1993 and 2005…according to the Pew Hispanic Center, annual illegal immigration from Mexico jumped 54% in the few years after the treaty was ratified, from 260,000 in 1994 to 400,000 a year from 1995 to 2000. And it has continued growing after that.[109]

One critic of the Mexican agricultural policy noted that Mexico's last experiment with free market ideas from the North ended in the Mexican Revolution of 1916: "This permanent [rural] underclass will represent a potentially explosive challenge to the political stability of the regime. Did Salinas consider the fate of Diaz?"

The promise of a "quick fix" for American labor through an explosion of exports to Mexico has not been fully realized: "in order for Mexico to become a dynamic market for American exports—thus providing 'good jobs for good wages' for US workers…it had to maintain an overvalued currency," which it proved unable to do.[110] Diana Negroponte was later to note that "the Washington Consensus fell into relative disrepute in the early 21st century."[111]

Education

The agreement, however, was said in 2007 to have produced a "smaller than expected impact on Mexican wages and income per head." Little had been done to provide alternatives to subsistence farming or to improve education, particularly secondary education. The *ejido* sector accounted for 43 percent of farmland and 60 percent of farmers but only 10 percent of agricultural production. The general educational level of the work force was well below that in most of the Far East.[112] As Kenneth Dam has observed: "to the extent that real wages of the unskilled have not grown, the remedy is to improve productivity through education and skills training or through the application of more capital to jobs." The chief relief program took the form of a stipend for mothers who had their children vaccinated and kept them in school; this had important public health effects.

Although Mexican manufacturing exports increased by 193 percent and agricultural exports (mostly vegetables) by 60 percent during the period 1993–9, there was increased income inequality within Mexico. The previously protected industries involved goods intensive in low-skilled labor. The close proximity of the northern areas to a newly opened American market reduced the comparative advantage of the Mexican South. There was a widening of returns for education, whereas little was done about the schooling deficit. Although primary education is universal in Argentina, Chile, and Uruguay, it is not achieved until the seventh income decile in the case of Mexico.[113] Between 1980 and 1996, Mexico increased its public expenditures on health eightfold, from 0.4 percent of the GDP to 3.2 percent of the GDP and was rewarded by an increase of nearly 15 years, to 75, in average life expectancy and a fall in infant mortality from 68 per thousand in 1988 to 32 per thousand in 1994, in part because of massive extension of vaccination programs. During the same period, public expenditures for education rose only from 3.2 percent to 4 percent, a rate far below that of the developing countries of the Far East, although higher than that in two of Negroponte's other posts, the Philippines and Honduras.[114] Education at the high school level is the weak link.[115] From 1980 to 1990, the average level of schooling increased by 2 years and the proportion of workers with secondary education rose from 26 percent to 39 percent; however, expenditures for research and development were far below those in the developing countries of the Far East.[116]

The ultimate success of NAFTA is dependent on major structural changes in the United States, particularly in its scientific and technical education. British Prime Minister Harold Macmillan had recognized this for his own country in his reaction to Hong Kong textile imports; Negroponte was later to focus on it in several speeches given as Director of National Intelligence. As one commentator observed, free-trade areas can lead to either upward or downward convergence of wages:

> It is evident that upward convergence of wages for Mexico and the United States for labor of similar skills depends primarily on US initiatives to restructure its own economy toward increased productivity and competitiveness…far more needs to be done to reverse the trend in real wages of the US underclass…. Migrants earn rents on the difference between wages at home and abroad. Investors earn rents from shifting production from high-wage to low-wage areas.[117]

Further, and even more alarmingly,

> Real wages especially for problematic regions sectors and occupational skills are continuing a downward trend. The US recession in the 90s is different from previous downswings. It reflects not merely the cyclical underemployment of existing capacity but the need to continue major structural adjustments of the economy and its workforce to meet the demands of increased international competition.[118]

The eminent international economist Gottfried Haberler, writing 40 years earlier, had urged caution in the application of economic models of free trade, especially static ones:

It is true, however, that if occupational and geographic mobility of factors of production is sharply restricted, a country will derive less advantage from its trading opportunities than if factors were fully mobile. Moreover, trade will then often produce sharp changes in the distribution of income as between the different immobile factors—a condition which may be undesirable in itself and is likely to lead to undesirable social reactions, to price rigidity, and unemployment, thus entailing deviation from the "ideal conditions."[119]

On both sides of the border, the educational limitations of the low-skilled labor force imposed sharp limitations on "occupational mobility." Haberler also found some merit in the "infant industry—import substitution" justification for protectionism, but only if it was pursued for the purpose of developing economies of scale allowing local industries to brave international competition: "The condition that protection can in the end be withdrawn is generally taken as a necessary though not always a sufficient criterion ... for success." With respect to both these qualifications of "free trade" principles, Haberler urged that "Economic history has more to offer than theoretical analysis for the solution of these problems." The economists and trade representatives on both sides who negotiated the NAFTA agreement were more doctrinaire and did not consider these refinements.

In 1995, only 46 percent of the eligible age group in Mexico was enrolled in secondary schools, as against 89 percent in the United States, 94 percent in Spain, and 96 percent in South Korea. In 1998, Mexican primary school teachers were paid $12,450 as against $15,789 in Thailand, $33,973 in the United States, and $39,921 in South Korea. An attempt to reform the school system against the wishes of the teachers' unions in the early 1990s is said to have been vitiated in implementation by union opposition. Latin American teachers' unions are as obstinate as their American counterparts; it is said that "Not a single case of significant alteration in any ... core policies has occurred anywhere in the region over the past decade and a half."[120]

The Embassy was "not able to create any big chunks of funding for educational exchange ... we worked on various schemes to create a sort of educational NAFTA."[121]

Trade Diversion from NAFTA

Whether NAFTA increased overall economic efficiency is open to debate because of the phenomenon of trade displacement. As Dam has put it, "diversion results in a less efficient (higher real cost) exporter getting the business and displacing a more efficient third party exporter." Thus, the free access to the US market enjoyed by Mexican maquiladora factories gave them benefits at the expense of the countries party to the earlier Caribbean Basin initiative. Similarly, the rules of origin provisions relating to textiles requiring that "yarn be produced, fabric made, and clothing sewn" within NAFTA benefited segments of the US textile industry at the expense of their Far Eastern competitors. Dam observes that "the office of the US Trade Representative rather proudly put in its 1999 annual report 'US firms have obtained more than an eight percentage point margin of preference [in Mexico] compared to non-NAFTA competition.'"[122] Public choice theory teaches that "trade-diverting products will very likely be included [in agreements] but trade-creating products may or may not be included ... it is politically easier for negotiating countries to include trade diverting products." The requirement of Article XXIV of the General Agreement on Tariffs and Trade (GATT) that PTAs include "substantially all" or more than 80 percent of trade has been honored in the breach.

Dam recognizes that PTAs, unlike GATT agreements, virtually eliminate barriers at one stroke and therefore may have dynamic effects. "The most important dynamic effect for Mexico may well be the Salinas internal economic liberalization reforms." However the complex web of preferential agreements between and among various countries, the so-called "spaghetti bowl," "plays directly into the hands of the industries who benefit."[123]

The standard critique of NAFTA is that of the economist Joseph Stiglitz, for a time a member of the Council of Economic Advisers: the agreement's benefits presuppose "perfect information, perfect risk-markets, perfect competition and no innovation." By introducing uncertainty, a possibly damaging shift on the part of investors from risky to nonrisky activities is stimulated. "The US keeps its agricultural subsidies and developing countries are not allowed to impose countervailing duties ... How could one expect a developing country to have much bargaining power when negotiating with the US?" Furthermore, rules of origin prohibited Mexico from fabricating Chinese goods for export to the United States, and intellectual property provisions insulated US drug companies from Mexican competition. It has been said of intellectual property protection that it "may skew research and development to favor practical inventions rather than more fundamental and theoretical ones, but it is not clear whether this kind of institutional arrangement is better suited to society."[124] A classic article by economists Paul Samuelson and Wolfgang Stolper was said to demonstrate that liberalization lowers the wages of unskilled workers in high-income countries (although with the qualification, not mentioned by Stiglitz, that "it is always possible to bribe the suffering factor by subsidy or other redistributive devices so as to leave all factors better off as a result of trade."[125] Stiglitz's prescription called for freer movements of labor and elimination of agricultural subsidies, a cause taken up without much success by Mexican President Vicente Fox. Mexican critics more mildly observed that

> Unless trade liberalization is complemented with other policies that can help increase productivity, develop more human capital (through education) and provide an adequate safety net for the losers in liberalized trade, the perceived association between economic growth and freer trade ... will weaken.[126]

The most comprehensive short critique of preferential trade agreements, Jagdish Bhagwati's *Termites in the Trading System*[127] notes that the NAFTA agreement, like most PTAs but unlike the European Union and Mercosur agreements (economic and political agreement among Argentina, Brazil, Paraguay, and Uruguay), contains no uniform external tariff. Salinas sold the agreement to the Americans with the observation that it would "lock in" his economic reforms, raising the question "Is it really democratic to have President Salinas (who signed NAFTA) tie the hands of future Mexican presidents in this way?" Bhagwati is dubious about inclusion in such agreements of what he regards as extraneous provisions dealing with intellectual property and environmental and labor standards at the behest of American lobbying groups. In his view, "royalty collection is not a trade issue." As for the environment, a quest for uniform standards may be unwise: "it may make perfect sense to Mexico to worry about polluted water and for the US to worry about polluted air." As for labor standards, given the decline of US private sector unions "it is truly ironic if US labor standards are to be the gold standard for its trading partners." PTAs give economically large and powerful countries an advantage that "they cannot secure at the WTO because the developing countries are there in greater numbers and can resist." NAFTA was "arguably even a mistake," leading to "trade fatigue" undermining the Doha Round of trade negotiation. Finally, PTAs can lead to trade diversion during economic crises; in the peso crisis of 1994 "external tariffs were raised on 502 items from 20% or less to as much as 35% while the NAFTA-defined reductions in Mexican tariffs on US and Canadian goods continued."[128]

The Immigration Issue

In May 1991 in a letter to Senator Lloyd Bentsen and Congressman Dan Rostenkowski, President George H.W. Bush excluded US immigration policy from the negotiations. This has been ascribed by Robert Earle to congressional weariness with immigration as a political issue; only five years had passed since the political convulsions accompanying enactment of the Simpson–Mazzoli Act, which reformed US immigration law, with its "amnesty" provisions. In addition to illegal immigration, about 20 percent of legal immigration into the United States was from Mexico. Negroponte, throughout his tenure, exhorted American consuls, contrary to their usual inclination, to construe the visa laws to facilitate immigration; it was better to have immigrants "on the books" rather than off them. He also dispatched additional manpower to consulates to eliminate the long lines of Mexicans surrounding them, which he viewed as demeaning to both successful and unsuccessful applicants.

Recalled William Jeffras Dieterich,

> We finally had to get away from making people wait outdoors by building this shelter, a roof over one of the parking lots with benches in it, that gave people a place to wait for their turn to go up to the window,[129]

The "family unification" provisions of US immigration law under which about two-thirds of immigrants are admitted perversely discriminate against skilled immigrants. The average Mexican immigrant had 7.6 years of schooling; 85 percent of them settled in California, Illinois, and Texas. Although immigration was excluded from the agreement, its premise was that "an economically healthy

Mexico helps to relieve illegal immigration and ward off political instability in Mexico."[130] The United States has not ratified the International Convention on the Rights of All Migrants and Their Families (1990),[131] which confers basic rights of due process, wage payment, access to education and emergency health services, and consular access on illegal immigrants.

According to President Salinas' version of events:

> President Bush repeatedly said that the Mexican oil industry had to be opened to the market and the process of private ownership. I said: 'No. But we do need these trade negotiations and this trade agreement to include the free movement of labor and workers.' And he said 'That's impossible. Because we would not be able to pass through the US Congress.' And I said 'Well, for us it's crucial to have the free movement of people.' And he said for us it's crucial to have private ownership of Mexican oil.' And my response was 'Let's go for the workers.' And he said 'Let's go for the oil'. And I said 'Let's go for the workers.' And that was it. No workers, no oil.[132]

A critic of the agreement, commenting on the Salinas-Bush dialogue, observed: "So much for David Ricardo, comparative advantage, and the Harvard, M.I.T. and Chicago-trained economics establishment."[133]

However, in an important respect, vital to the United States, NAFTA has been a disappointment:

> In the nine year period from 1994 when NAFTA went into effect through 2002 real GDP in Mexico has grown by about 3% a year—about half of what was needed for the necessary job creation.... If Mexico were able to achieve sustained high rates of GDP growth on the order of 6% a year for at least 10 to 15 years, this, coupled with the already declining birth-rates, would largely eliminate the unauthorized migration issue because Mexicans could find opportunities at home.[134]

From the American standpoint, the agreement was not an unalloyed blessing; contrary to predictions, "the initial capital inflows into Mexico generated exports which turned the bilateral trade flows into a US deficit by the late 1990s."[135] The negotiators were said to have assumed that the NAFTA agreement would have no effect on northward migration for five years, following which there would be a 25 percent reduction in the sixth through tenth years and a 50 percent reduction in the eleventh through fifteenth years.[136]

One unanticipated consequence of NAFTA was vastly increased illegal immigration into the United States; 1990 saw the first increase in border crossings since the American enactment of the Simpson–Mazzoli Immigration Act in 1986.[137] From a low of 950,000 border apprehensions in 1989, a drop from the 1.7 million in 1986, the number had risen to 1.26 million by 1992, and to 1.81 million by 2000, before falling off to 1.21 million in 2006.[138] The total number of unauthorized immigrants remaining in the United States was estimated at 8.5 million in 2000 and 11.6 million in 2006, of whom 4.68 million were conservatively estimated to be Mexican. The failure to deal with immigration issues at the time of the agreement was not an advantage for the United States; indeed, the Mexican government fostered migration to the United States in a variety of ways, including the offer of dual citizenship to migrants and the furnishing to them of identification cards and expanded consular services. Although a 6–7 percent growth rate would cause available jobs to equal the size of the Mexican workforce in about 10 years, it was not forthcoming, in part because of low tax yield in Mexico and consequent gross underinvestment in education. The only hopeful development as respects future migration pressure derives from a dramatic fall in the birth rate from 6.1 children per woman in 1974 to 2.4 children per woman in 1990. On the other hand, it has been observed that "Money sent back home by immigrants far outweighs development aid both in volume and in reaching the intended beneficiaries."[139]

In November 2007, as Deputy Secretary of State, Negroponte took part in a conference at Monterrey, at which President Felipe Calderón expressed his nation's grievances about America's insatiable demand for drugs, as well as money laundering and the flow of weapons into Mexico. Negroponte acknowledged that the proposed border wall "was not the optimal solution" but alluded to "the sovereign right of a country to control its border." He denied that there were significant links between drugs and terrorism in Mexico, unlike Afghanistan, and noted: "We are a country of immigrants. Not one single member of my immediate family, not even me, was born in the United States." In November 2007, Diana Negroponte lamented that

People oppose illegal immigrants, but still want their houses built, offices cleaned, lawns cut, children cared for and products consumed. We are becoming an inward-looking protectionist people with a mean streak≈rarely seen in America's history. It will take great leadership previously unseen to restore the generosity and outreach of the American people.[140]

Some cautionary words about the current American border-sealing project were voiced by the Mexican commentator Jorge Castenada:

An attempt to clamp down on immigration from the South by sealing the border…would make social peace untenable in the barrios and pueblos of Mexico…The US should count its blessings; it has dodged instability on its borders since the Mexican Revolution, now nearly a century ago. The warnings from Mexico are loud and clear. This time, it might be a good idea to heed them.[141]

A later American ambassador, Jeffrey Davidow, writing of immigration, observed that

the dual magnets of the booming American economy and large post-IRCA Mexican communities in the United States probably accounted for most of the influx. But clearly at least a portion of the outflow of former

Mexican factory workers and campesinos was stimulated by the inability of Mexican producers to compete with increasing and cheaper US imports entering the country as tariffs fell.[142]

As a Mexican writer said,

No country has ever attempted to develop an export manufacturing base by opening its borders so quickly and so indiscriminately to more efficient and lower-cost producers. No nation not even the US has so willingly sacrificed an industrial policy or an equivalent form of managed trade.[143]

The changes in the border towns are typified by the present situation in Agua Prieta, opposite Douglas, Arizona, one of the less populous and important such towns:

The town's current population is approximately 110,000 up from about 37,000 in 1990…37.7% of the town's population is economically active, and the town's unemployment rate is 30 percent. The average monthly base salary with benefits is approximately $515 in US dollars. As of 2005 there were 23 maquiladoras in Agua Prieta employing 7,425 workers…. The largest is Levolor Kirsch, a retail factory, which employs 1,800 workers, followed by Takata, an automotive factory, which employs 1,250 and MWC de Mexico, an automotive factory, which employs 1,100.[144]

NAFTA and Agriculture
Early in the NAFTA negotiations at Dallas,

Mexico would make concessions that according to a number of participants left the mouths of Canadian and US negotiators agape…in agriculture, investment, and financial services…. Opening agriculture across the board was probably the most important concession made by Mexico at Dallas since it meant placing maize on the agenda for the first time. This was a decision that would affect the lives of millions of Mexican peasants and consumers.[145]

As Kenneth Dam noted, "unilateral tariff reductions were used by Mexico during the Salinas administration. Only in the most developed countries does unilateral liberalization still seem odd."[146]

The elimination of the corn and bean tariffs over time was a major grievance of the leaders of the Zapatista rebellion in southern Mexico that broke out just after ratification of the NAFTA agreement. Not only were tariffs to be progressively reduced, but subsidies amounting to 44 percent of the value of production in 1991 were to be largely withdrawn or converted into welfare payments: "the most important sectoral effect of NAFTA is on maize farming…[there was] shoddy empirical work…on employment consequences."[147] In his thousand-page apologia for his program, written after he departed for exile in extradition-free countries after expiration of his term, Salinas had little to say about the agricultural sector, although noting that a reserve clause in the NAFTA agreement allowed Mexico to tax the export of products contained in the basic shopping basket, a somewhat moot point as Mexican corn and bean production was not internationally competitive. Salinas noted that social expenditures as a percentage of GDP increased from 7.1 percent in 1988 to 11.6 percent in 1994, most of the new expenditure taking the form of welfare payments to farmers who had lost their production subsidies. He acknowledged that no common market had been sought: "We only proposed free trade, not national absorption. We lost financial supports, but Mexico kept its capacity of decision-making on aspects fundamental to its life." He conceded that it had "not made sufficient progress in the area of the human and labor rights for our migrant workers in the United States" and that later there was a "collapse of agricultural production in 1996 and 1998 owing to a harsh drought Mexico suffered in those years and the drop in direct support to the campesinos."[148]

NAFTA did not inaugurate this Mexican policy toward agriculture. A left-wing critic observed:

[F]arm policy in the 1980s explicitly sought to drain off the rural population. A demographic purge was launched to remove some three million "unnecessary" workers from the congested Mexican countryside, freeing agriculture of more than 15 million "extra people".

Imports of grain rose from 52 million tons in 1987–93 to 90 million in 1994-9; corn imports from 17 million tons in 1987–93 to 30 million tons in 1994-9. By 2008, corn was to be totally liberated from tariffs; in fact the Minister for Economy established a tariff-free quota of 2.667 million tons above the NAFTA level at an earlier date.[149]

As a critic of the policy observed later: "A government that is genuinely reflective of Mexican interests and accountable to the Mexican people is much more likely to have a program that will target poverty and unemployment and thus reduce emigration."[150] As a bargaining counter, Salinas made occasional suggestions that Mexico would turn to Japan if its overtures to the United States were rebuffed.[151] His proposal for NAFTA was accompanied by other neoliberal measures, including the privatization of several industries including the telephone company,[152] the denationalization of banks, the curtailment of "featherbedding" at the national oil company,[153] and a measure allowing 100 percent foreign ownership of tourist facilities.[154]

There were estimates that the Mexican policies replacing fertilizer and equipment investments with income subsidies would drive 15 million peasants out of agriculture, fostering a northward migration like that of unskilled blacks from agricultural areas in the American South in the 1940s, 1950s, and 1960s. Other estimates of the number of displaced farmers ranged widely from 700,000 over 9 years to 10 million over 10 years. "No one argues that agriculture policy reforms will make Mexicans less likely to move to the US...As Mexican migrants move north, they are more likely to enter the US"[155] By 1995, remittances from "illegal" Mexican workers in the United States were estimated at $3 billion annually and one-fifth of the Mexican workforce was said to be in the United States. Cross-border migration had an especially dramatic impact in the United States because of the rough equality in size of the two nations' unskilled work forces despite the greater population of the United States: 8–10 million in Mexico as compared with 10–12 million in the United States.[156] By 2001, remittances were said to amount to $8.895 billion.[157]

In 2007, former Mexican President Vicente Fox bitterly reflected on the consequences of NAFTA combined with American agricultural subsidies:

> NAFTA was not so kind to the Mexican farmers. Hit hard by the peso devaluation, now they faced competition from the highly efficient and richly subsidized agribusiness of the US where the economic insanity of farm-price supports for millionaire growers and billionaire-run corporations persists even today. Suddenly Mexico was showered with cheap American corn, a boon to hard-pressed consumers in the big cities. But this was a threat to the Mexican farmer, who could not compete with US farmers' superior methods, equipment, capital, productivity and quality— all funded by the $16 billion in farm subsidies that Washington doles out every year. North America was an impossible goliath for the 3.5 million Mexican Davids who farmed the little *ejido* plots of ten to twelve acres allotted to them by the PRI.[158]

The malign effects of American farm subsidies were conceded by former US Trade Representative Carla Hills, writing in support of the Doha negotiations in 2005:

> Most Americans do not know how the huge subsidies that wealthy countries (including the United States) pay their farmers force more efficient producers in poor countries out of the market, nor do they know that 80% of US farm subsidies go to large agribusinesses, not to small family farmers.

Although the Mexican corn producers were not "more efficient," Fox was right that their plight was aggravated by American subsidies. American insistence that American subsidy cuts be paralleled by similar subsidy cuts in France, Germany, and Japan, whose subsidy programs have social and environmental dimensions lacking in the United States had more than a little to do with the failure of the Doha Round, whose ultimate proximate cause was fear in India and China of too-rapid agricultural change.[159]

The Petroleum Sector

Although the State Department was involved in the negotiation of only a limited number of segments of the NAFTA, one of them was the petroleum sector, sacrosanct to the Mexicans since the nationalization of the industry by the Lázaro Cárdenas government in 1938, the annual anniversary of the nationalization being a national holiday. At the outset of the negotiation, certain sectors of the industry were placed off limits to the negotiators, including

(1) no obligation to guarantee petroleum supplies (2) no investment in areas reserved to the Mexican state (3) no free trade in the energy sector reserved to the state (4) no risk contracts in the energy sector and (5) no foreign gasoline stations.

Notwithstanding these limitations, foreign companies were allowed to sell exploration services on a performance bonus but not on a risk-sharing basis; the petrochemical sector reserved to the government was limited to eight basic commodities; private electric plants selling current through the government-owned grid were allowed; some supply contracts were allowed; and 50 percent of Pemex's procurement, rising to 70 percent over 7 years was to be done through open international bidding. Even with respect to the petroleum industry, Mexico was "forced to put on the table purchasing agreements that had been used as a 'set-aside' to promote the Mexican capital goods industry."[160] Salinas, a convinced and doctrinaire free trader, is said not to have seriously resisted this, at one point allegedly telling American negotiators: "You guys keep pressing PEMEX for greater access."[161] When President George H.W. Bush attempted to improve on these concessions while attending a baseball game with President Salinas in San Diego, he was "discreetly advised by Ambassador ... Negroponte that the subject was off limits."[162] As a result of lack of investment, production by Pemex fell 22 percent between 2004 and 2009, and exports by it fell 35 percent during these years. Mexico's non-oil tax revenues amounted in 2009 to only 10.8 percent of the GNP, a percentage well below that in most developing countries, giving rise to underinvestment in infrastructure and the education system.[163]

One of the prices paid by the Clinton administration to secure enactment of the NAFTA was curtailment of a tax on airline and cruise ship passengers, the proceeds of which was to be devoted to the retraining of displaced American workers.[164] The Bush administration for its part had proposed a short-lived "Enterprise for the Americas" plan an overriding principle of which was that FTAs should impose no cost on the US budget. The plan proposed debt relief and a modest grant to the Inter-American Development Bank for infrastructure improvements, as well as to an environment trust to foster the creation of national parks in Latin America. Absent from it was any "comprehensive rural-focussed development strategy that emphasizes irrigation and education."[165] Existing institutions provide some relief to heavily impacted American regions:

the US at least insures regions against income shocks.... a one dollar reduction in a US region's per capita personal income triggers a 34 cent decrease in federal taxes and a 6 cent increase in federal transfers...the main concern of US legislatures is US infra-structure and development assistance, not NAFTA-generated problems in Mexico.[166]

The Mexican state will be left with responsibility for compensating the losers from NAFTA ... [the] role of the state [is] severely curtailed by privatization and deregulation and in the absence of a compulsory system of social security, this will be a difficult task to accomplish.[167]

By contrast, the ESF created first to address the problems of Southern Italy and later those of Greece, Spain, Portugal, and Ireland disbursed $119 billion over a 4-year period in support of EEC-required National Development Plans.[168] Later, Jorge Castañeda, Vicente Fox's foreign minister, unsuccessfully pressed for creation of a joint development bank. It has been noted, however, that the completely free movement of labor made possible by the Schengen Agreements, eliminating border controls within the EEC, was the product of 30 years of gradual development after the Treaty of Rome.[169] Another neglected area was the deficient protection of property and contract rights in Mexico; the remains of the *ejido* system and the prevalence of nonexistent land titles and squatter housing created a condition typical of Latin America, where 80 percent of property and 50–75 percent of the labor force is said to be outside the formal economy and therefore without the ability to borrow, insure, connect with public utilities, sue, or be taxed.[170]

Drugs

As for drugs,

> The United States went to war by proxy against a profitable business that it was impossible to halt…senseless war against the laws of supply and demand…engaging underdeveloped countries in a forceful reallocation of resources, the commitment of political capital, and the cession of civilian power to their military establishments…hurting individual rights and further weakening institutional safeguards against intrusive government…the war on terrorism…restricted the flow of people, capital and goods into the United States in recent years even further.[171]

One embarrassing episode involved the cross-border abduction by American bail bondsmen acting at the behest of the Los Angeles office of the DEA of Humberto Machaín, a Mexican doctor wanted as a defendant in an American drug case, which roused nationalist passions in Mexico.[172] The DEA had a grudge against Machaín because he had kept a captured DEA agent, Enrique Camarena, alive while the drug cartel tortured him. Wilkinson charged the DEA with "acting like cowboys…it was very hard to tell them anything." The American Justice Department stubbornly insisted in pressing forward with its prosecution beginning in May 1990 despite Mexican protests and American court reverses, the case ultimately going to the US Supreme Court;[173] the case ultimately resulted in an acquittal.[174] It was not until June 1993 that Secretary of State Warren Christopher moved to prevent further such abductions.[175]

> Because of its stake in NAFTA, the Mexican government restrained its impulse to expel the DEA and ordered the American agents to simply "suspend" activities in Mexico. Even this mild protest was rescinded a day later after prodding from the US Embassy and Mexico's own NAFTA negotiators.[176]

On another occasion, John Negroponte, for the only time in his diplomatic career, physically handed back to the Undersecretary of Foreign Affairs a note demanding suspension of DEA enforcement activities. The Macháin abduction was said to have been carried out by the Los Angeles office of the DEA as a reprisal for the death in Mexico of the DEA agent, Camarena, and without the prior authorization of either the State Department or the DEA director. Once apprehended, Macháin, an unsavory character, was difficult for the Americans to release; at one point Vice President Dan Quayle was sent to Mexico to smooth over tensions resulting from the episode.

A consequence of NAFTA was an upsurge in the illegal drug trade:

the pressures from increased competition under a market model make it more difficult for those who are economically displaced to resist the temptation of economic gains related to drug production and illegal migration [a phenomenon] perfectly in line with the dictates of neoclassical economic theory, which encourages countries to specialize in those exports that enjoy a comparative advantage.

Furthermore, "Social disruption and economic pressure from free market reforms have intensified in rural areas, fuelling the tendency to grow illicit crops as a household survival strategy."[177]

By the mid-1990s, Mexico was said to account for 70 percent of American cocaine imports, 80 percent of marijuana, and 20–30 percent of heroin, the total traffic amounting to $7 billion per year, much of it hidden in the increased truckloads of legal goods crossing the border.[178] Half of the imports were marijuana. Negroponte in congressional testimony was to acknowledge that its levels exceeded those of the 1990s.

The response to this problem was not a serious demand-side effort to address drug consumption in the United States, which would have entailed unpopular drug testing in schools and colleges like that previously successfully introduced in the military and workforce. Instead, it took the form of an increased and ominous militarization of drug enforcement on both sides of the border. The only hopeful response to the problem is found in the enactment in California and about a dozen other states of so-called "medical marijuana" laws, reminiscent of the "medicinal alcohol" exception to the Noble Experiment (Prohibition). These bid fair to transfer supply from the drug cartels to American home-based growers.

In the United States, the milestones in the march to militarization were an amendment of the Posse Comitatus Act in 1981 to allow military participation in international drug interdiction; further expansion of the military role in the omnibus drug control act in 1986; the designation of the Department of Defense as the lead agency for drug interdiction in 1989; and the appropriation of nearly a billion dollars for US military assistance in military Mexican border drug interdiction and technical assistance in 2007–8.

On the Mexican side, beginning in 1992, a federal preventive police with nearly 11,000 agents was created for drug interdiction. In 1996, the Mexican Supreme Court decided that the armed forces could participate in drug interdiction. By

2004, a commentator could write that "Practically all drug law enforcement operations have been handed over to military officers."[179] Wilkinson observed: "now the army is corrupted by the same contagion, simply because the pay in government is too bad and the money in drugs is too good."

In 2007–8, a conference at Mérida, Yucatán, planned for an expansion of both countries' military roles, together with a $500 million grant to Mexico by the United States and projected spending of another $900 million by the US military in Mexico and Central America, a development described by Diana Negroponte, who urged the necessity of careful debate and transparency in both the US and Mexican Congresses, although without speculation on the ultimate effect of these developments on civil–military relations in two nations that had hitherto been unusually successful in keeping their militaries out of politics.[180] Cárdenas, for the Mexican left opposition, characterized this policy as a choice by both countries to do battle on

> a battleground best known to the drug dealers and with weapons they choose … the US and Mexico spend too much of their energy and resources trying to intercept drugs and too little taking away sources of supply and reducing demand,

leading to "arbitrary coercion by drug lords and security authorities alike," the victims of which were "impoverished peasants in rural Mexico and South America … poor youths in US inner cities who use illegal substances for psychological escape or self-destruction," the trade amounting to "2% of gross domestic product."[181] Left to one side is the jaundiced view that "The evidence is overwhelming that US anti-drug efforts overseas have had virtually no impact on its problems with drugs at home, and probably never will."[182]

It has also been suggested that the political reporting and intelligence services of the American Embassy left something to be desired. The United States was allegedly "blindsided" by the Chiapas rebellion in Mexico's southernmost state, which began just after Negroponte's departure, by the peso devaluation and balance of payments crisis that shortly followed, and by the extent of drug corruption in Mexican society, extending to the Mexican president's brother. It has been suggested that "both the Bush and Clinton administrations exaggerated Mexico's successes in fighting drug trafficking in order to preserve its reputation and to negotiate NAFTA."[183] Early in his tenure, Negroponte observed that "I am convinced that President Salinas has wrought a sea-change" in narcotics cooperation. In October 1991, he persuaded a reluctant Salinas to attend a Latin American summit on drugs; Salinas sought assurances that this was not linked to free trade. At the end of 1991, there was an episode at Veracruz in which American customs officers witnessed a shootout between federal police and corrupt troops in which seven policemen died.[184] After the story broke in the Mexican press, Negroponte and Salinas' chief of staff, Jose Cordoba Montoya, announced that an impartial investigation would be conducted by the Mexican National Commission on Human Rights.[185] The report, issued on December 6, 1991, contained findings resulting in the imprisonment of a three-star Mexican general and five of his subordinates; however, it was also learned that a high officer of the Mexican drug agency who mediated the clash was himself involved with drug traffickers.

On March 10, 1992, Negroponte sent a ten-page dispatch to Washington that echoed his widely published May 1991 cable, a dispatch described by Leslie Fraser as "an impassioned call to gag the dissident DEA field agents."[186] In it, he regretted that

> leakage in the US press of insider information about the shooting of PGR agents by Mexican military personnel caused great consternation in the GOM [which might jeopardize] the NAFTA, the centrepiece of the new relationship with Mexico … a major impetus to modernization [leading to] a broad spectrum of closer relations with the United States [and] slow but steady convergence between Mexican and American views in international foreign affairs. Salinas and commerce secretary Jaime Serra spend a considerable amount of time emphasizing that NAFTA is not meant to be a closed bloc, but that Mexico like the US is interested in dropping trade barriers throughout Latin America and the world, and that eventual inclusion of other countries in Latin America in the free trade sphere is a possibility for the future. To this end, Mexico has taken a lead role in trade liberalization in Latin America … Mexico has considered itself to be a natural leader in Latin America and has recently expressed as a desire to lead the rest of Latin America into free market reforms and eventual economic prosperity.[187]

Earlier on November 21, 1991, Fraser had cautioned

> I would urge that we bear in mind that Mexican military now and in the future will play a lead role in narcotics eradication and interdiction. It would be unfortunate if through public comments we create lasting institutional resentments that make cooperation more difficult …. [The episode might] correct the deficiencies in Government of Mexico (GOM) military/Office of Attorney General (PGR) coordination which led to this type of situation.[188]

The bloodbath thus described as a "deficiency in coordination" was also characterized as a harbinger of better things: "both organizations stand to gain if a better working relationship results from this when all is said and done."[189]

Salinas. thereafter, allowed US assistance to the drug war to drop from $45 million to 0. The embassy reported that "The incident has given some impetus to 'Mexicanization' of our anti-narcotics cooperation, but this is a generally positive trend."[190] A critic from the Mexican left, Jorge Castenada, wrote that "All of what happened was warned of, written about, and clearly visible early on in the Salinas years: no one was watching, listening, or willing to read the writing on the thick white walls that criss-cross Mexico City."[191] In 1997, Negroponte was quoted as saying: "I don't think we ever doubted Salinas' personal integrity. He was a very disciplined guy. He always wore that Casio sports watch. He worked like hell." "Every American official who came through there met with the Mexicans involved with NAFTA. That was the prism through which the American Government was looking at the Mexican Government. We certainly felt that the reformers were in the ascendancy." A *New York Times* commentator observed:

> Those bright, English-speaking officials seemed to sustain an American faith: that the more Mexico opened up to competition, the more its government would have to scale back its economic role—and the less chance Mexican officials would have to demand bribes in return for waiving rules or awarding contracts.

An exception to this relative complacency took place in 1992, when American drug enforcers came upon a videotape showing cocaine traffickers consorting with a Mexican general, Javier Escobedo.

> Mr. Negroponte, the Ambassador, saw it as an unusual opportunity and he immediately delivered a copy to Mexico's Defense Minister.... General Escobedo chose neither to turn informant nor face a court martial. Instead...he drove to the grave of his father, who had also been an army general, and shot himself to death. The circumstances of his suicide were never disclosed.[192]

As Director of National Intelligence, in his threat assessment for 2006, Negroponte told the House Intelligence Committee that Mexico's July 2006 election "illustrated Mexico's polarization along socioeconomic lines." He declined to speculate in open session on what might provoke a mass migration northward, although noting, to the surprise of his questioner, that "there are essentially some ungoverned areas in the far north [of Mexico] where they really are not in control of the governors or the central government."

Negroponte regarded the NAFTA Treaty, along with the Montreal Protocol on ozone, as his greatest achievement, and declared that Mexico was his favorite posting, finding "a soft spot in my heart for the country of Mexico, extremely nice people, a big country, visited 32 states. NAFTA, I feel very proud of that accomplishment."[193] On his departure from Mexico, he said that in business and commercial terms "NAFTA [was] equal to what the end of the Cold War meant to our political relations."[194] In a speech in 2000, he lauded NAFTA's "predictability and continuity...[its] framework for removal of the remaining barriers...[and] region-wide investment strategies." He observed that "migratory equilibrium is not something likely to be achieved in any near-term horizon," although expressing the hope that Mexico would be able to avail itself of American special visa programs for information technology workers and that more liberal provision might be made for entry of temporary workers "by being so strict on temporary work permits, we have probably caused more rather than fewer Mexicans to immigrate." He also noted that there were "more Americans of Mexican descent than there were Mexicans at the time of revolution [1916]." He did not take up a suggestion of Cárdenas for "legally enforceable agreements to assure humane treatment for migrant workers."[195] As to law enforcement, "collaboration not sanctions should be the fundamental precept" in addressing movements of "narcotics to the north, weapons and stolen cars to the south."[196]

In 2007, he urged ratification of the FTA with Colombia, noting that it eliminated an average 12 percent tariff on three-fourths of American exports to Colombia and could give rise to an additional $1.1 billion in US exports annually.[197] He noted that liberalization of the Colombian economy had produced a 20 percent drop in the numbers of persons in poverty in 5 years, and that without ratification the "siren song of populism and authoritarianism grows louder." Negroponte held President Álvaro Uribe in high regard:

> He is probably the most impressive leader I know. You have to judge a leader in relation to the challenges he faces, the odds…persistence, clarity, integrity, hard work…these are the things that characterize great leaders, usually. Enormous energy. Enormous focus. Don't underestimate energy and health as really critical factors in these things—they make a difference. You wonder how Roosevelt did what he did being as sick as he was, toward the end of his life. He must have had huge willpower.[198]

Out of fear of American agricultural exports, Ecuador declined to enter into negotiations for a FTA. In 2008, Negroponte lauded the results of NAFTA: "jobs, energy security and lower prices," and looked toward a FTA of the Asia/Pacific, building on the World Trade Organization and its ongoing Doha Round, the Asia–Pacific Economic Cooperation Agreement, and US FTAs with Australia (2004), South Korea (2007), and Singapore.[199] Inspired by the example of NAFTA, the United States had also entered into bilateral agreements with Jordan (2000), Chile (2004), Bahrain (2004), Morocco (2004), Peru (2007), and Panama (2007) as well as a Central American Free-Trade Agreement (CAFTA). The CAFTA contained quotas on sugar and beef dairy, and peanut products to protect US producers, and textile products imported under the agreement had to be made from American yarn and fabrics. The scope for a FTA with the Southern cone countries differed from that applicable to Mexico. US investment in the Southern cone, $58 billion, was twice that in Mexico, although trade with the Southern cone was only 18 percent of that with Mexico; there was also no potential immigration problem with these distant Latin American countries.[200] On departing from Mexico, Negroponte had declared: "I don't think it's inconceivable to think by the next generation [of] an integration of all the countries of the hemisphere."[201] He urged a "systematic and deliberate investment in understanding each other's languages, cultures and institutions," and noted that "Not since Franklin Delano Roosevelt have we thought of the hemisphere on its own merits, rather than in terms of insulating it from the influences of imported totalitarianism."[202]

Thirty years before Negroponte's tour in Mexico, diplomat John Paton Davies, Jr., wrote a critique of America's well-meaning but frequently misdirected foreign assistance programs, under the title "Why Ouagadougou," reflecting the views of some wiser students of foreign policy:

needing no huge appropriations nor battalions of bureaucrats is international trade. This has been an area of relative neglect. What is needed here is the lowering of trade barriers and the stabilization of commodity prices. With these, the underdeveloped countries can begin to pay their own way, moving at their own pace in their own fashion—a wholesome thing for them, and a wholesome thing for us.[203]

Unlike trade, which encourages poor countries to boost production and develop new ideas, aid has often gone to leaders who run their countries into poverty instead of developing them, with additional resources going to those who can display the least development.[204]

For all its imperfections, Negroponte's NAFTA remains America's most notable implementation of this vision. The slide of the world into recession has led to prophecies that attempts at a global free-trade regime will collapse. The United States has been said to "combine an absolutist insistence on its own national sovereignty with a universalist claim to worldwide jurisdiction...ill-suited to the plural world which globalization has created." To those who, like John Gray, consider that "the instruments of economic life have become dangerously emancipated from social control and political governance,"[205] regional groupings like NAFTA may replace visions of a universal market and simplistic views of laissez-faire. NAFTA whatever its other consequences, has forced the United States and Mexico to jointly confront problems of education, crime, and drugs that otherwise would have remained separate national concerns but whose resolution now requires intense regional cooperation. The United States alone will not determine the terms of that cooperation; it is being forced by migration to reconsider its immigration and labor policies and by crime to reconsider its policies with respect to both firearms and drugs, most recently by the Report of the Latin American Commission on Drugs and Democracy.[206]

Negroponte's ambassadorship in Mexico was his most consequential office. Although the NAFTA treaty resulted from an initiative by the Salinas government, it is unlikely that it would have been picked up on without the support of the ambassador, particularly in light of the skepticism of the Trade Representative's office about bilateral and regional trade agreements. Mexico, no longer a "distant neighbor," is now a nation whose fate is inextricably and self-consciously linked to that of the United States. The future economic development of both nations is almost certainly dependent on their emulating the emphasis of various Far Eastern nations and France on scientific education. Their joint future is similarly dependent on renunciation of their current, criminal-law-based drug policies, which bid fair to militarize the one Latin American nation with firmly rooted traditions of civilian government and the United States in its train.

14

THE PHILIPPINES

Today you hear much talk of absolutes...people say that two systems as
different as ours cannot exist in the same world...that one is good and one
is evil, and good and evil cannot exist in the world. Good and evil have
existed in this world since Adam and Eve went out of the Garden of Eden.

The proper search is for limited ends which soon enough educate us in
the complexities of the tasks that face us. That is what all of us must learn
to do in the United States, to limit objectives, to get ourselves away from the
search for the absolute, to find out what is within our powers.... We must
respect our opponents. We must understand that for a long period of time
they will continue to believe as they do and that for a long long period of
time we will both inhabit this spinning ball in the great void of the universe.

— Dean Acheson, quoted in D. McLellan,
Dean Acheson: The State Department Years
(New York: Dodd Mead, 1976), 173–4

John Negroponte had begun to look for a job in the private sector after the Clinton
administration got off to a slow start in filling ambassadorships. In June 1993,
The New York Times ran an editorial lamenting the numerous unfilled embassies; by coincidence or for better reason, Negroponte was offered the Philippine
embassy on the following day. At the start of the Clinton administration, Carlos
Salinas reportedly called Bill Clinton asking him to retain Negroponte in Mexico.

Exit from Empire

Negroponte's service in the Philippines was uneventful; he found the post
much less high pressure than his earlier and later assignments. The United
States had exited from its two major Philippine bases, Clark Field and Subic
Bay, before his arrival. A treaty that would have allowed it to retain bases had
been defeated in the Philippine Senate in 1991, partly, it was said, because
of the abrasive style of Richard Armitage as the US negotiator. Thereafter, the
US Navy "pulled out everything that could float (including three dry docks)
and anything that could be unscrewed."[1] The outgoing ambassador, Richard
Solomon, had publicly stated that the 1950s era Mutual Defense Treaty, which
was still in force, "does not require a permanent US military presence on
Philippine soil." Clark Field had been largely destroyed by a volcanic eruption;

Subic Bay was converted into a recreational, industrial, and commercial complex. Although the remaining base facilities were said to have been looted by well-connected Filipinos,[2] the reconstruction at Subic Bay, including the last-minute demolition of thousands of houses occupied by "squatters," had been sufficiently completed by November of 1996, three months after Negroponte's departure, to allow the ASEAN Conference to be held there.[3]

Negroponte's tenure in the Philippines involved the renunciation of the remnants of America's imperial role and the placement of the relationship on new economic foundations. These are unusual in that the foundation of the Philippine economy is the export of skilled labor rather than economic development within the Philippines. This has resulted from America's mixed policies as a colonial power; it fostered a reasonably good education system while leaving virtually untouched an economic order resting on latifundia (pieces of property covering very large land areas), crony capitalism, and a politicized justice system. The Philippines have been outstripped in economic development by several Southeast Asian countries whose legal and economic institutions are in better shape and that have invested more heavily in education, while retaining advantages derived from a common language and long links with the United States.

The economic history of the Philippines prior to Negroponte's arrival has been succinctly summarized :

> Philippine elites so enjoyed the arrangements provided by the American colonial regime that they were loathe to make the transition to independence [which was] accompanied by provisions that were more clearly advantageous to the landed oligarchy that controlled the state (most of all a bilateral trade agreement ensuring continuing dependence on the American market).... [B]ecause the grantor of independence was a rising superpower, it was especially difficult for the Philippines to emerge as a truly sovereign nation.... [It had] external support to sustain an unjust, inefficient, and graft-ridden political and economic structure; Washington in turn received unrestricted access to two of its most important overseas military installations.... Marcos displayed a particularly keen insight into the nature of the neo-colonial bond—and knew that American strategic needs presented ample opportunity for private gain. Close relations with the United States assisted him in his efforts to cultivate closer relations with the IMF and World Bank...the departure of the US bases in 1992 had left the country feeling both more exposed and more aware of its surroundings...there was suddenly a greater tendency to look around the neighborhood.[4]

Administering an Embassy

On Negroponte's arrival, relations with the Philippines were at their nadir. The post, in addition to being perceived as of limited importance, was hot and humid, as well as being one of the largest embassies in the world, with nearly 2,000 employees. There were 100,000 holders of American passports in the Philippines and 2 million Filipinos in the United States. It was difficult to obtain good Foreign Service officers, so Negroponte resorted to a form of impressment, inviting Raymond Burghardt, a ranking member of his staff in Honduras to dinner with his wife while Burghardt was a diplomat in residence at City University of New York in New York City, a soft billet. Negroponte announced that Burghardt's help was needed in Manila and that refusal of such a posting was the sort of thing that "got around" and affected one's "corridor reputation." Burghardt went to Manila. There were, nonetheless, severe staffing problems there. Two successive consular chiefs, including one recruited by Negroponte, were dismissed for cause from the Foreign Service; one of them was indicted, but ultimately acquitted; the other was believed to have directly granted visa applications presented by a law firm that charged from $5,000 to $10,000 for presenting uncomplicated applications. The first had toured the islands, judging beauty contests and directly admitting some women who wound up in American massage parlors.[5] When questioned, the consular chief indicated that he was engaging in "outreach," leading Negroponte to observe that "every Filipino wants a visa. There is no place in the world where there is less need for outreach." In addition, a head of the security office and a commercial counselor were also dismissed for cause.

Issues relating to the costs of environmental cleanup at the bases lingered.[6] There were complaints by the Philippine government about the treatment of Filipino guest workers in the Northern Mariana Islands, an American commonwealth;[7] the exportation of manpower was a political issue in the Philippines, and there was pressure for additional American visas.[8] President Fidel Ramos visited the United States in November 1993, and President Bill Clinton visited the Philippines in November 1994, together with an enormous entourage; the ambassador was embarrassed when the entire Philippine political establishment was left wilting in the sun for several hours at a scheduled event because the president was operating on "Clinton Standard Time."[9]

Negroponte was cautioned by Clinton's aides not to let Clinton be photographed playing the saxophone, as they believed him to be overexposed in this respect. This object was foiled when Mme. Ramos at dinner told Clinton of a musical group in which she participated which he promptly joined, performing a much appreciated (and photographed) rendition of "Summertime." There was also a papal visit to the Philippines, an event in which Negroponte's wife Diana, a committed Catholic, participated. Negroponte also took part in elaborate commemorations of the battles attendant on liberation of the Philippines from the Japanese and was reminded that the Ambassador's summer residence at the city of Baguio was where the Japanese surrender of forces was signed.

As he had in Mexico, Negroponte invited biologist and conservationist Thomas Lovejoy to educate him about environmental issues. They visited the island of Palawan and two other islands in the southwestern part of the country. Negroponte's young family attracted significant attention in the Philippines by reason of the varied ages of his Honduran children.

Encouraging the Ramos Government

The new Ramos government carried out a program of trade liberalization and attacked some of the agricultural cartels. It succeeded in attracting some foreign investment; except for electronics, there were few high-value exports.

Preferential access to the American market for sugar had ended in 1974. Senior American officials liked Ramos. His primary emphasis was on the restoration of political freedom, and not social change. There was considerable devolution, decentralization, and deregulation. There had been a quite drastic reduction in American foreign aid; with the departure of the bases, the Philippine president no longer had immediate and rapid access to the US president. US aid amounted to $319 million over a two-year period out of a $2 billion international aid package.[10] During this period, the people of the Philippines were its most important export; expatriate workers accounted for $6 billion a year in remittances:[11] "lines form daily before dawn around the US Consulates...the Philippine elite still send child after child abroad for education and often permanent expatriation."[12]

One assessment of Ramos concluded that he "conducted a more coherent administration [than Corazon Aquino], made peace with the principal insurgents, directed a more prosperous economy, but failed to do much for most Filipinos."[13] Negroponte declared that among national leaders he had known, he was much impressed by Ramos: "He rolled up his sleeves and got things done."[14]

The Ramos government imposed closer control over the military and brokered settlements with some Moslem secessionists on the southern island of Mindanao. It provided tax concessions for exporters by a new law in 1995, and entered into an East Asian growth area including Brunei, Malaysia, and Indonesia. The Filipinos captured terrorists in the Ramzi Yousef group "just at the same time that we were reducing our humint capabilities, the Manila Central Intelligence Agency station being reduced by 50 percent."[15] Negroponte was instrumental in securing their immediate transfer to the United States where they were tried and imprisoned.

At the time of Negroponte's arrival, there were discussions looking toward military access agreements with nations in the area. Negroponte viewed the quest for such an agreement with the Philippines as a "mission impossible" in view of the nationalist feelings aroused by the controversy, leading to closing of the American bases. These new arrangements ranged from the formal access agreement negotiated with Singapore to arrangements under consideration with such countries as Malaysia, Australia, and Thailand."[16] "The time has come," President Corazon Aquino said, in declining the earlier arrangement to negotiate a new one, "to close the books on a colonial vestige";[17] proposals for a so-called "Acquisition and Cross-Servicing Agreement" relating to aviation were finally rebuffed in November 1994.[18] They had been acknowledged by Negroponte on November 10, just before President Clinton's visit and created an uproar. Signing of an agreement was initially deferred until March 1995 and then deferred indefinitely.[19]

Thus, however reluctantly, the United States wound up in the posture recommended 17 years earlier by George Kennan: "The American response to the situation that now exists should be, surely, the immediate, complete, resolute and wordless withdrawal of the facilities and the equipment they contain, leaving to the Philippine government the real estate, and only that."[20]

By 1996, the Philippines were on a growth path centered on the former complex at Subic Bay, which had become a regional hub for Federal Express.

Although per capita income was still 10 percent of that in Taiwan, a growth rate of 7 percent had been achieved.[21] One writer summarized the years of Negroponte's tenure as happy ones for the Philippines: 1994–7

> was an important period in Philippine economic history. It was an era of decisive reform in which there was a return to moderately good growth rates, peaking at almost 6% in the middle of the decade. There was a clear, if modest, reform dividend. Unfortunately, however, just as the country appeared set to rejoin the East Asian growth club, external factors [drought and the Asian debt crisis] intervened.[22]

During his tenure, in February 1995, Negroponte had told potential investors that the Philippines offered "the chance to get in on another Asian success story before lines begin queuing up," referring to $740 million in new US investment, an 18 billion peso budget surplus, a 5.5–6.5 percent growth rate and stable deficit levels in the budget; he saw a need for $50 billion in capital investments. There remained problems with the tax system and water supply: the "streamlining of government operations has a long way to go [and] cartel-like arrangements and other inefficiencies still burden many areas of the economy."[23] The government had remedied power shortages by erecting badly needed fossil fuel plants. Per capita gross domestic product had fallen from $870 in 1986 to $720 in 1991 as a result of the political turbulence of the Marcos and early Aquino years; it then began an accelerating rise. In a farewell speech before the Makati Business Club in August 1996, Negroponte noted that the Philippines had overcome its barnacles: "Twenty years of authoritarian rule. The land of natural and man-made disasters. The stifling power of the oligarchs." The two-way trade figures in 1996 were almost double those in 1992; "both our countries are now comfortable with the shift in emphasis from the military to the economic."[24]

In the Philippines, Diana Negroponte was said to be "perhaps the most visible of all the ambassadors' ladies...a real trouper." She was credited with spending much time in depressed areas in Tondo, as well as being "a tasteful interior decorator." She at least pretended to be fond of the Philippines, making an invidious comparison in its favor:

> The Mexican way of life is very different from the Philippine. The difference is between black and white. The only similarity is in the strength of the family and in the Catholic religion. Otherwise you are wonderful individualistic independent people.[25]

Mrs Negroponte was the recipient of much publicity in the Philippines. She was called upon to answer questions on delicate subjects: "On abortion: 'John and I are parents of five adopted children who would not have parents if it weren't for us and we love them deeply. That's the clearest statement we can ever make on that issue.'" "Would she and her husband consider adopting a Filipino child? Her clear blue eyes crinkled mischievously. 'No, I'm on the pill. I even told Cardinal Sin. He was speechless for once.' "[26] Negroponte participated in many ceremonies commemorating the 50th anniversary of World War II battles.

Mrs Negroponte was a serious Catholic from an Anglo-Catholic family of long standing; John Negroponte's Greek Orthodox affiliation was of a more nominal variety. On the evidence of their remarkable adopted family, their shared conviction was that of the General Thanksgiving in the Anglican Book of Common Prayer, "that we show forth thy praise not only with our lips but in our lives."

By 2008, the Philippines were heavily dependent on remittances from Filipinos abroad, these amounting to $12.3 billion for the first nine months of the year, a 17 percent increase from a year earlier. Remittances amounted to some 13 percent of the gross national product. The 8 million Filipinos working abroad were said to make up 25 percent of the nation's workforce.[27] In one respect, the level of remittances was a success story: the Filipino expatriate workers were more highly skilled than those from other countries by reason of a proliferation of nursing and caregiving schools. As in Latin America, the totality of the educational system left much to be desired. Per capita expenditures per pupil were said to be $138 per year, as against $853 in Thailand, $1,800 in Singapore, and $5,000 in Japan. Only 2.2 percent of the national budget was spent on education.[28] Goods exports were almost stagnant, but the overall economy grew by 7.2 percent in 2007 and was projected to grow by 3–4 percent in 2009.[29]

Resisting Chinese Encroachment

A significant flap arose over the Chinese seizure of a disputed atoll in the Spratly Islands known by the appropriate name of Mischief Reef, leading Burghardt to observe "if this were in a movie, people would boo." Negroponte perceived this as an exercise in Chinese bullying that should be nipped in the bud and encouraged vehement protests by both the Philippine and American governments. The dispute over the Spratleys had led to several dozen deaths in a clash between China and Vietnam; although the Chinese claim is thin and driven by offshore oil; it continues to this day.[30] It led to a slow revival of the US–Filipino military relationship, including joint exercises and ship visits. Burghardt credits Negroponte with mastery at the art of getting Washington to direct his own talking points. Negroponte displayed directness and bluntness in in-house discussions and declared, "you've got to believe in something otherwise you might just as well go sell insurance." He and Holbrooke were regarded as protégés of the outspoken Philip Habib and were sometimes jokingly referred to as the "New York school" of foreign policy, with a regard for field experience and a contempt for "staff weenies." Although he was a more subdued personality than Holbrooke, Negroponte could be argumentative, and occasionally lost his temper, a process referred to by subordinates as "throwing a Negroponte"; no grudges survived these occasional outbursts. This reputation stood Negroponte in good stead when as Deputy Secretary of State he had to recruit foreign service officers to accept unwanted assignments in Iraq.

A Summing Up

Looking back in 2009, Negroponte felt that

> Marcos, of course, was a disaster for the country. But they came through that and became more democratic than just about any other country in

East Asia...they have not yet fallen into a consistent pattern of political behavior. They certainly have a lot of assets. They have the English language. They got a lot of overseas workers sending back revenues. We left them a pretty good education system, but it's a bit frayed around the edges now.... [Ramos] probably impressed me as much as any leader I've ever had the opportunity to deal with. He was almost bicultural. He had an affinity for the United States while still being very Filipino. He stood head and shoulders above any political leader who had preceded him and actually that was sort of the high point of Philippine political and economic development [He] really rolled up his sleeves and got stuff done,

particularly during the electricity brownout crisis.[31] Frank Wisner was to take the view that the Filipinos in the post-Marcos era "have been able to prove that democracy is a good antidote at a time of economic crisis."[32] Wisner, a Vietnam colleague, was one of Negroponte's closest friends; Negroponte's oldest daughter, Marina, stayed with the Wisners for almost a year during one of Negroponte's foreign assignments.

By 2009, in addition to remittances from foreign workers, the Philippines enjoyed about 15 percent of the global call center business, as against 37 percent in India. Entry-level call center salaries were $3,858 annually, about those in India, whereas the average salary of information technology professionals was $10,730, about a third less than in India. Philippine call centers are said to have earned $6.8 billion in gross business in 2008.[33]

On Negroponte's departure, a Philippine commentator observed:

He represents the adaptation of US diplomacy to a diminished role in a former colony and to the reality that the contraction of US military deployment in Asia has also meant diminished power and influence...the diplomacy of consensus rather than dictation...establishing the basis for a more mature and equal relationship, devoid of false expectations.[34]

Negroponte's departure from the Philippines preceded a series of disasters, political, natural, and economic. The political disaster was the replacement of General Ramos by the bibulous President Joseph Estrada, a former film actor; the natural disaster was the tsunami that swept Southeast Asia; and the economic disaster was the Asian debt crisis that impacted the Philippines less than the more developed Asian countries, as its dependence on foreign loans had not gone as far. Negroponte's tenure was, nonetheless, successful in weaning the Philippines from colonial practices and preferences.

15

PANAMA

Stability, then, has commonly resulted not from a quest for peace but from a generally accepted legitimacy. "Legitimacy" as here used should not be confused with justice. It means no more than an international agreement about the nature of workable arrangements, about the permissible aims and methods of foreign policy.

— Henry A. Kissinger, *A World Restored*
(London: Gollancz, 1973), 1

In September 1995, President Bill Clinton agreed with President Ernesto Balladares of Panama to begin exploratory conversations about a continuing US presence at some bases after 1999. Under the 1977 Panama Canal Treaty negotiated by the Carter administration, the last US military personnel were to leave the American bases in the former Canal Zone by December 31, 1999. On October 11, 1996, just after Fort Amidor had reverted to Panamanian control, John Negroponte was named chairman of an interagency working group on the status of the bases, charged with forging a coherent negotiating position and with negotiating with the Panamanian government. Word of his appointment was leaked after the Clinton administration had been criticized for laxity in the "war on drugs" and after the Senate had passed a resolution asking that bases in Panama be retained after 1999. Negroponte had previously been involved in base negotiations in the Philippines and in discussions with the Mexican government about US military involvement in drug eradication. In mid-November 1996, the Panamanians said that the base issue was not on the negotiating table, and Balladares announced that Panama would begin the twenty-first century "without the presence of foreign military bases." Earlier, in July, Balladares had said that Panama might be willing to have Howard Air Force Base made into a multinational counternarcotics center without demanding payment "as part of our contribution to the drug war". However, "Brazil, Argentina, and Chile [were] nervous about exposing their armed forces to the risk of corruption." Panama at the time received only minor amounts of American military assistance, about $7 million in FY 1996, with $4.8 million budgeted for FY 1997.[1] As of October 1996, there were 6,900 US military personnel in Panama at Howard Air Force Base, Fort Kobbe, Rodman Naval Station, the Jungle Operations Training Center at Fort Sherman, a satellite communications facility at Galeta Island, and the

Southern Command Headquarters at Quarry Heights. The economic impact of base closures was estimated at about $1 billion over five to six years.

In preliminary talks not involving Negroponte, the United States had expressed a reluctance to pay for bases, since any payment would revive charges that the 1977 treaty was a "giveaway" to the Panamanians. In addition, numerous stateside bases were being closed, with loss of employment, rendering the opening of a new foreign base politically difficult. The State Department was initially dubious about the merits of retaining bases. Negroponte personally regarded the proposal as a "non-starter": The Panamanians "didn't have their heart in it" and "wanted to assert themselves." The negotiations were complicated by news that depleted uranium and chemical weapons had been tested at the Tropic Test Center in Panama. At the time of his designation as negotiator in October 1996, "Negroponte...ha[d] been kept waiting for months for a new assignment." His initially hopeful assessment of the possibilities of negotiation altered with the death of Panamanian Foreign Minister Gabrial Lewis on December 19, 1996. The designated Panamanian negotiator, Jorge Ritter, had been the Noriega government's ambassador to Colombia and was thought to be not innocent of knowledge of drug trafficking, whereas Negroponte's appointment, because of his history in Honduras, was said to "rankle the important leftist wing of Panama's ruling Democratic Revolutionary Party." "A lot of people on both sides said the negotiations would never go anywhere until both Ritter and Negroponte were fired.... [Their appointments] definitely got things off on the wrong foot." "Negroponte reminded Panamanians of the 'special relationship' during which Panama was Washington's neo-colony and subservient to US interests."[2] On April 28, 1997, it was announced that Negroponte would be retiring on June 1 "for personal reasons." This date was later extended to September 1. In July, formal negotiations began; by mid-August, Negroponte was said to have recommended withdrawing from negotiations. Only the Southern Command and the Drug Enforcement Agency had any enthusiasm for the project.[3]

> In January 1998, discussions began with Brazil, Colombia, and Mexico in an attempt to give a more convincing multilateral character to the project, but these talks broke down in June and the United States was obliged to look elsewhere for a base in Latin America to counter drug trafficking.[4]

Negroponte's successor as negotiator, Francis MacNamara, produced an onerous draft agreement that achieved no favor with the Panamanians. The American military was rapidly losing interest in the bases, General Wesley Clark reducing the number of proposed troops from 5,000 to 2,500 and the number of bases from 7 to 3.[5] The United States was disinclined to pay for rights it had just relinquished without compensation; the attitude of the American negotiators was summed up in a study by the American Enterprise Institute: "Panama has the right to fail—or succeed—on its competency and as a consequence of its own actions." "It must address issues of economic reform, privatization, and government efficiency—even if it means laying off thousands of non-productive government workers and ending subsidized services."[6] By 2008, one of the former base areas had sprouted more than 20 hotels and tall condominium buildings, catering to American tourists and expatriates, and there were areas in the country with a major building boom, tourism of the Panama Canal being undiminished. George Kennan had recommended surrender of the Panama Canal to the Panamanians but had given some further advice that appears yet to be taken:

> this government would be wise, should the canal be abandoned to the Panamanians…[to encourage] the development of alternative facilities…facilities for rapid handling of container traffic by rail from Texas ports to Southern California could pick up part of the load, as could similar facilities operating across southern Mexico.[7]

As of 2008, the railroad from Houston/Galveston to Los Angeles was single track in many places.

Although a congressional resolution sponsored by Senator Jesse Helms urged that the bases were necessary to the "war on drugs,"[8] this was disputed. A Southern Command spokesman acknowledged that given the availability of bases in the United States and Puerto Rico, the Panamanian facility was not vital, and indeed that the Howard radar facility was out of operation for 10 months during 1994.[9]

16

MCGRAW-HILL

When you sell a man a book you don't just sell him twelve ounces of paper and ink and glue, you sell him a whole new life.

— Christopher Morley, *Parnassus on Wheels*
(New York: Doubleday, 1917), Chapter 4

When it became clear that the Panama Canal negotiations were likely to be abortive, it was rumored that Negroponte was slated to be ambassador to Greece,[1] a prospect that some thought fell victim to the critics of his activities in Honduras. A series of critical articles about Negroponte had appeared in *The Baltimore Sun* in 1995; Negroponte had declined to be interviewed by the reporters, a decision which he later regretted. He ascribed the reluctance to offer him a more significant assignment to these articles. Richard Holbrooke, however, then declared that Negroponte "turned down an offer from Secretary [Madeleine] Albright to go to Greece as Ambassador." Negroponte states that he first learned of the possibility that he might be selected for Greece from an Al Kamen column in *The Washington Post*, and that he complained about this to the Deputy Secretary, Strobe Talbott. He was disappointed since he hoped to be selected for Korea, a post that instead went to Stephen Bosworth. On his entry into the Foreign Service, Negroponte's father had told him to resist any relegation to Greece, which would have the appearance of resting on something other than his qualifications as a diplomat. In explaining his refusal to accept the Greek assignment to his brother Nicholas, then an internationally known authority on computers, Negroponte asked him: "If you were offered the presidency of a small university in the midwest, would you accept it?"

Negroponte then undertook to repair his finances by becoming Executive Vice President for Global Markets of McGraw-Hill, the publishing company. His choice of occupation owed something to both circumstance and conviction. McGraw-Hill was not a convenient assignment for him, as the company was based in New York and his family remained in Washington, requiring him to remain three nights a week in an apartment in McGraw-Hill's office building in New York. His acceptance of this opportunity in preference to others rested in part on convictions about the importance of technical education and publishing to future development in both the United States and the Third World.

The company by multinational standards was not huge, having a foreign sales volume of less than a billion dollars a year at the beginning of Negroponte's four-years tenure there; its Chairman, Harold McGraw, was a leader in recognizing the impact on publishing of globalization and the new internet-based technologies.[2] International revenues accounted for about 20 percent of McGraw-Hill's sales and were growing at twice the speed of domestic sales.[3] Negroponte devoted himself to seeking new markets in China and the Far East, as well as Latin America. He made more than 40 trips abroad. Most of his effort was devoted to China and India, producing sales increases but not dramatic ones. McGraw-Hill and its Standard & Poor affiliate became subscribers to Oxford Analytica, an open-source information service founded by Negroponte's former National Security Council colleague, David Young. Negroponte's compensation at McGraw-Hill was said to be $850,000 annually, evenly divided between salary and bonus; a complicated severance package with a lump sum of $1 million and deferred compensation of $400,000 in five annual installments; and the financial disclosure process delayed his nomination as UN ambassador.[4] Although Harold McGraw assured him on his departure that he was welcome to return, Negroponte chose on his later retirement from government to remain in Washington for family reasons, one of his children being in school there; the depressed state of the publishing industry might have played a part in this judgment.

17

UNITED NATIONS

Once to every man and nation
Comes the moment to decide
In the strife of truth with falsehood
For the good or evil side
Some great cause, some great decision
Offering each the bloom or blight
And the choice goes by forever
twixt that darkness and that light.

— James Russell Lowell, 1845
(on the occasion of the Mexican War)

Appointment and Confirmation

John Negroponte had been recruited to serve as UN ambassador by Secretary of State Colin Powell. He had gone to see Powell in December 2000 and had indicated his readiness to accept another assignment in government. When after a month he had heard nothing, he wrote to Powell in late January. According to Powell, it took quite a bit of effort to get him the job, which was sought after by many people. He had a 20-minute interview with President George W. Bush, during which he was asked how he would deal with Russia: "seriously, carefully, with care—don't paint them into a corner." Powell wanted him because their prior association at the National Security Council (NSC) would make it difficult for the press to drive a wedge between the Secretary of State and the UN Ambassador. He assured Negroponte that Bush wanted to emphasize the role of the United Nations. Nicholas Rostow, later General Counsel to the New York State University System, was Powell's counsel at the United Nations. Negroponte's nomination as UN ambassador had languished for several months while the Senate Foreign Relations Committee investigated new allegations concerning Honduras. Negroponte had been offered the post only after it had been refused by several others, including Elizabeth Dole, because of its lack of cabinet rank.[1]

Negroponte found the United Nations the most intellectually stimulating of his assignments because of the intensity of the negotiations involved and the pleasure of close association with like-minded and realistic diplomatic professionals. The initial unanimous Security Council resolution relating to Iraq was no small diplomatic achievement; the same is also true of the first unanimous UN resolution upholding a "two state" solution in Palestine. The action of the United States in going to war without a second resolution is not an event for which he is personally chargeable, having been critical of the aspirations toward "nation-building" in Iraq and having sought more time for inspections. He can be criticized for remaining in office, where he exercised an important moderating influence on later events, having accepted a French resolution recognizing the temporary nature of the Anglo-American occupation.

Negroponte's predecessor, Richard Holbrooke, had departed on Inauguration Day, January 20, 2001; Negroponte was selected on March 6 and not formally nominated until May 14; the administration had agreed to wait until September for hearings. Holbrooke had negotiated a modus vivendi with South Carolina Senator Jesse Helms allowing renewal of UN funding by the United States.[2] At the hearings, Negroponte was supported in a written statement by Holbrooke and in testimony by Arizona Senator John McCain, who noted that "John knew my father when he was commander in chief of our Pacific forces," and by Alaska Senator Ted Stevens, who noted that "because our wives get along very well, we became dinner companions on many occasions."[3] Rhode Island Senator Lincoln Chafee observed: "So far as the US public is concerned, any one who wants this job is welcome to it." Negroponte referred to the United Nations as one of the international community's best tools for uniting to restrain violators of international law and declared that it "needs and deserves consistent support, including full and timely payment of our dues... Of the 43,000 UN peacekeepers deployed throughout the world today, only 44 troops are from the US, all but one in observer status." He also echoed Secretary Powell's misgivings about comprehensive economic sanctions against Iraq, declaring that there is no benefit to sanctioning purely civilian trade with the Iraqi people.[4]

Negroponte's nomination was denounced by the usual critics of his actions in Honduras (he had even been the subject of a hostile Norwegian film, *The Ambassador*, which made no attempt to be fair and balanced[5]) but was vigorously championed by others. Former Secretary of State George Shultz wrote a letter to the *Los Angeles Times* in defense of Negroponte that the paper declined to publish, "It's whether we want someone skillful to represent the US"[6] The columnist Richard Reeves referred to him as "one of the more impressive products of the Foreign Service" and observed of Honduras:

> Ronald Reagan approved the recommendations and gave the orders. Most of the charges are essentially true, including turning a blind eye to human rights abuses by the Honduran military... I would vote to confirm Ambassador Negroponte and investigate President Reagan."[7]

Journalist Arnaud de Borchgrave noted that "the Central American countries are now free under democratic governments.... The pro-Sandinista 'disinformers' have never forgiven Mr. Negroponte for the way he oversaw the first contra operations."[8]

The syndicated columnist Georgie Anne Geyer, with long credentials as a Latin American specialist, assessed the "Contra war":

I would venture that the role of the contras, always an imprecise instrument, in defeating Sandismo was over-rated. Yet Enrique Bolaños Geyer, the respected Liberal party candidate for next November's elections in Nicaragua, calls them "a necessary evil." When I asked him recently if the Sandinistas could have been defeated, as they were electorally in the elections of 1990, without the additional military pressure of the contras, he shook his head: "I doubt it very much." It seemed in the early and mid 80s that all Central America would become Marxist. In Nicaragua, the Sandinistas marched around in commando uniforms yelling "liberacion" and "revolucion" while looting the country, driving it into the ground economically, and violating human rights.[9]

She lauded Negroponte as one of

the couriers between cultures men and women who know the world sympathetically but, most important, realistically. In a world too often convulsed with absolute faiths and answers, they form and guide, often with quiet mastery, the gradual changes that are the true mark of the march of civilization.[10]

A minor embarrassment was caused by a $600,000 kitchen renovation in the ambassador's quarters at the Waldorf-Astoria, included in a published compendium of "all-American stupidity."[11] In fact, the renovation was necessitated by a desire to enlarge the kitchen and reconfigure the dining room for large receptions and did not alter the private living quarters.

Negroponte called on more than a hundred of his fellow ambassadors in recognition of the fact that many of the ambassadors from smaller countries did not have instructions from their governments, rendering personal relations important. This performance was unmatched since the tenure of the bachelor and diplomat Vernon Walters, who once proclaimed "I have to eat somewhere" in explanation for his own propensity to "dine around," and was in marked contrast to the insular practices of ambassadors like Jeane Kirkpatrick and John Bolton.

One of Negroponte's designated deputy ambassadors was a Cambodian refugee whom he had befriended.[12]

9/11 and its Aftermath

On September 11, 2001, Negroponte was at the State Department. When the building was cleared because of a supposed threat, he

drove home—very difficult to get there because a lot of streets were closed or jammed. I wanted to have an anchor. I have a pretty large family. I had three children in school in Washington. My wife was working that day, and so I just wanted to be at home.

Before Negroponte's confirmation, Resolution 1368 passed on September 12 recognized the right of self-defense in an introductory clause but authorized no use of force, whether by UN peacekeepers called Blue Helmets or by anyone else. It was not passed under the auspices of Chapter VII of the UN Charter, a prerequisite for authorizing military force.[13] In the view of Jean-David Levitte, French chairman of the Security Council on that date, the resolution was path breaking in that it recognized terrorist acts as acts of war and those equipping terrorists as guilty of acts of aggression—new departures in international law. The refusal of the Taliban government in Afghanistan to extradite terrorists was, in due course, recognized as justification for the war on Afghanistan.

Immediately after his confirmation, which was accelerated because of 9/11, Negroponte was successful in obtaining a unanimous UN resolution, Resolution 1373 of September 2001, pledging cooperation in suppressing terrorism and setting up a special Security Council committee under British chairmanship to monitor compliance, to make proactive steps against terrorism mandatory for all member states.[14] This was the foundation of global cooperation in impairing money flows of terrorists; it also contained paragraphs prohibiting safe havens and the supply of weapons of mass destruction. It was highly unusual for a permanent as distinct from nonpermanent member to be placed in charge of implementation. At Georgetown in 2002, Negroponte observed: "this was no instance where the United States had to lobby for votes…humanity was appalled; solidarity was complete." Negroponte referred to the United Nations as a unique partner in troubled times and to the resolution as the United Nations' single most powerful response. On October 7, he transmitted a formal notice of the United States' intention to exercise its right of self-defense under Article 51 of the UN charter with respect to the Taliban in Afghanistan.[15] The assertion expressly rested on the action of the Taliban in willingly harboring terrorists; it did not go so far as an earlier American statement suggesting that the presence of terrorists in another state justified invasion in the absence of complicity by the government.[16] The Irish president of the Security Council urged the United States to formally appear before the Security Council to announce its action. "Negroponte hesitated. The Bush administration did not want to suggest that it needed permission, but it finally agreed."[17]

An End to Humility

Up until this point, American foreign policy under the new Bush administration had appeared to be restrained in nature, designed to vindicate the president's campaign pledge of a more "humble" foreign policy. Many, including the writer and Negroponte, had supported Bush's election in the hope that it would bring about a more restrained foreign policy as compared with that of Madeleine Albright. Albright's conduct of foreign policy had been succinctly summarized by a left-of-center critic:

> Madeleine Albright explained, using 'exceptionalist' language last heard from McGeorge Bundy, 'If we have to use force, it is because we are America. We are the indispensable nation. We stand tall, we see farther into the future.' The issue of nuclear disarmament was neglected. The Russians were not engaged in this or any other positive way, instead the North Atlantic Treaty Organization (NATO) was enlarged to encircle it. In the absence of an agreement between Moscow and Washington,

the secondary nuclear powers did nothing and India and Pakistan tested nuclear devices. The failure to use Moscow and the Organization for Security and Cooperation in Europe (OSCE) structure to secure Serb withdrawal from Kosovo at Rambouillet led to massive bombing of Serbia and Kosovo but eventually the European allies insisted that Russian mediation to this end be obtained and it was this rather than the bombing that secured a result.[18]

The best commentary on this was supplied by the young Henry Kissinger in his first book:

Utopias are not achieved except by a process of leveling and dislocation which must erode all patterns of obligation. These are the two great symbols of the attacks on the existing order: the Conqueror and the Prophet, the quest for universality and for eternity, for the peace of impotence and the peace of bliss ... [In Metternich's time] unity was not yet equated with identity, nor the claims of the nation with the dictates of morality.

Kissinger declared that "the fundamental problem of politics, is not the control of wickedness but the limitation of righteousness."[19]

The expansion of NATO to the Russian frontier had been decried by George Kennan in 1997 on the basis that it would "influence the nationalistic, anti-Western and militaristic tendencies in Russian opinion [and] have an adverse effect on the development of Russian democracy"[20] but was defended in 2005 by Albright's collaborator Richard Holbrooke: "Kennan's warning that enlarging NATO would destabilize Europe—carried the dinner audience with its eloquence and sense of history. Events, of course, proved Bill Clinton right and Kennan and the bulk of the liberal intellectual community wrong."[21] This does not read so well in 2011.

After his confirmation as UN Ambassador, Negroponte urged economic assistance to Afghanistan, stating that the United States and the international community have an enormous obligation to not walk away as had been done in the past. Negroponte may have been thinking of the failure to maintain economic aid to Central America after the Salvadoran and Nicaraguan peace settlements in 1990; while out of government at McGraw-Hill in the period 1997–2001, he expressed his concern in that regard to me, alluding to a "food chain" of immigration northward extending all the way to Bolivia as a result of the absence of economic development. Negroponte's admonition as respects Afghanistan fell on deaf ears; having installed the Karzai government in 2002, the United States and its allies left it more or less for dead. In February 2002, Negroponte had warned that

personally looking back at my own Vietnam experience and remembering the problems we had, having started our Vietnamization program much too late, having too much of the burden of fighting ourselves, remembering the cardinal errors of our military strategy ... I would advocate trying to do as much as we can to improve the security capabilities of the Afghans

themselves and minimize the role of international security forces.... If you
look at the past record of international military forces and their effectiveness in Afghanistan, the record isn't too spectacular.[22]

Seven years later, the pertinence of this warning is glaringly apparent. At the
same time, he characterized 9/11 as a "criminal rather than religious act" and
alluded to the "economic tourniquet [the Israelis] have on the Palestinians." The
international community committed $4.5 billion to Afghanistan in 2002 and the
United States only $297 million of this figure. George Kennan expressed similar
concerns:

> I wonder why the Democrats have not asked the president right out,
> "What are you talking about? Are you talking about one war or two wars?
> And if it's two wars, have we really faced up to the competing demands
> of the two?"[23]

By October 2003, there were 130,000 American troops in Iraq and 11,000 in
Afghanistan, a country larger than Iraq.[24]

In the same speech, Negroponte was at pains to deny any necessary connection between poverty and terrorism:

> The fact is that the man who led Al Qaeda was fabulously wealthy...ter-
> rorism as we have known it over the last 40 years has not been a poor
> man's game [nor do people] suddenly lose their moral compass because
> they are poor.

Negroponte at the United Nations

As respected the convention on terrorism in process of development, Negroponte said that military personnel should not be covered but should continue to operate under the laws of war and that "liberation movements" should not be exempted. It was found after the revelations about Abu Ghraib that the United States had adhered to neither of these premises.[25]

Negroponte was vexed by the presence in New York of Elliott Abrams, who was widely seen as a protector of Israeli interests. On protesting to NSC Director Condoleezza Rice, he was told that it was better to have the well-connected Abrams on the inside rather than the outside.

UN Secretary General Kofi Annan is said to have regarded Negroponte as "a respected and tough-minded professional, though one with very little influence at the White House."[26] On September 12, 2002, Annan cautioned: "There is no substitute for the unique legitimacy provided by the United Nations."[27] French Ambassador Jean-David Levitte described Negroponte as "a very great professional." One commentator observed:

He never deviated from the Washington line—but he read the script with a good deal more elegance and urbanity than the neo-con warriors in Washington...[He has] the true diplomat's iron discipline. He never flaps, grandstands, or seeks glory for himself. He has a reputation for fairness and civility...he was subject to the three-line whip from Washington which gave him little role in formulating Iraq policy.[28]

In the wake of 9/11, Negroponte warned the Iraqi government not to take advantage of US involvement in Afghanistan, and announced that the United States reserved the right in self-defense to attack state sponsors of terrorism.[29] He was startled by the request from Washington that he "Go find the Iraqi ambassador and tell him if they take advantage we will blast them to smithereens," a request he viewed as coming from George H.W. Bush, Dick Cheney, and Donald Rumsfeld.

A letter to the U.N. over the signature of US ambassador John D. Negroponte contained inflammatory language about self-defense requiring action with respect to other states and organizations. The letter caused embarrassment to Negroponte who had seen the final draft before it left State and knew that language had not been in there. The words had been inserted by Stephen Hadley at the N.S.C.[30]

Negroponte identified as possible locales for intervention the Philippines, Indonesia, and Malaysia.[31] The first intimation that the British and others received that intervention against Iraq might be contemplated came, according to Sir Jeremy Greenstock, from a source in the Singapore government in February 2002. In March 2002, a memorandum from the British ambassador to Washington, later leaked to the *Sunday Times* in London, advised that the Americans were considering action in Iraq. In April 2002, Prime Minister Tony Blair visited Bush in Crawford, Texas, and in response to inquiries about the British attitude should the United States decide to proceed against Iraq said "I'm with you, George." Blair did not regard this as support for a specific course of action, nor was this statement communicated to Greenstock.

Warning the Administration

In a little-noticed interview given in January 2003 in the interval between the first and second debates on Security Council resolutions on Iraq, Negroponte expressed a view similar to that of French Foreign Minister Dominique Villepin to a reporter who, noting his experience in Vietnam and Honduras, observed that Negroponte "knows a thing or two about regime change":

> It is not for me to decide [whether to use force against Iraq]. It's the President's decision, he's our commander in chief…if you're asking me my view based on the most important experience I have with the use of force, which was Vietnam, it is one of caution. Regime change is really not something that's ever been dealt with in Security Council resolutions. It's not part of the purview of our UN policies.

In the same interview Negroponte credited the UN Chief Inspector Hans Blix, the target of brickbats from Washington neoconservatives, with "getting inspections started quicker than anyone expected":[32]

After his retirement in 2009, asked whether he favored the Iraq War, Negroponte noted that he had not "been sitting in the councils" of the Bush administration. He "would have advocated waiting—[putting] a lot of effort into the inspection regime—six months, a year." The administration was "in such of a hurry" and "might have found a more willing international community" had we waited. "Once we got in we had to manage as best you could." Powell and Deputy Secretary of State Richard Armitage had warned that we would "own" Iraq.[33]

Apart from this overlooked interview, Negroponte's misgivings were not publicly visible. The Canadian ambassador, Paul Heinbecher, observed: "If he had doubts, he never let them show." Greenstock observed: "Colin Powell was the good soldier, and John Negroponte was the good soldier to the good soldier." He was viewed as a nonpartisan pragmatist and credited or debited with an unflinching allegiance to his government's policies.[34] His ethic was that attributed to Ambassador Philip Habib:

> he epitomized the code of the diplomat: Follow orders. Go through channels. Keep your superiors informed. Give them your best analysis and honest opinions, then shut up and implement the policy decisions they make. Let them do the talking in public. Keep private disagreements private. Keep secrets secret. Keep your personal biases, politics and preferences out of the picture. If you don't like the policy, either get over it or get out.[35]

It was nonetheless understood that Negroponte was willing to leave more time to win the Security Council's unanimous approval to invade Iraq but was thwarted by Washington.[36]

At about the same time, the UN disarmament negotiator Hans Blix wrote in his diary for January 9, 2003:

> I doubt the US if it tried would even get a majority for a resolution author-izing armed force. And if it did not have such a resolution, going it alone would have much less support in American opinion and might not allow the United States to deploy from Turkey or Saudi Arabia.[37]

In this period, "the battle had not taken place; it had only been put off." The British Ambassador, Sir Jeremy Greenstock observed: "We entrenched ourselves in different interpretations of what the wording of Resolution 1441 meant."[38] Another commentator observed that

> the final draft resolution was a masterpiece of linguistic subterfuge that enabled the principal adversaries on the Council—the United States and France—to interpret its provisions as they wished .... The French appeared willing, with classic Hollywood style Gallic cynicism, to give the United States and Britain the legal cover to take out Saddam militarily—as long as they weren't seen as responsible.[39]

On January 9, Blix expressed the view that under the 1991 resolution, the next report of the inspectors was not due until March 31, 2003, a proposition denied by Negroponte on January 16.[40]

Executor of Policy

On September 12, 2002, President Bush delivered a speech to the General Assembly, the terms of which had been the subject of frantic discussions in Washington, continuing to the moment of delivery. In the speech, Bush suc-cumbed to Colin Powell's request, following requests by Blair, that UN author-ization be sought. In the speech as delivered, President Bush referred to "resolutions" in the plural; in the text as released, the singular was used: "We will work with the U.N. Security Council for the necessary resolutions."

By September, two writers in the *Financial Times* thought that the United States was backing off from early involvement in Iraq: "The expense of the oper-ation at a time when the US economy is weak has struck home." Negroponte, it was said, "has gained widespread respect from his fellow diplomats in spite of being forced to play a pugnacious role as Washington's messenger."[41]

Negroponte obtained from the Security Council a resolution, Resolution 1441, adopted on November 8, 2002, calling on Iraq to allow inspections for weapons of mass destruction to resume, although not without giving assurances that became significant later on:

> this resolution contains no "hidden triggers" and no "automaticity" with respect to the use of force. If there is a further Iraqi breach, reported to the Council by the United Nations Monitoring, Verification and Inspection Commission (UNMOVIC), the International Atomic Energy Agency (IAEA) or a member state, the matter will return to the Council for discussion as

required in paragraph 12. One way or another, Mr. President, Iraq will be disarmed. If the Security Council fails to act decisively in the event of further Iraqi violations, this resolution does not constrain any member state from acting to defend itself against the threat posed by Iraq or to enforce relevant UN resolutions and protect world peace and security.[42]

Greenstock also affirmed that there was no 'automaticity' without a further meeting of the Security Council; Levitte took the view that the meeting had to be provided for and the resolution had to be open to the interpretation that a further resolution was required to satisfy both France and Russia. The complaint of the Iraqi representative was all too accurate as a description of the position of some of Negroponte's political masters: "the US does not want the inspectors to come back because if they come back, they will prove the American lie."[43]

This initial resolution passed after a reference to "any necessary means," usually understood to be an authorization of armed force, had been deleted.[44] The United States was a reluctant participant in the negotiations, which had taken place at the behest of Powell and over the objections of Cheney, Paul Wolfowitz, and Rumsfeld. The British ambassador, Sir Jeremy Greenstock, later told the Chilcoat Committee, investigating Britain's entry into the Iraq War, that he might have had to resign if Britain went to war without a resolution resembling that adopted as Resolution 1441. Negroponte's initial instructions included the impossible demand that the inspectors be followed about by representatives of the military from each of the five permanent members of the Security Council. In the midst of the negotiations, Negroponte had to go to Johns Hopkins Hospital in Baltimore for a prostate operation. Thereafter discussions between Negroponte, Levitte, and Greenstock resumed during his rehabilitation process; there were also discussions among the Foreign Ministers, Powell, Jack Straw, and Dominique de Villepin, and also meetings with the Russian and German UN Ambassadors. The French Foreign Minister, Dominique de Villepin, later French president Jacques Chirac's premier, had cautioned against any commitment to regime change:

> recognizing the legitimacy of a change of regime would be creating instability on the international scene that would be endless. Where would we put the border between acceptable regimes for some and unacceptable ones for others?[45]

It was said that

> the French sought to secure the main point: to prevent the interpretation of the resolution as itself authorizing the use of force…the US came to a compromise very early…the US decided to accept the idea of a second meeting of the U.N. Security Council. The going-in US position had been that a resolution should be passed and then, if the Iraqis breached it, force should be used. The French for their part came to agree that there did not have to be two resolutions but there had to be two steps, which meant that if the Iraqis were in material breach, a second meeting of the Security

Council would have to decide what steps to take...the French, having decided to vote yes, did not want anyone else to vote no.[46]

The United States felt that it did not need a second resolution but sought one at the behest of Tony Blair. At the time of adoption of Resolution 1441, only Mexico expressed the view that a second resolution expressly authorizing military action was necessary. Greenstock thought that Resolution 1441 gave the subsequent military action legality but not legitimacy. The UN debates, in his view, made it easier for the United Nations to play a role in the postwar recovery of Iraq.[47] Negroponte had told the administration from the outset that a Security Council majority for such a resolution was unlikely.

On December 7, Negroponte, on receiving an incomplete Iraqi declaration concerning its Weapons of Mass Destruction (WMD) programs, announced that "Iraq has spurned its last opportunity to comply with its disarmament obligations." The British ambassador in Washington, Sir Christopher Meyer told Vice President Cheney's aide Lewis "Scooter" Libby, "It won't wash in the Security Council" as a violation of Resolution 1441.[48] The documents turned over by the Iraqis to the Americans were not given to the secretary general but only to the five permanent members of the Council, ostensibly because of nuclear security concerns, although detail about the arming of Saddam by the United States was said to have been excised.[49] Negroponte was to observe: "I've never been put under greater pressure from Washington on any single subject than to get a hold of that document," which was delivered to the United States and then copied by it for the other permanent members.[50]

The disquiet among responsible Europeans about American unilateralism did not have its origins in the second Bush administration. If one had to put a date on it, it might be the date that Madeleine Albright replaced Warren Christopher as Secretary of State, or perhaps the earlier date when she became ambassador to the United Nations. The independent British parliamentarian and foreign correspondent Martin Bell, writing in 2000 in the wake of the Kosovo War, observed:

> Since the cold war ended and especially from the mid-1990s onward, the Americans have seemed to be to be less a guarantee of our security than a potential threat to it. If there is a lesson to be learned from the Kosovo crisis, it is the need for a considered and concerted European defence policy as a counterweight to the Americans' tendency to blunder around the planet as if they own it.[51]

The French were wary of US intentions after a speech by Colin Powell on December 19, 2002, putting Iraq in material breach. Nonetheless, at that time, "the French government's expectation was that Saddam Hussein would commit a blunder in making life difficult for the returning inspectors and/or that weapons of mass destruction would be found." The French had made plans to contribute 15,000 men and 100 planes to the war, as they had in the first Gulf War. On January 7, Chirac had advised his military to assume a state of readiness; the aircraft carrier *Clemenceau* was sent toward the Suez Canal. Instead, there was passive cooperation by the Iraqis and no weapons found. The French concluded that the new inspections regime was useful in that the inspectors' presence constrained Saddam from using such weapons, and therefore a war was not necessary.

On January 14, following a meeting between Levitte and Condoleezza Rice, the French concluded that the United States was negotiating in bad faith, and that for the United States, war was a foregone conclusion: Rice had asked what the French would do when the war started in two more months or so. The *Clemenceau* was turned around, whether because of what was learned from Rice or because of escalating French domestic opposition to intervention is unclear.

According to Greenstock:

> On January 20 [at a special session on terrorism sought by the French], de Villepin made his statement that war could not be justified. [This was unexpected, since the session did not deal with Iraq.] This worsened the atmosphere.... Diplomacy seemed only for show. The US began advancing different reasons for going to war, weapons of mass destruction, wickedness of Saddam, etc.[52]

Sharp words were exchanged between Powell and Villepin at a luncheon following the meeting. Nonetheless, the United States sought a second resolution to help Tony Blair with his domestic political problems. On January 22, Chirac and Germany's Gerhard Schröder met and coordinated their governments' positions.

On January 27, Negroponte, on the occasion of a briefing by Hans Blix on the statement filed by the Iraqis, suggested that the statement provided a sufficient predicate for an immediate second resolution, "There is nothing in either presentation that would give us hope that Iraq has ever intended to fully comply."[53] A French delegate stated:

> Frankly, that shocked us because Resolution 1441 subsumed earlier resolutions that outlined a return to inspections over a period of months stretching into the summer of 2003. That was a complete change in the rules of the game. By mid-January, it was clear to us that Powell had only won a battle when he convinced Bush to take the issue of Iraq to the U.N. Security Council...we were not going to be railroaded into war on Rumsfeld's timetable.[54]

On February 21, Jean-David Levitte suggested to the Americans that the second resolution be dropped: "it would cause unnecessary damage...if the second resolution was rejected, it would split the Security Council and would make it patent that the United States was going to war illegally." In Kosovo, the United States had relied on earlier resolutions. "Stephen Hadley said he appreciated Levitte's arguments but that it was too late. The United States did not need the second resolution but Blair did, and the United States needed Blair."[55] The United States thought at this point that it had enough votes and that China and Russia would abstain, isolating the French.

Earlier in February, France, Belgium, and Germany refused to pledge contingent military aid if Turkey were attacked by Iraq; this precipitated a crisis within NATO. Germany had agreed to supply aid bilaterally, but the United States insisted on a formal guarantee: "Bush was determined to make life difficult for Schroeder." On February 21, National Security Advisor Rice is said to have told the Chilean Ambassador to the United Nations, Heraldo Munoz, that "We will go [into Iraq] with or, if needed, without the U.N. Security Council." On the same day, Mexican President Vicente Fox told Spanish Premier José Aznar that Mexico would oppose the resolution. On the following day, Bush is said to have repeated his language to Chilean President Ricardo Lagos,[56] as well as to Aznar: "If anyone vetoes, we'll go. Saddam Hussein isn't disarming. We have to catch him right now…. There are two weeks left. We can't allow Saddam Hussein to stall until summer…I won't go beyond mid-March."[57] In February, first the French and then the Germans suggested benchmarks for intensified inspections, such as increased aerial surveillance and inspections of road traffic. On March 5, the French, German, and Russian foreign ministers released a joint statement saying that "we will not let a proposed resolution pass that would authorize the use of force. Russia and France, as permanent members of the Security Council, will assume all their responsibilities on this point."[58]

On March 10, the British proposed a compromise resolution with a short 7 to 10 day ultimatum setting forth six tests to be met by the Iraqis. According to Negroponte, Greenstock worked "feverishly" with Blix to stave off a resolution authorizing war, going to the limit of and possibly beyond his instructions. The French on March 14 through Levitte said they would veto the text as it stood, or any resolution containing an ultimatum, but did not state that they would veto any resolution; the Iraqis rejected the six tests. Chirac more carelessly declared that France was opposed to military intervention "whatever the circumstances." Before the veto threat, Greenstock had eight of the nine necessary votes for his compromise. After the veto threat, nonaligned countries did not want to incur criticism at home for supporting an unsuccessful resolution. On March 1, the French had told the Chileans they would use the veto, a proposition reiterated to the Mexicans on March 9.[59] The promise to the Mexicans was given in a conversation between Presidents Fox and Chirac; Fox did not want to annoy the United States by supplying a decisive abstention to the French, and Chirac assured him that France's veto threat would make it clear that Mexico's abstention was not the decisive event. On March 15, Chile proposed a 30-day deadline, later reduced to three weeks, accepted by Chirac, but rejected by the United States, because of concerns about the Iraqi climate and its military timetable, the United States pressuring Mexico and other countries not to join in it. There was a view that if Saddam survived the spring season and the UN session that he would resume undetected military development. Against this, the French urged that American troops could easily spend the summer in air-conditioned comfort in Kuwait.

Blix found that Negroponte, Powell, and Rice "were mostly restrained and all contacts were perfectly civil"; he reproached Negroponte for raising concerns about cluster bombs, which had "a short but intense political life span," and obsolete drones held by the Iraqis.

When Negroponte, this time accompanied by Secretary of State Powell and Central Intelligence Agency director George Tenet, returned to the Security Council to obtain a second resolution, the US claims of continuing Iraqi violations were met with what proved to be justified skepticism. Negroponte had been skeptical about the wisdom of the presentation:

> It's not because I thought that there weren't any WMDs, but I thought we should do it at a hearing or in a speech. I didn't think you should tie up the Council. [Washington was] looking for a "Stevenson moment" and I didn't think much of that idea.[60]

Greenstock referred to "a catalogue of unresolved questions," and Negroponte to "an active program of denial and deception." The Mexican ambassador, writing of Powell's charts and photographs, observed: "this show wasn't for us. It was for an international audience, the US media."[61] When the French finally woke up to what was the real US intention they made the decision to threaten a veto rather than remain with an option of abstention. Chirac did not wish to set a precedent by which the UN Security Council would be put in a position of rubber stamping a US decision. Others thought that the French made mistakes by explicitly threatening a veto, thereby giving the British an alibi for not pressing forward with their resolution to buy a small amount of time; by not more fully mobilizing the European Union states other than Germany; and by refusing a guarantee to Turkey; this view seems less than persuasive.[62] The French for their part thought that US policy might have been different had Blair, instead of going to Washington alone, acted in concert with the French and the Germans.

Negroponte and Tenet, who flanked Powell in a famous photograph of Powell making his speech, were said to have "hooded eyes cast down on their laps like Benedictine monks at vespers."[63] In 2009, Negroponte continued to maintain "We all believed there were WMD. There was no effort to pull the wool over anybody's eyes, so far as I'm aware. [Powell] made a good faith effort [but] turned out to be wrong, so there we are."[64]

Foreign Minister Villepin demanded "Why go to war if there still exists an unused space in resolution 1441?"[65] He further declared: "we cannot accept an ultimatum as long as the inspectors are reporting progress in terms of cooperation. We are choosing how to define the world we want our children to live in."[66] In a response to Secretary of Defense Rumsfeld's denunciation of "old Europe," Villepin observed: "War is always the sanction of failure. This message comes to you today from an old country, France, from a continent like mine, Europe, that has known wars, occupation, and barbarity."[67]

Villepin's lament was a lament for the passing of the United States from a pacific to a revolutionary power, as once defined by Henry Kissinger:

> The distinguishing feature of a revolutionary power is not that it feels threatened ... but that nothing can reassure it. Only absolute security—the neutralization of the opponent—is considered a sufficient guarantee, and thus the desire of one power for absolute security means absolute insecurity for all the others.[68]

"Like Benedictine Monks at Vespers":
Negroponte and Tenet at the United Nations

After several days of frantic maneuvers, including pressure by Negroponte on the Mexican and Chilean foreign ministers to recall or instruct their ambassadors, alleged and undenied use of electronic eavesdropping by the American delegation,[69] and visits by Villepin to the Cameroons, and Guinea, French client states, and to Angola, it became obvious not only that the resolution faced a possible veto by three of the five permanent members, France, Russia, and China, but that it would not command a majority on the Security Council, the opposition of Germany, Mexico, and Chile being decisive. The United States enjoyed the firm support only of Britain, Spain,[70] and post-Communist Bulgaria. The sponsors of the resolution therefore withdrew it, blaming, and exaggerating, the alleged intransigence of the French and went to war in Iraq, creating a crisis of conscience for a number of figures in the American and British governments.

The British had warned through their ambassador in Washington, Sir David Manning, that apart from the effectiveness of further inspections, there had been insufficient preparation for the occupation of Iraq. "Greenstock tirelessly made the case for a resolution authorizing force. John Negroponte according to observers supported him but exhibited little of his British colleague's fervor or energy...London was desperate for it...." Chile's Juan Valdez recalled that "the main actor in the Council was Jeremy Greenstock, not John Negroponte. The British supplied all the main arguments." Negroponte's view was that

If the French had indicated that they would abstain, he was certain that Moscow and Beijing would have done the same and enough nonpermanent members would have voted with Washington to ensure passage of a second resolution. "It came down to what was going on in the mind of Jacques Chirac," he said later. "That was the game."[71]

Negroponte's last remarks to the Security Council were that "considering a work program at this time is quite simply out of touch with the reality that we confront.... Under the current circumstances, we have no choice but to set this work aside for the time being."[72]

Assessing a Defeat

Negroponte and Powell remained in office, Powell having lent his prestige to support of the abortive resolution though having warned President George W. Bush of the probable consequences of war. Negroponte eight years later was to say that he did not understand why Powell did not resign, as at that point he was bitter at his marginalization by Bush, Cheney, and Rumsfeld; he attributed Powell's reluctance to his code of military discipline. During the struggle in the Security Council, Greenstock, who wore a countenance even more mournful than that of Negroponte, did not resign, although he later did resign, allegedly by prearrangement, as Paul Bremer's deputy in Iraq. He was later discouraged by Foreign Minister Jack Straw from publishing a memoir critical of his nation's policy during the life of the Labor Government; although most of the manuscript was cleared for publication by the British Foreign Office, there were fears of a flareup of controversy over Iraq. Negroponte viewed him as something of a free spirit. In May 2003, Greenstock gave a speech at Harvard University in which he was quoted by the *Harvard University Gazette*:

The international debate over Iraq was as much about the role of a lone superpower in a globalized world, about the United Nations' place in that world, about non-proliferation of weapons of mass destruction, and about relations between the United States and Europe, as it was about Iraq, he said.

"You have to draw lessons, if you're wise, from all of that," Greenstock said.

The crisis highlighted the need for strong international institutions, Greenstock said, adding that Britain would not again join the United States in a go-it-alone venture. In fact, Greenstock said, it would be unwise for the United States to go it alone again because so many problems being faced today—from international terrorism to humanitarian crises to reconstruction in Afghanistan—require international cooperation to solve.

"The lesson that will and must be drawn by the United States is that you cannot go it alone," Greenstock said. "You may be the greatest power in history, but you cannot go it alone."[73]

After the debate was over, Army General Jay Garner described Negroponte as "look[ing] a hell of a lot more rested than Greenstock."[74]

The UN proceedings were described as "a diplomatic debacle of historic proportions. No U.N. resolution to bestow legitimacy, no grand coalition of western powers, no major Arab nations to supply regional cover, not even a northern front from Turkey."[75] Nonetheless, the neoconservative Richard Perle celebrated, with an article entitled "Thank God for the Death of the U.N."[76]

Twenty-odd Democrats in the Senate voted against the administration's war resolution; save for the full-throated opposition of West Virginia Senator Robert Byrd, their efforts to influence public opinion were best described as perfunctory. On the other side of the Atlantic, the Leader of the House of Commons, Robin Cook, a former foreign minister, resigned from the government;[77] the most notable speech in opposition to the war was given from the opposition benches by former Chancellor of the Exchequer Kenneth Clarke, one of the few dissenting Conservatives; it almost certainly cost him his party's leadership:

> The answer to the questions "Did Washington determine such actions many months ago?" and "Could the President seek reelection without war and the removal of Iraq's President?" is as obvious as the reply to "Does the emperor have clothes?" How many terrorists will we recruit in the greater long-standing battle? What will we do to the stability of Saudi Arabia, Pakistan, or Egypt? The next time a large bomb explodes in a Western city or an Arab or Moslem regime topples and is replaced by extremists, the Government must consider the extent to which the policy contributed to it.[78]

To American surprise but not that of Blix, in Ankara the Turkish Grand National Assembly voted against a government resolution authorizing participation in the war, several dozen government deputies voting with the opposition. This sort of legislative independence appeared to have disappeared from the Anglo-Saxon world.

In 2007, asked to admit that France was right on Iraq, Negroponte responded:

> I'm a professional diplomat [laughter]. My job is to, I've always felt my job is to play the cards that I'm dealt so I was, if you let me finish. Both at the U.N. and in Iraq I think that I played a role of trying to do the best to implement the policies of my government.[79]

The subdued eloquence of Blix is the best commentary on this sequence of events:

> It was not reasonable to maintain that individual members of the Security Council had the right to take armed action to uphold decisions of the Council when a majority of the Council was not yet ready to authorize that action.

> The right of self-defence if an armed attack occurs is recognized and necessary, as was the case in Iraq's attack on Kuwait in 1990. After September

11, the Bush administration maintained that in some situations a state must have the right to use armed force in anticipation of an attack—to take pre-emptive action…. The action taken against Iraq in 2003 did not strengthen the case for a right to pre-emptive action.

There was another option for the states that wished to take armed action against Iraq in the spring of 2003. They could have heeded the Council's request for more time for inspection. Support by the Security Council for pre-emptive armed action would have given the armed action legitimacy.

Instead, a greater price was paid for this action: in the compromised legiti-macy of the action, in the damaged credibility of the governments pursu-ing it, and in the diminished authority of the United Nations.[80]

In 2008, Blix observed, even more succinctly:

In 1945 the US helped to write into the UN Charter a prohibition of the use of armed force against states. Exceptions were made only for self-defense against armed attacks and for armed force authorized by the Security Council. In 2003 Iraq was not a real or imminent threat to any-body. Instead, the invasion reflects a claim made in the 2002 US national security strategy that the charter was too restrictive, and that the US was ready to use armed force to meet threats that were uncertain as to time and place—a doctrine of preventive war…. from the most powerful mem-ber of the UN it is a dangerous signal. If preventive war is accepted for one, it is accepted for all.[81]

The Iraq resolution was not the first time the United States had asserted a right to preemptive self-defense; a similar claim had been made in 1986 during Secretary George Shultz's tenure in support of the bombing of Libya.[82]

At a joint press conference after the withdrawal of the second resolution, Greenstock declared "There's a recognition this has not been a finest diplomat's hour," whereas Negroponte said that "We regret that in the face of an explicit threat to veto by a permanent member, the vote counting became a secondary consideration."[83]

Five days later, on March 22, the neoconservative Richard Perle published an article in *The Spectator* in London describing the Security Council as "a product of the liberal conceit of safety through international law administered through international institutions."[84] In response, in my own postmortem and prophecy concerning the affair, I published on April 5, 2003 a letter reading as follows:

Two Kinds of Conceit. It is startling that Richard Perle believes that the U.N. Security Council is a product of the 'liberal conceit of safety through international law administered through international institutions.' In fact, as Robert A. Divine has shown (Roosevelt and World War II, 1969), it was an attempt at a 'realistic peace based on an alliance of the great powers;' at a revival of the Holy Alliance. If there is now 'conceit,' it is on the part of those who believe that powers have ceased to be powers and that infantry is no longer important in war.[85]

One clear loser in this affair was the first Bush administration's vision of a "new world order" based not on the United Nations conceived of as a "world parliament" but on the five permanent members of the Security Council, functioning in concert as a new "Holy Alliance" or as Franklin Roosevelt's "Four [or five] Policemen."[86] A *New York Times* journalist noted of Vice President Cheney and his neoconservative allies that "Security Council inaction would help prove their point that the institution is losing its relevance."[87] Nicholas Fenton declared that the Security Council proceedings "allowed the other Great Powers to work cooperatively in order to circumscribe the actions of the US"[88] Forty years earlier, General Charles de Gaulle had observed of the United Nations that "the future of the U.N. depended upon the cooperation of the five major powers including China." He obviously meant Communist China.[89] It is important to remember, as his *Washington Post* interview suggests, that Negroponte avoided taking the most extreme positions during the UN debates:

> Negroponte did not refer to the administration's controversial National Security Strategy, which claimed an American unilateral right to use force at any time and place in anticipation of future threats. Rather they defended the intervention in terms of the continuing authority of U.N. resolutions and the failure of the Iraqi regime to comply with disarmament

---

Two kinds of conceit

From Mr George Liebmann
Sir: It is startling that Richard Perle ('United they fall', 22 March) believes that the UN Security Council is a product of the 'liberal conceit of safety through international law administered through international institutions'. In fact, as Robert A. Divine has shown (*Roosevelt and World War II*, 1969), it was an attempt at a 'realistic peace based on an alliance of the great powers'; at a revival of the Holy Alliance. If there is now 'conceit', it is on the part of those who believe that powers have ceased to be powers and that infantry is no longer important in war.
George W. Liebmann
Baltimore,
USA

THE SPECTATOR 5 April 2003   33

An Amateur's Comment

agreements. The Bush administration pulled back from the extreme unilateral brink: instead of asserting a new doctrine of preventive force, it couched its actions in terms of U.N. authority.[90]

A more benign interpretation of the effect on the United Nations' role is offered by Ian Hurd, assistant professor of political science at Northwestern University:

> There was never any serious suggestion that the General Assembly should have the capacity to force a collective outcome on a reluctant Great Power...the Council managed to contribute in three ways to its general goals of maintaining international peace and stability. First, the legitimacy of the Council made it worthwhile for the US to seek Council approval for its preferred policy on Iraq [and] forced the US to justify its position. Second, many third party countries such as Canada and Turkey looked to the Council to signal whether it was appropriate to support the mission. Third, the Council, by refusing to approve the operation accomplished both of its realistic but more modest goals when Great Powers disagree; it reinforced the legal principle of the Charter on the use of force, and it raised the political costs of unilateralism for the hegemon.[91]

The costs proved to be not only political but economic. The costs of the first Gulf war had been almost entirely paid for by America's allies, including countries such as France, Germany, Japan, and Canada. The costs of the Iraq war, which were about ten times as great as the Gulf war, in the vicinity of a trillion dollars, fell almost entirely on the United States.

A second loss was to any perception of the United States as a peace-loving country, with the immunities this had heretofore conferred. The 100-year-old George Kennan wrote one of his last letters to the historian John Lukacs:

> I am finishing this letter on the morning when, according to the press, the U.N. Security Council (weeping over the absence of the French) is supposed to take some action giving sanction to an early attack, almost exclusively by ourselves, on the present regime of Iraq. I take an extremely dark view of all this—see it, in fact, the beginning of the end of anything like a normal life for all the rest of us. What is being done to our country today is surely something from which we will never be able to restore the sort of a country you and I have known.[92]

UN Secretary General Kofi Annan thereafter convened a rare meeting of the ambassadors of the five permanent members to discuss the United Nations' further role. It was a measure of how far the United Nations had strayed from Roosevelt's design that such a meeting in the absence of the nonpermanent members of the Security Council was regarded as a novelty.

Negroponte, thereafter, staved off a Security Council resolution condemning the Anglo-American intervention, noting that the members of the Council "didn't want to incur the political cost or the political friction."[93] There was no love lost for the Iraqi government, however much what was seen as premature action was regretted.

Development Issues

As UN ambassador, Negroponte attended a conference on international development at Monterrey in Mexico where, along with Undersecretary for Economic Affairs Alan Larson, he resisted demands that developed nations earmark 0.7 percent of their Gross National Product for international assistance.[94] At the conference, the United States committed an additional $10 billion in aid over three years, leading Negroponte to tell an nongovernmental organization (NGO) representative, the economist Jeffrey Sachs, "You're getting what you asked for."[95] On March 28, after the invasion of Iraq, Negroponte walked out on a speech by the Iraqi ambassador.[96]

The "Negroponte Doctrine" and Israel

Negroponte vetoed resolutions that were critical of Israeli behavior on the Gaza strip, enunciating a principle that the United States would not support resolutions critical of Israel unless they also criticized the acts of Arabs that provoked Israeli reprisals; this became known as "the Negroponte doctrine."[97] One especially inglorious manifestation of this policy concerned a resolution calling for an investigation of the bombardment of the Jenin refugee camp in 2002 by Israel, which assertedly cost several hundred lives. After Negroponte threatened to veto a resolution, Israeli Foreign Minister Shimon Peres indicated that Israel would accept an investigation. Negroponte then sponsored a revised resolution providing for an investigation, which was adopted on April 19. Israel then adopted Fabian tactics, demanding the addition of military personnel to the investigating commission, insisting on control over testimony and documents, and demanding that a final report contain no public observations or conclusions. On April 29, National Security Adviser Rice told Prime Minister Ariel Sharon that the United States was "with you all the way" on these issues, leading a commentator to observe that "This may be the first time that a sponsor of a UN Security Council resolution ended up blocking its implementation within a matter of days."[98] Negroponte also vetoed a resolution urging Israel not to harm Palestinian leader Yassir Arafat at a time when Israel laid siege to his compound, although regretting that a rush to vote precluded modification of the resolution.[99]

A "Two-State Solution"

Negroponte later took satisfaction in successful sponsorship of the first UN resolution expressly looking toward a "two-state" solution in Palestine. He negotiated a version of Resolution 1397 affirming the right of existence of a Palestinian state, describing the negotiation as "a little bit like an all-night poker game."[100] The resolution skillfully embraced language from speeches by both Bush and Powell and was described by a European diplomat as "a completely new dance" for the Americans. As adopted (unanimously with the Syrian delegate abstaining) the resolution read as follows:

"The Security Council,

"Recalling all its previous relevant resolutions, in particular resolutions 242 (1967) and 338 (1973),

"Affirming a vision of a region where two States, Israel and Palestine, live side by side within secure and recognized borders,

"Expressing its grave concern at the continuation of the tragic and violent events that have taken place since September 2000, especially the recent attacks and the increased number of casualties,

"Stressing the need for all concerned to ensure the safety of civilians,

"Stressing also the need to respect the universally accepted norms of international humanitarian law,

"Welcoming and encouraging the diplomatic efforts of special envoys from the United States of America, the Russian Federation, the European Union and the United Nations Special Coordinator and others to bring about a comprehensive, just and lasting peace in the Middle East,

"Welcoming the contribution of Saudi Crown Prince Abdullah,

"1. *Demands* immediate cessation of all acts of violence, including all acts of terror, provocation, incitement and destruction;
"2. *Calls upon* the Israeli and Palestinian sides and their leaders to cooperate in the implementation of the Tenet work plan and Mitchell Report recommendations with the aim of resuming negotiations on a political settlement;
"3. *Expresses* support for the efforts of the Secretary-General and others to assist the parties to halt the violence and to resume the peace process;
"4. *Decides* to remain seized of the matter."

Opposing Scapegoating

In both 2002 and 2003, Negroponte also imposed conditions on peacekeeping forces absolving American participants from being subjected to the jurisdiction of the new International Criminal Court (ICC), declaring that

Our Declaration of Independence states that governments are instituted among men deriving their just powers from the consent of the governed.... We have built up in our two centuries of constitutional history a dense web of restraints on government and of guarantees and protections for our citizens.... The history of American law is very largely the history of that balance between the power of the government and the rights of the people. We will not permit that balance to be overturned by the imposition on our people of a novel legal system they have never accepted or approved, and which their government has explicitly rejected.[101]

At Negroponte's confirmation hearing, he had spoken somewhat more mildly about the ICC, noting the fiasco of the Slobodan Miloševic trial and observing "In some cases those efforts have not been so successful and I am hopeful we will be mindful of the lessons learned as progress is made toward establishing the Sierra Leone Special Court and the tribunal in Cambodia."[102] In July 2002, he threatened to withdraw US military personnel from the Bosnian peace keeping force if they were not provided with immunity from ICC jurisdiction by the UN authorizing resolution. Later, in testifying on fiscal 2005 appropriations before the House Subcommittee on Commerce, Justice, State, and the Judiciary, Negroponte said of the ICC that it was

> gravely flawed in the areas of accountability, due process, relationship to the Security Council and U.N. Charter, and jurisdiction. The risk of politicization is great. It does not recognize the principle that there shall be no double jeopardy except for its own decisions.

After the revelations about Abu Ghraib, Negroponte's successors were not successful in renewing the conditions in 2004.

At his confirmation hearing, he also defended US withdrawal from a UN conference on racism that was "overwhelmed by the negative rhetoric of recrimination and hate"; he also called for disbursement of the second tranche of funds for the United Nations in the amount of $582 million that had been agreed to by Senators Jesse Helms and Joe Biden in exchange for reforms at the United Nations.

Preparing an Iraqi Transition

In May 2003, after the invasion, Negroponte obtained Security Council approval of Resolution 1483 legitimating the occupation, lifting sanctions, and allocating $18 billion in blocked accounts to the allies.[103] The French gave their support on the premise that a viable Iraqi state was needed to contain Iran. Negroponte declared that "the liberation of Iraq has cleared the way for today's action" and described Saddam's Iraq as "unwilling adequately to feed its people, a state in which critical infrastructure projects were left to languish while luxurious palaces were built and a state in which free political expression was cruelly repressed and punished."[104] He readily agreed to a reference in the resolution to American responsibilities as an occupying power, reflecting "a sense of hubris on the part of the Americans." Cheney and Rice had opposed calling the situation an occupation and had opposed the time limit in the resolution, desiring maximum freedom of maneuver. The British were insistent on a defined and transparent legal basis.[105] Some of his colleagues in Washington with their demands for permanent military bases appear not to have realized what this implied.

On August 20, Negroponte sought a new resolution following the bombing of UN headquarters in Baghdad and the death of the chief UN representative, Sérgio Viera de Mello of Brazil. In October, acting on instructions, he resisted UN pressures for an interim government: "There is no evidence that installing an interim government right away would improve the security conditions in the country."[106] A Chilean proposal required a timetable for transition to be submitted by December 15. On October 16, a resolution was adopted, but France, Germany, and Russia indicated that, in view of inadequate provisions on transition, they would not send troops. By November 15, Paul Bremer and the Iraq Provisional Authority promulgated a schedule calling for a government to be formed by June 30, 2004, with final elections under a new constitution by December 31, 2005. This resolution was variously characterized. A critic of American policy said that it gave the United States "a formal writ as an occupying power." The neoconservative Max Boot said it created "a veiled protectorate...the Cromer not the Curzon model."[107] In January 2004, an Iraqi delegation asked to be heard by the Security Council, and Negroponte vigorously resisted ("By no means!") suggestions that Bremer be present, fearing that proceedings would turn into a trial of the Americans; in the final event, it was agreed that Bremer and Greenstock, by then the British representative in Iraq, would not be present.[108]

On May 19, following Negroponte's designation as ambassador to Iraq, he took part in an informal UN discussion of the interim government:

> We want to assist the interim government to gain ownership of the political process as soon as possible. This is my official mission statement and determination...To put it frankly, we don't want this new government to fall on its ass.

He is also said to have lamented that there was no President Karzai in sight.[109] He was successful in obtaining funding for the UN missions in Iraq and Afghanistan, agreeing to enhanced support of a UN agency headquartered in the Dominican Republic to obtain Latin American support. By June 1, the UN representative, Lakhdar Brahimi, had assembled an interim government, though not without some American influence. On June 6, a new resolution was drafted, the United States agreeing to inclusion of a paragraph referring to international law, another referring to "full responsibility and authority" for the interim government, and dates for its inception (June 30, 2004) and termination (December 31, 2005). At the conclusion of the effort, Negroponte declared "You know, this resolution actually represents the instructions for my diplomatic mission in Iraq. Everything is [in] here that I have to do and promote."[110] A commentator observed: "Not since the League of Nations gave Britain and France mandates over large parts of the Middle East in the 1920s had foreign countries had such sweeping powers in the region."[111]

Taking note of Sergei Lavrov's promotion to Foreign Minister and Jeremy Greenstock's presence in Baghdad, Negroponte observed: "When you are ambassador to the UN Security Council, you either go on to become the secretary of foreign relations of your country or they send you to Baghdad!"[112] (Greenstock was ultimately to resign from his position in Baghdad after having been marginalized by Bremer.)

Later, there were significant recriminations when it was discovered that the US National Security Agency (NSA), in cooperation with British intelligence, had been eavesdropping on several of the nonaligned delegations. The disclosure was a result of the leak of a January 31, 2003, NSA memorandum by a translator at the British Government Communications Headquarters.[113] When it was later reported that Secretary General Kofi Annan's conversations had also been transcribed, his office issued a statement of protest.[114]

Negroponte was a vigorous defender of the work of several of the United Nations' specialized agencies, most particularly the Commission on Refugees, the World Food Program, and United Nations International Children's Emergency Fund (UNICEF). He was credited with attempting to facilitate an NGO report to the Security Council on the Darfur crisis, being stymied by Washington: "Negroponte was, as always, cordial and accommodating, in glaring contrast to the abrasive John Bolton who followed."[115] Levitte paid tribute to his willingness to listen to his interlocutors and to his creativity in finding ways forward past disagreements. His eldest daughter spent 2 1/2 years working with the World Food Program, the last year and a half in a field office in India, before pursuing graduate studies.

Negroponte departed from the United Nations after having repaired some of the damages from the abortive second Iraq resolution and ensuing war. He did not, however, firmly implant in public understanding the "structure of peace" based on the five permanent members that Franklin Roosevelt had dreamed of and planned for and that also played a role in the thought of the first President Bush. His exceptionally close relationship with the British and French ambassadors, particularly before the replacement of Levitte by Jean-Marc De La Sabiere, as well as those of China, Russia, and Germany, provided a model for the future—a movement toward a permanent five-party conference of ambassadors to resolve or deflect developing international problems. He was almost certainly correct in his view, shared with James Baker, that only Secretary Powell's resignation, not his own, might have prevented American entry into the Iraq War.

18

IRAQ

If drunk with sight of power we loose
Wild tongues that have not Thee in awe
Such boastings as the Gentiles use
Or lesser breeds without the law
Lord God of Hosts, be with us yet
Lest we forget—lest we forget!

For heathen heart that puts her trust
In reeking tube and iron shard
All valiant dust that builds on dust
And guarding, calls not Thee to guard
For frantic boast and foolish word
Thy mercy on Thy People, Lord.

— R. Kipling, *Recessional* (1897)

Beginning in Iraq

John Negroponte effectively volunteered to be Ambassador to Iraq: "I would do it if you asked me." Looking back, he observed of the decision to enter Iraq:

> I was not party to the decision, but I saw it coming, and when we went in, and after we'd been there for a while, I felt, "We have to deal with the situation as it is, and we have to make the best of it." And I ended up making a personal contribution—volunteered to go.[1]

Others considered for the job included Robert Blackwill and US Deputy Secretary of Defense Paul Wolfowitz, both of whom were thought likely to present confirmation problems, and Thomas Pickering, former US ambassador to the United Nations. Negroponte was described by the *Washington Post* reporter Bob Woodward as being from "the old school of foreign service, there was almost no one like him any more…executors of programs and policies made by others…used to bad and ineffective governments." Asked by President George W. Bush, in what was said to be the only question asked him at his job interview, whether he thought democracy was possible in Iraq, Negroponte declared "I don't think it's beyond the wit of man." In an effort to improve civil–military coordination, Bush gave a dinner for Negroponte, General George Casey, former chief of staff of the US Army, and their wives. The National Security Policy Directive (NSPD) 36 of May 11, 2004, transferred authority from the Pentagon to the State Department over "all US government employees…except those under the command of an area military commander." On April 27, Negroponte assured the Senate Foreign Relations Committee that the interim government "would have no authority to sign long-term oil contracts."[2]

Negroponte engaged a public affairs officer in Mexico, and part-time speechwriter for him at the United Nations, Robert Earle, as a policy adviser in both Iraq and at the Directorate of National Intelligence. Earle was charged to think about "to start with, who is the enemy. Everyone says something different." He declared to Earle that "he'll have latitude. The people at the White House know that they've made a mess of things." Earle was an admirer of Negroponte and was close to him in his thinking. He subsequently published a memoir that was flattering to Negroponte, but did so without reference to his reticent subject; in consequence, they were not on speaking terms for a year afterward. Six diplomats of ambassadorial rank agreed to serve under Negroponte. On arrival, he declared his credo:

> our mission in Iraq is to support the sovereign democratic rights of the Iraqi people to govern themselves, defend their country and rebuild their economy. Iraq's future is in Iraqi hands. America's policy is to be Iraq's respectful and supportive friend.[3]

Negroponte and Casey "as a symbolic affirmation…sat down together and wrote two mission statements, each two pages long. Each man signed both documents."[4] Notwithstanding the displeasure of neo conservatives with statements by the UN representative for Iraq, Lakhdar Brahimi, that were critical of Israel, Negroponte declared that cooperation with the UN was in America's "strategic interest" in organizing elections. Brahimi had declared that "The great poison in the region is this Israeli policy of domination and the suffering imposed on the Palestinians [and the] equally unjust support of the US for this policy."[5]

His first act, fully accomplished after Congressional approval on September 30, 2004, barely three months after his arrival, was to release $2.2 billion to the military to reinforce security, allowing it to immediately hire Iraqis. This

> doubled the size of the Iraqi security budget that had been advocated by Ambassador Paul Bremer and increased the police force by 40 percent. It would be a year though before the funding increase resulted in trained Iraqis on the streets…. Money wouldn't put effective Iraqi soldiers on the streets in Ramadi and Fallujah as long as the insurgents were the intimidators fighting with the blessings of the Sunni imams.[6]

"He thought Garner and Bremer had been a little starry-eyed in thinking that they could reconstruct the country quickly; the first order of business had to be re-establishing central authority in the Iraqi government."[7] This, and the elections, Negroponte regarded as his greatest achievement in Iraq; he regarded the second battle of Fallujah as essential to the assertion of authority. A second later budgetary reallocation in December 2004 supplied $246 million additional funds for security in four contested cities; a third reallocation supplied $225 million additional for security in Baghdad and $607 million for operation and maintenance of oil, electric, and water facilities, an unglamorous subject neglected in the preexisting allocations of the Coalition Provisional Authority (CPA). In all, Negroponte's budget reallocations left oil, transport, and health allocations more or less untouched, while increasing allocations for security by 55 percent, for private sector employment by 359 percent, for justice and public safety by 47 percent, and for education and refugee aid by 40 percent. Because many electric and water projects could not be safeguarded or constructed on a timely basis, allocations for electrical projects were reduced by 21 percent and for water projects by 49 percent.

By January 2005, 42 of 45 National Guard battalions were at least of 70 percent strength; they had been in disarray on his arrival. In the summer of 2004, more accurate measurements of the number of Iraqi personnel had been instituted, the number shown as "on duty" as of June 15, 2004, being restated to show 47,255 persons actually "trained and equipped" as of August 25, 2004. The new Iraqi security forces performed well at the January 2005 elections, although it was alleged that "The large expansion of the police payroll during Ambassador Negroponte's tenure and beyond stemmed in part from the growth of new [Iraq Police Service] patronage networks," such as the Kurdish Pashmerga and the Shii Badr Corps, both said to be "ridden with corruption and sectarian interests."[8]

A later US Strategic Studies Institute review concluded that "Ambassador Bremer embraced transformation, seeking open governance and free markets in a society without the most basic level of security. Not only were the two not properly sequenced, they were antithetical...."[9]

Negroponte relied on Patrick Kennedy to set up the embassy, a role Kennedy, now Undersecretary for Management at the State Department, also performed at the Directorate of National Intelligence. The transition with Paul Bremer, US ambassador to Iraq, was handled by the Deputy Ambassador James Jeffrey (later ambassador to Turkey). Jeffrey, who had been ambassador to Albania, preceded Negroponte to Iraq by six weeks. On Negroponte's arrival, "Jeffrey showed him a map of Baghdad locating a week's worth of about 100 insurgent attacks. The main issue was security, Jeffrey said. 'We don't have it.'"[10] "We're standing up an embassy for this crazy goddamn CPA thing in the midst of this burlesque palace, being shelled every day, a really bad nightmare."[11] Before leaving for Baghdad, Negroponte had told Paul Wolfowitz "I'm afraid we may have made the same mistake that we did in Vietnam where we didn't start Vietnamization until it was too late."[12] Negroponte viewed Bremer, who had no recent experience in the Third World, as not well suited to the Iraqi assignment. Henry Kissinger was Bremer's major patron; he owed his appointment to Secretary of State Donald Rumsfeld. Negroponte viewed his own role model as Ellsworth Bunker, whose performance in Vietnam he admired, for his austere dignity and aplomb.

As ambassador to Iraq, Negroponte's greatest regret "is that we were never able to dissuade the Sunni politicians from their boycott of those elections... in January 2005."[13] "From the beginning of the insurgency in 2003, he believed, the administration had underestimated its size and miscalculated its motivations. Worse, they were still doing it. It was not a surprise that the Pentagon would put out optimistic reports."[14] He urged Robert Richer, a CIA division chief in Baghdad, to be vocal in telling Bush that the insurgency was gaining strength and that Iraq was on the verge of civil war,[15] only to be reproached by Richer for merely telling Bush "We've got some hiccups," Negroponte rejoined, defending his use of nonconfrontational language, "I get my message across." Richer later joined the security contractor, Blackwater, for a time, later resigning from it in the course of a controversy over bribery of Iraqi officials, which he opposed.[16]

Inheriting a Debacle

On his appointment, Richard Holbrooke had said of Negroponte: "He is far more qualified than Bremer. John is subtle, Bremer is black and white. John understands ambiguity." Early on, Negroponte observed: "you can't just outlaw evil…you've got to be ready for it and deal with it where you find it."[17] Henry Kissinger said "He brings great steadiness and solidity. He has the patience and subtlety to bring it off," while UN Secretary General Kofi Annan referred to him as "an outstanding professional, a great diplomat, and a wonderful ambassador." A journalist speculated that policy would not be "kinder and gentler," but that Negroponte would "sand down some rough edges in foreign policy." In June 2004, before going to his new post, he secured unanimous Security Council approval for the new arrangements creating a sovereign Iraqi government but continuing international control over security forces; the latter provision seriously qualified Iraqi sovereignty.[18] Bremer had left in haste and without ceremony advancing the transfer of power from the Provisional Authority to the Iraqi government by two days to avoid insurgent attack. Unlike Bremer, Negroponte had no power to rule by decree. On his way out of the door, Bremer, under the influence of the neoconservatives in Washington, unleashed a shower of last-minute decrees in addition to a draft constitution, which astonish by their *naïveté* and presumptuousness. Even more remarkably, they appear to deviate from President Bush's understanding when the United States entered the war. Bush told Spanish Premier José Aznar on February 22, 2005, "we're already putting into effect a post-Saddam Iraq, and I believe there's a good basis for a better future. Iraq has a good bureaucracy and a civil society that's relatively strong. It could be organized into a federation." President Bush, however, grossly underestimated the cost of the war, telling Aznar that if it were somehow avoided "that would be the best solution. Besides, it would save us $50 billion."[19]

Bremer's ukases included:

CPA Order 1, May 16, 2003, de-Ba'athification of Iraqi Society, requiring the discharge of as many as 85,000 state employees.
CPA Order 2, May 23, 2003, Dissolution of Iraqi Entities, disbanding the 385,000-man armed forces, 285,000 staff members of the Ministry of Interior, and 50,000 members of presidential security units. These two orders appear not to have been "staffed out" in Washington; one writer suggests that the only authorization for them may have come from Vice President Richard Cheney's office.[20]

CPA Order 37, September 19, 2003, limiting individual and corporate taxes to 15 percent not only for 2004 but for subsequent years, and exempting all coalition contractors and subcontractors.

CPA Order 38, September 19, 2003, imposing a 5 percent import levy, with coalition contractors and subcontractors exempt.

CPA Order 39, September 19, 2003, allowing 100 percent foreign ownership of all business in Iraq other than those in the natural resources, banking and insurance sectors and allowing 100 percent repatriation of profits. Discrimination against foreign investors was prohibited; discrimination in their favor permitted.

CPA Order 40, September 19, 2003, permitting opening of six foreign banks by the end of 2008 and providing that there would be no limit thereafter, and allowing 50 percent foreign ownership of Iraqi banks.

CPA Order 94, June 2004, abolishing the limits on foreign banks and foreign bank ownership in CPA Order 40.[21]

Other June 2004 orders related to compensation of victims of Saddam's regime, money laundering, and financial management.

The first two orders were passed without consultation with the British, notwithstanding that British staff was in the same office as the American staff. Although this policy determination was not prearranged with Rumsfeld, it is supported to this day by Rumsfeld's assistant and Director of Special Plans Douglas Feith, and the British assert that Bremer was on the telephone with Rice and Rumsfeld for long periods each evening and was unlikely to have acted on his own.

More than two years earlier, the State Department had prepared a 13-volume "Future of Iraq" project. Bremer explained in his memoirs that he had largely ignored this document, as it was a study, not a plan. The document nonetheless was prophetic:

> The question of the Ba'ath Party is at the heart of the transition it is not possible to equate party membership with criminalization.... The period immediately after regime change might offer criminals an opportunity to engage in acts of killing, plunder, looting, etc.

The Democratic Principles Working Group would warn against a policy of total de-Ba'athification without the reintegration of former Ba'athists into society.

> Many participants sent the message that the USG needs to prepare for a stay of five to ten years...rapid reform and training of a new police force to deal with both the normal routine preservation of law and order and the exceptional circumstances of popular acts of vengeance as well as to combat the further development of criminal syndicates...ex military personnel, not associated with torture and corruption in police activities, could play a part in recruiting and training new police members.

> De-Ba'athification would not consist of the total abolition of the current administration, since, in addition to its role of social control, that structure does provide a framework for social order. Those former Ba'athists who

are not reintegrated into society, most notably members of the Iraqi army, may present a destabilizing element, especially if they are left without work or ability to get work.

The CPA discontinued support to state-owned enterprises supplying fertilizer, chlorine, and cement, without considering resulting coordination problems. Negroponte increased funds for the agricultural sector from a meager $5 million to $72 million.[22] A majority of CPA reconstruction contracts were awarded to major US companies, including KBR, a subsidiary of Halliburton, which in 2003 received a $2.4 billion no-bid reconstruction contract from the Army.

David Kay, the former Chief Inspector of the Iraq Survey Group, said that the State Department study, "it was not a plan to hand to a task force and say 'go implement.'" Retired Colonel Paul Hughes, who had served as chief of the Special Initiatives Office for the Office of Recovery and Humanitarian Assistance (ORHA) and as the director of the Strategic Policy Office for the CPA, concurred, adding that while "it produced some useful background information it had no chance of really influencing the post-Saddam phase of the war." The Pentagon's favorite exiles, including Ahmed Chalabi, neither liked nor agreed with the study. British Ambassador Jeremy Greenstock blamed Chalabi's influence for the total de-Ba'athification directed by Bremer, and took the view that the basic error was not putting the military in control of pacification; the military in Bremer's time was operating separately from the CPA.[23]

> [T]he new American team had a withering term for the optimistic approach of their predecessors ... "the illusionists" for their conviction that America could create a Jeffersonian democracy on the ruins of Saddam Hussein's medieval brutalism.[24]

Negroponte viewed the restoration of security as Iraq's pre-eminent need, and viewed with disdain the notion that the Americans' role was to win hearts and minds by "saying hello to people and playing the guitar." "By the time [the CPA] closed, most US military leaders viewed it as only slightly less onerous than the insurgency itself."[25] The legacy of the CPA was imposed on the new government, since it required a consensus of the president and prime minister and other officials to over-turn CPA edicts, numerous Americans with terms ending in 2009 were left in charge of government commissions, and the Embassy controlled a large portion of the Iraqi budget.[26]

Negroponte denies being influenced by a Rand Corporation study of Iraqi reconstruction.[27] This urged that departure not be tied to artificial deadlines, urged creation of a consultative framework including all of Iraq's neighbors, stressed the importance of coordination between civil, military, and economic authorities, predicted that the oil sector would not be able to finance the cost of reconstruction, discouraged dumping of foreign agricultural products, and estimated security needs as 520,000 troops to 2005, 258,000 in 2005, and 145,000 in 2008. Its recommendations that only the Republican Guard be immediately demobilized, that elections not be rushed, and that international burden-sharing be established at the outset had been overtaken by events.

In setting up the Embassy, Negroponte heeded recommendations of Frank Ricciardone (now Ambassador in Ankara) and Michael Kicklighter, Inspector General at the Pentagon. He had weekly dinners with Casey and Allawi; Allawi's dinners were given outside on a porch with fans, in what Allawi considered the cool of the evening: 100–110° Fahrenheit. His weekly dinners with Iraqi Deputy Prime Minister Saleh featured fresh vegetables, a commodity denied to the embassy, whose supplies came from Kuwait.

Negroponte's principal instruction from the State Department was to eliminate or reduce visible American corruption in Baghdad, or in Powell's words, to "get control of the money." Robert Earle observed to Negroponte that "the CPA just sort of fell over before my eyes as soon as Jerry [Bremer] left," leading Negroponte to respond "It's amazing he kept it upright as long as he did." "Money," Earle said. Negroponte responded: "I'm going to review all that…. I'm going to go through the whole 18 billion reconstruction fund and see what it looks like here, not what people say it looks like in Washington."

Negroponte concluded that "we've got an economic dimension that's detached from the security dimension. If we don't deal with the enemy, we get nowhere and the military will be disengaged." He declared to Earle apropos of the Sunni insurgents: "you've just told me they're dug in and have us surrounded. That's how things stand, isn't it?" Earle observed: "he's furious at the negligence that has led to this situation." Negroponte declared, apropos of the American offensive at Second Fallujah: "we need to break his will first. We need to hurt him into rethinking his strategy."[28] "We have to bring the politics and security together, through diplomacy and the military. There's no politics without security, or any reconstruction." "Why don't you simply say that all aspects of the reconstruction program will be subordinated to and supportive of the counterinsurgency effort. One sentence." Earle observed: "his unstated motto could be 'don't fail and you will succeed.' "[29]

> Richard Armitage said that the State Department grew increasingly worried by the tone of life inside the zone. "I defined it as the bar scene from Star Wars", he said in 2005. "The people running to and fro, young people in very heady positions, they didn't have a clue what they were doing." State was so alarmed that one of the orders given to John Negroponte and his aides was "Clean up that goddamn Green Zone" Armitage's instructions to Ambassador James Jeffrey, the number-two American diplomat in Baghdad were, "I don't want to see people running around with arms out there drinking beer; I don't want to see people I don't know who they are carrying weapons; clean up this freaking place; send people home."
>
> "As soon as we got Negroponte out there, and got State involved, everything changed" said Armitage…. "We had reporting, it was orderly, things started to run." Under the new team, "we started getting reams of reporting, so we got the texture of society, we got the debate of society, we got all of it."[30]

It was said that $8.8 billion in Coalition Provisional Authority funds were unaccounted for or misspent and that Iraq had become a "hunting ground for the world's shadier characters."[31]

Second Fallujah

The most debated decision made on Negroponte's watch was that leading to the bloody re-conquest of Fallujah. The first battle of Fallujah in March 2004 had taken place on Bremer's watch, after the lynching of several American contractors there, Bremer was cheered on by the neo conservatives in Washington; the loss of 600 civilian lives and destruction did much to antagonize the Sunni population, and the conflict ended with a truce which effectively restored the city to insurgent control.[32] The operation had been rushed: "the US Marines and the CPA wanted a slow, careful approach, but Bremer, Rumsfeld, President Bush and Abizaid insisted that the city be taken, and taken immediately."[33] The reconquest of Fallujah in November 2004 cost at least 1,000 insurgent casualties as well as 52 American dead and 425 wounded and left the city virtually destroyed; it was justified as a necessary precursor to the elections, "undercutting the ability of the insurgents to launch attacks to block the January 2005 election."[34] Powell viewed Fallujah as "a hotbed of insurgent activity... [a] safe haven, totally out of control." As related by President Bush's then press secretary, Scott McClellan, "Bush and his team [Abizaid, Casey, and Negroponte] had decided that [the insurgents] must be defeated for once and for all before the forthcoming elections." The ensuing insurgency in Mosul led Fallujah to be derided as an application of the "whack-a-mole" theory of counter-insurgency.[35]

Negroponte was credited with cooperation with the military, replacing the fraught relationship between Bremer and General Sanchez.[36] "A reassuring convergence of leadership in a single mission. Trust."[37] He and General Casey had adjacent offices in the Green Zone.

Negroponte's performance was criticized by an Iraqi historian of the conflict: "Image frequently overwhelmed substance as the USA. set one symbolic goal after another... within the tight constraints of artificial dates and deadlines." Negroponte's return of Ba,athists into public service and efforts to rebuild the Iraqi security forces "fell foul of the limited time available for the Interim Government to consolidate itself, the milestone of the upcoming elections, and the existence of empowered Shia groups." He had been presented by Bremer with a schedule that gave only a limited three-day role to a National Conference which otherwise might have helped to render elections more legitimate.

On inheriting this mess, he may have reflected on the cautionary words of the 98-year-old George Kennan in an interview in 2002:

> I have seen no evidence that we have any realistic plans for dealing with the great state of confusion in Iraqian affairs which would presumably follow even after the successful elimination of the dictator.... I fear that any attempt on our part to confront that latent situation by military means alone could easily serve to aggravate it rather than alleviate it.[38]

Two weeks earlier Kennan had warned, in an interview with *The Hill*, a publication widely read in Congress:

> war has a momentum of its own and it carries you away from all thoughtful intentions when you get into it. Today, if we went into Iraq, like the President would like us to do, you know where you begin—you never know where you're going to end.[39]

Curbing Sadr

In another episode, like Second Fallujah driven by the impending elections,

> Negroponte was calling for a decisive blow against Moqtada al Sadr. He
> was backed by his superiors in Washington even though certain reports
> claimed the US Marines were responding to local challenges rather than
> implementing part of a detailed political plan.

An ensuing settlement negotiated by the Shii cleric Sistani had Sadr's forces
evacuate a town and mosque, while living to fight another day, causing the
Americans to appear as "an irresolute force that lacked subtlety in its approach
to changed issues." The commentator William Pfaff stated: "When Negroponte
was informed that Sadr was summoning help, he 'decided to pursue the
case.'...Sadr was turned into a national leader." "A policy of attacking Iraqi
cities with armor, artillery, and air power in order to seize individuals defies
reason. The only chance of minimizing current costs is to do everything possible to lend legitimacy to the interim government and its chaotically formed new
national assembly."[40] Negroponte undertook to deflect criticism by observing

Negroponte and Family: 2002

that "there is only one quarterback and his name is Allawi"; the American military was praised for its skill in avoiding damage to the mosque.[41] Negroponte believed that this military encounter helped divert the Sadr movement into political channels. Patrick Cockburn, a critic of American policy, concedes that thereafter Sadr was "wary of fighting the US Army for a third time…the dissecting of Iraq has probably gone too far for the country to exist as more than a loose federation." A companion of Sadr, a Dr. Ruboie, alleged an assassination plot in connection with a truce to be signed in Sadr's father's house in Najaf: "I went berserk with both Casey and the Ambassador. They denied they knew of a trap and said they would investigate but he heard nothing more from them."[42]

Preparing Elections

By some accounts, Negroponte's policy of hastening elections aborted with "the failure of the secularists and nationalists to perform in the elections of January 2005."[43] He was under heavy pressure from both Bush and Sistani not to postpone elections, even though the UN representative Brahimi as well as Secretary General Kofi Annan and the interim president Allawi urged postponement; his own conclusion is said by Woodward to have been that doing so would not have made much difference:

> The Shiis were already the winners. They would prevail. The only question was how the US could help shape things—which was different from determining them. It was time to take our hands off…if we had ten years, then we could do it another way…I'm with Rumsfeld on the training wheels now. We're just going to have to take them off.[44]

"Iraqi politicians say they aren't ready, they're scared, they're not in control, but I still can't think of another way forward."[45] General Casey was said to be against postponing elections, while Negroponte at least toyed with the idea.[46] Whatever doubt he had was dispelled by clear marching orders from President Bush given at a meeting of the NSC in which Negroponte participated by teleconference.

The elections when held were conducted using party lists and a nationwide constituency rather than geographic districts. This was a result of decisions made by Bremer and the UN. Their timing had been discussed at a meeting of Secretary General Annan, Greenstock, Bremer, and Negroponte at the UN in January 2004. This almost certainly produced a more polarized legislative body, and was characterized by one commentator as "a huge mistake." Bremer had contended that there was insufficient time to lay out districts. In addition "small non-geographically based parties would have had difficulty winning seats…these minor parties figured to be among the strongest advocates of democracy."[47] The use of a nationwide constituency made it impossible to postpone elections in troubled areas only, and drove the effort to pacify Fallujah and Najaf before the elections; it also "mobilized the electorate along ethnic and professional lines."[48] There were an impressive 8.5 million voters, few of whom were Sunnis. Negroponte was philosophical about the lack of Sunni participation: "they'll see this too. That will have its own impact if they decided to sit it out and end up watching everyone else exercise their rights."[49] Two million expatriates were allowed to vote, though only a small number did so. On his departure from Iraq in March 2005, The elections came off in an orderly fashion though with little Sunni participation because of fear of reprisals. Systematic disruption was avoided by Casey's order banning vehicular traffic for three days before the election.

Negroponte declared "The job is far from done. What is begun well ends well and the January 30 election was certainly a good beginning."[50] The later elections in December 2005 were organized with provincial constituencies using the same lists that had been pronounced inadequate for that purpose earlier in the year. By comparison with his successor, Negroponte is said to have "shined by his discretion…[Zalmay] Khalizad does not deny having provided fully written parts of the Constitution to the Iraqis."[51] To the extent that the present Iraqi government is our own creation, its defense is open to Hans Morgenthau's objection

> we have contracted with ourselves and I do not regard this as a valid foundation for intervention…it would be very difficult for us to win a military victory, and even if we win it, it means nothing politically.[52]

Fostering Iraqi Politics

Fouad Ajami, a writer sympathetic to the Bush policies, noted:

> As I observed [Negroponte] in August, there was mastery and skill to his performance; understated and calm, he seemed determined to stay in the background and to let the Iraqi leaders assume greater burdens and higher visibility. He was no doubt aware that Bremer had had a heavy touch and he wanted it known that the time of the American regency had come to an end…. The consensus was that this was in truth a viceroy keen to carry himself as an ambassador and to observe with the strictest fidelity the transition to Iraqi sovereignty.

Columnist Georgie Anne Geyer declared that he "constantly insisted that the Iraqis take the lead, in part out of pragmatism, in part out of a show of respect." He was opposed to creating or reinforcing dependencies, a central problem in Vietnam, and was opposed to the Washington mind set, manifest in domestic politics as well as foreign policy, in favor of command and control approaches rather than those vesting discretion in those assisted. Similarly, he avoided efforts to micro-manage the military. Bob Woodward observed:

> There was almost no one like him any more. His role models were Ellsworth Bunker and Henry Cabot Lodge…he believed ambassadors were the executors of programs and policies made by others…. The first order of business had to be re-establishing central authority in the Iraqi government.

Negroponte expressed the fear that "I'm afraid we may have made the same mistake that we did in Vietnam, where we didn't start Vietnamization until it was too late."[53]

His methodology was described by Robert Earle: "Stupidities that infuriate me don't agitate him at all...[he] will listen more than speak, won't reveal his state of mind." Negroponte declared that

> my task is to make sure that the people we have working with us out here don't abandon us when we make changes because they think we wouldn't listen to them.... He's almost delicate as he meets and focuses on each dignitary,

> His whole thought is complete when he writes; he doesn't write as he thinks...when he deletes a sentence or a paragraph, he strikes it out with a single pen stroke, offering no explanation...the absence of neurotic fearful quibbling astonishes me as always.... His attic has no cobwebs.[54]

Elsewhere, Ajami referred to him as "the hands-off John Negroponte, who didn't stick around long enough to make a difference at any rate."[55]

Another critic credited Negroponte with purging Bremer's faithful Republicans but charged the staff with knowing nothing about the Kurds: "the American operation seemed to be running like a temp agency."[56]

"[T]he new US ambassador John Negroponte no longer sat at the head of the table during meetings, as Jerry Bremer had...he deliberately took a seat off to one side." On his arrival, on a day when Bremer made an unheralded departure, he eschewed press briefings and undertook to make himself as invisible as possible.[57] This approach was not appreciated by frustrated journalists, one of whom wrote that Negroponte "rarely spoke to the press or developed personal relations with many Iraqi politicians." If approached by a carpet salesman, this *New York Times* reporter wrote, Khalizad would have enthusiastically bargained for a carpet, while

> "Bremer, a catastrophe as civil administrator, would have ordered the carpet shop closed down, forced it to modernize, restructured its workforce, and ended up offending the workers as well as the owner and his entire family. Negroponte wouldn't have bothered shopping for carpets at all."[58]

Large cost-plus contracts to American multi nationals were in some measure replaced by fixed-price contracts for smaller Iraqi firms. When Negroponte took office, only $1 billion of the $18 billion allocated for reconstruction had been spent, and fewer than 10 percent of the 2,800 planned projects were under way. Much of the reconstruction money he had shifted away from large projects to the provision of security,[59] which also helped reduce unemployment. One of his first acts was to secure control of the reconstruction funds previously administered by the military.[60] "It made little sense to build electrical towers and oil pipelines when the guerrilla fighters kept blowing them up."[61] There were "simplified acquisition rules requiring fewer bids and less cost data for contracts of less than $500,000.... The change in reconstruction strategy ultimately proved beneficial and began to reduce costs."[62]

His approach was to step back in favor of the Iraqis, who unfortunately had limited experience with operations and equipment maintenance. Large scale

American corruption was thus replaced by smaller-scale Iraqi corruption, an effect ultimately sought to be mitigated by the creation of joint provincial reconstruction teams, which were slow getting under way because of disagreements between the State Department and military about how they were to be protected.[63] He also in October sought waivers of 20 onerous American procurement rules that delayed reconstruction.[64] He brought in Bill Taylor, a military man and former ambassador with experience in Afghanistan to supervise reconstruction and replace huge cost-plus contracts with multinationals with smaller fixed-price contracts with Iraqi firms.

> Taylor thought it was foolish to believe that the US aid would reduce the insurgency by buying new friends. It didn't happen in Vietnam and it wasn't going to happen in Iraq…. The principal motivation was to reconstruct so that stability, economic growth, security and political growth could evolve.[65]

His predecessor Paul Bremer, in an op-ed piece in January 2006 timed to coincide with the publication of his book, paid Negroponte a considerable compliment by writing that two of his own worst mistakes were excessive emphasis on large-scale projects rather than daily needs and failure to seek exemption from procurement rules.[66]

Negroponte defined his three priorities as military training for the Iraqis, elections, and reconstruction. He rejected efforts by the Sunnis and Kurds to postpone the elections, being over optimistic about Sunni participation in them and under considerable pressure from Sistani and the majority Shiis to get them under way.[67]

The American aspiration for one-man, one-vote democracy in Iraq, as distinct from some system that would limit central government in favor of local elites, led William F. Buckley, Jr., to inquire: "are we traveling at a rate so ideologically prepossessing as to scorn human and cultural experience?"[68]

Five Years

Negroponte helped alter the President's rosy perspective on the war.

> I told the President in November [2004]…that we weren't winning, and he was shocked', a former administration official recalled in an interview. "And John Negroponte backed me up. I called John and said "I told the president this and I want you to know it, so if you've got a different view"…and he said no."[69]

He opposed caricatured views of Shiis as Iranian agents and Sunnis as enemies. Efforts were made to assist and co-opt some of the Shii militias, notably the Badr army, a process extended to Sunni groups after his departure. His view at the end of 2004 was that the United States was neither winning nor losing. Even so, he dissented from what he viewed as an overly pessimistic CIA report in December 2004.[70] The CIA representative, Robert Richer, was bitter about this: "he pulled his punches rather than frankly convey the peril of Iraq's situation. Negroponte didn't call it like it is. He wants to be secretary of state." He tried at times to use Richer as a foil for bad news: "no one would give a dissenting view. If you do, you are ostracized."[71] He supported an amnesty designed to partially undo the effects of Bremer's overwide "de-Ba'athification" but, with an eye toward the politics of Washington, opposed any amnesty for anyone who had assaulted or killed American troops.[72]

Contrary to Richer's assumption, Negroponte had Earle prepare a long memorandum, whose pessimism and long time frame was not well received by the president: "to be more exact, he's after the election on Sunday."[73]

> [Negroponte] talks about something he has learned in the Third World: change requires time, it can't all be rushed. 'His focus is on the next five to ten years.' 'This is not getting better', he says, "It's getting worse. His judgment is cool to the point of being chilling. He has seen huge national efforts—Vietnam—not work. This might not work either. He wants to get that message to the top. Our policy is failing."

Negroponte wanted the memorandum to

> describe what we can and should do, in concert with the Iraqis and the international community over a recognizable time frame, let's say five to ten years... make it about the Iraqis. What's their role.... What about [the lack of Iraqi] banking. Think of the corruption and theft that invites.

He does not find time oppressive because it is the only dimension in which trial and error can resolve practical and psychological complexities into change."[74]

> The worst thing is when you try to bumper sticker people. Give them room to develop their own thoughts within the larger scheme of your analysis. Just give it two or three years. It isn't only the physical work, it's the set of social relations, normalcy, stability. Engineers can't fix this country. You need them but they're not enough. That's the mistake. Time, Robert, time.[75]

The memorandum called for "patience and persistence. As an order of magnitude, five years is the right time frame for its crucial, initial phase." It began with a fairly blunt declaration:

> Democracy is possible in Iraq, but Iraq is a postconflict failed state. Every key sector—from health to education to transportation to water, electricity, and oil—is run down and dilapidated.... Some goals are being met (in Najaf and Fallujah, for example) but far from all.... We are still thinking about the problem at hand in terms that were rough estimates, not based on dynamic ground realities, when they were proposed. This insurgency and foreign terrorism... will remain an enemy of freedom and democracy in Iraq well beyond... the election of another Iraqi government.... At a minimum, we need to make a comprehensive, five-year commitment... public confidence and support is crucial, especially in the area of intelligence.

"Iraq's security forces are still in their fledgling state. Few of them have independent capability."

> We should ... get on with building an upper-echelon command structure, responsive to civilian authority. That's as important as anything we can do in the field of military training; it needs more emphasis than that currently assigned to it. A substantial IMET [International Military Education and Training] program is in order, with training in the states, and perhaps elsewhere. This challenge will impose fewer demands on us in five years if we get things right now, given the current state of Iraqi Security Forces.

The inadequacies of the South Vietnamese General Staff provided the obvious background for this recommendation.

The memorandum called for "reducing US military presence in a way that will facilitate our training equipping and mentoring role while also providing Iraq with a sense of strategic reserve." It did not urge a "surge," matters not having reached the parlous state they did two years later.

It also urged "additional regional security arrangements, perhaps through the Gulf Cooperation Council, that make its non-aggressive, self-defense security posture fully transparent." The declassified memorandum's only redacted sentence, probably dealing with Iran, followed here.

In a stillborn suggestion, the memorandum urged a NATO (North Atlantic Treaty Organization) role in Iraq: "Iraq is an anomalous necessity in the NATO sphere now because it actually lies in the heart of the global War on Terror."

The experience of European Union (EU) countries with centralized police forces led Negroponte to suggest "that we should explore the EU's active involvement in the critical police dimension of Iraq's security efforts."

A diplomatic noninterference pact among Iraq's neighbors was suggested. These internationalizing measures, almost all stillborn, could be carried out "without the Security Council's further blessing."

As for economic aid, Negroponte thought the World Bank should lead with respect to the agriculture sector, a suggestion not favorably viewed in Washington. He gave priority to modernization of the banking sector. Further,

> Given the damage and disruption the insurgency has caused to our reconstruction program, over the five year time frame envisioned additional reconstruction funds will be required. We have to do as good a job in stimulating the international donor community as we have done in the foreign debt reduction effort. Iraq ... is a failed state, and a big one.

"Iraq's democratic future and its political identity will be fought out around two poles: federalism and Islamism. These poles are not necessarily antithetical. Each will have to be present."

> [W]e are in a deep hole with the Iraqi people. They hold us accountable for not delivering better services, more security, and a swifter reduction of forces.... The sources of this antipathy run deeper than our engagement here, however. Victimization and helplessness are endemic themes in this part of the world, spawning hopeless dependency at one extreme and terror at the other.

This plan … will begin driving the insurgents and terrorists out of the political, economic and social space—as well as the geographic space—they
seek to colonize through violence …. We will need all five years to get that
dynamic on track and rolling …. But if we are clear and explicit enough it
will not take five years to enlist more help in this mission … more international involvement is critical. Otherwise we won't be deriving maximum
benefit from our investments and sacrifices to date while losing our foot-
ing not only in Iraq but the global War on Terror at large.[76]

The memorandum precipitated a visit from a delegation including Secretary of
State Condoleezza Rice's counselor Philip Zelikow and Ambassador Richard Jones.
This may have accelerated Negroponte's departure from Iraq. Earle said of the visitors: "this boarding party is CPA redux." Negroponte issued a mission statement
before the group's arrival, though the mission statement purposefully avoided
urging greater foreign involvement in reconstruction. Earle had urged involvement of the French, Germans, and Russians, described by Negroponte as "all my
negative friends at the U.N." Earle urged that "their contractors would have come
here; they would have been attacked; and they would have told Paris and Berlin
and Moscow to protect them." "Too late for that now," Negroponte said, although
there is no reason to think that he did not join in Earle's view of the "huge diplomatic blunder Bush made in this largely unilateral war."[77] Earle's suggestion that
Iraqi agricultural development be confided to the World Bank was met by Zelikow
with the observation that "the United States is the world's leading agricultural
exporter and the Department of Agriculture wants to be a bigger player here."[78]
    Negroponte believed that the chief problem was violence in Baghdad, which
might be "dampened down, over time."

    with the adequate deployment of Iraqi and US forces, with the continued
    efforts to train and improve the Iraqi Security Forces, particularly, their
    army …. I would hope that our forces can take more of a support role and
    training role and fall more into the background.

During most of his tenure, four-star General David Petraeus was in charge of
training the Iraqi army, in which capacity he got mixed reviews. On returning to
the United States, Petraeus drafted the much-praised Counter-Insurgency Field
Manual and displayed a MacArthurian mastery of press relations.
    Negroponte stated that

    getting out, just leaving, seems to me not to be an option … one of the
    risks then would be that it would become a safe haven for al-Qaeda to
    carry out its plans to spread Islamic extremism, its version of Islam to other
    parts of the Middle East and then to Western Europe and elsewhere and
    use it as a platform. That's what [was said] in [a] famous letter to Zarqawi
    [militant Islamist] about 1.5 years ago.

Negroponte was to return to this letter as a theme in later congressional testimony given while he was Director of National Intelligence,[79] and again in a
speech given while Deputy Secretary of State.[80]

The large embassy under construction costing $700 million was large because "a lot of people at the Embassy are security personnel … it was also important that we get out of the Republican Palace … which is of course symbolic of the past Iraqi history." At the time, it was said that 2,500 of the 3,700 embassy employees were security personnel, and 500 were members of the CIA.[81] An inspector general's report in 2005 noted that Negroponte as ambassador had signed off on personnel size estimates in October 2004, and found the estimates of 731 US personnel in 2007–8 and 461 US personnel in 2010–12 to be justified. The estimate for the earlier period included 187 regional affairs officers and 280 training officers; the latter were to be phased out over time.[82] As for "de-Ba'athification," his approach differed from that of his predecessor Paul Bremer "we're focused at the moment and the Iraqi judicial system is focused on the worst offenders." Negroponte was leery of a purge of schoolteachers, professors, and doctors. He did not oppose the execution of Saddam, given that there were "some Sunni extremists … under the illusion that they may be fighting to bring Mr. Saddam back to power."

Blackwater

Negroponte did not find Baghdad an agreeable assignment, notwithstanding the intensive security supplied by Blackwater, the embassy's private security contractor. This included 36 personal protection specialists, two K-9 teams, and three MD 530 Boeing helicopters with pilots. In one instance, an Italian journalist was killed by guards at a temporary roadblock erected because bad weather forced him to drive rather than fly to a meeting with General Casey.[83] Negroponte's secretary was photographed wearing a helmet and flak jacket while working in the Green Zone, and he was said to have remonstrated against the high-handed treatment of Iraqi civilians by his bodyguards. The conditions of his life were described by Robert Earle:

> His movements will be unpredictable. He'll send his car ahead in a convoy as if he were in it and follow later in a little helicopter. He'll make arrangements to meet in one place and then arrange through separate channels to meet elsewhere … he'll always be followed by a security detail and he'll never walk into a room before the security detail has checked it out, even his own office …. If his security team follows him too closely or gets rough with by-standers, he'll press his hands palm down and say "Please" in a way they don't ignore.[84]

A less-than-sympathetic account of the Blackwater contingent declared that they were

> loaded to the hilt with pistols and M-14s, chiseled like bodybuilders and wore tacky wraparound sunglasses … looked like caricatures, real, life action figures, or professional wrestlers. Their haircuts were short and they sported security earplugs and lightweight machine guns … ran Iraqi cars off the road or fired rounds at cars if they get in the way of a Blackwater convoy.[85]

Blackwater abuses were evident even at the time of Negroponte's confirmation hearing, where apropos of private contractors, he said "I don't know the full extent of my responsibilities, but I will find them out."[86] An inspector general's report in January 2009 recommended greater supervision of Iraq security contractors, who were exercising "inherently governmental functions," while finding that "The security footprint…is a legacy of the Coalition Provisional Authority period."[87] The humility of American contractors had not been enhanced by a blanket immunity from Iraqi law given them by Bremer in CPA Order 17.

A happier memory came about when Negroponte heard an unusual amount of gunfire at night and visited a monitoring post equipped with TV screens and monitored by seven or eight Blackwater personnel. The screens disclosed an unusual number of Iraqis running about discharging weapons. "What's going on?" Negroponte inquired. "Iraq defeated Portugal, 4-3," was the reply.

Later, as Deputy Secretary of State, Negroponte was to negotiate an agreement with the military leaving State Department security contractors under State Department jurisdiction and immune from extraterritorial criminal punishment: Defense "won't hire them, they won't fire them," while at the same time requiring 24 hours' notice to the military of personnel movements by contractors and limiting use of force to that "reasonable in intensity, duration and magnitude." The agreement required annual training of contractors, and required them to withdraw when encountering force; it was vague on the ultimate legal accountability of contractors, the two departments agreeing to work together to establish a framework.[88] As part of the reaction to Blackwater abuses, Negroponte replaced the State Department's director of diplomatic security.[89] He did not address a larger menu of reforms suggested by a critic of military privatization several years before Blackwater's time in Iraq:

> The currently high monitoring threshold for notification of pending contracts should be lowered…the Military Extraterritorial Jurisdiction Act could be expanded to include the activities of US based Private Military Forces (PDF) and/or PDF employees who are US citizens working abroad, regardless of their client. Presently the Act only applies to civilian contractors working directly for the US Department of Defense on US military bases; it does not apply to contractors working outside US facilities, those working for another US agency (such as the CIA) nor to US nationals working overseas for a foreign government or organization…. market-based sanctions are also not a sufficient deterrent for controlling actions by individual PDF employees.[90]

An human rights group criticized the agreement as falling

> far short of US military "control" over or even effective coordination of non-DOD [Department of Defense] private security contractors, does very little to address the issue of impunity, and only highlights the extent to which the mission of private security contractors (PACS) has become dangerously intertwined and confused with our military missions.[91]

The difficulty arose from the fact that the protection of civilian employees and contractors was not part of the military's assigned mission; security costs therefore accounted for 16.7 percent of contract prices.[92]

Some of the enhanced American training for Iraqi security forces was alleged to involve "Special Forces teams to advise, support, and possibly train Iraqi squads, most likely hand-picked Kurdish Pashmerga fighters and Shii militiamen to target Sunni insurgents and their sympathizers." This was referred to by Negroponte's traditional critics as "the Salvador option," although it was acknowledged that to the extent this approach was initiated, it predated his arrival.[93] The allegations were dismissed by him as "utterly gratuitous." Following his departure, and with the rise in influence of General David Petraeus, American efforts could no longer be characterized as anti-Sunni; they were devoted to building up neighborhood security and appeared directed toward an ultimate federal solution of the sort urged by former Ambassador Peter Galbraith and Senator Joseph Biden.

Departure from Iraq

"I've got to get out of there. I want to get out of Baghdad as soon as possible," he is said to have told a colleague, according to a *New York Times* story, though he denies such a conversation. "They want me to come back for something, but I want to do the private sector."[94] His commitment to President Bush was for one year, though his wife, with three teenage children, one at home, on hand, was not sorry to have him home sooner, particularly since Negroponte had had a heart episode while in Iraq. In an interview with George Stephanopoulos in January 2005, Negroponte, in a much-quoted statement about the possible American response to an Iraqi government request for withdrawal of troops, declared:

> Well, none of them have done so, so you're asking me a hypothetical question. But I think the basic answer to your question is that if, at some point, the government of Iraq decides that it no longer believes that our forces are necessary here for their own security, we will comply with that wish. That's made clear, actually, in Security Council Resolution 1546.[95]

That provision had been included in the resolution at the insistence of the French. The resolution had the effect of abrogating the interim constitution, with its guarantees to the Kurds; it almost certainly also abrogated the continuing effect of Bremer's decrees, or empowered the new Iraqi government to do so. Earle observed that "Negroponte won't sign on to anything as provocative as various proposals for creating a Kurdish state."[96]

The elections had been accompanied by a Sunni boycott; Ali al-Sistani's Shii allies had 140 of 275 seats, the Kurdish Alliance 75, and the secular Iraqi 40. Sunni representation was negligible. According to former US Assistant Secretary of State for Inter-American affairs Bernard Aronson of the State Department, "before the election Negroponte defeated a plan to send consultants to head off too big a victory by Shiis. Negroponte 'had the courage to say no,' arguing that American meddling could undermine the legitimacy of the vote."[97] In Robert Earle's words: "His strong preference is to see if the Iraqis can do it on their own...resisting those who were eager for him to settle things by playing king maker."[98] He found the UN election office under a Colombian, Carlos Valenzuela, extremely helpful in organizing the elections. Election Day began with eight or nine car bombs in Baghdad, but thereafter Negroponte was heartened by the lines at the polls he observed from a helicopter. Cell phones made a major difference; early voters informed their friends that it was safe to vote. In an interview with John Simpson of the British Broadcasting Corporation on January 21, 2005, Negroponte declared: "We have not provided assistance toward the election of any specific slate or candidate"; he also again stressed that Resolution 1546 stated that the Anglo-American "mandate could be ended sooner if requested by the government of Iraq." He declined to take a position on the much-disputed question as to the number of civilian deaths since the beginning of the war.

There was wrangling over ministries in the transitional government, not resolved until after Negroponte's departure in March 2005; his successor, Zalmay Khalizad, an Afghan-American who had signed several of the neoconservative manifestos in the runup to the Iraq War, did not arrive until late June; his appointment was reportedly delayed by administration displeasure at statements contradicting policy. In the intervening period an overburdened James Jeffrey had to perform the two jobs of ambassador and deputy ambassador; it was said, "the new government was busily packing its ministries with Shia militiamen and writing a constitution that would enshrine Islamic law and increase the centrifugal forces in Iraq."[99] Khalizad did not escape criticism: "Khalizad had three deputies. Three. He had no bench. Plus Khalizad loved to negotiate.... His staff didn't have the depth or the talent to execute assignments."[100] Khalizad was seen as being a temperamental "lone ranger"; under his tenure, the situation in Baghdad steadily deteriorated.

> While Negroponte was content to allow the Iraqis to make their own decisions, however long it took, Khalizad tried to intervene in the constitutional negotiations. There was little he could do, however, since he had no votes in the committee; he simply ended up with his fingerprints on the murder weapon of Iraq's united future. As a Sunni himself, Khalizad's efforts were interpreted as hostility by some Shia Arabs. Sunni Arabs would have been won over only by success...to Khalizad's activism goes the final great miscalculation of this period...Khalizad backed by Washington pressed the Iraqis to finish on schedule. With no time for compromise, the Shia Arabs and Kurds did the only thing they could, outvote the Sunnis and write their own constitution.

> "The diplomats with long experience in discussing and contending with the world's most intractable political morasses were the social Darwinists with respect to Iraqi politics and sovereignty...strategic success in Iraq would only arrive as a result of serial Iraqi tactical failures.[101]

Negroponte's tenure produced creditable statistical benchmarks. Electrical production when he came was 3621 MW, as against a prewar level of 4,075 MW; on his departure, it was 4,262 MW, falling to 3,475 MW by the time of the departure of Zalmay Khalizad. Oil production was flat during his tenure. Iraqi forces increased in number from 87,000 to 171,300. The number of land lines surpassed prewar levels; the number of mobile phones increased more than fivefold, to 2.422 million; it was to nearly quadruple again during Khalizad's tenure. Eight hundred and eighty three American soldiers lost their lives during Negroponte's tenure, as against 862 previously and 1,503 in the somewhat longer tenure of Khalizad. Although only $366 million of reconstruction funds had been spent when Negroponte arrived, when he left nine months later, 1/3rd of the funds had been disbursed and 3/4th of them obligated; 1,000 projects had been completed and there were 1,000 under way employing 180,000 Iraqis. The Inspector General for Iraqi Reconstruction credited Negroponte's regime with "short-term results in support of a counter-insurgency campaign.... Investment in Iraq's security forces began to pay dividends." The first two lessons of Iraqi reconstruction according to the Inspector General were the two stressed by Negroponte: "Security is necessary.... Developing the capacity of people and systems is important." Another military commentator declared that it was "striking to see Casey and Negroponte essentially fill what had been a policy and strategy void with a defined course of action after arriving in Baghdad." The course defined included elimination of terrorist safe havens and a focus on the 14 leading cities in the runup to the elections.[102]

Later Assessments

For Negroponte, the low point in Iraq came well after his departure, with the bombing of the Samarra mosque in February 2006. He considered Iraq to be in a terrible mess during his tenure, notwithstanding the fact that he is fondly remembered by at least some Iraqi politicians. Looking back in 2009, he observed

> I hope it doesn't fall apart once we leave, but it sure is a lot better than people expected a couple of years ago. We were all holding our heads ... after the bombing of the Samarra mosque That was terrible. The sectarian violence that ensued in Baghdad was just—tragic. And alarming. Somehow we weathered that.[103]

In March 2009, he observed "my nightmare [is] that we get out too quickly and sort of pre-emptively give up."[104]

In April 2006, Negroponte told the National Press Club that there were by then 100 functioning Iraqi battalions, as against not more than two or three upon his arrival in Iraq in June 2004. In a speech to the US Chamber of Commerce's National Security Business Forum in July 2006, Negroponte acknowledged that opportunities for American business in Iraq was quite limited, except for construction, engineering, and security. Later, in a speech at the John F. Kennedy School of Government at Harvard University, in December 2006, Negroponte was to recognize that "Many Sunnis view the Shia as Iranian controlled and regard the current government as predatory," while expressing the view that Iraq now had "a democratic constitution that could allow Iraqis to settle their differences peacefully." The final elections in December 2005 had likewise been a disaster for the secular parties; the Shii groups had 128 seats, including 32 held by Sadr's faction, the Sunni groups 55, the Kurds 53, and Allawi's secular grouping 25.

> It was only after Allawi and Ahmed Chalabi did so badly in the election on December 15, 2005 (Chalabi did not win a single seat) that the US seems

to have appreciated the weakness of the secular anti-Saddam leadership which it had cultivated for so long.[105]

This was a charge that might have been good against Khalizad but not against Negroponte, who had recognized the fact of Shii dominance. Chalabi, it was said, was "detested by the CIA and the State Department."[106]

In September 2006, the administration released excepts from a previously leaked report on Iraq concluding that terrorists were "spreading in number and geographic diffusion…the underlying factors fueling the spread of the movement outweigh its vulnerabilities and are likely to do so for the next five years."[107]

In January 2007, testifying before the Senate Intelligence Committee as part of the Annual Threat Assessment, Negroponte conceded there was currently a greater presence of Al Qaeda in Iraq than before the war. He "wouldn't say there's been a widespread growth of Islamic extremism beyond Iraq." He also gave the assessment that "Iran doesn't want Iraq to fall apart" though it had recently adopted "a more aggressive posture." These statements, in response to Democratic questioning, cannot have delighted the administration. Nor did they pass unnoticed; commentator Bruce Hoffman observed

> In contrast to both long-standing White House claims and the prevailing conventional wisdom, the Annual Threat Assessment presented by Negroponte to the Senate Select Committee on Intelligence painted a disquieting picture of a terrorist movement on the march rather than on the run.[108]

However, Negroponte also reiterated the administration view that "a precipitous withdrawal could lead to collapse of security forces" and again referred to the intercepted Zawahiri letter announcing a design to acquire terrorist sanctuaries first in Iraq and then in the Levant. He told the corresponding House committee that Iraqi oil output was below prewar levels, that there was serious inflation, no progress in securing an agreed sharing-out of oil revenues, and severe power shortages.

Later, in 2008, Negroponte stated that in March 2005 on his departure from Iraq he had estimated that it would require five years for Iraqi security forces to be strong enough to stabilize the country without the use of US fighting men.[109] In December 2007, in a press conference in Baghdad after visits to nine locations in eight days, including Basra, Fallujah, and Ramadi, he indicated that American support of Sunni "Awakening" personnel was not intended to give rise to another militia. He saw benefits from a new Iraqi pension law, deflected questions about Blackwater by reference to an Federal Bureau of Investigation examination of abuses, and welcomed an enhanced role for the UN refugee organization and temporary postponement of a referendum on the status of Kirkuk promised by Article 140 of the Iraqi Constitution.[110] One writer on the problems in the Balkans and Iraq arising from the Versailles conference has foreseen

> a return to…small, ethnically and religiously homogeneous micro states…small people today are by no means weak anymore. New tactics of terrorism and new weapons of mass destruction have equalized the balance between small and large.[111]

The problems of oil sharing and mixed populations in Baghdad and Kirkuk have hindered fulfillment of such a vision in Iraq, though there has already been ethnic separation through massive refugee flows. Negroponte considered that the final resolution would be the product of political bargaining among the newly empowered Iraqi politicians, not an American-imposed solution of the sort sought to be fostered in different ways by Bremer and Khalizad. This vision, though not capturing the imagination of Washington, is being fulfilled by events.

Negroponte's counsel in Iraq was the counsel of realism. Security must precede "nation-building"; as the great Judge Learned Hand put it, few things have done more to bring people from the abyss than the habit of acquiescence to the law as it is. The character of a nation's government cannot be determined or enforced from abroad; it will reflect habit and history and ultimately must be negotiated among a nation's political actors. All that foreigners can do is provide a short framework for such discussions and tests of strength. Negroponte shared adviser and diplomat George Kennan's view that even despotic rulers have "as Gibbon once pointed out, a certain identity of interest with those who are ruled." He also held the view that military force could not be used lightly, or inserted with an eyedropper, and that its collateral effects on opinion were more important than its direct effect on territory and resources. The creation of political institutions required time and mutual accommodation. Negroponte exhibited courage in defying the desire of both the Defense Department and congressional Democrats for a rushed exit while separating himself from neo-conservative advocates of a permanent American imperium, recognizing the authority of the Iraqi government to require withdrawal of the occupiers.

Negroponte, in his role as Director of National Intelligence (DNI), was present at the meetings deciding on a "surge" but was not a policy advocate. The promoters of the surge were President George W. Bush himself and General Petraeus. Negroponte thought that the improved conditions in Iraq were at least equally due to the growth in the number of trained Iraqi soldiers and to new financial support of the "Sunni Awakening."

At the close of Negroponte's tenure in Iraq,

> In his office in Baghdad he had a very serious photo of him with Bush with their arms around each other looking very stoic and then next to it there's a photo of him and his wife with plastic spy glasses and a plastic spy beard, also very fitting for his new job—a very disarming sense of humor.[112]

On the announcement of his appointment as DNI, his brother Michel, with whom he frequently argued about politics, sent a telegram to his brothers John, Nicholas, and George: "Do you think if Mom had been nicer to John, we would have this problem?"

19

DIRECTOR OF NATIONAL INTELLIGENCE

While the Houses were employing their authority thus, it suddenly passed out of their hands. It had been obtained by calling into existence a power which could not be controlled. In the summer of 1647, about twelve months after the last fortress of the Cavaliers had submitted to the parliament, the parliament was compelled to submit to its own soldiers.

— T. Macaulay, *The History of England from the Accession of James I*
(London: E. H. Butler, 1849), 91

As Director of National Intelligence (DNI), Negroponte took on a highly responsible job in which he almost certainly would have been made a scapegoat for any successful terrorist episodes. His task was to construct and regulate new institutions, although he was accorded limited budgetary powers and being subjected to willful obstruction by the Defense Department. In a period of institutional threats to civil liberty, he successfully insisted that incarceration of terrorists take place subject to the constraints imposed by the military or civil justice systems, and he encouraged congressional legislation in this sphere. Pitched turf battles and difficulties with some members of Congress rendered this a less-than-happy assignment but one that created useful institutions dealing with open intelligence and interagency cooperation, as well as the training of intelligence staff.

As DNI, Negroponte said in December 2006 that he expected to serve for the remainder of the Bush term until January 2009, an expectation not realized. Bush had told him on his appointment that "this will be the capstone assignment for your career."[1] Bush had said that he was looking for "a work horse, not a show horse"; the position had been offered to Robert Gates, who declined it; others mentioned included General Tommy Franks and former Governor of New Jersey Tom Kean.[2] Negroponte had been shortlisted for the World Bank, a position that went first to Paul Wolfowitz and then, following Wolfowitz's embarrassing departure, to Robert Zoellick.

At his confirmation hearing, Negroponte was lauded by Senator John D. Rockefeller IV of West Virginia as "a tough and disciplined man with self-esteem and with the willingness to make decisions and to tell truth to power."[3] He was confirmed on May 18, after pledging to be assertive in his relations with the Department of Defense and warding off the familiar criticisms of his service in

A Sign of Bureaucratic Growth: The President's Cipher Clerk in 1900

Honduras,[4] having previously arranged for Patrick Kennedy and Mary Margaret Graham (who he had earlier known as the CIA station chief in New York) to be his two deputies and for David Shedd to be his chief of staff. These appointments were controversial among the more extreme neoconservatives: Graham was said to be "a staggering appointment for one who had barely cut her teeth in the clandestine service" and it was said that Porter Goss' staff "suspected [her] of being at the center of personnel leaks"; she was also denounced for revealing the total amount of spending on intelligence, surely a matter that should be public knowledge in a democracy[5] and that had been the subject of general disclosures during the Clinton administration. He also brought in Thomas Fingar, who had been intelligence director at the State Department and who had dissented from the National Intelligence Estimate (NIE) relating to Iraq's possession of weapons of mass destruction; Negroponte selected him in part to "make a statement." Other principal appointments included Army General Ron Burgess who had been head of intelligence (G2) for the Joint Chiefs of Staff and who later served as head of the Defense Intelligence Agency (DIA) in charge of requirements or customer requests, Ambassador Kenneth Brill as head of the National Counterproliferation Center, and Scott Redd, a retired admiral, as head of the National Counterterrorism Center and Ben Powell as his counsel. At his confirmation hearing, Negroponte was asked about his willingness to disclose the total budget, such disclosure having been called for by the Senate version of the bill. His response suggested that Graham's disclosure may have been an authorized one: "The President made clear his opposition to declassification of the aggregate intelligence budget. If confirmed, I would always be willing to study any issues of concern to the Congress and discuss the results of my efforts

Appointment as Director of National Intelligence

with the President."[6] He also quite bluntly told the Senate committee that "Our policies in the Middle East feed Islamic resentment."[7]

The most rabid member of the neoconservative group, the journalist Kenneth Timmerman, who during a 2000 Maryland Senate campaign urged American overthrow, inter alia, of the governments of Egypt, Iraq, Iran, Pakistan, Syria, and Saudi Arabia, accused Negroponte of operating "a refugee camp for those who have not been happy with this [George W. Bush] administration."[8]

Negroponte had played no part in the drafting of the statute creating the Office of National Intelligence (ONI), which, like the statute creating the perhaps equally misbegotten Department of Homeland Security, had been a congressional initiative. Later, he referred to it as the product of a "demand for political expediency at the expense of deliberation," while voicing doubt that the intelligence community could survive another reorganization.[9] The administration "could've made the old system work," there were "five or so key agencies," and it "comes down to personalities."[10] He "believe[d] in playing the cards I'm dealt" and wanted to "take the first six months of next year [2007] to look at what changes we might recommend."[11] He later spoke of "distancing myself some-what from the idea" and said that the administration, which accepted the idea.[12]

He saw the need to build up human intelligence and analytic capability, which had been degraded at the end of the Cold War, and envisaged a 5- to 10-year building process. Because his tenure lasted only until February 2007, this process was not complete upon his departure. Later, he expressed regret about the splintering of intelligence operations into more than a dozen agen-cies, which he saw as an impulse to White House staff control of intelligence. Fewer agencies might have strengthened cabinet government, which he pre-ferred to the "imperial presidency" dominated by staffers who were not directly responsible to the Senate.

The columnist Georgie Anne Geyer declared that his appointment meant "a profound re-emphasis on pragmatic intelligence, a downgrading of the neocon cult and a most welcome rise and return of the old professionals"; Professor Anne-Marie Slaughter of Princeton University, referring also to the appoint-ments of Robert Gates as Defense Secretary and Robert Zoellick to the World Bank declared that he was one of "three seasoned moderates for important positions."[13] Another writer noted that Negroponte began with "no office, no staff, no budget.... He's never worked the political angles. But in this kind of job, he'll need political backing. This isn't just diplomacy any more."[14] The legislation creating the new office, however, expressly freed it from National Security Council and White House staff control: it "shall not be located in the Executive Office of the President." Another commentator, though describing Negroponte as "shy, introverted, and brilliant," observed "The Honduran job gave him the reputation in some circles of being a conservative stalwart. He was not...someone who was about to 'break the china' as Goss was doing."[15] The legislation creating the DNI job sought to grease the way for appointment of Goss as DNI by waiving the requirement of Senate confirmation in the event of promotion of the current CIA director; the president did not take the bait.

Shortly after assuming his post Negroponte was presented with a road map for reform by the Robb–Silberman Commission appointed to investigate the intelligence failures before the Iraq War. Unlike many national commissions, the commission did not focus on muckraking but produced a long and constructive report with 74 recommendations, 70 of which were implemented by Negroponte. However, Silberman, who became socially friendly with Negroponte, was dis-tressed that Negroponte took into DNI the existing intelligence community man-agement staff at CIA, which Silberman thought was staffed with bureaucratic discards. Silberman would also have preferred to see a smaller DNI office, modeled after that of the Joint Chiefs of Staff, composed of officials temporarily seconded from agencies and rewarded with promotions on their return.

Initially, Negroponte's office was in the Old Executive Office Building in the White House compound; then in a building across the street next to Blair House, and then at Bolling Air Force Base, the agency ultimately moving into more purpose-built headquarters near Tyson's Corner in Virginia. Bush told him that General Michael Hayden would be his deputy, Hayden's condition being a fourth star. He focused on integrating the work of the 16 intelligence agen-cies.[16] Negroponte regarded as one of the most important accomplishments of

Negroponte and Family: 2005

the first year and a half of his tenure as being the strengthening of a National Counterterrorism Center, the director of which

> hold[s] a video teleconference with all the different agencies, three times a day, every day to compare notes about the latest threat information that's come in. There's a video teleconference at eight in the morning, at one in the afternoon I think or at three in the afternoon and again, at one in the morning, every single day.[17]

Negroponte had a staff of about 1,250; the agencies were estimated to have 100,000 employees and a budget of $44 billion.[18]

Negroponte was also instrumental in creating an Open Source Center to improve the analysis of publicly available information.[19] This used both internal research and contracts and subscriptions with organizations like Oxford Analytica, which synthesized research on current international problems by some 1,500 academics and independent scholars. For George Kennan, this should be the core function of any intelligence agency:

> scholarly study of the rest of the world, and of what's happening in the world generally on the basis of legitimate sources. We discovered many years ago, those of us in the Russian field, that when we made such a careful study of conditions in Russia in the way that any other scholar would—on the basis of material that was available to us in legitimate ways, either in the press, or through legitimate sources of observation—as a rule we knew much more than do the gumshoe agents who try to find out things through secret operations.[20]

Kennan also noted in the first volume of his memoirs that the most valuable course he took at Princeton was one in economic geography. Negroponte was very taken by the economic geography course he took in the first semester of his freshman year at Yale. The trade scholar Jagdish Bhagwati has noted that "university departments of geography have been increasingly shut down and fewer graduates in the subject are available to teach geography in schools."[21]

As a means to foster cooperation among agencies, the first-ever community-wide security badge was introduced. FBI agents were assigned to take the basic course given by the CIA to its own agents. Service outside one's home agency was rendered a prerequisite to promotion for intelligence executives. A National Digital Intelligence Library was created. Ninety CIA agents were assigned to the new National Counterterrorism Center, which had at least a dozen persons on hand at all hours of the day and night. He was later to deplore a 20 percent staff cut for the Center in the Intelligence Authorization Act of 2010. A Summer Hard Problems Workshop was instituted, and global futures partnerships were entered into with private-sector actors to investigate particular long-range problems. "What I found were a lot of people with pent-up frustration that said we need some change."[22]

The CIA proved unexpectedly reluctant to accept its role in coordinating all human intelligence, whereas the FBIs new counterintelligence section was slow to get off the ground. There was also a lack of uniformity in personnel policies, some agencies, for example, required polygraph tests whereas others did not.

In September 2005, Negroponte told the International Association of Chiefs of Police "A loss of confidence in government is the second wave of any terrorist attack. Mitigating the impact of that second blow is essential." Later in the same month, he urged upon the Joint Military Intelligence College the importance of the study of languages, particularly Chinese and Arabic: "interest in that was a bit stronger in my generation." A joint initiative including the State and Defense Departments was begun to support high school teaching of critical languages; it has made modest headway. In February 2006, he more soberly reflected on the nation's declining relative position, alluding to "competition for energy, the gap between rich and poor [nations], drug trafficking, and pandemics."[23]

In April 2006, he spoke before the Anti-Defamation League, and expressed some general views about Islamic terrorism, seeing it as

> less to drive America out [of the Middle East] than to provoke mainstream Muslims into buying into their political ideology...we should not think of the Muslim world as one thing—it is not. Communism was ostensibly universalist; jihadism is in fact exclusionist.... [It is] not backed by an enormous military machine, as was communism.... By contributing to efforts to improve the lives of the economically disadvantaged, we succeed where the terrorists fail. By ignoring insults...refusing to change the way we go about our daily lives, and most importantly, by choosing not to be afraid, we can make sure that the terrorists lose.... [It is] an ideology that perverts a great religion.

This sort of rhetoric was not forthcoming in this period from any other Bush administration spokesman; administration language tended to overstate the terrorist threat, as with the color-coded alert levels disseminated by the Department of Homeland Security. Sir Robert Thompson years earlier had described terrorism as a weapon of the weak, going so far as to declare that the outbreak of terrorism in Saigon "would be an admission of defeat" by the Vietcong.[24] Negroponte did not view the threat of subway bombings by suicide bombers as in any sense an existential threat, elsewhere declaring that "a terrorist attack using a WMD is less likely than a conventional attack and would be far less lethal than a WMD attack carried out by a state."[25]

Elsewhere, however, Negroponte gave greater credence to the suggestion that Al Qaeda was a movement with more focused political objectives: he repeatedly referred to a memorandum from Zawahiri to Zarqawi the authenticity of which has been a matter of some dispute, in which the writer cautions against attacks on Shias and methods, such as beheadings, that incite revulsion and goes on to urge: "do not rally except against an outside occupying enemy, especially if the enemy is first Jewish and secondly American,"[26] the objective being said to be the expulsion of Americans from Iraq, domination of its Sunni areas, subversion of neighboring Sunni states, and ultimately an attack on Israel.

Organizing an Agency

In an op-ed published in September 2006, Negroponte pointed to some major achievements: The majority of those who organized the 9/11 attacks had been captured or killed. The Counterterrorism Center and Counter-proliferation Center had been brought together at one location. Thousands of FBI personnel had been given new access to the Counterterrorism Center's secret-level database. One hundred joint terrorism task forces had been set up, as had state and regional fusion centers, and efforts were being made to fuse these into a national network. The National Clandestine Service had been established, as had a WMD innovation fund. What was unfortunately not discussed were the limits and safeguards imposed on these developments.[27] The Clandestine Service remained under the CIA as a result of a White House decision; the Silberman–Robb commission had wanted it moved to the National Counterterrorism Center and National Nonproliferation Center.[28] Although the improved coordination provided by the National Counterterrorism Center was necessary and welcome, the explosion in the size of federal law enforcement and intelligence agencies is less so, each now employing about 100,000 persons. Nearly 40 years earlier, the author had helped instigate successful opposition to drastic expansion of the federal criminal code, cautioning against chartering a national police force[29] and echoing Justice Robert Jackson's warning that "the potentialities of a federal centralized police system for ultimate subversion of our system of free government is very great."[30]

In October, Negroponte defined the new intelligence problem presented by "loose dynamic networks that form and dissolve rapidly to accomplish their goals." The events of 9/11 was said to be "the cardinal public event of your collective lifetime," on a par with Pearl Harbor and the fall of the Berlin Wall. He lauded adoption of a merit pay system, making pay depend on "how well you perform, not how long you've been around." In November, in a speech to the Overseas Security Advisory Council, he pointed with pride to the appointment of an information sharing environment program manager and of a civil liberties protection officer and noted that his chief information officer was a position of sufficient importance to require confirmation by the Senate. In a speech at the Kennedy School of Government at Harvard University in December 2006, Negroponte referred to the problems presented by "rapidly expanding and poorly integrated enclave immigrant Muslim communities" in Western Europe, and urged that new migrants be formally welcomed and that efforts be made to educate them in the values of tolerance, freedom of religion, and freedom of speech. Asked whether he felt that public confession of past errors by the government was useful, Negroponte said "I think that is very situationally dependent." Asked about Vice President Cheney's alleged "1 percent doctrine" justifying suppression of risks of terrorism, he urged "a measured view—in fact the appropriate one, rather than one based on exaggerated fears." The most important factor in the nonoccurrence of terrorist incidents after 9/11 was "having gone on the offensive…a factor that I would cite as the most important one." Asked which of his jobs he found most interesting, he said that "Ambassador to the UN [was] one of the most interesting if not the most interesting…negotiating Security Council resolutions is extremely interesting." As for assassination of terrorist leaders, "if you can capture them alive then I think that is the preferable course if only for the intelligence value you would get."

Warning on Science and Language Education

In a speech before the Woodrow Wilson International Center for Scholars in Washington, DC, on September 25, 2006, Negroponte lauded a report, *Rising Above the Gathering Storm*, recently issued by the National Academy of Sciences, the National Academy of Engineering, and the Institute of Medicine under the chairmanship of Norman R. Augustine, the former chief executive officer of Lockheed Martin, decrying the inadequacy of American education in science and technology. Negroponte noted that foreign graduate students receive 34 percent of American doctoral degrees in the natural sciences and 56 percent of those in engineering. As for American undergraduates, only 15 percent took degrees in science-related subjects, as against 67 percent of the same cohort in Singapore, 50 percent in China, 47 percent in France, and 38 percent in South Korea. The American balance of trade in high-technology goods had swung in a short time from a positive balance of $30 billion annually to a negative balance of the same dimension. When, shortly thereafter, I attended a Bush administration White House briefing for heads of state-level think tanks, I alluded to the concerns expressed by the DNI and inquired as to why the administration had allowed the proposals inspired by the Augustine Report to die a quiet death in Congress. The response I received from a White House economic aide included the observation that the DNI's remarks were "beyond his job description."

Negroponte had also spoken of this subject a few days earlier before the Oxford Analytica International Conference. He alluded to the rise as industrial powers of China, India, Indonesia, and Brazil and noted that rapid economic progress usually derived from "investment in integrating and applying new technology, as opposed to investing in new technology." Technology, he said, "has left the traditional linear discovery path and moved onto the exponential curve of Moore's Law." Radicalization, he noted, "can arise out of severe socio-economic alienation in even the most advanced democratic states." During the question-and-answer period, when asked about Guantanamo and CIA deten-tions, Negroponte said he was "happy that the whole issue—the detention of these terrorists—has come out in the open and been the subject of discussion before our legislature." This happiness was not universally shared within the Bush administration.

In January 2007 at a press conference, Negroponte outlined further improve-ments: Collectors and analysts of intelligence were being encouraged to work together. There was greater intelligence sharing with allies such as Britain, Canada, and Australia.[31] The president had promulgated guidelines on intelli-gence sharing and an implementation plan had been promulgated. Recruitment of employees focused more on ethnic groups and on persons with competence in languages and natural sciences. At Negroponte's confirmation hearing, he had noted that "the language skills, for example, in the CIA are substantially lower than those you would find in the State Department, for example."[32] In making these not-inconsiderable changes, Negroponte had done something to speak to the concerns of Roger Morris, one of his former colleagues on Kissinger's staff on Vietnam, who had resigned at the time of the Cambodia incursion (and who was, by improbable coincidence, one of the writer's college roommates during the first term of his freshman year):

Changing the system in the law firm, the company, the State Department or Pentagon would have to wait for the power that eventually came with playing the game carefully. The problem for too many, though, was at the top, convictions were somehow more expendable than ever, compromise more necessary. And there was never quite enough power or time to change the way it all worked. By middle age, bureaucratic politics was after all one of the most familiar and predictable elements in the lives of such men. The crippling force of the organizational ethic was familiar enough in other areas of American life, but few critics saw its pervasive frequently decisive influence on the nation's foreign policy. Men who had mainly earned selection by an experience that discouraged intellectual rigor were called to deal with problems of immense complexity and rapid change. To manage and master a bureaucracy of legendary recalcitrance presidents called principally on an elite of bureaucrats whose distinction derived in large part from their tractability.[33]

Presidential Briefings

Negroponte participated each morning from 8 to 8:30 in the briefing of the President when he was in Washington; these were not one-on-one briefings, including also "the Vice President, the Chief of Staff Mr. Joshua Bolten and Mr. Stephen Hadley, the National Security Advisor, so there's six of us in the room every morning" including a DNI official designated to present the day's briefing.

He told the National Press Club in April 2006 that he "began serving as principal adviser to the President on intelligence matters on my first day on the job."

> I read the material that's going to be presented to the President and some-
> times, although not very often, have some comments of my own as to the
> suitability of the material … I get an advanced copy of it the night before,
> so I read it then and then I usually give it another read just an hour or
> so before the President is briefed at eight o'clock in the morning to make
> sure that I've got the facts at my fingertips.[34]

We "try to make sure that the threats are evaluated as well as they possibly can
before we surface them … to try to make sure that people don't overreact to particular situations." This role was previously performed by the head of the CIA,
former Congressman Porter Goss, a former classmate of Negroponte at Yale,[35]
who is said to have resented being replaced in this capacity.[36] Some thought
that Negroponte perceived himself as chief analyst more than manager and that
he devoted too much time to the presidential briefing function. The Silberman–
Robb commission had been explicit in saying that "we do not believe that
the DNI ought to prepare, deliver, or even attend, every briefing." The briefing process, however, allowed Negroponte to exert a moderating influence on
administration policy toward terrorism, its earlier reactions having verged on the
hysterical when a handful of American citizens were detained for some six years
without formal hearings of any kind.

Negroponte was credited with forcing and fostering long-delayed presidential decisions on intelligence matters. Just before Negroponte's appointment,
a national commission had criticized the quality of the daily briefing given to
the president and had stressed the need for noting of dissenting views in it.[37]
Negroponte insured that the briefings included non-CIA sources and a separate
daily threat assessment.[38] Defending his role in a CNN interview in December
2005, Negroponte said that the two hours per day that the briefings and preparation for them required were well spent. Of President Bush, he observed

> He took his briefing very seriously…. It was kind of hard to tell Mr. Bush
> much he didn't know. He knew all these leaders very well—he placed a
> great deal of value on his personal relationships…. [He is] a very smart
> man.[39]

In this period, I commended to Negroponte the reflections on terrorism in a
book published 50 years earlier, Vannevar Bush's *Modern Arms and Free Men*:

> there is a fascination in fear. There is a vortex that surrounds the con-
> cept of doom. When there is stark terror about, men magnify it and rush
> towards it. Those who have lived under the shelter of a wishful idealism
> are most prone to rush into utter pessimism when the shelter fails. No ter-
> ror is greater than the unknown, except the terror of the half-seen…. Fear
> cannot be banished, but it can be calm and without panic, and it can be
> mitigated by reason and evaluation.

I presented John with my copy, after removing all indicia of original ownership, and suggested he pass it on to whomever he wanted. There was a bit of
reproachfulness in this; as the former Counterterrorism Coordinator Richard
Clarke later observed: "careful analysis could have replaced the impulse [of
the Bush administration] to break all the rules...this zeal stemmed in part from
concerns about the US presidential election."[40]

Warrantless Eavesdropping

Negroponte was involved in controversy over a program of warrantless eavesdropping embarked on by the National Security Agency without recourse to the
FISA court established during the Ford Administration on the recommendation
of Attorney General Edward H. Levi. Negroponte stated that briefing on the
program had been confined to the leaders of the Senate and House and of the
Intelligence Committees from both parties—eight congresspersons in all—by
direction of President Bush and Vice President Cheney. In fact, only four of
the eight, the intelligence committee persons, had been briefed, as Negroponte
acknowledged in a letter to Speaker Hastert in May 2006.[41] The program assertedly involved recording of the origin and destination of calls in the manner
of a pen register, not listening to their substance, permitting Negroponte to
contend "This was not about domestic surveillance...[it] was about dealing
with the terrorist threat in the most agile and effective way possible." The
Foreign Intelligence Surveillance Act (FISA) court had granted a blanket warrant
authorizing pen register recording not including the substance of calls. Admiral
Hayden was said to have been reluctant to disclose the fact that "most international communications pass through US switches, rendering them vulnerable to
NSA's eavesdropping."[42] Negroponte stressed that the program "involves monitoring telephone calls—international telephone calls—these are not domestic
telephone calls—where at least one end of the phone conversation takes place
outside the United States." Asked by Senator Russell Feingold whether there
were other "intelligence collection" programs that had not been revealed to the
full Intelligence Committees, Negroponte avoided a misleading denial: "Senator,
I don't know if I can comment on that in open session."

In May 2006, more details emerged about the eavesdropping program.
Negroponte had described it three days before a congressional hearing as
"about international terrorism and telephone calls between people thought to
be working for international terrorism and people here in the United States."
It was disclosed that the majority of domestic call records had been accessed,
leading to the charge that administration witnesses had been "parsing their
words with care and limiting comments to the portion of the program that had
been confirmed by the President in December." It was also asserted that Deputy
Intelligence Director Hayden had argued against a proposal by Vice President
Cheney for eavesdropping not authorized by the FISA court on domestic telephone calls and emails.[43] Negroponte also was said to have resisted eavesdropping on US citizens.[44] The issue is said to have involved follow-on investigations
of persons who had taken part in international calls. Taken in all, Negroponte
was much less perturbed about irregularities involving wiretapping than those
involving alleged torture. It has been clear since the advent of the automobile

that Fourth Amendment protections apply only in an attenuated way to those who call to their aid modern techniques of transportation and communication.

Negroponte's testimony in January 2007 in connection with the 2007 threat assessment likewise was not a model of candor. Asked whether all surveillance was under the statute and not under claimed inherent presidential power, Negroponte said this was the case "as far as the program that was described to you by the President of the United States." Pressed further, he said: "If you're referring to the program that we have described here—I'm not aware of any other. All the activity of NSA will be conducted under the Executive Order 12333 or from FISA court warrants." Negroponte had been instructed by the White House to avoid discussing wireless interceptions. A program relating to monitoring of certain bank transfers was subsequently revealed; it was not explained why either that program or the "pen register-type" program, recording phone numbers dialed by an instrument, should have come as a surprise to any reasonably imaginative terrorist. In July 2007, Negroponte contradicted statements of Attorney General Alberto Gonzales that the warrantless surveillance program had not been discussed at a meeting in March 2004.[45] He was usually a skeptic about exaggerated claims for secrecy, taking the view that in Washington, most matters would ultimately be disclosed.

Torture and Detention

Another inherited controversy involved what Negroponte's successor admitted were well-founded allegations of "waterboarding" and torture of certain Arab prisoners previously held by the CIA at secret locations, including one in Poland. There had been no "waterboarding" since 2003, before Negroponte's arrival. As a result of a report by the Inspector General of the CIA, John Helgerson, issued in May 2004, CIA Director Tenet had ordered earlier methods halted.

In November 2005, it was stated that

> US Intelligence czar John Negroponte reportedly has opted out of the Bush administration's effort to exempt the CIA from an anti-torture bill. Negroponte dodged the issue during a meeting last month with Senators. "It's above my pay grade," he said. Negroponte also declined to answer senators' questions on whether torture could ever produce useful information.[46]

In September 2006, Negroponte published an op-ed article in *USA Today* urging Congress to apply to CIA interrogations standards "mirroring the Detainee Treatment Act...well established in US law as determined by US courts": "we must ensure our laws provide clarity on the vague standards contained in Common Article 3 [of the Geneva Conventions] such as 'outrages upon personal dignity.'" At his confirmation hearing, Negroponte noted that the DNI

> legislation directs that the Director of the CIA report to the office for which I have been nominated.... I would expect the DNI would oversee all such activities at the strategic level...not only is torture illegal and reprehensible, but even if it were not so, I don't think it's an effective way of producing useful information.[47]

The language of the Detainee Treatment Act prohibited all agencies from utilizing "cruel inhuman or degrading" techniques prohibited by the 5th, 8th, and 14th amendments to the Constitution, as defined in the US Reservations to the UN Convention Against Torture of December 10, 1984; additionally, the Department of Defense was denied "any treatment or technique of interrogation not authorized by or listed in the US Army Field Manual on Intelligence Interrogation." Negroponte also sought legislation to ensure that "sensitive intelligence sources and methods…are not provided to the terrorists themselves," a problem in light of the Confrontation Clause of the Sixth Amendment.[48] In an interview with Fox News, Negroponte noted that the CIA at that time held no prisoners, they having all been moved to Guantanamo Bay in the summer of 2006 but continued to push the administration position after the Supreme Court decision in the *Hamdan v. Rumsfeld* case, which held that Common Article 3 of the Geneva Conventions was violated, applying the Third Geneva Convention to all detainees that statutory "clarification" was required, even though it had not been provided in the conflict with the Vietcong. Terrorism "was a different kind of war [involving] illegal enemy combatants." The *Hamdan* ruling, he said had curtailed interrogations: "the tough techniques may be kind of problematic because of the uncertainty introduced." The Fox interview was later quoted out of context by the commentator Mark Thiessen to imply that Negroponte had furnished a blanket endorsement of the techniques previously used by the CIA;[49] Negroponte did say that CIA questioning was "one of the most valuable, if not the most valuable source of human intelligence with respect to Al Qaeda," but the full interview makes clear Negroponte's receptivity to congressional restrictions codifying and limiting permitted techniques.[50]

In late 2006, Assistant Attorney General Steven Bradbury issued an opinion allowing virtually all the disputed techniques save waterboarding. In February 2007, the State Department's legal advisor, John Bellinger, who before 2003 had approved the disputed techniques but had had a change of heart, reportedly threatened to resign if the techniques were reinstituted. The transfer of CIA prisoners to Guantanamo is said to have been the upshot of an National Security Council (NSC) meeting in mid-August 2006 attended by Bush, Cheney, Rumsfeld, Condoleezza Rice, Hadley, Hayden, Bolten, and Negroponte in the Roosevelt Room of the White House; Rice favored and Cheney opposed closing of the sites.[51] In July 2007, after the departure of Negroponte as DNI, President Bush decided to keep the sites open, although no one was then confined in them, and new guidelines were issued for the CIA prohibiting forced nudity and curtailing sleep deprivation; Secretary Rice disassociated herself from this decision without opposing it. The CIA detention facilities were abolished by the Obama administration two days after it took office, and in April 2009 a direction was issued that the physical facilities be disposed of. The Bradbury opinion was withdrawn; shortly before leaving office, Bradbury himself withdrew several opinions issued by his predecessors.[52] Negroponte's view was that incarceration was appropriately a military or Justice Department function, not one for the intelligence agencies; if the CIA did it "Justice and military are off the hook."

When the requested statutory "clarification" was forthcoming, it was immediately vitiated by a so-called presidential signing statement by which the administration asserted the right to continue to engage in practices not authorized by Congress pursuant to a theory of presidential "inherent power." This theory had been presaged by the controversial assertions of the Lyndon Johnson administration about its authority to engage in the Vietnam War.[53] Senators John McCain of Arizona and John Warner of Virginia thereupon issued a statement in response to the signing statement: "The Congress declined when asked by administration officials to include a presidential waiver of the restrictions included in our legislation. Our committee intends through strict oversight to monitor the administration's interpretation of the new law." Senator Lindsey Graham of Florida, another cosponsor, issued a stronger statement: "I do not believe that any political figure in the country has the ability to set aside any…law of armed conflict that we have adopted or treaties that we have ratified."[54] In February 2008, the administration's compliant Acting Assistant Attorney General Steven Bradbury stated that the statute had changed the previous legal position, that the administration did not currently engage in waterboarding and that he had not determined whether the new statute prohibited it. At the same time, the administration threatened to veto an even more explicit prohibition of the practice. In January 2008, Negroponte confirmed that waterboarding had been used after 9/11, but said that "waterboarding hasn't been used in years. It wasn't used when I was DNI nor even for a few years before that."[55] Negroponte's perception was that "Bush and Cheney weren't going to change things beyond certain limits." He regarded the vociferous opposition to policy changes sought by the Obama administration as the product of concern by some members of the outgoing administration about possible criminal and other liabilities.

The sweeping nature of the claims of presidential authority had been forecast in the last published writing of George Kennan, a letter in *The Washington Post* for March 25, 2003, written at the age of 99,

> I am extremely concerned about the shameful, almost total passivity of Congress during the period of preparations for our military attack on Iraq. Congress' inaction is a dangerous precedent in executive-legislative relations. In light of this precedent, future Presidents will be tempted to seize virtually dictatorial powers under the title of commander-in-chief, and nothing in our history rules out the possibility of their yielding to that temptation. This seems to be the meaning of the recent crisis.

The most damning refutation of the Bush administration position on these matters is found in the writings of Sir Robert Thompson, one of the architects of British strategy in Malaya and a consultant to the Nixon administration on the Vietnam War. In 1974, Sir Robert had written

> Prisoners of war are held…to prevent them from fighting again and such detention is a humane alternative to their being killed or enslaved as in earlier times. Enemy civilians are also interned for the duration of the war not necessarily for anything they may have done, but to prevent them committing any hostile act…Even citizens of the country

itself who have committed no treasonable act but are considered to sympathize with the enemy may be detained

[T]he problem of charging a person in court is obvious. Some of the sources of evidence may be delicate from an intelligence point of view and require to be safeguarded as being of more value in the future rather than being blown to secure one conviction. To some extent the problem can be solved by making it a criminal offence to be caught in certain circumstances where only the factual evidence at the time of arrest is enough to secure a conviction...carrying arms, ammunition or explosives without a license, breaking a curfew...such harsh laws have to be used sparingly and chiefly against hard core terrorists known to have committed bestial acts against the civilian population...a government must be seeking eventual reconciliation with the main body of terrorist supporters. This is unlikely to be achieved by a policy of wholesale revenge through hangings and heavy prison sentences...

The decision whether to charge in court or to detain is an executive act, as is any order of detention itself which is made under powers approved by the legislature. Detention is not a sanction. The original order may be for a certain period, but it can be reviewed or renewed on the merits of each case.

A successful policy will depend almost entirely on the treatment not only of those who surrender but also of those who are captured or arrested, because the distinction may easily be blurred by terrorist propaganda.... This general approach by the government, quite apart from moral considerations, eliminates any question of torture or harsh treatment as being completely counter-productive.... I have always argued very strongly against the use of terror or torture or indeed of any act not sanctioned by law.[56]

Eight years earlier, Thompson had addressed questions of procedure in greater detail:

If the power to arrest and detain is clearly laid down within certain limits and the individual is given a full opportunity to appear, represented by counsel, before a tribunal presided over by a judge which advises the government whether the case against the detainee is adequate then there are sufficient safeguards to prevent the power being used for purely arbitrary arrests. It should be the firm policy of the government [to bring] all persons who have committed an offense to public trial...showing that justice is being done...spotlighting the brutality of terrorist crimes.

Trials in camera, martial law, and military tribunals can never be satisfactorily justified. They are in themselves a tacit admission that responsible government has broken down. In the long term adherence to the law is a great advantage to the government. It helps to make all officers and civilian officials responsible and accountable for their actions. It puts torture and the shooting of captured terrorists in their proper place; however great the provocation, both are crimes and the latter is murder.... It puts the government in a position in which it is represented as a protector of those who are innocent and it puts the terrorists in the position of criminals.[57]

Notwithstanding these cautionary words, detainees, including some American citizens, were denied any hearings at all, even administrative hearings, for periods sometimes exceeding seven years, and there were "disappearances" of "enemy combatants" at CIA sites. "Inherent powers" were asserted and rights of legislative and judicial supervision were denied. The classic response to those who would put "terrorists" beyond legal protection was that given by the arch-conservative British parliamentarian J. Enoch Powell on the occasion of deaths in custody in Kenya in 1957:

In general, I would say that it is a fearful doctrine which must recoil on the heads of those who pronounce it, to stand in judgment on a fellow human being and to say "Because he was such and such, therefore the consequences which would otherwise flow from his death shall not flow." Nor can we ourselves pick and choose where and in what parts of the world we shall use this or that kind of standard. We cannot say "We will have African standards in Africa, Asian standards in Asia and perhaps British standards here at home". We have not that choice to make. We must be consistent with ourselves everywhere. All government, all influence of man on man rests upon opinion. What we can do in Africa, where we still govern and where we no longer govern, depends upon the opinion which is entertained of the way in which this country acts and the way in which Englishmen act. We cannot, we dare not, in Africa of all places, fall behind our once highest standards in the acceptance of responsibility.[58]

Similar statements had been made by Lord George Curzon, Viceroy of India, about the administration of justice in India[59] and by Winston Churchill during the House of Commons debate on the Amritsar massacre.[60]

At a hearing in February 2006, Negroponte echoed some of the administration's rhetoric:

We assess that should the jihadists thwart the Iraqis' efforts to establish a stable political and security environment, they could secure an operational base in Iraq and inspire sympathizers elsewhere to move beyond rhetoric to attempt attacks against neighboring Middle Eastern nations, Europe, and even the United States.[61]

In the same month, Negroponte told the Marine Corps Intelligence Association that the CIA had detained and questioned a small number of high-value terrorists:

"questioning is consistent with US law, subject to congressional oversight, and scrutinized by the Department of Justice." The last two statements were literally correct; the "oversight" involved disclosure to the four Congressional leaders, not the full complement of the intelligence committees, and the Justice Department in the notorious Bybee Memorandum, signed by Assistant Attorney General Jay Bybee in 2002, which was later withdrawn at the instance of Assistant Attorney General Jack Goldsmith, had blessed almost any conceivable tactic and was to do so again in memoranda approved by Acting Assistant Attorney General Steven Bradbury not released until April 2009. It was later acknowledged by Negroponte's successor in early 2008 that waterboarding had been applied to three of those questioned; it is virtually impossible to make the case that this was "consistent with US law," although it was clear that it had been authorized by the president and vice president. Officials like Negroponte and, after him, Attorney General Michael Mukasey, went through contortions denying the obvious to avoid incriminating the leaders of the government during their terms of office. Negroponte warned against any destruction of records of interrogations;[62] it was later confirmed that the CIA had destroyed 92 such records,[63] and in November 2010 a special prosecutor, John Durham, announced that there would be no resultant prosecutions.

Of a piece with this was Negroponte's acquiescence in the administration's redefinition of the objectives of his agency as including "fostering the growth of democracies," an interventionist rather than defensive mission,[64] although he was at pains to deny that it gave "new authority to undermine" foreign governments.[65] However, he was insistent on evidence, ordering a special study on terrorism's influence on Iraq.[66] Unlike the neoconservatives, Negroponte avoided careless language about "Islamofascism," stressing the importance of the debates among Muslims about the future,[67] and warned against efforts to demand the impossible of the Pakistani government.[68] He was charged, however, with "hyping" the discovery of an alleged "network of Islamic extremists" in Lodi, California.[69]

Turf Battles with Defense and Justice

John Negroponte was involved in some large and important turf battles, with mixed results. At his confirmation hearing, he made clear that "the Director of the CIA will report to me, as the law states and as the President also reaffirmed."[70]

[Y]esterday there was a reference to an effort to bring together the different intelligence components of the Pentagon and have them all report through Under Secretary [Stephen] Cambone with regard to dealing with the DNI. I see my authority under the law in no way will preclude my ability to deal directly with such agencies as the NSA, the National Reconnaissance Office and so forth.[71]

The DNI was given a voice in selecting the head of a new National Security Division of the FBI and was given influence over about a third of the FBI budget.[72] In June 2005, the president rejected a recommendation of the Silberman–Robb

Commission that would have allowed the Pentagon to conduct covert operations.[73] After great pressure from Secretary of Defense Rumsfeld, this judgment
was later quietly reversed. In October 2005, both the FBI and the Pentagon
were permitted to gather human intelligence; the DNI's role was limited to the
setting of rules to limit interagency conflicts.[74] The justification for this on the
part of the Pentagon was the need to "prepare the battlefield." In anticipation
of this grant of authority, a "special operations command" under General Bryan
O. Brown had been established by Rumsfeld in March 2004; by March 2006,
there were "special operations" troops attached to a dozen embassies.[75] More
ominously, the Pentagon enlarged its intelligence activities in the United States
as part of a new misleadingly entitled "Northern Command," mining databases
and tracking antiwar protests, while allegedly only "receiving" rather than "collecting" intelligence.[76] A counterintelligence field activity rapidly acquired 290
analysts, more than the 200 at the State Department; it was ultimately shut down
and its functions transferred to a defense counterintelligence and human intelligence center in August 2008.[77] The 2006 Intelligence Authorization bill gave the
Defense Department some access to FBI databases, but it required approvals by
the DNI and reports to Congress.

Proposals for a domestic intelligence agency on the lines of Britain's MI-5
were, however, rebuffed in favor of reorganization of the FBI; the objections
to these proposals were well set out in a letter written by former FBI Director
Louis Freeh,[78] responding to an article by Judge Richard Posner of the US Court
of Appeals for the Seventh Circuit in Chicago in *The Wall Street Journal*.[79]
Negroponte had been given authority to reassign 100 Defense Department intelligence personnel; Rumsfeld then issued an order purporting to require the con-
currence in these reassignments of Stephen Cambone, the Assistant Secretary
of Defense for Intelligence. "We look at these people as intelligence people,
and the Secretary [Rumsfeld] certainly looks upon these as DOD [Department of
Defense] folks," Negroponte observed.[80]

Replacing Goss and Boeing

In May 2006, Negroponte became more assertive. Porter Goss was ousted
at Negroponte's instance as head of the CIA, as was his military deputy and
his third in command, Kyle Foggo. Goss' ouster had also been urged by federal judge Laurence Silberman, cochairman of the commission investigating
the intelligence failures before the Iraq War and by members of the Foreign
Intelligence Advisory Board. Goss, who had once proclaimed: "I don't do personnel," was perceived as being in over his head. Foggo had been under
investigation by the FBI and the CIA inspector general because of his friendship with military contractors implicated in a congressional bribery scandal.
Goss had resisted the firing of Foggo. General Michael Hayden was installed
as head of the CIA and Stephen Kappes, a veteran official who had been
in eclipse under Goss, became his deputy.[81] Goss was said to have never
had a strong relationship with Bush because of an "inability to master details
of intelligence activities"; there had been a great deal of personnel turnover
under Goss' tenure, including the replacement of the head of the clandestine
service, two deputies, and a dozen department heads.[82] Another account laid

Goss' departure to two causes: conflict with Negroponte, who wanted the lead analytical role to be played by the DNI's office, who wanted the CIA to focus primarily on human spying, and who was annoyed at Goss' recalcitrance at assigning agents to the Counterterrorism Center and Goss' failure to comply with a Negroponte ultimatum to fire Foggo, or leave himself. The FBI was said to be investigating allegations that a lobbyist "threw poker parties attended by prostitutes at the Watergate Hotel for members of Congress and top-ranking CIA officials. Foggo has acknowledging attending the poker games but denied anything improper occurred."[83] He later pled guilty to an indictment. Goss felt that Negroponte was micromanaging the clandestine service, "wants all my people," and "maintained a regal manner."[84] Negroponte was said to have indicated to the White House that Goss had signaled an intention to leave at the end of 2006, prompting his inclusion in the wave of replacements of personnel sought to be carried out at one stroke by the new White House chief of staff, Josh Bolten.[85] At a press conference announcing the change, Negroponte said: "Porter had talked for some time about the possibility of leaving public service … had talked about himself being a transitional leader."[86] Negroponte thought that Goss displayed poor judgment in purging Kappes and a colleague who Negroponte viewed as the most experienced people in the agency, and in temporizing rather than dealing with the Foggo situation. He was also more than annoyed at Goss' noncooperation in providing analysts for the new National Counterterrorism Center, which Negroponte viewed as the linchpin of the office of DNI. Nonetheless, Negroponte did not enjoy the Goss episode, both because of his former friendship with Goss and because of the attacks on him in the press inspired by Goss and his supporters. The departure of Michael Hayden as Negroponte's deputy also made his job more difficult.

Negroponte also took a keen interest in the spy satellite program, a $25 billion project that was five years behind schedule, and $5 billion over budget, reallocating an important contract covering half the project relating to telescope-like electrical lenses from Boeing to Lockheed.[87] Boeing had no experience with spy satellites and had previously been allowed to monitor its own contract. The Boeing contract was said by Director Kennedy to be "killed, dead, buried, stake in the heart."[88] The reallocation was opposed by Boeing's congressional protectors, including Congresswoman Jane Harman of California.[89]

Negroponte introduced important safeguards into the preparation of National Intelligence Estimates, requiring that all the participating agencies voice confidence in the sources used.[90] CIA station chiefs were instructed to forward copies of their reports to the DNI.[91] Thomas Fingar, a State Department official who had dissented from the much-criticized prewar NIE on Iraq was placed in charge of a new estimate of conditions there. This was done both to "make a statement" and because Negroponte held him in high esteem.

Iran and a National Intelligence Estimate

On his appointment, Negroponte was the subject of sardonic comment by the Clinton servitor Sidney Blumenthal, who observed that the "discrepancy between the reckless record of John Bolton and the anodyne promises of John

Negroponte is not the only factor that points to [Bush's] cognitive dissonance." Blumenthal continued with what he thought were a series of rhetorical questions with negative answers:

> Has the administration commissioned an NIE for military options against Iran? Has the new DNI, John Negroponte, assured the intelligence community that its objectivity and integrity will be protected from any political pressure? Will the DNI prominently raise caveats from intelligence analysts where there are disagreements? Will any new NIE be shared with Congress in a timely fashion before any debate of any action is undertaken?[92]

In February 2006, Negroponte earned the displeasure of the neoconservatives by publicly expressing the view that Iran was at least five years away from being able to produce nuclear arms,[93] though there was a possibility that it could acquire them from another country. On April 20, he told the National Press Club that "we believe that it is still many years off before they are likely to have enough fissile material to assemble into, or to put into, a nuclear weapon; perhaps into the next decade." In June, he told the BBC that estimates were that Iran would have a nuclear bomb "between the beginning of the next decade and the middle of the next decade." He reiterated this in a National Public Radio interview on September 1. The interviewer asked him "four and ten years from now" and Negroponte responded "Five to ten years from now." He said with assurance that Israel's more pessimistic assessment of two years was not based on different data, but that the Israelis "will give you the worst-case assessment." In September, he told Oxford Analytica that "Our intelligence community assessment is that Iran is determined to acquire a nuclear weapon I think for state purposes, not to make any of those materials available to non-state actors." In December 2006, at the Kennedy School, he declared that Iran "probably has not produced or acquired sufficient fissile material." On December 3, 2007, after his departure as DNI, a formal National Intelligence Estimate, concurred in by all 16 intelligence agencies confirmed this view; after leaks to the press, a redacted version of the report was published, effectively terminating any rationale for military action against Iran during the remaining time left to the Bush administration:

> we judge with moderate confidence Iran probably would be technically capable of producing enough high explosive ordinance (HEO) for a weapon sometime during the 2010–15 time frame (IND [State Department Bureau of Intelligence and Research] judges Iran is unlikely to achieve this capability before 2013 because of foreseeable technical and programmatic problems). All agencies recognize the possibility that this capability may not be attained until after 2015. We judge with high confidence that Iran will not be technically capable of producing and reprocessing enough plutonium for a weapon before about 2015.[94]

Negroponte was later to say that this document "failed to communicate the requisite uncertainty."[95]

The neoconservatives charged that a Democratic congressional aide, previously fired by the White House aide Bill Luti, had gotten a copy from Negroponte's office, and hurled brickbats at several Negroponte appointees, including DNI deputy for analysis, Thomas Fingar, formerly head of intelligence and research at the State Department, who had committed the additional sin of opposing the confirmation of John Bolton as ambassador to the United Nations. Negroponte was annoyed by the leak, whose timing did not aid efforts to enhance European pressure on Iran.

This affair was described by the journalist William Pfaff as a virtual mutiny of the intelligence, foreign affairs, and defense bureaucracies, determined to ensure that no factual predicate existed for the Bush administration acting to go to war with Iran without further congressional authorization.[96] In February 2008, as Deputy Secretary of State, Negroponte reiterated the conclusion of the NIE: "it's only the work on the warhead that's stopped, not the missile and delivery system." After leaving office, Negroponte declared in March 2009 that Iran wanted nuclear weapons, and declared of his estimate of a date between 2010 and 2015: "I don't believe that that assessment has essentially changed." "I think that's what they want, I think that's what they're headed towards, I think that's what they're going to get."

> I think we can delay them through sanctions, through import restrictions, through working with other countries. But definitively stop them? Even if you used coercive means, I think it would be quite difficult by now.... Iran is a big country with a substantial scientific community [which has] aspired to nuclear capability since the time of the shah.[97]

The UN Disarmament chief, Mohamed El Baradei noted in his memoirs that Negroponte's view was in accord with that of the UN inspectors and that Negroponte repeated "this view in public, perhaps as a way to fend off the Israelis and hard-liners who were beating the drum for military action."[98]

Negroponte saw no appetite within the administration for a war with Iran, the administration having been chastened by the Iraq experience; by contrast, Dick Cheney, Donald Rumsfeld, and Paul Wolfowitz had been pressing for intervention in Iraq since immediately after 9/11. Vice President Cheney in his memoirs noted that "The NIE itself precluded us from considering as robust a range of options as we might have otherwise considered.[99]

In the same interview, he discouraged as a "provocation" a proposed Taiwan referendum on UN membership, and suggested that Taiwan's just grievances at the United Nations could be assuaged by Taiwan's making liberal use of UN provisions allowing participation by nonstate actors.[100]

Troubles with Congress

Negroponte had on several occasions found the need to fight off congressional criticism. After clamor from neoconservatives asserting that the CIA was suppressing evidence that Saddam Hussein actually possessed weapons of mass destruction,[101] Negroponte caused 48,000 relevant documents pointing to the opposite conclusion to be posted on the DNI website.[102] In April 2006, he was criticized by the chairman and the ranking member of the House Intelligence Committee for the alleged creation of a bureaucratic overlay above the intelligence agencies,[103] while Senator Susan Collins of Maine charged that he had not done enough to assert his authority over the NSA, the National Reconstruction Office, the National Geospatial Intelligence Office, and the National Counterterrorism Center.[104] In July 2006, a House Intelligence subcommittee released a bipartisan report decrying a lack of urgency in addressing "groupthink" and inadequate coordination among agencies. Senator Collins recognized, however, that Negroponte was under enormous pressure: "He can't afford to fail because the threats are too dire and the consequences too great."[105] Less respectable criticism came from the ex-Watergate conspirator E. Howard Hunt:

under Negroponte's watch, we have now failed to predict that Hamas would win the Palestinian elections and that Iran would be able to enrich uranium so soon…any changes made by Negroponte will take time to prove themselves.[106]

Another commentator observed:

One is tempted to conclude that Ambassador Negroponte discovered what many critics of the Intelligence Reform and Terrorism Act of 2004 had already sadly observed, that in terms of executive authority the DNI was little more than the old chief of the intelligence community staff with a few more medals and epaulets.[107]

A particularly egregious example of congressional sniping came when

the vice-chairman of the Senate Select Committee on Intelligence, Sen Rockefeller [said] the new national DNI has already failed his "first test," in addressing the vulnerabilities exposed by 9/11. But classification, says Rockefeller, forbids him from saying what that "first test" is.[108]

Departure from DNI

In February 2007, Negroponte was replaced as DNI and became Deputy Secretary of State.[109] The possibility of this change had been broached by Secretary Rice in May 2006; Bush did not want to make the change until a suitable replacement was found as DNI. Negroponte was perceived as being uncomfortable with his managerial responsibilities at DNI:

tilting too far toward [advising] would risk losing the time to manage: the preference that dogged Negroponte…. The DNI spends his days waiting outside the Oval Office for the President, trying to manage the community on his blackberry.[110]

Rice had not gotten along with Robert Zoellick as US Deputy Secretary of State; Zoellick had wanted to go to either Treasury or the World Bank and was appointed to the World Bank after the demise of Paul Wolfowitz. Negroponte received a call on New Year's Eve while on vacation in Naples, Florida, asking that he take the Deputy Secretary job and agreed to do so.

In the spring of 2006, Negroponte was not happy with his role as DNI. The controversy leading to Goss' dismissal had been personally wrenching, and he was at loggerheads with the Chairman of the House Intelligence Committee, Congressman Peter Hoekstra of Michigan. By the end of the year, Negroponte had reconciled with Hoekstra and expected to finish his term as DNI. His successor, Admiral Mike McConnell enjoyed Negroponte's confidence; Negroponte had unsuccessfully tried to recruit him as his deputy. McConnell, who had been head of intelligence for the Joint Chiefs of Staff during the first Gulf war, was also Cheney's candidate.

Shortly before leaving as DNI, Negroponte circulated a multipage directive to analysts admonishing that analysis "must be objective and independent of political considerations," "must be as transparent as possible," and "must identify intelligence gaps and provide precise guidance to collectors."[111] Only a month before this change was announced, Negroponte had given an interview to Walter Pincus of *The Washington Post*, who was perhaps more familiar with his career than any other reporter, indicating that he intended to stay on as DNI until the end of the administration, a possible effort to head off any change.[112] Two commentators speculated that he had "grown particularly weary of clashes with members of Congress"; and that he moved because he felt "barred from policymaking" as DNI.[113] The change drew criticism from Senator Jay Rockefeller, who declared "I think he walked off the job, and I don't like it" and from the intelligence commentator Robert Hutchings, who characterized the change as "quite irresponsible." Congressman Hoekstra was troubled by the fact that, by reason of his departure, the principal intelligence agency was all in the hands of military men; Senator Susan Collins expressed distress because he was "making progress."[114]

A later Inspector General's report issued in 2008 following Negroponte's departure found that between 2006 and 2007, the number of ODNI employees reporting a high level of respect for senior leaders declined by 10 percent and the number reporting satisfaction with their policies declined by 10 percent, suggesting that Negroponte's departure was not viewed as a positive development. The report also noted continued recalcitrance in cooperation among agencies. A Working Group established by Negroponte in 2005 to adopt uniform rules relating to collection of data on American citizens still had not formulated rules three years later. Similarly, a Negroponte request for a memorandum of understanding between the FBI and the Department of Homeland Security relating to the operation of Fusion Centers remained unsigned even after three years.[115]

Looking back at his experience as DNI, Negroponte wrote in 2010 that he deplored the later replacement of McConnell and Hayden as weakening the career ethos, and expressed the view that the DNI like the FBI Director should have a fixed 10-year term, though remaining removable by the President. He was in agreement with a July 2008 executive order resolving uncertainties by giving the DNI a voice in removal of agency chiefs. He noted the vexing lack of clarity as to whether the DNI's covert action authority extended to the conduct of operations and whether non-CIA personnel could be station chiefs, an issue on which the Obama administration sided with the CIA. He was skeptical about the value of national centers like the NCTC for assessing the behavior of state actors, which requires less tactical intelligence and more stress on "the quality of the analysts themselves, and necessitates a centralized focus on language training, foreign area studies, and the tradecraft of challenging preconceptions and communicating uncertainties."[116]

His appointment at State won general praise, except from the neoconservative militant Frank Gaffney, who foresaw a future of "insubordination" and "sabotage" of the Bush administration's campaign against Iran. A widely published interview and article by Seymour Hersh of the New Yorker alleged that Negroponte was displeased by back-channel funding of Sunni insurgents in Lebanon asserted to be aligned with Al Qaeda as part of an American effort to resist expansion of the "Shii crescent":

> Q. Your bottom line is that Negroponte was aware of this, obviously, and he wanted to distance himself from it? That's why he decided to give up that position and take the number two job at the State Department? A. That's one of the reasons, I was told. Negroponte also was not in tune with Cheney. There was a lot of complaints about him because he was seen as too much of a stickler, too ethical for some of the operations the Pentagon wants to run…. Negroponte was very sensitive to the [arms for hostages] issue that took place 20 years ago. He did not want a repeat of it.[117]

Negroponte had no personal animosity toward Cheney, who he viewed as a hard worker, but one with a fixed mind-set that screened out unwelcome information. The conclusion that Cheney had drawn from the Ford administration and the collapse in Vietnam was that executive supremacy was essential and that Congress was the enemy. Negroponte viewed the Vietnam failure as a function of a failure to be forthright with Congress and the public, and even the military, as to costs and benefits. Negroponte's staff had no high regard for Cheney's deputy Scooter Libby, who was viewed as overbearing and arrogant, as was Secretary Rumsfeld, who displayed little interest in intelligence briefings, which were frequently interrupted or broken off by him.

Libby, according to some of the testimonial letters presented at his sentence hearing on perjury charges, including that of Congressman Christopher Cox, had been the architect of the most far-reaching of the administration's "power grabs": an effort to effectively repeal the Posse Commitatus Act to allow the military to supplant state authority in the wake of terrorist outrages. This proposal, embodied in a "stealth amendment" to an annual Defense Authorization bill was actually enacted by Congress but was repealed a year later after protests from all 50 state governors; the administration tried to stave off repeal by vetoing one version of the repealing legislation.[118]

In another article, Hersh attributed to a former senior intelligence officer, now a Pentagon consultant the statement

> Negroponte said, "No way. I'm not going down that road with the NSC running operations off the books, with no finding." Negroponte shared

the White House's policy goals but wanted to "do it by the book." There was a sense at the senior ranks level that he wasn't fully on board with the more adventurous clandestine initiatives [and] had problems with this Rube Goldberg policy contraption for fixing the Middle East.[119]

He also did not adhere to the view that the problem of terrorism would be with us forever; it "doesn't have to be forever...out there for quite a while."[120] Negroponte had no personal difficulties with Cheney, whom he had known since a visit by Cheney to Vietnam while Cheney was a congressman from Wyoming. He regarded Rumsfeld's departure from the administration after the 2006 elections (which Cheney opposed) as something of a turning point. Rumsfeld, though personally charming, was anything but a good listener and frequently arrived at meetings without having read the underlying papers. Powell, who was asked to leave after the 2004 elections, was said to have bitterly resented Bush's failure to secure Rumsfeld's resignation at that time. Powell's failure to resign when Bush, against his advice, took the decision to go into Iraq, has been much criticized; in the course of the deliberations of the Iraq Study Group (the so-called Baker-Hamilton Commission), former Secretary of State Baker is said to have observed of Powell: "He's the one guy who perhaps could have prevented this from happening."[121]

Negroponte's departure as DNI was more commonly ascribed to frustrations arising from his lack of budget authority and affirmative pull from Secretary Rice and former colleagues at the State Department. The only condition that Negroponte attached to his acceptance of the job as Deputy Secretary was that Bush attend his swearing in, to dispel any impression of a lack of confidence; Bush did so.

Negroponte had no problem with quite far-reaching legislation relating to interception of communications and even relating to questioning of terrorists and the use of military commissions. But he also appeared to share three principles enunciated by Justice Jackson in response to threats of terrorism by totalitarian states far more powerful than Al Qaeda:

men have discovered no technique for long preserving free government except that the Executive be under the law, and the law be made by parliamentary deliberations...emergency powers are consistent with free government only when their control is lodged elsewhere than in the Executive that exercises them.... Procedural due process must be a specialized responsibility within the competence of the judiciary on which they do not bend before political branches of the government, as they should on matters of policy.[122]

20

DEPUTY SECRETARY OF STATE

Even England's experience in ruling subject nations will not enable it to
found and maintain a world empire and a world civilization like that of
Rome. The material interests and the national character of the peoples of
the earth are too discordant for this.

> — Count Johann von Bernstorff, "The New Diplomacy,"
> *Neue Frei Presse*, Vienna, May 30, 1920, reprinted in 306
> *Living Age*, 133 (July 17, 1920)

Liberal democracies, unlike tyrannies, by their very natures cannot generate continuous counter-frightfulness for any length of time, at least
in dependent territories. So it was in Palestine, in Cyprus, in Kenya, in
Batavia, in Algiers.

> — Isaiah Berlin, "Zionist Politics in Wartime Washington,"
> in H. Hardy (ed.), *Isaiah Berlin, Letters, 1928–46*
> (Cambridge: Cambridge University Press, 2004), 663, 689–90

At his confirmation hearings, Negroponte defended administration pressures on
Iran and was cautioned by Senator Barack Obama of Illinois: "We do not want
to see precipitous actions that have not been thought through, have not been
discussed, have not been authorized." He also acknowledged the existence of
problems in Latin America: "democracy is not necessarily delivering the kinds
of results that people had hoped for." He was praised by Senator Chuck Hagel
of Nebraska as "one of the pre-eminent diplomats of our time" and was also
praised by Senators Ted Stevens of Alaska and Joe Lieberman of Connecticut,
who appeared as witnesses. The hearings were interrupted by a heckler who
declared: "This man is not a man of peace. This man is not going to help get us
get out of Iraq.... This man is a war criminal...."

Negroponte agreed that violence in Iraq was increasing in "scope, complexity, and lethality." He declared a purpose to redeploy several hundred diplomats from Western Europe to less-developed nations, alluding to the value of
one-man posts such as the one he had once occupied in Hue. Asked whether
he considered that the United States had legal authority to attack Iran, he
dodged: the question put him in a "difficult position" vis-à-vis Secretary of

State Condoleezza Rice, "I'd be reluctant to substitute [my judgment] for hers." The United States should be "prepared to broaden our diplomatic activity if they were to take that first step of stopping their enrichment program." As for Latin America, Negroponte urged on Mexico more privatization of the oil industry: "how as a state-owned corporation can you mobilize sufficient investment?" At Negroponte's swearing in, President George W. Bush declared that he "understands the importance of fighting the extremists with all elements of national power." Amid laughter, Bush exhorted young Foreign Service officers to "get on his calendar so he can explain to you how best to do your job. I did the same thing." Bush declared "It doesn't hurt that he can play a mean game of poker." A reference to Negroponte's notoriety for card playing gained while at Yale. On assuming office, Negroponte exhorted younger diplomats to seek difficult posts in underdeveloped countries. He noted the limited time remaining to the administration: "there are big issues out there. But radical new departures? I think it would be unrealistic."[1]

At a conference on democracies in Mali, Negroponte cautioned, in language with some American as well as African resonance, against "leaders [who] have sought to use their mandate from the voters to eliminate checks and undermine democratic institutions. Democracy is rule by laws and institutions, not by individuals. It does not concentrate power in one person or office."[2] The United States is said to have downplayed the significance of the conference of the Community of Democracies, a Clinton administration creation, by withholding representation at the Foreign Minister level; it also insisted on representation of the Iraqi and Afghan governments, which in the final event did not come.[3]

It was said that Secretary Rice wanted to concentrate on North Korea, Iran, and Israel–Arab relations, and that "Negroponte could handle the rest of the globe."[4] Neither at Stanford as provost nor at the State Department was Rice famed for her interest in the details of administration. Her advent, and that of Negroponte, gave rise to greater moderation and greater coherence to American foreign policy, the strains of the Rumsfeld–Powell era being past. This ironically vindicated the observation of former Ambassador to El Salvador Robert White, no Reagan–Bush favorite, in 1992:

> The fatal mistake was made by Kennedy. The reason the NSC is powerful is because of its physical location. As long as there is another foreign policy center in the White House, then for all practical purposes the only solution to that is to have the Secretary of State always be the President's best friend.[5]

Negroponte joined President Bush on many foreign visits; Bush had a joking relationship with him and referred to him as "Ponte," a more respectful and dignified sobriquet than those given to most members of his administration.

Kennan and "Open Intelligence"

Shortly before his departure as DNI, Negroponte was presented with the George F. Kennan Award by the National Committee on American Foreign Policy. In his acceptance speech, he gave voice to some of Kennan's values, referring to Kennan as "the quintessential all-source analyst, a man of prodigious learning, bottomless curiosity, and absolute intellectual integrity." He noted Kennan's emphasis on confronting adversaries with "diplomatic, economic, and political strength": "At times he felt that the containment doctrine had become overly militarized. American intervention in Vietnam was a case in point." Kennan's career illustrated the importance of a "middle path" and provided a warning against the "fallacy of the single alternative." Kennan "mastered 7 languages"; he took "intellectual risks" and provided "challenges to conventional wisdom"; he gave weight to "deep-seated, often opaque, cultural and historical factors." His career, and particularly the famous Long Telegram, Kennan's reply to the US Treasury Department, showed that "field reporting, based on a broad frame of reference remains the critical backbone of intelligence analysis ... open source material, cultural research [and] on the ground study." The intelligence community, he declared, was "doing more than ever before to tap the expertise of outside intellectuals"; unlike the bi-polarity of Kennan's time, it confronted "greater flux, [a] plethora of dangerously empowered state and non-state actors."

Negroponte did not share Kennan's antipathy to what the elder statesman viewed as gratuitous intervention for humanitarian ends in Africa, urging greater Chinese involvement in Darfur and pointing with pride to America's AIDS programs and its role in Liberia and Sierra Leone. Kennan had condemned US intervention in Somalia before American troops were driven out, observing that Somalia's problems were "partly the result of drought, partly of overpopulation, and partly ... of the absence of any governmental authority. What we are doing holds out no hope of coming to terms with any of those situations."[6] Negroponte also visited several of the Francophone countries, including Mali and Cote d'Ivoire, and referred without apparent criticism to the US military's creation of a new Africa Command based in Europe,[7] though it has been said that he was deeply skeptical about this initiative.

Defending Iraq Policy

As Deputy Secretary of State, Negroponte wrote an op-ed piece defending the administration position opposing any deadline for troop withdrawals from Iraq: "deadlines would stiffen the obstructionists." He painted a rosy picture of developments in Iraq, asserting that "we are on track to double the number of provincial reconstruction teams from 10 to 20" and that 84 percent of reconstruction funds for 11 sectors had been spent. He conceded that "some key ministries like oil have not performed well," but contrasted the situation with that which had existed two years before when he arrived as Ambassador:

> the country had no permanent government, no Council of Representatives, no constitution, no IMF stand-by agreement, no hydrocarbon laws in draft or otherwise, no willingness to cut subsidies, no International Compact with Iraq, and no forum for constructive dialogue with its neighbors. Now all that exists .... Iraq has cut fuel subsidies, increased hard currency reserves to 18 billion dinars and mitigated currency pressures by appreciating the Iraqi dinar.[8]

Although he was an advocate of a continued commitment to Iraq, he was not among those urging that a "surge" of more troops be sent. The improvement in conditions in Iraq was in no small measure due to US financial support of some of the Sunni militias: to baksheesh, not bullets; and to training of Iraqi soldiers.

Latin America

In May 2007, Negroponte visited his former posting in Ecuador, which had a new populist government that had ordered the closing of an airfield used by the United States for drug control and had ousted the Occidental Petroleum Company. Negroponte had a lengthy meeting with the new president of Ecuador, lasting an hour and a half. Asked by the press to comment on the statement by Hugo Chavez of Venezuela that he and President Bush should "be tried and thrown in prison for the rest of their days,"[9] he mildly observed "I don't think I have ever personally criticized Mr. Chavez." Later, he observed: "I think one of the great things Mr. Bush did was not give Hugo Chavez the satisfaction of reacting to his various provocations. My sense is that that bothered Chavez. I don't think Mr. Bush ever mentioned his name."[10] Negroponte admired Álvaro Uribe of Colombia: "really nothing short of amazing...a fabulous success story."[11]

Law of the Sea

In June, he published an op-ed article robustly urging ratification of the law-of-the-sea treaty. This had been negotiated in 1973–82 and had come into force in 1994 after being modified to accommodate Reagan administration objections to its deep-sea mining provisions. No narrow nationalist, Negroponte lauded "more robust international partnership in all domains—partnerships essential to meeting today's global and trans-national security challenges."[12] Exceptionally thinly reasoned oppositions to ratification were thereafter published by Professors Jack Goldsmith of Harvard University and Jeremy Rabkin of George Mason University School of Law, and by the shrill neoconservative propagandist Frank Gaffney, objecting to the adjudication by international arbitration of ship seizure cases provided by the treaty, but minimizing the significance of the treaty's exception for military activities.[13] In September, Negroponte told a congressional committee that "we cannot just go out and negotiate another treaty, much less one that is more favorable."[14]

> We have more to gain from legal certainty and public order in the world's oceans than any other country.... Currently as a non-party the US is not in a position to maximize its sovereign rights in the Arctic or elsewhere.... It is implausible and unwise to think that the US can rely on military power alone to enforce its rights, particularly economic rights.... [the treaty] actually increases the area over which a country exercises sovereign rights.[15]

Foreign Aid and the Far East

In July 2007, Negroponte delivered an address to the Business Council for International Understanding, pointing with pride to the doubling of foreign assistance levels during the Bush administration and to the fact that since the 1960s exports had risen from 6 percent of GDP to 16 percent and imports from

5 percent of GDP to 21 percent. He referred to more than 40 bilateral investment treaties, to efforts to stimulate private investment in Pakistan, Iraq, and
Mindanao in the Philippines, and to proposals for free-trade zones in Pakistan
border regions. He expressed the hope that progress in North Korea nuclear
negotiations might lead to a definitive peace treaty and a new framework in the
Far East. Similarly, he noted that the Free-Trade Agreement with South Korea
had led to expressions of interest by Japan in a Free-Trade Agreement: "we all
know about some of the kinds of barriers that exist in terms of access to the
Japanese economy that hopefully would be dealt with in a free trade discussion." He endorsed a deepening of economic dialog with Russia similar to a
deepening of economic dialog with China. Further, "I, as a Greek-American, am
a strong advocate personally of Turkish membership in the European Union,"
rejection of which "could be a serious setback for the forces of modernization
in that country."[16]

In February 2008, speaking before the Japan Society, Negroponte lauded the
Japanese government's pledge of expenditures of $30 billion to reduce "global
warming" problems: "reducing greenhouse gases, an accessible good for all
countries, both industrialized and developing." In October 2007, he told the
American Enterprise Institute that "a major weakness of the Kyoto protocol was
its exclusion of the two largest developing countries."

Pakistan Crisis

In November 2007, Negroponte traveled to Pakistan, where he urged an end
to the state of emergency, the relinquishment by General Pervez Musharraf of
his uniform, and parliamentary elections in January to restore civilian rule. His
effort to marry the interests of Benazir Bhutto and Musharraf occasioned criticism of "a desperate State Department—with John Negroponte as the ghoulish
go-between and British Prime Minister Gordon Brown as the blushing brides-
maid."[17] Negroponte was said to have known

> it was a marriage made in hell, between two politicians whose hatred of
> each other went back years. But the hope was that the deal would take the
> passion out of the anti-Musharraf protests and buy some time. Washington
> could point to a democratic transition and still have Musharraf at the other
> end of the phone … an unstable political deal dressed up as a strategy.[18]

The Pakistani government acceded to these suggestions, though the elections
were postponed to February 2008 by reason of the turmoil following the assassination of former Prime Minister Benazir Bhutto after her return to Pakistan.
He also met at length with Musharraf's deputy, General Ashfaq Kayani, reportedly exhorting him to "use your influence: you can help save Pakistan."[19] Later,
after the elections resulted in a coalition antimilitary government, Negroponte
returned to Pakistan on the day the new government was sworn in, a juxtapo-
sition of events that was criticized in Pakistan. He was upbraided by lawyers
angry at lack of American support for restoration of the Chief Justice ousted by
Musharraf. One interlocutor asked him: "How is Pakistan different to Honduras?"
Negroponte reportedly responding: "You have put me on the spot." He also

failed to respond to the question "What do you know about our Chief Justice that we don't know?" Negroponte noted that the new parliament had pledged to deal with the judiciary within 30 days, leading to the retort: "you can't build a Parliament on the debris of the judiciary." Negroponte drew the line at nego-tiations with extremists: "Security measures are obviously necessary when one is dealing with irreconcilable elements who want to destroy our very way of life...I don't see how you can talk with those kinds of people," as distinct from "reconcilable elements [who] can be persuaded to participate in the democratic political process." As for Musharraf, "any debate or any disposition as regards his status will have to be addressed by the internal Pakistani political process."[20] Later, Negroponte lauded the outcome of the Pakistan elections, with their suc-cess for moderate parties, and the declining support for religious extremism in Pakistan. A British commentator, Godfrey Hodgson, referred to him as "a pro-consul...the hardest of the hard. Negroponte occupies a position in imperial affairs today comparable to that of John J. McCloy or Averell Harriman at the height of the Cold War."[21]

In April and May of 2008, Negroponte gave a series of speeches and inter-views, stating two central concerns.

First, "our real challenge remains in the Middle East." He supported the direct talks between Israel and Abu Mazen (Mahmoud Abbas), discouraging Hamas involvement, his vision being of an agreement which would ultimately be put to a Palestinian referendum. He encouraged the building-up of Palestinian security forces. It was up to the Israelis and Abu Mazen to talk to Hamas if they wished to do so. However, "it's not going to be resolved satisfactorily until this vision of a Palestinian state is realized."[22]

Deepening Relations with China

Negroponte's other overriding concern was with China. In 2000, while he was out of government, he gave an address to an Asia House dinner in Hong Kong, where he in his youth had spent "two formative years." He declared that he was greatly influenced by an article by Robert S. Ross of Boston College, "The Geography of Peace: East Asia in the 21st Century."[23] He did not see the United States as moving toward isolationism. Its success in the Cold War was popu-lar; it was prosperous, "the pressure in the defense area is to spend more, not less; the strong constitutional role of the President in foreign policy vis-à-vis domestic policy created an executive bias toward foreign involvement. Demographic shifts within the US were giving rise to greater interest in the Far East. If Korea were re-unified, the rationale for American presence there would diminish, but there might be an impulse toward greater Japanese militarization". He saw a danger of military competition: "Japan probably could not rival China [a view not shared by others, including George Kennan and William Pfaff], but without a US guarantee, there would be pressure for military competition." As to Taiwan: "let cooler heads prevail and leave time for a Taiwan solution to ripen." According to his former subordinate, Raymond Burghardt, the head of the American liaison office with Taiwan, he became somewhat legendary in the State Department for the matter-of-factness of his rebuff of Chinese protests of high-ranking US–Taiwan meetings: "So what? We've done it for years!" There was need for development in East Asia of cooperative economic and security arrangements on the European model, but the overall picture was hopeful, because of the end of colonialism and the Cold War, and the spread of democracy and globalization.[25] He was "concerned about the PRC's continued military build-up" and with "national modernization that will inevitably be accompanied by unpredictable social changes." He sought in discussions with the Chinese "a China which sticks to reform and development and stays on the path of peaceful development." The world clearly does not need a Chinese Admiral Alfred von Tirpitz, and there is ground for concern about China's interest in building an aircraft carrier and enlarging its fleet. He was concerned with "the lack of transparency about their intentions." He welcomed the fact that China was "coming out of its shell and engaging more." "At the moment China's in very much of an export mode. But sooner or later their own people are going to be demanding increases in their standard of living." In February 2008, Negroponte noted a 20 percent increase in US exports to China in the preceding year: "as the Chinese seek to find a way to grow their domestic economy, increase domestic consumption, and as they look to perhaps lower their own savings rates to the benefit of the Chinese citizenry." He had a Senior Dialog with his counterpart in the Chinese Foreign Ministry, and there were 50 working groups on specialized subjects.[25] He was careful to balance Japanese and Chinese interests, recognizing Japan as America's primary Far Eastern ally and China as its primary source of imports. In late January, he spoke to the Japan Society:

> Formal institutions for peace and security in Asia, particularly Northeast Asia, are not as developed as they are in other regions. [There is] potential to use the Six Party Talks [with North Korea] as the beginning of a more lasting multi-lateral structure.[26]

Mexico Revisited

In the same month, Negroponte gave an interview to Televisa, a Mexican media outlet. He declared that the new Mérida Initiative for cooperation on drug enforcement would not involve any American military presence, which "will not take place here, no way … I know why not. And surely you also know it." He noted that 60 percent of drug enforcement funds would go to civilian agencies rather than the Mexican military. He also denied that the United States would have undercover DEA agents in Mexico not listed to the Mexican government. As to immigration law, he was "not very optimistic between now and the end of the administration" as to the prospects for change. Mexican drug enforcement would not be subject to a certification process, which had previously outraged Mexican nationalists. He expressed concern about "insecurity in the border area [which] prevents economic development," and expressed hope that increased employment in Mexico would stem the movement of migrants.[28] In 1999, while out of government, Negroponte had expressed concern about the involvement of the military in drug enforcement, alluding to the corruption of the Panamanian Defense Force under General Manuel Noriega. Negroponte saw nothing wrong with the use of the military to destroy marijuana crops but thought that military involvement should largely be confined to circumstances where traffickers were using military means such as vessels and aircraft. He saw use of the military as confined to a temporary period, "several years, ten years," although that enforcement should be "as close to the source as possible" but cautioned "if all you have is assisting the Latin American military in combating drugs—sooner or later that policy is going to founder."[29] The drug problem, for him, was a problem for US domestic policy.

Return to Iraq

In December, Negroponte visited Iraq and pressed parliamentary leaders to agree on de-Ba'athification and oil revenue-sharing laws; in February 2008, the Iraqi parliamentarians agreed on limits to the purge of Ba'athists and to a one-year agreement on division of revenues, as well as on measures to strengthen provincial governments.[29] In January 2008, Negroponte visited Vietnam, where he was told by some of his interlocutors that he spoke Vietnamese with a Saigon accent; he was impressed by the large attendance at a mass in the Saigon cathedral, and by the cordiality of the welcome he received there.

Farewell to Foreign Service

Negroponte was given a retirement reception in 2009 at the State Department in the week preceding the end of the Bush administration. Secretary of State Rice spoke of him with evident warmth. Henry Kissinger was in attendance; an attendance that might have been explained by the fact that he was to attend a luncheon with Rice immediately following the ceremony. Almost immediately thereafter, the 86-year-old Kissinger reacted violently to an interview Negroponte had given to Jay Nordlinger of *National Review*, which was implicitly critical of Kissinger's stance at the Paris peace talks; a heated letter by Kissinger prompted a reply by Negroponte. Negroponte supported the proposed expansion of the State Department, alluding to the explosion in the number of independent foreign countries from 60 to nearly 200 and the need for greater midcareer training of Foreign Service officers along the lines of the War Colleges; he lamented the fact that there was no "training float" in the Foreign Service. At his retirement, only 10 of the top 50 positions in the Department were occupied by career diplomats, a serious embarrassment to the rational conduct of foreign policy, notwithstanding some exceptional noncareer ambassadors. The remarkable means by which America chooses ambassadors had been described by L. Anthony Motley of the State Department in his oral history:

> The process then and now which I believe to be wrong was for the Department to put up a candidate, then the Office of Presidential Personnel would put up a candidate for every job. This committee would then decide between the two.[30]

Only one Foreign Service officer, Lawrence Eagleburger, had risen to be Secretary of State; there had been three postwar Deputy Secretaries who had risen from the Foreign Service: Eagleburger, Walter Stoessel, and Negroponte himself.[31] Negroponte found the Deputy Secretary's role as the selector of career ambassadors one of the more satisfying parts of his service. After a three-year freeze on new positions, he was successful in obtaining 500 new positions for the State Department in the 2009 budget, exploiting his good relations with Senators Stevens and Daniel Inouye of Hawaii and Representatives John Murtha, Jane Harman, and Peter Hoekstra.

It may be due to Negroponte's restraining influence, in the last two years of the second Bush administration, that America pulled back from the project of an attack on Iran with its further disruption of the international order. If so, Americans owe him a considerable debt for sparing them the working out of Henry Kissinger's prophecy: "order, once shattered, can be restored only by the experience of chaos."[32] After his retirement, Negroponte said of Iran that "military action was not the way to go" and that he had "thought this for a long time—even more so for Israel." He was skeptical of the Iranians' willingness to negotiate unless their "isolation deepens." He saw "no harm in talking...in opening a bilateral channel if we go into it with our eyes open" not expecting an "instant result." What was needed was unity of the large powers, not a "least common denominator" in their dealings with Iran, achieving this required "enhancement of dialogue with Russia."[33]

Negroponte's recent career navigated the shoals of an era in which, as British author Peter Calvocoressi has put it, "witnessed...an intensification of intolerant religious fundamentalism in the Islamic Middle East, among Christians in the United States, in Judaism, and in Hinduism."[35] In a valedictory speech at Trinity College, Dublin, two months before the end of his tenure, Negroponte declared a view of Iraq and Afghanistan that accentuated the positive to a degree that may shortly be belied by history, stressing the expulsion of Al Qaeda from Anbar province, a 9 percent economic growth rate, Iraqi-led security in 13 of 18 provinces, and a ceasefire with al Sadr, though acknowledging unsolved problems involving the division of oil revenues and northern cities and the professionalization of security forces. "Iraq...will not be a client state of Iran, and it will not be a theocracy."

Afghanistan, though beset by "ongoing violence, narco-trafficking and widespread corruption" had increased children at school from 900,000 to 6 million, including 1.5 million girls previously denied education; healthcare was available to 65 percent of the population, as against 8 percent previously. Both examples presumed the success of a unitary state in multiethnic nations that may not prove ready for it, given their populaces' inexperience with limited government and the resultant conviction, in Judge Learned Hand's words, that "an alien master is worst of all," as well as the fact that in both Pakistan and Afghanistan the majority of the population was illiterate. Although providing verbal support for the Bush administration's aspirations, he is said to have regarded the problems of Pakistan and Afghanistan as indivisible and did not favor a war against Moslem fundamentalism so long as havens for terrorists were not provided. In a memorial tribute to diplomat Richard Holbrooke in December 2010, Negroponte observed: "he wanted to try to help maneuver the situation toward a negotiated outcome. But I think we all recognize that the pieces don't yet seem to be in place."[35] More convincingly, he affirmed his central faith: "I am convinced of the benefits of a US-led international order based on good governance, economic freedom, and open trade," while acknowledging that "[d]omestic financial troubles in the United States and elsewhere are affecting the real economies of other countries and rendering developing states more vulnerable to the fluctuations of commodity price shocks and reductions in trade financing."[36] These developments impair his vision of US leadership but not his central vision, which must now be carried on by multipolar institutions some of which he helped nurture.

Later, Negroponte praised the Obama administration for its allocation of $1.5 billion for Pakistan: "a new order of magnitude…catching up with reality." He thought the new administration had gotten off to a "terrific start" and that as to Iraq its time frame was consistent with "withdrawal in a responsible way." He praised a "shift to greater multi-lateralism," having witnessed two wars, Vietnam and Iraq, in which the United States had led itself into different forms of economic ruin by conducting conflicts against the wish and without the financial support of most of its normal allies. Whether greater consultation among Franklin Roosevelt's "five policemen," the United States, Britain, the Soviet Union, France, and China, would have avoided the wars and war scares involving perceived trespasses on each other's spheres of interest he did not explore, although this question has a bearing on the wars in Central America, Vietnam, Afghanistan, and Angola, the rushed decolonization of Africa, the wars in the Horn of Africa, the near apocalypse resulting from missiles in Turkey and Cuba, and the failed states following in the wake of these conflicts. Negroponte saw at last a "fairly benign global geopolitical environment [with] no real tension among the greater powers." His worldview was free of apocalyptic talk about "clashes of civilizations." He did not "think we can go it alone in this world," though the United States was "still the leading nation." Not enough attention had been given to cybersecurity and the security of space satellites, matters that required more attention and transparency. There was an "arc of instability" from Gaza to Iran, and he expressed no opinion about the possibilities of a "grand bargain" in the Middle East.[37] His valedictory remarks omitted comment on three failures of domestic policy on which he had commented elsewhere: drug policy, agricultural dumping, and inadequate science education in the nation's high schools.

In directing the State Department, Negroponte had the task of recovering from an era in which it had been effectively marginalized. While Colin Powell had paid much more attention to the organization and morale of the Foreign Service than his immediate predecessors, the marginalization of its role in the Iraq War decisions had not helped its morale. The Foreign Service had much to recover from, including an extraordinary year in the Albright era in which it took in no recruits, a heedless action with a devastating effect on recruitment by universities of serious students of international relations and foreign languages. Negroponte sought to expand the role of the Foreign Service in the efforts at "nation-building" in Iraq and Afghanistan; these could only benefit from professional and detached advice. At a conference in the State Department in late 2010, he deplored the fact that since the glory days of AID in Vietnam, we had "atomized our assistance efforts in such a way that it's very hard to direct them towards a strategic purpose." He noted that he had "always been pounding the table for the Iraqization, the Afghanization." He carried out the

State Department's part in the deepening of relations with China, an initiative for which Secretary of the Treasury Paulson deserves much credit. He also recognized that the Pakistanis would have to make their own political choices, but also recognized, as he had in Iraq, the importance of sustaining security institutions. Toward the end of his tenure, according to one of the "Wikileaks" documents, he emphatically warned Armenia against arms shipments to Iran.[38] His most enduring achievement was a long-overdue enlargement of the Foreign Service.

After retirement from the State Department, Negroponte became vice-chairman of McLarty and Associates, an international consulting firm, as well as a one-day-a-week lecturer in Yale's strategic studies program run by Paul Kennedy and John Lewis Gaddis. While at Yale, his advice was asked on whether the university press, in a book about the controversy generated by Danish cartoons deemed by some Moslems to blaspheme the Prophet Mohammed, should republish the cartoons. His advice was against doing so, viewing publication as a "gratuitous act":

> how much of the academic purpose of this book is stymied by the fact of not publishing the cartoons. I don't think it's stymied at all since the images are accessible elsewhere, especially on line … the American newspapers took the decision not to publish the images back in 2005.[39]

In August 2010, after the withdrawal of the last American combat troops from Iraq, Negroponte noted that "the specter of sectarianism poisoning the ranks of Iraqi military and police forces remains the single most serious threat to be guarded against, and urged "congressional support for funding requests … [t]oo often in the past we have tired of an international undertaking when our military role has finished." He expressed the view that "the days of backroom political deals brokered by the US Embassy in Baghdad will be fewer and further between."[40]

CONCLUSION

Events we have already witnessed in the cold war could easily have caused actual war in the nineteenth century or even in the earlier parts of the twentieth...If nations keep up contacts, keep discussing, then time will finally erode their hesitation and resistance. Impatience, especially as regards important problems between large groups of powers, is unnecessary and harmful. If the last 15 years' experience has saved us now from the deadlock created by the idea that face-to-face discussions are futile, then all these years have not passed in vain.

> — Ismet Inonu, "Negotiations and the National Interest,"
> in Carnegie Endowment for International Peace,
> *Perspectives on Peace, 1910–1960*
> (Westport, CT: Praeger, 1960), 135, 150

John Negroponte, although a Democrat at the beginning of his career and a Republican at the end of it, was no partisan. His initial party affiliation was a function of his admiration for the conduct of foreign affairs by Franklin D. Roosevelt and Harry S. Truman.

Negroponte had begun his career in the waning hours of the Dwight Eisenhower administration; in an interview given shortly after his retirement, he professed respect for the prudence of Eisenhower and John Foster Dulles. It is likely that he recalled their refusal to intervene in Indochina after Dien Bien Phu, the failure to exploit whatever opportunities were presented by the Hungarian Revolution in 1956, the settlement on inglorious but workable terms of the long war in Korea, the refusal to support a last gasp of imperialism at Suez, the fiscal conservatism and refusal to perceive "missile gaps," and relaunch arms races. The administration of Eisenhower, to be sure, had done little to educate the public about foreign policy. It had retired fine public servants like George Kennan and John Paton Davies, although saving Charles Bohlen from their fate. It had prevented the elections contemplated by the Geneva Agreement; supported the erection of a Catholic refugee government in South Vietnam; refused to recognize Red China; and finally, in what was more a blunder than an act of policy, allowed the Francis Gary Powers U-2 spy plane affair to blow up the Four-Power Conference that Winston Churchill had sought as his last political act. The Eisenhower administration was not adverse to covert actions; under it, the coup in Guatemala had been sponsored and early preparations made for the Bay of Pigs, but the wars it planned were "proxy wars"; it had ended or forestalled wars, not started them. Its rhetorical reliance on "massive retaliation" at least did not indulge the illusion that limited wars could be rendered cost free.

Negroponte professed no such respect for the administration of John F. Kennedy and Robert Kennedy, to whom he usually referred conjunctively. Its venture into Vietnam had been undertaken without clear definition of a political object, in apparent reaction to Khrushchev's bluster at Vienna, and with illusions that the Green Berets and counterinsurgency were a cure-all. While Negroponte was at Stanford, he was critical of the notion that limited commitments were sufficient to win limited wars; he was equally critical of the Bush–Rumsfeld effort to run the Iraq war on the cheap. The Kennedy administration brought down a Vietnamese government while giving inadequate thought to what would succeed it. Negroponte did not proffer a further indictment, which might have included the Bay of Pigs; the failure to withdraw Jupiter missiles in Turkey before,[1] rather than after, a crisis that came perilously close to a nuclear exchange,[2] the disgrace that was Operation Mongoose[3] CIA covert operations in Cuba developed during the early years of Kennedy's administration, the relaunching of an arms race through perception of a fictitious missile gap,[4] the beginnings of budget deficits and one-way Keynesianism, the rhetorical extravagances of the inaugural speech, the purging of senior members of the Foreign Service, pressure for rushed decolonization by the British and French, and a well-intentioned approach to foreign aid to Latin America, Asia, and Africa that produced few positive results, urging land reform and grand projects while neglecting education, taxation, and justice systems. To his credit, Kennedy did have the Nuclear Test Ban Treaty, an early environmental agreement, although he was, in considerable measure, led into it by British Prime Minister Harold Macmillan and Lord Hailsham, the British science minister and treaty negotiator.

Lyndon Johnson's decision to enter into Vietnam negotiations and not to seek reelection Negroponte viewed as courageous and as cutting his losses. For Nixon, he had a grudging respect, owing to the openings to Russia and China and his empowerment of Henry Kissinger. Negroponte believed that an opportunity had been lost at the close of the Vietnam negotiations to secure North Vietnamese withdrawal from the South, and was uncertain as to whether the indecent haste in which they were concluded was ascribable to Nixon or to Kissinger, although he tended to blame the latter. He made no reported comment on Gerald Ford or Jimmy Carter, although Negroponte supported and helped to foster their generosity toward Indochina's refugees.

Negroponte admired Reagan and changed his party affiliation because of him. Ronald Reagan cut his losses in Lebanon and avoided war in Panama and Central America while pushing back through surrogates at what he perceived as aggression in Central America and Afghanistan and striving to limit nuclear arms. Reagan was also more supportive of environmental initiatives than is generally appreciated. The elder George Bush supported Negroponte when he embraced the vision of enhanced trade with Mexico; in addition, Bush intelligently fostered détente in Europe and avoided pushing Mikhail Gorbachev too hard. About Bill Clinton, Negroponte had little to say; he owed Clinton two not very important assignments in the Philippines and Panama and the offer of one in Greece, but had reason to feel himself pushed to the sidelines, and retired to go to McGraw-Hill.

Negroponte's return to high office in the second Bush administration and his navigation of its shoals for eight years was itself no small diplomatic achievement. He did not share the mind-set of some of its leading members. Although Negroponte professed respect for President Bush's intelligence and credited him with good questions and appropriate curiosity, he saw in George W. Bush and Richard Cheney two men who were traumatized and thrown off their intellectual moorings by 9/11. He viewed Donald Rumsfeld as arbitrary and inattentive, and found his views naïve about the swift and surgical use of military force. Negroponte cautioned the administration about entry into the Iraq War, won an unexpected unanimous UN resolution according added time for negotiation but was obliged to carry out instructions with respect to a second resolution that transgressed his view that some more time for inspections would have been appropriate.

Negroponte's mission in Iraq was that of picking up the pieces, and making the best of a bad thing. He felt it necessary to use force to initially assert authority over the Sunni Moslems and Moquada al Sadr, but looked to elections, however imperfect, to provide legitimate leadership and a forum in which differences could be negotiated. He carried back to Washington a message, unwelcome to both Rumsfeld and the Democrats, that preparing a decent departure would take both time and cost money.

As DNI Negroponte sought, without being disloyal to the administration, to curb its worst indecencies, in which many saw an "abandonment of law and history" providing precedents for an incipient fascism.[5] The somewhat overwrought reaction of the Bush administration, and more particularly Vice President Cheney, to 9/11 called to mind the reflections of British Ambassador to Germany Horace Rumbold on the character and deeds of Franz von Papen, vice chancellor of Germany under Adolf Hitler:

> Other motives than solely consideration for law and order compelled them to act. [He] is convinced that in some mysterious way he possesses a popular mandate to govern the country and even to reform the Constitution and that the real desire of the country is for authoritative government, the limitation of parliamentary government, and the reform of institutions.... A lightweight gentleman rider in his youth, he displayed the characteristics which might have been expected from him when he took office.... Not only did he take every political fence at a gallop, but he seemed to go out of his way to find fences that were not in his course—incessant challenges to the political parties, the Federal States.[6]

Although fairness requires the recognition that the powers assumed were not used against the administration's domestic critics or to interfere with two elections the results in which were not to the administration's liking, the joint warning of Justices of the Supreme Court Robert Jackson, Felix Frankfurter, and

Owen Roberts remains pertinent to its malign precedents: "Evil men are rarely given power; they take it over from better men to whom it had been entrusted."[7]

Negroponte emptied the CIA's prisons, admitted what had happened in them prior to his arrival, and declared that legislative definition of rules was to be welcomed. He supported a subordinate who disclosed the intelligence budget. Negroponte similarly joined with others in curbing domestic eavesdropping excesses. He discharged a political CIA director, Porter Goss, restored control of the agency to professionals, and safeguarded the integrity of National Intelligence Estimates while providing for a coordinated National Counterterrorism Center. He also unsuccessfully cautioned against the destruction of interrogation records and corrected misleading statements by Attorney General Alberto Gonzales.

In his last assignment as Deputy Secretary of State, Negroponte attempted to foster a return to civilian government in Pakistan that would not be disastrous to security interests. He greatly deepened diplomatic relations with China by proliferating meetings of experts, a commitment also of Secretary of the Treasury Henry Paulson. As his final, and most heartfelt, act Negroponte secured appropriations for a long-deferred substantial enlargement of the Foreign Service. The fiscal 2009 budget provided for 1,100 additional Foreign Service officers and 300 new Agency for International Development (AID) personnel.

It is hard, without caricature, to describe the difficulties under which Negroponte labored for the last eight years of his tenure, particularly for the first six of them. The president had a Wilsonian bent; foreign policy had, over the objections of Secretary of State Colin Powell, fallen under the control of a group whose most articulate exponent was the Deputy Secretary of Defense, Paul Wolfowitz, one of the few colleagues whom Negroponte criticized in conversations with friends. A sympathetic biography of Wolfowitz accurately describes his major premises:

> First, idealism, particularly his long-standing quest to promote democracy overseas.
>
> Second, he saw a unipolar world in which the United States had become the global custodian by virtue of its military superiority. Although not a veteran, he evidenced a belief in the efficacy of American military power. He looked to the military as a key American tool in dealing with other nations.
>
> Third, he manifested an optimistic assessment of US capabilities in terms of money and commitment. He sought to use America's military and diplomatic positions to promote US interests, keep the US on the initiative and not simply react to the world as America found it…Wolfowitz believed that the US could pre-empt perceived threats to its security, domestically and overseas.
>
> He saw that the energy-rich world of the Middle East eclipsed everything else on the list of US geopolitical concerns. US military strength would make it fruitless and financially disastrous for any nation (or group of nations) to compete with the US in the global arena. As a corollary, he thought that the United States ought to be reluctant to enter into agreements

or make accommodations with other nations such as China … looking to multilateral institutions only when it served US interests.

For good measure, Wolfowitz was said to believe that "the use of force to liberate people is very different from the use of force to suppress or control them or even to defeat them" and to further stress "the danger of foreign and national security policy centered on the notion of equilibrium."[8]

An even more astonishing expression of the neoconservative faith was that tendered by writers William Kristol and Lawrence Kaplan in the runup to the Iraq War, lauding "the tactic of military preemption, the objective of regime change and a vision of American power that is fully engaged and never apologetic." Diplomats were derided for "poring over maps and position papers." It was proclaimed that "Repudiation of Europe is after all America's main excuse for being." "Arms control agreements, international treaties, and an aversion to the use of force" were derided. Diplomats like Negroponte were condemned for addressing themselves to "the roof of the world over Patagonia where there is a hole in the ozone layer … confusing these worries with actual threats." "A campaign to uproot tyranny and export democracy" was called for in place of the "luxury of mere containment." "A coalition so broad that its effect is to hamper the US from carrying out this mission is not a coalition worth having."

Kristol and Kaplan proclaimed "that things might be worse … is of course a possibility. But given the status quo in Iraq, it is difficult to see how." Five million internal and two million external refugees from the Iraq War might disagree with them.

Furthermore,

> Powell and others have argued that if the US alienates Iraq's Sunnis, Iraq could be plunged into chaos. (During the war in Afghanistan, Powell made the same point—wrongly as it turned out—about overthrowing the ethnic Pashtuns who led the Taliban.)

These maledictions upon Powell do not read too well today. The book holds up to scorn a virtual anthology of prophetic quotations from, among others, James Baker, Zbigniew Brzezinski, Jimmy Carter, Steve Chapman, Chuck Hagel, Carl Levin, Brent Scowcroft, and Anthony Zinni.

As for the costs of adventurism, Kristol and Kaplan assured us that the

> task will be made considerably easier by Iraq's vast oil resources … initially as many as 75,000 US troops may be required to police the war's aftermath at a cost of $16 billion a year … probably be drawn down to several thousand soldiers after a year or two.

All that was needed was

> $100 billion per year above current defense budgets … American pre-eminence cannot be maintained from a distance. The US should conceive

of itself as at once a European power, an Asian power, and of course a Middle Eastern power...missile defense is about preserving America's ability to wield power abroad.[9]

To this grandiosity, Negroponte opposed the humbler diplomatic virtues, as once defined by U. Alexis Johnson: "keeping those who need to know informed, listening seriously to their opinions so no one feels ignored, preserving their confidences, never lying, always trying to expand the areas of agreement, finding and maximizing overlapping areas of common interest," together with respect for the essential "three Cs of democratic government: communication, coordination and consensus." "With the rest of the world prostrate," diplomat Alexis Johnson declared, "we were lords of virtually all we surveyed to the point that we began to have illusions of omnipotence."[10] Johnson urged that we "stop confusing foreign policy with theology," a conviction Negroponte upheld by precept and example.

Negroponte's vision was of the United States as a leading power in a world unified by the trade fostered by international agreements, in which developing environmental and health problems, the product of economic externalities, required cooperative action among nations. He viewed America's ethnic diversity as an asset in the world. In this vision, US military power was necessary but far from sufficient. Unilateralism carried with it heavy economic costs, present in the second Iraq War, absent in the first...He was mindful of the effect of excessive militarization of foreign policy on twentieth century Germany and Japan, which contrasted with Britain's success in maintaining worldwide influence with an historically small standing army—an influence resting on good intelligence and training, local knowledge and the willingness to limit objectives, exercise indirect control, and cut losses.

More broadly, Negroponte held the view, as to both domestic and foreign issues, of Charles Evans Hughes, a seriously underappreciated Secretary of State to Warren Harding and Calvin Coolidge:[11]

> There is no lack of schemes for the regeneration of society, schemes not infrequently of a sort which would not be needed by a society capable of freely adopting them. The construction of a theoretical paradise is the easiest of human efforts. The familiar method is to establish the perfect or almost perfect state, and then to fashion human beings to fit it. This is a far lighter undertaking than the necessary and unspectacular task, taking human nature as it is and is likely to remain, of devising improvements that are workable.

Negroponte's career was unusual in its time for the self-control he displayed throughout it. He was subjected to much criticism on various issues both from disinformation purveyors on the left and the highly orchestrated propagandists on the neoconservative right. He never rose to the bait, responding to criticism only when required to do so at confirmation hearings. He was, in general, a bad source for journalists; when he made unexpected disclosures, they were usually facts necessary to correct a misleading record. In an age of personal self-indulgence, he exemplified self-control and self-discipline. He belonged to no cliques; his emotional outlet was manifestly his family, immediate and extended. Dean Acheson's tribute to Harry Truman fully applies to Negroponte: "He did not let his ego get between himself and his work"; he was not one of the "foolish tawdry moths who fly at publicity's consuming fire" of whom Justice Learned Hand wrote in his eulogy of Justice Benjamin Cardozo. He exemplified the diplomat's code, founded at its best on recognition that other people have interests and ambitions, and that flexibility in the conduct of personal and international relations is a good in itself. This limited his influence and the reach of his voice; he was no tribune of the people and some of his causes suffered thereby. It is the author's hope that this work will be of assistance to the wise and displace attention now given to the noisy.

GEORGE W. LIEBMANN, a Baltimore lawyer and native New Yorker grew up in the same apartment building as John Negroponte and was a classmate of his for several years. After their paths diverged at the age of about ten, Liebmann attended a variety of schools, public and private, concluding at the Riverdale Country School in New York. He then went to Dartmouth, graduating with high distinction in government, and then to the University of Chicago Law School, where he was a managing editor of the Law Review. He then moved to Baltimore to be law clerk to the then Chief Judge of the Maryland Court of Appeals, Frederick W. Brune (best known as the author of the 1958 Report of the Council of Chief Justices criticizing several Warren Court Supreme Court decisions). After brief service as an enlisted reservist in the Army and as an inactive law officer in Navy JAG, he joined a Baltimore law firm.

During the period 1968–72, Liebmann was involved in four major national political controversies. He was the organizer and secretary of the Coalition against the Supersonic Transport, which was successful in its purpose. As an Assistant Attorney General of Maryland and counsel to its Department of Social Services, he successfully argued in the Supreme Court the case of *Dandridge v. Williams*, which effectively brought an end to efforts to constitutionalize welfare rights. He organized the defense by state attorneys general of cases attacking the constitutionality of school financing systems; his brief on behalf of 34 state governments was cited in both the majority and dissenting opinions in *San Antonio v. Rodriguez* in which the Supreme Court warded off federal constitutional attacks on such systems. Shortly thereafter, Liebmann wrote a series of influential articles in the *ABA Journal*, *Business Lawyer*, and other publications opposing extensive expansions of the federal criminal code proposed by both the Johnson and Nixon administrations; these opposition efforts were ultimately successful.

His private practice at various times involved constitutional and appellate litigation, private antitrust litigation, and real estate, environmental, and bankruptcy law.

In 1980–91, Liebmann served as Executive Assistant to Governor Harry Hughes of Maryland and was the principal draftsman of legislation regulating land use around the Chesapeake Bay.

In 1981, he started his own law practice, Liebmann and Shively, P.A. He served as chairman of governors' commissions on medical malpractice and on local government antitrust liability and wrote extensively on land use and local government issues. In 1993, he was a Simon Industrial and Professional Fellow at the University of Manchester, England, and in 1996 first became a Visiting Fellow at Wolfson College, Cambridge, England, to which he has frequently returned.

Liebmann is the author of a trilogy of books on sublocal governments and their potential, including *The Little Platoons* (1995), *The Gallows in the Grove* (1997), and *Solving Problems without Large Government* (2000), reprinted as *Neighborhood Futures* (2002). He is also the author of three books of biographical sketches, *Six Lost Leaders* (2002), *The Common Law Tradition: A Collective Portrait of Five Legal Scholars* (2004), and *Diplomacy between the Wars: Five Diplomats and the Shaping of the Modern World* (2007).

Since 2001, he has been the volunteer executive director of the Calvert Institute for Policy Research, a state-level think tank, and editor of a compendium of its papers, *The Trimmer's Almanac: Ten Years of the Calvert Institute* (2007). He is president of the Library Company of the Baltimore Bar, a life member of the American Law Institute, and a permanent member of the Federal Judicial Conference for the Fourth Circuit.

GLOSSARY OF ACRONYMS

AID	Agency for International Development
AIDS	Acquired Immunity Deficiency Syndrome
APROH	Association for the Progress of Honduras
ARVN	Army of (South) Vietnam
ASEAN	Association of Southeast Asian Nations
BATF	Bureau of Alcohol, Tobacco, and Firearms
CFC	Chlorofluorocarbons
CIA	Central Intelligence Agency
CNN	Cable News Network
CPA	Coalition Provisional Authority
DAS	Deputy Assistant Secretary
DCM	Deputy Chief of Mission
DEA	Drug Enforcement Administration
DIA	Defense Intelligence Agency
DMZ	Demilitarized Zone
DNI	Director of National Intelligence
DRV	Democratic Republic of (North) Vietnam
ECA	Economic Cooperation Administration
EEC	European Economic Community
EPA	Environmental Protection Agency
EU	European Union
FBI	Federal Bureau of Investigation
FDN	Nicaraguan Democratic Force (Contras)
FISA	Foreign Intelligence Surveillance Act
FMLN	Salvadoran National Liberation Front
FPA	Fisherman's Protective Act
FTA	Free-Trade Agreement
FUSADES	Foundation for Economic and Social Development
GATT	General Agreement on Tariffs and Trade
GDP	Gross Domestic Product
GOES	Government of El Salvador
GOH	Government of Honduras
GOM	Government of Mexico
GSV	Government of South Vietnam

GVN	Government of (South) Vietnam
HEO	High Explosive Ordnance
IAEA	International Atomic Energy Agency
ICRC	International Committee of the Red Cross
IMF	International Monetary Fund
INS	Immigration and Naturalization Service
IRS	Internal Revenue Service
MACV	Military Assistance Command Vietnam
NAFTA	North American Free-Trade Agreement
NATO	North Atlantic Treaty Organization
NGO	Nongovernmental Organization
NIE	National Intelligence Estimate
NLF	National Liberation Front (Viet Cong)
NSA	National Security Agency
NSC	National Security Council
NSDD	National Security Decision Directive
NSPD	National Security Presidential Directive
NSSM	National Security Study Memorandum
NYU	New York University
OAS	Organization of American States
OECD	Organization for Economic Cooperation and Development
OES	Office of Oceans, Environment, and Scientific Affairs
ONI	Office of National Intelligence
ORHA	Office of Reconstruction and Humanitarian Assistance
OSCE	Organization for Security and Cooperation in Europe
PACS	Private Security Contractors
PAN	National Action Party
PEMEX	Mexican Petroleum
PGR	Office of the Attorney General
POW	Prisoners of War
PRI	Institutional Revolutionary Party
PTA	Preferential Trade Agreement
SALT	Strategic Arms Limitation Treaty
SEC	Securities Exchange Agreement
SST	Supersonic Transport
UNHCR	United Nations High Commissioner for Refugees
UNICEF	United Nations International Childrens' Emergency Fund
UNMOVIC	United Nations Monitoring, Verification and Inspection Commission
USG	United States Government
VAT	Value Added Tax
VC	Vietcong
WMD	Weapons of Mass Destruction
WTO	World Trade Organization

NOTES

Acknowledgments

1 A. Feininger, *New York in the Forties* (New York: Dover, 1978), 1.
2 D. Wakefield, *New York in the Fifties* (Boston: Houghton Mifflin, 1992), 3, 6.
3 A. De Conde, "Forward," in K. Jones (ed.), *US Diplomats in Europe, 1919–41* (Santa Barbara, CA: ABC Clio, 1981), xiv.

Chapter One

1 Transcript of December 3, 2006, C-Span, *Question and Answer with JN*, available at www.politics.stephaniedray.com/?q=node/183
2 Department of State, Opening Ceremony for Global Classrooms DC Model UN, April 28, 2008.
3 Transcript of December 3, 2006, www.politics.stephaniedray.com/?q=node/183
4 P. Calvocoressi, *Threading My Way* (London: Duckworth, 1994), Chapters 1 and 2.
5 I. Theotokas and G. Harloftis, *Leadership in World Shipping: Greek Family Firms in International Business* (New York: Palgrave Macmillan, 2009), 238, 288.
6 "Greek Women's Heroism Recalled as Underground Pleads for Aid," *New York Times*, February 4, 1943, 26: 2.
7 J. Nordlinger, "Negroponte at Large," *National Review Online*, March 24, 2009.
8 N. Hoplin, et al., *Funding Fathers: The Unsung Heroes of the Conservative Movement* (Washington: Regnery, 2008), 64.
9 R. Cornwell, *The [London] Independent*, July 3, 2004.
10 Nordlinger, "Negroponte at Large."
11 J. Nordlinger, "Negroponte Speaks," *National Review*, March 23, 2009, 19.

Chapter Two

1 Department of State (DOS), Theodore Heavner Oral History, May 28, 1997.
2 DOS, Opening Ceremony for Global Classrooms DC Model UN, April 28, 2008.
3 FRUS 1961–3, vol. IX (Washington: GPO, 1995), 459.
4 F. Snepp, *Decent Interval: The American Debacle in Vietnam and the Fall of Saigon* (London: Allen Lane, 1980).
5 Ibid., 141–4.
6 FRUS, Northeast Asia, 1961–3, vol. XXII (Washington: GPO, 1996), 687; Green to State Department, June 22, 1962.
7 M. Castells (ed.), *The Shek Kip Mei Syndrome: Economic Development and Public Housing in Hong Kong and Singapore* (London: Pion, 1990).

Chapter Three

1 Gibson to Secretary of State, January 27, 1949, National Archives, Record Group 84, Entry 3344, Box 1.
2 J. Kennedy, *The Strategy of Peace* (New York: Harper, 1960).

3   C. Sulzberger, *A Long Row of Candles: Memoirs and Diaries 1934–54* (New York: Macmillan, 1969), 1016.

4   The Gibson memorandum, together with those of Young and Heath, appears at FRUS, vol. XXII, 1952–4 (Washington: GPO, 1982), 2330.

5   http://en.wikipedia.org/wiki/Michigan_State_University_Vietnam_Advisory_Group

6   Jack Lydman to Robert Hoey, July 26, 1954, in National Archives, Office of Southeast Asian Affairs, Cambodia and Vietnam, Entry UD51, Box 3, Folder 404.2 (Record Group 59/250/51/26).

7   "Round-Up of Events in Vietnam Political Crisis, 9/1-24/54," in National Archives, Office of Southeast Asia Affairs, Cambodia and Vietnam, Entry UD51, Box 3, Folder 361.21 (Record Group 59/250/51/26).

8   C. Sulzberger, *The Last of the Giants* (New York: Macmillan, 1970), 118.

9   Ibid., 172.

10 P. Calvocoressi, *World Politics, 1945–2000* (New York: Pearson, Longman, 2000), 537.

11 Ibid., 538.

12 R. Turner, "Reassessing the Causes: Gulf of Tonkin Incident Not the Real Start," *Washington Times*, August 2, 2009, citing an article said to have appeared in the *Vietnam Courier* for May 1984 recounting a decision to open the Ho Chi Minh trail said to have been made by the Lao Dong Party on May 19, 1959.

13 See R. Beisner, *Dean Acheson: A Life in the Cold War* (New York: Oxford, 2006), Chapter 11.

14 Gibson to Acheson, September 16, 1949, National Archives, Record Group 84, Entry 3344.

15 Article in the London Observer, quoted in C. Hitchens, *Why Orwell Matters* (New York: Basic Books, 2002), 27.

16 National Archives, Office of Southeast Asian Affairs, Cambodia and Vietnam, Entry UD51, Box 3, Folder 362.2 (Record Group 59/250/51/26).

17 Quoted in G. Loescher and J. Scanlan, *Calculated Kindness: Refugees and America's Half-Open Door, 1945 to the Present* (New York: Free Press, 1986), 104.

18 Quoted in D. Lancaster, *The Emancipation of French Indo-China* (Oxford: Oxford University Press, 1961), 347.

19 J. Buttinger, *Vietnam: A Dragon Embattled* (New York: Praeger, 1967), 251.

20 W. Bundy, Notes on the Republican White Paper on Vietnam, August 24, 1965, in National Archives, Entry 5305, Box 2, Chron file August–December 1965.

21 Memorandum, June 28, 1965, in ibid.

22 K. Bird, *The Color of Truth: McGeorge Bundy and William Bundy, Brothers in Arms* (New York: Simon and Schuster, 1998), 256.

23 P. Honey, "Vietnamese Notebook," 21 Encounter No. 6, 64, 65, 66 (December 1963).

24 R. Morris, *Uncertain Greatness: Henry Kissinger and American Foreign Policy* (London: Quartet Books, 1977), 34.

25 US Department of State, US Chiefs of Mission, 1778–1973 (Washington: Department of State, 1973).

26 J. Davies, *Foreign and Other Affairs* (New York: Norton, 1964), 175–6.

27 Ibid., 198.

28 The first quotation is quoted in A. Preston, *The War Council: McGeorge Bundy, the NSC and Vietnam* (Cambridge: Harvard University Press, 2006), 30; the second in "The Use of Power with a Passion for Peace," *Time*, June 25, 1965, 26–7, both in G. Goldstein, *Lessons in Disaster: McGeorge Bundy and the Path to War in Vietnam* (New York: Times Books, 2008), 15–16.

29 NSC Minutes, January 8, 1954, FRUS, Indochina, Part 1, 947–55 (Washington: GPO, 1982), quoted in Goldstein, *Lessons in Disaster*, 50.

30 Transcript of December 3, 2006, C-Span, *Question and Answer with JN*, available at www.politics.stephaniedray.com/?q=node/183

31 DOS, James Rosenthal Oral History, May 24, 1996.

32 G. Geyer, "A New Breed of White House Diplomats" (syndicated column), February 28, 2005.

33 DOS, Robert Oakley Oral History, July 7, 1992; LBJ Library, Ellsworth Bunker Oral History, December 12, 1980.

34 U. Johnson, *The Right Hand of Power* (Englewood Cliffs, NJ: Prentice Hall, 1984), 532.

35 Nomination of Ambassador John D. Negroponte to be Ambassador to the United Nations, Hearing before the Senate Foreign Relations Committee, 107th Congress, 1st Session, September 13, 2001 (hereafter "U.N. Hearings"), 11.

36 R. Cornwell, *The [London] Independent*, July 3, 2004.

37 Saigon A-64, July 23, 1964, National Archives, Record Group 59, Box 2937.

38 Saigon A-99, August 12, 1964, National Archives, Record Group 59, Box 2938. See also Manfull to State Department, July 6, 1964, attaching a report to the same effect on a visit from June 17 to 22, 1964, National Archives, Record Group 59, Box 2926, Folder Pol. 2.

39 Saigon A-125, August 17, 1964, National Archives, Record Group 59, Box 2938.

40 Saigon A-188, September 11, 1964, National Archives, Record Group 59, Box 2938.

41 Saigon A-255, October 1, 1964, National Archives, Record Group 59, Box 2938.

42 Saigon A-331, October 27, 1964, National Archives, Record Group 59, Box 2938.

43 Saigon A-394, November 21, 1964, National Archives, Record Group 59, Box 2938.

44 Saigon A-684, March 9, 1965, National Archives, Record Group 59, Box 2938.

45 Saigon A-9, A-11, A-12, May 25, May 30, and June 17, 1965, National Archives, Record Group 59, Box 2939.

46 Saigon A-76, July 30, 1965, National Archives, Record Group 59, Box 2938.

47 Saigon A-234, October 6, 1965, National Archives, Record Group 59, Box 2939.

48 National Archives, DOS Assistant Secretary of State, Far East, 1961–74, Entry 5408, Box 9, Memoranda dated October 26 and 27, 1965.

49 DOS, Philip Habib Oral History, May 24, 1984.

50 Saigon A-305, November 15, 1965, National Archives, Record Group 59, Box 2938.

51 A. Dommen, *The Indochinese Experience of the French and Americans* (Bloomington, IN: University of Indiana, 2001), 653.

52 DOS, David Lambertson Oral History, August 31, 2004.

53 Johnson, *The Right Hand of Power*, 226.

54 DOS, Robert Oakley Oral History, July 7, 1992, available at memory.loc.gov

55 JN, "What's Really Going on Out There?," October 30, 1969.

56 DOS, John Helble Oral History, April 5, 1996.

57 DOS, William Harrison Marsh Oral History, December 3, 1997.

58 M. Belaud and D. Schoen, *What Makes You Tick: How Successful People Do It and What You Can Learn from Them* (New York: Harper, 2009), 165.

59 DOS, Joseph P. O'Neill Oral History, May 19, 1998, available at memory.loc.gov

60 Negroponte to State Department, Hue 225, sent as Saigon 4437, National Archives, Record Group 59, Box 2876.

61 Bird, *The Color of Truth*, 328, 333.

62 DOS, David Nes Oral History, November 10, 1982.

63 Chalmers Wood to Nolting, April 4, 1963, National Archives, Vietnam Working Group, Record Group 59, Entry 5305, Box 1, Folder ORG 1.

64 DOS, Kenneth Rogers Oral History, October 21, 1997.

65 DOS, William Jeffras Dieterich Oral History, October 19, 1999.

66 DOS, John Sylvester Oral History, April 6, 1993.

67 LBJ Library Oral History, Walt Rostow, March 21, 1969.

68 Pentagon Papers, vol. II, 55 (Boston: Beacon Press, 1971), 55, quoted in Goldstein, *Lessons in Disaster*, 54–5.

69 Quoted by E. Hammer, *A Death in November: America in Vietnam, 1963* (New York: Dutton, 1987), 121, as quoted in Goldstein, *Lessons in Disaster*, 72.

70 Taylor to State Department, Vietnam, January–June 1965 (Washington: GPO, 1996), 554, 561, quoted in Goldstein, *Lessons in Disaster*, 121.

71 LBJ Library Oral History, William Colby, June 2, 1981.

72 Negroponte memorandum, January 15, 1966, National Archives, Record Group 59, Box 2876.

73 National Archives, Vietnam South, Pol. 27, Airgram A505, March 1, 1966, quoted in W. Gibbons, *The US Government and the Vietnam War* (Princeton: Princeton University Press, 1995), 267.

74 V. Walters, *Silent Missions* (New York: Doubleday, 1978), 566.

75 See J. Mc Allister, "Only Religions Count in Vietnam: Trich Tri Quang and the Vietnam War," *Modern Asian Studies*, vol. 42 (2008), 751.

76 N. Ky, *Buddha's Child* (New York: St Martin, 2003), 89–90.

77 Lodge to State Department, September 21, 1965, National Archives, Record Group 59, Box 2931, Folder Pol. 13-6.

78 Hue 197, April 26, 1965; Saigon A-393, December 17, 1965; Saigon 3371, March 17, 1966; Saigon 4128, April 21, 1966; Negroponte memorandum, December 7, 1965, all in National Archives, Record Group 59, Box 2876.

79 Lodge to Secretary of State, April 9, 1966, National Archives, Record Group 59, Box 2924, Folder Pol. 1/1/66.

80 McGeorge Bundy to Lyndon Johnson, February 1965; William P. Bundy Chron File 2/65, National Archives.

81 DOS, Richard Teare Oral History, July 31, 1998.

82 Johnson, *The Right Hand of Power*, 404.

83 M. Higgins, *Our Vietnam Nightmare* (New York: Harper, 1965); R. Critchfield, *The Long Crusade: Political Subversion in the Vietnam War* (New York: Harcourt Brace, 1968); R. Shaplen, *The Lost Revolution* (New York: Harper, 1965); M. Moyar, *Triumph Forsaken: The Vietnam War 1954–65* (Cambridge: Cambridge University Press, 2006), 216–18; M. Moyar, "Political Monks: The Militant Buddhist Movement During the Vietnam War," *Modern Asian Studies*, vol. 38 (2004), 749.

84 See McAllister, "Only Religions Count in Vietnam," 751.

85 Moyar, *Triumph Forsaken*, 277. See also R. Topmiller, *The Lotus Unleashed: The Buddhist Peace Movement in South Vietnam* (Lexington, KY: University of Kentucky, 2002).

86 JN Memo re HAK Visit July 10–29, 1966, A-285 to DOS, July 29, 1966, in National Archives, DOS Assistant Secretary of State, Far East, 1961–74, Entry 5408, Box 9.

87 D. Duncanson, *Government and Revolution in Vietnam* (Oxford: Oxford University Press, 1968), 415 n.377.

88 Negroponte to State Department, December 5, 1966, National Archives, Record Group 59, Box 2876.

89 DOS, David Lambertson Oral History, August 31, 2004.

90 Bunker to Johnson, May 3, 1967, in D. Pike, The Bunker Papers: Reports to the President from Vietnam, 1967–73 (hereafter "Bunker Papers"), 3.

91 Ibid., 23.

92 William Bundy to Porter, December 29, 1966, National Archives, Record Group 59, Box 5414, Folder 18.

93 Bunker Papers, 75.

94 Bunker Papers, 82.

95 Bunker Papers, 135, 153, 139.

96 H. Maurer, *Americans in Vietnam, 1945–75: An Oral History* (New York: Holt, 1989).

97 L. Sorley, *A Better War: The Unexamined Victories and Final Tragedy of America's Last Years in Vietnam* (New York: Harcourt Brace, 1999), 2, 5.

98 Roche to Johnson, May 1, 1967, National Archives, Record Group 59, Box 5408, Folder 10.

99 Johnson, *The Right Hand of Power*, 522.

100 Sorley, *A Better War*, xiv.

101 Holdridge to Kissinger, October 16, 1969, in National Archives, Nixon Collection, Miscellaneous Institutional Files, NSC Administrative Files, Box H-308.

102 P. Hofmann, "For 2 US Aides, Fluent in Vietnamese, Paris is a Place to Talk," *New York Times*, February 17, 1969, 3: 4.

103 JN Oral History, The Cold War, Liddell Hart Military Archive, Kings College, London, March 31, 1997, Number 29/130.

104 J. Stacks, *James B. Reston and the Rise and Fall of American Journalism* (Boston: Little Brown, 2002), 246.
105 J. Schecter, "The Education of a Hawk," *Esquire*, January 1984.
106 C. Etchison, *The Rise and Demise of Democratic Kampuchea* (Boulder, CO: Westview, 1984), 96; see T. Tho, *Cambodian Incursion* (Washington: US Army Center for Military History, 1979), 171–3.
107 Telephone interview, October 29, 1976, quoted in W. Shawcross, *Sideshow: Kissinger, Nixon and the Destruction of Cambodia* (London: Andre Deutsch, 1979), 269.
108 DOS, John Sylvester Oral History, April 6, 1993.
109 Lake and Morris to Kissinger, draft, April 29, 1970, in National Archives, Nixon Collection, Anthony Lake Chron Files, 6/69-10/70, Box 1046.
110 Holbrooke, "Political Settlement in South Vietnam: How Can the Powers be Shared," June 18, 1969; Morris and Lake to Kissinger, October 21, 1969, in National Archives, Nixon Collection, Anthony Lake Chron Files, 6/69-10/70, Box 1046.
111 T. White, *In Search of History: A Personal Adventure* (New York: Harper, 1978), 396.
112 FRUS, Vietnam 1964–8, vol. VI (Washington: GPO, 2002), 285, 329, 334.
113 DOS, Philip Habib Oral History, May 24, 1984.
114 Luu Van Loi, *Fifty Years of Vietnamese Diplomacy, 1945–95* (Hanoi: The Gioi Publishers, 2000), 193.
115 D. Mc Lellan, *Cyrus Vance* (Totowa, NJ: Rowman and Allenhold, 1985), 17.
116 L. Berman, *No Peace, No Honor* (New York: Simon and Schuster, 2001), 68.
117 DOS, Philip Habib Oral History, May 24, 1984.
118 This is the common view of American historians, shared by the North Vietnamese. Van Loi, *Fifty Years of Vietnamese Diplomacy*, 197.
119 FRUS, Vietnam 1964–8, vol. VIII (Washington: GPO, 2003), 7, 26, 34, 58, 119, 184, 287.
120 A. Schlesinger, *Journals 1952–2000* (New York: Penguin, 2007), 268 (entry for January 28, 1969).
121 *New York Times*, February 17, 1969, 3: 4.

Chapter Four

1 US Department of State, Donald Norland Oral History, December 15, 1992.
2 J. Negroponte, "The Negotiated Solution," September 21, 1969.
3 J. Negroponte, "Language," September 23, 1969.
4 J.D. Negroponte, "Celebrating the Sixtieth Anniversary of the Foreign Service Institute," *DISAM Journal*, December 2007.
5 D. Gilmour, *The Ruling Caste: Imperial Lives in the Victorian Raj* (New York: Farrar Straus, 2005).
6 J. Negroponte, "Our Bureaucracy in Vietnam: A Portrait of American Efficiency," September 27, 1969.
7 J. Negroponte, "The Nature of the War," September 29, 1969.
8 J. Negroponte, "Vietnam and the Concept of Limited War: Is a Reappraisal in Order?" March 1970.
9 Quoted in G. Liebmann, *Diplomacy Between the Wars: Five Diplomats and the Shaping of the Modern World* (London: I.B.Tauris, 2008), 16.

Chapter Five

1 "US and USSR Urge Geneva Conference to Give Priority to Treaty Banning Weapons on Ocean Floor," *The New York Times*, June 17, 1970, 7: 7; "Geneva Conference Ends," *The New York Times*, September 4, 1970, 1: 4. A memorandum on the issues, of unknown authorship but in a style resembling that of Negroponte, dated April 18, 1969 appears in Foreign Relations of the United States, 1969–76, vol. E-2, Documents on Arms Control, 1969–72 (Washington: GPO, 2007).
2 Analytical Summary Prepared by John Negroponte of the National Security Council, June 22, 1971, in Foreign Relations of the United States, 1969–76, vol. E-1, Documents

on Global Issues, 1969–72, Document 400 (Washington: GPO, 1990), available at http://www.state.gov/r/pa/ho/frus/nixon/e1/53201.htm

3 While Negroponte was thus engaged, I made one of my occasional contributions to contemporary history, arguing the case of *Dandridge v. Williams* in the Supreme Court, a case summarized in the *Encyclopedia of the American Constitution* with the statement: "After *Dandridge*, it became futile to argue to the Supreme Court either that welfare subsistence was a fundamental interest or that wealth discrimination implied a suspect classification. Since 1970, the court has regularly shied away from decisions that would place the judiciary in the position of allocating state resources." 397 US 471 (1970), see 2 L. Levy, et al. (eds.), *Encyclopedia of the American Constitution* (New York: Macmillan, 1986), 534.

4 V. Walters, *Silent Missions* (New York: Doubleday, 1978), 513–14, 531.

5 Department of State, Winston Lord Oral History, April 28, 1998.

6 D. Young, "The Spiritual Dimension of the Exercise of Political Power," available at www.oxan.com/events/speecharchive/2000-10-05

7 Department of State, Robert Duemling Oral History, April 11, 1989.

8 W. Isaacson, *Kissinger: A Biography* (London: Faber and Faber, 1992), 426 ff. See also Luu Van Loi, *Fifty Years of Vietnamese Diplomacy, 1945–95* (Hanoi: The Gioi Publishers, 2000), 235.

9 H. Kissinger, *White House Years* (London: Weidenfeld and Nicolson, 1979), 1493 n.3.

10 H. Brandon, *The Retreat of American Power* (London: Bodley Head, 1972), 57.

11 R. Morris, *Haig: The General's Progress* (London: Robson, 1982), 198.

12 Ibid., 204.

13 Van Loi, *Fifty Years of Vietnamese Diplomacy*, 116.

14 Ibid., 129.

15 Ibid., 148.

16 G. Aiken, *Aiken: Senate Diary, January 1972–January 1975* (Brattleboro, VT: Stephen Greene Press, 1976), 13, 327 (entries for February 5, 1972 and September 28, 1974).

17 A. Haig, *Inner Circles* (New York: Warner Books, 1992), 296.

18 National Archives, Record Group 59, Lot D481, Box 14, Folder Pol. 15.

19 Kissinger, *White House Years*, 1033.

20 National Archives, Nixon Collection, NSC Papers, Name Files, Harriman, Box 817, Folder 8, Memcon, June 14, 1969; Harriman Comments on Mr. Robert Shaplen's Memorandum for Dr. Kissinger, July 8, 1969; Memcon, September 19, 1969; Letter Harriman to Kissinger, September 22, 1969.

21 Memorandum of Conversation, Harriman, Kissinger, David R. Young, February 24, 1971, in National Archives, Nixon Collection, NSC Name Files, Harriman, Box 817, Folder 8.

22 Lodge to Rusk and McNamara, May 14, 1964, National Archives, Record Group 59, Box 2933, Folder Pol. 15.

23 W. Bundy, *A Tangled Web: The Making of Foreign Policy in the Nixon Presidency* (New York: Hill and Wang, 1998).

24 D. Pike (ed.), *The Bunker Papers: Reports to the President from Vietnam, 1967–73* (Berkeley, CA: Institute for East Asian Studies, 1990).

25 A. Isaacs, *Without Honor: Defeat in Vietnam and Cambodia* (Baltimore: Johns Hopkins, 1983).

26 Bunker Papers, vol. 3, 850.

27 Brandon, *The Retreat of American Power*, 62.

28 Department of State, William Stearman Oral History, April 15, 1992.

29 National Archives, Nixon Collection, NSC Files, President/HAK Memcons, Box 1025, Folder 37, October 8, 1971.

30 Isaacson, *Kissinger*, 381.

31 J. Negroponte to Kissinger, February 16, 1972, in National Archives, Nixon Collection, POW/MIA, Box 3, John Negroponte Negotiations Files 1972–3.

32 J. Kimball, *The Vietnam War Files: Uncovering the Secret History of Vietnam War Strategy* (Lawrence, KS: University Press of Kansas, 2004), 450 n.54.

33 J. Negroponte to Kissinger, March 30, 1972, POW/MIA, Box 3, John Negroponte Negotiations Files 1972–3, National Archives, Nixon Collection.

34 Foreign Relations of the United States, Soviet Union, 1969–76, vol. XIV, October 1971–May 1972 (Washington: GPO, 2006), 92, 99, 139.

35 T. Szulc, *The Illusion of Peace: Foreign Policy in the Nixon Years* (New York: Viking, 1978), 544.

36 Foreign Relations of the United States, Soviet Union, vol. XIV, 632.

37 Ibid., 654. The document referred to is in National Archives, Nixon Presidential Materials, NSC Files, Kissinger Office Files, Box 21, HAK's Secret Moscow Trip Apr 72, TOHAK/HAKTO File [1 of 2], see Ibid., 409 n.2. The memo is unsigned but attributed to Negroponte at Ibid., 655 n.4. It spoke of flexibility in provisions for troop withdrawals and a political settlement.

38 Ibid., 409 n.2.

39 Foreign Relations of the United States, Soviet Union, vol. XIV, 1047; see Isaacson, *Kissinger*, 426.

40 S. Hersh, *The Price of Power: Kissinger in the Nixon White House* (New York: Summit Books, 1983), 584.

41 Foreign Relations of the United States, Soviet Union, vol. XIV, 1078.

42 Ibid., 1081.

43 Hersh, *The Price of Power*, 523.

44 Foreign Relations of the United States, Soviet Union, vol. XIV, 755.

45 W. Thomson and D. Frizzell (eds.), *The Lessons of Vietnam* (New York: Crane, Russak, 1977), 151, 153.

46 Hersh, *The Price of Power*, 523.

47 J. Prados, *Keepers of the Keys: A History of the National Security Council from Truman to Bush* (New York: Morrow, 1991), 331, quoting to R. Nixon, *RN: Memoirs* (New York: Simon and Schuster, 1978), 81.

48 LBJ Library, Walt Rostow Oral History, March 21, 1969.

49 U. Johnson, *The Right Hand of Power* (Englewood Cliffs, NJ: Prentice Hall, 1984), 439.

50 Ball to Rusk, April 11, 1964; Bohlen to Ball, April 13, 1964, in National Archives, Record Group 59, Box 19 of General Records of the Department of State, Formerly Top Secret Central Policy Files, 1964–6.

51 Bohlen to Ball, December 31, 1965, in National Archives, Record Group 59, File Pol. 27.

52 National Archives, Nixon NSC Files, Name File, De Gaulle.

53 Thomson and Frizzell, *The Lessons of Vietnam*, 167.

54 S. Herrington, *Silence Was a Weapon: The Vietnam War in the Villages* (San Francisco: Presidio Press, 1982), 19, reprinted as *Staking the Vietcong* (New York: Ballasting, 1982); D. Andrae, *Ashes to Ashes: The Phoenix Program and the Vietnam War* (Lexington, MA: Lexington Books, 1990); D. Valentine, *The Phoenix Program* (New York: Morrow, 1990).

55 Transcript of December 3, 2006, C-Span, *Question and Answer with JN*, available at www.politics.stephaniedray.com/?q=node/183

56 Foreign Relations of the United States, Soviet Union, vol. XIV, 766.

57 Hersh, *The Price of Power*, 527.

58 J. Negroponte to Kissinger, July 14, 1972, POW/MIA, Box 3, John Negroponte Negotiations Files 1972–3, National Archives, Nixon Collection.

59 Ibid., 575.

60 J. Negroponte to Kissinger, July 27, 1972, and J. Negroponte Memorandum, September 19, 1971, in Nixon NSC Files, National Archives, Box 828, Folder 17.

61 Kissinger to Nixon, August 3, 1972; Nixon to J. Negroponte, August 4, 1972, in Nixon NSC Files, National Archives, Box 828, Folder 17.

62 Ibid.

63 Memcon, Presidential Palace Saigon, August 18, 1972, Nixon NSC Files, National Archives, POW/MIA, Box 3, John Negroponte Negotiations Files 1972–3.

64 Memcon, Presidential Palace Saigon, August 17, 1972, Nixon NSC Files, National Archives, POW/MIA, Box 3, John Negroponte Negotiations Files 1972–3.

65 J. Negroponte Oral History, The Cold War, Liddell Hart Military Archive, Kings College, London, March 31, 1997, Number 29/130.

66 www.gwu-edu/~nsarchiv/NSAEBB/NSAEBB193/HAK%206-20.72pdf

67 L. Berman, *No Peace, No Honor* (New York: Simon and Schuster, 2001), 156–7.

68 A. Dommen, *The Indochinese Experience of the French and the Americans: Nationalism and Communism in Cambodia, Laos, and Vietnam* (Bloomington, IN: Indiana University Press, 2001), 829 ff.

69 W. Haygood, "Ambassador with a Big Portfolio," *Washington Post*, June 21, 2001.

70 J. Negroponte Oral History, The Cold War, Liddell Hart Military Archive, Kings College, London, March 31, 1997, Number 29/130.

71 Szulc, *The Illusion of Peace*, 626.

72 T. Szulc, "How Henry Did It in Vietnam," *Foreign Policy*, Summer 1974, summarized in 103 *Time* 41 (June 10, 1974).

73 G. Goldstein, *Lessons in Disaster: McGeorge Bundy and the Path to War in Vietnam* (New York: Times Books, 2008), 16.

74 Kissinger, *White House Years*, 1493 n.3.

75 S. Karnow, *Vietnam: A History* (London: Century Publishing, 1983), 648.

76 Kissinger, *White House Years*, 1345.

77 "Some Thoughts on Where We Stand on Negotiations," in Folder, Sensitive Camp David, vol. XIX, Box 856, For the President's Files (Winston Lord) in NPMP (Nixon Presidential Materials Project) and NSCF (National Security Council Files), Archives, College Park, quoted in Kimball, *The Vietnam War Files*, 287.

78 H. Kissinger, *White House Years* (Boston: Little Brown, 1979), 1358.

79 Berman, *No Peace, No Honor*, 164.

80 Hersh, *The Price of Power*, 593.

81 Isaacson, *Kissinger*, 449.

82 Kimball, *The Vietnam War Files*, 340–7.

83 Szulc, *The Illusion of Peace*, 664–5.

84 Haig, *Inner Circles*, 295.

85 M. and B. Kalb, *Kissinger* (Boston: Little, Brown, 1974), 357.

86 Thomson and Frizzell, *The Lessons of Vietnam*, 125.

87 Foreign Relations of the United States, Soviet Union, vol. XIV (Memorandum of Conversation, October 13, 1972). See J. Kimball, *Nixon's Vietnam War* (Lawrence, KS: University Press of Kansas, 1998), 340.

88 J. Ehrlichman, *Witness to Power* (New York: Simon and Schuster, 1982), 314.

89 H. Haldeman, *The Haldeman Diaries: Inside the Nixon White House* (New York: Putnam, 1994) (entry for October 12, 1972, 516).

90 R. Nixon, *RN: The Memoirs of Richard Nixon* (New York: Simon and Schuster, 1978), 705.

91 Van Loi, *Fifty Years of Vietnamese Diplomacy*, 254.

92 Ehrlichman, *Witness to Power*, 313.

93 Haig, *Inner Circles*, 202–3.

94 Kimball, *Nixon's Vietnam War*, 347.

95 Prados, *Keepers of the Keys*, 335, citing N. Hung and J. Schechter, *The Palace File* (New York: Harper, 1986), 386.

96 Nixon to Thieu, November 14 and 18, 1972, in Thieu, Box 16, White House Special Files, Nixon Presidential Materials Project.

97 LBJ Library, Ellsworth Bunker Oral History, December 12, 1980.

98 *The New York Times*, May 1, 1975, 1 and 6. On their illegitimacy, see M. Bundy, "Vietnam, Watergate, and Presidential Powers," *Foreign Affairs*, vol. 58 (1980), 397.

99 Isaacson, *Kissinger*, 485.

100 K. Clymer, *The United States and Cambodia, 1969–2000* (London: Routledge, 2004), 59–60.

101 Ehrlichman, *Witness to Power*, 315.

102 J. Negroponte Oral History, The Cold War, Liddell Hart Military Archive, Kings College, London, March 31, 1997, Number 29/130, 13.

103 Quoted in Kissinger, *White House Years*, 1443, quoted in I. Gaiduk, *The Soviet Union and the Vietnam War* (Chicago: Ivan Dee, 1996), 242.

104   Kimball, *Nixon's Vietnam War*, 347, citing Kissinger to Haig, November 23, 1972 in HAK Paris Trip, 18–25 November file, HAKTO, Box 26, Nixon Presidential Materials Project.

105   *The New York Times*, December 17, 1972, 1:6.

106   P. Asselin, *A Bitter Peace: Washington, Hanoi and the Making of the Paris Agreement* (Chapel Hill: University of North Carolina, 2002), 115, quoting Negroponte memorandum for Kissinger, "Alternate Proposal for Bilateral US-DRV Agreement," 15 November 1972, John Negroponte Negotiations Files, 1972–3, vol. 1; Jon Howe Vietnam Subject Files, Box 5, Nixon Presidential Materials Project, College Park.

107   Haig to Colonel Guay, December 15, 1972, in National Archives, Nixon Collection, NSC Files, Haig Chronological File, Box 997.

108   Karnow, *Vietnam*, 653.

109   Kimball, *Nixon's Vietnam War*, 365.

110   Kissinger, *White House Years*, 1467.

111   Memcon, Kissinger and Ivy League Presidents, May 17, 1972, National Archives, Nixon Collection, President/HAK Mem Cons, Box 1026.

112   See also Hung and Schecter, *The Palace File*, 146, 502 n.1.

113   L. Gardner, *Pay Any Price: Lyndon Johnson and the Wars for Vietnam* (Chicago: Ivan Dee, 1995), 342, quoting Hung and Schechter, *The Palace File*, 146. See also Asselin, *A Bitter Peace*, 178, citing S. Ambrose, *Nixon: Ruin and Recovery, 1973–90* (New York: Simon and Schuster, 1989).

114   Isaacson, *Kissinger*, 483.

115   Haig, *Inner Circles*, 299.

116   Ibid., 290 ff.

117   Isaacson, *Kissinger*, 483.

118   Van Loi, *Fifty Years of Vietnamese Diplomacy*, 190.

119   Thomson and Frizzell, *The Lessons of Vietnam*, 104 ff.

120   R. Thompson, *Peace Is Not at Hand* (London: Chatto and Windus, 1974), 119–20.

121   J. Schecter, "The Education of a Hawk," *Esquire*, January 1984.

122   Neil Sheehan Papers, Library of Congress, Note for December 11, 1973, cited in R. Dallek, *Nixon and Kissinger: Partners in Power* (London: Allen Lane, 2007), 470.

123   Ibid.

124   Ibid.

125   Hung and Schecter, *The Palace File*, 98.

126   L. Berman, *No Peace, No Honour: Kissinger, Nexon and Betrayal in Vietnam* (New York: Simon and Schuster, 2001).

127   Hung and Schecter, *The Palace File*.

128   Berman, *No Peace, No Honor*, 257.

129   Select Committee on POW/MIA Affairs, US Senate, Deposition of John Negroponte, 51, cited in B. Hendon and E. Stewart, *An Enormous Crime: The Definitive Account of American POWs Abandoned in Southeast Asia* (New York: St. Martin's, 2007), 493 n.10.

130   Asselin, *A Bitter Peace*, 180.

131   Thompson, *Peace Is Not at Hand*, 92.

132   Thomson and Frizzell, *The Lessons of Vietnam*, 278.

133   Asselin, *A Bitter Peace*, 165.

134   LBJ Library, William Colby Oral History, June 2, 1981.

135   Ibid.,181.

136   M. Maclear, *The Ten Thousand Day War: Vietnam, 1945–75* (New York: St. Martin's, 1981), quoted in D. Brinkley, *Tour of Duty* (New York: Morrow, 2004), 426.

137   J. Negroponte Oral History, The Cold War, Liddell Hart Military Archive, Kings College, London, March 31, 1997, Number 29/130.

138   Van Loi, *Fifty Years of Vietnamese Diplomacy*, 267.

139   Le Duc Tho, Vietnam Courier, June 1985, quoted in W. Duiker, *The Communist Road to Power in Vietnam*, 2nd ed. (Boulder, CO: Westview, 1996), 325.

140   Thompson, *Peace Is Not at Hand*, 110.

141   Johnson, *The Right Hand of Power*, 537.

142   F. Snepp, *Decent Interval: The American Debacle in Vietnam and the Fall of Saigon* (London: Allen Lane, 1980), 86.

143   Kissinger to W. Rostow, January 5, 1973, in National Archives, Record Group 59, Box 832.

144   LBJ Library, William Colby Oral History, June 2, 1981.

145   Johnson, *The Right Hand of Power*, 538.

146   LBJ Library, Ellsworth Bunker Oral History, December 12, 1980.

147   *London Times*, June 3, 1953, 8; see P. Calvocoressi, *World Politics, 1945–2000* (New York: Penguin, 2001), 53, 117, 121.

148   Special Inspector General for Iraqi Reconstruction: Hard Choices: The Iraq Reconstruction Experience (Washington: GPO, 2009), 160.

149   Kissinger to Nixon, September 18, 1971, National Security Files, Subject Vietnam, Alexander Haig Special File, quoted by W. Hammond, *US Army in Vietnam: Public Affairs: The Military and the Media* (Washington: Center for Military History, 1996), 119; Ehrlichman, *Witness to Power*, 316.

150   Thompson, *Peace Is Not at Hand*, 126.

151   Berman, *No Peace, No Honor*, 2.

152   National Archives, Nixon Collection, Oral Histories, Box 2, Elliot Richardson Oral History, May 31, 1988.

153   Department of State, William Stearman Oral History, April 15, 1992.

154   Ibid.

155   Bundy, *A Tangled Web*, 495–6.

156   J. Willbanks, *Abandoning Vietnam: How America Left and South Vietnam Lost Its War* (Topeka: University Press of Kansas, 2008), 169.

157   Ibid., 269.

158   Ibid., 266.

159   National Archives, Nixon Collection, Oral Histories, Box 2, Jerrold Schecter Oral History, February 24, 1988, 8.

160   H. Kissinger, *Years of Renewal* (New York: Simon and Schuster, 1999), 541, 542, quoted in A. Horne, *Kissinger, 1973: The Crucial Year* (New York: Simon and Schuster, 2009), 392.

161   G. Kennan, *The Cloud of Danger* (Boston: Little, Brown, 1977), 94.

162   G. Kennan, "Interview with Eric Sevareid" (1975), in T. Jespersen (ed.), Interviews with George F. Kennan (Jackson, MS: University Press of Mississippi, 2002), 149, 157.

163   Berman, *No Peace, No Honor*, 269 ff.

164   Calvocoressi, *World Politics*, 537.

165   R. Lowenthal, "The Vietnamese Agony: A Reply to Critics," *26 Encounter*, January 1966, 54, 57–8.

166   Bundy, *A Tangled Web*, 516.

167   Memorandum of Robert Barnett, July 28, 1971, in National Archives, Department of State, East Asian Division, Entry 5408, Box 15.

168   William Stearman Oral History, April 15, 1992.

169   M. Green, *Indonesia: Crisis and Transformation, 1965–9* (Washington: Compass, 1990), 152–3, cited in K. Bird, *The Colour of Truth: McGeorge Bundy and William Bundy, Brothers in Arms* (New York: Simon and Schuster, 1998), 254, 453–5.

170   Foreign Relations of the United States, Vietnam 1964 (Washington: GPO, 2006), 484, quoted in Goldstein, *Lessons in Disaster*, 140.

171   D. Halberstam, *The Making of a Quagmire* (New York: Random House, 1965), 315, quoted in Goldstein, *Lessons in Disaster*, 269 n.5.

172   R. Nixon, *RN: Memoirs* (New York: Simon and Schuster, 1978), 743.

173   Kimball, *Nixon's Vietnam War*, 370.

174   Asselin, *A Bitter Peace.*, at 181, quoting Kissinger, *White House Years*.

175   Thompson, *Peace Is Not at Hand*, 128.

176   Kimball, *Nixon's Vietnam War*, 371.

177   Telcon McNamara/Kissinger, January 3, 1973, in Kissinger Telsons, available at www.gwu.edu/~nsarchiv/.

178   Snepp, *Decent Interval*, 488.

179 Van Loi, *Fifty Years of Vietnamese Diplomacy*, 285.

180 Department of State, John Sylvester Oral History, April 6, 1993.

181 Snepp, *Decent Interval*, 488.

182 L. Sorely, *A Better War: The Unexamined Victories and Final Tragedy of America's Last Years in Vietnam* (New York: Harcourt Brace, 1999), 379–80.

183 Calvocoressi, *World Politics*, 539.

184 Department of State, John Sylvester Oral History, April 6, 1993.

185 Ehrlichman, *Witness to Power*, 316.

186 J. Webb, *A Time to Fight: Reclaiming a Just and Fair America* (New York: Broadway Books, 2008), 204.

187 See W. Hixson, "Containment on the Perimeter: George F. Kennan and Vietnam," in W. Hixson (ed.), *Leadership and Diplomacy in the Vietnam War* (New York: Garland, 2000), 259.

188 Isaacson, *Kissinger*, 489.

189 J. Margolin, "Vietnam and Laos: The Impasse of War Communism," in S. Courtois et al., *The Black Book of Communism: Crimes, Terror, Repression* (Cambridge, MA: Harvard University Press, 1999), 565, 570, 572.

190 G. Loescher and J. Scanlan, *Calculated Kindness: Refugees and America's Half Open Door, 1945 to the Present* (New York: Free Press, 1986), 121.

191 Department of State, US Asia-Pacific Council, April 11, 2008.

192 Moynihan to Nixon, April 22, 1973, National Archives, Nixon National Security Council Files, Name File, Moynihan.

193 Schecter, "The Education of a Hawk"

194 Prados, *Keepers of the Keys*, 334. Prados inaccurately states that Negroponte left the NSC staff "a year after Kissinger's negotiation." In fact, he left at the end of February 1973, when implementation of the Paris Agreement had scarcely begun.

195 S. Shane, "Poker-Faced Diplomat; Negroponte is Poised for Role as Spy Chief," *The New York Times*, March 29, 2005, 14.

196 Department of State, Peter Rodman Oral History, May 22, 1994.

197 Department of State, Peter Swiers Oral History, June 6, 1999

198 Department of State, Curtis Jones Oral History, March 29, 1994.

199 M. Belaud and D. Schoen, *What Makes You Tick: How Successful People Do It and What You Can Learn from Them* (New York: Harper, 2009), 165.

200 See C. Villiers, *Start Again, Britain* (London: Quartet Books, 1984).

201 J. Villiers, *Granny Was a Spy* (London: Quartet Books, 1988).

202 J. Negroponte Oral History, The Cold War, Liddell Hart Military Archive, Kings College, London, March 31, 1997, Number 29/130, 14–19.

203 Transcript of December 3, 2006, C-Span, *Question and Answer with JN*, available at www.politics.stephaniedray.com/?q=node/183.

204 C. Trueheart, "Style," *Washington Post*, May 3, 1988, D7.

Chapter Six

1 See Quito 00607, January 28, 1974; 5954, September 9, 1974; 7005, October 27, 1974; 5836, October 12, 1975; 3620, May 23, 1975.

2 *The New York Times*, May 20, 1973, 8: 1; November 9, 1974, 2: 3; December 9, 1974, 57: 1; January 26, 1975, III, 48: 3.

3 *The New York Times*, October 6, 1973, 1.

4 Quito 00566, January 22, 1975.

5 D. Corkill and D. Cubitt, *Ecuador: Fragile Democracy* (London: Latin America Bureau, 1988), 25 ff.

6 J. Negroponte to Department of State, September 14, 1973, A-120; in the National Archives, General State Department Records, Box 2245, Folder Pol. 12.

7 Quito 0643, January 1975.

8 Quito 0617, January 1975.

9 Quito 1397, February 1975.

10 Nixon to Lara, March 8, 1974, in National Archives, Nixon Collection, Miscellaneous Institutional Files, NSC Administrative Files, Box H-308.

11 Guayaquil 456, March 1975.

12 *The New York Times*, September 2, 1975, 1: 7; September 3, 1975, 2: 4.

13 *The New York Times*, November 12, 1975, 43: 3 (C.L. Sulzberger), November 21, 1975 (reply).

14 *Foreign Relations of the United States*, 1969–76, vol. IV (Washington: GPO, 2002), 397; Kissinger, National Security Study Memorandum 131, June 23, 1971; *The New York Times*, August 10, 1973, 37: 2. See generally H. Brands, "Richard Nixon and Economic Nationalism in Latin America: The Problem of Expropriations, 1969–74," *Diplomacy and Statecraft*, vol. 18 (2007), 215.

15 Department of State, Douglas Watson Oral History, January 17, 2000.

16 Negroponte to Kissinger, April 14, 1975, P87054-0748, Department of State Review Authority Case No. 20083282, March 18, 2009, see P. Agee, *Inside the Company: CIA Diary* (New York: Stonehill, 1975).

17 See H. Kissinger, *Years of Upheaval* (New York: Little Brown, 1982), 393, 403, 407; compare http://www.gwu.edu/~nsarchiv/NSAEBB/NSAEBB255/index.htm; L. Qureshi, *Nixon, Kissinger and Allende: US Involvement in the 1973 Coup in Chile* (Lanham, MD: Lexington Books, 2008).

Chapter Seven

1 *The New York Times*, January 23, 1975, 36: 2.

2 *The New York Times*, March 29, 1975, 6: 3.

3 See Thessaloniki 54, February 2, 1975 (bus strike); 648, November 6, 1975 (Pollution Exhibition); 666, November 25, 1975 (Karamanlis); 659, November 18, 1975 (demonstration); 655, November 11, 1975 (PLO office); 653, November 11, 1975 (Mavros visit); 696, December 16, 1975 (lignite).

4 W. La Feber, *Inevitable Revolutions: The United States in Central America* (New York: Norton, 1993), 310. The embassy had 116 members; there were 300–400 American military personnel.

5 B. Hayes, *Midnight Express* (New York: Warner Books, 1977).

Chapter Eight

1 *The New York Times*, August 29, 1979, 7: 1; August 29, 1979, 7: 1; September 1, 1979; September 5, 1979, IV, 20: 3; September 13, 1979, II, 22: 4; September 16, 1979, IV, 18: 4.

2 Nomination of John D. Negroponte to be Ambassador to the United Nations, Hearings before the Senate Foreign Relations Committee, September 13, 2001 (hereafter "UN Hearings").

3 J. Wang, *Handbook on Ocean Politics and Law* (Westport, CT: Greenwood, 1992), 142 ff.

4 W. Warner, *Distant Water: The Fate of the North Atlantic Fisherman* (New York: Penguin, 1983), 309, 320, 322, 323, 327.

5 Department of State, Richard J. Smith Oral History, July 30, 1996.

6 *The New York Times*, February 15, 1979, 25: 1; March 30, 1979, 7: 1; July 5, 1979, 12: 1; April 16, 1980, 4: 3; June 15, 1980, 12: 1; March 2, 1981, 3: 4; March 11, 1981, 10: 3; March 13, 1981, 11: 3.

7 *The New York Times*, June 3, 1980, 10: 4; March 7, 1981, 3: 1.

8 *The New York Times*, May 3, 1981, 60: 3.

9 Delimitation of Maritime Boundary in Gulf of Maine Area, ICJ Reports No. 67, *USA. v. Canada*, 1984, see Wang, *Handbook on Ocean Politics and Law*, 142 n.66.

10 *The New York Times*, July 27, 1980, 13: 1; October 22, 1981, 28: 6; August 2, 1981, V, 6: 5.

11 Analytical Summary Prepared by John Negroponte of the National Security Council, June 22, 1971, in Foreign Relations of the United States, 1969–76, vol. E-1, Documents on Global Issues, 1969–72, Document 400 (Washington: GPO, 19), available at http://www.state.gov/r/pa/ho/frus/nixon/e1/53201.htm

Chapter Nine

1 S. Hurst, *The Carter Administration and Vietnam* (London: Macmillan Press, 1996), 112. See also L. Stern, *Defense Relations Between the United States and Vietnam: The Process of Normalization, 1977–2003* (Jefferson, NC: McFarland, 2005).

2 M. Haas, *Genocide by Proxy, Cambodian Pawn on a Superpower Chessboard* (Westport, CT: Praeger, 1991), 117.

3 N. Chanda, *Brother Enemy: The War After the War* (New York: Harcourt Brace, 1986), 86.

4 J. Garner, "The Reagan Administration's Southeast Asia Policy," in J. Hsuiung (ed.), *The National Security Paradox* (Westport, CT: Praeger, 1983), 121. See Negroponte's testimony in Human Rights in Asia: Communist Countries, Hearings before the Subcommittee on Asia and Pacific Affairs, House Foreign Affairs Committee, 96th Congress, 2nd Session, October 1, 1980, 11–23.

5 Ibid.

6 Documents on American Foreign Policy 1977–80 (Washington: US Department of State, 1982), Document 606.

7 D. Anderson, *An American in Hanoi: America's Reconciliation with Vietnam* (White Plains, NY: East Bridge, 2002).

8 Association for Diplomatic Studies and Training, Foreign Affairs Oral History Project, Interview with Ambassador Daniel A. O'Donohue, May 28, 1996.

9 A. Haig, *Caveat: Realism, Reagan, and Foreign Policy* (London: Weidenfeld and Nicolson, 1984), 30.

10 Association for Diplomatic Studies and Training, Foreign Affairs Oral History Project, Interview with Ambassador Daniel A. O'Donohue, May 28, 1996.

11 N. Easton, *Gang of Five: Leaders at the Center of the Conservative Ascendancy* (New York: Simon and Schuster, 2000), 165 ff.; see also B. Bradlee, *Guts and Glory: The Rise and Fall of Oliver North* (London: Grafton, 1988), 154.

12 E. Hobsbawm, *The Age of Extremes* (New York: Pantheon, 2000), 457.

13 Garner, "The Reagan Administration's Southeast Asia Policy," 123.

14 J. Mann, *About Face: A History of America's Curious Relationship with China from Nixon to Clinton* (New York: Knopf, 1999).

15 G. Kennan, *The Cloud of Danger* (Boston: Little, Brown, 1977), 94–5.

16 Negroponte's testimony in Human Rights in Asia, 11.

17 J. Hein, *From Vietnam, Laos and Cambodia* (New York: Twayne, 1995), 46–7.

18 W. Robinson, *Terms of Refuge: The Indochinese Exodus and the International Response* (London: Zed, 1995), 295.

19 Department of State, Robert Oakley Oral History, July 7, 1992.

20 Department of State, Lacy Wright Oral History, January 6, 1998.

21 P. Koehn, *Refugees from Revolution: US Policy and the Third World* (Boulder, CO: Westview, 1991).

22 Hein, *From Vietnam, Laos and Cambodia*, 46–7; J. Tollefson, *Alien Winds: The Re-education of America's Indochinese Refugees* (Westport, CT: Praeger, 1989), xiv; P. Strand and W. Jones, *Indochinese Refugees in America: Problems of Adaptation and Assimilation* (Durham, NC: Duke University Press, 1985), 77; G. Kelly, *From Vietnam to America: A Chronicle of the Vietnamese Immigration to the United States* (Boulder, CO: Westview, 1977); P. Koehn, *Refugees from Revolution: US Policy and the Third World* (Boulder, CO: Westview, 1991).

23 D. Davies, "Time to Encourage the Vietnamese Titoists," *Far Eastern Economic Review*, July 17, 1981, 30; R. Nations, "The Saigon Cowboys Will Not Give Up," *Far Eastern Economic Review*, July 17, 1981, 32.

24 C. Bon Tempo, *Americans at the Gate: The US and Refugees During the Cold War* (Princeton: Princeton University Press, 2008), 146–7.

25 G. Loescher and J. Scanlan, *Refugees and America's Half-Open Door, 1945 to the Present* (New York: Free Press, 1986), 123–4.

26 Ibid., 138.

27 Kelly, *From Vietnam to America*, 18.

28 W. Shawcross, *The Quality of Mercy: Cambodia, Holocaust, and Modern Conscience* (New York: Simon and Schuster, 1984), 293, 348.

29 S. Henley, "Honoring an 'Aggressive Interventionist': Ambassador Morton Abramowitz," *Foreign Service Journal*, July/August 2006.
30 Loescher and Scanlan, *Refugees and America's Half-Open Door*, 200.
31 Department of State, Theodore Wilkinson Oral History, January 11, 1999.
32 In re Coconut Oil Antitrust Litigation, M.D.L. 474 (N.D. Cal., 1983).
33 R. Bonner, *Waltzing with a Dictator: The Marcoses and the Making of American Policy* (London: Macmillan Press, 1987), 174–5, 290, 329, 334, citing In re Coconut Oil Antitrust Litigation, Multidistrict Litigation Panel: State 034796, February 10, 1981.
34 J. Taft, "Fleeing Our Responsibilities: The US Owes Succor to Iraqi Refugees," *Washington Post*, June 24, 2007.

Chapter Ten

1 Department of State, David Miller Oral History, January 6, 2003.
2 Quoted without citation in R. Donner, *Weakness and Deceit: US Policy and El Salvador* (London: Hamish Hamilton, 1985), 251.
3 C. Krauss, *Inside Central America: Its People, Politics and History* (New York: Simon and Schuster, 1991), 194.
4 Department of State, James Maack Oral History, March 20, 2004.
5 Department of State, Fernando Rondon Oral History, June 4, 1997.
6 C. Arnson, *Crossroads: Congress, the Reagan Administration and Central America* (New York: Pantheon, 1989), 51.
7 Department of State Curtin Winsor Oral History, February 29, 1988.
8 R. Pastor, *Condemned to Repetition: The United States and Nicaragua* (Princeton: Princeton University Press, 1987), 251.
9 B. Bradlee, *Guts and Glory: The Rise and Fall of Oliver North* (London: Grafton, 1988), 216.
10 Ibid., 146.
11 Department of State, Laurence Pezzulo Oral History, February 24, 1989.
12 "The Quiet One," *London Economist*, September 5, 1981, 48.
13 National Security Decision Directive 17, December 1, 1981, available at www.gwu. edu/~nsarchiv, see Arnson, *Crossroads*, 72 ff.
14 Negroponte to Motley, September 20, 1983.
15 Department of State, Curtin Winsor Oral History, February 29, 1988.
16 Negroponte to Kirkpatrick, February 15, 1983.
17 B. Rubin, *Secrets of State: The State Department and the Struggle Over US Foreign Policy* (New York: Oxford University Press, 1985), 226 ff.
18 Ibid., 225–6.
19 W. Pfaff, *Barbarian Sentiments: America in the New Century*, 2nd ed. (New York: Hill and Wang, 2000), 175–6.
20 W. Lake, *Third World Radical Regimes: US Policy Under Carter and Reagan* (New York: Foreign Policy Association, 1985), 12–13.
21 Department of State, Robert White Oral History, June 10, 1992.
22 Arnson, *Crossroads*, 72.
23 J. Brecher, et al., "A Secret War for Nicaragua," *Newsweek*, November 8, 1982, reprinted in P. Rosset and J. Vandermeer (eds.), *The Nicaragua Reader: Documents of a Revolution Under Fire* (New York: Grove, 1983), 208–13.
24 Tegucigalpa 9683, Negroponte to Shultz, November 3, 1982.
25 Tegucigalpa 9544, Negroponte to Shultz, November 30, 1982.
26 Quoted in J. Le Moyne, "Testifying to Torture," *New York Times*, June 5, 1988.
27 D. Dent, *The Legacy of the Monroe Doctrine: A Reference Guide to US Involvement in the Caribbean and Latin America* (Westport, CT: Greenwood, 1999), 244.
28 Tegucigalpa 9619, Negroponte to Shultz, November 2, 1982.
29 Negroponte to Graham, November 12, 1982.
30 Peter R. Rosenblatt to Madeleine Edmondson, February 1, 1983.
31 S. Emerson, *Secret Warriors: Inside the Covert Military Operations of the Reagan Era* (New York: Putnam, 1988), 90–3.

32 "US Is Said to Plot Against Sandinistas," *New York Times*, November 1, 1982; "US Backing Raids Against Nicaragua," *New York Times*, November 2, 1982.

33 C. Dickey, *With the Contras: A Reporter in the Wilds of Nicaragua* (New York: Simon and Schuster, 1985), 239.

34 J. Prados, *Safe for Democracy: The Secret Wars of the CIA* (Chicago: Ivan Dee, 2006), 515.

35 W. Leo Grande, *Our Own Backyard: The United States in Central America, 1977–92* (Chapel Hill: University of North Carolina Press, 1998), 298.

36 T. Barry, et al., *Dollars and Dictators: A Guide to Central America* (Albuquerque, NM: Resource Center, 1982), 171.

37 Tegucigalpa 214, Negroponte to Shultz, January 11, 1982.

38 Tegucigalpa 403, Negroponte to Shultz and others, February 19, 1982.

39 W. Lafeber, *Inevitable Revolutions: The United States in Central America* (New York: Norton, 1993).

40 A. Riding, "Hondurans Upset at Civilian Rule," *New York Times*, November 9, 1982.

41 Tegucigalpa 4201, Negroponte to Shultz, May 19, 1982.

42 R. Woodward, *Veil: The Secret Wars of the CIA, 1981–87* (New York: Simon and Schuster, 1987), 231.

43 R. Gutman, *Banana Diplomacy: The Making of American Policy in Nicaragua* (New York: Simon and Schuster, 1988), 136.

44 Rubin, *Secrets of State*, 228.

45 L. Jenkins, "Diplomats Overshadowed by Officer Influential in Latin Region," *Washington Post*, January 3, 1984.

46 Rubin, *Secrets of State*, 91–2.

47 Department of State, Anthony Motley Oral History, March 7, 1991.

48 Department of State, John A. Ferch Oral History, September 27, 1991.

49 Rubin, *Secrets of State*.

50 M. Rosenberg, "Honduras: Bastion of Stability or Quagmire?" in D. Schulz and D. Graham (eds.), *Revolution and Counterrevolution in Central America and the Caribbean* (Boulder, CO: Westview, 1984), 340.

51 Gutman, *Banana Diplomacy*, 103.

52 Latin America Regional Reports, July 9, 1982, 6.

53 D. Schulz and D. Sundloff Schulz, *The United States, Honduras, and the Crisis in Central America* (Boulder, CO: Westview, 1994), 75–7.

54 Department of State, Theodore Wilkinson Oral History, January 11, 1999.

55 *The New York Times*, April 3, 1983, I, 1: 3, see also April 7, 1983, II, 16: 1.

56 T. Leonard, *Central America and the United States: The Search for Stability* (Athens, GA: University of Georgia, 1991), 197.

57 J. Gibson, *The Perfect War: Techno War in Vietnam* (Boston: Atlantic Monthly Press, 1986), 457–8.

58 W. Blanchard, *Neocolonialism, American Style* (Westport, CT: Greenwood, 1996), 79.

59 Department of State, Curtin Winsor Oral History, February 29, 1988.

60 R. McGehee, "Deadly Deceits," 44 Facts on File 470 (1984); R. Mc Gehee, "The CIA and the White Paper on El Salvador," *The Nation*, April 11, 1981, 425.

61 Tegucigalpa 4201, Negroponte to Shultz, May 19, 1982.

62 Tegucigalpa 3277, Negroponte to Shultz, April 18, 1982.

63 Tegucigalpa 4849, Negroponte to Shultz, June 9, 1982.

64 Tegucigalpa 7317, Negroponte to Shultz, August 30, 1982.

65 J. Morris, *Honduras: Caudillo Politics and Military Rulers* (Boulder, CO: Westview, 1983), 116.

66 G. Shultz, *Turmoil and Tradition* (New York: Scribner, 1993), 288.

67 Tegucigalpa 9850, Negroponte to Shultz, November 8, 1982.

68 Tegucigalpa 3864, Negroponte to Shultz, May 6, 1982.

69 JN to State Department, June 8, 1983, Tegucigalpa 5881.

70 Tegucigalpa 4068, Negroponte to Shultz, April 27, 1983.

71 Schulz and Sundloff Schulz, *The United States, Honduras*, 77.

72 J. Duarte, "Eyewitness to History: Retired Diplomat Recalls Service in Latin America," available at www.Sthelenastar.com/articles/2008/06/19/news/local/doc4859c5600634b690614870 (June 19, 2008).

73 *Wall Street Journal*, March 9, 1984.

74 Department of State, William Jeffras Dieterich Oral History, October 19, 1999.

75 Tegucigalpa 3456, April 8, 1983.

76 Prado, *Safe for Democracy*, 516.

77 Department of State, Robert Duemling Oral History, April 11, 1989.

78 Negroponte to Motley, Clark and Casey, July 29, 1983.

79 Tegucigalpa 7600, Negroponte to Shultz, July 20, 1983.

80 Tegucigalpa 6944, Negroponte to Shultz, July 1, 1983.

81 *Los Angeles Times*, August 12, 1983.

82 *The New York Times*, January 12, 1982.

83 *London Times*, October 31, 1983, 6.

84 "Pilot Killed Landed in Nicaragua," *Washington Post*, January 4, 1984; S. Kinzer, "Copter Strayed in Strong Wind, Official Asserts," *Toronto Globe and Mail*, January 14, 1984; R. McCartney, "All Details to be Re-examined," *Washington Post*, January 20, 1984.

85 *The New York Times*, April 29, 1984, I, 66: 1, see also *New York Times*, April 20, 1984.

86 "US Rejection of Nicaraguan Envoy Credited to CIA Influence," *San Diego Union Tribune*, April 2, 1984.

87 D. Negroponte, "Work Among Refugees Is Purely Humanitarian," *Miami Herald*, June 12, 1983, 6E.

88 Negroponte to Shultz, March 18, 1982.

89 Schulz and Sundloff Schulz, *The United States, Honduras*, 77–8.

90 "Plaza 'Diana Negroponte' Construivan en Tegucigalpa," *El Heraldo*, May 25, 1985.

91 Arnson, *Crossroads*, 58.

92 Ibid., 84.

93 M. Danner, *The Massacre at El Mozote* (New York: Vintage, 1994), 136, see also G. Astor, *Presidents at War: From Truman to Bush: The Gathering of Military Powers to the Commander in Chief* (New York: Wiley, 2006), 203.

94 Arnson, *Crossroads*, 99.

95 Department of State, Anthony Motley Oral History, March 7, 1991.

96 *London Times*, April 11, 1983, 6.

97 Negroponte to Casey, Clark, and Enders, May 13, 1983.

98 *The New York Times*, April 3, 1983.

99 See generally J. Kruckewitt, "US Militarization of Honduras in the 1980s and the Creation of CIA-Backed Death Squads," in M. Cecilia and N. Rodriguez (eds.), *When States Kill: Latin America, the US and the Technologies of Terror* (Austin: University of Texas, 2005), Chapter 7.

100 A. Armony, "Transnationalizing the Dirty War: Argentina in Central America," in G. Joseph (ed.), *In from the Cold, Latin America's New Encounter with the Cold War* (Durham, NC: Duke University Press, 2008).

101 "Interview with Duane Clarridge," available at http://www.gwu.edu/~nsarchiv/cold-war/interviews/episode-18/clarridge3.html

102 J. Binns, *The United States in Honduras: An Ambassador's Memoir, 1980–81* (Jefferson, NC: Mc Farland, 2000), 13–14, 33, 51.

103 Ibid., 320 n.12. 322 n.12, 25.

104 Department of State, Theodore Wilkinson Oral History, January 11, 1999.

105 Tegucigalpa 405, Negroponte to Abrams and Bosworth, January 18, 1982.

106 U.N. Hearings, 69, 72, 39.

107 S. Menzel, *Dictators, Drugs and Revolution: Cold War Campaigning in Latin America, 1965–89* (New York: Author House, 2006), 141–3.

108 Tegucigalpa 2854, Negroponte to Shultz, April 2, 1982.

109 Barry, et al., *Dollars and Dictators*, 166.

110 Menzel, *Dictators, Drugs and Revolution*, 143.

111 Tegucigalpa 8233, Negroponte to American Embassy, London, September 23, 1982. The letter appeared in the Economist for October 23, 1982.

112 US Department of State, Country Reports on Human Rights (1982), 609–15, see "Special Report—Battalion," 316, *Baltimore Sun*, June 11–18, 1995.

113 Nomination of Ambassador John D. Negroponte to be Director of National Intelligence, Hearings before the Select Committee on Intelligence, United States Senate, 109th Congress, 1st Session, April 12, 2005 (hereafter "DNI Hearings"), 161.

114 J. Mann, *About Face: A History of America's Curious Relationship with China from Nixon to Clinton* (New York: Knopf, 1999), 103, citing R. Cohen, "People's Republic of China: The Human Rights Exception," *Human Rights Quarterly*, 9 (1987), 478–9.

115 Rubin, *Secrets of State*, 181–2.

116 Department of State, Anthony Motley Oral History, March 7, 1991.

117 D. Negroponte, *Conflict Resolution at the End of the Cold War: The Case of El Salvador, 1989–94* (Ann Arbor: University Microfilms, 2006).

118 Arnson, *Crossroads*, 96.

119 Astor, *Presidents at War from Truman to Bush*, 203.

120 22 USC. Secs 2151n and 2304.

121 P. Rodman, *More Precious Than Peace: The Cold War and the Struggle for the Third World* (New York: Scribner, 1994), 247.

122 G. Shultz, *Turmoil and Triumph: My Years as Secretary of State* (New York: Scribner, 1993), 291.

123 Foreign Relations of the United States, 1950, vol. II (Washington: GPO, 1976), 598–624.

124 R. Cornwell, *The [London] Independent*, July 3, 2004.

125 J. Negroponte, "Honduras Is Well Worth Saving," *Los Angeles Times*, August 12, 1983, II, 7.

126 Tegucigalpa 8401, Negroponte to Shultz, September 28, 1982.

127 Tegucigalpa 9849, Negroponte to Shultz, November 8, 1942.

128 U.N. Hearings, 18.

129 "Sistema Judicial Es El Punto Debil de Honduras," *Tiempo*, August 13, 1984, 13; "Tendencia de Impartir Justicia en Honduras es Positiva: Negroponte," *La Prensa*, April 1, 1985.

130 Tegucigalpa 01818, Negroponte to Shultz, February 8, 1985.

131 National Commissioner for the Protection of Human Rights in Honduras, The Facts Speak for themselves: Preliminary Report (New York: Center for Justice and International Law/Human Rights Watch, 1994), 212, 225.

132 Leo Grande, *Our Own Backyard*, 298 and authorities cited.

133 Prados, *Safe for Democracy*, 526.

134 UN Hearings, 18, 70.

135 A. Mc Coy, "Torture in the Crucible of Counterinsurgency," in L. Gardner and M. Young (eds.), *Iraq and the Lessons of Vietnam, or How Not to Learn from the Past* (New York: New Press, 2007), 256.

136 Cornwell, *The [London] Independent*.

137 Amnesty International, Honduras Human Rights Violations in the 80s (London: Amnesty International, 1988), 18. See also the statistics of assassinations and disappearances in R. Lapper and J. Painter, *Honduras: State for Sale* (London: Latin American Bureau, 1985), 87.

138 Le Moyne, "Testifying to Torture."

139 Central Intelligence Agency. Inspector General, Report of Investigation, Selected Issues Relating to CIA Activities in Honduras in the 1980s (Washington: Central Intelligence Agency, 1997), 126, available at www.gwu.edu/~nsarchiv/latin_america/honduras/cia_ig_report/03-01.htm

140 Ibid., 299, citing J. Le Moyne, "CIA Accused of Tolerating Killings in Honduras," *New York Times*, February 14, 1986.

141 Leo Grande, *Our Own Backyard*, 299.

142 Dickey, *With the Contras*, 125.

143 K. De Young, "Former Ambassador in Line for UN Post," *The Washington Post*, February 17, 2001, 4; C. Lynch, "Bush Names Negroponte to UN Post," *The Washington Post*, March 7, 2001, 20; *The New York Times*, February 18, 2001; May 28, 2001, 5: 5; June 14, 2001, 1: 2; June 15, 2001, 2: 3; August 18, 2001, 14: 1; September 14, 2001, B3: 1; September 15, 2001, B2: 6.

144 R. Byrd, *Losing America: Confronting a Reckless and Arrogant Presidency* (New York: Norton, 2004), 125–6.

145 S. Kinzer, "Our Man in Honduras," *New York Review of Books*, vol. 48, no. 14 (September 20, 2001).

146 Binns, *The United States in Honduras*, 49–50, 201–2, 205, 207–8.

147 "An Exchange on John Negroponte," *New York Review of Books*, vol. 48, no. 16 (October 18, 2001).

148 Le Moyne, "Testifying to Torture," 47.

149 Inter-American Court of Human Rights, Series C, No. 4 (1988), In re Velasquez Rodriguez, Order of January 15, 1988, 9 HRLJ 104 (1988); 9 HRLJ 105 (1988); Judgment of July 21, 1988, 28 ILM 291 (1989), 9 HRLJ 212 (1988); Judgment of July 21, 1989 (damages), 11 HRLJ 127 (1990), 12 HRLJ 14 (1991).

150 Quoted in J. Nordlinger, "John Negroponte," *National Review*, June 25, 2001, 40.

151 UN Hearing, 57.

152 Cf. G. Black, "The Many Killers of Father Carney," *The Nation*, January 23, 1988, 84–5; J. Carney, *To Be a Revolutionary* (New York: Harper One, 1985).

153 CIA Stipulations to Facts Regarding Honduran Military Activities and US Intelligence in Honduras in the 1980s, available at www.mayispeakfreely.org/nodev/index.php?gSec=doc&doc_id=121

154 S. Shane, "Poker-Faced Diplomat; Negroponte Is Poised for Role as Spy Chief," *New York Times*, March 29, 2005, 14.

155 M. Lacey, "Central American Fallout Stalls U.N. Pick," *New York Times*, June 4, 2001, 1: 2.

156 Perspectives on World History and Current Events, John Negroponte: Career of a Conservative Idealist.

157 UN Hearings, 29–30.

158 *The New York Times*, July 22, 1984, IV, 5: 1.

159 Alvarez was said to be associated with the Unification Church of the Rev. Sun Moon. J. Weiss, "National Identity, Repression, and Popular Response," in J. Kirk and G. Schuyler (eds.), *Development and Change in Central America* (Westport, CT: Praeger, 1988), 47.

160 Leo Grande, *Our Own Backyard*, 394–5.

161 Lapper and Painter, *Honduras*, 107.

162 Schulz and Sundloff Schulz, *The United States, Honduras*, 137 n.3.

163 Department of State, Ward Barman Oral History, July 27, 1998.

164 Ibid., 92.

165 Schulz and Sundloff Schulz, *The United States, Honduras*, 79.

166 Ibid., 106.

167 Ibid., 396.

168 Leo Grande, *Our Own Backyard*, 357–63.

169 Tegucigalpa 11971, Negroponte to Shultz, September 24, 1984.

170 Tegucigalpa 13843, December 16, 1983.

171 Negroponte to Motley, September 20, 1983.

172 Leo Grande, *Our Own Backyard*, 353.

173 C. Menges, *Inside the National Security Council: The True Story of the Making and Unmaking of Reagan's Foreign Policy* (New York: Simon and Schuster, 1988), 161 ff.

174 Poindexter to McFarlane, "A Proposal for Resolving Inter-Agency Conflict," November 23, 1984 in Iran-Contra Hearings, vol. 100–8, pp. 414–17, cited at Leo Grande, *Our Own Backyard*, 362 n.82.

175 Leo Grande, *Our Own Backyard*, 363.

176 R. Pardo-Maurer, *The Contras, 1980–89: A Special Kind of Politics* (Westport, CT: Praeger, 1990), 86.

177 Menzel, *Dictators, Drugs and Revolution*, 165; see also T. Greentree, *Crossroads of Intervention: Insurgency and Counterinsurgency Lessons from Central America* (Westport, CT: Praeger, 2008), 116.

178 Menzel, *Dictators, Drugs and Revolution*, 191.

179 T. Draper, *A Very Thin Line: The Iran-Contra Affairs* (New York: Hill and Wang, 1991), 108, citing *The Washington Post*, April 12, 1989.

180 Leo Grande, *Our Own Backyard*, 391.
181 Draper, *A Very Thin Line*, 109.
182 McFarlane Memorandum, Recommended Telephone Call, April 25, 1985, available at www.gwu.edu/~nsarchiv/
183 Iran-Contra Report, Findings, Para. 63, available at www.gwu.edu/~nsarchiv
184 Ibid., 395.
185 Email North to Poindexter, September 17, 1986, available at www.gwu.edu/~nsarchiv/. See Iran-Contra Report, Finding 102.
186 Director of National Intelligence Hearing, 18.
187 J. Omang, "Two Ambassadors to Central America Expected to be Replaced," *The Washington Post*, January 5, 1984.
188 M. Perry, *Eclipse: The Last Days of the CIA* (New York: Morrow, 1992), 394, citing R. Weekes, "CIA's Friend Sent Into Exile," *Manchester Guardian*, April 8, 1984.
189 Leo Grande, *Our Own Backyard*, 315.
190 Gutman, *Banana Diplomacy*, 191.
191 L. Chavez, "Reagan's Man in Honduras Is Having Some Back Talk," *The New York Times*, July 22, 1984.
192 Tegucigalpa 00416, Negroponte to Shultz, January 10, 1985.
193 Ibid., 180, 213–15.
194 Pardo-Maurer, *The Contras, 1980–89*, 34.
195 J. Omang, "Transfer Planned for Envoy to El Salvador," *The Washington Post*, December 12, 1984 (Motley); R. Greenberger, "Some Conservatives Claim They Blocked Political Purge at State Department," *Toronto Globe and Mail*, December 20, 1984 (Negroponte and Reagan); "Reagan Administration Is Considering Diplomatic Appointments to Latin America," *Latin America Weekly Report*, January 25, 1985 (Democratic Senator); T. Waldo, "Shake-Up of US Diplomatic Corps," *San Francisco Chronicle*, March 13, 1985 (Shultz).
196 Perry, *Eclipse*, 122.
197 Department of State, Ward Barman Oral History, July 27, 1998.
198 Tegucigalpa 11100, Negroponte to San Jose Embassy, October 11, 1983.
199 Leo Grande, *Our Own Backyard*, 590.
200 "US Presence Provokes Misgivings in Honduras," *New York Times*, February 9, 1984.
201 Waldo, "Shake-Up of US Diplomatic Corps."
202 Prados, *Safe for Democracy*, 526.
203 Perry, *Eclipse*, 396.
204 Leonard, *Central America and the United States*, 197.
205 D. Moreno, *The Struggle for Peace in Central America* (Miami: University of Florida Press, 1994), 40.
206 Krauss, *Inside Central America*, 217.
207 *The New York Times*, February 18, 1984, I, 22: 3, disputing a column by John Oakes, appearing on January 28, 1984; *The New York Times*, August 4, 1984, I, 22: 4, disputing an article appearing on July 27, 1984; Tegucigalpa 6639, Negroponte to Shultz, August 9, 1982, responding to an article by former Ambassador to Salvador Robert White which appeared in the magazine for July 18, 1982. See Oakes' later column, J. Oakes, "Treating the Honduras as a Vassal State," *The New York Times*, January 11, 1985.
208 *The New York Times*, September 12, 1982.
209 *London Times*, September 26, 1984, 6.
210 *London Times*, October 2, 1984.
211 "McFarlane Ends Trip to Five Nations," *The Washington Post*, January 20, 1985.
212 Prados, *Safe for Democracy*, 526.
213 *The New York Times*, March 30, 1985, I, 3: 3.
214 *Dallas Morning News*, April 28, 1985, 39a.
215 Krauss, *Inside Central America*, 217–18.
216 *The New York Times*, February 14, 1989; April 16, 1989, I, 5: 1; April 19, 1989, 23: 4; May 23, 1989, I, 24: 5.
217 UN Hearing, 49.
218 *The New York Times*, May 1, 1989, I, 12: 6.

219 D. Ryan, *US-Sandinista Diplomatic Relations: Voice of Intolerance* (Macmillan Press, 1995), 100–4.
220 *United States v. Oliver North*, in the United States District Court for the District of Columbia, Criminal No. 88-0080-02 GAG, Government Stipulations 44, 60, 63, 102.
221 Lapper and Painter, *Honduras*, 87.
222 R. Kagan, *A Twilight Struggle: American Power and Nicaragua, 1977–90* (Glencoe, IL: Free Press, 1996), 394–5, citing Negroponte to State Department, Tegucigalpa 6693, May 18, 1985.
223 B. Shore, "Panel OKs Two Nominees for Important Latin Posts," *San Diego Tribune*, June 9, 1989.
224 Leonard, *Central America and the United States*, 194.
225 Congressional Research Service, Foreign Policy Budget for 2007 (revised February 17, 2006) (Washington: Congressional Research Service, 2006), 30.
226 S. Murshed, (ed.), "Global Integration and Growth in Honduras and Nicaragua," in *Globalization, Marginalization, and Development* (London: Routledge, 2002), 226.
227 R. Kaplan, "Was Democracy Just a Moment," *Atlantic*, December 1997; see R. Kaplan, *The Coming Anarchy: Shattering the Dreams of the Post Cold War* (New York: Random House, 2000).
228 M. Vargas Llosa, "Global Village or Global Pillage," *Reason*, July 2001.
229 See Toronto Globe and Mail, May 31, 1985 (appointment of Ferch); "McFarlane Ends Trip to Five Nations," *The Washington Post*, January 20, 1985 (departure of Gorman); *Seattle Times*, July 1, 1986 (departure of Ferch); "US Probes Embassy Goofs in Nicaragua," *Seattle Times*, June 3, 1985, excerpted from Foreign Policy, Summer 1985.
230 "Human Rights Commission Asks for Negroponte Expulsion," *Latin American Weekly Report*, May 17, 1985.
231 T. Farer, "Why Contadora States Oppose US Policy in Central America," *San Francisco Chronicle*, July 10, 1985.
232 Gates to Casey, December 14, 1984, available at www.gwu.edu/_nsarchiv/. A marking indicates the document was superseded by a revised document dated December 18 not in the released archive.
233 J. Lehman, *Command of the Seas* (New York: Scribner, 1988).
234 J. Adams, *A Foreign Policy in Transition: Moscow's Retreat from Central America and the Caribbean, 1985–92* (Durham, NC: Duke University Press, 1992).
235 "Interview with Yuri Pavlov," available at http://www.gwu.edu/~nsarchiv/coldwar/interviews/episode-18/pavlov3.html
236 Transcript of December 3, 2006, C-Span, *Question and Answer with JN*, available at www.politics.stephaniedray.com/?q=node/183
237 W. Hagood, "Ambassador with Big Portfolio: John Negroponte Goes to Baghdad with a Record of Competence and Controversy," June 21, 2004, C-01.
238 "Profile: John Negroponte: Ringmaster for the Big US Spy Showdown," *Sunday Times [London]*, February 20, 2005.
239 "Diana Negroponte, Madre de una Hondurena," *La Prensa*, May 7, 1983.
240 UN Hearings, 33.
241 H. Kissinger, *A World Restored: Metternich, Castlereagh and the Congress of Vienna* (London: Gollancz, 1973).
242 U.N. Hearing, 59.
243 U.N. Hearing, 17.
244 Report of the President's National Bipartisan Commission on Central America (New York: Macmillan, 1984), 84, 86; see A. Schlesinger, *Journals, 1952–2000* (New York: Penguin, 2007), 484 (entry for September 17, 1983).
245 Ibid., 113.
246 JN Oral History, The Cold War, Liddell Hart Military Archive, Kings College, London, October, 1997, Number 27/162.
247 P. Calvocoressi, *World Politics 1945–2000* (New York: Pearson-Longman, 2001), 825.
248 JN, CNN Interviews, September and October 1997.
249 R. Leiken, *Why Nicaragua Vanished: A Story of Reporters and Revolutionaries* (Lanham, MD: Rowman and Littlefield, 2003), 148.

250 G. Garvin, *Everybody Had His Own Gringo: The CIA and the Contras* (Washington: Brassey's USA, 1992), xv.

251 UN Hearings, 69.

252 Schulz and Sundloff Schulz, *The United States, Honduras*, 321.

253 B. Bradley, *Time Present, Time Past: A Memoir* (New York: Knopf, 1996), 54.

254 Calvocoressi, *World Politics, 1945–2000*, 824.

255 D. Bonior, "The Wright Speakership," in US House of Representatives, The Cannon Centenary Conference: The Changing Nature of the Speakership, House Document No. 108-204 (Washington: GPO, 2004), 52.

256 A. Chardy, "Abrams Under Fire for US Policy Failure in Panama," *Houston Chronicle*, May 6, 1988.

257 Schulz and Sundloff Schulz, *The United States, Honduras*, 234–5.

258 *Associated Press*, May 16, 1988; N. Kempster and R. Ostrow, "A New Deal for Noriega," *St. Petersburg Times*, May 17, 1988; E. Sciolino, "A Latin Specialist Quits the White House," *New York Times*, May 17, 1988; "Race for Key State Department Post Sets Capital Abuzz," *Associated Press*, January 14, 1989.

259 Schlesinger, *Journals, 1952–2000*, 616 (entry for May 17, 1991).

260 "Interview with Nathaniel Davis," available at http://www.gwu.edu/~nsarchiv/coldwar/interviews/episode-18davis3.html

261 "Interview with Duane Clarridge," available at http://www.gwu.edu/~nsarchiv/coldwar/interviews/episode-18/clarridge3.html

262 Garvin, *Everybody Had His Own Gringo*, 127–8.

263 Department of State, Anthony Motley Oral History, March 7, 1991, citing J. Martin, "Sea Mines in Nicaragua," Proceedings of the US Naval Institute, September 1990.

264 F. Castro, *My Life* (London: Allen Lane, 2007), 265.

265 Department of State, Joseph P. O'Neill Oral History, May 19, 1998.

266 F. Castro, Chavez and the Americas' Bright Future, February 3, 2006, available at www.cubasolidarity.com

267 G. Kennan, *The Cloud of Danger: Current Realities of American Foreign Policy* (Boston: Little, Brown, 1977), 67.

268 Negroponte, *Conflict Resolution at the End of the Cold War*.

269 Ibid., 115–16.

270 Ibid., 401.

271 Ibid., 87.

272 Ibid., 218, 220.

273 Ibid.

274 Ibid., 11.

275 Ibid., 44 and n.25.

276 Ibid., 206–7.

277 Ibid., 143, 165.

278 Ibid., 168.

279 Ibid., 402.

280 Ibid., 405.

281 Ibid., 406.

282 Ibid., 329.

283 Ibid., 20.

284 Ibid., 8, 172, citing J. Dunkerley, *The Pacification of Central America* (New York: Verso, 1994), Appendices A and B.

285 Calvocoressi, *World Politics 1945–2000*, 827.

286 R. Woodward, *Central America: A Nation Divided* 3rd ed. (New York: Oxford University Press, 1999), 272.

287 T. Carothers, *In the Name of Democracy: US Policy Toward Latin America in the Reagan Years* (Berkeley: University of California, 1991).

288 J. Nordlinger, "Negroponte at Large," *National Review Online*, March 24, 2009, available at http://article.nationalreview.com/?q=ODA0YTU2YjQxYjg5ODEwYWRhYzViZWM4NDExOGJmZjU

289 Department of State, William Harben Oral History, 1998.

290 J. Dunkerley, *Power in the Isthmus: A Political History of Central America* (London: Verso, 1988), 563 ff.

291 Woodward, *Central America*, chapter 8.

292 A. Thorpe, "Honduras, the New Economic Model, and Poverty," in V. Bulmer-Thomas (ed.), *The New Economic Model in Latin America and Its Impact on Income Distribution and Poverty* (London: Macmillan Press, 1996), 223 ff.

293 A. Arana, "The New Battle for Central America," *Foreign Affairs*, November/December 2001, 88.

294 L. Schmaltzbauer, *Striving and Surviving: A Daily Life Analysis of Honduran Transnational Families* (London: Routledge, 2005).

295 S. Kinzer, *Overthrow: America's Century of Regime Change* (New York: Times Books, 2007), 102.

296 Ibid., 91, 99.

297 T. Judt (ed.), "Whose Story Is It? The Cold War in Retrospect," in *Reappraisal, Reflections on the Forgotten Twentieth Century* (New York: Penguin, 2008), 372.

298 Department of State, J. Negroponte Interview with Charlie Rose, April 25, 2008.

299 J. Negroponte, Address to Organization of American States, June 3, 2008.

300 The 1980 figures are from Barry, et al., *Dollars and Dictators*, 163.

301 D. Negroponte, "You Can't Go Home Again? Zelaya's Bid to Return could Trigger a Desperate Gamble," *Washington Times*, July 2009.

302 (Washington: Brookings, 2009), 4, 10, 14, 22. 54, 64, 73.

Chapter Eleven

1 P. Shabecoff, "The Environment as a Diplomatic Issue," *The New York Times*, December 25, 1987, I, 24: 4.

2 "International Science Gains Higher Profile," *Science*, vol. 231 (March 14, 1986), 1240.

3 L. Cannon, "Reagan Hears GOP Senators' Complaints," *Washington Post*, June 13, 1985.

4 J. Negroponte, State Department Perspective on International Environmental Issues, Current Policy 1008, in National Archives, ARC 1488627, Folder 4310 (1987); J. Negroponte, The Environmental Agenda and Foreign Policy, Current Policy 949, in National Archives, ARC1488555, Folder 4215 (1987).

5 J. Negroponte, *Current Developments in US Oceans Policy* (Washington: DOS, 1986); J. Negroponte, *Who Will Protect Freedom of the Seas* (Washington: DOS, 2006).

6 J. Gray, *False Dawn: The Delusions of Global Capitalism* (New York: New Press, 1998), 80–1.

7 *The New York Times*, June 30, 1987 (Perle); August 15, 1987, 26: 4 (Negroponte response).

8 Hearings before the Subcommittee on International Scientific Cooperation, House Committee on Science, Space and Technology, June 25, 1987 (Current policy Release 997, Bureau of Public Affairs, Department of State), quoted in Y. Richmond, *Cultural Exchange and the Cold War: Raising the Iron Curtin* (University Park, PA: Penn State University Press, 2003), 210–11.

9 "US Policy on Exchanges with the Soviets Called in Shambles," *Science*, vol. 237 (July 3, 1987), 18.

10 Hearings to Examine US-Soviet Science and Technology Exchanges before the Subcommittee on International Scientific Cooperation, House Committee on Science, Space and Technology, June 23, 1987, 68.

11 Weekly Compilation of Presidential Documents, vol. 20, no. 26, 946 (1984).

12 G. Kennan, *The Cloud of Danger* (Boston: Little, Brown, 1977), 223.

13 J. Negroponte, US-Soviet Scientific Exchanges, Current Policy 997, in National Archives, ARC1488607, Folder 4285 (1987).

14 Department of State, Suzanne Butcher Oral History, April 11, 2000.

15 Circular 175: Request for Authority to Negotiate a Protocol to the Convention for the Protection of the Ozone Layer, Negroponte to Wallis, in US House of Representatives, Committee on Energy and Commerce, Hearings, March 9, 1987, 119–29.

16 J. Nordlinger, "Negroponte at Large," *National Review Online*, March 24, 2009, available at http://article.nationalreview.com/?q=ODA0YTU2YjQxYjg5ODEwYWRhYzViZ WM4NDExOGJmZjU

17 S. Roan, *Ozone Crisis: The 15-Year Evolution of a Sudden Global Emergency* (New York: Wiley, 1989), 155.

18 "US Says Progress Made in World Limits on Ozone Depleting Chemicals," *Associated Press*, January 28, 1987.

19 R. Benedick, *Ozone Diplomacy: New Directions in Safeguarding the Planet* (Cambridge, MA: Harvard University Press, enlarged ed. 1998), 101.

20 "President Must Decide: State Department Pushes Radical Ozone Treaty," *Human Events*, June 20, 1987.

21 Benedick, *Ozone Diplomacy*, 197 ff.

22 J. Gribbin, *The Hole in the Sky: Man's Threat to the Ozone Layer* (London: Corgi Books, 1988), 138.

23 S. Anderson and K. Sarma, *Protecting the Ozone Layer: The U.N. History* (London: Earthscan, 2002), 351–64; P. Haas, "Banning Chlorofluorocarbons: Epistemic Community Efforts to Protect Stratospheric Zone," *International Organization*, vol. 46 (1992), 187, 191; see J. Negroponte, "Protecting the Ozone Layer," Department of State Bulletin 2123 (June 1987), 59.

24 M. Hoffmann, *Ozone Depletion and Climate Change: Constructing a Global Response* (Albany, NY: SUNY Press, 2005), 92–4, citing Negroponte's testimony in Hearings before the Senate Committee on Environment and Public Works on Ozone Depletion, the Greenhouse Effect, and Global Climate Change, 100th Congress, 1st Session, January 28, 1987, at 45.

25 N. Harrison (ed.), "From the Inside Out: Domestic Influences on Global Environmental Policy," in *Climate Change and American Foreign Policy* (New York: St. Martin's, 2000), 108.

26 P. Michaels and R. Balling, *Climate of Extremes: Global Warming Science They Don't Want You to Know* (Washington: Cato Institute, 2009), 20.

27 L. Dotto and H. Schill, *The Ozone War* (New York: Doubleday, 1978), see E. Conway, *High Speed Dreams: NASA and the Technopolitics of Supersonic Transportation* (Baltimore: Johns Hopkins University Press., 2005), 130–1; J. Lear, "Teaching in the Big School," *Saturday Review*, January 2, 1971, 63; L. Carsson, "Organization Formed to Fight SST," *Baltimore Evening Sun*, November 12, 1970.

28 Kissinger to Nixon, April 25, 1969, in National Archives, Nixon Collection, NSC Files, Box 397, Folder 7.

29 G. Kennan, *The Cloud of Danger: Current Realities of American Foreign Policy* (Boston: Little, Brown, 1977), 28.

30 E. Lane, "Report from Antarctica," *Newsday*, December 15, 1985; Letter to the Editor, North Jersey Record, March 6, 1986.

31 J. Negroponte, Success of Antarctic Treaty, Current Policy No. 937 (1987), in National Archives, ARC1488549, Folder 4207.

32 D. Israelson, "Has PM Put Issue of Acid Rain on Hold?," *Toronto Star*, September 29, 1986; "US Denies Agreement on Acid Rain Controls," *Toronto Globe and Mail*, October 21, 1987, A16.

33 Department of State, Richard J. Smith Oral History, July 30, 1996.

34 "Sorting Out Answers to Nuclear Accident Questions," *Dallas Morning News*, May 4, 1986.

35 Department of State Secretary, State 140173, May 1986.

36 J. Negroponte, Nonproliferation and the Future Uses of Nuclear Energy, Current Policy 959, in National Archives, ARC1488572, Folder 4238 (1987).

37 J. Negroponte, International Prospects for Civil Nuclear Power in the Post-Chernobyl Era, Current Policy 887, in National Archives, ARC1488572, Folder 4238 (1986).

38 Department of State, Theodore Wilkinson Oral History, January 11, 1999.

39 Department of State, Nancy Ostrander Oral History, May 14, 1986.

40 National Archives, Record Group 59, Stack Area 490, Row 56, Compartment 12, Shelf 03-04, Boxes 1–4, Bureau of Oceans, etc., AIDS, 1973–81.

41 C. Freeman and J. Negroponte, "Information Memorandum re AIDS and the Death of Modern African Societies," Cohen Files, OA 92241, Box 2, Folder 'AIDS in Africa' 2 of 2, Ronald Reagan Presidential Library, quoted in J. Brier, *Infectious Ideas: US Political Responses to the AIDS Crisis* (Chapel Hill: University of North Carolina Press, 2009).

42 SINE 70/1-87, Sub-Saharan Africa: Implications of the AIDS Pandemic (June 1987), 15.

43 Department of State, Thomas Macklin, Jr. Oral History, September 27, 2000.

44 Department of State, J. Negroponte remarks to Washington International Renewable Energy Conference, March 4, 2008; J. Negroponte remarks to Japan Society, January 31, 2008.

45 J. Nordlinger, "Negroponte at Large," *National Review Online*, March 24, 2009, available at http://article.nationalreview.com/?q=ODA0YTU2YjQxYjg5ODEwYWRhYzViZWM4NDExOGJmZjU

Chapter Twelve

1 C. Powell, *A Soldier's Way* (London: Hutchinson, 1995).

2 DNI Hearings, "Hearings on the Nomination of John D Negroponte to be Director of National Intelligence before the Senate Select Committee on Intelligence," January 20, 1965, 9.

3 Department of State, Robert Oakley Oral History, July 7, 1992.

4 *The New York Times*, May 17, 1988, I, 10: 4.

5 *The New York Times*, May 30, 1988, 1: 1.

6 G. Shultz, *Turmoil and Tradition* (New York: Scribner, 1993), 1051.

7 T. Leonard, *Central America and the United States: The Search for Stability* (Athens, GA: University of Georgia, 1991), 283.

8 L. Murillo, *The Noriega Mess: The Drugs, the Canal, and why America Invaded* (New York: Video Books, 1995), 602.

9 F. Kempe, *Divorcing the Dictator: America's Bungled Affair with Noriega* (London: I.B. Tauris, 1990), 256 ff.

10 R. Pear and N. Lewis, "The Noriega Fiasco: What Went Wrong," *The New York Times*, May 30, 1988.

11 Kempe, *Divorcing the Dictator*, 307.

12 Pear and Lewis, "The Noriega Fiasco."

13 Ibid., 122 ff.; citing S. Christian, *Nicaragua: Revolution in the Family* (New York: Vintage, 1986), 311–13.

14 Ibid., 289.

15 J. Prado, *Keepers of the Keys: A History of the National Security Council from Truman to Bush* (New York: Morrow, 1991), 655; L. Carman and G. Wilson, "Strike on Iran Oil Platforms," *Washington Post*, April 19, 1988, A3.

16 D. Brinkley (ed.), *The Reagan Diaries* (New York: Harper, 2007), 599, 661.

17 *The New York Times*, December 1, 1987.

18 *The New York Times*, November 14, 1988, II, 7: 5; "State Department: For Diplomats, Time to Read the Tea-Leaves," *The New York Times*, January 10, 1989.

Chapter Thirteen

1 El Porvenir, June 11, 1989, 7A.

2 *The New York Times*, February 14, 1989, I, 15: 1. February 19, 1989, IV, 2: 4; "Acceptance of US Ambassador Stirs Anger in Mexico," *St. Petersburg Times*, February 10, 1989.

3 P. Russell, *Mexico Under Salinas* (Austin, TX: Mexico Resource Center, 1994), 312, citing Excelsior, February 8, 1989, 1A, 30A.

4 "Mexicans Cool to Envoy Choice," *Dallas Morning News*, February 2, 1989; *Associated Press*, March 3, 1989; A. Golden, "Even Critic of US Policy Lauds Bush Choice for Mexico Envoy," *San Diego Union Tribune*, February 4, 1989; *Associated Press*, February 7, 1989; M. Miller, "Bush's Choice of Envoy Sparks Furor in Mexico," *Los Angeles Times*, February 9, 1989; M. Moffett, "Stresses Growing Between Mexico

and Washington," *Wall Street Journal*, February 15, 1989; Jack Anderson, Syndicated Column, February 24, 1989.

5   "Trouble Brews for Donald Gregg," *Economist*, May 27, 1989.

6   Department of State, Robert Pastorino Oral History, March 6, 1998.

7   D. Negroponte, *Conflict Resolution at the End of the Cold War: The Case of El Salvador, 1989–94* (Ann Arbor: University Microfilms, 2006), 251, citing an oral interview with John Negroponte and "Arms for the FMLN: The Mexican Connection," Mexico City 10248, April 20, 1990; Digital National Security Archive, George Washington University.

8   E. Krauze, "Looking at Them: A Mexican Perspective on the Gap with the United States," in F. Fukuyama (ed.), *Falling Behind: Explaining the Development Gap between Latin America and the US* (New York: Oxford University Press, 2008), 48, 62.

9   *San Diego Union Tribune*, December 24, 1989, 1.

10 T. Barry, et al., *The Great Divide: The Challenge of U. S.-Mexican Relations in the 1990s* (New York: Grove Press, 1994), 439 n.150.

11 Negroponte to Secretary of State, Mexico 19843, August 1989, Mexico 24683, September 1989.

12 C. Salinas, "A New Hope for the Hemisphere," *New Perspective Quarterly* (Winter 1991), 128, quoted in J. Gray, *False Dawn: The Delusions of Global Capitalism* (New York: New Press, 1998), 47.

13 J. Dominguez and R. de Castro, *The United States and Mexico: Between Partnership and Conflict* (London: Routledge, 2001), 123.

14 UN Hearing, supra.S5 1990, 43.

15 S. Dryden, *Trade Warriors: USTR and the American Crusade for Free Trade* (New York: Oxford, 1995), 370.

16 S. Aguayo, *Myths and Misperceptions: Changing US Elite Visions of Mexico* (La Gelechia: Center for US-Mexican Studies, UCSD, 1998), 238; Barry, et al., *The Great Divide*, 376, 377, 382, quoting Carlos Phiz, "Conclusion de Negroponte: con el Tratado de Libre Comercio, Mexico Quedaria a Disposicion de Washington," *Proceso*, May 13, 1991.

17 J. Contreras, *In the Shadow of the Giant: The Americanization of Mexico* (New Brunswick, NJ: Rutgers University Press, 2009), 40–2.

18 W. Mead, "Bushism Found: A Second-Term Agenda Hidden in Trade Agreements," *Harper's Magazine*, vol. 285 (September 1992), 37.

19 J. Negroponte, Interview, United Press International, September 4, 1993.

20 Negroponte, *Conflict Resolution at the End of the Cold War*, 253–4.

21 S. Ellis, "Bilateralism and the Future of International Trade," *Essays in International Finance*, vol. 5 (Summer 1945), reprinted in American Economic Association, Readings in the Theory of International Trade (Philadelphia: Blakiston, 1950), 408.

22 R. Sally, *New Frontiers in Free Trade: Globalization's Future and Asia's Rising Role* (Washington: Cato Institute, 2008), 76.

23 B. Lindsey, "Protectionist Racket: Misconceptions about the NAFTA," *Reason*, November 1993.

24 A. Vargas Llosa, *Liberty for Latin America: How to Undo Five Hundred Years of State Oppression* (New York: Farrar, Straus and Giroux, 2005), 29.

25 Ibid., 31.

26 Ibid., 39.

27 Ibid., 49.

28 Ibid., 52, 54.

29 Ibid., 67.

30 Ibid., 98.

31 Ibid., 113.

32 Ibid., 117.

33 Ibid., 124.

34 K. Dam, *The Law-Growth Nexus: The Rule of Law and Economic Development* (Washington: Brookings, 2006), 78.

35 Ibid., 115, citing D. Furnish, "Judicial Review in Mexico," *Southwestern Journal of Law and Trade in the Americas*, vol. 7 (2000), 235.

36 Ibid., quoting R. Kossick, "The Rule of Law and Development in Mexico," *Arizona Journal of International and Comparative Law*, 21 (2004), 715.

37 F. Fukuyama (ed.), *Falling Behind: Explaining the Development Gap between Latin America and the US* (New York: Oxford University Press, 2008), 286.

38 Ibid., 154.

39 Ibid., 181–2.

40 Ibid., 186.

41 Ibid., 237.

42 S. Hanks and S. Walters, "Economic Freedom, Prosperity, and Equality: A Survey," *Cato Journal*, vol. 18 (1999), 335.

43 N. Botawa, "Why Institutions Matter: Fiscal Citizenship in Argentina and the United States," in F. Fukuyama (ed.), *Falling Behind: Explaining the Development Gap between Latin America and the US* (New York: Oxford University Press, 2008), 262.

44 Fukuyama, *Falling Behind*, 211.

45 C. Heredia, "NAFTA and Democratization in Mexico," *Journal of International Affairs*, vol. 48 (1994), 13, citing P. Wu, "Mexican-US Meeting Hits Roadblock," *Journal of Commerce* (July 11, 1991).

46 J. Mazza, *Don't Disturb the Neighbors: The United States and Democracy in Mexico, 1970–95* (New York: Routledge, 2001), 66 and n.21 and 22, citing a 1997 interview with Negroponte.

47 Mazza, *Don't Disturb the Neighbors*, 75, 87–8, citing L. Robinson and J. Bussed, "Can Salinas Troika Work?," *US News and World Report*, December 3, 1990, 51.

48 Mazza, *Don't Disturb the Neighbors*, 83.

49 P. Calvocoressi, *World Politics 1945–2000* (New York: Pearson-Longman, 2001), 181.

50 J. Duarte, "Eyewitness to History: Retired Diplomat Recalls Service in Latin America," available at www.Sthelenastar.com/articles/2008/06/19/news/local/doc4859c5600634b690614870 (June 19, 2008).

51 E. Hobsbawm, *The Age of Extremes* (New York: Pantheon, 2000), 357.

52 E. Espinosa, "NAFTA in Mexico," in P. Coffey (ed.), *NAFTA: Past, Present and Future* (Boston: Kluwer, 1999), 69.

53 G. Grayson, *The North American Free Trade Agreement: Regional Community and the New World Order* (Lanham, MD: APPRAISE of America, 1995).

54 Mazda, *Don't Disturb the Neighbors*, 70, citing a 1997 interview with JN.

55 W. Branigin, "Mexico Eyes Pact with US, Canada," *Washington Post*, May 24, 1990, E1.

56 Quoted in H. von Bertrab, *Negotiating NAFTA: A Mexican Envoy's Account* (Westport, CT: Praeger, 1997), 128.

57 W. Orme, *Understanding NAFTA: Mexico, Free Trade, and the New North America* (Austin: University of Texas, 1996), 47.

58 *The New York Times*, July 15, 1989, 20: 1; July 25, 1989, 1: 5; July 28, 1989, 1: 4; February 5, 1990, 1: 1.

59 *The Washington Post*, February 26, 1992, 2: 5; March 22, 1992, 29: 1.

60 *The Washington Post*, February 6, 1993, C6; 6.

61 *The New York Times*, August 29, 1998, 15: 1.

62 V. Bulmer-Thomas, et al., (eds.), "Who Will Benefit," in *Mexico and the North American Free Trade Agreement: Who Will Benefit?* (London: Macmillan Press, 1994), 221–2; *The Washington Post*, July 14, 1993, 17: 1; July 15, 1993, 1: 6.

63 *The Washington Post*, November 29, 1991, 1: 6; December 2, 1991, 22: 4; May 31, 1993, 21: 5; August 15, 1993, C2: 1; August 27, 1993, 25: 4.

64 P. Lumsdaine, "US Military Involvement in Mexico's Quagmire Deepens," *Flashpoint! Electronic Magazine*, available at www.webcom.com/hrin/magazine/april96/mexico.html; see also L. Freeman and J. Sierra, "Mexico: The Militarization Trap," in C. Youngers and E. Rosin (eds.), *Drugs and Democracy in Latin America: The Impact of US Policy* (Boulder, CO: Lynne Rienner, 2005), 263.

65 Ibid., 133.

66 T. Golden, "For an Envoy, A Fond Adios from Mexico," *The New York Times*, September 5, 1993, I, 9: 1.

67 Russell, *Mexico Under Salinas*, 352.

68 Mazza, *Don't Disturb the Neighbors*, 66–88, 148, 159.

69 Quoted in El Proceso, May 13, 1991, 7.

70 C. Cárdenas, "Misunderstanding Mexico," *Foreign Policy*, vol. 78 (1990), 113, 116.

71 von Bertrab, *Negotiating NAFTA*, 82.

72 C. Reynolds, "Mexico's Development Challenges," in K. Middlebrook and E. Zepeda (eds.), *Confronting Development: Assessing Mexico's Economic and Social Policy Challenges* (Stanford, CA: Stanford University Press, 2003), 598–9.

73 L. Bresser-Pereira, et al., *Economic Reforms in New Democracies: A Social Democratic Approach* (Cambridge: Cambridge University Press, 1993), 207 ff.

74 Ibid., 161, 163, 167, 205, 208.

75 A. De Witt, "Challenge and Response: Mexico in a Changing World," *New Leader* (May/June 2002), 9.

76 E. Peters, *Polarizing Mexico: The Impact of Liberalization Strategy* (Boulder, CO: Lynne Rienner, 2002), 210 ff.

77 Gray, *False Dawn*, 45.

78 Op. cit. note 73 supra., 158.

79 Ibid., 160.

80 Ibid., 186.

81 Ibid., 198.

82 Ibid., 212.

83 D. Beechy, "US Ambassador Says That Relations with Mexico Are Now at Critical Mass," *Houston Chronicle* (August 14, 1991).

84 D. Dresser, "Post-NAFTA Politics in Mexico," in C. Wise (ed.), *The Post-NAFTA Political Economy: Mexico and the Western Hemisphere* (University Park, PA: Penn State University Press, 1999), 245.

85 B. Bradley, *Time Present, Time Past: A Memoir* (New York: Knopf, 1996), 349–51.

86 E. Malkin, "Nafta's Promise Unfulfilled: After 15 Years the Pact Has Had Mixed Results," *The New York Times*, March 24, 2009, B1.

87 Orme, *Understanding NAFTA*, 70–1.

88 Calvocoressi, *World Politics 1945–2000*, 812, 815–16.

89 Malkin, "Nafta's Promise Unfulfilled," B1.

90 R. Pastor, "The Future of North America: Replacing a Bad Neighbor Policy," *Foreign Affairs* (July–August 2008), 84.

91 Fukuyama, *Falling Behind*, 63–4.

92 P. Andrews, "Liberalizing and Criminalizing Flows Across the US-Mexican Border," in C. Wise (ed.), *The Post-NAFTA Political Economy: Mexico and the Western Hemisphere* (University Park, PA: Penn State University Press, 1999), 212; see Aldo K. Kopinak, "The Maquiladorization of the Mexican Economy," in R. Grinspun and M. Cameron (eds.), *The Political Economy of North American Free Trade* (London: Macmillan Press, 1993), 143.

93 C. Reynolds, "The NAFTA and Wage Convergence," in R. Belous and J. Lemco (eds.), *NAFTA as a Model of Development: The Benefits and Costs of Merging High and Low Wage Areas* (Albany: SUNY Press, 1995), 24–5.

94 K. Appendini, "Agriculture and Farmers Within Nafta," in V. Bulmer-Thomas, et al. (eds.), *Mexico and the North American Free Trade Agreement: Who Will Benefit?* (London: Macmillan Press, 1994), 62 ff.

95 *The Washington Post*, November 8, 1991, 27: 1.

96 V. Bulmer-Thomas, *The New Economic Model in Latin America and Its Impact on Income Distribution and Poverty* (London: Macmillan Press, 1996), 219.

97 Espinosa, "NAFTA in Mexico," 107.

98 R. Wise, "Labor and Migration Policies Under Vicente Fox," in G. Otero (ed.), *Mexico in Transition: Neoliberalism, Globalism, the State and Civil Society*, 2nd ed. (London: Zed, 2004), 152.

99 Department of State, Theodore Wilkinson Oral History, January 11, 1999.

100 E. Hollings, "Reform Mexico First," *Foreign Policy*, vol. 93 (1993–4), 91.

101 R. Grinspun and M. Cameron, *The Political Economy of North American Free Trade* (London: Macmillan Press, 1993), 19.

102 M. Reid, *Forgotten Continent: The Battle for Latin America's Soul* (New Haven: Yale University Press, 2007), 296.

103 Commission on the Skills of the American Workforce: America's Choice: High Skills or Low Wages (Washington: GPO, 1990).

104 R. Rothstein, "The NAFTA and Downward Wage Pressure," in R. Belous and J. Lemco (eds.), *NAFTA as a Model of Development: The Benefits and Costs of Merging High and Low Wage Areas* (Albany: SUNY Press, 1995), 41–5.

105 K. Middlebrook and E. Zepeda, *Confronting Development: Assessing Mexico's Economic and Social Policy Challenges* (Stanford, CA: Stanford University Press, 2003), Figures 7.1, 11.2; Tables 7.1, 2.12, 4.1, 8.2, 14.9.

106 Bresser-Pereira, et al., *Economic Reforms in New Democracies*, 205 ff.

107 Sally, *New Frontiers in Free Trade*, 79–80.

108 J. Stiglitz, "Lessons from Cancun and Recent Financial Crises," in E. Zedillo (ed.), *The Future of Globalization: Explorations in Light of Recent Turbulence* (London: Routledge, 2008), 70–1.

109 J. Judis, "Trade Secrets: The Real Problem with NAFTA," *New Republic*, April 9, 2008, 10.

110 J. Castañeda, *The Mexican Shock: Its Meaning for the US* (New York: New Press, 1995), 32.

111 D. Negroponte, *The Merida Initiative and Central America: The Challenges of Containing Public Insecurity and Criminal Violence* (Washington: Brookings, 2009), 9.

112 Reid, *Forgotten Continent*, 296 ff.

113 F. Bean and B. Lowell, "NAFTA and Mexican Migration to the United States," in S. Weintraub (ed.), *NAFTA's Impact on North America: The First Decade* (Washington: Center for Strategic and International Studies, 2004), 263.

114 Peters, *Polarizing Mexico*, 2.

115 A. Urquidi, "Mexico's Development Challenges, 1991–2000," in K. Middlebrook and E. Zepeda, *Confronting Development: Assessing Mexico's Economic and Social Policy Challenges* (Stanford, CA: Stanford University Press, 2003), 562.

116 L. Lever and R. Gomez, "Education and Development in Mexico," in K. Middlebrook and E. Zepeda (eds.), *Confronting Development: Assessing Mexico's Economic and Social Policy Challenges* (Stanford, CA: Stanford University Press, 2003).

117 C. Reynolds, "Will a Free Trade Agreement Lead to Wage Convergence: Implications for Mexico and the United States," in J. Bustamente, et al. (eds.), *US-Mexico Relations: Labor Market Interdependence* (Stanford, CA: Stanford University Press, 1992), 477 ff.

118 Ibid., 478–81.

119 G. Haberler, "A Survey of International Trade Theory," in *Selected Essays* (Cambridge, MA: MIT Press), 1985), 55, at 96, 98, 108 n.69.

120 Fukuyama, *Falling Behind*, 22, 83, 287, 291.

121 Department of State, William Jeffras Dieterich Oral History, October 19, 1999.

122 K. Dam, *The Rules of the Global Game: A New Look at US International Policymaking* (Chicago: University of Chicago, 2001), 137.

123 Ibid., 138–9, 142, 147.

124 J. Chauffour, *The Power of Freedom: Uniting Development and Human Rights* (Washington: Cato Institute, 2009), 99.

125 W. Stolper and P. Samuelson, "Protection and Real Wages," *Review of Economic Studies*, vol. 9 (1941), 58, reprinted in *American Economic Association, Readings in the Theory of International Trade* (Philadelphia: Blakiston, 1950), 333.

126 J. Stiglitz, "Fair Trade," *The National Interest*, No. 95, May–June 2008, 19, 21, 23; J. Castañeda and P. Naria, "New Priorities for Latin America," *Current History*, vol. 107, no. 709 (May 2008), 213.

127 J. Bhagwati, *Termites in the Trading System: How Preferential Agreements Undermine Free Trade* (New York: Oxford, 2008).

128 Ibid., 20, 45, 47, 53, 59, 81, 87, 93.

129 Department of State, William Jeffras Dieterich Oral History, October 19, 1999.

130 Dam, *The Rules of the Global Game*, 38.
131 The text is available at www2.ohchr.org/english/law/cmw.htm
132 Salinas in LatinFinance, June 1998, quoted in J. MacArthur, *The Selling of "Free Trade": NAFTA, Washington, and the Subversion of American Democracy* (New York: Hill and Wang, 2000), 119.
133 Ibid.
134 S. Weintraub, "Trade, Investment, and Economic Growth," in *NAFTA's Impact on North America: The First Decade* (Washington: Center for Strategic and International Studies, 2004), 3–7, 18.
135 R. Pomfret, *Economics of Regional Trading Arrangements* (Oxford: Clarendon, 1997), 291.
136 J. Bustamente, "Nafta and Labor Migration to the US," in V. Bulmer-Thomas, et al. (eds.), *Mexico and the North American Free Trade Agreement: Who Will Benefit?* (London: Macmillan Press, 1994), 79.
137 *Washington Post*, October 6, 1990, 2: 5; June 24, 1991, 13: 1.
138 Department of Homeland Security, Office of Immigration Statistics, Annual Statistical Reports. In all relevant years, 92–6 percent of those apprehended were Mexican. See also Department of Homeland Security, Office of Immigration Statistics, Estimates of the Unauthorized Immigrant Population Residing in the United States, January 2006 (Washington: Department of Homeland Security, August 2007).
139 Chauffour, *The Power of Freedom*, 44.
140 Mexico Institute, The US Elections and the Future of US-Mexico Relations, June 12, 2008.
141 Castañeda, *The Mexican Shock*, 46.
142 J. Davidow, *The US and Mexico: The Bear and the Porcupine* (Princeton: Markus Wiener, 2004), 116.
143 Castañeda, *The Mexican Shock*, 48.
144 City of Douglas, Douglas, Arizona (Douglas, AZ, 2008), 3.
145 M. Cameron and B. Tomlin, *The Making of NAFTA: How the Deal Was Done* (Ithaca, NY: Cornell University Press, 1990), 91, 107, 110.
146 Dam, *The Rules of the Global Game*, 74.
147 Pomfret, *Economics of Regional Trading Arrangements*, 295.
148 C. Salinas de Gortari, *Mexico: The Policy and Politics of Modernization* (Barcelona: Plaza and Jane Editores (trans. P. Hearn and P. Rosas), 1992), 15, 519, 1157, 1243.
149 A. Bartra, "Rebellious Cornfields: Toward Food and Labor Self-Sufficiency," in G. Otero (ed.), *Mexico in Transition: Neoliberalism, Globalism, the State and Civil Society* 2nd ed. (London: Zed, 2004).
150 R. De la Garza and G. Szekely, "Policy, Politics and Emigration: Re-examining the Mexican Experience," in F. Bean, et al. (eds.), *At the Crossroads: Mexico and US Immigration Policy* (Lanham, MD: Rowman and Littlefield, 1997), 221–2.
151 *The Washington Post*, November 2, 1993, 7: 1; 19: 3.
152 *The New York Times*, September 21, 1998, E 1: 2.
153 *The Washington Post*, May 3, 1990, 33: 5; September 3, 1991, E1: 1; April 18, 1992, 15: 1.
154 *The New York Times*, October 31, 1998, 16: 1.
155 P. Martin, "Do Mexican Agricultural Policies Stimulate Emigration?," in F. Bean, et al. (eds.), *At the Crossroads: Mexico and US Immigration Policy* (Lanham, MD: Rowman and Littlefield, 1997), 89.
156 Reynolds, "Will a Free Trade Agreement Lead to Wage Convergence," 480.
157 Wise, "Labor and Migration Policies Under Vicente Fox," 145.
158 V. Fox, *Revolution of Hope: The Life, Faith and Dreams of a Mexican President* (New York: Viking, 2007), 151.
159 C. Hills, "The Stakes of Doha," *Foreign Affairs*, December 2005.
160 von Bertrab, *Negotiating NAFTA*, 97.
161 Grayson, *The North American Free Trade Agreement*, 82.
162 von Bertrab, *Negotiating NAFTA*, 58–9.

163   R. Cyran and M. Hutchinson, "Mexico's Fiscal Woes," *The New York Times*, November 27, 2009.

164   Grayson, *The North American Free Trade Agreement*, 217. See generally M. Trebilcock, et al., *Trade and Transitions: A Comparative Analysis of Adjustment Policies* (London: Routledge, 1990).

165   Grayson, *The North American Free Trade Agreement*, 243.

166   W. Gruben and J. Welch, "Is NAFTA More Than a Free Trade Agreement?," in V. Bulmer-Thomas, et al. (eds.), *Mexico and the North American Free Trade Agreement: Who Will Benefit?* (London: Macmillan Press, 1994), 191, 196.

167   V. Bulmer-Thomas, et al., *Mexico and the North American Free Trade Agreement: Who Will Benefit?* (London: Macmillan Press, 1994), 208.

168   R. Hoffmann, "Can the EC Social Charter be a Model for the NAFTA?," in R. Belous and J. Lemco (eds.), *NAFTA as a Model of Development: The Benefits and Costs of Merging High and Low Wage Areas* (Albany: SUNY Press, 1995), 188 ff.

169   F. Bean, et al., *At the Crossroads: Mexico and US Immigration Policy* (Lanham, MD: Rowman and Littlefield, 1997), Introduction.

170   H. De Soto, "Missing Ingredients of Globalization," in E. Zedillo (ed.), *The Future of Globalization: Explorations in Light of Recent Turbulence* (London: Routledge, 2008), 20.

171   Ibid., 71, 76, 78.

172   N. Lewis, "White House Tries to Quiet Storm over Court's Ruling on Right to Kidnap Suspects Abroad," *The New York Times*, June 16, 1992, 8.

173   *US v. Alvarez-Machain*, 504 US 655 (1992).

174   *The Washington Post*, April 18, 1990, 22: 1; April 20, 1990, 24: 1; April 21, 1990, 18: 1; April 27, 1990, 33: 1; May 2, 1990, 1: 3; May 4, 1990, 3: 5; May 10, 1990, 30: 1; May 19, 1990, 2: 5; May 26, 1990, 2: 5; July 21, 1990, 4: 2; August 11, 1990, 3: 5; December 9, 1992, 25: 2; December 15, 1992, 1: 5; December 16, 1992, 10: 1.

175   *The Washington Post*, June 22, 1993, 15: 5.

176   Orme, *Understanding NAFTA*, 97.

177   T. Barry, et al., *Crossing the Line: Immigrants, Economic Integration and Drug Enforcement on the US-Mexican Border* (Albuquerque, NM: Resource Center Press, 1994).

178   Andrews, "Liberalizing and Criminalizing Flows Across the US-Mexican Border," 201 ff.

179   M. Toro, "Mexican Policy Against Drugs: From Deterring to Embracing the US," in S. Weintraub (ed.), *NAFTA's Impact on North America: The First Decade* (Washington: Center for Strategic and International Studies, 2004).

180   D. Negroponte, "The Merida Initiative: Time for a Healthy Public Debate," available at www.brookings.edu/opinions/2007/1106_mexico_negroponte.aspx; Negroponte, *The Merida Initiative and Central America*.

181   Cárdenas, "Misunderstanding Mexico," 113.

182   P. Hakim, "Clinton and Latin America: Facing an Unfinished Agenda," 92 *Current History* 97 (March 1992).

183   J. Chabat, "Mexico's Foreign Policy after NAFTA," in R. de la Garza and J. Velasco (eds.), *Bridging the Border: Transforming Mexico-US Relations* (Lanham, MD: Rowman and Littlefield, 1997), 39 ff.

184   Mexico City 180362, November 8, 1991, cited in L. Fraser, "NAFTA and the War on Drugs as Competing National Security Agendas in 1990–2: The Triumph of Neo-Liberalism and the Quest for US-Mexican Integration," *Journal of Iberian and Latin American Studies*, vol. 9 (2003), 1.

185   Mexico City 257044, November 21, 1991, see also Mexico City 245423, November 20, 1991; 246658, November 20, 1991; 390228, December 13, 1991; 427572, December 19, 1991; 346921, December 6, 1991, cited in Fraser, "NAFTA and the War on Drugs."

186   Fraser, "NAFTA and the War on Drugs," 17.

187   Mexico City 255832, March 10, 1992.

188   Mexico City 257044, November 21, 1991; Fraser, "NAFTA and the War on Drugs," 28.

189   Mexico City 265753, November 22, 1991.

190 R. Parker, "Bush, Clinton Inaction Let Cartels Flourish," *abqjournal News*, "Mexico on the Edge: The Drug Cartel Threat," *abqjournal News*, available at www.abqjournal.com/news/drugs/1drug3-5.htm

191 Castañeda, *The Mexican Shock*, 32ff.

192 T. Golden, "Mexico and Drugs: Was US Napping?," *The New York Times*, July 11, 1997.

193 Department of State, Opening Ceremony for Global Classrooms DC Model UN, April 28, 2008.

194 M. Witoshynsky, "Changing of the Guard," *Business Mexico*, vol. 3, no. 8 (August 1993).

195 Cárdenas, "Misunderstanding Mexico," 113.

196 J. Negroponte, "US-Mexico Relations," Address to Ibero-Americana University, September 2000, in DNI Hearings, 81–7.

197 J. Negroponte, "Trade Accord with Colombia a Plus for Like-Minded US," *San Antonio Express-News*, April 8, 2008.

198 J. Nordlinger, "Negroponte at Large," *National Review Online*, March 24, 2009, available at http://article.nationalreview.com/?q=ODA0YTU2YjQxYjg5ODEwYWRhYzViZWM4NDExOGJmZjjU

199 Department of State, J. Negroponte Remarks to US Asia-Pacific Council, April 11, 2008.

200 F. de la Balze, "Finding Allies in the Back Yard: NAFTA and the Southern Cone," *Foreign Affairs*, vol. 80 (July–August 2001), 7.

201 *The News [Mexico City]*, September 5, 1993.

202 J. Negroponte, "U.S-Mexican Relations are Definitely Better," *[Mexico City] News*, June 30, 1993, 26.

203 J. Davies, *Foreign and Other Affairs* (New York: Norton, 1964), 37–8.

204 Chauffour, *The Power of Freedom*, 68.

205 Gray, *False Dawn*, 235.

206 Available at www.drugsanddemocracy.org/files/2009/02/declaracao_ingles_site.pdf

Chapter Fourteen

1 A. Dovonila, "The First Post-Bases US Envoy," *Philippine Daily Inquirer*, July 26, 1996.

2 D. Kirk, *Looted: The Philippines After the Bases* (London: Macmillan Press, 1998).

3 *The Washington Post*, November 13, 1993, 19: 1; May 21, 1995, 24: 3; November 17, 1996, 20: 1; November 24, 1996, 33: 1.

4 A. Balisacun and H. Hill, *The Philippine Economy: Development, Policies, and Challenges* (New York: Oxford University Press, 2003), 47.

5 C. Fiel, "M. Dulce Extranjero," *Philippine Daily Inquirer*, February 12, 1995.

6 *The Washington Post*, November 12, 1994, 18: 4; June 20, 1995, 18: 4; M. Satchell, "Toxic Legacy: What the Military Left Behind," US *News and World Report*, January 24, 2000, 30–1.

7 *The Washington Post*, August 29, 1994, 1: 4; December 18, 1994, 44: 1.

8 *The Washington Post*, November 21, 1995, 16: 3; November 25, 1995, 12: 2.

9 *The Washington Post*, November 11, 1993, 45: 1; November 12, 1994, 17: 1

10 "US to Stress Trade, Less Aid," *Philippine Times-Journal*, June 30, 1994.

11 Remittances were said to have amounted to 4.24 billion in 1996. P. Kelly, *Landscapes of Globalization: Human Geographies of Economic Change in the Philippines* (London: Routledge, 2000), 38.

12 D. Steinberg, *The Philippines: A Singular and a Plural Place* 4th ed. (Boulder, CO: Westview, 2000), 194 ff.

13 P. Calvocoressi, *World Politics, 1945–2000* (New York: Pearson-Longman, 2001), 566.

14 J. Nordlinger, "Negroponte Speaks," *National Review*, March 23, 2009, 19.

15 Director of National Intelligence Hearings, 31.

16 US Secretary of Defense, Report to the President and Congress, January 1994, Part II, 21.

17 *Financial Times*, September 18, 1991.

18 *The Washington Post*, November 23, 1994, 15: 1.

19 D. Schirmer, "US Bases by Another Name: ACSA in the Philippine," February 1995, available at www.sjsu.edu/depts/sociology/living/ramos-950200.html

20 G. Kennan, *The Cloud of Danger* (Boston: Little, Brown, 1977), 98.

21 "The Newest Asian Tiger," *Newsweek*, vol. 128 (December 2, 1996), 45.

22 Balisacun and Hill, *The Philippine Economy*, viii.

23 "US Sees Philippine Adjustment Picture Brighter," *Asian Economic News*, February 20, 1995.

24 J. Negroponte, "Renewed Partners," *Makati Business Club*, August 1, 1996.

25 "To Be an Ambassador's Wife," *Business World*, Manila, January 15, 1996, 28.

26 L. Kalaw-Tirol, "The Other Ambassador," *Philippine Daily Inquirer Sunday Magazine*, October 9, 1994, see also "The Ambassador's Fair Lady," *Philippine Star*, January 29, 1995.

27 S. Mydans, "Filipinos Lament How Far They Haven't Come," *The New York Times*, August 20, 2009.

28 S. Mydans, "Little Space as Filipinos Overwhelm the Schools," *The New York Times*, August 27, 2009.

29 J. Hookway, "Manila Banks on Its Expats," *The Wall Street Journal*, December 5, 2008, A12.

30 Available at http://oai.dtic.mil/oai/oai?&verb=getRecord&metadataPrefix=html&identifier=ADA309432 for an American War College study.

31 J. Nordlinger, "Negroponte at Large," *National Review Online*, March 24, 2009, available at http://article.nationalreview.com/?q=ODA0YTU2YjQxYjg5ODEwYWRhYzViZWM4NDExOGJmZjU

32 Department of State, Frank Wisner Oral History, March 22, 1998.

33 J. Hookway and J. Cuneta, "Philippine Call Centers Ring Up Business," *The Wall Street Journal*, May 30, 2009.

34 A. Dovonila, "The First Post-Bases US Envoy," *Philippine Daily Inquirer*, July 26, 1996.

Chapter Fifteen

1 M. Sullivan, "CRS Issue Brief: Panama-US Relations: Continuing Policy Concerns," January 2, 1997, available at http://www.fas.org/man/crs/92-088.htm

2 P. Sanchez, "Panama: A 'Hegemonized' Foreign Policy," in J. Hey (ed.), *Small States in World Politics: Explaining Foreign Policy Behavior* (Boulder, CO: Lynne Rienner, 2003), 71.

3 "Negroponte Returns," *The Washington Times*, October 14, 1996; *Economist*, March 29, 1997; "US Point Man for Panama to Step Down," *Agence France Presse*, April 26, 1997; House Committee on Government Reform, Subcommittee on Criminal Justice, Hearings: "Losing Panama," May 4, 1997; "Panama-US Negotiations on Ancillary Center to Begin Soon," *Inter Press Service*, July 16, 1997; "John Negroponte Will Recommend Withdrawing from Negotiations," *Emerging Markets Report*, August 19, 1997; G. Garvin, "Talks on US Troops in Panama May Be Failing," *Miami Herald*, August 24, 1997; "Negroponte Replaced," *Associated Press*, September 12, 1997.

4 C. Sanders, *America's Overseas Garrisons: The Leasehold Empire* (New York: Oxford University Press, 2000), 140.

5 J. Poland, *Emperors in the Jungle: The Hidden History of the US in Panama* (Durham, NC: Duke University Press, 2003), 131–2.

6 M. Falcoff, *Panama's Canal: What Happens When the US Gives a Small County What It Wants* (Washington: AEI Press, 1998).

7 G. Kennan, *The Cloud of Danger* (Boston: Little, Brown, 1977), 57.

8 S.Con.Res.14, 104 Congressional Record page S9983, September 5, 1996.

9 A. Isacson, *Update: The Panama Canal Base Negotiations*, October 31, 1996, available at www.ciponline.org/1030pana.htm

Chapter Sixteen

1 N. Munoz, "Rights Honduras Accusations Fly Against Bush Designee," *Inter Press Service*, March 13, 2001.
2 "Publishers Bullish in Outlook for 1999," *Publishers' Weekly*, December 21, 1998; H. McGraw, 66 Vital Speeches No. 2, 655 (2000); Statement by Harold McGraw, Market News Publishing, March 7, 2001.
3 "Publishing Stocks: August Performance," *Publishers' Weekly*, September 8, 1997; "Salary Survey," *Publishers' Weekly*, July 5, 1999, July 3, 2000, July 9, 2001.
4 M. Lacey, "Central American Fallout Stalls U.N. Pick," *The New York Times*, June 4, 2001, 1: 2; J. Ellenburg, "Somebody Wasn't Watching the Store," *National Journal*, June 2, 2001.

Chapter Seventeen

1 J. Ellenburg, "Somebody Wasn't Watching the Store," *National Journal*, June 2, 2001.
2 D. Chollet and R. Orr, "Reclaiming Success at the United Nations," *Washington Quarterly*, vol. 24 (Autumn 2001), 7.
3 Hearings on the Nomination of John D. Negroponte to be Ambassador to the United Nations, Senate Foreign Relations Committee, September 13, 2001, 9.
4 UN Hearing, 13, 15, 19.
5 R. Grossman, Review of E. Borgen, The Ambassador, 63–3 The Americas 507 (2007).
6 J. Nordlinger, "Dirty Wars," *National Review*, June 25, 2001.
7 R. Reeves, "In the Matter of John Negroponte," *Tulsa World*, June 21, 2001.
8 A. de Borchgrave, "Stalled Nominations," *The Washington Times*, May 1, 2001.
9 G. Geyer, "Contra Past Hobbles Nominees," *The Washington Times*, July 30, 2001.
10 G. Geyer, "Negroponte Embassy Evolving Attitudes at U.N.," *The Washington Times*, December 7, 2007.
11 K. Petras and R. Petras, *Unusually Stupid Americans: A Compendium of All-American Stupidity* (New York: Villard, 2003), 64.
12 S. Siv, *Golden Bones: An Extraordinary Journey from Hell in Cambodia to a New Life in America* (New York: Harper, 2008), 280.
13 P. Bennis, *Challenging Empire: How People, Governments and the UN Defy US Power* (Northampton, MA: Olive Branch Press, 2006), 201.
14 K. Kitfield, *War and Destiny: How the Bush Revolution in Foreign and Military Affairs Redefined American Power* (Washington: Potomac Books, 2001), 75.
15 C. Greenwood, "International Law and the War Against Terrorism," *International Affairs*, vol. 78 (2002), 301.
16 M. Byers, "Pre-emptive Self-Defense: Hegemony, Equality, and Strategies of Legal Change," *Journal of Political Philosophy*, vol. 11 (2003), 171.
17 D. Bosco, *Five That Rule Them All: The U.N. Security Council and the Making of the Modern World* (New York: Oxford University Press, 2009), 210.
18 R. Blackburn, "The Imperial Presidency, the War on Terrorism, and the Revolutions of Modernity," *Constellations*, vol. 9 (2002), 3, 9.
19 H. Kissinger, *A World Restored: Metternich, Castlereagh and the Congress of Vienna* (London: Gollancz, 1973), 316, 319, 206.
20 G. Kennan, "A Fateful Error," *The New York Times*, February 5, 1997.
21 R. Holbrooke, "The Paradox of George F. Kennan," *The Washington Post*, March 21, 2005.
22 L. Sanchez, "Ambassador Suggests U.N. Inspections Resume in Iraq," *The San Diego Union-Tribune*, February 19, 2002; Interview, San Diego Union Tribune, March 3, 2002.
23 "Hill Profile: George F. Kennan," *The Hill*, September 25, 2002.
24 H. Munoz, *A Solitary War: A Diplomat's Chronicle of the Iraq War and Its Lessons* (Golden, CO: Fulcrum, 2008), 20, quoting Lt. Gen. David Barno.
25 R. Dannheiser, "Negroponte: Fighting Terror Must Be Key Focus for US," U.N., Department of State Washington File, February 11, 2002, available at http://usinfo.org/wf-archive/2002/020211/epf108.htm

26 J. Traub, *The Best Intentions: Kofi Annan and the U.N. in the Era of American World Power* (London: Picador, 2007), 177.

27 Munoz, *A Solitary War*, 26.

28 R. Cornwell, *The [London] Independent*, July 3, 2004.

29 *The New York Times*, October 10, 2001, B5: 5; C. Lynch, "US Reserves Right to Attack State Sponsors of Terrorists: Acts of Self-Defense, Envoy Says," *Washington Post*, October 9, 2001, 13.

30 J. Prados, *Hoodwinked: The Documents That Reveal How Bush Sold Us on War* (New York: New Press, 2004), 167.

31 *The New York Times*, October 9, 2001, B5: 6; October 10, 2001, 1: 1.

32 C. Lynch, "UN Ambassador Emerges as Voice of Caution on Iraq," *The Washington Post*, January 14, 2003, 17.

33 Interview, April 7, 2009, available at www.charlierose.com/view/interview/10199

34 S. Shane, "Poker-Faced Diplomat, Negroponte Is Poised for Role as Spy Chief," *The New York Times*, March 29, 2005, 14.

35 J. Borkin, *Cursed Is the Peacemaker: The American Diplomat Versus the Israeli General, Beirut 1982* (New York: Applegate Press, 2002), 22.

36 "Bush Picks Negroponte for Iraq Post," *Los Angeles Times*, April 20, 2004.

37 H. Blix, *Disarming Iraq: The Search for Weapons of Mass Destruction* (London: Bloomsbury, 2004), 115.

38 C. Cogan, *French Negotiating Behavior: Dealing with La Grande Nation* (Washington: US Institute of Peace, 2003), 203.

39 R. Hoyle, *Going to War: How Misinformation, Disinformation and Arrogance Led America into Iraq* (New York: Thomas Dunne, 2008), 299, 300.

40 Munoz, *A Solitary War*, 30.

41 C. Hoyos and Q. Peel, "A Test of the Permanent Five," *Financial Times*, September 28, 2002.

42 UN Doc, S/PV 4644, November 8, 2002, 190.

43 C. Hoyos, "Bush Sets Out Hardline Stance on Iraqi Arms," *Financial Times*, October 17, 2002.

44 R. Ramesh, *The War We Could Not Stop* (London: Thunder's North Press, 2004).

45 "Bush's Step Toward UN Is Met by Warm Welcome: Council Seems Ready to Act," *New York Times*, September 13, 2002, quoted in N. Fenton, *Understanding the UN Security Council: Consent or Coercion* (Aldershot, UK: Ashgate, 2004), 186 n.21.

46 Cogan, *French Negotiating Behavior*, 203.

47 "Iraq Inquiry—Live," available at http://www.guardian.co.uk/politics/blog/2009/nov/27/iraq-iraq.

48 P. Gordon and J. Shapiro, *Allies at War: America, Europe and the Crisis Over Iraq* (New York: McGraw-Hill, 2004), 116–17.

49 J. Hancock, *Human Rights and US Foreign Policy* (London: Routledge, 2007).

50 Bosco, *Five That Rule Them All*, 219.

51 M. Bell, *An Accidental MP* (London: Viking, 2000), 155.

52 Munoz, *A Solitary War*, quoting a talk by Jeremy Greenstock at the Center for European Studies.

53 T. Purdon, *A Time of Our Choosing* (New York: Times Books, 2003), 68.

54 Kitfield, *War and Destiny*, 115.

55 Gordon and Shapiro, *Allies at War*, 149.

56 Munoz, *A Solitary War*, 10–12.

57 *El País*, September 26, 2001, quoted in M. Danner, "The Moment Has Come to Be Rid of Saddam," in R. Silvers (ed.), *The Consequences to Come: American Power After Bush* (New York: New York Review Books, 2008), 52–8.

58 Ibid., 43.

59 Ibid., 64–5.

60 Bosco, *Five That Rule Them All*, 222.

61 K. De Young, *Soldier: The Life of Colin Powell* (New York: Knopf, 2006), 448.

62 J. Howarth, "France: Defender of International Legitimacy," in R. Fawn and R. Hinnebusch (eds.), *The Iraq War: Causes and Consequences* (Boulder, CO: Lynne Rienner, 2006, 49 ff.

63 E. Margolis, *American Raj: Liberation or Domination* (New York: Key Porter Books, 2008), 53.

64 J. Nordlinger, "Negroponte Speaks," *National Review*, March 23, 2009, 19.

65 UN Document S/PV 4701, February 5, 2003.

66 UN Document S/PV 4714, March 7, 2003.

67 B. Burrough, et al., "The Rush to Invade Iraq: The Ultimate Inside Account," *Vanity Fair*, May 2004.

68 Kissinger, *A World Restored*, 2.

69 M. Mitchell, *The Spy Who Tried to Stop a War: Katherine Gun and the Secret Plot to Sanction the Iraq Invasion* (London: Polipoint Press, 2008), 57.

70 D. Sanger, "US May Abandon UN Vote on Iraq, Powell Testifies," *The New York Times*, March 14, 2003.

71 Bosco, *Five That Rule Them All*, 228, 229.

72 Munoz, *A Solitary War*, 76.

73 *Harvard Gazette*, Harvard University, May 8, 2003.

74 B. Woodward, *State of Denial* (London: Simon and Schuster, 2006), 136.

75 Kitfield, *War and Destiny*, 118.

76 Munoz, *A Solitary War*, 79; citing *The Guardian*, March 21, 2003.

77 401 Parliamentary Debates (Commons), 6th Series, cols. 226–8 (March 17, 2003).

78 400 Parliamentary Debates (Commons), 6th Series, cols. 293–5 (February 26, 2003).

79 Department of State, French-American Foundation, May 16, 2007.

80 Blix, *Disarming Iraq*, 274.

81 H. Blix, "A War of Utter Folly," *The Guardian*, March 20, 2008.

82 J. Anderson and G. Ikenberry, *The End of the West? Crisis and Change in the Atlantic Order* (Ithaca, NY: Cornell University Press, 2008), 191.

83 March 17, 2003, available on US State Department website.

84 R. Perle, "United They Fall," *The Spectator*, March 22, 2003.

85 G. Liebmann, "Two Kinds of Conceit," *The Spectator*, April 5, 2003, 33.

86 See J. Divine, *Roosevelt and Foreign Policy* (Harmondsworth: Penguin, 1969); R. Dallek, *FDR and US Foreign Policy*, 1932–45 (Oxford: Oxford University Press, 1995), 342, 389, 434.

87 Sanger, "US May Abandon UN Vote on Iraq, Powell Testifies."

88 Fenton, *Understanding the UN Security Council*, 204.

89 C. Bohlen to G. Ball, December 31, 1965, in National Archives, Record Group 59, Box 19 of General Records of the Department of State, Formerly Top Secret Central Policy Files, 1964–6.

90 G. Ikenberry, *Liberal Order and Imperial Ambition: Essays on American Power and World Politics* (Cambridge, UK: Polity, 2006), 265.

91 I. Hurd, *After Anarchy: Legitimacy and Power in the U.N. Security Council* (Princeton: Princeton University Press, 2007), 191–2.

92 J. Lukacs, *George Kennan: A Study of Character* (New Haven: Yale University Press, 2007), 187.

93 L. Fasulo, *An Insider's Guide to the U.N.* (New Haven: Yale University Press, 2005), 92.

94 A. De Witt, "Challenge and Response: Mexico in a Changing World," *The New Leader*, May/June 2002, 9.

95 J. Sachs, *The End of Poverty: Economic Possibilities for Our Time* (New York: Penguin, 2005), 218.

96 C. Lynch, "US Envoy Walks Out During Iraq Ambassador's Speech," *The Washington Post*, March 28, 2003, 36.

97 *New York Times*, December 21, 2002, 10: 4; *The Washington Post*, October 6, 2004, 20.

98 S. Zunes, "The Swing to the Right in US Policy toward Israel and Palestine," *Middle East Policy*, vol. 9 (2002), 45, 58.

99 M. Turner, "US Vetoes U.N. Resolution on Arafat," *Financial Times*, September 17, 2003, 11.

100 Department of State, Opening Ceremony for Global Classrooms DC Model UN, April 28, 2008.

101 Explanation of Vote, 12 July 2002, quoted in J. Ralph, *Defending the Society of States: Why America Opposes the International Criminal Court and Its Vision of World Society* (New York: Oxford University Press, 2007).

102 Nomination of John D. Negroponte; Testimony before the Committee on Foreign Relations, United States Senate, September 13, 2001.

103 F. Barringer, "UN Reaction to Resolution Seems Positive but Reserved," *The New York Times*, May 10, 2003.

104 W. Shawcross, *Allies: The US, Britain, Europe and the War in Iraq* (New York: Public Affairs Press, 2004).

105 Munoz, *A Solitary War*, 85.

106 Ibid., 101.

107 A. Shadid, *Night Draws Near: Iraq's People in the Shadow of America's War* (New York: Holt, 2005), 197; M. Boot, "Reality Check: This Is War," in G. Rosen (ed.), *The Right War? The Conservative Debate on Iraq* (Cambridge: Cambridge University Press, 2005), 94–5.

108 Ibid., 108.

109 Ibid., 119.

110 Ibid., 143.

111 Shawcross, *Allies*, 177.

112 Ibid., 148.

113 Mitchell, *The Spy Who Tried to Stop a War*, 57.

114 Ibid., 172–3.

115 J. Egelund, A Billion Lives: An Eyewitness Report from the Frontiers of Humanity (New York: Simon and Schuster, 2008), 89.

Chapter Eighteen

1 J. Nordlinger, "Negroponte Speaks," *National Review*, March 23, 2009, 19.

2 J. Foster, *Naked Imperialism: The US Pursuit of Global Dominance* (New York: Monthly Review Press, 2006), 130.

3 R. Earle, *Nights in the Pink Hotel: An American Strategist's Pursuit of Peace in Iraq* (Annapolis: Naval Institute Press, 2008), 1, 2, 21.

4 K. De Young, *Soldier: The Life of Colin Powell* (New York: Knopf, 2006), 507.

5 D. Phillips, *Losing Iraq: Inside the Postwar Reconstruction Fiasco* (New York: Basic Books, 2005), 2066 ff., citing W. Strobel, "Negroponte: Cooperating with the U.N. in 'Strategic Interest' of US," Knight-Ridder-Tribune News Service, April 28, 2004; W. Safire, "Brahimi's Two Mistakes," *The New York Times*, April 26, 2004, 19.

6 B. West, *No True Glory: A Frontline Account of the Battle for Fallujah* (New York: Bantam, 2005), 236, 245.

7 B. Woodward, *State of Denial* (London: Simon and Schuster, 2006), 307.

8 Special Inspector General for Iraq Reconstruction, Hard Lessons: The Iraq Reconstruction Experience (Washington: GPO, 2009), 202.

9 S. Metz, *Learning from Iraq: Counterinsurgency in American Strategy* (Carlisle, PA: US War College, 2007), 87.

10 Woodward, *State of Denial*, 280.

11 Ibid., 324.

12 Ibid., 310.

13 Transcript of December 3, 2006 C-Span Question and Answer with J. Negroponte, available at www.politics.stephaniedray.com/?q=node/183

14 Woodward, *State of Denial*, 477.

15 Ibid., 383.

16 *The New York Times*, November 11, 2009, 1.

17 Earle, *Nights in the Pink Hotel*, 24.

18 *The New York Times*, April 28, 2005, 9: 1; May 21, 2005, 18: 1; June 8, 2005, 11: 5; June 9, 2005, 1: 5; R. Wright, "Bush Picks U.N. Envoy as Ambassador to Iraq," *The Washington Post*, April 20, 2004, 1, 17; W. Hapgood, "Ambassador with a Big Portfolio: JN Goes to Baghdad with a Record of Competence and Controversy," *The Washington Post*, June 21, 2004, C1.

19 El Pais, September 26, 2001, quoted in M. Danner, "The Moment Has Come to Be Rid of Saddam," in R. Silvers (ed.), *The Consequences to Come: American Power After Bush* (New York: New York Review Books, 2008), 52–8.

20 J. Pfiffner, "US Blunders in Iraq: De-Ba'athification and Disbanding the Army," *Intelligence and National Security*, vol. 25 (2010), 26.

21 E. Herring and G. Rangwala, *Iraq in Fragments: The Occupation and Its Legacy* (London: Hurst, 2006), 226–9. The CPA Orders and Regulations are found at www.iraqcoalition.org/regulations/index

22 Special Inspector General for Iraq Reconstruction, Hard Lessons: The Iraq Reconstruction Experience (Washington: GPO, 2009), 283, 327.

23 "Sir Jeremy Greenstock at the Iraq War Inquiry," *Guardian*, December 15, 2009.

24 J. Burns, "If It's a Civil War, Do We Know It?" *The New York Times*, July 24, 2005.

25 J. Kitfield, *War and Destiny: How the Bush Revolution in Foreign and Military Affairs American Power* (Washington: Potomac Books, 2005), 351.

26 S. Zunes, "The United States in Iraq: The Consequences of Occupation Policy," *International Journal of Contemporary Iraqi Studies* (January 2007), 57.

27 J. Dobbins (ed.), *America's Role in Nation-Building from Germany to Iraq* (Santa Monica: Rand Corporation, 2003), cited in R. Brigham, *Is Iraq Another Vietnam* (New York: Public Affairs, 2006), 73.

28 Earle, *Nights in the Pink Hotel*, 51, 61, 80.

29 Ibid., 61, 81, 93.

30 T. Ricks, *Fiasco: The American Military Adventure in Iraq* (New York: Penguin, 2006), 208, 391.

31 P. Cockburn, *The Occupation: War and Resistance in Iraq* (London: Verso, 2006), 173.

32 *The New York Times*, November 28, 2004, 1: 1; Ricks, *Fiasco*, 330–5, 341–3; see W. Kristol, "After Fallujah," *Weekly Standard*, April 12, 2004.

33 Herring and Rangwala, *Iraq in Fragments*, 29; West, *No True Glory*, 58–62; Kristol, "After Fallujah," April 12, 2004.

34 Ricks, *Fiasco*, 398–406; for a contrasting view, see Herring and Rangwala, *Iraq in Fragments*, 35–6.

35 S. Mc Clellan, *What Happened: Inside the Bush White House and Washington's Culture of Deception* (Washington: Public Affairs, 2008), 241.

36 B. Graham, "General and Ambassador Working Closely to Coordinate Military, Diplomatic Efforts," *The Washington Post*, November 30, 2004, 12.

37 Earle, *Nights in the Pink Hotel*, 145.

38 J. Mayer, "A Doctrine Passes," *The New Yorker*, October 14, 2002.

39 "Hill Profile: George F. Kennan," *The Hill*, September 25, 2002.

40 W. Pfaff, "When the Marines Make Policy, Iraq Burns," *International Herald-Tribune*, August 21, 2004.

41 C. Fair, et al., *Treading on Hallowed Ground: Counterinsurgency Operations in Sacred Places* (New York: Oxford, 2008), 162.

42 P. Cockburn, *Moqtada Al Sadr and the Fall of Iraq* (London: Faber, 2008), 196–7, 202, 207.

43 A. Allawi, *The Occupation of Iraq: Winning the War, Losing the Peace* (New Haven, CT: Yale University Press, 2007), 327–33, 397 ff.

44 Woodward, *State of Denial*, 307–8, 312, 382, 477–8.

45 Earle, *Nights in the Pink Hotel*, 140.

46 G. Jaffe and D. Cloud, *The Fourth Star: Four Generals and the Epic Struggle for the Future of the US Army* (New York: Crown, 2009), 184.

47 R. White, *The Morass: United States Intervention in Central America* (New York: Harper, 1984), 268.

48 K. Papagianni, "State Building and Transitional Politics in Iraq: The Perils of a Top-Down Transition," *International Studies Perspectives*, vol. 8 (2007), 253.

49 Earle, *Nights in the Pink Hotel*, 195.

50 R. Worth, "US Envoy Leaves Iraq," *The New York Times*, March 17, 2005.

51 Corne Lesnes, in Le Monde, August 24, 2005.

52   Quoted in G. Goldstein, *Lessons in Disaster: McGeorge Bundy and the Path to War in Vietnam* (New York: Times Books, 2008), 196.

53   Woodward, *State of Denial*, 308, 310.

54   Earle, *Nights in the Pink Hotel*, 51, 71, 137, 208.

55   F. Ajami, *The Foreigner's Gift: The Americans, the Arabs, and the Iraqis in Iraq* (New York: Free Press, 2006), 261, 309.

56   Q. Lawrence, *Invisible Nation: How the Kurds' Quest for Statehood Is Shaping Iraq and the Middle East* (New York: Walker and Co., 2008), 248.

57   *The New York Times*, June 29, 2004, 1: 6; W. Pincus, "Process of Transferring Power Is Going to be Evolutionary, Negroponte Says," *The Washington Post*, April 28, 2004, 15.

58   R. Engel, *War Journal: My Five Years in Iraq* (New York: Simon and Schuster, 2008), 218–19.

59   *The New York Times*, August 31, 2004, 9: 1; D. Cloud, "US Diplomat Wants More Funds for Iraqi Security," *The Wall Street Journal*, August 30, 2004, A1.

60   *The New York Times*, May 16, 2004, 18: 1.

61   T. Miller, *Blood Money: Wasted Billions, Lost Lives, and Corporate Greed in Iraq* (New York: Little, Brown, 2006), 209–11, 224, 235.

62   Special Inspector General for Iraq Reconstruction, Hard Lessons: The Iraq Reconstruction Experience (Washington: GPO, 2009), 177.

63   Lawrence, *Invisible Nation*, 260–1.

64   *The New York Times*, October 17, 2004, 14: 1.

65   Miller, *Blood Money*, 209–12.

66   *The New York Times*, January 13, 2006, 21: 1. For other Bremer post-mortems, see P. Bremer, "The Right Call," *The Wall Street Journal*, January 12, 2005, A10; P. Bremer, "Personal Satisfaction," *The Wall Street Journal*, February 23, 2005, A16; for General Jay Garner's reflections, see J. Garner, "After the Vote," *The Wall Street Journal*, February 1, 2005, A12.

67   *The New York Times*, November 28, 2004, 1: 1; December 1, 2004, 14: 1; January 19, 2005, 10: 1; G. Kessler and R. Wright, "Negroponte's Move to Iraq Calculated to Ease Transition; He Plans to Focus on Nation's Elections, Reconstruction," *The Washington Post*, June 20, 2004, 18; S. Wilson, "US Envoy Says Iraq Vote on Track; Negroponte Is Firm on January Despite November Death Toll," *The Washington Post*, December 1, 2004, 1.

68   W. Buckley, "Iraq: Framing a New Constitution!" *The New York Sun*, July 27, 2005.

69   Ricks, *Fiasco*, 408.

70   *The New York Times*, December 7, 2004, 1: 6; B. Bender, "Top Spy Chief Softened Early Assertiveness; Some Wonder How Loyalty Will Play Out," *Boston Globe*, February 19, 2005.

71   L. Robinson, *Tell Me How This Ends: General David Petraeus and the Search for a Way Out of Iraq* (New York: Public Affairs, 2008), 9.

72   *The New York Times*, August 4, 2004, 1: 2; see Herring and Rangwala, *Iraq in Fragments*, 86–7.

73   Earle, *Nights in the Pink Hotel*, 183.

74   Ibid., 149, 158.

75   Ibid., 166.

76   Baghdad to Secretary of State, December 2004, "A Plan for Dealing with the Next Government of Iraq," Baghdad 002048, declassified September 24, 2009, Case ID: 2009 06579.

77   Earle, *Nights in the Pink Hotel*, 49, 200, 212.

78   Ibid., 216.

79   *The New York Times*, October 12, 2005, 6: 5; February 3, 2006, 16: 5.

80   "Negroponte Fears Al Qaeda Expansion," Financial Times.com, May 17, 2007.

81   J. Scahill, *Blackwater: The Rise of the World's Most Powerful Mercenary Army* (London: Serpent's Tail, 2007), 288.

82   Department of State, Office of the Inspector General…, Review of Staffing Process for Embassy Baghdad's new Embassy Compound, Report No. 1QO-05-61, July 2005.

83 *The New York Times*, March 11, 2005, 10: 1; J. Glantz, "Italian Was Killed at Checkpoint Set Up for US Ambassador's Trip," March 12, 2005, 9: 2.

84 Earle, *Nights in the Pink Hotel*, 23.

85 J. Scahill, *Blackwater: The Rise of the World's Most Powerful Mercenary Army* (London: Serpent's Tail, 2007), 71.

86 The Nomination of Hon. John D. Negroponte to be US Ambassador to Iraq, Hearing before the Committee on Foreign Relations, United States Senate, 108th Congress, Second Session, April 27, 2004, 43.

87 US Department of State..., Office of Inspector General, Review of Diplomatic Security's Management of Personal Protective Services in Iraq, Report No. MERO 1QO-09-02, January 2009, 1, 19.

88 D. Sands, "Pentagon, State to Restrict Private Contractors," *The New York Times*, December 6, 2007, A15; K. De Young, "State Department Contractors in Iraq Are Reined In," *The Washington Post*, December 6, 2007.

89 K. De Young, "Negroponte Ousts State Department Chief of Security," *The Washington Post*, October 25, 2007.

90 P. Singer, *Corporate Warriors: The Rise of the Privatized Military Industry* (Ithaca, NY: Cornell University, 2003), 240 ff.

91 Human Rights First, Private Security Contractors at War: Ending the Culture of Impunity (Washington: Human Rights First, 2008), 20.

92 Special Inspector General for Iraq Reconstruction, Hard Lessons: The Iraq Reconstruction Experience (Washington: GPO, 2009), 179.

93 Ibid., 288 ff., see R. Dreyfuss, "Phoenix Rising," *American Prospect*, January 1, 2004; M. Hirsh and J. Barry, "The Salvador Option: The Pentagon May Put Special Forces Led Assassination or Kidnapping Teams in Iraq," *Newsweek*,
January 8, 2005; see R. Kaplan, "Supremacy by Stealth," *Atlantic Monthly*, July–August 2003, 78.

94 D. Jehl and E. Bumiller, "Bush Picks Envoy to Iraq to Be New Overseer of Spy Agencies," *The New York Times*, February 17, 2005.

95 Department of State Press Archives, "Ambassador John Negroponte on ABC's This Week with George Stephanopoulos," June 23, 2005, available at http://statelists.state.gov/scripts/wa.exe?A2=ind0501d&L=dospress&P=917

96 Earle, *Nights in the Pink Hotel*, 158.

97 S. Shane, "Poker Faced Diplomat: Negroponte Is Poised for Role as Spy Chief," *The New York Times*, March 29, 2006, 14.

98 Earle, *Nights in the Pink Hotel*, 237.

99 L. Robinson, *Tell Me How This Ends: General David Petraeus and the Search for a Way Out of Iraq* (New York: Public Affairs, 2008), 9.

100 B. West, *The Strongest Tribe: War, Politics and the Endgame in Iraq* (New York: Random House, 2008), 75.

101 T. Maule, *Hope Is Not a Plan: The War in Iraq from Inside the Green Zone* (Westport, CT: Praeger, 2007), 10, 116.

102 B. Graham, *By His Own Rules: The Story of Donald Rumsfeld* (New York: Public Affairs Press, 2009), 492.

103 Nordlinger, "Negroponte Speaks," 19.

104 Ibid.

105 Cockburn, *The Occupation*, 95.

106 Ibid., 29.

107 "Bush Hits Political Leaks, Discloses Key Conclusions in Terror Report," *New York Times*, September 23, 2006, A1.

108 B. Hoffman, "The Global Terrorist Threat: Is Al Qaeda On the Run or On the March?" *Middle East Policy*, vol. 14 (June 2007), 44.

109 Department of State, J. Negroponte Interview with Charlie Rose, April 25, 2008.

110 Department of State, J. Negroponte Press Conference, Baghdad, December 2, 2007.

111 D. Andelman, *A Shattered Peace: Versailles 1919 and the Price We Pay Today* (New York: Wiley, 2008), 202, 204.

112 Y. Dreazen, NPR Interview, *Weekend Edition*, March 26, 2005.

Chapter Nineteen

1   B. Woodward, *State of Denial* (London: Simon and Schuster, 2006), 390 ff.

2   D. Eisenberg, "Bush's New Intelligence Czar," *Time*, February 28, 2005.

3   DNI Hearing, supra, 4.

4   *New York Times*, April 13, 2005, 14: 1; April 11, 2005, 12: 5; April 13, 2005, 14: 1; April 22, 2005; M. Fletcher, "Negroponte Named National Intelligence Chief," *Washington Post*, February 18, 2005, 1; D. Priest, "Relationship with Bush Will Be Key," *Washington Post*, February 18, 2005, 8; M. Dobbs, "Negroponte's Time in Honduras at Issue," *Washington Post*, March 21, 2005, 1; M. Dobbs, "Papers Illustrate Negroponte's Contra Role," *Washington Post*, April 12, 2005, 4; 19: 1; W. Pincus, "Negroponte Intends to Remain to End of Bush's Term," *Washington Post*, December 3, 2006, 6; Profile, *Financial Times*, June 25, 2004, 8a; D. Clud, "Negroponte Named Intelligence Chief," *Wall Street Journal*, February 18, 2005, A2; C. Robbins, "Negroponte Has Tricky Mission," *Wall Street Journal*, April 27, 2004, A4; Y. Dreazen, "Another Big Handover Looms for Iraq," *Wall Street Journal*, March 23, 2005, A4.

5   K. Timmerman, *Shadow Warriors: The Untold Story of Traitors, Saboteurs and the Party of Surrender* (New York: Crown Forum, 2007), 199, 241.

6   DNI Hearing, 174.

7   Quoted in C. Patten, *Cousins and Strangers: American, Britain and Europe in a New Century* (New York: Holt, 2006), 197.

8   Ibid., 380 n.30.

9   J. Negroponte and E. Wittenstein, "Urgency, Opportunity and Frustration: Implementing the Intelligence Reform and Terrorism Prevention Act of 2004," *Yale Law and Policy Review*, vol. 28 (2010), 379.

10   JN, Interview, National Public Radio, January 13, 2010.

11   W. Pincus, "Negroponte's First Job Is Showing Who's Boss," *Washington Post*, March 1, 2005, 13; D. Ignatius, "A Czar's Uncertain Clout," *Washington Post*, March 4, 2005, 21; H. Rosin, "Clique and Dagger: The Jocks and Nerds of Spy High Are Getting a New Principal," *Washington Post*, April 12, 2005, C1; W. Pincus, "Negroponte Stresses Mandate for Change," *Washington Post*, April 13, 2005, 4; W. Pincus, "Nomination of Negroponte Deputy Backed," *Washington Post*, April 15, 2005, 6; D. Ignatius, "Can the Spy Agencies Dig Out," *Washington Post*, April 15, 2005, 25; W. Pincus, "Top Intelligence Officials Name Deputies," *Washington Post*, May 7, 2005, 8; P. Dreazen, "Panel Blasts Intelligence Community Failures," *Wall Street Journal*, April 1, 2005, A4; J. Solomon, "Bush Team Takes Steps to Address US Security Gaps," *Wall Street Journal*, July 13, 2005.

12   J. Negroponte, "Intelligence System Is Getting Better," *National Public Radio*, January 13, 2010.

13   G. Geyer, "A New Breed of White House Diplomats," *Syndicated Column*, February 28, 2005; A. Slaughter, "Partisans Gone Wild," *Washington Post*, July 29, 2007.

14   B. Drogin, "Diplomatic Skill May Not Be Enough," *Los Angeles Times*, February 20, 2005.

15   Timmerman, *Shadow Warriors*, 227.

16   K. De Young, "GAO Faults Agencies' Sharing of Terror Data," *Washington Post*, April 19, 2006, 3.

17   W. Pincus, "Negroponte Seeks Better Communication," *Washington Post*, July 20, 2005, 4; W. Pincus, "Negroponte Cites Innovations in Intelligence," *Washington Post*, April 21, 2005, 7.

18   *New York Times*, September 30, 2005, 2: 4; April 21, 2006, 21: 6.

19   *New York Times*, November 9, 2005, 14: 5.

20   G. Kennan, "Interview with Foreign Policy Magazine, Summer 1972," in T. Jespersen (ed.), *Interviews with George F. Kennan* (Jackson, MI: University Press of Mississippi, 2002), 156.

21   J. Bhagwati, *Termites in the Trading System: How Preferential Agreements Undermine Free Trade* (New York: Oxford, 2008), 75.

22   "Playing Defense," 141 US News and World Report No. 17, November 6, 2006 and 141 US News and World Report No. 17, November 13, 2006.

23 "Oil Price Rises Strengthen Our Enemies: Negroponte," *Financial Times*, February 3, 2006.

24 Memorandum of Meeting, April 4, 1963, President, Thompson, Ormsby-Gore, in National Archives, General State Department Records, Box 2245, Folder, Pol. 7.

25 I. Litwak, *Regime Change: US Strategy through the Prism of 9/11* (Baltimore: Johns Hopkins University Press, 2007), 299.

26 W. Pincus, "US Will Not Flee Iraq, Bush Says: President Responds to Letter Attributed to Al Qaeda Leader," *Washington Post*, October 16, 2005; S. Glasser and W. Pincus, "Seized Letter Outlines Al Qaeda Goals in Iraq," *Washington Post*, October 12, 2005, A13.

27 J. Negroponte, "Yes, We Are Better Prepared," *Washington Post*, September 10, 2006.

28 M. Mazzeti, et al., "Spy Czar Gains Clou," *Los Angeles Times*, June 30, 2005; P. Jehl, "Intelligence Chief Gains Authority," *International Herald Tribune*, July 1, 2005; S. Gorman, "Coordination Said to Be Lacking in Spy Chief's Office," *Chicago Tribune*, October 16, 2005.

29 G. Liebmann (ed.), "Chartering a National Police Force," *American Bar Association Journal*, vol. 56 (1970), 1070, 1176; "A Dangerous Explosion: The Proposed Federal Criminal Code," *Trial*, vol. 9, no. 5 (1973), 21; "Economic Crimes: The Proposed Federal Criminal Code," *Business Lawyer*, vol. 27 (1971), 177; "The Proposed Federal Criminal Code: What Does It Mean for Business Corporation Law Review," vol. 3 (1979); "Antitrust and the Proposed Revision of Federal Criminal Laws: Penalties," *Antitrust Law Journal*, vol. 43 (1974), 409; Hearings before the Subcommittee on Criminal Laws, Senate Judiciary Committee, 92nd Congress, First Session, Reform of Federal Criminal Laws, Part I, February 10, 1971, 113–28; see also Ibid., Part VII, 93rd Congress, First Session, April 13, 1978, 1116–30; for the history of the controversy see R. Gainer, "Federal Criminal Code Reform: Past and Future," *Buffalo Criminal Law Review*, vol. 2.1:45 (1998), 131–2.

30 P. Kurland, "Robert H. Jackson," in L. Friedman and F. Israel (eds.), *The Justices of the United States Supreme Court, 1789–1969* (New York: Chelsea House, vol. 4, 1969), 2543, 2565.

31 *Time*, May 15, 2006.

32 DNI Hearing, 34.

33 R. Morris, *Uncertain Greatness: Henry Kissinger and American Foreign Policy* (London: Quartet Books, 1977), 26–7.

34 W. Pincus, "CIA to Cede President's Brief to Negroponte," *Washington Post*, February 19, 2005, 15.

35 *New York Times*, February 18, 2005, 1: 3; February 20, 2005, 22: 1; D. Priest, "CIA Moves to Second Fiddle in Intelligence Work," *Washington Post*, February 27, 2005, 9.

36 Timmerman, *Shadow Warriors*, 226.

37 *New York Times*, April 1, 2005, 1: 1.

38 *New York Times*, July 26, 2005, 18: 4.

39 J. Nordlinger, "Negroponte Speaks," *National Review*, March 23, 2009, 19.

40 R. Clarke, "The Trauma of 9/11 Is No Excuse," *Washington Post*, May 31, 2009.

41 B. Gellman, *Angler: The Cheney Vice Presidency* (New York: Penguin Press, 2008), 454, citing Negroponte to Hastert, May 17, 2006.

42 J. Bamford, *The Shadow Factory: The Ultra-Secret NSA from 9/11 to the Eavesdropping on America* (New York: Doubleday, 2008), 282.

43 D. Eggen, "Negroponte Had Denied Domestic Call Monitoring: Administration Won't Comment on NSA Logs," *Washington Post*, May 15, 2006. See also *New York Times*, February 3, 2006, 16: 5; D. Milbank, "He Could Tell You But Then He'd Have to Kill You," *Washington Post*, April 25, 2006, 2; Eggen, "Negroponte Had Denied Domestic Call Monitoring," 3.

44 R. Sale, www.sicsempertyrannis, 5 July 2006.

45 Editorial, "Growing Tired of Obfuscation," *Knight-Ridder Business News*, July 30, 2007.

46 www.sciencedaily.com/upi/?feed=TcpN...-negroponte.xml

47 DNI Hearing, 14.

48 J. Negroponte, "Support US Intelligence: Clarifying Our Treaty Obligations Would Not Harm Nation's Troops," *US News*, September 19, 2006, 12A.

49 M. Thiessen, *Courting Disaster: How the CIA Kept America Safe and How Barack Obama Is Inviting the Next Attack* (New York: Perseus, 2010), 10.

50 www.foxnews.com/story/0,2933,214203,00.html

51 E. Bumiller, *Condoleeza Rice: An American Life* (New York: Random House, 2007), 297.

52 M. Mazzetti and S. Shane, "Interrogation Debate Sharply Divided Bush White House," *New York Times*, May 4, 2009, A1.

53 See William Bundy to Abrahan Chayes, June 23, 1964, National Archives, General State Department Files, East Asian Division, Folder, Pol. 27; L. Meeker, The Legality of US Participation in the Defense of Vietnam, Department of State Bulletin, March 4, 1966.

54 C. Savage, *Takeover: The Return of the Imperial Presidency and the Subversion of American Democracy* (Boston: Little Brown, 2007), 276–7.

55 R. Mikkelsen, "US Used Waterboarding But No More: Ex Spy Chief," *Reuters*, January 28, 2008.

56 R. Thompson, *Peace Is Not at Hand* (London: Chatto and Windus, 1974), 48–9.

57 T. Thompson, *Defeating Communist Insurgency* (London: Chatto and Windus, 1966), 53–4.

58 Parliamentary Debates (Commons), November 27, 1957.

59 Curzon to Alfred Lyttleton, August 29, 1900; Curzon to Knollys [Secretary to The King], 14 December 1902, quoted in K. Rose, *Superior Person: A Portrait of Curzon and His Circle in Late Victorian England* (London: Weidenfeld and Nicolson), 1969.

60 Parliamentary Debates (Commons), August 7, 1920.

61 S. Shane, "Senate Session on Security Erupts un Spying Debate," *New York Times*, February 3, 2006, available at www.nytimes.com/2006/02/03/politics/03threats.html?_ r=1&oref=slogin; W. Pincus, "Iraq Just One Factor, Negroponte Says," *Washington Post*, September 26, 2006, 3.

62 M. Isikoff and M. Hosenball, "Tracking a Paper Trail: A Memo from a Top Intelligence Official Warned the CIA Not to Destroy Its Interrogation Tapes," *Newsweek*, December 24, 2007.

63 M. Mazetti, "C.I.A. Destroyed 92 Interrogation Tapes," *New York Times*, March 2, 2009.

64 W. Pincus, "Director Highlights Fostering Growth of Foreign Democracies," *Washington Post*, October 27, 2005, 9.

65 "Negroponte Unveils New Spy Priorities," in B. Bender (ed.), *Boston Globe*, October 27, 2005.

66 W. Pincus, "Negroponte Orders an Update on Terrorism's Influence on Iraq," *Washington Post*, August 5, 2006, 7.

67 W. Pincus, "Muslims' Own Debates Called Key to Future," *Washington Post*, February 18, 2006, 16.

68 W. Pincus, "Pakistan Will Have to Reckon with Tribal Leaders; Negroponte Pessimistic on Afghanistan and Neighbor," *Washington Post*, December 15, 2006, 26.

69 I. Lustick, *Trapped in the War on Terror* (Philadelphia: University of Pennsylvania, 2006), 44.

70 DNI Confirmation Hearing, 41.

71 DNI Hearing, 22, 26, 31.

72 *New York Times*, June 12, 2005, 1: 6; June 30, 2005, 1: 6; W. Pincus, "Spy Chief Gets More Authority Over FBI," *Washington Post*, June 30, 2005, 1; W. Pincus, "Negroponte to Review Intelligence Changes," *Washington Post*, July 2, 2005, 19; A. Squeo, "Justice Department Faces White House Overhaul," *Wall Street Journal*, June 13, 2005, A4.

73 D. Jehl, "White House Is Said to Reject Panel's Call for a Greater Pentagon Role in Covert Operations," *New York Times*, June 28, 2005, 6: 1.

74 *New York Times*, October 14, 2005, 16: 1; W. Pincus, "CIA, Pentagon Seek to Avoid Overlap," *Washington Post*, July 4, 2005, 2.

75 *New York Times*, March 8, 2006, 1: 6; May 10, 2006, 1: 5. See http://www.usdoj.gov/opa/documents/olc-memos.htm

76 R. Block, "Pentagon Steps Up Intelligence Efforts Within US Borders, Mining Large Databases, Tracking Antiwar Protests, Collecting vs. Receiving," *Wall Street Journal*, April 27, 2006, A1.

77 W. Pincus, "Pentagon Expands Its Domestic Intelligence Activity," *Washington Post*, November 27, 2005, A06; J. Warrick, "Intelligence-Gathering Program May Be Halted," *Washington Post*, April 2, 2008, A08; "Unit Created by Rumsfeld Shut Down," in Reuters (ed.), *Gulf Times*, August 6, 2008.

78 L. Freeh, "Former FBI Director Says US Doesn't Need a National Police Force," *Wall Street Journal*, March 19, 2007, A13.

79 R. Posner, "Time to Rethink the FBI," *Wall Street Journal*, March 19, 2007, A13.

80 W. Pincus, "Some Lawmakers Doubt DNI Has Taken Intelligence Reins," *Washington Post*, February 2, 2006, 9; "Negroponte's Battle for Authority," *New York Times*, March 6, 2006, A13; W. Pincus, "House Approves Intelligence Measure: Provision Barring Transfers Between Agencies Without Approval of Congress is Removed," *Washington Post*, June 22, 2005, 6.

81 *New York Times*, May 6, 2006, 1: 6; May 9, 2006, 1: 6.

82 W. Pincus and D. Kinzer, "Bush Ends Goss' Stormy Tenure as Director of C.I.A.," *Washington Post*, May 6, 2006.

83 S. Gorman and J. Hirsch, "Goss Resigns as C.I.A. Chief," *Baltimore Sun*, May 6, 2006.

84 R. Scarborough, *Sabotage: America's Enemies Inside the CIA* (Washington: Regnery, 2007).

85 Timmerman, *Shadow Warriors*, 289.

86 JN, News Briefing on CIA Changes, May 8, 2006.

87 W. Pincus, "Spy Satellites Are Under Scrutiny," *Washington Post*, August 16, 2005, 11; J. Karp, "Negroponte Signals His Desire for Greater Say Over Satellites," *Wall Street Journal*, September 19, 2005, B4; *New York Times*, September 30, 2005, 17: 1.

88 US News and World Report, November 13, 2006.

89 A. Badiru, *Step Project Management: Guide for Science, Technical and Engineering Projects* (Washington: CRC, 2009), 334.

90 *New York Times*, July 29, 2005, 1: 1.

91 W. Pincus, "CIA Station Chiefs Are Instructed to Include Negroponte in Reporting," *Washington Post*, May 13, 2005, 4.

92 S. Blumenthal, *How Bush Rules* (Princeton, NJ: Princeton University Press, 2006), 175–6, 254.

93 *New York Times*, February 3, 2006, 4: 3.

94 DNI, *Iran: Nuclear Intentions and Capabilities* (Washington: DNI, 2007), available at http://www.dni.gov/press_releases/20071203

95 Negroponte and Wittenstein, "Urgency, Opportunity and Frustration," 379.

96 W. Pfaff, "The *Coup d'État* Against Bush," January 17, 2008, available at www.williampfaff.com

97 Nordlinger, "Negroponte Speaks," 19.

98 M. El Baradei, *The Age of Deception: Nuclear Diplomacy in Treacherous Times* (New York: Metropolitan Books, 2011), 193.

99 R. Cheney, In My Time (New York: Threshhold Books, 2011), 479.

100 JN Interview with Bill McMahon, Council for Foreign Relations, February 1, 2008.

101 "Need to Know: John Negroponte's Dismissive Attitude Toward the Saddam Tapes," *Weekly Standard*, February 27, 2006; "Bush: Get Stuff Out," *Weekly Standard*, March 20, 2006; "Senators Question Posting of Iraqi Nuclear Papers," *New York Times*, November 5, 2006; see also Timmerman, *Shadow Warriors*, 264–71.

102 *New York Times*, March 28, 2006, 1: 3; W. Pincus, "US Releases First of Seized Iraqi Papers," *Washington Post*, March 17, 2006, 15.

103 W. Pincus, "Intelligence Director's Budget May Near $1 billion, Report Finds," *Washington Post*, April 20, 2006, 11.

104 *New York Times*, April 20, 2006, 1: 3; Pincus, "Some Lawmakers Doubt DNI Has Taken Intelligence Reins," 9; D. Rogers, "Pelosi Plans Panel to Oversee Spy Agency Funds," *Wall Street Journal*, December 14, 2006, A3.

105 S. Shane, "In New Job, Spymaster Draws Bi-Partisan Criticism," *New York Times*, April 20, 2006, 1.

106 E. Hunt, *American Spy: My Secret History* (New York: Wiley, 2007). 331.

107 F. Hitz, *Why Spy? Espionage in an Age of Uncertainty* (New York: Thomas Dunne, 2008), 174–5.

108 *Washington Post*, February 2, 2006, A9, quoted in T. Gup, *Nation of Secrets: The Threat to Democracy and the American Way of Life* (New York: Doubleday, 2007), 2.

109 L. Blumenfeld, "For Negroponte, Move to State Department is a Homecoming," *Washington Post*, January 29, 2007, 1; see also W. Pincus, "Negroponte Calls Intelligence Restructuring a Work in Progress," *Washington Post*, January 20, 2007, 8; W. Pincus, "Office Overseeing Spy Agencies Emphasizes Lessons Learned," *Washington Post*, February 26, 2007, 13.

110 G. Treverton, *Intelligence for an Age of Terror* (Cambridge: Cambridge University Press, 2009), 97.

111 *Knight Ridder Business News*, March 1, 2007, 1.

112 W. Pincus, "National Intelligence Director Says He'll Stay On," *Washington Post*, December 3, 2006, A6.

113 M. Mazzetti and D. Sanger, "Departing Intelligence Chief Felt Uncomfortable as Top Spy," *New York Times*, January 5, 2007, A1; M. Mazzetti and D. Sanger, "Speculation Surrounds Choice by Spy Chief to Step Back," *New York Times*, January 5, 2007.

114 Mazzetti and Sanger, "Departing Intelligence Chief Felt Uncomfortable as Top Spy," A1; K. De Young and W. Pincus, "Negroponte Moves to Job Considered Crucial at State Department," *Washington Post*, January 5, 2007, A5.

115 ODNI, Office of the Inspector General, Critical Intelligence Community Management Challenges, November 12, 2008.

116 Negroponte and Wittenstein, "Urgency, Opportunity and Frustration," 379.

117 "Seymour Hersh on John Negroponte, America funding Sunni groups (outside of Iraq) to foment civil war and contain Hezbollah," morganucadon.com The Whole World is Watching, February 25, 2007, available at http://morganucadon.com/node/296; G. Kessler, "Negroponte to Leave Job to Be State Department Deputy," *Washington Post*, January 4, 2007, 11; A. Kamen, "Negroponte to State: You Heard It Here First," *Washington Post*, January 5, 2007, 15; De Young and Pincus, "Negroponte Moves to Job Considered Crucial at State Department," A5.

118 See Conclusions, Note 7, infra.

119 S. Hersh, "The Redirection: Is the Administration's New Policy Benefiting Our Enemies in the War on Terrorism," *New Yorker*, March 3, 2007.

120 DOS, JN Interview with Charlie Rose, April 25, 2008.

121 B. Woodward, *The War Within* (New York: Simon and Schuster, 2008), 52.

122 United States ex rel Shaughnessy v. Mezei, 345 US 206 (1953) (Jackson, J., dissenting); Youngstown Sheet and Tool Co v. Sawyer, 343 US 579 (1952).

Chapter Twenty

1 "Choice for No. 2 at State Department Defends Bush's Stance on Iran," *The New York Times*, January 31, 2007; "Radical Populism on Negroponte's List," *The Washington Times*, January 31, 2007, A13; T. Shanber, "Negroponte Advises New Diplomats to Seek Challenging Posts," *The New York Times*, February 21, 2007, A10.

2 Department of State, Community of Democracies Inaugural Session, November 15, 2007.

3 J. Traub, *The Freedom Agenda: Why America Must Spread Democracy [Just Not the Way George Bush Did]* (New York: Farrar Straus, 2008), 205–6.

4 G. Kessler, *The Confidante: Condoleezza Rice and the Creation of the Bush Legacy* (New York: St. Martin's, 2007), 246.

5 Department of State, Robert White Oral History, June 10, 1992.

6 G. Kennan, "Somalia: Through a Glass, Darkly," *The New York Times*, September 30, 1993.

7 Department of State, J. Negroponte Interview with Charlie Rose, April 25, 2008.

8 J. Negroponte, "What's Going Right in Iraq," *The Wall Street Journal*, May 4, 2007, 15.

9 "Chavez Attacks Bush," *The New York Times*, February 2, 2007, 8.

10 J. Nordlinger, "Negroponte Speaks," *National Review*, March 23, 2009, 19.

11 Ibid.

12 JN, "Reap the Bounty: US Should Join International Law of the Sea Convention," *The Washington Times*, June 13, 2007, A17.

13 J. Goldsmith and J. Rabkin, "A Treaty the Senate Should Sink," *The Washington Post*, July 2, 2007; F. Gaffney, "LOST Runs Silent, Runs Deep," *The Washington Times*, October 30, 2007, 14; F. Gaffney, "The U.N.'s Big Power Grab," *The Washington Times*, October 2, 2007.

14 "White House Pushes Sea Treaty," *The Washington Times*, September 28, 2007.

15 L. Murkowski, "Law of Sea Treaty Crucial to US," *Anchorage Daily News*, November 8, 2007; J. Abrams, "White House Warming to Law of Sea Treaty," *Oakland Tribune*, October 5, 2007; Testimony before the Senate Foreign Relations Committee, September 27, 2007.

16 Department of State, Deputy Secretary John D. Negroponte at the Business Council for International Understanding, July 19, 2007.

17 T. Ali, *The Duel: Pakistan on the Flight Path of American Power* (New York: Scribner, 2008), 159.

18 D. Sanger, *The Inheritance: The World Obama Confronts and the Challenges to American Power* (New York: Harmony Books, 2009), 238–9.

19 *The Washington Times*, November 23, 2007; *Asian News International*, November 21, 2007.

20 J. Perlez, "A Chill Ushers in a New Diplomatic Order in Pakistan," *The New York Times*, March 28, 2008, A8.

21 G. Hodgson, "Washington Discovers Islamabad," *Open Democracy*, November 28, 2007.

22 Department of State, J. Negroponte Interview with Charlie Rose, April 25, 2008; Department of State, J. Negroponte Address to French-American Foundation, May 16, 2007.

23 23 International Security No.4, 81 (1999), also in M. Brown, et al. (eds.), *The Rise of China* (Cambridge, MA: MIT Press, 2000), 167–204.

24 J. Negroponte, Address to Asia House Dinner, Hong Kong, October 18, 2000, in Director of National Intelligence Hearing, 88–96.

25 Department of State, J. Negroponte Interview with Charlie Rose, April 25, 2008; Testimony before the Senate Foreign Relations Committee, May 15, 2008; J. Negroponte Press Roundtable, Beijing, January 17, 2008.

26 J. Negroponte, Address to Japan Society, January 31, 2008.

27 J. Negroponte, Interview with Televisa, November 6, 2007.

28 J. Negroponte, The Role of Land Forces in Drug Interdiction: The Need for Caution in a Pragmatic Struggle, George Bush School, Texas A&M University, 1999, in Director of National Intelligence Hearing, 75–80.

29 P. von Zielbauer, "US Urges Iraq to Take Advantage of Lull," *The New York Times*, December 3, 2007.

30 Department of State, Anthony Motley Oral History, March 7, 1991.

31 H. Kopp, et al., *Career Diplomacy: Life and Work in the US Foreign Service* (Washington: Georgetown University, 2008). The listing in this work omits Reginald Bartholomew, as well as Joseph Grew and Sumner Welles among earlier officials.

32 H. Kissinger, *A World Restored: Metternich, Castlereagh and the Congress of Vienna* (London: Gollancz, 1973), 207.

33 Interview, April 7, 2009, available at www.charlierose.com/view/interview/10199

34 P. Calvocoressi, *World Politics 1945–2000* (New York: Pearson-Longman, 2001), 183.

35 Available at www.pbs.org/newshour/bb/remember/july-dec10/holbrooke2_12-14.html

36 JDN Remarks at Trinity College, Dublin, November 17, 2008, available at www.state.gov/s/d/2008/111961.htm

37   Interview, available at www.charlierose.com/view/interview/10199

38   Negroponte to Yerevan Embassy, December 23, 2008, EO 12958, available at www. guardian.co.uk/world/us-embassy-cables-documents/184879

39   P. Needham, "Q. and A.: Negroponte Discusses Cartoons," *Yale Daily News*, August 28, 2009.

40   Available at www.foreignpolicy.com/articles/2010/08/19/the_beginning_of_ the_end?

Conclusion

1   P. Nash, *The Other Missiles of October* (Chapel Hill: University of North Carolina, 1997).

2   M. Dobbs, *One Minute to Midnight: Kennedy, Khrushchev, and Castro on the Brink of Nuclear War*, 3rd ed. (New York: Knopf, 2008).

3   D. Bohning, *The Castro Obsession: US Covert Operations in Cuba, 1959–1965* (Washington: Potomac Books, 2005).

4   C. Preble, *John F. Kennedy and the Missile Gap* (Chicago: Northern Illinois University Press, 2004).

5   W. Pfaff, "American Fascism," *International Herald Tribune*, April 21, 2009; N. Wolf, "Fascist America in 10 Easy Steps," *Guardian*, April 24, 2007; J. Lukacs, *Democracy and Populism: Fear and Hatred* (New Haven: Yale University Press, 2006). See the amendment to 10 USC. sec.333 enacted by stealth as sec.1076 of Public Law 109-364, the Defense Authorization Act of 2007 authorizing the use of the military in domestic law enforcement, repealed after protests from all 50 state governors by the Defense Authorization Act of 2008, Public Law 110-18, sec. 1068, see the letter of the 50 governors of August 6, 2006, available at www.nga.org. See also Secretary Donald Rumsfeld's earlier proposal, implemented in the proposed legislation, for making the Department of Defense the lead agency, and "the NORTHCOM Commander…the principal USG official for…'catastrophic event[s]' " Rumsfeld to General Dick Myers, September 20, 2005, "USG's Ability to Deal with Catastrophic Events–Natural or Terrorist," available at http://library.rumsfeld.com/doclib/sp/383/2005-09-20%20 to%20 Myers%20re%20The%20USGs%20Ability%20to%20Deal%20With%20 Catastrophic%20Events-Natural%20or%20Terrorist.pdf#search="National   Guard". The Cox letter describing Libby's efforts is at www.thesmokinggun.com/file/ scooter-libby-love-letters?page=19-21

6   Rumbold to Foreign Office, July 19, 1932.

7   *Screws v. United States*, 325 US 91 (1945).

8   L. Solomon, *Paul D. Wolfowitz: Visionary Intellectual, Policymaker and Strategist* (Westport, CT: Praeger, 2007), 1–2, 4.

9   L. Kaplan and W. Kristol, *The War over Iraq: Saddam's Tyranny and America's Mission* (San Francisco: Encounter Books, 2003), ix, 48, 56, 60, 75, 92, 93, 98, 123.

10   U. Johnson, *The Right Hand of Power* (Englewood Cliffs, NJ: Prentice Hall, 1984), 406, 625, 633.

11   A. Cohrs, *Unfinished Peace After World War I: America, Britain, and the Stabilization of Europe* (Cambridge, UK: Cambridge University Press, 2006).

INDEX